Lecture Notes in Computer Science

T0218479

Lecture Notes in Computer Science

Vol. 49: Interactive Systems. Proceedings 1976. Edited by A. Blaser and C. Hackl. VI, 380 pages. 1976.

Vol. 50: A. C. Hartmann, A Concurrent Pascal Compiler for Minicomputers. VI, 119 pages. 1977.

Vol. 51: B. S. Garbow, Matrix Eigensystem Routines – Eispack Guide Extension. VIII, 343 pages. 1977.

Vol. 52: Automata, Languages and Programming. Fourth Colloquium, University of Turku, July 1977. Edited by A. Salomaa and M. Steinby. X, 569 pages. 1977.

Vol. 53: Mathematical Foundations of Computer Science. Proceedings 1977. Edited by J. Gruska. XII, 608 pages. 1977.

Vol. 54: Design and Implementation of Programming Languages. Proceedings 1976. Edited by J. H. Williams and D. A. Fisher. X, 496 pages. 1977.

Vol. 55: A. Gerbier, Mes premières constructions de programmes. XII, 256 pages. 1977.

Vol. 56: Fundamentals of Computation Theory. Proceedings 1977. Edited by M. Karpiński. XII, 542 pages. 1977.

Vol. 57: Portability of Numerical Software. Proceedings 1976. Edited by W. Cowell. VIII, 539 pages. 1977.

Vol. 58: M. J. O'Donnell, Computing in Systems Described by Equations. XIV, 111 pages. 1977.

Vol. 59: E. Hill, Jr., A Comparative Study of Very Large Data Bases. X, 140 pages. 1978.

Vol. 60: Operating Systems, An Advanced Course. Edited by R. Bayer, R. M. Graham, and G. Seegmüller. X, 593 pages. 1978.

Vol. 61: The Vienna Development Method: The Meta-Language. Edited by D. Bjørner and C. B. Jones. XVIII, 382 pages. 1978.

Vol. 62: Automata, Languages and Programming. Proceedings 1978. Edited by G. Ausiello and C. Böhm. VIII, 508 pages. 1978.

Vol. 63: Natural Language Communication with Computers. Edited by Leonard Bolc. VI, 292 pages. 1978.

Vol. 64: Mathematical Foundations of Computer Science. Proceedings 1978. Edited by J. Winkowski. X, 551 pages. 1978.

Vol. 65: Information Systems Methodology, Proceedings, 1978. Edited by G. Bracchi and P. C. Lockemann. XII, 696 pages. 1978.

Vol. 66: N. D. Jones and S. S. Muchnick, TEMPO: A Unified Treatment of Binding Time and Parameter Passing Concepts in Programming Languages. IX, 118 pages. 1978.

Vol. 67: Theoretical Computer Science, 4th GI Conference, Aachen, March 1979. Edited by K. Weihrauch. VII, 324 pages. 1979.

Vol. 68: D. Harel, First-Order Dynamic Logic. X, 133 pages. 1979.

Vol. 69: Program Construction. International Summer School. Edited by F. L. Bauer and M. Broy. VII, 651 pages. 1979.

Vol. 70: Semantics of Concurrent Computation. Proceedings 1979. Edited by G. Kahn. VI, 368 pages. 1979.

Vol. 71: Automata, Languages and Programming. Proceedings 1979. Edited by H. A. Maurer. IX, 684 pages. 1979.

Vol. 72: Symbolic and Algebraic Computation. Proceedings 1979. Edited by E. W. Ng. XV, 557 pages. 1979.

Vol. 73: Graph-Grammars and Their Application to Computer Science and Biology. Proceedings 1978. Edited by V. Claus, H. Ehrig and G. Rozenberg. VII, 477 pages. 1979.

Vol. 74: Mathematical Foundations of Computer Science. Proceedings 1979. Edited by J. Bečvář. IX, 580 pages. 1979.

Vol. 75: Mathematical Studies of Information Processing. Proceedings 1978. Edited by E. K. Blum, M. Paul and S. Takasu. VIII, 629 pages. 1979.

Vol. 76: Codes for Boundary-Value Problems in Ordinary Differential Equations. Proceedings 1978. Edited by B. Childs et al. VIII, 388 pages. 1979.

Vol. 77: G. V. Bochmann, Architecture of Distributed Computer Systems. VIII, 238 pages. 1979.

Vol. 78: M. Gordon, R. Milner and C. Wadsworth, Edinburgh LCF. VIII, 159 pages. 1979.

Vol. 79: Language Design and Programming Methodology. Proceedings, 1979. Edited by J. Tobias. IX, 255 pages. 1980.

Vol. 80: Pictorial Information Systems. Edited by S. K. Chang and K. S. Fu. IX, 445 pages. 1980.

Vol. 81: Data Base Techniques for Pictorial Applications. Proceedings, 1979. Edited by A. Blaser. XI, 599 pages. 1980.

Vol. 82: J. G. Sanderson, A Relational Theory of Computing. VI, 147 pages. 1980.

Vol. 83: International Symposium Programming. Proceedings, 1980. Edited by B. Robinet. VII, 341 pages. 1980.

Vol. 84: Net Theory and Applications. Proceedings, 1979. Edited by W. Brauer. XIII, 537 Seiten. 1980.

Vol. 85: Automata, Languages and Programming. Proceedings, 1980. Edited by J. de Bakker and J. van Leeuwen. VIII, 671 pages. 1980.

Vol. 86: Abstract Software Specifications. Proceedings, 1979. Edited by D. Bjørner. XIII, 567 pages. 1980

Vol. 87: 5th Conference on Automated Deduction. Proceedings, 1980. Edited by W. Bibel and R. Kowalski. VII, 385 pages. 1980.

Vol. 88: Mathematical Foundations of Computer Science 1980. Proceedings, 1980. Edited by P. Dembiński. VIII, 723 pages. 1980.

Vol. 89: Computer Aided Design - Modelling, Systems Engineering, CAD-Systems. Proceedings, 1980. Edited by J. Encarnacao. XIV, 461 pages. 1980.

Vol. 90: D. M. Sandford, Using Sophisticated Models in Resolution Theorem Proving.
XI, 239 pages. 1980

Vol. 91: D. Wood, Grammar and L Forms: An Introduction. IX, 314 pages. 1980.

Vol. 92: R. Milner, A Calculus of Communication Systems. VI, 171 pages. 1980.

Vol. 93: A. Nijholt, Context-Free Grammars: Covers, Normal Forms, and Parsing. VII, 253 pages. 1980.

Vol. 94: Semantics-Directed Compiler Generation. Proceedings, 1980. Edited by N. D. Jones. V, 489 pages. 1980.

Vol. 95: Ch. D. Marlin, Coroutines. XII, 246 pages. 1980.

Vol. 96: J. L. Peterson, Computer Programs for Spelling Correction: VI, 213 pages. 1980.

Vol. 97: S. Osaki and T. Nishio, Reliability Evaluation of Some Fault-Tolerant Computer Architectures. VI, 129 pages. 1980.

Vol. 98: Towards a Formal Description of Ada. Edited by D. Bjørner and O. N. Oest. XIV, 630 pages. 1980.

Vol. 99: I. Guessarian, Algebraic Semantics. XI, 158 pages. 1981.

Vol. 100: Graphtheoretic Concepts in Computer Science. Edited by H. Noltemeier. X, 403 pages. 1981.

Vol. 101: A. Thayse, Boolean Calculus of Differences. VII, 144 pages. 1981.

Vol. 102: J. H. Davenport, On the Integration of Algebraic Functions. 1–197 pages. 1981.

Vol. 103: H. Ledgard, A. Singer, J. Whiteside, Directions in Human Factors of Interactive Systems. VI, 190 pages. 1981.

Vol. 104: Theoretical Computer Science. Ed. by P. Deussen. VII, 261 pages. 1981.

Vol. 105: B. W. Lampson, M. Paul, H. J. Siegert, Distributed Systems – Architecture and Implementation. XIII, 510 pages. 1981.

Vol. 106: The Programming Language Ada. Reference Manual. X, 243 pages. 1981.

Lecture Notes in
Computer Science

Edited by G. Goos and J. Hartmanis

137

International Symposium on Programming

5th Colloquium
Turin, April 6–8, 1982
Proceedings

Edited by M. Dezani-Ciancaglini and U. Montanari

Springer-Verlag
Berlin Heidelberg New York 1982

Editors
Mariangiola Dezani-Ciancaglini
ISI
C.so M.D'Azeglio 42, 10125 Torino, Italy

Ugo Montanari
ISI
C.so Italia 40, 56100 Pisa, Italy

AMS Subject Classification (1980): 68B05, 68B10, 68B20
CR Subject Classification (1981): 4.20, 5.24

ISBN 3-540-11494-7 Springer-Verlag Berlin Heidelberg New York
ISBN 0-387-11494-7 Springer-Verlag New York Heidelberg Berlin

Printed in Germany

Printing and binding: Beltz Offsetdruck, Hemsbach/Bergstr.
2145/3140-543210

FOREWORD

The 25 papers contained in this volume have been selected among 75 submitted papers for presentation at the V-th International Symposium on Programming (Torino, April 6-8, 1982). The previus four colloquia were held in Paris in 1974, 76, 78 and 80.

The Program Committee consisted of J.ARSAC, Université P.et M.Curie, Paris; G.AUSIELLO, Università di Roma; M.DEZANI, Università di Torino; P.HENDERSON, Oxford University; C.GIRAULT, Université P. et M.Curie, Paris; D.GRIES, Cornell University, Ithaca (NY); A.MARTELLI, Università di Torino; U.MONTANARI (Chairman), Università di Pisa; M.NIVAT, Université Paris 7, Paris; M.PAUL, Technische Universität, Munich; B.ROBINET, Université P. et M.Curie, Paris; M.SINTZOFF, Mble Research Laboratory, Bruxelles.

The Organizing Committee consisted of I.Margaria, S.Ronchi della Rocca, F.Sirovich, M.Zacchi, Istituto di Scienze dell'Informazione, Torino.

The editors feel very grateful to the other members of the Program Committee and to the following referees: L.Aiello, A.Albani, V.Ambriola, P.Ancillotti, A.Arnold, E.Astesiano, F.Baiardi, R.Barbuti, H.Barendregt, M.Bellia, J.Berstel, O.Carvalho, P.Chretienne, M.Coppo, P.Degano, G.De Michelis, R.De Mori, S.Eichhole, K.Elhardt, M.Fontet, H.Ganzinger, G.Gardarin, M.C.Gaudel, R.Giegerich, R.Gnatz, F.Grandoni, P.Greussay, J.Guessarian, G.Guiho, C.Herzog, B.Hoferer, W.Lahner, G.Levi, G.Longo, B.Lorho, H.Lovenich, F.Luccio, A.Maggiolo-Schettini, D.Mandrioli, I. Margaria, M.Martelli, G.Mauri, P.Miglioli, C.Montangero, L.Nolin, M. Ornaghi, G.Pacini, H.Partsch, P.Pepper, J.F.Perrot, A.Pettorossi, G.Pujone, V.von Rhein, G.Roncairol, S.Ronchi, E.Saint-James, P.Sallé,

M.Simi, F.Sirovich, M.Somalvico, P.G.Terrat, F.Turini, G.Vaglini, M. Vanneschi, B.Venneri, M.Venturini-Zilli, H.Vogel, A.Widery, M.Wirsing, M.Zacchi.

Moreover we acknowledge the financial support provided by the following institutions and firms:

C.N.R. - Comitato per le Scienze Matematiche

C.N.R. - G.N.A.S.I.I.

C.N.R. - Progetto Finalizzato Informatica - Obiettivo CNET - Unità ISI Pisa e Torino.

Cassa di Risparmio di Torino

Comune di Torino

Regione Piemonte - Assessorato alla Cultura

Olivetti S.p.A.

A.I.C.A.

Mariangiola Dezani-Ciancaglini
Istituto di Scienze dell'Informazione
Università di Torino

Ugo Montanari
Istituto di Scienze dell'Informazione
Università di Pisa

CONTENTS

APPLICATIVE COMMUNICATING PROCESSES IN FIRST ORDER LOGIC

Marco Bellia, Pierpaolo Degano and Giorgio Levi
Istituto di Scienze dell'Informazione
Università di Pisa, Italy

Enrico Dameri
Systems & Management SpA, Area Tecnologie Software
Pisa, Italy

Maurizio Martelli
Istituto CNUCE - C.N.R., Pisa, Italy

ABSTRACT

We describe a first order applicative language for the specification of deterministic systems of communicating computing agents à la Kahn-MacQueen. Both the sequential and parallel interpreter we give are based on lazy evaluation, are demand driven and can handle infinite streams and non-terminating procedures. An equivalent least fixed-point semantics is then presented which neatly copes with the above features of the language. It is worth noting that computations in our logical based model can be considered as formal proofs, thus making formal reasoning about programs easier.

1. INTRODUCTION

The aim of this paper is to give a model of distributed computing based on an applicative first order logic language. The communicating computing agents we describe are essentially those modelled by Kahn and MacQueen /12, 13/, i.e. processes whose data are streams and which exchange information through one-way (single writer and multiple readers) channels. Since we want our language to be applicative, the agents we model are stateless, and the basic computation step consists in a reconfiguration of a <u>system of computing agents</u> (SCA).

The language we propose is a modification of PROLOG /14/. Any SCA is modelled by a set of atomic formulas, each corresponding to a single agent. Distributed programs are represented as sets of procedurally interpreted Horn clauses, each being a process definition. Channels which connect two or more agents are modelled by the presence of the same variable in the corresponding atomic formulas. In order to limit ourselves to statically defined one-way channels, we restrict PROLOG by statically distinguishing the input arguments of an atomic formula from its output arguments. This restriction to PROLOG limits its expressive power as far as problem solving is concerned, e.g. it forbids invertibility. On the other hand, PROLOG has been extended to cope with infinite streams, which require our language to have non-strict processes and lazy constructors. In spite of the above outlined modifications, the simple and clear logical concepts which underly PROLOG need to be only slightly modified to provide a fixed-point semantics of our language. Remarkably enough, the semantics is defined in terms of a least fixed-point construction, even in the presence of non-terminating processes.

Finally, let us note that our language can be seen as a proper extension of term rewriting systems, when Horn clauses are interpreted as rewrite rules extended to provide more than one output. Thus, we argue that relevant properties and proof techniques of term rewriting systems, such as Church-Rosser property and Knuth-Bendix completion algorithm, can be generalized and used here.

In Sections 2 and 3 we will introduce the syntax of the language we use to talk about agents and channels. Then, we will discuss the behaviour of SCA's in terms of lazy system transformations. Finally, we will define a fixed-point semantics, related to the model theoretic semantics of logic theories.

2. BASIC SYNTACTIC CONSTRUCTS

Our language is a many sorted first order language, which allows to express the behaviour of SCA's in terms of rewriting systems.

The language alphabet is $\mathcal{A} = \{S, C, D, V, F, R\}$, where:

S is a set of identifiers. Given S, we define a sort s which is:

i) simple if $s \in S$,

ii) functional if $s \in S^* \rightarrow S$,

iii) relational if $s \in S^* \rightarrow S^*$.

C is a family of sets of constant symbols indexed by simple sorts.

D is a family of sets of data constructor symbols indexed by functional sorts.

V is a family of denumerable sets of variable symbols indexed by simple sorts.

F is a family of sets of function symbols indexed by functional sorts.

R is a family of sets of predicate symbols indexed by relational sorts.

The basic construct of the language is the atomic formula, wich corresponds to the agent, the basic component of a SCA.

An atomic formula is:

i) a data atomic formula of the form $d(t_1,\dots,t_m)=v$, such that $t_1,\dots,t_m$ are data terms of sorts $s_1,\dots,s_m$, v is a variable symbol of sort s and $d \in D$ has sort $s_1 \times \dots \times s_m \rightarrow s$, or

ii) a functional atomic formula of the form $f(t_1,\dots,t_m)=v$, such that $t_1,\dots,t_m$ are data terms of sorts $s_1,\dots,s_m$, v is a variable symbol of sort s and $f \in F$ has sort $s_1 \times \dots \times s_m \rightarrow s$, or

iii) a relational atomic formula of the form $r($**in:** $t_1,\dots,t_m$; **out:** $v_{m+1},\dots,v_n)$, such that $t_1,\dots,t_m$ are data terms of sorts $s_1,\dots,s_m$, $v_{m+1},\dots,v_n$ are variable symbols of sorts $s_{m+1},\dots,s_n$ and $r \in R$ has sort $s_1 \times \dots \times s_m \rightarrow s_{m+1} \times \dots \times s_n$.

A data term of sort s ($s \in S$) is:

i) a constant symbol of sort s,

ii) a variable symbol of sort s,

iii) a data constructor application $d(t_1,\dots,t_m)$ such that $t_1,\dots,t_m$ are data terms of sorts $s_1,\dots,s_m$ and $d \in D$ has sort $s_1 \times \dots \times s_m \rightarrow s$.

A system formula (s-formula) is either:

i) an atomic formula, or

ii) a formula of the form c_1, c_2 such that c_1 is an atomic formula and c_2 is a s-formula. The s-formula c_2 is said to be the inner s-formula of c_1.

An input (output) variable is a variable that occurs in the in (out) parameter part of a relational atomic formula, or in the left (right) hand side of a functional atomic formula.

S-formulas are used to combine functional and relational atomic formulas. They define a local environment which is shared by (and allows the interaction among) its components.

The s-formula concept allows us to talk about SCA's. Each atomic formula corresponds to an agent, and its variables can be seen as channels connecting different agents. Input and output variables represent the inputs and the outputs of agents. The producer-consumer relationships are modelled by the occurence of the same variable among the output variables of an atomic formula (the producer), and the input variables of a different atomic formula (the consumer).

An example of s-formula, and the corresponding SCA, follows.

$f_1(v_1,v_4)=y_1$,
r_1(**in:** $d_1(v_2,v_3)$; **out:** y_2,y_3),
r_2(**in:** $d_2(v4)$; **out:** v_1,v_2),
r_3(**in:** c; **out:** v_3,v_4).

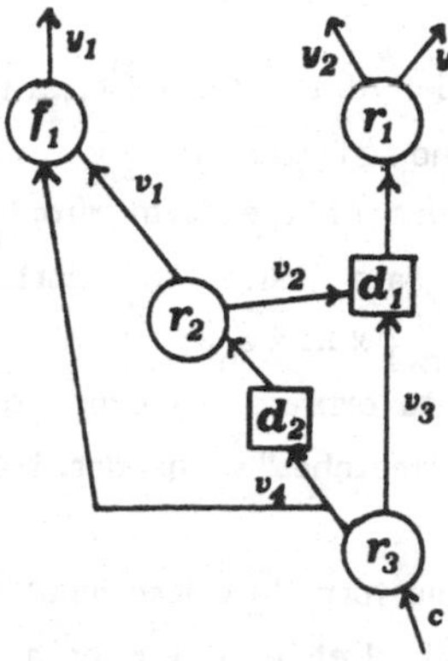

Fig.1

The agents (represented as nodes of the graph) are modelled by the atomic formulas; the producer-consumer relationships (represented by directed arcs) are modelled by the presence of the same variable in the output and input parts of different atomic formulas. Square nodes denote data atomic formulas.

The s-formulas defined so far can express a larger class of systems than SCA's, therefore we will introduce some constraints on their form.

Let $M_{in}(\mathbf{a})$ ($M_{out}(\mathbf{a})$) be the multiset of the input (output) variables of an atomic formula **a**.

Condition 1. For each s-formula $S = \mathbf{a}_1,\mathbf{a}_2,\ldots,\mathbf{a}_n$ the multiset $\bigsqcup_{i=1,..,n} M_{out}(\mathbf{a}_i)$ must be a set.

This condition, i.e. the absence of multiple output occurrences of a variable in a s-formula, ensures that every variable is computed by only one atomic formula. In the SCA framework, this means that for each channel, there is at most one producer.

Condition 2. For each atomic formula $\mathbf{a}_i$ in a s-formula, each variable belonging to $M_{in}(\mathbf{a}_i)$ must belong to $M_{out}(\mathbf{a}_k)$, where $\mathbf{a}_k$ is an atomic formula occurring in the inner s-formula of $\mathbf{a}_i$.

This condition forbids to write s-formulas whose input variables do not occur as output variables of any of its inner s-formulas. With this limitation, for any consumer there exists exactly one producer, and the whole SCA results to be a directed acyclic graph.

Note that output variables of a s-formula which are not input variables for any formula, model SCA outputs.

3. REWRITE RULES

This Section is concerned with the definition of the rewrite rules which define SCA transformations.

A set of procedures is a set of declarations and rewrite rules.

The set of declarations gives sorts to the objects occurring in the rewrite rules.

A rewrite rule is a formula of the form **l→r**, such that its left part **l** is a header and its right part **r** is either empty or has the form of a s-formula, consisting of functional or relational atomic formulas.

A header is either:

i) a functional header of the form $f(t_1,\dots,t_m)=t$, such that $t_1,\dots,t_m,t$ are data terms of sorts $s_1,\dots,s_m,s$ and $f\in F$ has sort $s_1 \times \dots \times s_m \to s$, or

ii) a relational header of the form $r($**in:** $t_1,\dots,t_m$; **out:** $t_{m+1},\dots,t_n)$, such that $t_1,\dots,t_m, t_{m+1},\dots,t_n$ are data terms of sorts $s_1,\dots,s_m,s_{m+1},\dots,s_n$ and $r\in R$ has sort $s_1 \times \dots \times s_m \to s_{m+1} \times \dots \times s_n$.

Rewrite rules allow us to express the dynamics of SCA's. In fact, a rewrite rule allows to rewrite any agent which "matches" its header, leading to the set of agents corresponding to the rule right part.

Let **f** be an atomic formula whose input data terms and output variables are $(t_1,\dots,t_m)$ and $(v_1,\dots,v_n)$ respectively. Let $\mathbf{e}:\mathbf{l}\to\mathbf{r}$ be a rewrite rule, such that **f** and **l** have the same function (or predicate) symbol, and let $(\tau_1,\dots,\tau_m)$, $(\sigma_1,\dots,\sigma_n)$ be the input and the output data terms of the header **l**. The atomic formula **f** can be rewritten by **e** if there exists an instantiation λ of variable symbols to data terms, such that $[(\tau_1,\dots,\tau_m)]_\lambda = (t_1,\dots,t_m)$.

Note that the variable symbols occuring in the t_i's cannot be instantiated, since they represent channels connected to an existing producer.

If such an instantiation exists, **f** can be replaced by a set of atomic formulas, obtained by applying λ to the rewrite rule right part **r** (a renaming is performed on the variables that interconnect the atomic formulas of the rewrite rule right part, thus establishing the internal producer-consumer relationships).

We are now left with the problem of properly establishing the correspondence between the output channels of **f** and $[\mathbf{r}]_\lambda$. This correspondence is defined by the instantiation μ, such that $[(v_1,\dots,v_n)]_\mu = [(\sigma_1,\dots,\sigma_n)]_\lambda$.

Note that the occurrence of data constructor symbols in the input and the output data terms of the header **l**, may involve data atomic formulas in the rewriting process, in both the replaced and the replacing structures. The occurrence of a data constructor symbol in the input of the header corresponds to a selection on the input channel of **f**. If λ exists, such a channel is connected to the output of a suitable data atomic formula, which therefore must be included in the replaced structure.

On the other hand, the occurrence of a data constructor symbol in the output of the header, corresponds to a data construction operation on some output channel of $[\mathbf{r}]_\lambda$. Hence a suitable data atomic formula must be inserted in the replacing structure.

As an example, consider the SCA of Fig. 1, where agent r_2 is rewritten using the rule

$e_1 : r_2(\textbf{in: } d_2(x); \textbf{ out: } y, d_3(z)) \rightarrow f_2(w, d_3(x))=z\ ,\ r_4(\textbf{in: } x; \textbf{ out: } y, w).$

Figures 2a and 2b show the replaced and replacing structures, while Figure 2c shows the rewritten SCA, corresponding to the s-formula:

$f_1(v_1,v_4)=y_1\ ,\ r_1(\textbf{in: } d_1(d_3(z'),v_3); \textbf{ out: } y_2,y_3)\ ,$

$f_2(w',d_3(v_4))=z'\ ,\ r_4(\textbf{in: } v_4; \textbf{ out: } v_1,w')\ ,\ r_3(\textbf{in: } c; \textbf{ out: } v_3,v_4).$

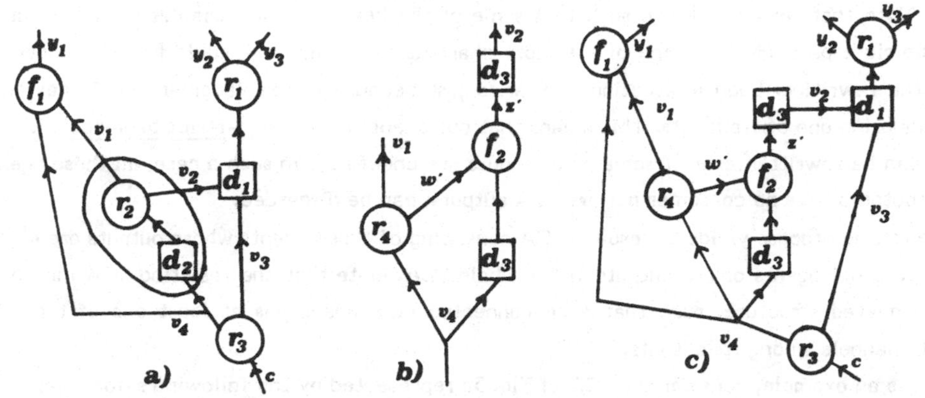

Fig. 2

The above definition of rewrite rule is inadequate, since the s-formula obtained by a rewriting could represent an illegal SCA, i.e. the s-formula could violate condition 1 or 2. Hence corresponding conditions must be imposed on rewrite rules. In order to give some insight into the meaning of the conditions, we will informally use operational arguments.

Let $\mathbf{h} \rightarrow \mathbf{a}_1,\mathbf{a}_2,\ldots,\mathbf{a}_n$ be a rewrite rule.

<u>Condition 3</u>. Multiset $M_{in}(\mathbf{h})$ must be a set.

The absence of multiple occurrences of a variable in the header (corresponding to the left-linearity property of term rewriting systems /11/) is related to the Church-Rosser property.

<u>Condition 4</u>. $\bigcup_i M_{out}(\mathbf{a}_i)$ is a set and for each $\mathbf{a}_i$, $M_{in}(\mathbf{h}) \cap M_{out}(\mathbf{a}_i) = \emptyset$.

In a rewrite rule, absence of multiple occurrences of output variables, and disjointness of the sets of header input variables and of atomic formulas output variables, rule out the case of multiple producers.

<u>Condition 5</u>.

<u>5.1</u>. All variable symbols occurring in $M_{out}(\mathbf{h})$ and $M_{in}(\mathbf{a}_i)$, must belong either to $M_{in}(\mathbf{h})$ or to $M_{out}(\mathbf{a}_k)$, where $\mathbf{a}_k$ is in the inner s-formula of $\mathbf{a}_i$.

<u>5.2</u>. For each $\mathbf{a}_k$ in a right part, $M_{out}(\mathbf{a}_k)$ must contain at least one variable symbol

belonging either to $M_{out}(\mathbf{h})$ or to $M_{in}(\mathbf{a}_i)$, where $\mathbf{a}_k$ is in the inner s-formula of $\mathbf{a}_i$.
The first part of this condition means that, during the application of the rewrite rule to a specific atomic formula, all the input variables of the right part will be properly bound. In fact, either they will be bound to the outputs of some atomic formula non occurring in the s-formula (i.e. they belong to $M_{in}(\mathbf{h})$), or to output variables of an atomic formula in the inner s-formula.
In the SCA framework, this ensures that for any consumer there exists a producer. Moreover, the way the atomic formulas corresponding to the consumers and the producers are nested, ensures that the SCA modelled by the rewrite rule right part is acyclic.

The second part of the condition constrains the output variables to be either output of the header, or input for an atomic formula in the s-formula, i.e. for any producer there exists at least a consumer.

Note that we allow rules, such that some of the header input variables do not occur in the rule right part. Hence, some of the input channels of an agent A could be non connected after the rewriting. Such a situation may arise just because the replacement of A may take place ignoring one of its inputs. This means that our agents have a non-strict behaviour, i.e. an agent can be rewritten even if some of its inputs are undefined. In such a case, all those agents whose outputs have no consumer nor are SCA outputs, can be discarded.
The rewriting process yields as result a SCA consisting of those agents whose outputs are either inputs to other agents or are outputs of the whole SCA. Note that the resulting SCA may be a non connected structure, such that each connected component has at least one of the SCA output channels among its outputs.

As an example, consider the SCA of Fig. 3a represented by the following s-formula:
$f_1(v_1,v_2,v_3)=v_4$, $f_2(v_5)=v_6$, $f_3(a)=v_1$, $f_4(c)=v_3$, r(**in:** b; **out:** v_2,v_5)
where we rewrite $f_1(v_1,v_2,v_3)=v_4$ according to the following rules
$\mathbf{e}_2 : f_1(x,y,z)=w \rightarrow f_5(x)=w;$ $\quad$ $\mathbf{e}_3 : f_4(c)=x \rightarrow f_4(c)=x.$
The resulting SCA is shown in Fig. 3b.

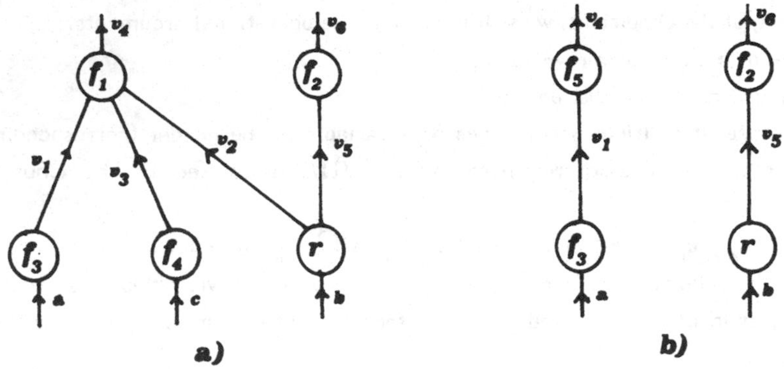

Fig. 3

The conditions we have defined so far are concerned with a single rewrite rule and with the rewriting process. If we want to limit ourselves to deterministic systems, we need a final global condition on sets of rewrite rules.

Condition 6. (determinism) Let E be a set of rewrite rules. For each pair of rules $e_i, e_j \in E$, $e_i : l_i \to r_i$, $e_j : l_j \to r_j$, such that the headers l_i and l_j have the same function or predicate symbol, the tuple of input data terms $(t_i^1,...t_i^m)$, $(t_j^1,...t_j^m)$ of l_i and l_j are such that there exists no instantiation λ of variable symbols to data terms, such that $[(t_i^1,...t_i^m)]_\lambda = [(t_j^1,...t_j^m)]_\lambda$.

The above condition ensures that any atomic formula in a s-formula can be rewritten at most by a single rewrite rule.

4. OPERATIONAL SEMANTICS

The language described in Sections 2 and 3 has several semantics aspects that are worth to be discussed before going into the description of the interpreter. Some of these aspects are concerned with the operational semantics only, while a few of them affect also the mathematical semantics.

a) The language needs an external evaluation rule, since defined procedures are allowed to be non-strict.

b) The language leads naturally to a call by need /24, 23/ interpreter, i.e. an interpreter based on call by name and structure sharing. In fact, our language allows to express structure sharing (which cerresponds to multiconsumer channels), thus making it something more than a mere implementation aspect.

c) Our interpreter is based on a lazy evaluation rule /7, 10 /, i.e. it allows data structure incremental evaluation. This can be achieved letting the data constructors to be non-strict (at least in some of their arguments). Our data constructors are intrinsically lazy in all of their arguments (see how data constructors are handled by the matching process within a rewriting). As a consequence of lazy constructors, data on our channels are not forced to be ground data terms (i.e. terms not containing any variable symbol), but are allowed to be suspensions, i.e. partially evaluated data structures.

d) Lazy constructors allow us to cope with infinite data structures (streams /15/) and with non-terminating procedures having streams as inputs and/or outputs. Agents having streams on their input or output channels correspond, in our applicative framework, to the intuitive notion of process.

e) The sequential interpreter can easily be modified to provide an equivalent parallel interpreter. The construction of the parallel interpreter from the sequential one is similar to the one given by Kahn and MacQueen /13/.

We will first give an informal description of the sequential interpreter, which will be then extended to parallelism. A complete formalization of the operational semantics is too tedious and lengthy to be given here and is essentially the same as the semantics given in /2/.

The interpreter's goal is computing the output of the whole SCA. Therefore, an attempt is made to rewrite those agents which produce the outputs of the whole SCA. Matching a header against an agent A may require the instantiation of an input variable of A. This situation mirrors the fact that on some input channels of the agent under rewriting there is no sufficient information. Then, one recursively attempts to rewrite exactly those agents whose outputs are needed to perform the previous step. Note that an agent is rewritten to approximate its outputs as much as it is required and that an agent is rewritten only once, since any other agent which uses its outputs will find exactly the needed and already computed information on the proper channels.

It is worth noting that the evaluation of a SCA possibly terminates with one rewriting of all the agents which produce SCA outputs. This behaviour corresponds to the lazy evaluation strategy consisting in allowing the producers to compute only what is needed to proceed in the computation. Unfortunately, this same strategy is not satisfactory for the top-level producers, from which we expect a complete output computation. Therefore, we model the external environment (which consumes the SCA outputs) by means of a PRINT agent, which causes recursive evaluation of the top-level agent, in order to print the results of the complete output computation.

Parallelism can be achieved by allowing concurrent rewritings of agents. Concurrent rewritings are possible in the following cases:

a) there exist several agents computing distinct outputs of the SCA;
b) the matching process involves more than one input term (i.e. both the header and the agent have several input terms). Term matchings can be handled concurrently, possibly leading to concurrent rewritings.

It is worth noting that our interpreter, unlike Kahn-MacQueen's parallel interpreter /13/, is demand-driven even in the parallel version, i.e. useless rewritings are never performed.

Example

type NAT **is** 0, s(NAT) ;

type STREAM-OF-NAT **is** nil, cons(NAT, STREAM-OF-NAT).

```
int : NAT ──► STREAM-OF-NAT ;
odd :     ──► STREAM-OF-NAT ;
sqr :     ──► STREAM-OF-NAT ;
sqr1 : NAT x STREAM-OF-NAT ──► STREAM-OF-NAT ;
odd1 : STREAM-OF-NAT ──► STREAM-OF-NAT ;

int(x)=cons(x,y)  ──►  int(s(x))=y ;
odd()=x  ──►  odd1(y)=x , int(0)=y ;
      odd1(cons(x,cons(y,z)))=cons(y,w)  ──►  odd1(z)=w ;
sqr()=x  ──►  sqr1(0,y)=x , odd()=y ;
      sqr1(x,cons(y,z))=cons(t,u)  ──►  sqr1(t,z)=u , +(x,y)=t ;
+(0,x)=x ──►   ;   +(s(x),y)=s(z)  ──►  +(x,y)=z .
```

The above set of procedures contains the following functions:

- int, which generates the infinite increasing sequence of natural numbers starting from the value of its argument.
- odd, which generates the infinite increasing sequence of odd numbers.

- sqr, which computes the infinite increasing sequence of all the squares of positive numbers. The square of n is obtained as the sum of the first n odd numbers.
- oddl, sqrl are auxiliary functions and + has the standard interpretation.

Figure 4 shows some systems of agents as derived by the parallel interpreter, starting from the system corresponding to the s-formula sqr()=out.

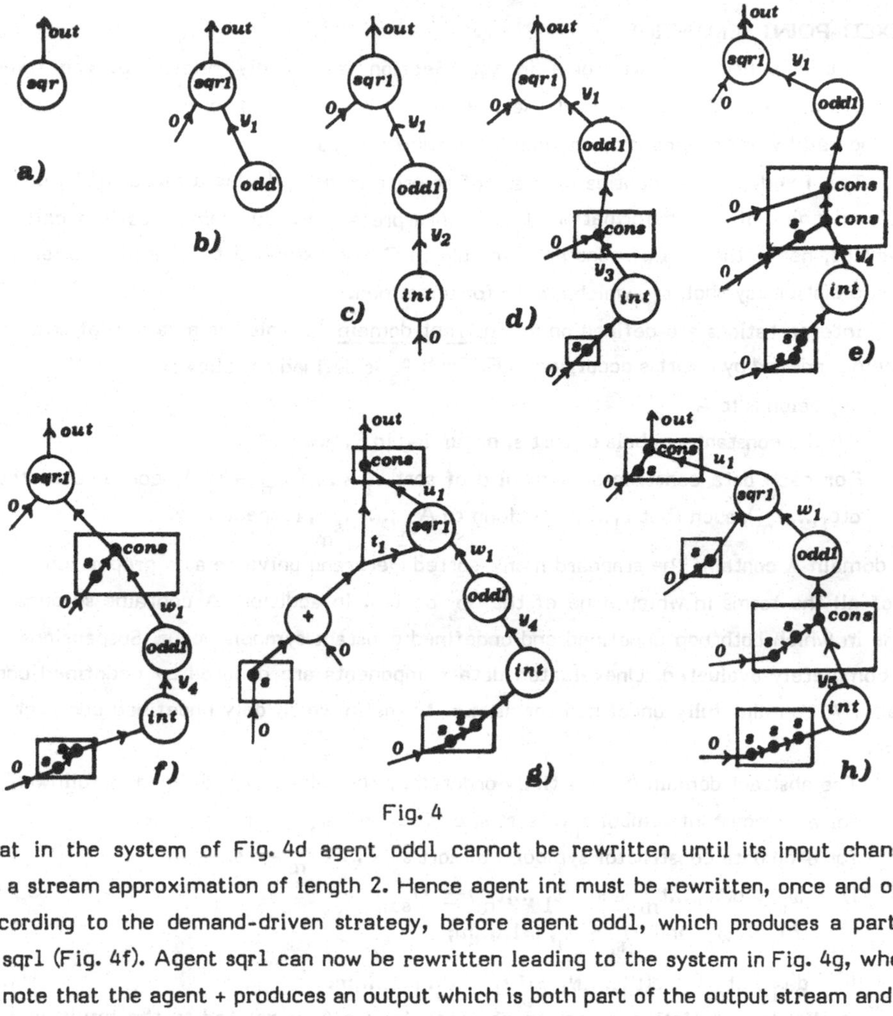

Fig. 4

Note that in the system of Fig. 4d agent oddl cannot be rewritten until its input channel contains a stream approximation of length 2. Hence agent int must be rewritten, once and only once according to the demand-driven strategy, before agent oddl, which produces a partial input to sqrl (Fig. 4f). Agent sqrl can now be rewritten leading to the system in Fig. 4g, where one can note that the agent + produces an output which is both part of the output stream and an input to agent sqrl. The last rewriting step we show in Fig. 4 results from parallel rewriting of agents + and int, as required by the existence of two top level output channels (labelled t_1 and w_1 in Fig. 4g). Let us finally note that the system in Fig. 4h produces the very first output stream approximation cons(s(0),u_1), i.e. a stream whose first component is the square of the natural number 1.

Some of the aspects pointed out at the beginning of this Section are only concerned with implementation (i.e. operational semantics). Namely, structure sharing and parallelism are only features of the interpreter. Similar considerations apply to data structure incremental evaluation, provided infinite data structures (streams) are not allowed.

On the other hand, non-strict procedures and streams must be reflected in any semantics definition. The above aspects are exactly those which make our calculus different from PROLOG, even if a computation, i.e. a sequence of rewritings, can still be viewed as a formal proof (each s-formula being a logical implication of the set of procedures).

5. FIXED-POINT SEMANTICS

The semantics we will give in this Section is strongly related to the fixed-point semantics given in /21/ for Horn clauses. However, a non trivial extension is needed to cope with the call by name semantics and lazy constructors /2, 17/.

The fixed-point semantics of a set of rewrite rules $E=\{\mathbf{e}_i\}$ is a model of E, obtained as the fixed-point of a transformation Φ_E on interpretations. Our semantics is a call by name semantics, hence the sets of constant symbols in C are extended to contain, for each simple sort s, a distinct symbol ω_s, which stands for undefined.

Interpretations are defined on an <u>abstract domain</u> A, which is a family of sets A_s, each set being indexed by a sort s occurring in E. Each A_s is defined as follows:

i) ω_s belongs to A_s.

ii) All the constant symbols of sort s, occurring in E, are in A_s.

iii) For each data constructor symbol d of sort $s_1 \times \dots \times s_m \rightarrow s$, A_s contains all the terms $d(t_1,\dots,t_m)$, such that $t_1,\dots,t_m$ belong to $A_{s_1},\dots,A_{s_m}$, respectively.

The domain A contains the standard many-sorted Herbrand universe as a proper subset, i.e. the set of all the terms in which none of the ω_s occurs. In addition, A contains suspensions, i.e. terms in which both non undefined and undefined constant symbols occur. Suspensions are data not completely evaluated. Unevaluated data components are denoted by undefined constants. Finally, A contains fully undefined terms, i.e. terms in which only undefined constant symbols occur.

The abstract domain A is partially ordered by the relation $\precsim$ defined as follows:

1) for each constant symbol c_i of sort s, $c_i \precsim c_i$ and $\omega_s \precsim c_i$;

2 for each data constructor symbol d of sort $s_1 \times \dots \times s_m \rightarrow s$,

  i) $\omega_s \precsim d(t_1,\dots,t_m)$ and $d(t_1,\dots,t_m) \precsim \omega_s$ if $t_i \precsim \omega_{s_i}$ and $\omega_{s_i} \precsim t_i$, $i=1,\dots,m$;

  ii) $d(t_1,\dots,t_m) \precsim d(t'_1,\dots,t'_m)$ if $t_i \precsim t'_i$, $i=1,\dots,m$.

The partial ordering relation $\precsim$ on the abstract domain A, is related to the intuitive notion of suspension approximation as introduced by the lazy constructors. As an example, the relation $cons(1,\omega) \precsim cons(1,cons(2,\omega))$ mirrors the fact that $cons(1,cons(2,\omega))$ is a refinement of $cons(1,\omega)$.

Interpretations are defined as subsets of the interpretation base B. The <u>interpretation base</u> B is a set of atomic formulas defined as follows:

i) For each function symbol f (occurring in E) of sort $s_1 \times \dots \times s_m \rightarrow s$, B contains all the formulas $f(t_1,...,t_m)=t$ such that $t_1,...,t_m$ and t have sorts $s_1,...s_m,s$ respectively, and $t \preceq \omega_s$ does not hold.

ii) For each predicate symbol r (occurring in E) of sort $s_1 \times ... \times s_m \longrightarrow s_{m+1} \times ... \times s_n$, B contains all the formulas $r($**in:** $t_1,...,t_m$; **out:** $t_{m+1},...,t_n)$, such that $t_1,...,t_m,t_{m+1},...,t_n$ have sorts $s_1,...,s_m,s_{m+1},...,s_n$ respectively, and there exists at least one of the terms t_i, $i= m+1,...,n$, such that $t_i \preceq \omega_{s_i}$ does not hold.

The interpretation base B is the set of all the ground atomic formulas, i.e. formulas not containing variable symbols. Each formula in B assigns specific ground output terms to the application of function (or predicate) symbols to ground input terms. Two atomic formulas are <u>colliding</u> if they assign different output terms to the same function or predicate application.

B is partially ordered by the relation $\subseteq$, such that $\mathbf{f}_i \subseteq \mathbf{f}_j$ if and only if $\mathbf{f}_i$ and $\mathbf{f}_j$ are colliding, and for each pair of output terms (t_{i_k},t_{j_k}) of $\mathbf{f}_i$ and $\mathbf{f}_j$, $t_{i_k} \preceq t_{j_k}$.
Intuitively, $\mathbf{f}_i \subseteq \mathbf{f}_j$ reflects that at least one of the outputs of $\mathbf{f}_j$ is a refinement of the corresponding output of $\mathbf{f}_i$.

Since our language is deterministic, the semantics of a set of rewrite rules cannot contain colliding atomic formulas. Hence an <u>interpretation</u> is any subset of B not containing colliding atomic formulas.
The set of interpretations $\{\xi_i\}$ can be partially ordered by the relation $\leq$, defined as follows: $\xi_i \leq \xi_j$, if and only if for each formula $\mathbf{f}_{i_k} \in \xi_i$, there exists a formula $\mathbf{f}_{j_h} \in \xi_j$, such that $\mathbf{f}_{i_k} \subseteq \mathbf{f}_{j_h}$.

Roughly speaking, an interpretation assigns output values to applications of functions and relations to ground input values. All the other applications have only undefined outputs. Note that the partial ordering relation $\leq$ on interpretations corresponds to an intuitive notion of better approximation. In fact, if $\xi_i \leq \xi_j$, then either ξ_j assigns output values to some applications that in ξ_i had only undefined outputs, or ξ_j refines some output value of ξ_i.

Let ξ_i and ξ_j be interpretations and $\xi'_i(\xi'_j)$ be the subsets of $\xi_i(\xi_j)$ such that each formula in $\xi'_i(\xi'_j)$ has no colliding formula in $\xi_j(\xi_i)$.
The diadic operator $\bigcup$ on interpretations is defined as follows:
i) all the formulas in ξ'_i belong to $\xi_i \bigcup \xi_j$,
ii) all the formulas in ξ'_j belong to $\xi_i \bigcup \xi_j$,
iii) for each pair of colliding formulas $\mathbf{f}_k \in \xi_i$ and $\mathbf{f}_h \in \xi_j$, $\xi_i \bigcup \xi_j$ contains $\mathbf{f}_k$, if $\mathbf{f}_h \subseteq \mathbf{f}_k$, $\mathbf{f}_h$ otherwise.

Note that $\xi_i \bigcup \xi_j$ is an interpretation, such that $\xi_i \leq \xi_i \bigcup \xi_j$, and $\xi_j \leq \xi_i \bigcup \xi_j$.

We will now introduce the transformation Φ_E which maps interpretations onto interpretations and will be used to define the semantics of a set of rewrite rules E.

Let ξ_i be any interpretation and $\mathbf{e}_k : H(\mathbf{e}_k) \rightarrow G(\mathbf{e}_k)$ be a rewrite rule of E. The rewrite rule $\mathbf{e}_k$ defines a transformation Φ^k which maps ξ_i onto the interpretation $\xi^k_i = \Phi^k(\xi_i) = \xi_i \bigcup \xi^{k'}_i$, where $\xi^{k'}_i$ is defined as follows.
For each instantiation λ of variables to terms of A, the formula $[H(\mathbf{e}_k)]_\lambda \in \xi^{k'}_i$, if

1) at least one output variable of $[H(e_k)]_\lambda$ is not undefined, and

2) for each atomic formula a_j in $G(e_k)$ either

2.1) $[a_j]_\lambda \in \xi_i$, or

2.2) all the output variables of $[a_j]_\lambda$ are undefined.

Note that λ must instantiate a variable v of sort s to a term belonging to A_s, and that if $G(e_k)$ is empty, condition 2 is satisfied for any instantiation λ.

Note also that $\xi^{k'}_i$ is an interpretation, since with a single equation we cannot derive colliding atomic formulas. Furthermore, ξ^k_i is always defined, since for each formula $f_r \in \xi_i$ such that there exists a colliding formula $f_q \in \xi^{k'}_i$, $f_r \subseteq f_q$, as a consequence of condition 6 (determinism). Hence ξ^k_i is an interpretation such that $\xi_i \leq \xi^k_i$.

The transformation Φ_E is the transformation defined by all the rewrite rules of E according to the above definition, i.e.

$$\xi_{i+1} = \Phi_E(\xi_i) = \bigcup_{e_k \in E} \Phi^k(\xi_i).$$

It can be proven that transformation Φ_E on the set of interpretations partially ordered by $\leq$ is monotonic and continuous. Hence, there exists the least fixed-poit interpretation ξ^* such that $\xi^* = \Phi_E(\xi^*)$, which can be obtained by iteratively applying Φ_E, starting with the empty subset of B, which is the bottom element of the partially ordered set of interpretations.

The equivalence between the fixed-point semantics and the operational semantics defined in Section 4 is related to the completeness of first order logic. In fact, if the fixed-point interpretation of a set of rewrite rules E contains a ground atomic formula $f(t_1,...,t_m)=t$ (r(**in:** $t_1,...,t_m$; **out:** $t_{m+1},...,t_n$)) then the interpreter, given the s-formula $f(t_1,...,t_m)=x$ (r(**in:** $t_1,...,t_m$; **out:** $x_{m+1},...,x_n$)) will produce the value t $(t_{m+1},...,t_n)$ on the system output channel(s). A formal proof of the equivalence can be obtained by a straightforward extension of the proof of a similar result /17/.

6. RELATED WORK

An accurate tutorial on models for distributed computing is presented in /18/. Our model is strongly related to the Kahn-MacQueen's stream processing model, even if some features (data-driven computation, streams, etc.) are similarly handled by DATA FLOW languages /6/and by LUCID /1/.

The main difference between our language and Kahn-MacQueen's model is the nature of agents which, in our case, are applicative. Kahn-MacQueen's agents can be seen as static processes with state, even if dynamic process activation can be obtained by means of system reconfiguration. System reconfiguration is the only computation mechanism provided in our language. The applicative nature of agents allows us to take a logical approach to the definition of semantics. The resulting mathematical semantics is very simple, while operational semantics can be interpreted as an inference system which provides sound bases for proving properties of systems.

Modelling distributed systems in terms of first order logic is being pursued by several authors, through suitable extensions to PROLOG. Namely, coroutining, parallel processes and lazy evaluation have been obtained by adding to pure PROLOG a suitable control language /5/, with the aim of defining efficient execution (proof) strategies. A similar approach is taken in /9/, where PROLOG is extended with primitives for defining evaluating rules, which include coroutining à la Kahn-MacQueen. /22/ gives a formulation of the Kahn-MacQueen's model in first order logic extended with streams and non-terminating processes. Such a proposal is different from ours in the use of channels and in the mathematical semantics. Namely, no distinction between input and output channels is statically imposed. Moreover, the extensions to the Herbrand universe and to the transformation on interpretations which are needed to cope with infinite streams and non-terminating processes, lead to a greatest fixed-point construction.

Finally, our language is a proper extension of algebraic abstract data type specification languages /16, 3, 8, 20, 4/, concerned with multi-output procedures (relational rewrite rules), while systems in algebraic specification languages are connected tree-structured SCA's, whose agents have a single output and such that for each producer there exists at most one consumer.

7. CONCLUSIONS

The language we have defined can be considered as the applicative counterpart of Kahn-MacQueen's model. Interpreting systems of communicating processes as logical theories allows us to define a rather simple fixed-point semantics which gives a denotation to non-terminating procedures (processes). Moreover, we conjecture that several proof techniques originally developed for first order theories, algebraic data types and term rewriting systems can be applied to our language as well. This is one research direction for future work.

Another aspect we would like to describe in our language is nondeterminism. The semantics of nondeterminism as it was given for PROLOG /21/ is unsatisfactory to our purposes, since it gives a single model (a set) as the denotation of a nondeterministic program. We think that a mathematical characterization of nondeterminism should be based on tree-structured models similar to Milner's models /19/.

The final aspect we are currently investigating is related to the pragmatics of our language, when considered as a specification language. In other words, we are trying to understand which classes of problems can naturally be specified and how real life state based distributed problems can be handled.

REFERENCES

1. E.A. Ashcroft and W.W.Wadge - LUCID, a Nonprocedural Language with Iteration - C.ACM 20 (1977), 519-526.
2. M. Bellia, P. Degano and G. Levi - A Functional plus Predicate Logic Programming Language - Proc. Logic Programming Workshop, Debrecen (Hungary) (1980), 334-347.
3. R.M. Burstall and J.A. Goguen - Putting Theories together to Make Specifications - Proc. 5th Int'l Joint Conf. on Artificial Intelligence, Cambridge (1977), 1045-1058.
4. R.M. Burstall, D.B. MacQueen and D.T. Sannella - HOPE: an Experimental Applicative Language - Proc. LISP Conference, Stanford (1980).
5. K. Clark and F. McCabe - IC-PROLOG Language Features - Proc. Logic Programming Workshop, Debrecen (Hungary) (1980), 45-52.
6. J.B. Dennis - First Version of a Data Flow Procedure Language - Proc. Symposium on Programming, Paris (1974), Springer Verlag, 362-376.
7. D. Friedman and D. Wise - CONS Should not Evaluate its Arguments - Automata, Languages and Programming, S. Michaelson ed., Edinburgh Univ. Press (1976), 256-284.
8. J.A. Goguen and J.J. Tardo - An Introduction to OBJ: a Language for Writing and Testing Formal Algebraic Specifications - Proc. IEEE Conf. on Specifications of Reliable Software, Los Angeles (1979), 170-189.
9. A. Hansson, S. Haradi and S.Å. Tärnlund - Some Aspects on a Logic Machine Prototype - Proc. Logic Programming Workshop, Debrecen (Hungary) (1980), 53-60.
10. P. Henderson and J.H. Morris - A Lazy Evaluator - 3rd ACM Symp. on Principles of Programming Languages (1976), 95-103.
11. G. Huet and D.C. Oppen - Equations and Rewrite Rules: A Survey - in: Formal Languages: Perspectives and Open Problems, R. Book ed., Academic Press (1980)
12. G. Kahn - The Semantics of a Simple Language for Parallel Programming - Information Processing 74, North-Holland (1974), 471-475.
13. G. Kahn and D.B. MacQueen - Coroutines and Networks of Parallel Processes - Information Processing 77, North-Holland (1977), 993-998.
14. R.A. Kowalski - Predicate Logic as Programming Language - Information Processing 74, North-Holland (1974), 569-574.
15. P. Landin - A Correspondence between ALGOL 60 and Church's Lambda Calculus - C.ACM 8, (1965), 89-101.
16. G. Levi and F. Sirovich - Proving Program Properties, Symbolic Evaluation and Logical Procedural Semantics - Proc. MFCS'75. LNCS 32, Springer Verlag (1975), 294-301.
17. G. Levi and A. Pegna - Top-down mathematical semantics and symbolic execution - to be published in RAIRO Informatique Theorique.
18. D.B. MacQueen - Models for Distributed Computing - in: La Conception de Systèmes Reparties, INRIA (1978), 139-174.
19. R. Milner - A Calculus of Communicating Systems - LNCS 92, Springer Verlag (1980).
20. D.B. Musser - Abstract Data Types in the AFFIRM System - Proc. IEEE Conf. on Specifications of Reliable Software, Los Angeles (1979), 47-57.
21. M.H. vanHemden and R.A. Kowalski - The Semantics of Predicate Logic as a Programming Language - J.ACM 23 (1976), 733-742.
22. M.H. vanHemden, G.J. de Lucena and H. de M. Silva - Predicate Logic as a Language for Parallel Programming - CS-79-15, Univ. of Waterloo, Dept. of Comp. Science, Nov. 1980.
23. J. Vuillemin - Correct and Optimal Implementations of Recursion in a Simple Programming Language - J.CSS 9 (1974).
24. C. Wadsworth - Semantics and Pragmatics of the Lambda-Calculus - PhD. Thesis, Oxford, 1971.

A MACHINE-LEVEL SEMANTICS FOR NONDETERMINISTIC, PARALLEL PROGRAMS*

David B. Benson
Computer Science Department
Washington State University
Pullman, WA 99164 USA

1. Introduction.-- Consider the following flowchart:

(1)

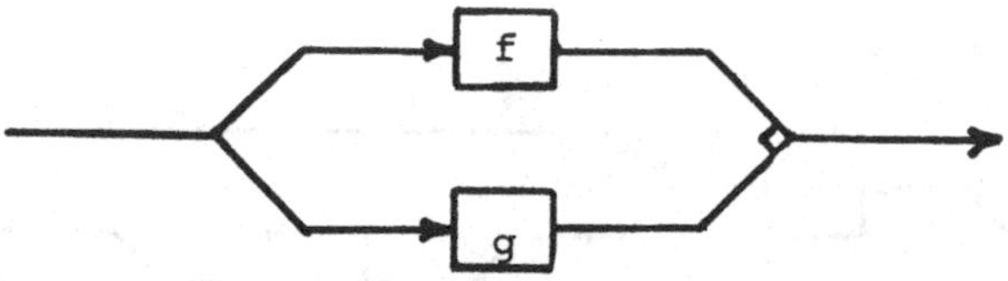

consisting of a control line coming in on the left; a fork into two control lines; two noncommunicating programs, each with a single entrance and single exit; a join of the two control lines into one and the single control line exit. In section 2 we formalize the action of the fork-join combination of f and g as in flowchart (1). The mathematics depends crucially on the existence of a single (nondeterministic) input state at entrance to the entire flowchart to treat race conditions, [Karp & Miller, 1969].

To handle more complex situations arising in the study of communicating processes, consider the flowchart

(2)

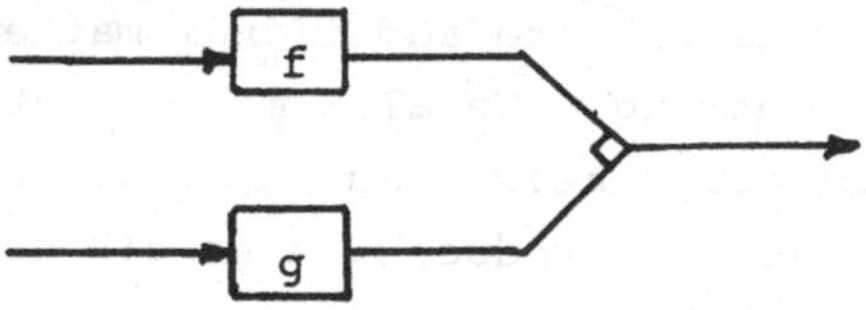

where the two input control lines may carry different states. This occurs in situations where two parallel processes converge on a critical section or message exchange:

(3)

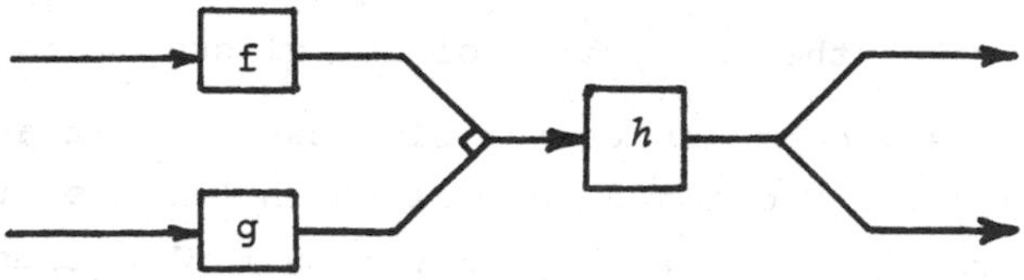

*Research partially supported by National Science Foundation grant MCS-8003433.

In flowchart (3), we suppose the processor following the top control path needs access to a critical resource controlled by the processor following the bottom control path. The granting of access to the critical resource is a join of the two processes. The critical section operations are in h, whereupon the top processor reemerges and the bottom process goes off to look for other processors requiring access to the critical resource.

To give a more complete example, suppose there is a producer P, and consumer C, and a single cell buffer between them with critical sections W (write into the buffer) and R (read from the buffer). The complete diagram is

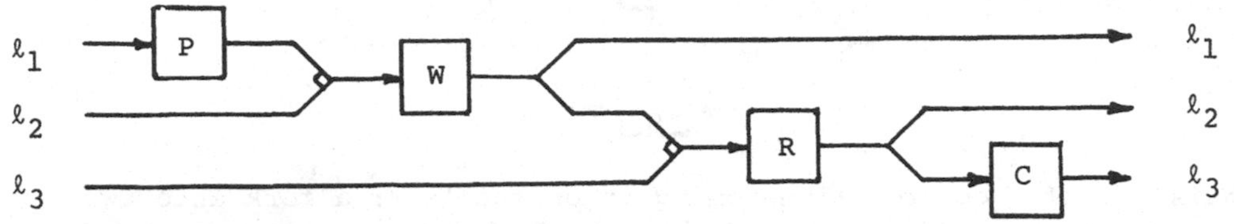

in which each of ℓ_1, ℓ_2, and ℓ_3 loop back to the beginning.

In sections 3 and 4 we give a more abstract mathematical treatment of the join operator which is a strict generalization of the fork-join case, and which provides a multilinear semantics for critical sections. In section 5 we point out that denotational semantics for such nondeterministic, parallel programs already exist. These denotational semantics are required to solve the loop equations which result from flowcharts such as flowchart (4). We make no attempt to consider history semantics such as in [Francez, et al., 1980; Rounds & Brookes, 1981], as message passing will require additional mathematical apparatus within the multilinear setting. We also make no attempt to consider infinite sequences of computations as in, e.g., [Park, 1980, 1981]. We conceive of the computation as producing a single nondeterministic result at this level of abstraction.

Nondeterminism is treated here as a formal sum $\Sigma r_i \sigma_i$ where r_i denotes the multiplicity with which state σ_i occurs. The r_i lie in a commutative semiring R so that $\Sigma r_i \sigma_i + \Sigma s_i \sigma_i = \Sigma (r_i + s_i) \sigma_i$ and $t(\Sigma r_i \sigma_i) = \Sigma (t r_i) \sigma_i$ make the collection of formal sums into a module over the semiring R. Any commutative semiring can be used as the base semiring in this analysis. Section 2 is written in terms of the semiring of natural numbers, $\mathbb{N}$. In this case the multiplicities count the number of paths reaching the states, [Benson, 1982]. Other typical examples are the boolean semiring $\mathbb{B}$, any distributive lattice, and multiplicity semirings, [Elgot, 1979].

2. Nondeterministic semantics of the fork-join situation.-- The semantics of fork appears easy: if S is any state-space the fork produces two copies of the state-space, $\Delta: S \to S \times S: s \mapsto \langle s,s \rangle$. This works if S is a deterministic state space, but in section 3 we will discover that an essentially different notion is required for fork.

With two copies available, two completely independent programs may run in parallel, producing two independent outcomes, viz: $f \times g: S \times S \to S \times S: \langle s_1,s_2 \rangle \mapsto \langle f(s_1), g(s_2) \rangle$.

Combining the results at the join is the interesting part. The two independent programs must record their results in a single common store.

The write to common store is a binary operation, join, of the form $\nabla: S \times S \to S$ in which S is now forced to be a nondeterministic store. To determine the possible race conditions, it will be necessary to record which locations each program may attempt to write.

The fork-join combination of f and g, flowchart (1), is in general $f \diamond g = \Delta \cdot (f \times g) \cdot \nabla$ but in this section we do not give a separate semantics for ∇.

Formally, let Sv be a set of storable values and Loc be a countable set of locations. Let Store = [Loc $\to$ Sv] be the set of possible stores, functions from locations to storable values. For each set X, let $F(X)$ be the set of finite subsets of X. An active location set L is a finite set of locations, $L \in F(\text{Loc})$. An active location set models the set of locations into which a program may write. All locations in Loc-L will not be written by any program with active location set L.

The active stores are pairs, consisting of a store and an active location set: $A = \{\langle s,L \rangle \mid s \in \text{Store}, L \in F(\text{Loc})\}$.

Let $s_0 \in$ Store be a distinguished store. The subset of active stores based on s_0 is $A(s_0) = \{\langle s,L \rangle \mid \ell \notin L \Rightarrow s(\ell) = s_0(\ell)\}$. The intent is to codify the possible stores which may arise in

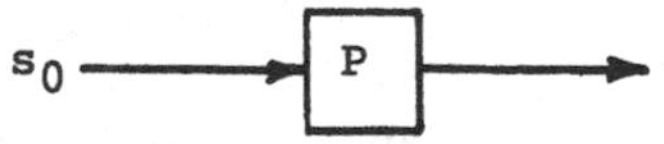

by the action of a program P with active location set L upon input s_0.

Nondeterminism may be handled by counting the number of different ways a nondeterministic program may give rise to a particular store. For $s_0 \in$ Store, let $D(s_0)$ be the free $\mathbb{N}$-module generated by $A(s_0)$. $D(s_0)$ is the nondeterministic domain based on s_0. Define the domain D to be the free $\mathbb{N}$-module generated by the entire set of active stores A. Each $D(s_0)$ is a submodule of D and indeed,

2.1 Lemma. $D = \sum_{\langle s,L\rangle \in A} D(s)$.

The task is to formalize a multiplication of nondeterministic domains as the semantics of the join operation. The join gives rise to nondeterminism due to race conditions. The crucial definition is: For $a_i = \langle s_i, L_i \rangle \in A(s_0)$, $i = 1,2$, and $s \in$ Store: $s \in I(a_1,a_2)$ iff

$$\forall \ell \in \text{Loc:} \quad s(\ell) = \begin{cases} s_0(\ell) & \text{if } \ell \notin L_1 \cup L_2 \\ s_1(\ell) & \text{if } \ell \in L_1 - L_2 \\ s_2(\ell) & \text{if } \ell \in L_2 - L_1 \end{cases}$$

$$\text{and } s(\ell) \in \{s_1(\ell), s_2(\ell)\} \text{ if } \ell \in L_1 \cap L_2.$$

$I(a_1,a_2)$ is the set of all stores which agree with the base store wherever a_1 and a_2 are not active, agree with s_i wherever a_i is the only active store, $i = 1,2$, and agree with either a_1 or a_2 -- or both if they agree -- wherever both a_1 and a_2 are active.

N.B.: Each program p_i statistically determines its active location set L_i. All we require here is that p_i writes to no location in $\text{Loc}-L_i$. At any particular invocation it may write to none, some or all the locations in L_i.

To enable semantical composition to be defined, i.e., the semantics of single entrance-single exit programs to be functions from D to D, we define the multiplication on each $D(s_0)$ and then lift the definition to the functions representing program behavior.

2.2 Definition. For $a_i = \langle s_i, L_i \rangle \in A(s_0)$, $i = 1,2$, define $\diamond: A(s_0) \times A(s_0) \to D(s_0)$ by $a_1 \diamond a_2 = \sum_{s \in I(a_1,a_2)} \langle s, L_1 \cup L_2 \rangle$. Extend the definition to all of $D(s_0)$, $\diamond: D(s_0) \times D(s_0) \to D(s_0)$, by linearity: $(\Sigma m_i a_i) \diamond (\Sigma n_j b_j) = \sum_i \sum_j m_i n_j (a_i \diamond b_j)$.

2.3 Theorem. The algebraic system $\langle D(s_0), +, \diamond \rangle$ is a commutative semiring with zero $0 = \Sigma 0 a_i$ and the active store $i = \langle s_0, \emptyset \rangle$ as the semiring identity. Furthermore, $A(s_0)$ is an idempotent basis for $D(S_0)$ as $a \diamond a = a$ for all $a \in A(s_0)$.

The main thesis is that nondeterministic, parallel program behaviors can be viewed as certain linear transformations of the module

D. By linear transformation here we mean any function $f: D \to D$ such that

$$f(na + mb) = nf(a) + mf(b)$$

for $n,m \in \mathbb{N}$ and $a,b \in D$. The restriction to linear transformations arises for reasons given in [Benson, 1982; Lorentz & Benson, 1980]. Axiom P1 below formalizes the fact tha no program segment knows what locations were modified by previous program segments. Axiom P2 guarantees that no program can modify the value stored at a location outside its active location set.

P1: $f\langle s,L\rangle = f(s)$, i.e., $\forall a_1,a_2 \in A$: $a_i = \langle s,L_i\rangle$, $i = 1,2$, imply

$$f(a_1) = f(a_2).$$

P2: $\forall\langle s,L\rangle \in A$: $f\langle s,L\rangle = \Sigma n_i\langle s_i,L_i\rangle$ implies if $n_i \neq 0$ then

$$\forall \ell \notin L_i: \quad s_i(\ell) = s(\ell).$$

2.4 Definition. The linear endomorphisms of D satisfying P1 and P2 are said to be P-computable functions. The set of such is denoted by P.

Because of P1, we may abuse the notation and write, for $a = \langle s,L\rangle$, $f(s)$ instead of $f(a)$.

We now lift the definition of the join multiplication, $\diamond$, to P. This requires two steps, as so far $\diamond$ is only defined on $D(s_0)$, separately for each $s_0 \in$ Store.

Note that for each $a_0 \in A$, $a_0 = \langle s_0,L_0\rangle$, and for each $f \in P$, $f(a_0) = f(s_0) \in D(s_0)$. Thus the following is well-defined:

(*) $$f\diamond g(a_0) = f(s_0) \diamond g(s_0) \in D(s_0).$$

As a notational convenience, for $\Sigma n_i a_i \in D$, let the index set run over the a_i for which $n_i \neq 0$. Now each $a_i = \langle s_i,L_i\rangle$ determines $D(s_i)$. So for each pair $f,g \in P$, $f\diamond g(a_i)$ is defined by (*) and, in fact, so is $f\diamond g(n_i a_i) = n_i f\diamond g(a_i) = n_i(f(s_i)\diamond g(s_i)) \in D(s_i)$

Now as $D(s_i) \subseteq D$ for all i,

(**) $$f\diamond g(\Sigma n_i a_i) = \Sigma n_i(f\diamond g(a_i))$$

By this, we may well-define

2.5 Definition. $\diamond: P \times P \to P$ is defined by (**).

2.6 Theorem. The algebraic system $\langle P,+,\diamond\rangle$ is a commutative semiring, where $f+g(d) = f(d)+g(d)$, with the always zero function as 0 and the function <u>id</u>$(s) = \langle s,\emptyset\rangle$ as the semiring identity.

The interpretation of these data is: $f+g$ is the behavior of the nondeterministic combination $(f \underset{\sim\sim}{or}\ g)$, while $f\diamond g$ is the behavior of the parallel (fork-join) combination of f and g.

It only remains to consider the composition of program behaviors. Because of the active location considerations, this is not just the functional composition of the linear transformations in P. If $f_{i+1}\langle s_i,L_i\rangle = f_{i+1}(s_i) = \langle s_{i+1},L_{i+1}\rangle$, $i = 0,1$, then define

$$f_1 \blacksquare f_2\langle s_0,L_0\rangle = \langle s_2,L_1\cup L_2\rangle$$

as the composite program may actively store anywhere in $L_1\cup L_2$. By linearity we have

2.7 Definition. For $f_1,f_2 \in P$, $f_1\blacksquare f_2$ is determined as follows: If $f_1(s_0) = \sum_i m_i\langle s_i,L_i\rangle$ and $f_2(s_i) = \sum_{j_i} n_{j_i}\langle s_{j_i},L_{j_i}\rangle$ then

$f_1\blacksquare f_2(s_0) = \sum_i \sum_{j_i} m_i n_{j_i}\langle s_{j_i},L_i\cup L_{j_i}\rangle$.

2.8 Theorem. The operation $\blacksquare: P\times P \to P$ is associative and the function $\underline{id}(s) = \langle s,\emptyset\rangle$ is an identity for it.

We now have that both $\langle P,+,\diamond\rangle$ and $\langle P,+,\blacksquare\rangle$ are semirings with common identity element. Little seems to be known about such paired semirings.

3. Nondeterministic semantics of the join operation.-- The smooth development of the previous section depended crucially on keeping everything based to obtain only finite formal sums. This was possible because the locations outside of $L_1\cup L_2$ were known to contain values undisturbed from a single base store s_0. A join of two arbitrary control lines will not have this pleasantness, leading to infinities in attempting to formalize the possible race conditions.

Our idea is to stay as finite as possible, but to record the infinities in an appropriate algebraic system when they occur. A nondeterministic state is then a pair consisting of a finite part and an infinite part.

To this end, let A be as before and define, for $a_1,a_2 \in A$ and $s \in$ Store: $s \in J(a_1,a_2)$ iff

$$\ell \in \text{Loc:}\qquad s(\ell) = \begin{cases} s_1(\ell) & \text{if } \ell \in L_1-L_2 \\ s_2(\ell) & \text{if } \ell \in L_2-L_1 \end{cases}$$

and

$$s(\ell) \in \{s_1(\ell), s_2(\ell)\} \quad \text{if} \quad \ell \notin L_1 \cup L_2 \quad \text{or if} \quad \ell \in L_1 \cap L_2.$$

We write $J(a_1,a_2) \in F$ if $J(a_1,a_2)$ is a finite set.

Let R be a commutative semiring and let F be the left R-module freely generated by A. This is the finite part. Let K be a commutative semiring and let C be a left K-module which is countably complete with respect to addition in C and generated by A. This is the infinite part. Let $\tau: R \to K$ be a semiring homomorphism.

A typical example of this structure is obtained by: $R = \mathbb{N}$, $K = \mathbb{B}$, $\tau: \mathbb{N} \to \mathbb{B}$ sends zero to zero and everything else to one. The free left $\mathbb{B}$-module generated by A is countably complete. Information about the number of paths is lost when passing from the finite part to the infinite part.

Now C is a left R-module by defining $\bar{\tau}: R \times C \to C$ as $\tau(r,\beta) = \tau(r)\beta$. Therefore $F \times C$ is a left R-module with scalar multiplication $r\langle\alpha,\beta\rangle = \langle r\alpha, \tau(r)\beta\rangle$. Note that setting $K = 0$ recovers section 2 for semiring R.

3.0 Proposition. $F \times C \cong F \bullet C$.

Let $D = F \bullet C$ and define $\nabla: F^2 \to D$ by linear extension from $\nabla: A^2 \to D$ which is given by: For $a_i = \langle s_i, L_i\rangle \in A$, $i = 1,2$,

$$a_1 \nabla a_2 = \begin{cases} \langle \sum_{s \in J(a_1,a_2)} \langle s, L_1 \cup L_2\rangle, 0\rangle & \text{if } J(a_1,a_2) \in F \\ \langle 0, \sum_{s \in J(a_1,a_2)} \langle s, L_1 \cup L_2\rangle\rangle & \text{if not.} \end{cases}$$

3.1 Lemma. The function $\nabla: F^2 \to D$ is commutative.

However, $\nabla: F^2 \to D$ is not a homomorphism from the R-module F^2 to D. Instead we have

3.2 Lemma. $\nabla: F^2 \to D$ is a bilinear map:

$$(\alpha_1+\alpha_2)\nabla\beta = \alpha_1\nabla\beta + \alpha_2\nabla\beta.$$

$$\alpha\nabla(\beta_1+\beta_2) = \alpha\nabla\beta_1 + \alpha\nabla\beta_2,$$

$$r\alpha\nabla\beta = \alpha\nabla r\beta.$$

We will need the operation $\blacklozenge: A^2 \to C$:

$$a_1 \blacklozenge a_2 = \langle 0, \sum_{s \in J(a_1,a_2)} \langle s, L_1 \cup L_2\rangle\rangle$$

where $a_i = \langle s_i, L_i\rangle$, $i = 1,2$.

Now we may define $\nabla: C^2 \to D$ and $\nabla: F \times C \to D$ by linear extension from the generators: For $a \in A$ (viewed either as a generator of C or of F) and $\beta = \Sigma \ell_i a_i \in C$,

$$a\nabla\beta = \Sigma\ell_i(a\bullet a_i)$$

where $\ell_i<0,\gamma> = <0,\ell_i\gamma>$.

Finally in this line of definitions, $\nabla\colon D^2 \to D$ is given by

$$\begin{aligned} &<\Sigma r_i a_i,\beta_1> \nabla <\Sigma s_j a_j,\beta_2> \\ &= \Sigma r_i a_i \nabla \Sigma s_j a_j \\ &\quad + \Sigma\tau(r_i)(a_i\nabla\beta_2) \\ &\quad + \Sigma\tau(s_j)(\beta_1\nabla a_j) \\ &\quad + \beta_1\nabla\beta_2. \end{aligned}$$

3.3 Lemma. $\nabla\colon D^2 \to D$ is a bilinear map.

As before, only some of the linear endomorphisms on D denote single-entrance, single-exit programs. First, axioms P1 and P2 hold for all generators A. In addition, we require continuity,

P3: $\Sigma\ell_i a_i \in C$: $f(\Sigma\ell_i a_i) = \Sigma\ell_i f(a_i)$

and the additional axiom P4, given after some explanation. Every endomorphism $f\colon D \to D$ is the biproduct of two endomorphisms $f_F\colon F \to D$ and $f_C\colon C \to D$, $f = f_F \oplus f_C$. Intuitively, the behavior of a program on infinite data is an extension of its behavior on finite data. To this end, axiom P4 requires that the infinite part, f_C, agrees with the finite part, f_F, wherever possible: Notice that $\hat{\tau}\colon F \to C$: $\Sigma m_i a_i \mapsto \Sigma\tau(m_i)a_i$ is a linear transformation of R-modules.

P4: For $f = f_F \oplus f_C$,

$$\begin{array}{ccc} F & \xrightarrow{\quad f_F \quad} & F \oplus C \quad D \\ {\scriptstyle\hat{\tau}}\downarrow & & \downarrow{\scriptstyle \hat{\tau}\oplus C} \\ C & \xrightarrow[\quad f_C \quad]{} & F \oplus C \quad D \end{array}$$

commutes.

3.4 Definition. The linear endomorphisms of D satisfying P1, P2, P3 and P4 are said to be P-computable functions. The set of such is denoted by P.

Consider defining the fork-join combination of P-computable functions by $f\diamond g = \Delta\cdot(f\times g)\nabla$, where Δ is the diagonal map, $\Delta(d) = d\oplus d$.

3.5 Proposition. If f, g have only finite output for input s, i.e., $f(s) = <\Sigma n_i a_i,0>$ and similarly for $g(s)$, then $f\diamond g$ has only finite output.

3.6 Theorem. The algebraic system $<P,+,\diamond>$ satisfies all the axioms for a commutative semiring except that it lacks an identity for $\diamond$.

The problem arises from the use of the diagonal map, Δ. This causes a loss of information in that individual active stores are no longer paired and, for instance, $id \diamond id \neq id$. We remedy this situation by using tensor products as the semantics of multiple control lines.

4. Tensor Algebra for Join. -- If M is an R-module for commutative semiring R, the tensor product M⊗M is the set of congruence classes determined by the bilinearity equations

$$<\alpha_1+\alpha_2,\beta> \equiv <\alpha_1,\beta> + <\alpha_2,\beta>,$$
$$<\alpha,\beta_1+\beta_2> \equiv <\alpha,\beta_1> + <\alpha,\beta_2>,$$
$$r<\alpha,\beta> \equiv <r\alpha,\beta> \equiv <\alpha,r\beta>,$$

on the free module with generators M^2. Now every bilinear map f: $M^2 \to M$ gives rise to a unique linear map f: M⊗M → M such that with the canonical bilinear map b: $M^2 \to$ M⊗M, $f = b \cdot \hat{f}$. We drop the hat notation in, e.g., ∇: D⊗D → D.

4.1 Definition. The function $\diamond$: P×P → P is given by $f \diamond g = \Delta \cdot (f \otimes g) \cdot \nabla$, where Δ is the tensor diagonal map, $\Delta<\alpha,\beta> = <\alpha,\beta>\otimes<\alpha,\beta>$.

4.2 Theorem. The algebraic system <P,+,$\diamond$> is a commutative semiring with identity id(s) = <s,∅>∈F. Furthermore, if K = 0 this system is exactly the system of theorem 2.6.

The composition of program behaviors is similar to that for the fork-join situation. There is, however, a pleasant description within the tensor algebra: Define the function

$$u(<s,L>,<s',L'>) = <s,L\cup L'>$$

on the set of active stores, A, and extend this definition bilinearly to u: D⊗D → D, i.e., so that for example we have

$$u(<s_1,L_1> + <s_2,L_2>,<s,L>) = <s_1,L_1\cup L> + <s_2,L_2\cup L>,$$
$$u(<s,L>,<s_1,L_1> + <s_2,L_2>) = <s,L\cup L_1> + <s,L\cup L_2>,$$
$$u(ra_1,a_2) = u(a_1,ra_2) \text{ for } a_1,a_2\in A, r\in R.$$

This uniquely determines u: D⊗D → D. Let s: R → D: r ↦ r<s,∅> ∈ F be the given map for each state s.

4.3 Lemma. u is associative, $(u\otimes id_D)\cdot u = (id_D\otimes u)\cdot u$, while for each s, $(id_D\otimes s)\cdot u \cong id_D$, so that D is a quasi-R-algebra with product $a_1a_2 = u(a_1\otimes a_2)$ and multiplicative right units s(1) for each s.

4.4 Lemma. If f and g are P-computable endomorphisms of D, then $f\cdot\Delta\cdot(g\otimes id)\cdot u$ is also P-computable.

Therefore we have

4.5 Definition. The composition of P-computable functions, $\blacksquare : P\times P \to P$, is given by the functional composition, $f\blacksquare g = f\cdot\Delta\cdot(g\otimes\underline{id})\cdot u$.

4.6 Theorem. The algebraic system $\langle P,+,\blacksquare\rangle$ is a semiring with identity $\underline{id}(s) = \langle s,\emptyset\rangle \in F$. Furthermore, if $K = 0$ this system is exactly the system of Theorem 2.8.

The critical section of flowchart (3) is $\nabla\cdot h\cdot\Delta\colon D\otimes D \to D\otimes D$, a linear transformation. The entire flowchart is $(f\otimes g)\cdot\nabla\cdot h\cdot\Delta\colon D\otimes D \to D\otimes D$, which is again a linear transformation. However, even if f, g, and h are P-computable, neither $\nabla\cdot h\cdot\Delta$ nor $(f\otimes g)\cdot\nabla\cdot h\cdot\Delta$ are P-computable as axiom P1 fails. This is directly due to the race conditions in the join, ∇. Therefore, the behaviors of programs formed from P-computable functions together with join and fork form a proper superset of the P-computable functions.

5. Conclusion.-- The semantics presented handles a relatively narrow, but still interesting, class of nondeterministic, parallel programs. The deficiency is the lack of a suitable semantics for the confluence of two control lines. Confluence, in the presence of multiple processors, results in several processors on the same control line. This requires an essential addition to the concepts presented here, [Main & Benson, 1982].

If one can otherwise ensure that two processors on the same control path never interact or that there never is more than one processor on a control path, then the nondeterminism represented by sum is an adequate semantics for confluence, [Benson, 1979].

With this proviso, there are at least three techniques to solve the recursion equations which arise in specifying the behavior of fully looping programs such as flowchart (3). The first is to note that the endomorphisms in question may be represented as pairs of (infinite) matrices, the first over the semiring R, the second over K. The iterative matrix equations resulting from the looping constructs may or may not have solutions, depending upon the structure of the matrices in question and the structure of R, [Benson, 1982]. The second method is the least fixed point techniques in [Poigné, 1981], provided the base semirings R and K are idempotent. The third is the extremely general method of [Benson & Guessarian, 1981] for finding canonical solutions to recursion schemes in any universal algebra. In this technique, solutions will always exist irrespective of the structure of R and K.

Acknowledgments.-- I appreciate the aid of Dr. Hai Joon Kim in formulating section 2 and Mr. Michael G. Main for fruitful discussions resulting in many improvements.

REFERENCES

D. B. Benson (1979), In Scott-Strachey style denotational semantics, parallelism implies nondeterminism, to appear in Math. Sys. Theory, v. 15. (Tech. Rpt. CS-79-054).

D. B. Benson (1982), Counting paths: nondeterminism as linear algebra, WSU Comput. Sci. Tech. Rpt. CS-82-084.

D. B. Benson and I. Guessarian (1981), Algebraic solutions to recursion schemes, WSU Comput. Sci. Tech. Rpt. CS-81-079.

C. C. Elgot (1979), The multiplicity semiring of a Boolean ring, IBM Research Report RC 7450.

N. Francez, D. J. Lehmann, A. Pnueli (1980), A linear history semantics for distributed languages, IEEE Conf. Record of 21st FoCS Symp., 143-151.

R. M. Karp and R. E. Miller (1969), Parallel program schemata, J. Comput. Sys. Sci. 3, 147-195.

R. J. Lorentz and D. B. Benson (1980), Deterministic and nondeterministic flowchart interpretations, WSU Comput. Sci. Tech. Rpt. CS-80-066.

M. G. Main and D. B. Benson (1982), An algebra for nondeterministic, distributed processes, WSU Comput. Sci. Tech. Rpt. CS-82-087.

D. Park (1980), On the semantics of fair parallelism, LNCS 86, Springer-Verlag, 509-526.

D. Park (1981), Concurrency and automata on infinite sequences, LNCS 104, Springer-Verlag, 167-183.

A. Poigné (1981), Using least fixed points to characterize formal computations of non-deterministic equations, LNCS 107, Springer-Verlag, 447-459.

W. C. Rounds and S. D. Brookes (1981), Possible futures, acceptances, refusals and communicating processes, IEEE Conf. Record of 22nd FoCS Symp., Nashville, TN.

A FORMALIZED PROOF SYSTEM FOR TOTAL CORRECTNESS OF WHILE PROGRAMS

J.A. Bergstra
Department of Computer Science
University of Leiden
Wassenaarseweg 80
2333 AL Leiden

J.W. Klop
Department of Computer Science
Mathematical Centre
Kruislaan 413
1098 SJ Amsterdam

ABSTRACT

We introduce datatype specifications based on schemes, a slight generalization of first order specifications. For a schematic specification $(\Sigma, \mathbb{E})$, Hoare's Logic $HL(\Sigma, \mathbb{E})$ for partial correctness is defined as usual and on top of it a proof system $(\Sigma, \mathbb{E}) \vdash p \rightarrow S \downarrow$ for termination assertions is defined. The system is first order in nature, but we prove it sound and complete w.r.t. a second order semantics. We provide a translation of a standard proof system $HL_T(A)$ for total correctness on a structure A into our format.

0. INTRODUCTION

In this note we will present a formalized proof system for total correctness of while-programs. Its merits should be first of all that it acts as a first order proof system (although we can, at this moment, only prove a soundness result w.r.t. a second order semantics which allows fewer models for a specification than the usual first order semantics would do). The advantage of having a formalized proof system $(\Sigma, \mathbb{E}) \vdash p \rightarrow S \downarrow$ for program termination which is just as first order as Hoare's logic $HL(\Sigma, \mathbb{E}) \vdash \{p\}S\{q\}$ for partial correctness is both the possibility of mechanisation and the effect of giving a firm basis for a logical (proof theoretic) investigation of the system.

An essential point is that we want to base our proof system on a specification $(\Sigma, \mathbb{E})$ rather than on a structure A, which is done by most authors. For Hoare's Logic there is no strict need either to consider HL(A) for a fixed datastructure A, and the more general case of $HL(\Sigma,E)$ is clearly of substantial importance.

In various fairly standard approaches to total correctness, such as in HAREL [7] and [8] for deterministic sequential processes and in APT & OLDEROG [1] and GRÜMBERG et al. [6] for fair parallel computation the essence of using a fixed domain A is in the assumption that certain parts of A, as a many-sorted algebra, are well-ordered. This gives rise to quite natural proof rules like the system $HL_T(A)$ that we explain in section 1.1 in order to compare it with our system.

Instead we will develop a device called *schemes* which constitutes a slight generalization of the first order predicate logic. For a specification with schemes we write $(\Sigma, \mathbb{E})$ (whereas (Σ,E) denotes a specification with $E \subseteq L(\Sigma)$). Using schemes we can work in quite a flexible way with signature extensions, a method that proved to be useful and to be of first order character in BERGSTRA & KLOP [2]. Thus we obtain a proof system for termination assertions $(\Sigma, \mathbb{E}) \vdash p \to S \downarrow$ on top of a logic for partial correctness, in the same way as in BERGSTRA & KLOP [2] proof systems for program inclusion are obtained from a partial correctness logic.

We will now sum up the main notations and results.

For a specification $(\Sigma, \mathbb{E})$ with $\mathbb{E}$ a set of schemes, the logic of partial correctness $HL(\Sigma, \mathbb{E})$ brings nothing new. A proof system $(\Sigma, \mathbb{E}) \vdash p \to S \downarrow$ is then defined such that soundness can be shown for a semantics $\models_S$ in Lemma 5.

As a relation of $(\Sigma, \mathbb{E})$, p and S, $\vdash$ is recursively enumerable, thus deserving its denotation as a proof system.

Given a fixed A let $\mathbb{E}_A$ be the set of all schemes Φ over Σ_A that are true in A in the sense of $\models_S$. There is the following completeness result:

<u>THEOREM</u> (9.2) $(\Sigma_A, \mathbb{E}_A) \vdash p \to S \downarrow \iff A \models p \to S \downarrow$.

In order to compare our system with a usual formalism using well-ordered sets we take the notation [p] S [q] for total correctness (i.e. $[p]\ S\ [q] \equiv \{p\}\ S\ \{q\}\ \&\ p \to S \downarrow$) and define a system $HL_T(A) \vdash [p]\ S\ [q]$ for datastructures A with a fixed well-ordering $\leq$ on it. Then we define a canonical specification $(\Sigma_A, \mathbb{E}_A^{<})$ of such A and state the following result:

THEOREM (11.1) $HL_T(A) \vdash [p]\ S\ [q] \Rightarrow HL(\Sigma_A, \mathbb{E}_A^{<}) \vdash \{p\}\ S\ \{q\}$ and $(\Sigma_A, \mathbb{E}_A^{<}) \vdash p \to S \downarrow$.

This result says that the proposed formalism can be used to represent methods using well-ordered sets.

Some final remarks should be made. First of all it would be nice to have a logic for total correctness which is of a first order nature and which is sound and complete for a semantics of specifications and programs which is of first order nature as well. For partial correctness the corresponding problem was solved in BERGSTRA & TUCKER [5]. There a so called axiomatic semantics for <u>while</u>-programs is given such that HL is sound and complete for it in a most general and first order way. It is not clear to us whether or not a similar result can be obtained for total correctness. Anyhow, if we consider simultaneously first order semantics for specifications and the operational semantics (which is not first order) for programs, a proof system $\mathrel{|\!\sim}$ for $(\Sigma,E) \mathrel{|\!\sim} p \to S \downarrow$

is either not sound or trivial. This follows immediately from the Compactness Theorem.

Secondly it should be noticed that in principle it is possible to produce a sophisticated proof theory of $(\Sigma, \mathbb{E}) \vdash p \to S \downarrow$. Indeed, for one structure A already many different and plausible specifications $(\Sigma, \mathbb{E}_i)$ can be found which have different proof theoretic properties. Of course a similar line of investigation is possible for methods using well-ordered sets, but that will require replacing the well-ordering by a better one from time to time. Essentially this involves a modification of the datastructure which seems less attractive from a theoretical point of view.

1. SCHEMES

A scheme will be a generalization of an assertion. Next to the usual predicate-logical symbols a scheme may also contain symbols φ_i^n. The φ_i^n function syntactically as n-ary relation symbols (although their semantics is quite different); the n will mostly be omitted. Formally:

DEFINITION 1.1. The set $Sch(\Sigma)$ of *schemes over the signature* Σ, with typical variable Φ , is inductively defined by:

$$\Phi ::= P_i^n(t_1,\ldots,t_n),\ t_1 = t_2,\ \varphi_i^n(t_1,\ldots,t_n)\ (\text{all } n,i) \mid$$

$$\Phi_1 \vee \Phi_2,\ \Phi_1 \wedge \Phi_2,\ \neg\Phi\ ,\ \forall x\Phi,\ \exists x\Phi.$$

Here the P_i^n are n-ary predicate symbols from Σ, $t_i \in Ter(\Sigma)$ (the set of Σ-terms) and the φ_i^n are *scheme variables*. The latter are not part of Σ, but will be considered to be standardly included in the language (as logical symbols), just like the ordinary variables x,y,... . Note that $Ass(\Sigma) \subseteq Sch(\Sigma)$, where $Ass(\Sigma)$ is the set of assertions over Σ.

EXAMPLE 1.2. (i) The induction scheme IND $\equiv [\varphi(0) \wedge \forall x(\varphi(x) \to \varphi(Sx))] \to \forall x\varphi(x)$.
(ii) $\varphi_1 \to (\varphi_2 \to \varphi_1)$, a scheme with 0-ary scheme variables.

NOTATION 1.3. If Φ is a scheme containing precisely the scheme variables $\varphi_1,\ldots,\varphi_n$, we write $\Phi \equiv \Phi(\varphi_1,\ldots,\varphi_n)$.

2. SUBSTITUTION IN SCHEMES

The intended meaning of the scheme variables is that one may substitute assertions for them. For technical reasons it is convenient to allow even substitution of schemes for the scheme variables.

DEFINITION 2.1. Let $\Phi, \Psi \in Sch$. Then $\Phi[\Psi/\varphi(x_1,\ldots,x_n)]$ is the result of replacing each occurrence of the form $\varphi(t_1,\ldots,t_n)$ $(t_i \in Ter)$ in Φ, by $\Psi[t_1,\ldots,t_n/x_1,\ldots,x_n]$. ('Ordinary' substitution $[\vec{t}/\vec{x}]$ in a scheme is defined just as for assertions.)

EXAMPLE 2.2. (i) Let $\Phi \equiv$ IND and $\Psi \equiv x+y = y+x$. Then $\mathrm{IND}[\Psi/\varphi(x)] \equiv \Psi[0/x] \wedge \forall x(\Psi[x/x] \rightarrow \Psi[Sx/x]) \rightarrow \forall x\Psi[x/x] \equiv 0+y = y+0 \wedge \forall x(x+y = y+x \rightarrow Sx+y = y + Sx) \rightarrow \forall x\ x+y = y+x$.
(ii) Let $\Phi \equiv \varphi_1 \rightarrow (\varphi_2 \rightarrow \varphi_1)$. Then $\Phi[\varphi(x)/\varphi_1][\varphi(x)/\varphi_2] \equiv \varphi(x) \rightarrow (\varphi(x) \rightarrow \varphi(x))$.

3. SEMANTICS OF SCHEMES

The most important one of the definitions below is no. (iii) where $A \models_s \Phi$ is defined: A is a standard model of Φ.

DEFINITION 3.1. (i) Let $\Phi \in Sch(\Sigma)$ and let $\Phi \equiv \Phi(\vec{\varphi})$. Then $\Phi \upharpoonright \Sigma = \{\Phi[\vec{p}/\vec{\varphi}] \mid \vec{p} \in Ass(\Sigma)\}$. (E.g., IND $\upharpoonright \Sigma_{PA}$ is the set of all induction axioms over the signature of Peano's Arithmetic.)
(ii) Let $A \in Alg$. Then $A \models \Phi$ abbreviates $A \models \Phi \upharpoonright \Sigma_A$. (E.g. we have $A \models$ IND for every model A of PA.)
(iii) $A \models_s \Phi \Longleftrightarrow \forall A' \geq A : A' \models \Phi$. Here $A' \geq A$ means: A' is an *expansion* of A (i.e. A plus added 'structure'). In words: Φ is schematically true in A. (E.g. $N \models_s$ IND. As a contrast, consider a nonstandard model N^* of PA. Then $N^* \models$ IND, but not $N^* \models_s$ IND.)
(iv) If $\mathbb{E} \subseteq Sch(\Sigma)$, we call $(\Sigma, \mathbb{E})$ a *scheme specification*. (Cf. an ordinary specification (Σ, E) where $E \subseteq Ass(\Sigma)$.) Example: $(\Sigma_{PA}, \mathbb{PA})$, i.e. Peano plus the scheme IND.
(v) Let $\Sigma' \geq \Sigma$. Then $(\Sigma, \mathbb{E})_{\Sigma'} = (\Sigma', \mathbb{E} \upharpoonright \Sigma')$. Here $\mathbb{E} \upharpoonright \Sigma' = \{\Phi[\vec{p}/\vec{\varphi}] \mid p \in Ass(\Sigma'), \Phi(\vec{\varphi}) \in \mathbb{E}\}$. (So, by attaching Σ' as subscript the scheme specification is transformed to an ordinary specification.)
(vi) Let $A \in Alg(\Sigma)$. Then $A \models (\Sigma, \mathbb{E})$ abbreviates $A \models (\Sigma, \mathbb{E})_\Sigma$.
(vii) Let $A \in Alg(\Sigma)$. Then: $A \models_s (\Sigma, \mathbb{E}) \Longleftrightarrow A \models_s \Phi, \forall \Phi \in \mathbb{E}$.
(viii) $Alg_s(\Sigma, \mathbb{E}) = \{A \in Alg(\Sigma) \mid A \models_s (\Sigma, \mathbb{E})\}$. (E.g. $Alg_s(\Sigma_{PA}, \mathbb{PA}) = \{N\}$.)
(ix) $Alg_s(\Sigma, \mathbb{E}) \models_s \Phi \Longleftrightarrow \forall A \in Alg_s(\Sigma, \mathbb{E})\ A \models_s \Phi$. Instead of the LHS we will also write simply $(\Sigma, \mathbb{E}) \models_s \Phi$.

4. DERIVABILITY OF SCHEMES

DEFINITION 4.1. $(\Sigma, \mathbb{E}) \vdash \Phi$ is defined as the usual derivability of an assertion from a specification (to this end the φ_i^n are treated as n-ary predicate symbols) plus the *substitution rule:*

$$\frac{\Phi_1}{\Phi_1[\Phi_2/\varphi(\vec{x})]}$$

for all $\Phi_1, \Phi_2 \in Sch(\Sigma)$ and all scheme variables φ.

PROPOSITION 4.2. $(\Sigma, \mathbb{E}) \vdash p \Leftrightarrow (\Sigma, \mathbb{E})_\Sigma \vdash p$, *for all* $p \in Ass(\Sigma)$.

PROOF. ($\Leftarrow$) trivial; ($\Rightarrow$) induction on the length of the proof of $(\Sigma, \mathbb{E}) \vdash p$. (This amounts to commutativity of substitution and derivability in the usual sense.) □

The following lemma presents a useful soundness result:

LEMMA 5. $(\Sigma, \mathbb{E}) \vdash \Phi \Rightarrow (\Sigma, \mathbb{E}) \models_s \Phi$.

PROOF. Assume $(\Sigma, \mathbb{E}) \vdash \Phi$ and consider a structure A with $A \models_s (\Sigma, \mathbb{E})$. We show that $A \models_s \Phi$. Therefore consider $A' \geq A$ with $A' \models (\Sigma, \mathbb{E})$ and $\Sigma' = \Sigma_{A'}$.
The following sequence of implications establishes $A' \models \Phi$:

$$\begin{aligned}
&(\Sigma, \mathbb{E}) \vdash \Phi(\vec{\varphi}) \Rightarrow \\
&(\Sigma', \mathbb{E}) \vdash \Phi(\vec{\varphi}) \Rightarrow \\
&(\Sigma', \mathbb{E}) \vdash \Phi(\vec{p}) \text{ for all } p \in Ass(\Sigma') \Rightarrow (4.2) \\
&(\Sigma', \mathbb{E})_{\Sigma'} \vdash \Phi(\vec{p}) \text{ " " " " " } \Rightarrow \\
&(\Sigma, \mathbb{E})_{\Sigma'} \vdash \Phi(\vec{p}) \text{ " " " " "}
\end{aligned}$$

Of course $A' \models (\Sigma, \mathbb{E})$ implies $A' \models (\Sigma, \mathbb{E})_{\Sigma'}$ and consequently

$$A' \models \Phi(\vec{p}) \text{ for all } p \in Ass(\Sigma')$$

which is $A' \models \Phi$. □

REMARK 5.1. The corresponding completeness result fails. To see this let us consider the example $(\Sigma_{PA}, \mathbb{P}\mathbb{A})$. Completeness of $\vdash$ w.r.t. $\models_s$ would entail

$$(\Sigma_{PA}, \mathbb{P}\mathbb{A}) \vdash \Phi \Leftrightarrow (\Sigma_{PA}, \mathbb{P}\mathbb{A}) \models_s \Phi$$

for all Φ, and especially for all $p \in Ass(\Sigma_{PA})$: $(\Sigma_{PA}, \mathbb{P}\mathbb{A}) \vdash p \Leftrightarrow (\Sigma_{PA}, \mathbb{P}\mathbb{A}) \models_s p$.
Now $Alg_s(\Sigma_{PA}, \mathbb{P}\mathbb{A}) = \{N\}$ and we find $(\Sigma_{PA}, \mathbb{P}\mathbb{A}) \vdash p \Leftrightarrow N \models_s p$.
From 4.2 and $(\Sigma_{PA}, \mathbb{P}\mathbb{A})_{\Sigma_{PA}} = (\Sigma_{PA}, PA)$ this leads to $PA \vdash p \Leftrightarrow N \models_s p$

which contradicts Gödel's incompleteness theorem.

DEFINITION 6. The schematic theory $\mathbb{E}_A$ of a structure A is defined as the set of all schemes $\Phi \in Sch(\Sigma_A)$ such that $A \models_s \Phi$.

LEMMA 6.1. *The following are equivalent:*

(i) $(\Sigma_A, \mathbb{E}_A) \vdash \Phi$

(ii) $(\Sigma_A, \mathbb{E}_A) \models_s \Phi$

(iii) $A \models_s \Phi$.

PROOF. (i) ⇒ (ii) according to Lemma 5. (ii) ⇒ (iii) ⇒ (i) are evident from the definitions. □

DEFINITION 7. A^s is the maximal (full) expansion of A, i.e. A^s is a structure (with presumably an uncountable signature) which contains a name for each possible relation function or constant on it.

The following property follows easily:

PROPOSITION 7.1. $A \models_s \Phi \Longleftrightarrow A^s \models \Phi$.

A^s will be used in the proof of Theorem 9.2. Moreover, in sections 10 and 11 we will use the partial correctness logic $HL(\Sigma, \mathbb{E})$ for schematic specifications.

DEFINITION 7.2. $HL(\Sigma, \mathbb{E}) \vdash \{\varphi\}\ S\ \{\psi\}$ is Hoare's logic over $(\Sigma, \mathbb{E})$.

Syntactically one requires that $S \in WP(\Sigma)$ and $\varphi, \psi \in Sch(\Sigma)$. Its axioms and rules are exactly the same as usually for HL, the only difference being that schemes may occur at the position of assertions in the original system.

8. TERMINATION ASSERTIONS

DEFINITION 8.1. (i) Let $p \in Ass(\Sigma)$ and $S \in WP(\Sigma)$. Then $p \to S\downarrow$ is a termination assertion.

(ii) (Semantics:) If $A \in Alg(\Sigma)$ then: $A \models p \to S\downarrow \Longleftrightarrow$ S converges on every input $\vec{a} \in A$ such that $A \models p(\underline{\vec{a}})$.

The next definition is based on the concept of 'prototype proof' $\pi(S)$ as defined in BERGSTRA & KLOP [2]. This is roughly a scheme of which every ordinary proof of $\{p\}S\{q\}$ is a substitution instance. To this end we view a proof of $\{p\}S\{q\}$ as an 'interpolated statement', i.e. a statement in which assertions may occur; see Example 8.5 of a $\pi(S)$. For the precise details we refer to BERGSTRA & KLOP [2].

Simply speaking a prototype proof $\pi(S)$ is obtained by using scheme variables as precondition, postcondition, intermediate assertions and invariants. Let $\varphi \ldots \psi$ be the scheme variables occurring in $\pi(S)$ in linear order. Then the logical information that is required about $\varphi \ldots \psi$ is a scheme $\varphi \overset{S}{\leadsto} \psi$ which incorporates all implications that are used in applications of the rule of consequence.

<u>DEFINITION 8.2</u>. Let $S \in \mathcal{WP}(\Sigma)$. Then $\varphi \overset{S}{\leadsto} \psi$ abbreviates the scheme $\forall(\bigwedge \kappa(\{\varphi\}\pi(S)\{\psi\}))$, where $\pi(S)$ is the prototype proof of S, κ denotes the set of implications used in $\{\varphi\}\pi(S)\{\psi\}$, and $\forall$ denotes the universal closure. Here φ,ψ are scheme variables different from those in $\pi(S)$. (As in BERGSTRA & KLOP [2] and in Example 8.5, we will denote the scheme variables in $\pi(S)$ by $r_1, r_2, \ldots$.)

Now we have the following proposition; the proof is routine and therefore omitted.

<u>PROPOSITION 8.3</u>. (i) $\varphi \overset{S_1;S_2}{\leadsto} \psi \vdash \varphi \overset{S_1}{\leadsto} r \wedge r \overset{S_2}{\leadsto} \psi$ *for some* r.
(ii) $\varphi_1 \overset{S}{\leadsto} \psi_1 \wedge \varphi_2 \overset{S}{\leadsto} \psi_2 \vdash \varphi_1 \wedge \varphi_2 \overset{S}{\leadsto} \psi_1 \wedge \psi_2$.
(iii) $HL(\Sigma, \mathbb{E}) \vdash \{\varphi\}S\{\psi\} \Leftrightarrow (\Sigma, \mathbb{E}) \vdash \varphi \overset{S}{\leadsto} \psi$ *for some proof scheme* $\varphi \overset{S}{\leadsto} \psi$.

(In fact we must write $\varphi(\vec{x})$, $\psi(\vec{x})$ *etc. instead of* φ,ψ *where* $\vec{x}$ *is a list of the relevant variables.)*

The next definition is crucial.

<u>DEFINITION 8.4</u>. Let $p \to S\downarrow$ be a termination assertion. Then $\Phi(p \to S\downarrow)$ is the corresponding *termination scheme*, defined by:

$$\Phi(p \to S\downarrow) \equiv (\{p \wedge \varphi(\vec{x})\} \overset{S}{\leadsto} \{\underline{\text{false}}\}) \to \neg \exists\vec{x}(p \wedge \varphi(\vec{x})).$$

Here $\vec{x}$ is a list of the free variables in p and the variables in S.

<u>EXAMPLE 8.5</u>. Let S ≡ <u>while</u> x ≠ 0 <u>do</u> x:= P(x) <u>od</u>, in the signature of PA; P is the predecessor function.

```
Now   π(S) ≡
      {r0(x)}
      {r1(x)}
while x ≠ 0 do
        {r1(x) ∧ x ≠ 0}
        {r2(Px)}
   x:= P(x)
        {r2(x)}
        {r1(x)}
od
        {r1(x) ∧ x = 0}
        {r3(x)}.
```

Let us determine the termination scheme $\Phi(\underline{\text{true}} \to S\downarrow)$.

$\varkappa(\{\underline{\text{true}} \wedge \varphi(x)\}\ \pi(S)\{\underline{\text{false}}\}) =$

$\{\ \underline{\text{true}} \wedge \varphi(x) \to r_0(x),$
$\quad r_0(x) \to r_1(x),$
$\quad r_1(x) \wedge x \neq 0 \to r_2(Px),$
$\quad r_2(x) \to r_1(x),$
$\quad r_1(x) \wedge x = 0 \to r_3(x),$
$\quad r_3(x) \to \underline{\text{false}}\}.$

Now $\Phi(\underline{\text{true}} \to S\downarrow) = \sigma \to \neg\, \exists x\ \varphi(x)$, where σ is the universal closure of the conjunction of the six implications above.

Note that $\Phi \equiv \Phi(\underline{\text{true}} \to S\downarrow)$ is none other than IND, to be precise: $(\Sigma_{PA}, \mathbb{P}\mathbb{A}) \vdash \Phi \leftrightarrow \text{IND}$. Here $\Phi \to \text{IND}$ follows by the substitution $\varphi(x) \equiv r_0(x) \equiv r_1(x) \equiv r_2(x)$ in Φ and by deriving from σ that $\neg\, \varphi(0) \wedge \forall x(\neg\varphi(x) \to \neg\, \varphi(Sx))$ (where S denotes the successor function).

<u>NOTATION 8.6</u>. We will write often $(\Sigma, \mathbb{E}) \vdash p \to S\downarrow$ instead of $(\Sigma, \mathbb{E}) \vdash \Phi(p \to S\downarrow)$.

9. Before formulating the main theorem we need the following proposition, whose routine proof is omitted.

<u>PROPOSITION 9.1</u>. $A^S \models \Phi(p \to S\downarrow) \Longleftrightarrow A^S \models p \to S\downarrow$.

<u>THEOREM 9.2</u>. *The following are equivalent:*

(i) $(\Sigma_A, \mathbb{E}_A) \vdash \Phi(p \to S\downarrow)$

(ii) $A \models_s \Phi(p \to S\downarrow)$

(iii) $A \models p \to S\downarrow$.

<u>COMMENT</u>: This result indicates the completeness of $(\Sigma, \mathbb{E}) \vdash \Phi(p \to S\downarrow)$ as a logic for total correctness.

<u>PROOF</u>: (i) $\Longleftrightarrow$ (ii) by Lemma 6.1. (ii) $\Longleftrightarrow$ (iii):

$A \models_s \Phi(p \to S\downarrow) \Longleftrightarrow$ (by Proposition 7.1)
$A^S \models \Phi(p \to S\downarrow) \Longleftrightarrow$ (by Proposition 9.1)
$A^S \models p \to S\downarrow \Longleftrightarrow$ (trivially)
$A \models p \to S\downarrow$. $\square$

10. $(\Sigma_{PA}, \mathbb{P}\mathbb{A})$, AN EXAMPLE IN DETAIL

Let N be the structure $(\omega,+,\cdot,S,P,0)$ and let $\mathbb{P}\mathbb{A}$ be a suitable version of Peano's arithmetic on N with a scheme for induction as indicated in the example in 1.2

We will list here some properties of the partial and total correctness logics based on $(\Sigma, \mathbb{P}\mathbb{A}) = (\Sigma_{PA}, \mathbb{P}\mathbb{A})$.

As a matter of fact $(\Sigma, \mathbb{P}\mathbb{A}) \vdash p \to S\downarrow$ is incomplete for total correctness on N. This is easily seen from the fact that the set of programs S with $(\Sigma, \mathbb{P}\mathbb{A}) \vdash \underline{true} \to S\downarrow$ is Σ^0_1 whereas on the other hand $N \models \underline{true} \to S\downarrow$ is a complete Π^0_2 predicate of programs S. The example 8.5 shows, however, that $(\Sigma, \mathbb{P}\mathbb{A})$ proves the termination of nontrivial programs.

11. RELATIONS WITH A STANDARD PROOF METHOD

Let A be a data structure containing a binary relation $<$ which is in fact a well ordering of A with smallest element $o \in |A|$. For A we have a system of proving total correctness $HL_T(A)$ and a canonical specification $(\Sigma_A, \mathbb{E}^{<}_{A})$. After detailed definitions we prove the following result which indicates that $HL_T(A)$ can be formalized via $(\Sigma_A, \mathbb{E}^{<}_{A})$ and its total and partial correctness logic.

<u>THEOREM 11.1</u>. *If*

$$HL_T(A) \vdash [p]S[q]$$

then

$$HL(\Sigma_A, \mathbb{E}^{<}_{A}) \vdash \{p\}S\{q\}$$

and

$$(\Sigma_A, \mathbb{E}^{<}_{A}) \vdash p \to S\downarrow .$$

The system $HL_T(A)$ is nothing new, versions of it appeared in [1], [5], [6] and [7] and various other places. The intended meaning of $[p]S[q]$ is: $\{p\}S\{q\}$ & $p \to S\downarrow$.

<u>DEFINITION 11.2</u>. $HL_T(A)$ has the following rules:

(i) $$[p[t/x]]\ x:= t\ \ [p]$$

(ii) $$\frac{[p]S_1[q] \quad [q]S_2[r]}{[p]S_1;S_2[r]}$$

(iii) $$\frac{[p \wedge b]S_1[q] \qquad [p \wedge \neg b]S_2[q]}{[p]\ \underline{if}\ b\ \underline{then}\ S_1\ \underline{else}\ S_2\ \underline{fi}\ [q]}$$

(iv) $$\frac{A \models p \to p' \quad [p']S[q'] \quad A \models q' \to q}{[p]S[q]}$$

(v) $$\frac{[I(\alpha) \wedge b]S[\exists\beta < \alpha\ I(\beta)] \quad A \models I(0) \to \neg b}{[I_0]\ \underline{while}\ b\ \underline{do}\ S\ \underline{od}\ [I_0 \wedge \neg b]}$$

where $I_0 \equiv \exists\alpha\, I(\alpha)$ and $\alpha,\beta \notin VAR(S)$.

11.3. $(\Sigma_A, \mathbb{E}^{<}_A)$ consists of E_A, the theory of A in $Ass(\Sigma_A)$, and the scheme $\mathbb{E}^{<}$ of induction along $<$:

$$\forall\beta[(\forall\alpha(\alpha < \beta \to \varphi(\alpha))) \to \varphi(\beta)] \to \forall\alpha\, \varphi(\alpha).$$

11.4. We can now prove the theorem. The first part concerns partial correctness. This is a straightforward induction on program depth, except in the case of the <u>while</u> rule. We will consider this case.

Suppose that

$$[I_0]\ \underline{\text{while}}\ b\ \underline{\text{do}}\ S_0\ \underline{\text{od}}\ [I_0 \wedge \neg b]$$

has been deduced from

$$[I(\alpha) \wedge b]S_0[\exists\beta < \alpha\ I(\beta)],\ A \models I(0) \to \neg b$$

with $I_0 \equiv \exists\alpha\, I(\alpha)$.

From the induction hypothesis we find (in $HL(\Sigma_A, \mathbb{E}^{<}_A)$):

$$\vdash \{I(\alpha) \wedge b\}\ S_0\ \{\exists\beta < \alpha\ I(\beta)\}$$

using the rule of consequence then

$$\vdash \{I(\alpha) \wedge b\}\ S_0 \{I_0\}$$

and with existential generalization on the precondition

$$\vdash \{I_0 \wedge b\}\ S_0\ \{I_0\}$$

then with the <u>while</u> rule

$$\vdash \{I_0\}\ \underline{\text{while}}\ b\ \underline{\text{do}}\ S_0\ \underline{\text{od}}\ \{I_0 \wedge \neg b\}.$$

11.5. The second part of the proof involves showing $(\Sigma_A, \mathbb{E}_A) \vdash p \to S\downarrow$. We abbreviate $(\Sigma_A, \mathbb{E}^{<}_A)$ to $(\Sigma, \mathbb{E})$ in this part of the proof. Of course we use induction on the structure of the proof of $[p]S[q]$. With X we denote the variables occurring free in p, S, q.

Suppose that $[p]S[q]$ was obtained by applying the rule of consequence to $[p']S[q']$, then by the induction hypothesis $(\Sigma, \mathbb{E}) \vdash p' \to S\downarrow$; an easy logical calculation then shows $(\Sigma, \mathbb{E}) \vdash p \to S$ because $\mathbb{E} \vdash p \to p'$.

For the case $S \equiv x := t$ we explain the argument in detail.

$$(\Sigma, \mathbb{E}) \vdash \forall X(p \wedge \varphi \to \underline{\text{false}}) \supset \neg\, \exists X\ p \wedge \varphi$$

because this is a tautology. Then

$$(\Sigma, \mathbb{E}) \vdash (\forall X(p \wedge \varphi \rightarrow r[t/x]) \wedge \forall x(r \rightarrow \underline{false})) \rightarrow \neg \exists X\, p \wedge \varphi\ .$$

thus

$$(\Sigma, \mathbb{E}) \vdash [p \wedge \varphi \overset{x:=t}{\rightsquigarrow} \underline{false}] \rightarrow \neg \exists X\, p \wedge \varphi$$

$$(\Sigma, \mathbb{E}) \vdash \varphi(p \rightarrow S\downarrow)$$

$$(\Sigma, \mathbb{E}) \vdash p \rightarrow S\downarrow .$$

The argument in case [p]S[q] was obtained from an application of the conditional rule 11.2 (iii) is entirely straightforward and is therefore omitted.

The harder cases of composition and iteration remain and we treat composition here. Let $S \equiv S_1;S_2$. Assume $HL_T(A) \vdash [p]S[q]$. Choose an assertion u with

$$HL_T(A) \vdash [p]S_1[u], HL_T(A) \vdash [u]S_2[q].$$

We show that $(\Sigma, \mathbb{E}) \vdash p \rightarrow S\downarrow$. It is sufficient to derive, working in $(\Sigma, \mathbb{E})$, $\neg\exists X\, p \wedge \varphi$ from $p \wedge \varphi \overset{S}{\rightsquigarrow} false$. So assume $p \wedge \varphi \overset{S}{\rightsquigarrow} \underline{false}$. Then for some r: $p \wedge \varphi \overset{S_1}{\rightsquigarrow} r$ and $r \overset{S_2}{\rightsquigarrow} \underline{false}$.

Because of $HL(\Sigma, \mathbb{E}) \vdash \{p\}S_1\{u\}$ (part (i) of this theorem) one obtains a proof scheme $p \overset{S_1}{\rightsquigarrow} r$, combining this one with $p \wedge \varphi \overset{S_1}{\rightsquigarrow} u$ one obtains using Proposition 8.3 $p \wedge \varphi \overset{S_1}{\rightsquigarrow} r \wedge u$; from $r \overset{S_2}{\rightsquigarrow} \underline{false}$ one immediately obtains $r \wedge u \overset{S_2}{\rightsquigarrow} \underline{false}$.

Now using the induction hypothesis on S_2 we know that $(\Sigma, \mathbb{E}) \vdash \Phi(r \rightarrow S_2\downarrow)$ thus $(\Sigma, \mathbb{E}) \vdash (r \wedge \Phi \overset{S_2}{\rightsquigarrow} \underline{false}) \rightarrow \neg\exists X r \wedge \varphi$. Substituting u for φ and applying modus ponens we obtain $\neg\exists X r \wedge u$. After applying the rule of consequence on $p \wedge \varphi \overset{S_1}{\rightsquigarrow} r \wedge u$, $\forall X(r \wedge u) \rightarrow \underline{false}$ we find $p \wedge \varphi \overset{S_1}{\rightsquigarrow} \underline{false}$. The induction hypothesis on S_1 then immediately yields $\neg\exists X\, p \wedge \varphi$.

The case that $S \equiv$ <u>while</u> b <u>do</u> S_0 <u>od</u> is similar but tedious and will be omitted. It occurs in detail in [3]. □

REFERENCES.

[1] APT, K.R. & E.R. OLDEROG, *Proof rules dealing with fairness*, Bericht Nr. 8104, March 1981, Institut für Informatik und Praktische Mathematik, Christian Albrechts-universität Kiel.

[2] BERGSTRA, J.A. & J.W. KLOP, *Proving program inclusion using Hoare's Logic*, Mathematical Centre, Department of Computer Science, Research Report IW 176, Amsterdam 1981.

[3] BERGSTRA, J.A. & J.W. KLOP, *A formalized proof system for total correctness of while programs*, Mathematical Centre, Department of Computer Science, Research Report IW 175, Amsterdam 1981.

[4] BERGSTRA, J.A. & J.V. TUCKER, *Hoare's Logic and Peano's Arithmetic*, Mathematical Centre, Department of Computer Science, Research Report IW 160, Amsterdam 1981.

[5] BERGSTRA, J.A. & J.V. TUCKER, *The axiomatic semantics of while programs using Hoare's Logic*, manuscript May 1981, definitive version in preparation.

[6] GRÜMBERG, O., N. FRANCEZ, J.A. MAKOWSKY & W.P. DE ROEVER, *A Proof Rule for fair Termination of Guarded Commands*, Report RUU-CS-81-2, Vakgroep Informatica Utrecht.

[7] HAREL, D., *First Order Dynamic Logic*, Springer Lecture Notes in Comp. Sc. 68, 1979.

[8] HAREL, D., *Proving the correctness of regular deterministic programs: a unifying survey using dynamic Logic*, T.C.S. 12(1) 61-83.

AUTOMATIC PROGRAM TRANSFORMATION VIEWED AS THEOREM PROVING

Ernesto J. F. Costa
Dept. Engenharia Electrotécnica
Universidade de Coimbra
P-3000 Coimbra,PORTUGAL

Abstract

We identify the problem of automatic recursion removal using the unfold/fold methodology (2) to the problem of finding a ε-pattern-matcher σ for two terms t and s, i.e.so that $\sigma t =_{\varepsilon} s$. We propose a new method to solve this equation based on a technique of dynamic completion of a term rewriting system for the property $t =_{\varepsilon} s \implies t \xrightarrow{*}_{R} s$. This method presentssome advantages because it enables us to work with incomplete theories and limits the number of superpositions we must do during the process of completion.

1.Introduction

Program transformations are now widely accepted as a powerful tool to design correct and efficient programs (1,2,4). The idea is to start with a simple and correct program ignoring any question of efficiency and then try to improve it using correctness preserving transformations. This methodology originated some systems which,interactively,help programmersin developing their programs. One of the best known is due to Burstall and Darlington (2). It is based on the heuristic use of few and simple transformation rules and can do many optimizing transformations such as combining loops re-use storage,recursion removal or even synthesising implementations for abstract data types (4). In this paper we consider only the problem of recursion removal. Our aim is to show how we can fully automatize this transformation for the class of linear recursive definitions. For this purpose we have develloped a new technique for using term rewriting systems which,in our case,is more efficient than the traditional Knuth-Bendix (9) technique.

2.Recursion removal using Burstall-Darlington methodology

In Burstall-Darlington system recursion removal is based on the use of a sequence of three transformation rules,named unfold,laws and fold,and defined as follows:

(i) unfold: if $E \Leftarrow E'$ and $F \Leftarrow F'$ are equations and there is some occurrence in F' of an instance of E,replace it by the corresponding instance of E' obtaining F", then add the equation F $\Leftarrow$ F";

(ii) laws: we may transform any equation by using on its right hand expression any we have about the base functions (associativity,commutativity,etc.);

(iii) fold: it is the reverse of the unfold transformation.

Removing recursion relies on the user's ability to invent a new (auxiliary) function -- called "eureka" by Burstall-Darlington -- and on his intuition for finding a tail-recursive definition for it.

Example 1

Consider the following linear recursive definition (x,n $\in$ N and n $\geq$ 0):

```
F(x,n) == if n=0 then 1
          else if even(n) then F(x,n÷2)**2                          (1)
               else (F(x,(n-1)÷2)**2)*x fi fi
```

In order to remove this non tail-recursion the user must provide the system with the auxiliary function:

```
G(g1,g2,g3,g4) == (F(g1,g2)**g3)*g4                                 (2)
```

which can be used to compute F(x,n) because

```
F(x,n) = G(x,n,1,1)                                                 (3)
```

The next problem to solve is to find a tail-recursive definition for G. This is achieved by the system (under user's guidance) by unfolding once the F call in (2), using (1) and rewriting the unfolded expression in such a way that finally it can be folded using (2):

```
G(g1,g2,g3,g4) == (if g2=0 then 1
                   else if even(g2) then F(g1,g2÷2)**2
                        else (F(g1,(g2-1)÷2)**2)*g1 fi fi)**g3)*g4
```

by unfolding F in (2).

Assuming that the if-then-else-fi is naturally extended (10) this can be rewrited as:

```
== if g2=0 then (1**g3)*g4
   else if even(g2) then ((F(g1,g2÷2)**2)**g3)*g4
        else (((F(g1,(g2-1)÷2)**2)*g1)**g3)*g4 fi fi
```

In order to simplify the presentation we consider the rewriting of each branch of the if-then-else-fi separately. For the first one we have:

(1**g3)*g4 → 1*g4 → g4

by using the rules ∀x,1**x = 1 and ∀x,1*x = x.

For the second one:

((F(g1,g2÷2)**2)**g3)g4 → (F(g1,g2÷2)**(2*g3))*g4

by using the rule ∀x,y (x**y)**z = x**(y*z).

For the third one:

(((F(g1,(g2-1)÷2)**2)*g1)**g3)*g4 → (((F(g1,(g2-1)÷2)**2)**g3)*(g1**g3))*g4 →

((F(g1,(g2-1)÷2)**(2*g3))*(g1**g3))*g4 → (F(g1,(g2-1)÷2)**(2*g3))*((g1**g3)*g4)

by using the rules ∀x,y,z (x*y)**z = (x**z)*(y**z),(x**y)**z = x**(y*z),(x*y)*z = x*(y*z). By putting all these partial results together we obtain:

```
== if g2=0 then g4
   else if even(g2) then (F(g1,g2÷2)**(2*g3))*g4
        else (F(g1,(g2-1)÷2)**(2*g3))*((g1*g3)*g4) fi fi
```

which can be folded using (2) giving:

```
G(g1,g2,g3,g4) == if g2 = 0 then g4
                  else if even(g2) then G(g1,g2÷2,2*g3,g4)          (4)
                       else G(g1,(g2-1)÷2,2*g3,(g1**g3)*g4) fi fi
```

(4) is a tail recursive definition of G which,together with (3),enables us to compute (1) iteratively.

If we want fully automatize this technique the system must be able to produce (2) and to choose a rule at each step of the rewriting so that a final fold with (2) is possible in all branches involving F. The first problem can be solved using a first--order generalisation technique (see (1)). Our aim in this paper is to solve the second one.

3.Formalization of the problem

Let *V* be a countable set of variables and *F* a finite or countable set of functions.

We define a term as either a variable x or f(t1,...,tn) where f is an n-ary function and t1,...,tn are terms. We denote by T the set of all terms. The set of all variables in a term t is denoted by $\nu(t)$.

Let $\Phi(t)$ denote the set of occurrences of t defined as:

(i) $\Lambda \in \Phi(t)$;

(ii) $u \in \Phi(ti) \Longrightarrow iu \in \Phi(f(t1,\ldots,tn)) \quad \forall i,\ 1 \leq i \leq n.$

It follows that the set of all occurrences may be partially ordered by:

$$u \ll v \Leftrightarrow \exists w:\ v=uw$$

Two occurrences are said to be disjoint iff $u \not\ll v$ and $v \not\ll u$. $\bar{\Phi}(t)$ is the set of occurrences which do not correspond to a variable.

We call substitution a mapping σ from V to T, with $\sigma(x)=x$ almost everywhere. They are noted σ,ρ,η and can be extended as morphisms of T by:

$$\sigma(f(t1,\ldots,tn)) = f(\sigma(t1),\ldots,\sigma(tn))$$

Given two terms t and s, one calls t=s an equation. Let ε be a set of equations. One defines an equational theory, noted $=_\varepsilon$, as the smallest congruence containing all elements of ε and closed under substitution.

Given two terms t and s the problem of finding all substitutions σ so that $\sigma(t)=_\varepsilon \sigma(s)$ is called the ε-unification problem of $=_\varepsilon$. If we are looking for all σ so that $\sigma(t)=_\varepsilon s$, we call it ε-pattern-matching problem. These problems are, in general, undecidable (see (7)). But we can characterize a class of theories for which these problems are decidable (see (9)). To define these classes we must introduce the notion of canonical (or complete) term rewriting system. A term rewriting system (t.r.s.) R is a set of pairs of terms (γ,δ), so that $\nu(\delta) \subseteq \nu(\gamma)$. Let t/u denote the subterm ot t at occurrence u. We can associate to a t.r.s. a binary relation over T named reduction relation: giving a t.r.s. R and two terms t and s we say that s reduces to t in u, and we write $s \rightarrow_R t$, iff

$$\exists (\gamma,\delta) \in R,\ \exists u \in \Phi(s),\ \exists \eta : s/u=\eta\gamma \text{ and } t=s\ [\, u \leftarrow \eta(\delta)\,]$$

i.e. t is obtained by replacing the subterm s/u by $\eta(\delta)$.

If we consider $\overset{*}{\leftrightarrow}$ i.e. the transitive and reflexive closure of $\rightarrow_R$ we define an equational theory $=_R$. Reciprocally to every equational theory $=_\varepsilon$ we can associate a t.r.s. R so that $=_R\ =\ =_\varepsilon$. A t.r.s. R is said to be noetherian iff for every term t there is no infinite sequence:

$$t=t0 \rightarrow_R t1 \rightarrow_R t2 \rightarrow_R \ldots$$

If for every terms t,t1,t2 so that $t \xrightarrow{*}_R t1$ and $t \xrightarrow{*}_R t2$ there is a term t* so that $t1 \xrightarrow{*}_R t^*$ and $t2 \xrightarrow{*}_R t^*$ the t.r.s. is said to be confluent. A complete t.r.s. is one which is noetherian and confluent.

A term t is in $\longrightarrow_R$-normal form iff there is no t' so that $t \longrightarrow_R t'$. If $s \xrightarrow{*}_R t$ and t is in $\longrightarrow_R$-normal form we say that t is a $\longrightarrow_R$-normal form of s. An important property of a complete t.r.s. *R* is that each term t has a unique normal form t*. Using this property we have:

$$\eta(t) =_R \eta(s) \Longleftrightarrow \eta(t)^* = \eta(s)^*$$

and the ε-unification problem is decidable (see(5,8)).

Let us return now to our problem. We start from a definition G(x) == Ti which we unfold once giving new terms T_c^0=(1**g3)*g4,T_c^1=((F(g1,g2÷2)**2)**g3)*g4 and T_c^2=(((F(g1,(g2-1)÷2)**2)*g1)**g3)*g4. Then,we try to apply some rules to those which contain F in such a way that each of these terms could fold with G(x) == Ti. In other words,we try to find substitutions η_j:

$$\eta_j Ti =_\varepsilon T_c^j \quad \text{for } j=1,2. \qquad (5)$$

where $=_\varepsilon$ is the theory associated with the rewriting rules. Our problem is then equivalent to the ε-pattern-matching problem. But the usual formal technique is not useful for pratical problems (see (6)). As a matter of fact:

(i) present algorithms give the set of all ε-pattern-matchers (which can be infinite) for every unrelated terms;

(ii) the t.r.s. may not be complete even if we apply the Knuth-Bendix's completion algorithm;

In our case:

(iii) we only need one particular ε-pattern-matcher because the two terms T_c^j and Ti are related: T_c^j is a functional duplication of Ti;

(iv) we want to work with equational theories for which neither complete nor ε-pattern-matching algorithms exist.

For these reasons we start transforming our original problem (5) into

$$T_c^j \xrightarrow{*}_R \eta_j Ti \quad \text{for } j=1,2. \qquad (6)$$

To solve this problem we use a backtracking algorithm,together with heuristics (implied by (iii)) in order to reduce the combinatorial explosion and to insure finite termination. The heuristic part is fully described in (3). Here we discuss how (iv) may be achieved.

4. Dinamic completion of a t.r.s.

If a theory $=_R$ is such that $t=_R s \Longrightarrow t \overset{*}{\longrightarrow}_R s$ a backtracking algorithm (assuming that R is noetherian) will be complete. But this may not be the case. Our aim is then to transform R into a new t.r.s. R' so that $=_{R'} = =_R$ and

$$t=_{R'}s \Longrightarrow t \overset{*}{\longrightarrow}_{R'} s \tag{7}$$

R' must necessary contain the effect of an equation. Consider for instance the term t=h1(h2(h3(F(x)))) and the <u>equations</u> $\vec{e1}$ == h2(h3(x1)) = h4(h5(x1)),e2 == h1(h4(x2)) = h2(h4(x2)). The only <u>rule</u> we can apply is $\vec{e1}$ at occurrence 1 (the arrow indicates the direction of application) and we have:

$t \dashrightarrow_R t'$=h1(h4(h5(F(x))))

But we can now apply $\vec{e2}$ at occurrence Λ :

$\dashrightarrow_R t''$=h2(h4(h5(F(x))))

and still apply $\overleftarrow{e1}$,i.e. the same equation but in the reverse direction,yielding:

$\dashrightarrow_R t'''$=h2(h2(h3(F(x)))).

This is a new term we cannot obtain only by using the t.r.s. R ={$\vec{e1}$,$\vec{e2}$}(note that $\vec{e2}$ cannot be applied to t). This is the only situation where we may need to use an equation because when $\vec{e1}$ <u>and</u> $\vec{e2}$ may be applied to t we can arrive to t''' using only one rewriting by $\vec{e2}$ (see (3) for the proof). In that situation we transform our initial t.r.s. R into a new one R' equal to R plus the rule $\vec{sr12}$ == h1(h2(h3(x3))) $\dashrightarrow$ h2(h2(h3(x))).

So,our primitive backtracking algorithm is modified in such a way that,after producing all normal forms from a term t,it considers all the rules that have been applied to t and tries to obtain new rules from these. If it does not find any of these new rules it stops. If it finds them it starts the backtracking process with the new set R'. As we easily see from the example the new rules are an equational consequence of the other rules and so $=_R = =_{R'}$.

Let us now give more formally,the way these new rules are constructed.Let $\vec{ei}$ == li $\dashrightarrow$ri and $\vec{ek}$ == lk $\longrightarrow$ rk be two rewriting rules with ν(li) $\cap$ ν(lk) = $\emptyset$. We must consider two cases:

(i) <u>a</u> $\exists$ ui $\in$ $\bar{\Phi}$(ri), $\exists\sigma$: σN=σlk with σ minimum and ri/ui=N

<u>b</u> $\not\exists$ui' $\in$ $\bar{\Phi}$(li) : $\exists\sigma'$,σ'N'=σ'lk with li/ui'=N'

<u>c</u> We have the derivation

$M = \sigma li \dashrightarrow M' = \overrightarrow{ei}(M) \dashrightarrow M'' = \overrightarrow{ek}(M') \dashrightarrow M''' = \overleftarrow{ei}(M'')$

Then we introduce the new rule $\overrightarrow{srik}$ so that $M''' = \overrightarrow{srik}(M)$. This rule is constructed as follows. We have

$M = \sigma li \dashrightarrow M' = \sigma ri \dashrightarrow M'' = (\sigma ri)$ [$ui \leftarrow\!\!- \sigma rk$]

As we can apply $\overleftarrow{ei}$ to M'':

$\exists \sigma''$: $M''/ui=\sigma rk=\sigma''N$.

Also, if Xi is the set of variables $xi \in \nu(ri)$ at occurrence vi, such that vi and ui are disjoint, then $\sigma''|Xi=\sigma$ (where $\sigma|V$ means the restriction of σ to V). So $M''= \sigma''ri$ and $M'''=\sigma''li$. In conclusion

$\overrightarrow{srik}$ == $\sigma li \dashrightarrow \sigma li$ (8)

(ii) a $\exists uk \in \bar{\Phi}(lk)$: $\exists \sigma$, $\sigma N=\sigma ri$ with σ minimum and $lk/uk=N$
b $\nexists uk' \in \bar{\Phi}(lk)$: $\exists \sigma$, $\sigma N'=\sigma li$ with $lk/uk'=N'$
c We have the derivation

$M = \sigma(lk$ [$uk \leftarrow\!\!- li$] $) \dashrightarrow M'=\overrightarrow{ei}(M) \dashrightarrow M''=\overrightarrow{ek}(M') \dashrightarrow M'''=\overleftarrow{ei}(M'')$

Then we introduce the new rule

$\overrightarrow{srki}$ == $\sigma(lk$ [$uk \leftarrow\!\!- li$] $) \dashrightarrow \sigma''(rk$ [$uk' \leftarrow\!\!- li$] $)$ (9)

with $M''=\sigma rk$, $\exists uk' \in \bar{\Phi}(rk)$: $M''/uk'=\sigma N=\sigma''ri$ and $\sigma''|Xk=\sigma$.

In both cases the conditions a and b mean that the rule $\overrightarrow{ek}$ can be applied because of the privious application of $\overrightarrow{ei}$. Condition c simply means that we use an equation in the derivation.

Example 2

Let us consider the following function (over N):

F(x) == <u>if</u> c0(x) <u>then</u> a(x)
<u>else</u> <u>if</u> c1(x) <u>then</u> h4(F(b1(x)),d1(x)) (10)
<u>else</u> h1(h2(F(b2(x)),d2'(x)),d2''(x)) <u>fi</u> <u>fi</u>

and the set of rewriting rules:

$\vec{e}1 == h4(h4(x,y),z) \longrightarrow h4(x,h4(y,z))$; $\vec{e}2 == h2(h2(x,y),z) \longrightarrow x$; $\vec{e}3 == h1(h2(x,y),z) \longrightarrow h2(h3(x,z),y)$; $\vec{e}4 == h3(h4(x,y),z) \longrightarrow h3(h5(x,y),z)$; $\vec{e}5 == h5(h1(x,y),z) \longrightarrow h4(h2(x,z),y)$; $\vec{e}6 == h1(x,\alpha1) \longrightarrow x$; $\vec{e}7 == h2(x,\alpha2) \longrightarrow x$; $\vec{e}8 == h4(x,\alpha4) \longrightarrow x$; $\vec{e}9 == h4(h5(x,y),z) \longrightarrow h4(h5(x,z),y)$.

Using a standard technique (see (1)) we introduce the auxiliary function:

$$G(x,y,z,w) == h1(h2(h4(F(x),y),z),w) \qquad (11)$$

$$\text{and } F(x) = G(x,\alpha4,\alpha2,\alpha1) \qquad (12)$$

To find a tail recursive definition for (11) we follow the process of section 2:

$$\begin{aligned} G(x,y,z,w) == \; & \underline{if}\ c0(x)\ \underline{then}\ h1(h2(h4(a(x),y),z),w) \\ & \underline{else}\ \underline{if}\ c1(x)\ \underline{then}\ h1(h2(h4(h4(F(b1(x)),d1(x)),y),z),w) \\ & \quad \underline{else}\ h1(h2(h4(h1(h2(F(b2(x)),d2'(x)),d2''(x)),y),z),w)\ \underline{fi}\ \underline{fi} \end{aligned} \qquad (13)$$

The first recursive branch can be transformed by rule 1 into

$$h1(h2(h4(F(b1(x)),h4(d1(x),y)),z),w) \qquad (14)$$

and can be folded using (11). On the contrary there is no composition of rules $\vec{e}1,\ldots,\vec{e}9$ such as the second branc can be folded using (11). In a tree-like simplified presentation we have the derivations:

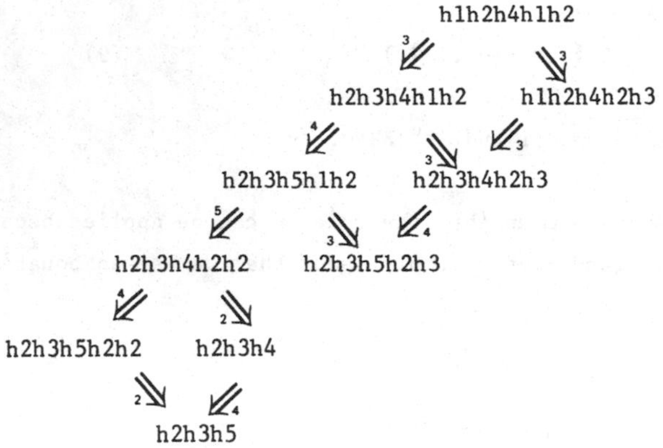

Pairs of rules satisfying conditions _a_ and _b_ are (3,4),(4,5),(5,4) and (5,2). But only (3,4) verifies also _c_ giving the new rule

$$\vec{sr}34 == h1(h2(h4(x,y),z),w) \longrightarrow h1(h2(h5(x,y),w),z) \qquad (15)$$

Now the second branch can successively be rewritten in:

$\longrightarrow$ h1(h2(h5(h1(h2(F(b2(x)),d2"(x)),d2'(x)),y),w),z) $\longrightarrow$

h1(h2(h4(h2(h2(F(b2(x)),d2"(x)),d2'(x)),w),z) $\longrightarrow$ h1(h2(h4(F(b2(x)),d2'(x)),w),z)

using rules $\vec{sr34}$ at occurrence Λ ,$\vec{e5}$ at occurrence 11 and $\vec{e2}$ at occurrence 111. This last expression can be folded using (11) and we obtain the tail-recursive definition for (10):

G(x,y,z,w) == <u>if</u> co(x) <u>then</u> h1(h2(h4(a(x),y),z),w)
<u>else</u> <u>if</u> c1(x) <u>then</u> G(b1(x),h4(d1(x),y),z,w) (16)
<u>else</u> G(b2(x),d2'(x),w,z) <u>fi</u> <u>fi</u>

The reader can easily check that the Knuth-Bendix completion algorithm cannot terminate with all the rules $\vec{e1},\ldots,\vec{e9}$.

5.Conclusion

We have related the problem of automatic recursion removal with the problem of finding an ε-pattern-matcher for two terms t and s. For <u>pratical reasons</u>,we have proposed a new method to solve this last problemwhich combines an heuristic approach (not described here) and a formal technique of dynamical completion of a t.r.s. for the property $t =_R s \Longrightarrow t \xrightarrow{*}_R s$.This technique enables us to work with <u>incomplete theories</u> for which the standard Knuth-Bendix technique is not usable. The rules produced are obtained by a superposition process similar to that of Knuth-Bendix,but here again we have the advantage of limiting the number of superpositions by considering only the pairs of rules that have been effectively applied. Our method is now under implementation in order to be included in the Burstall-Darlington's program transformation system.

6.References

(1) J. Arsac and Y. Kodratoff: "Some methods for transforming recursive procedures into iterative ones",to appear ACM ToPLaS.
(2) R. Burstall and J. Darlington: 1977,"A transformation system for developping recursive programs",J.ACM,vol.24,n°1.
(3) E. Costa: 1981,"Dérecursivation automatique en utilisant des systèmes de réécriture de termes",thèse de 3ème cycle,Univ. de Paris VI.
(4) J. Darlington: 1981,"The synthesis of implementations for abstract data types", Nato Summer School on Automatic Program Construction,Bonas,France.

(5) M. Fay: 1979,"First-order unification in an equational theory",Proc. of the 4th Workshop on Automated Deduction,Austin,Texas.
(6) P. Gloess and J.-P. Laurent: 1980,"Adding dynamic paramodulation to rewrite algorithms",Proc. of the 5th Conference on Automated Deduction,Les Arcs,France.
(7) G. Huet and D. Oppen: 1980,"Equations and rewrite rules.a survey",SRI International Technical Report CSL-111.
(8) J. Hullot. 1980,"Compilation des formes canoniques dans des théories équationnelles",thèse de 3ème cycle,Univ. de Paris-Sud.
(9) D. Knuth and P. Bendix: 1970,"Simple word problems in universal algebras", in "Computational problems in abstract algebra",ed. J. Leech,Pergamon Press.
(10) Z. Manna,S. Ness and J. Vuillemin: 1973,"Inductive methods for proving properties of programs",C. ACM,vol.16,nº8.

AN ENLARGED DEFINITION AND COMPLETE AXIOMATIZATION OF OBSERVATIONAL CONGRUENCE OF FINITE PROCESSES

Ph. DARONDEAU

IRISA
Campus de Beaulieu
35042 RENNES CEDEX (FRANCE)

Abstract.

The paper is addressed to determine an adequate notion of observational equivalence of finite processes, and to give a complete axiomatization of the associated congruence. We begin with establishing the fact that recursive equivalence of processes as it has been defined in the work of Milner and his colleagues is not a fully observational equivalence, in that it is much more restrictive than it should be to agree in all cases with the judgement of an effective observer. Inspiring from CCS, an alternative syntax is proposed for processes, bringing forward n-ary guarding operators. Given p and q in that syntax, which allows invisible actions to be expressed, p and q are said equivalent iff after any common experiment, they both react by identical answers or absence of answer to any ambiguous communication offer that the observer may present. It is shown that this equivalence is also a congruence ; a finite set of equational axioms is given for the congruence, which we prove to be a complete proof system by argumenting over canonical forms of programs. In a second time, our language is enriched by adding it the necessary operators for expressing the parallel composition of processes and the renaming of their actions. The definition of the observational equivalence is extended accordingly, and it is shown that we still obtain a congruence, for which a complete proof system is finally given.

1. INTRODUCTION

The basic notation introduced by R. Milner in [1] for expressing asynchronous behaviours has given rise to a series of programming languages, or behaviour algebras, which have been intensively studied regarding operational congruence of programs [2] [3] [4] [5] . All these languages incorporate the idea that communication is synchronized and takes place along lines. Differences between languages lay in the following points : behaviours may be only finite or they may be infinite, communication may engage the passing of values or it may be pure synchronization, elementary communication events may be restricted to occur one at a time or communications may be forced to be simultaneous. According to [2], two programs are operationally congruent if they may be exchanged with one another in any larger program " without affecting the behaviour of the latter", which bears evidence of the practical interest of proof systems for operational congruence. The present paper is motivated by the opinion that the precise notion of recursive equivalence which has been used in the above referenced studies as a basis for defining the operational congruence of programs is more restrictive than needed if the only constraint to be respected is model realism. We argue that even in the simple case of finite processes without internal actions, the recursive equivalence of Milner discriminates between processes which cannot be distinguished from one another by any effective observer, for every potentialities of an ambiguous process cannot be experimented in a single run (such is the case for instance with processes p_1 and p_2 pictured in fig.1). The above statement leads us to suggest an extended definition of a "fully observational" equivalence of processes as an alternative to Milner's equivalence which is not thoroughly practical. As it has been done in [2], the paper restricts to finite processes with pure synchronization. The basic algebra of processes, excluding parallel composition and renaming operators from its signature, is introduced and discussed in section 2. Observational equivalence of processes is defined in section 3, and it is shown that such an equivalence justifies the relational representation of processes in the form of labelled trees. Section 4 gives a complete set of equational axioms for the congruence, which is found identical to the equivalence. Parallel composition and renamings are introduced in section 5 in the form of equationally defined operators upon basic processes, and it is finally shown that the equivalence studied so far is still a congruence for the extended signature.

2. BASIC PROCESSES

Let $M = L \cup \{\tau\}$, where L is an arbitrary enumerable set, the elements λ of which will be called observable action labels, $\tau \notin L$ being the unobservable action label. For any finite integer $n \geq o$, let $G_n = M^n$, the set of n-ary guarding operators, with $G_o = \{(\ )\} = \{NIL\}$. Our algebra of basic processes is W_Σ, the word-algebra over $\Sigma = \bigcup_{n \geq o} G_n$. The intuitive meaning is as follows. NIL is the program which has no potential actions ; $(\lambda_1, \ldots, \lambda_n).(p_1, \ldots, p_n)$ waits for some set of action demands $\{\lambda'_1, \ldots, \lambda'_k\}$ such that at least one λ'_j equals at least one λ_i, and subsequently signals acceptance of one such λ_i, taken arbitrarily, before entering the corresponding p_i ; $(\mu_1, \ldots, \mu_n).(p_1, \ldots, p_n)$, if at least one of μ_i s equals τ, waits for an unforeseeable delay for some set of action demands $\{\lambda'_1, \ldots, \lambda'_k\}$ such that at least one λ'_j equals μ_i for some i, and then either behaves as above if such a demand occurs within that delay or else enters one arbitrary p_i such that $\mu_i = \tau$ for the corresponding i. It should be noticed that our algebra is somewhat different from what would be expected in the line of Milner's work, since no magic operator is provided for constructing an ambiguous process without explicitly guarding its alternatives. This slight distinction is in fact essential to our results.

3. OBSERVATIONAL EQUIVALENCE OF BASIC PROCESSES

For any $\lambda \varepsilon L$, let $\overset{\lambda}{\rightarrow}$ be the following binary relation over $P_f(W_\Sigma)$, the set of finite parts of W_Σ.

$$\{NIL\} \overset{\lambda}{\rightarrow} \emptyset$$

$$\{(\mu_1, \ldots, \mu_n).(p_1, \ldots, p_n)\} \overset{\lambda}{\rightarrow}$$

$$\{p_i/\mu_i = \lambda\} \cup \bigsqcup_{\mu_j = \tau} F_j/\{p_j\} \overset{\lambda}{\rightarrow} F_j$$

$F \cup G \overset{\lambda}{\rightarrow} F' \cup G'$ <u>if</u> ($F \neq \emptyset$ <u>or</u> $G \neq 0$) <u>and</u>
($F = \emptyset = F'$ <u>or</u> $F \overset{\lambda}{\rightarrow} F'$) <u>and</u> ($G = \emptyset = G'$ <u>or</u> $G \overset{\lambda}{\rightarrow} G'$)

For any non empty $\Lambda \varepsilon P_f(L)$, let $\downarrow \Lambda$ be the following property, defined on elements of $P_f(W_\Sigma)$.

$\{NIL\} \downarrow \Lambda$

$\{(\mu_1, \ldots, \mu_n).(p_1, \ldots, p_n)\} \downarrow \Lambda$ <u>iff</u>

$(\forall i)$ ($\mu_i \neq \tau$ <u>and</u> $\mu_i \notin \Lambda$) <u>or</u> $(\exists i)$ ($\mu_i = \tau$ <u>and</u> $\{p_i\} \downarrow \Lambda$)

$F \cup G \downarrow \Lambda$ <u>if</u> ($F \neq \emptyset$ <u>and</u> $F \downarrow \Lambda$) <u>or</u> ($G \neq \emptyset$ <u>and</u> $G \downarrow \Lambda$)

Let the equivalence $\sim$ over $P_f(W_\Sigma)$ be recursively defined as follows :

$F \sim G$ <u>iff</u>

i) $\forall \Lambda \varepsilon P_f(L) \setminus \emptyset$ $F \downarrow \Lambda$ <u>iff</u> $G \downarrow \Lambda$

ii) $\forall \lambda \varepsilon L$ ($F \overset{\lambda}{\rightarrow} F'$ and $G \overset{\lambda}{\rightarrow} G'$) <u>imply</u> $F' \sim G'$.

Our observational equivalence $\sim$ over W_Σ is the derived equivalence $p \sim p'$ <u>iff</u> $\{p\} \sim \{p'\}$.

Namely, processes p and p' are equivalent iff the following conditions are fulfilled :

- for any sequence $S = (\Lambda_1 \rightarrow \lambda_1)(\Lambda_2 \rightarrow \lambda_2) \ldots (\Lambda_n \rightarrow \lambda_n)$ in which the observer has submitted demands Λ_i and received corresponding agreement answers $\lambda_i \varepsilon \Lambda_i$ in the order, then S is a possible experiment with p iff it is a possible experiment with p' ;

- for any such S, any possible answer that the observer may obtain from p, including the absence of answer, when he has submitted a new demand after experiment S, might equally have been got from p' after identical experiment (and vice-versa).

Although our equivalence is still recursively defined as was Milner's one, recursion bears rather here on the language of experiments than on the internal structure of the programs which make them feasible. It has been mentioned by one of the referees that the definition of the equivalence bears strong connection with the concept of "failure sets" given in [6], where identical ideas were presented first.

The definition of $\sim$ makes it clear that for any context $\mathcal{C}[.]$, the following properties hold :

$$\mathcal{C}[(\mu_1, \mu_2, \mu_3, \ldots, \mu_n).(p_1, p_2, p_3, \ldots, p_n)]$$

$$\sim \mathcal{C}[(\mu_2, \mu_1, \mu_3, \ldots, \mu_n).(p_2, p_1, p_3, \ldots, p_n)]$$

$$\mathcal{C}[(\mu_1, \mu_2, \mu_2, \ldots, \mu_n).(p_1, p_2, p_2, \ldots, p_n)]$$

$$\sim \mathcal{C}[(\mu_1, \mu_2, \ldots, \mu_n).(p_1, p_2, \ldots, p_n)].$$

Those properties justify the relational representation of processes in the form of labelled trees. For instance, letting equivalent processes p_1, p_2, p_3 be defined as

$$p_1 = (\lambda_1, \lambda_1).((\lambda_2).(\lambda_4).(NIL), (\lambda_2).(\lambda_3).(NIL))$$

$$p_2 = (\lambda_1).(\lambda_2, \lambda_2, \lambda_2).((\lambda_3).(NIL), (\lambda_3).(NIL), (\lambda_4).(NIL))$$

$$p_3 = (\tau).(\lambda_1).(\tau, \tau).((\lambda_2).(\lambda_3).(NIL), (\lambda_2).(\lambda_4).(NIL)),$$

their respective tree images are shown in the below figure 1. None of p_1, p_2, p_3 may be found equivalent to process $q = (\lambda_1).(\lambda_2).(\lambda_3, \lambda_4).(NIL, NIL)$.

Three equivalent processes

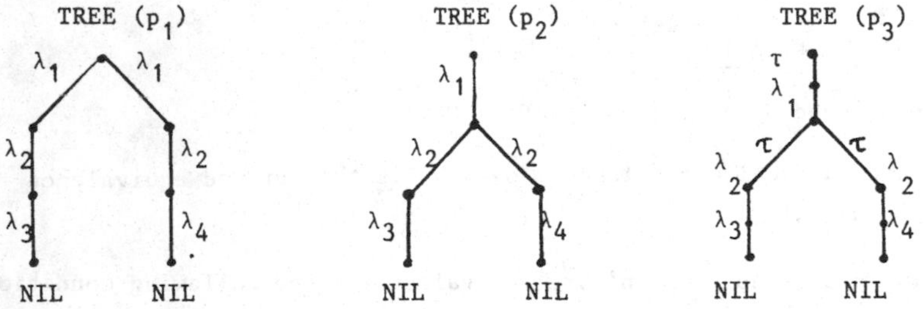

- figure 1 -

4. AXIOMATIZING THE EQUIVALENCE AND THE CONGRUENCE.

To begin with, let us recall the definition of observational congruence $\simeq$ over W_Σ.

Definition. $p \simeq p'$ iff for any program context $\mathcal{C}[.]$, the following equivalence holds: $\mathcal{C}[p] \sim \mathcal{C}[p']$

The first property that we shall prove is the following

Proposition 1. The observational congruence $\simeq$ over W_Σ is just the equivalence $\sim$.

Proof. We have to establish that for any $p, p' \in W_\Sigma$, $p \sim p'$ implies $\mathcal{C}[p] \sim \mathcal{C}[p']$.
We proceed by induction on tree $(\mathcal{C}[.])$, the tree image of the program context $\mathcal{C}[.]$.

Induction basis. If $\mathcal{C}[.]$ is the empty context, then $\mathcal{C}[p] = p \sim p' = \mathcal{C}[p']$.

Induction step. We have to prove that for any context $\mathfrak{C}[.] = (\mu_1, \mu_2, \ldots, \mu_n).(\bullet, p_2, \ldots, p_n)$, $p_1 \sim p'_1 \Rightarrow \mathfrak{C}[p_1] \sim \mathfrak{C}[p'_1]$. From the definition of $\sim$, the proof is immediate for n = 1. Turning now to the other cases where n>1, let process $q = (\mu_2, \ldots, \mu_n).(p_2, \ldots, p_n)$, and for any $\lambda \in L$, let $\{q\} \overset{\lambda}{\rightarrow} Q_\lambda$.

From the definition of $\downarrow\Lambda$, $\mathfrak{C}[p_1]\downarrow\Lambda$ iff

$(\forall i \in [1,n])\ (\tau \neq \mu_i \notin \Lambda)$ or $(\mu_1 = \tau$ and $\{p_1\}\downarrow\Lambda)$ or $(\exists\, i>1)\ (\mu_i = \tau$ and $\{p_i\}\downarrow\Lambda)$,

which is equivalent to $\mathfrak{C}[p'_1]\downarrow\Lambda$ since $p_1 \sim p'_1$ implies

$(\forall\Lambda)\ \{p_1\}\downarrow\Lambda$ iff $\{p'_1\}\downarrow\Lambda$.

Now, for $\lambda \in L$, let P_λ and P'_λ be defined as follows :

if $\mu_1 = \lambda$ then $P_\lambda = \{p_1\}$ else if $\mu_1 = \tau$ then $\{p_1\} \overset{\lambda}{\rightarrow} P_\lambda$ else $P_\lambda = \emptyset$;

if $\mu_1 = \lambda$ then $P'_\lambda = \{p'_1\}$ else if $\mu_1 = \tau$ then $\{p'_1\} \overset{\lambda}{\rightarrow} P'_\lambda$ else $P'_\lambda = \emptyset$.

Clearly, $p_1 \sim p'_1$ implies $P_\lambda \sim P'_\lambda$ in any case.

From the definition of $\overset{\lambda}{\rightarrow}$, it is easily shown that

$\{\mathfrak{C}[p_1]\} \overset{\lambda}{\rightarrow} P_\lambda \cup Q_\lambda$ and $\{\mathfrak{C}[p'_1]\} \overset{\lambda}{\rightarrow} P'_\lambda \cup Q_\lambda$.

In order to complete the proof, there remains to show $P_\lambda \cup Q_\lambda \sim P'_\lambda \cup Q_\lambda$ which is established in the following lemma. ■

Lemma 1 : For any $P, P', Q \in P_f(W_\Sigma)$,
$P \sim P'$ implies $P \cup Q \sim P' \cup Q$.

From proposition 1, we know that any axiom system which is complete for $\sim$ is also a proof system for the congruence. In order to axiomatize $\overset{\sim}{-}$, we shall therefore content ourselves with axiomatizing $\sim$. Some suitable notational conventions are now introduced before undertaking that job.

Notations. For any $\mu_i \in M$, $p_i \in W_\Sigma$, we let $(\mu_i\ p_i)$ stand for $(\mu_i).(p_i)$, $(\sum_{i=n}^{m} \mu_i\ p_i)$ stand for $(\mu_n, \mu_{n+1}, \ldots, \mu_m).(p_n, p_{n+1}, \ldots, p_m)$.

- notice the use of brackets -

In the sequel, we shall also make free use of the following identities, where $m_o \leq m_1 \leq m_2 \ldots \leq m_n$:

$$\mu_i\ p_i \equiv \sum_{j=i}^{i} \mu_j\ p_j$$

$$\sum_{i=m_o}^{m_1} \mu_i p_i + \sum_{i=m_1}^{m_2} \mu_i p_i + \ldots + \sum_{i=m_{n-1}}^{m_n} \mu_i p_i \equiv \sum_{i=m_o}^{m_n} \mu_i p_i$$

- notice the absence of brackets in the above forms -

We are now ready to tackle the axiomatization of $\sim$. Our first result will be to establish the soundness of the following schemes of formulae A1-A7, where $f \overset{+}{\sim} f'$ stands for

$$\left(\sum_{i=1}^{n_1} \mu'_i\, p'_i + f + \sum_{j=1}^{n_2} \mu''_j\, p''_j \right) \sim \left(\sum_{i=1}^{n_1} \mu'_i\, p'_i + f' + \sum_{j=1}^{n_2} \mu''_j\, p''_j \right)$$

<u>A1</u> - $\mu_1\, p_1 + \mu_2\, p_2 \overset{+}{\sim} \mu_2\, p_2 + \mu_1\, p_1$

<u>A2</u> - $\mu\, p + \mu\, p \overset{+}{\sim} \mu\, p$

<u>A3</u> - $(\tau).(p) \sim (p)$

<u>A4</u> - $\mu \left(\sum_{i=1}^{n} \mu'\, p_i \right) \overset{+}{\sim} \sum_{i=1}^{n} \mu\, (\mu'\, p_i)$

<u>A5</u> - $\tau NIL + \sum_{i=1}^{n} \mu_i\, p_i \overset{+}{\sim} \tau NIL + \tau \left(\sum_{i=1}^{n} \mu_i\, p_i \right)$

<u>A6</u> - $\sum_{i=1}^{n} \mu_i\, p_i + \tau\left(\sum_{j=1}^{m} \mu_j\, q_j\right) \overset{+}{\sim} \tau\left(\sum_{i=1}^{n} \mu_i p_i\right) + \tau\left(\sum_{j=1}^{m} \mu_j\, q_j\right)$ <u>if</u> $1 \leq m \leq n$

<u>A7</u> - $\sum_{i=1}^{n} \mu_i\, p_i + \tau\left(\sum_{j=1}^{m} \mu_j\, q_j\right) \overset{+}{\sim} \left(\sum_{i=1}^{n} \mu_i\, (\tau p_i + \tau q_i) + \sum_{j=n+1}^{m} \mu_j\, q_j\right)$ <u>if</u> $1 \leq n \leq m$

<u>Proposition 2.</u> Any interpretation of one of the schemes A1-A7 is a sound formula. (proof omitted).

Our next aim is to show that {A1-A7}is a complete axiom system for the observational equivalence $\sim$(and thus for the observational congruence).Another more explicit formulation is given below.

Let $\backsim$ be the least equivalence over W_Σ for which properties i and ii are satisfied :

i) $p \backsim p'$ <u>if</u> $p \sim p'$ is a possible interpretation of one of schemes A1-A7

ii) $\mathcal{C}\,[p] \backsim \mathcal{C}[p']$ <u>if</u> $p \backsim p'$

Knowing from propositions 1 and 2 that $p \backsim p' \Rightarrow p \sim p'$, we shall try to establish the reverse implication $p \sim p' \Rightarrow p \backsim p'$.

From now on, let B1-B7 denote schemes obtained from A1-A7 when replacing symbol $\sim$ with symbol $\backsim$. The method that we shall use to establish the above implication is to prove that for any program p, there exists a canonical form can $(p) \equiv$ can $(\text{can}(p)) \backsim p$ such that for any $p' \sim p''$ which verify $\text{can}(p') \equiv p'$ and can $(p'') \equiv$

p'', p' and p" must have identical tree-image (that is $p' \backsim p''$ can be proved using B1 and B2 only). Our objective will effectively be reached if such a canonical form is found, since $[q \backsim can(q) \Rightarrow q \sim can(q)]$ entails $[p \sim p' \Rightarrow p \backsim can(p) \sim can(p') \backsim p'] \Rightarrow p \backsim can(p) \backsim can(p') \backsim p' \Rightarrow p \backsim p'$.

The approach towards the construction of canonical forms will be cut into two successive steps. The first step is to show that for any $p \in W_\Sigma$, there exists $\hat{p} \backsim p$ such that for any sub-program q of $\hat{p}$ and for any $\lambda \in L$, $\{q\} \xrightarrow{\lambda} Q_\lambda$ implies Q_λ is a singleton set or $Q_\lambda = \emptyset$. The second step is to draw can (p) from $\hat{p}$. We now come to the first step.

Definition

For $\mu \in M$, let $\xrightarrow{\mu}$ be the following relation over W_Σ:
$(\mu_1, \ldots, \mu_n).(p_1, \ldots, p_n) \xrightarrow{\mu} p_i$ for any i s.t. $\mu_i = \mu$. For $m \in M^+$, $m = \mu_1.\mu_2. \ldots .\mu_n$ with $n \geq 1$, let $\xrightarrow{m}$ be the following relation over W_Σ:

$p \xrightarrow{m} p'$ iff there exist $p_o, p_1, \ldots, p_n$ in W_Σ which verify
$p = p_o \xrightarrow{\mu_1} p_1 \xrightarrow{\mu_2} p_2 \ldots \xrightarrow{\mu_n} p_n = p'$.

Then p' is a sub-program of p iff p = p' or there exists $m \in M^+$ s.t. $p \xrightarrow{m} p'$. o

Definition

For any $p, p' \in W_\Sigma$, p and p' are tree-equivalent ($p \overset{t}{\backsim} p'$) if $p \backsim p'$ may be proved from B1 and B2 only, that is if p and p' have identical tree-image. o

In the sequel, tree-equivalent processes will not be distinguished any more from one another, and the ambiguous notation $(\sum_{i \in [1,n]} \mu_i p_i)$ will consequently be used to designate any one of processes which are tree-equivalent to $(\sum_{i=1}^{n} \mu_i p_i)$. Some lemmas are now needed for defining $\hat{p}$.

Lemma 2.

let $p = (\sum_{i=1}^{n} \mu_i p_i)$ and let $\Lambda = \{\lambda \in L / \{p\} \xrightarrow{\lambda} F_\lambda \neq \emptyset\}$,

then $p \backsim (\sum_{\mu_i = \tau} \tau p_i + \sum_{\lambda \in \Lambda} \lambda (\sum_{p' \in F_\lambda} \tau p'))$

Lemma 3.

let $\{q\} \xrightarrow{\lambda} \{q_1\} \cup Q$, then

$\tau q + \lambda (\sum_{i=1}^{n} \tau q_i) \overset{+}{\backsim} \tau q [(\sum_{i=1}^{n} \tau q_i) /_\lambda q_1] + \lambda (\sum_{i=1}^{n} \tau q_i)$ comes from lemma 4

where $f [g_1 /_\lambda g_2]$ is obtained by substituting g_2 for g_1 in f at every occurence g of g_1 such that
$f \xrightarrow{\tau^m \lambda} g$ for some m.

Lemma 4.

Taking $m \geq 1$ and $s'_o \equiv \sum_{i=1}^{n} \tau q_i$, let $v'_m \equiv (\tau(\ldots(\tau(\lambda q_1 + s'_1) + s'_2)\ldots + s'_m)$, and $v''_m \equiv (\tau(\ldots(\tau(\lambda(s'_o) + s'_1) + s'_2)\ldots) + s'_m)$,

then $\tau v''_m \overset{+}{\approx} \tau(\tau v'_m + \tau v''_m)$.

Definition.

For $p \in W_\Sigma$, p is a <u>uniform program</u> (unif (p)) <u>iff</u> for any sub-program q of p and for any $\lambda \in L$, $\{q\} \overset{\lambda}{\to} Q_\lambda$ implies that Q_λ is a singleton set or $Q_\lambda = \emptyset$. o

Proposition 3.

For any $p \in W_\Sigma$, there exists a uniform program $\hat{p} \approx p$.

Proof.

We use induction on the maximal length l of experiments which are feasible with p.

Induction basis.

Let $l = 0$. Then the proposition is verified with taking $\hat{p} \equiv p$, since $(\forall \lambda \in L)(\{p\} \overset{\lambda}{\to} \emptyset)$.

Induction step.

Supposing that the proposition holds for $l \leq m-1$, let us consider the case $l = m \geq 1$ (whence $p \not\equiv NIL$).
let $p \equiv (\mu_1, \ldots, \mu_n).(p_1, \ldots, p_n)$, let $\Lambda = \{\lambda_1, \ldots, \lambda_k\} = \{\lambda \in L / \{p\} \overset{\lambda}{\to} F_\lambda \neq \emptyset\}$ and let $\sigma_j \equiv (\sum_{p' \in F_{\lambda_j}} \tau p')$.

From lemma 2, one has

$$p \approx (\sum_{\mu_i = \tau} \tau p_i + \sum_{j=1}^{k} \lambda_j \sigma_j).$$

Now let $f[\![\lambda_j \blacktriangleright \sigma_j]\!]$ denote the result obtained from simultaneously replacing with σ_j every sub-program g of f s.t. $f \overset{\tau^*\lambda_j}{\longrightarrow} g$, and that for any $j \in [1,k]$. Then $p \approx (\sum_{\mu_i = \tau} \tau p_i [\![\lambda_j \blacktriangleright \sigma_j]\!] + \sum_{j=1}^{k} \lambda_j \sigma_j)$ comes from repeated application of lemma 3.

For any $j \in [1,k]$, the maximal length of experiments feasible with σ_j is less than m, which implies by induction hypothesis that there exists a uniform program $\hat{\sigma}_j \approx \sigma_j$. One has finally
$p \approx \hat{p} \equiv (\sum_{\mu_i = \tau} \tau p_i [\![\lambda_j \blacktriangleright \hat{\sigma}_j]\!] + \sum_{j=1}^{k} \lambda_j \hat{\sigma}_j)$ which is a uniform program. ∎

As it has been announced earlier, our next aim is to obtain a canonical form for uniform programs, which is the object of the following definition.

<u>Definition</u>

Let p be a uniform program.

let $\Lambda = \{\lambda_1, \ldots, \lambda_n\} = \{\lambda \in L / \{p\} \xrightarrow{\lambda} P_\lambda \neq \emptyset\}$, and for $i \in [1,n]$, let $\{p\} \xrightarrow{\lambda_i} \{p_i\}$.

Let $\bar{\Lambda}_1, \ldots, \bar{\Lambda}_k$ be the maximal subsets Λ' of Λ for which $p \not\downarrow \Lambda'$; for $j \in [1,k]$, let $\Lambda_j = \Lambda \setminus \bar{\Lambda}_j$, and let $\Lambda_o = \Lambda \setminus \cup\{\Lambda_j, j \in [1,k]\}$.

Then p is a <u>canonical program iff</u> $p \overset{t}{\backsim} \tilde{p}$, given the following recursive definition of $\tilde{p}$:

- if $(p \not\downarrow \Lambda)$ then $\tilde{p} \equiv (\tau NIL + \sum_{i=1}^{n} \lambda_i \tilde{p}_i)$, else

$$\tilde{p} \equiv \left(\sum_{\lambda_i \in \Lambda_o} \lambda_i \tilde{p}_i + \sum_{j=1}^{k} \tau\left(\sum_{\lambda_i \in \Lambda_j} \lambda_i \tilde{p}_i\right) \right)$$ o

Noticing that for any p, $\tilde{p}$ is a canonical program, we shall now try to show that $p \backsim \tilde{p}$. Several lemmas are still necessary.

<u>Lemma 5.</u>

let $q \equiv (\tau,\tau)$ (NIL,p) where p is a canonical program. Then $q \backsim \tilde{q}$, and $\tilde{q}$ verifies

$(\forall \lambda \in L) (\tilde{q} \xrightarrow{\tau * \lambda} q_\lambda$ <u>iff</u> $p \xrightarrow{\tau * \lambda} p_\lambda \overset{t}{\backsim} q_\lambda)$.

<u>Lemma 6.</u>

$s + \tau(s' + \tau p + \tau p') \overset{+}{\backsim} s + s' + \tau p + \tau p'$

where s,s' stand for any Σ-forms.

<u>Lemma 7.</u>

Let $q = (\tau,\tau)(p,p')$ be a uniform program, whose sub-programs p and p' are canonical programs, both of which different from NIL. Then $q \backsim \tilde{q}$, and $\tilde{q}$ verifies:

$(\forall \lambda \in L)(\tilde{q} \xrightarrow{\tau * \lambda} q_\lambda \Rightarrow p \xrightarrow{\tau * \lambda} p_\lambda \overset{t}{\backsim} q_\lambda$ or $p' \xrightarrow{\tau * \lambda} p'_\lambda \overset{t}{\backsim} q_\lambda)$.

<u>Lemma 8.</u>

Let $q = (\tau,\tau, \ldots, \tau)(q_1, q_2, \ldots, q_k)$, with $k \geq 2$, be a uniform program whose sub-programs q_i are canonical programs. Then $q \backsim \tilde{q}$ and $\tilde{q}$ verifies :

$(\forall \lambda \in L)(\tilde{q} \xrightarrow{\tau * \lambda} q_\lambda \Rightarrow (\exists i \in [1,k])(q_i \xrightarrow{\tau * \lambda} p'_\lambda \overset{t}{\backsim} q_\lambda))$.

Lemma 9.

Let $q = (\lambda_{i_1}, \ldots, \lambda_{i_k}, \tau)(\tilde{p}_{i_1}, \ldots, \tilde{p}_{i_k}, p')$ be a uniform program whose sub-programs $\tilde{p}_{i_j}$ and p' are canonical programs. Then $q \approx \tilde{q}$, and $(\forall \lambda \in L)$ $(\tilde{q} \overset{\tau^*\lambda}{\to} q_\lambda \Rightarrow q \overset{\tau^*\lambda}{\to} p_\lambda \overset{t}{\approx} q_\lambda)$.

Proposition 4.

For any uniform program p, $p \approx \tilde{p}$ and $(\forall \lambda \in L)$ $(\tilde{p} \overset{\tau^*\lambda}{\to} p_\lambda \Rightarrow p \overset{\tau^*\lambda}{\to} p'_\lambda \approx p_\lambda)$.

(proof omitted).

Leaning on propositions 1 to 4, we shall now establish the main result of the section, which is that{A1 ...A7} is a complete proof system for the observational equivalence.

Lemma 10.

For $p \in W_\Sigma$, let can (p) denote any canonical program p' such that $p \approx p'$. Then can (p) exists for any p.

Lemma 11.

For $p, p' \in W_\Sigma$, $p \sim p' \Rightarrow can(p) \overset{t}{\approx} can (p')$.

Corollary.

For $p \in W_\Sigma$, can (p) is defined up to the tree equivalence $\overset{t}{\approx}$, and can (can(p)) $\overset{t}{\approx}$ can(p).

Theorem 1.

{A1, ... A7 }is a complete proof system for either the observational equivalence $\sim$ or for the observational congruence $\tilde{=}$ over W_Σ.

Proof.

Let $p \sim p'$, then $p \approx can(p) \approx can(p') \approx p'$ holds from lemmas 10 and 11, thus $p \approx p'$.

As $p \approx p' \Longrightarrow p \sim p'$ also holds from proposition 2, one may conclude $\sim \equiv \approx$ and{A1, ... A7} is a complete proof system for the observational equivalence, and therefore for the observational congruence (from proposition 1).

⊠

5. PARALLEL COMPOSITION AND RENAMINGS

Following [2], we shall now add to our signature Σ a binary operator which represents the parallel composition of programs, together with a set of unary renaming operators whose purpose is to modify the observable action labels of programs. Our final objective is to establish an equivalent of theorem 1 for the new signature, let $\mathbf{\Sigma}$.

From now on, the set L of observable action labels is assumed to be the union of disjoint subsets Δ and $\overline{\Delta}$ which are connected to one another by reciprocal bijections "$\overline{\ }$" : $\alpha \in \Delta \to \overline{\alpha} \in \overline{\Delta} \to \overline{\overline{\alpha}} = \alpha \in \Delta$. If p = (u/v), where "/" denotes parallel composition, then communication between components u and v of p will be possible iff there exists $\lambda \in L = \Delta \cup \overline{\Delta}$ such that λ and $\overline{\lambda}$ are observable action labels of u and v respectively. Recalling that $M = L \cup \{\tau\}$, let now M^M be the set of partial functions s from M to M which verify the following properties i to iii, where $\perp \notin M$ represents the undefined action label :

i) $s\mu = \tau$ iff $\mu = \tau$ ii) $s^{-1}(\lambda) \in P_f(L)$ for $\lambda \neq \tau$

iii) $(\forall \lambda \in L)\ (s(\overline{\lambda}) = \overline{s(\lambda)}$ or $s(\lambda) = \perp = s(\overline{\lambda}))$.

If p = (u [s]), where $s \in M^M$ and [s] is the corresponding unary operator, then p will have some action labelled λ' iff $s(\lambda) = \lambda'$ for some action label λ of u.

Given the above definitions, let $\mathcal{S} = \{[s]/s \in M^M\}$. Our new signature is $\mathbf{\Sigma} = \Sigma \cup \{/\} \cup \mathcal{S}$, and our algebra of extended programs is $W_{\mathbf{\Sigma}}$, the word algebra over $\mathbf{\Sigma}$. As it has been done for Σ in section 3, our first work with $W_{\mathbf{\Sigma}}$ is to define the observational equivalence of programs, let $\approx$. As Σ is included in $\mathbf{\Sigma}$, a possible short cut is to associate any extended process $p \in W_{\mathbf{\Sigma}}$ with an image πp in the set W_Σ of basic processes, and to take $p \approx p'$ iff $\pi p \sim \pi p'$. Such an indirect way is used in the following definition of the observational equivalence $\approx$ where we make abundant use of results from [2] without justifying them again.

Definition.

For $p \in W_{\mathbf{\Sigma}}$, the "$\Sigma$- image" of p is the basic process πp with $\pi : W_{\mathbf{\Sigma}} \to W_\Sigma$ defined up to the $\overset{t}{\sim}$ equivalence by the following recursive rules, where we let $(\sum_{i \in \emptyset} \mu_i\, p_i) = \emptyset$.

R1 . $\pi(\sum_i \mu_i\, p_i) = (\sum_i \mu_i \pi p_i)$

R2 . $\pi((\sum_i \mu_i p_i)\ [s]) = (\sum_{s\mu_i \neq \perp} s\mu_i\ \pi(p_i\ [s]\ ))$

R'2. $\pi(p\ [s]) = \pi((\pi p)\ [s]\ )$ if p is not a Σ form

R'3. $\pi(p/q) = \pi(\pi p/\pi q)$ if either p or q is not a Σ form

R 3. If $p = (\sum_i \mu_i p_i)$ and $q = (\sum_j \nu_j\ q_j)$ then $\pi(p/q) =$

$$(\sum_i \mu_i\ \pi(p_i/q) + \sum_j \nu_j\ \pi(p/q_j) + \sum_{\mu_i = \overline{\nu}_j} \tau\pi\ (p_i/q_j)).$$

o

Definition.

For p, q εW_Σ, p and q are observationally equivalent ($p \approx q$) iff their Σ-images are equivalent ($\pi p \sim \pi q$). ○

From the above definitions and from theorem 1, it can be easily shown that each of the following schemes of formulae S1, ..., S8 is sound for every interpretations.

<u>S1.</u> $\mu_1 p_1 + \mu_2 p_2 \overset{+}{\approx} \mu_2 p_2 + \mu_1 p_1$

<u>S2.</u> $\mu p + \mu p \overset{+}{\approx} \mu p$

<u>S3.</u> $(\tau).(p) \approx p$

<u>S4.</u> $\mu(\sum_{i\varepsilon I} \mu' p_i) \overset{+}{\approx} (\sum_{i\varepsilon I} \mu\mu' p_i)$ <u>if</u> $I \neq \emptyset$

<u>S5.</u> $\sum_{i\varepsilon I} \mu_i p_i + \tau(\sum_{j\varepsilon J} \mu_j q_j) \overset{+}{\approx} \tau(\sum_{i\varepsilon I} \mu_i p_i) + \tau(\sum_{j\varepsilon J} \mu_j q_j)$ <u>if</u> $J \subseteq I \neq \emptyset$

<u>S6.</u> $\sum_{i\varepsilon I} \mu_i p_i + \tau(\sum_{j\varepsilon J} \mu_j q_j) \overset{+}{\approx} \tau(\sum_{i\varepsilon I} \mu_i (\tau p_i + \tau q_i) + \sum_{j\varepsilon J\setminus I} \mu_j q_j)$

<u>if</u> $\emptyset \neq I \subseteq J$

<u>S7.</u> $(\sum_{i\varepsilon I} \mu_i p_i)[s] \approx (\sum_{s\mu_i \neq \perp} s\mu_i (p_i [s]))$

<u>S8.</u> If $p = (\sum_{i\varepsilon I} \mu_i p_i)$ and $q = (\sum_{j\varepsilon J} \nu_j q_j)$ then $p/q \approx$

$(\sum_{i\varepsilon I} \mu_i (p_i/q) + \sum_{j\varepsilon J} \nu_j (p/q_j) + \sum_{\mu_i = \overline{\nu_j}} \tau(p_i/q_j))$

We shall now try to establish that equational schemes S1 to S8 are a complete proof system for the observational equivalence $\approx$ and for the associated congruence $\underline{\approx}$. The method that we shall use here again is to prove first that $\approx$ and $\underline{\approx}$ are identical before establishing that S1-S8 are a proof system for $\approx$.

Lemma 12.

Let $\mathcal{C}[.] = (\mu_1, \mu_2, \ldots, \mu_n)\ (\bullet, p_2, \ldots, p_n)$, with $n \geq 1$, then $u \approx v \Rightarrow \mathcal{C}[u] \approx \mathcal{C}[v]$.

Lemma 13.

For u and v εW_Σ and s $\varepsilon \mathcal{S}$, $u \approx v \Rightarrow u\,[s] \approx v\,[s]$.

Lemma 14.

For u, v, p εW_Σ,
$u \approx v \Rightarrow (p/u) \approx (p/v)$ and $(u/p) \approx (v/p)$.

Proposition 5.

For p, q εW_Σ, let $p \underline{\approx} q$ iff
$(\forall \mathcal{C}[.] \varepsilon W_{\Sigma \cup \{.\}})\ (\mathcal{C}[p] \approx \mathcal{C}[q])$.

Then the observational congruence $\underline{\approx}$ over W_Σ is just the observational equivalence $\approx$.

Proof.

We have to establish that for any p, qε W_Σ, $p \approx q \Rightarrow \mathcal{C}[p] \approx \mathcal{C}[q]$. We proceed by induction on the term structure of $\mathcal{C}[.]$.

Induction basis.

If $\mathcal{C}$ is the empty context, then $\mathcal{C}[p] = p \approx q = \mathcal{C}[q]$.

Induction step.

We have to prove that for $\mathcal{C}[.]$ in any one of forms $(\mu_1, \ldots, \mu_n)$. $(\bullet, p_2, \ldots, p_n)$ or $(\bullet)\ [s]$ or $(\bullet/r)$ or $(r/\bullet)$, $p \approx q \Rightarrow \mathcal{C}[p] \approx \mathcal{C}[q]$. We proceed by case to case verification.

Case 1.

$\mathcal{C}[.] = (\mu_1, \ldots, \mu_n).(\bullet, p_2, \ldots, p_n)$. Then $p \approx q \Rightarrow \mathcal{C}[p] \approx \mathcal{C}[q]$ by lemma 12.

Case 2.

$\mathcal{C}[.] = (\bullet)\ [s]$

$\pi(\mathcal{C}[p]) = \pi(p\,[s]) = \pi((\pi p)[s])$ for any p, since $p = \pi\, p$ if pε W_Σ. The same way, one has $\pi(\mathcal{C}[q]) = \pi((\pi q)\ [s])$ for any q.

Now, $p \approx q \Rightarrow \pi p \approx \pi q$, where $\pi p, \pi q \varepsilon W_\Sigma$, and therefore $\pi((\pi p)\ [s]) \sim \pi((\pi q)\ [s])$ by lemma 13, that is still $\mathcal{C}[p] \approx \mathcal{C}[q]$.

Case 3.

$\mathcal{C}[.] = (\bullet/r)$

$\pi(\mathcal{C}[p]) = \pi(p/r) = \pi(\pi p/\pi r)$

$\pi(\mathcal{C}[q]) = \pi(\pi q/\pi r)$

Now, $p \approx q \Rightarrow \pi p \sim \pi q$, $\pi p = \pi(\pi p)$, and $\pi q = \pi(\pi q)$, thus $\pi(\pi p) \sim \pi(\pi q)$ which entails $\pi p \approx \pi q$.

By lemma 14 : $\pi p \approx \pi q \Rightarrow (\pi p / \pi r) \approx (\pi q / \pi r)$

$\Rightarrow \pi(\pi p / \pi r) \sim \pi(\pi q / \pi r)$

$\Rightarrow \mathcal{E}[p] \approx \mathcal{E}[q]$.

Case 4.

$$\mathcal{E}[\cdot] = (r/\bullet)$$

similar to case 3. ⊠

The final result of the paper may now be stated before some conclusions are drawn.

Theorem 2.

Equational schemes { S1, ..., S8 } are a complete proof system for either the observational equivalence $\approx$ or for the observational congruence $\underline{\approx}$ over $W_{\boldsymbol{\Sigma}}$.

Proof.

Let p and q ε $W_{\boldsymbol{\Sigma}}$ such that $p \approx q$ (or equivalently $p \underline{\approx} q$).

As ($u \approx v \Rightarrow \mathcal{E}[u] \approx \mathcal{E}[v]$)holds from proposition 5, one can easily verify, using structural induction over terms of $W_{\boldsymbol{\Sigma}}$, that for any r ε $W_{\boldsymbol{\Sigma}}$, $r \approx \pi r$ may be proved by a finite number of applications of axioms S7, S8.

Therefore, ($p \approx \pi p$) and ($q \approx \pi q$) can be given proofs in the axiomatic system {S1 ... S8}.

Let u and v ε W_{Σ} such that $u \approx v$.

$\pi u = u$ and $\pi v = v \Rightarrow u \sim v$ (from the definition of $\approx$).

By theorem 1, there exists a proof of $u \sim v$ in the axiomatic system{A1 ... A7}. Clearly, for any such proof $\mathcal{P}_{\sim}$, there exists a corresponding proof $\mathcal{P}_{\approx}$ of ($u \approx v$) in the axiomatic system {S1 , ..., S6} .

Therefore, ($\pi p \approx \pi q$) can be proved from {S1, ..., S8} since πp and $\pi q \varepsilon W_{\boldsymbol{\Sigma}}$.

⊠

6. CONCLUSIONS

In the paper, we have expressed the opinion that processes p and q are equivalent iff identical answers or absence of answer may be obtained from p and q for any ambiguous communication offer that the observer may present to either p or q after any identical sequence of interactions with the observed processes. We have established that the observational equivalence so defined is also a congruence, and that for two different signatures : Σ (n-ary guarding operators), and $\boldsymbol{\Sigma}$ (guarding operators, renaming operators, and parallel composition). Complete proof systems have been exhibited for the corresponding equivalences $\sim$ and $\approx$, given in the form of finite sets of equational axiom schemas. Technical developments which appear in the paper moreover show a possible strategy for efficient mechanized proofs : in order to prove $p \sim q$, a possible way is to prove can $(\pi p) \overset{t}{\sim}$ can (πq) through the following steps 1 to 4 :

1. From p and q, derive πp and πq using S7 and S8 ;
2. From πp and πq, derive uniform programs $\tilde{\pi} p$ and $\tilde{\pi} q$, using constructive versions of prop. 3 and lemmas 2-4 ;
3. From $\tilde{\pi} p$ and $\tilde{\pi} q$, derive can (πp) and can (πq), using constructive versions of prop. 4 and lemmas 5-9 ;
4. Verify that can (πp) and can (πq) have identical tree-image, using S1 and S2.

Although our signature Σ slightly differs from signature Σ_3 which has been considered in [2] , our congruence $\sim$ may appear as a proper extension of Hennessy-Milner's congruence $\underline{\sim}_3$ over $W_{\Sigma 3}$: if p and $q \in W_{\Sigma}$ can be translated into programs of $W_{\Sigma 3}$ by applying them the syntactical transformation trans : $(W_{\Sigma} \rightarrow W_{\Sigma 3}) : (\mu_1, \ldots, \mu_n)(p_1, \ldots, p_n) \overset{trans}{\rightarrow} (\mu_1 p_1 + (\mu_2 p_2 + (\ldots \mu_n p_n)\ldots))$, then trans (p) $\underline{\sim}_3$ trans (q) $\Rightarrow p \sim q$. In fact, every axiom which has been given for $\underline{\sim}_3$ can be shown to derive from S1-S8 up to syntactical translation.

As was remarked in [3], "the initial algebra for laws{ S1,...,S8} gives a possible denotational semantics for W_{Σ}, which is fully abstract with respect to the operational semantics". To the opposite, it seems not so easy to construct a direct denotational semantics of programs in the domain of labelled trees, although tree (can (πp)) is univoquely determined for $p \in W_{\Sigma}$. Another difficulty is to extend our results to infinite processes, which is our next objective, without neglecting the issue of fairness : it is our opinion that a suitable model cannot be obtained in that case with still reducing concurrency to nondeterminism as it has been done here for finite processes.

Acknowledgements

Thanks are due to P. Le Guernic for helpful discussions and advices.

References.

(1) Milner R. (1978). Synthesis of Communicating Behaviour. Proc. 7th MFCS Conference. Zakopane Poland. Springer-Verlag LNCS Vol. 64,pp. 61-83.

(2) Hennessy M. & Milner R. (1980). On observing nondeterminism and concurrency. ICALP'80. Noordwijkerhout. Springer-Verlag LNCS Vol. 74.

(3) Hennessy M. & Plotkin G. (1980). A term model for CCS. Proc. 9th MFCS Conference. Rydzyna Poland. Springer-Verlag LNCS Vol. 88, pp. 261-274.

(4) Milner R. (1980). A calculus of Communicating Systems . Springer-Verlag LNCS Vol. 92, (170 pp.)

(5) Milner R. (1980). On relating synchrony and asynchrony. University of Edinburgh Report CSR 75-80, (December 1980).

(6) Hoare C.A.R., Brookes S.D., Roscoe A.W. (1981). A theory of Communicating Sequential Processes. Programming Research Group - Oxford OX2 6PE.

PERLUETTE : A Compilers Producing System using Abstract Data Types

Ph. Deschamp, INRIA
Domaine de Voluceau
BP 105 78153 LE CHESNAY

ABSTRACT

Real compilers are usually ad hoc programs. They are costly to write and maintain, and too much complex to be proved correct. This paper presents the compilers producing system Perluette. This system is based upon a formal semantics of programming languages. Programming languages are considered to be algebraic data types. Then it becomes possible to specify and prove their implementations as representations of an algebraic data type into another one.

This formal approach has many advantages ; among these are : the modularity of the compilers specifications ; the independance between the source language and the target language descriptions.

This paper gives an example of compiler specification and describes the implementation of the system in its current state.

INTRODUCTION

Compilers are extensively used in the computer scientist's daily life and all users rely heavily on them. Moreover new programming languages as well as new computers spring up every year. It is thus fundamental to reduce the cost of compiler-producing, while enabling the compiler-writers to prove that the result of their work is correct.

Our approach to compiler specification is based on algebraic abstract data types. We present here the first implementation of our compiler generator, Perluette.

In the first part of this paper we introduce the overall structure of Perluette. The second part shows how we specify compilers, by way of a small example. The last part of the paper describes the implementation we have chosen for the compilers produced by the current version of the system.

I. - COMPILER PRODUCTION : Structure of Perluette

Many techniques are known which try to automate compiler-writing [Gri 71, AU 77]. In particular, with respect to the source language :

- lexical and syntactic analyses can be performed by table-driven programs ;

the analysis tables are usually produced from a grammar in BNF or from regular expressions ;

- the contextual constraints on source programs can be checked using two-level grammars, affix grammars or attributes [Knu 68];

- the ways to specify how to associate a semantic value with source programs are less agreed-upon, since they are not really well-suited to compilation - we can mention axiomatic semantics [Hoa 69], denotational semantics [Ten 76], algebraic semantics [CN 76], ...

As for the target code, much research is being devoted to the problem of producing "good" (efficient, reliable) code as easily as possible. This has led to a variety of techniques ; they usually use an internal form of the source program to be translated (trees or tuples).

The most conventional way to write compilers uses none of the techniques above : each compiler is an ad hoc program ; source language dependencies and target language dependencies are scattered through the body of the compiler. Such compilers are difficult to modify or maintain ; moreover they are not readily adapted to accept another source language, or to produce another kind of target code.

Thus it is necessary, in order to achieve the goals of cost-reduction and correctness-proof, to produce compilers from independent descriptions of the source and target languages specifications, as suggested by F.L. Morris [Mor 73]. This leads to the following "ideal" schema, where all the dirty work is automated :

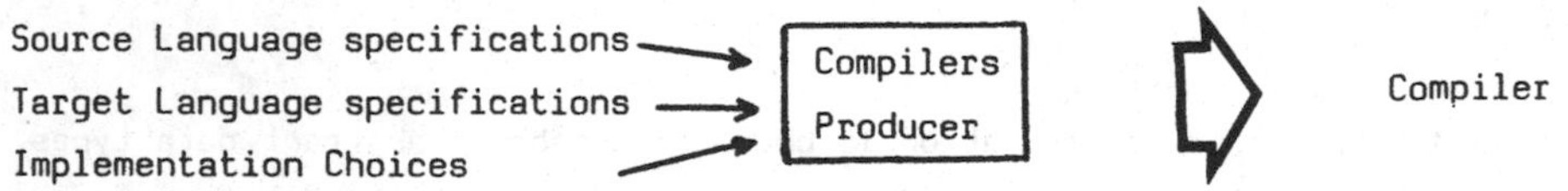

The implementation choices specification describe the kind of implementation the compiler designer chooses for each object of the source language - e.g. one needs to specify if arrays are implemented row-wise or column-wise. In our opinion this is an essential part in the design of compilers, and these implementation choices must be rigorously specified and proven correct.

Our compilers Producer System,named Perluette, works basically along these lines : the source language and target language are specified by algebraic abstract data types [GH 78, GHM 78] - abridged to ADT in the sequel - ; the implementation choices are specified as a representation of the source ADT by the target ADT, allowing to make use of the results of research on representations of ADTs [GTW 78]. The intermediate forms manipulated by the compilers are the terms of those ADTs, so that any compiler produced by Perluette has the following behaviour :

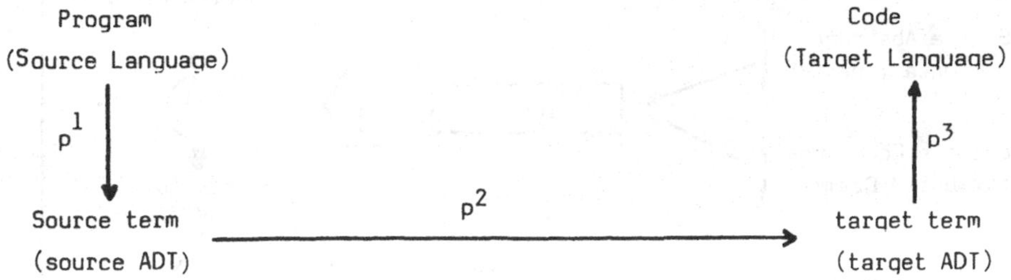

p^1 consists of lexical and syntactic analyses, symbol-table creation, context-dependent checks and source term production ;

p^2 is the translation from source to target terms, as a matter of fact a mere rewriting of the source term ;

p^3 is the code-generation phase ; at the moment we consider it as a top-down traversal of the object term, driven mainly by pattern-matching, but a great deal of evolution has been made provision for.

The first and third phases (p^1 and p^3) match respectively the front end and the back end of modern compilers. The front end is implemented by way of some of the techniques we mentioned earlier : automatic lexical and syntaxic analyses and attributes manipulation.

These three phases are produced by three (nearly) independent modules of the Perluette system. The overall schema of the whole processes of compiler definition, construction and use is given below.

In the next section we give the reader some of the flavour of the various specifications, by way of a small example. This example is treated at length in [Des 80], together with the validity proof of our implementation choices. A more realistic source language has been described using our formalism in[GDM 78] and has been used for the testing of our experimental version of Perluette.

The last section presents the implementation chosen for the three modules of the compilers produced by Perluette.

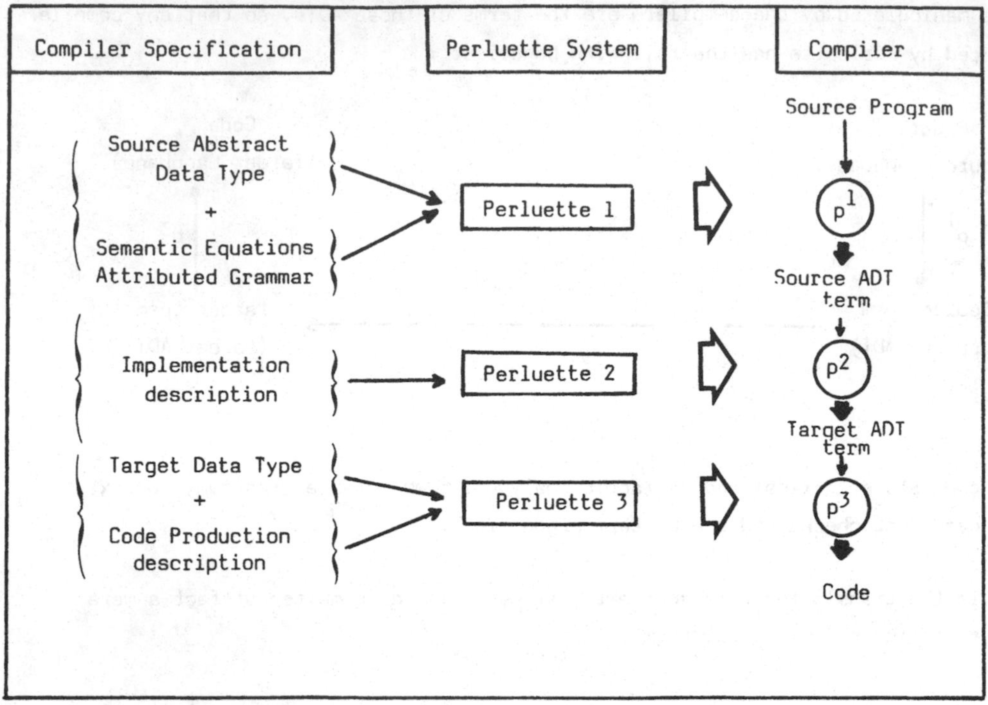

II. - COMPILER SPECIFICATION : A small example

A compiler specification is made up of three parts : source language definition, target language definition and implementation choices description.

II.1. - Source Language Specification

The small source language we want to describe here as an example allows to use integer variables and integer vectors, the lower and upper bounds of which are defined when they are declared - i.e. at compile-time.

Its syntax is immaterial here and will not be given. Suffice it to say that traditional statements on arrays are available : one can have access to the value of an array element or change this value ; of course usual operations on integers can be used, such as addition or multiplication. For simplicity sake we do not introduce any block-structure in this language, and we consider only correct programs - without so-called compile-time errors -. This increases the legibility of the semantic equations, since many tests may be omitted.

The semantic definition of a source language is divided into two parts :

- the presentation of the corresponding abstract data type ;

- the definition of the semantic functions, which give a meaning for each kind of sentence in the language (as a term of the ADT).

We shall here consider first the semantics of the expressions of our language, then the semantics of statements.

II.1.1. - Semantics of expressions

II.1.1.1. - Sorts for expressions

First of all we must consider the sort Integer : we specify that four operations on Integers can be used :

```
Type Integer :
    Op(Integer,Integer) → Integer : Add,Sub,Mult,Div
  End Integer ;
```

This declaration of the four operations is all the Perluette System needs : we are now able to construct terms of the sort Integer - as we denote any constant by its text, enclosed between apostrophes, following its sort name (e.g. "Integer '0'").

If we wanted to prove our compiler correct we would have to associate a semantics to the Integer sort, by way of axioms. In the scope of this paper however we shall deal only with the compiler construction, and not with its validity proof, so that only the syntactic part of the ADT is given.

In our language identifiers can be used, which refer to integer values :

```
Type Int-id :
    Op(Int-id) → Integer : Value
  End Int-id ;
```

There are also identifiers which give access to arrays :

```
Type Array-id :
    Op(Array-id,Integer) → Integer : Value-ith ;
    Op(Array-id)         → Integer : Lwb, Upb
  End Array-id ;
```

The operations Lwb and Upb give, for any array identifier, the value of its lower and upper bounds.

We now are able to define the terms we want to associate with the expressions that can occur in our language. For example, assuming some suitable declarations, to the expression

T[X[I+3]]

we want to associate the term

```
Value-ith(Array-id'X',
          Value-ith(Array-id'X',
                    Add(Value(Int-id'I'),Integer'3')))
```

We of course do not want to do this by hand, nor do we wish that our compiler users see it. This is an intermediate text manipulated by the compiler, produced by attributes that the Perluette System constructs from the semantic equations given below.

II.1.1.2. - Semantic function for expressions

We shall call this function "V" ; it yields, for each expression of our language, a term of the sort Integer. It is defined by equations such as :

```
V⟦E+T⟧  = Add(V⟦E⟧,V⟦T⟧)
V⟦NUMBER⟧ = Integer 'NUMBER'
V⟦id⟧  = Value(Int-id'id')
V⟦id [ E]⟧= Value-ith(Array-id'id',V⟦E⟧)
V⟦(E) ⟧ = V⟦E⟧
```

These equations specify exactly how to obtain, from the text of an expression, the corresponding term.

II.1.2. - Semantics of statements

II.1.2.1. - Sort for statements

In order to give the semantics of statements we introduce a new sort, Stmt. (The semantics of this sort would not be given by way of axioms, but by way of "predicate transformers", as statements alter the axioms of the ADT. For example, the result of the elaboration of "I:=0" is to introduce the property "Value(Int-id'I') = Integer '0'" and to suppress any property contradicting it ; thus the operation Value changes - see [Gau 80] for a complete introduction to this concept).

The operations of the sort Stmt, besides the obvious sequence statement, are Declare-integer and Declare-array, Assignment, which alters the operation Value, and

Change-ith, which modifies the operation Value-ith :

```
   Type Stmt :
       Op(Int-id)                         →    Stmt : Declare-integer ;
       Op(Int-id,Integer)                 →    Stmt : Assign ;
       Op(Array-id,Integer,Integer)       →    Stmt : Declare-array ;
       Op(Array-id,Integer,Integer)       →    Stmt : Change-ith ;
       Op(Stmt,Stmt)                      →    Stmt : Seq ;
   End Stmt ;
```

II.1.2.2. - Semantic function for statements

The semantic function "S" enables us to construct the terms corresponding to source programs. It is defined by semantic equations, among which are :

$S[\![id := E]\!] = Assign(Int\text{-}id'id', V[\![E]\!])$

$S[\![id[E_1] := E_2]\!] = Change\text{-}ith(Array\text{-}id'id', V[\![E_1]\!], V[\![E_2]\!])$

II.1.3. - Example

Using the S and V functions, we can obtain the semantic value associated to any correct program. Let us consider for example the following source program (which will be used throughout this paper)

```
   integer I ; integer J ;
   array [0..1]T ; array [1..4] X ; ...
       I:=1 ;
       X[4]:=0 ;
       ...
       J:=T[X[I+3]]...
```

The associated source term will be the following formula :

```
   Seq(Seq(Seq(...
       Declare-integer(Int-id'I')                            "Declaration of I"
       ,...
       , Declare-array(Array-id'T',Integer'0',Integer'1'     "Declaration of T"
       ...
       ,Seq(Seq(...                                          "Semicolons"
       Assign(Int-id'I',Integer'1')                          "I:=1"
       ,...
       ,Assign(Int-id'J',                                    "J:=
               Value-ith(Array-id'T',                        "   T[       "
                       Value-ith(Array-id'X',                "      X[    "
                               Add(Value(Int-id'I'),         "        I+  "
                                   Integer'3'))))))          "          3]] "
```

II.2. - Target language specification

The target language is described by an abstract data type and a code production specification ; we chose here a very simple language, in order to be able to describe it shortly : as well as registers, this language manipulates values and addresses where these values can be stored (as "contents") :

```
type contents = union(value,address) :
    op(value, value) → value      : add,sub,mult,div ;
    op(address)      → contents   : mc ;              (*memory contents*)
    op(address,value)→ address    : index
  end contents ;
type register :
    op(register) → contents : rc                       (*register contents*)
  end register ;
type stmt :
    op(register,contents) → stmt : load ;
    op(address,contents)  → stmt : store ;
    ...
    op(stmt,stmt)         → stmt : seq ;
    op()                  → stmt : nop
  end stmt ;
```

This target ADT is very simple indeed, and its description readily understood. Even so, code production has to be described in a rigorous way. This is done by way of a recursive function, the operand of which is the target term to produce code for - this is the converse of what is done in the first phase of the compiler, only much easier - ; for example, in the case of the "store" statement :

```
Code(store(<address> ,<contents>)) is
   case <address> of
   address ad : case <contents>of
                rc(register r) : STORE,r ad.          (*simplest case.*)
                  other        : ≠INCR (≠SAVE)        (*we need room.*)
                                 STORE,A ≠SAVE        (*save accumulator.*)
                                 code(store(register'A',<contents >)) (*these two*
                                 STORE,A ad            *statements do it.*)
                                 LOAD,A ≠SAVE         (*previous value.*)
                                 ≠DECR (≠SAVE).       (*give back space.*)
    index(address ad,< value>) : (*same thing, but indexed store*)
                                 ...
```

One can see from this example that "code" thus traverses the term in an "outside-in" fashion, using a kind of pattern-matching process for each subterm. We shall see in section III.3 how this is achieved in the compiler.

II.3. - Implementation choices specification

We describe the most simple implementation of our source language : every integer variable is represented by an address and every array variable by the address of its first element.

An implementation is specified by giving

. for each source type :

- the target type used to implement it ;
- the way to implement constants of this type when applicable ;

. for each source operator, the target term which represents it.

```
Type Integer : value ; (*integers are represented by values*)
   repr Integer'N' = value'DEC-TO-HEX(N)'(*integers are decimal,
                                            values are hexadecimal*)
Type Int-id:address ;
   repr Int-id'I' = address'FETCH-ADDRESS(I)'
                    (*see the representation of Declare-integer below*)
Type Array-id : address ;
   repr Array-id'X' = address'FETCH-ADDRESS(X)'

Type Stmt : stmt ; (*there are no constants of type Stmt*)

repr Op(Integer i, Integer j)→ Integer : Add =
       add(repr i, repr j) (*the target term is built from the terms which
                             represent the source sub-terms*)
...
repr Op(Int-id k)→ Integer : Value =
        mc(repr k)          (*remember that the representation of an identifier
                             is the address of its location*)
...
repr Op (Int-id var, Integer exp) →Stmt : Assign =  (*var:=exp*)
         store(repr var,repr exp)

repr Op (Int-id'id')→ Stmt : Declare-integer =
       (≠        (*here we perform compile-time computations*)
           ALLOCATE-INTEGER(id)   (*so that FETCH-ADDRESS may get
                                     the location*)
       ≠)        (*end of compile-time*)
       nop()     (*this is the term yielded by Declare-integer : as variables are
                   "allocated" at compile time, nothing need be done at run-time*)
...
```

The header of the representation of Declare-integer calls for some explanation. A "constant" occurs in it : as can be deduced from the semantic equations of the source ADT, that operation has only constants as operands in the terms we build ; we are thus able to state that these constants are not to be represented. This feature makes it possible to clearly separate what has to be done in the representation phase from what is done in the first phase (no allocation is performed in the first phase).

II.4. - Example of compiler throughput

We can now use the specification given in the previous section to rewrite any source term obtained from a source program : we just proceed from the inside of the term towards the outside, except for the subterms beginning with Declare-integer (or Declare-array), the subterms of which are not to be rewritten.

Let us use again the program given in II.1.3. with the corresponding source term. It is fairly easy to rewrite that term, using the set of rules of II.3.. We thus obtain immediately the target term :

```
seq(seq(seq(...
    nop()                                   (*But ALLOCATE-INTEGER(I) has been
                                                                  evaluated*)
    ,...
    ,seq(seq(...
    store(address'0',value'1')              (*If FETCH-ADDRESS(I)=>0*)
    ,...
    ,store(address'1',                      (*For J:=T[X[I+3]]*)
           mc(index(address'2'
                    sub(mc(index(address'4',
                                 sub(add(mc(address'0'),
                                         value'3',
                                     value'1'))),(*lower bound of X*)
                  value'0'))))))    (*lower bound of T*)
```

Remember that this is a target term, and as such not supposed to be legible. Some inefficiencies appear here, due to array indexing, which can be easily removed in the code production process.

Our compiler specification is now complete - as a matter of fact we would have to supply Perluette with such functions as ALLOCATE-INTEGER or FETCH-ADDRESS in order to obtain a running compiler. We are now going to describe the way this compiler is implemented by our system.

III.1. - Implementation of the first phase

As we mentionned earlier (section I), the context sensitive aspects of the source language are dealt with by attributes. We use for syntax analysis the SYNTAX system ; this system comprises a LALR(1) parsers constructor which generates very efficient analysers - with a very powerful parameterised error-recovery strategy [Bou 80] -. Coupled to SYNTAX is DELTA, an attributes processing system [Lor 75].

One of the consequences of our choice of LISP is that the attributes for contextual checks have to be specified in LISP, as well as the semantic functions. To simplify the work of compiler writers, a preprocessor to DELTA accepts as input descriptions of these semantic functions not too far from the form we gave, and produces as output a full description, in LISP, of the attributes to compute.

Thus what we gave in II.1.1.2. as V⟦id⟧ = Value(Int-id'id') will be translated by that preprocessor into :

```
(setq V(<id>)(list(quote Value)
                 (list(quote Int-id)
                      (quote PTEXT(id)))))
```

where PTEXT is the DELTA-standard attribute giving access to the string associated with a lexical unit.

When the first phase of the compiler encounters in a source program an integer identifier occuring in a expression, it evaluates this attribute definition. For example, compiling "...I..." produces the term (LISP-expression) : (Value(Int-id I)).

III.2. - Implementation of the second phase

As we have pointed out previously, this phase rewrites the source term computed by the first phase. This is done by evaluating it : each subterm is a function call, the result of which is the translation of this subterm. Those functions are used in a call-by-value scheme, except for the constants : these are, stricly speaking, nullary operations, but they are actually parameterised by their texts, which must not be evaluated.

This is best explained using an example : in order to rewrite the term given above, we need to define the functions Value and Int-id. We gave for Value the following representation :

repr op (Int-id k) → Integer : Value = mc(repr k)

The Perluette-2 module (see the diagram at the end of section I) produces this function definition for Value :

```
(lambda(k)
    (list(quote mc)k))
```

As for the constants, we use the "nlambda" feature of LISP : a nlambda function receives its arguments un-evaluated. Moreover, in order to be able to reach the texts of identifiers - this is used for example in the representation of Declare-integer (see II.3.) - we systematically keep them in the target terms : any constant of the target term is made up of three parts : its type, its denotation, the text of the source constant it comes from.

This explains the definition Perluette 2 deduces from the representation of Int-id :

```
(nlambda(I)
    (list(quote address)
         (FETCH-ADDRESS I)
         I))
```

Thus when the source term (Value(Int-id I)) is evaluated in this environment, it delivers the following target term :

```
(mc(address 0 I)
```

The second phase of the compilers produced by the Perluette System thus consists of definitions of lambda and nlambda expressions such as the above ; these definitions can be compiled for further efficiency.

III.3. - Implementation of the third phase

The target term is also considered as a LISP "program". The function calls which occur in this program produce code, depending on their operands, which are un-evaluated ; these functions are therefore defined as nlambdas.

This means that the LISP produced by Perluette from the code description of "store" (given in II.2.) results in this definition for store :

```
(nlambda(address contents)
    (let(match(car address))
        (cond((eq match(quote address))
              (let(ad(cadr address))
                  (let(match(car contents))
                      (cond((and(eq match(quote rc))
                                (eq(caadr contents)(quote register)))
                            (let(r(cadadr contents))
                                (STORE,r ad)))
                           (T(progn(≠INCR ≠SAVE)
                                  ...))))))
             ((and(eq match(quote index))
                  (eq...)
                  ...)
              (let(value(caddr address))
                  ...)))))
```

This is a straightforward translation of the code definition given in II.2.. As all other LISP programs composing the compilers, this is intended for the underlying LISP system and the compiler writer does not have to worry about it.

IV. - CONCLUSION

This system is a typical example of an application of theoretical methods to a practical compilers producing system. The advantages of this formal approach are obvious ; the modularity of the compiler specification facilitates the use of the system ; the source and the target languages are independently defined and the corresponding parts of the compiler (p^1 and p^3) can be used in several compilers.

The whole Perluette system is now running on Multics. The formal definition of a realistic programming language and the specification of an implementation have been used as a test case for the first two phases [GMD 81]. The third phase is being used with a description of the DEC 11 machine language. A code generator for Multics will be described later on.

The high quality of the compilers produced by Perluette has been our main aim throughout the development of the system. Efficiency considerations thus motivate our choice of LISP as host language for these compilers, while attributes provide the user with a powerful mean to perform compile-time computations.

Acknowledgements

M.C. Gaudel and C. Pair designed the theoretical approach upon which Perluette is based. M. Mazaud and R. Rakotozafy are co-implementors of the current version of the system. It is pleasure to thank them for our numerous and fruitful discussions.

BIBLIOGRAPHY

[AU 77] Aho A.V., Ullman J.D., Principles of Compiler Design Addison-Wesley, Reading, Mass., 1977.

[Bou 80] Boullier P., Génération automatique d'analyseurs syntaxiques avec rattrapage d'erreurs. Journées francophones sur la production assistée de Logiciel, Genève, 1980.

[CN 76] Courcelle B., Nivat M., Algebraic Families of Interpretations 17th Symposium on Foundations of Computer Science, Houston, 1976.

[Des 80] Deschamp Ph., Production de Compilateurs à partir d'une Description Sémantique des Langages de Programmation : le système Perluette. Thèse de Docteur-Ingénieur, INPL, 1980.

[GAU 80] Gaudel M.C., Génération et preuve de Compilateurs basées sur une sémantique formelle des langages de programmation. Thèse d'Etat, INPL, 1980.

[Gri 71] Gries D., Compiler Construction for Digital Computers. John Wiley and sons, New York, 1971.

[GDM 78] Gaudel M.C., Deschamp Ph., Mazaud M., Semantics of procedures as an algebraic abstract data type. Laboria Report n° 334, 1978.

[GDM 81] Gaudel M.C., Deschamp Ph., Mazaud M., Compilers Construction from high-level specifications. in Automatic Program Construction Techniques, MacMillan Publishing Co, 1981.

[GH 78] Guttag J.V., Horning J.J., The Algebraic Specification of Abstract Data Types. Acta Informatica, vol. 10, n°1, 1978.

[GH 81] Griss M.L., Hearn A.C., A Portable LISP Compiler Software-Practice and Experience, vol. 11, 1981.

[GHM 78] Guttag J.V., Horowitz E., Muser D.V. Abstract Data Types and Software Validation CACM 21, n° 12, 1978.

[GTW 78] Goguen J.A., Thatcher J.W., Wagner E.G., Abstract Data Types as Initial Algebras and the Correctness of Data Representations. in Current Trends in Programming Methodology 4, Prentice Hall, 1978.

[Hoa 69] Hoare C.A.R.,
An Axiomatic Basis of Computer Programming
CACM 12, n° 10, 1969.

[Knu 68] Knuth D.E.,
Semantics of Context Free Languages,
Mathematical Systems Theory 2, 2, 1968.

[Lor 75] Lorho B.,
Semantic Attributes in the system DELTA.
Symposium on Implementations of Algorithmic Languages,
Novossibirsk, USSR, 1975.

[Mor 73] Morris F.L.,
Advice on Structuring Compilers and proving them correct,
Symposium on Principles of Programming Languages, Boston, 1973.

[Ten 76] Tennent R.D.,
The Denotational Semantics of Programming Languages, CACM 19,
n° 8, 1976.

A WEAKEST PRECONDITION SEMANTICS FOR COMMUNICATING PROCESSES

by:

Tzilla Elrad[1] and Nissim Francez[2]

Dept. of Computer Science
Technion - IIT
Haifa 32000, Israel

SUMMARY

A weakest precondition semantics for communicating processes is presented, based on a centralized approach. Semantic equations are given for the CSP constructs. The representation of delay is discussed. Several examples of applying the rules are given.

Key Words and Concepts:
Weakest precondition, semantics, communicating processes, distributed programming, nondeterminism, termination, deadlock.

CR Categories: 5.24, 4.32.

---

(1) The work of the first author was supported by NSF grant MCS-80-17577.

(2) The work of the second author was supported by a grant by IBM-Israel.

I. INTRODUCTION

The importance of the axiomatic approach to formal definitions of the semantics of concurrent programming languages is by now widely recognized [OG,AFR1,FS,LS,LG].

The purpose of this paper is to investigate the use of WP (Weakest Precondition) semantics as a tool for the formal definition of the semantics of languages for concurrent and distributed programming.

As far as we know, all the previous attempts to use WP semantics were by means of reduction to sequential nondeterminism [LS,FS]. Here we aim at a direct concurrent semantics, preserving the processes structure of the program.

Due to recent developments in the technology of micro-processors, there is an increasing trend towards the use of languages supporting distributed activity involving communication, e.g. CSP [H], PLITS [FE], Distributed Processes [BH] and, recently, ADA [ADA].

As a model language for our investigation, CSP has been chosen. This language already has been given other formal definitions [FHLR], [FLP], [CH], [AFR1], [CC], [CM], [LG], [P] and attracted considerable attention.

An important feature of CSP is its emphasis on terminating concurrent programs, as opposed, to [MM] or [MI], for example, where non-termination is the rule. This fits nicely with the use of WP which also emphasizes termination.

In the denotational semantics already given for CSP [FHLR], [FLP], [CC], as well as in the various proof rules for partial correctness, no attempt was made to characterize properly terminating programs.

We show that properties like freedom of deadlocks are also naturally reflected in a WP semantics.

Some aspects of CSP which need to be clarified by formal definition of their semantics, are:

a) Stress on simultaneity rather than on mutual exclusion as the synchronization means.
b) The function of the communication primitives of input and output (traditionally known as send and receive) as a choice mechanism and repetition control mechanism. This is an extension of Dijkstra's guarded commands language [D] allowing two kinds of non-deterministic resolutions: local (within a process) and global (among several processes).
c) The distributed termination convention, by means of which the global property of termination (depending on the state of the whole program) is distributed to the various processes. By this convention a process will either terminate by itself, or its termination will be induced by other processes with which it communicates.

In principle, one can envisage two approaches to a WP semantics. According to the first approach, some a priori semantics is attributed to each process, and then those meanings are bound together to yield the semantics of the whole program. This approach was used in [FHLR], [FLP] and [MI], [MM] in the denotational setting. In previous attempts by Apt, de Roever and Francez (unpublished) this approach was tried in a WP setting, and caused the use of complicated states involving histories. Even there, a proper weakest precondition semantics for a process turned to be impossible, since such a semantics records only positive information, about successful computations, and disregards unsuccessful paths, which still may match with another process' failing path and thus create a global failure. Here we have chosen the second approach, where a centralized semantics is given directly to the whole program, thereby avoiding the consideration of histories as part of the state.

II. THE SEMANTIC EQUATIONS

We start with some preliminaries. Let $P:: [P_1 \| \ldots \| P_i \| \ldots \| P_n]$ be a program with (variable disjoint) communicating processes P_i, $i=1,\ldots,n$. The symbol " $\|$ " denotes concurrent composition. We refer the reader unfamiliar with CSP to [H] for an informal and detailed description of the language. Let Q be a predicate over the disjoint union of all the states of the P_i's.

We denote by Λ an empty process (with no instructions). We assume that each non-empty process is structured as $P_i:: S_i; P_i'$, with P_i' possibly Λ. We call P_i' the rest of process P_i, and its has a major significance in the definition of the "rest of the (whole) program", a central concept in what follows.

We denote by SEQ all non-empty sequential program sections, i.e. those sections which contain no communication. We assume WP[S,Q] as known [D] for $S \in$ SEQ.

We denote by IF all guarded selection statements. For notational convenience, we shall assume that each guard g has two components: a boolean b (we take $b \equiv$ true if it is not included) and a communication c (we take, by convention, $c \equiv$ skip, in case it was not included [LG]). Thus, if $S_i \in$ IF, S_i has the form

$$S_i:: [b_i^1;\ c_i^1 \rightarrow T_i^1 \ \square \ \vdots \ \square \ b_i^{n_i};\ c_i^{n_i} \rightarrow T_i^{n_i}].$$

Also, DO denotes the set of all repetitive statements. A subscript in a statement denotes the index of the process to which the statement belongs.

For convenience, we use the following syntactic (meaning preserving) transformation:

$$P_j?x \Rightarrow [P_j?x \rightarrow \text{skip}]$$
$$P_j!x \Rightarrow [P_j!x \rightarrow \text{skip}]$$

and thus have to consider i/o commands only as guards. We consider this to be a simpler solution (to the problem of the double role of i/o commands) then the distinction between weak and strong guarding as in [P].

We also use the (syntactic) predicate $\mu(c_i,c_j)$ where c_i,c_j are i/o commands.

$$\mu(c_i,c_j) = \begin{cases} \text{true} & c_i = [P_j?x]_i,\ c_j=[P_i!y]_j,\ \text{type}(x)=\text{type}(y) \\ \text{false otherwise.} \end{cases}$$

$\mu(c_i,c_j)$ means that c_i and c_j are <u>syntactically matching</u> communication commands taken from S_i and S_j respectively. Note that this definition hints that messages are strongly typed, and communication is always to named target processes, determined syntactically (at compile time), which are important features of CSP. We use also the notation target(c), where

$$\text{target}(P_j?x) = \text{target}(P_j!y) = j.$$

Also, by convention, target $([\text{skip}]_j) = j$.

We would like to extend the weakest precondition semantics for nondeterministic sequential programs [D] to deal with communicating processes. Obviously, we need to add a basic definition of the meaning of a single communication. We define:

<u>Global assignment-rule</u>: for $1 \leq i \neq j \leq n$

$$WP[[P_j?x]_i \| [P_i!y]_j, Q] = \begin{cases} Q^x_y & \mu(P_j?x, P_i!y) \\ \text{false} & \sim\mu(P_j?x, P_i!y), \end{cases}$$

where Q^x_y is the predicate obtained by substituting y for all free occurrences of x in Q. Operationally, this means that a single communication acts as a global assignment, relating variables of two (disjoint) processes.

Assume that for some $1 \leq \ell \leq n$, $S_\ell \in SEQ$, so S_ℓ contains no input/output commands. In that case S_ℓ might unconditionally be chosen for execution. An execution of S_ℓ should result in a state which satisfies the weakest precondition for a successful execution of the rest of the program in such a way that Q will hole at the end.

Thus we must have

$$WP[P,Q] \supset WP[S_\ell, Q']$$

where

$$Q' = WP[P_1 \| \ldots \| P'_\ell \| \ldots \| P_n, Q].$$

It can be proved that we can define: for some $1 \leq \ell \leq n$, $S_\ell \in SEQ$

$$WP[P,Q] = WP[S_\ell, WP[P_1 \| \ldots \| P'_\ell \| \ldots \| P_n, Q]]\ .$$

i.e. giving preference to sequential segments preserves the meaning. Recall that P'_ℓ is the rest of process P_ℓ, whose first section was sequential. But what if there is no $1 \leq \ell \leq n$: $S_\ell \in SEQ$? Then, the program is in a state in which each of the processes (not yet terminated) is willing to communicate; some of the communication commands serve as iteration guards, and some others as selection guards. In such a situation the following three properties must hold for any state belonging to the WP:

Property a: Execution of any of the passable guarded commands will result in a state which satisfies the weakest precondition for successfully executing the rest of the program, with respect to the same post condition Q.

Property b: Any exit from a loop should result in a state satisfying the weakest precondition for successfully executing the rest of the program, with respect to Q.

Property c: At least one of the guards is passable, or at least one of the loops must terminate.

None of the three alternatives holding means that the program is in a deadlock-state. In that case we must have WP[P,Q] = false.

We proceed by giving a formal presentation of properties a, b and c.

Property a: Communication commands as a choice mechanism

Since for all $1 \leq i \leq n$ S_i is either a selection (IF) command or an iteration (DO) command, all S_i's have the form:

$$S_i :: \begin{array}{l}[b_i^1 \, ; \, c_i^1 \rightarrow T_i^1 \\ \Box b_i^2 \, ; \, c_i^2 \rightarrow T_i^2 \\ \vdots \\ \Box b_i^{n_i} ; \, c_i^{n_i} \rightarrow T_i^{n_i}]\end{array} \quad \text{or} \quad S_i :: \begin{array}{l}*[b_i^1 \, ; \, c_i^1 \rightarrow T_i^1 \\ \Box b_i^2 \, ; \, c_i^2 \rightarrow T_i^2 \\ \vdots \\ \Box b_i^{n_i} ; \, c_i^{n_i} \rightarrow T_i^{n_i}]\end{array}$$

Our centralized approach enables us to determine (syntactically) all possible matching communications. The predicate $\mu(c_i^k, c_j^{k'}) \wedge b_i^k \wedge b_j^{k'}$ means that the corresponding communication path can be followed. In this case the guards $b_i^k \, ; \, c_i^k$ (in S_i) and $b_j^{k'} \, ; \, c_j^{k'}$ (in S_j) are said to be passable.

The following will define the meaning of the communication primitives as a choice mechanism and express global nondeterminism:

$$\bigwedge_{i,j,k,k' : \, \mu(c_i^k, c_j^{k'})} b_i^k \wedge b_j^{k'} \supset WP[c_i^k \parallel c_j^{k'}, WP[\tilde{P}_{i,j}, Q]]$$

whose meaning is: For any passable pair of matching guards, the execution of the communication commands will result in a state satisfying the weakest precondition for successfully executing the rest of the program (denoted by $\tilde{P}_{i,j}$) with respect to Q. An exact definition of $\tilde{P}_{i,j}$ follows below.

The condition $(c_i^k = \text{skip}) \wedge b_i^k$ indicates that process S_i is ready to choose some guard with no communication request, i.e. the guard b_i^k ; skip (in S_i) is passable. Here we have local nondeterminism:

$$\bigwedge_{i,k : \, c_i^k = \text{skip}} b_i^k \supset WP[\text{skip}, WP[\tilde{P}_i, Q]]$$

whose meaning is:

For any local nondeterministic choice, passing this guard will successfully end satisfying the weakest precondition of the rest of the program with respect to a.

We still have to define $\tilde{P}_{i,j}$ (and $\tilde{P}_i$), which represent the "rest of the program". The ability to consider this "rest of the program" is a major difference from the two-leveled approaches, which consider one process at a time.

Note that so far we did not care whether the c_i^k's are taken from an IF command or from a DO command. This distinction is expressed in the definition of $\tilde{T}$. We let, for $1 \leq i \neq j \leq n$

$$\tilde{P}_{i,j} = [P_1 \| \ldots \| \tilde{T}_i^k ; P_i' \| \ldots \| \tilde{T}_j^{k'} ; P_j' \| \ldots \| P_n]$$

$$\tilde{P}_i = [P_1 \| \ldots \| \tilde{T}_i^k ; P_i' \| \ldots \| P_n]$$

where

$$\tilde{T}_i^k = \begin{cases} T_i^k & S_i \in IF \\ T_i^k ; S_i & S_i \in DO . \end{cases}$$

The definition of $\tilde{T}_i^k$ reflects the usual meaning of a loop as once executing the loop body and then again the whole loop, as is usual in definitions using the least fixed point approach. However, the definition reflects also the fact that between two consecutive executions of a loop S_i, statement in some P_j, $j \neq i$, may be executed.

Property b: Distributed Termination

A loop S_i terminates either because all b_i^k's are false or because all the target processes referred to in its guard have terminated, or a combination of both.

The termination condition for a loop S_i (denoted by LE_i) can be expressed as follows:

$$LE_i = \bigwedge_{k:P_{target(c_i^k)} \neq \Lambda} \sim b_i^k$$

LE_i means: each of the guards of S_i is either non-passable (having b_i^k = false) or is trying to communicate with a terminated target process. Property b can be formally expressed as:

$$\bigwedge_{i:S_i \in DO} (LE_i \supset WP[P_1 \| \ldots \| P_i' \| \ldots \| P_n, Q]).$$

For each of the loops which satisfies LE_i (i.e. are ready to terminate) the program is in a state which satisfies the weakest precondition for successfully executing the rest of the program with respect to Q. Here the rest of the program is obtained by deleting S_i completely from the program.

Property c: Freedom from Deadlock

The predicate

$$BB_1 = \bigvee_{i,j,k,k':\ \mu(c_i^k,c_j^{k'})} b_i^k \wedge b_j^{k'}$$

means: at least one pair of matching communications is passable. Also, the predicate

$$BB_2 = \bigvee_{i,k:c_i^k = \text{skip}} b_i^k$$

means: at least one of the local nondeterministic guards is passable.

Let $\qquad BB = BB_1 \vee BB_2$.

BB means: at least one guard is passable (either a global nondeterministic choice can be made, or some local nondeterministic choice is possible).

In case of $\sim BB$ we must require that at least one of the loops is ready to terminate, as denoted by:

$$\bigvee_{i:S_i \in DO} LE_i .$$

Deadlock freedom can be thus expressed by:

$$BB \vee \bigvee_{i:S_i \in DO} LE_i \vee \bigvee_{i:S_i \in SEQ} \text{true}.$$

Formal presentation of the semantic equations

We sum up the preceding discussion with the following equations defining WP[P,Q] by cases:

WP EQUATIONS FOR CSP

0) Λ-rule.

$$WP[\Lambda \| \ldots \| \Lambda, Q] = Q$$

1) SEQ-rule

For some $1 \leqslant \ell \leqslant n$, $S_\ell \in SEQ$:

$$WP[P,Q] = WP[S_\ell, WP[P_1 \| \ldots \| P'_\ell \| \ldots \| P_n, Q]] \quad .$$

2) Communication-rule

For no $1 \leqslant \ell \leqslant n$, $S_\ell \in SEQ$:

$$WP[P,Q] = $$

$$\text{(E)} \qquad \bigwedge_{i:S_i \in DO} (LE_i \supset WP[P_1 \| \ldots \| P'_i \| \ldots \| P_n, Q])$$

$$\wedge$$

If BB then

$$\text{(CC)} \qquad [\bigwedge_{i,j,k,k':\ \mu(c_i^k,c_j^{k'})} (b_i^k \wedge b_j^{k'} \supset WP[c_i^k \| c_j^{k'}, WP[\tilde{P}_{i,j}, Q]])$$

$$\wedge$$

(C)		$\bigwedge_{i,k:c_i^k = \text{skip}} (b_i^k \supset WP[\text{skip}, WP[\tilde{P}_i,Q]])$
(ND)	else	$\bigvee_{i:S_i \in DO} LE_i$

Note: In case there are no loops

$$\bigwedge_{i:S_i \in DO} (LE_i \supset WP[P_1\|\ldots\|P_i'\|\ldots\|P_n,Q]) = \bigwedge_{\phi} = \text{true}$$

and

$$\bigvee_{i:S_i \in DO} LE_i = \text{false}.$$

Therefore, we obtain:

IF-Theorem If for all $1 \leq i \leq n$, $S_i \neq \Lambda \supset S_i \in IF$

$$WP[P,Q] =$$

$$BB$$

$$\wedge \quad (CC) \quad \bigwedge_{i,j,k,k':\, \mu(c_i^k,c_j^{k'})} b_i^k \wedge b_j^{k'} \supset WP[c_i^k\|c_j^{k'}, WP[\tilde{P}_{i,j},Q]]$$

$$\wedge \quad (C) \quad \bigwedge_{i,k:c_i^k = \text{skip}} b_i^k \supset WP[\text{skip},WP[\tilde{P}_i,Q]].$$

Thus, in case there are no loops the communication-rule is reduced to this expected IF-Theorem, which is a natural extension of the SEQ-IF rule in [D].

We may also prove the following:

COM-Theorem The COM-rule is equivalent to the following rule:

for no ℓ $1 \leq \ell \leq n$: $S_\ell \in SEQ$

$$WP[P,Q] = \underline{\text{if}} \bigvee_{i:S_i \in DO} LE_i \ \underline{\text{then}} \bigwedge_{S_i \in DO} (LE_i \supset WP[P_1\|\ldots\|P_i'\|\ldots\|P_n,Q])$$

$$\underline{\text{else}}$$

$$[BB$$

$$\wedge \bigwedge_{i,j,k,k':\, \mu(c_i^k,c_j^{k'})} (b_i^k \wedge b_j^{k'} \supset WP[c_i^k\|c_j^{k'}, WP[\tilde{P}_{i,j},Q]])$$

$$\wedge \bigwedge_{i,k:c_i^k = \text{skip}} (b_i^k \supset WP[\text{skip},WP[\tilde{P}_i,Q]])$$

$$].$$

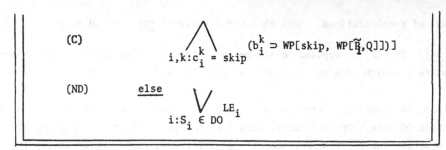

The operational meaning of this theorem is that in case some loop is terminating, then its termination can be given priority over communications. The reason for this is that a loop exit can only reveal new communication capabilities, but cannot cause any loss of communications. Note that the inverse is not a valid rule!

Remarks-1: In CSP, as opposed to sequential programs, it is possible for a loop to be in a state in which none of its guards is passable and the termination condition is false.

Thus, we should not expect to have a DO-rule which is a simple extention of the sequential DO-rule. Operationally, we attribute this property to delaying the process containing the loop. Thus, our semantic equation adequately characterizes the notion of delay, which has a highly operational meaning and is hard to capture abstractly.

-2: The semantic equations, as defined above have an operational meaning of preference of actions according to the following order:

1. sequential transitions
2. loop exits
3. communication.

In [E], and in a full version of the paper, it will be shown, that as far as WP is concerned, this semantics is equivalent to another one, giving equations that do not induce any preferences. It will also be shown that the WP semantics is equivalent to a natural operational semantics.

-3: Finally, the full version of the paper will contain a proof of the continuity of the above defined equations, justifying the existence and uniqueness of the defined WP predicate transformer.

III. EXAMPLES

We present some small examples of applying the rules. More extensive and complicated examples will appear in [E] (and in a full version of the paper).

Example: This example clarifies the way the communication-rule deals with loops.

a.1 Non terminating loops

Let $P::[P_1 \| P_2]$, where $P_1::*[\text{true}; P_2?x \rightarrow \text{skip}]$

and $P_2::*[\text{true}; P_1!y \rightarrow \text{skip}]$

Let $Q \equiv \text{true}$.

$WP[P_1 \| P_2, \text{true}] =$

using the communication-rule.

(E) $\text{false} \supset WP[\Lambda \| P_2, \text{true}]$

$\wedge$

$\text{false} \supset WP[P_1 \| \Lambda, \text{true}]$

$\wedge$

(BB) if true then

$\text{true} \wedge \text{true} \supset WP[P_2?x \| P_1!y, WP[\tilde{P}_{1,2}, Q]]$

$\wedge$

(C) $\bigwedge_{\phi} \cdots$

$\underline{\text{else}}$

(ND) $\sim$true $\vee$ $\sim$true.

Simplifying this (with $\bigwedge_{\phi} \equiv$ true) we obtain:

$$A = WP[P_2?x \| P_1!y, WP[\tilde{P}_{1,2},Q]].$$

By the definition of $\tilde{P}_{1,2}$ for a DO command:

$$WP[\tilde{P}_{1,2},Q] = WP[\text{ skip};P_1 \| \text{skip};P_2,Q].$$

Using the SEQ-rule twice

$$= WP[P_1 \| P_2,Q].$$

Substituting back the value of $WP[\tilde{P}_{1,2},Q]$ we obtain:

$$WP[P_1 \| P_2,Q] = WP[P_2?x \| P_1!y, WP[P_1 \| P_2,Q]] .$$

The least fixed point of this equation is false. So:

$$\underline{\underline{WP[P_1 \| P_2, \text{true}] = \text{false}.}}$$

<u>Terminating Loops</u>

Let $P::[P_1 \| P_2]$ where $P_1::*[\text{true}; P_2?x \rightarrow \text{skip}]$
and $P_2:: [\text{true}; P_1!y \rightarrow \text{skip}]$.

Let $Q \equiv x = y$

$WP[P_1 \| P_2,x = y] =$

Using the communication-rule

(E) false $\supset WP[\Lambda \| P_2,x = y]$

$\wedge$

(BB) $\underline{\text{if}}$ true $\wedge$ true $\underline{\text{then}}$

(CC) true $\wedge$ true $\supset WP[P_2?x \| P_1!y, WP[\tilde{P}_{1,2},Q]]$

$\wedge$

(C) $\bigwedge_{\phi}$ ...

(ND) $\underline{\text{else}}$ true.

After simplification, we obtain:

$$= WP[P_2?x \| P_1!y, WP[\tilde{P}_{1,2},Q]].$$

Using the definition of $\tilde{P}_{1,2}$:

$$WP[\tilde{P}_{1,2},Q] = WP[\text{ skip};P_1 \| \text{skip}, x=y]$$

(note the difference between the IF command and the DO command).

Using the SEQ-rule twice

$$= WP[P_1 \| \Lambda, x = y].$$

Using again the Communication-rule

$=$

(E) $true \supset WP[\Lambda \| \Lambda,\ x = y]$

$\wedge$

(BB) <u>if</u> false <u>then</u>

(CC) $\bigwedge_{\phi} \ldots$

$\wedge$

(C) $\bigwedge_{\phi} \ldots$

(ND) <u>else</u> true

And by simplification:

$= WP[\Lambda \| \Lambda,\ x = y].$

By using Λ-rule, we finally get:

$= x = y.$

Substituting back the value of $WP[\tilde{P}_{1,2}, Q]$ we obtain

$$WP[P_1 \| P_2,\ x = y] = WP[P_2?x \| P_1!y,\ x = y]\ .$$

And by using the Global-assignment-rule and the Λ-rule

$= true$

so:

$$WP[P_1 \| P_2\ x = y] = true.$$

IV. CONCLUSION

We have presented a definition of weakest precondition semantics (WP) for communicating processes as expressed in CSP. The approach is a centralized one, where the whole concurrent program is at hand, as opposed to two leveled approaches first defining separate meaning to processes, and then binding the separate meaning to a joint one. The weakest precondition semantics presented is capable of representing delays and deadlocks.

A similar approach was used to define WP semantics for shared variables concurrency using critical regions with the <u>with</u>...<u>when</u>...<u>do</u> construct.

We would like to stress again the fact that in both cases of concurrency considered, a centralized approach was needed to facilitate a weakest preconditioning semantics. We believe this property is pertinent to the relationship between weakest preconditions and concurrency: there does not seem to be any natural method by which the predicate transformer corresponding to a collection of interacting processes will be functionally defined in terms of the transformers corresponding to the processes rather then by the processes themselves. This is a deviation from the sequential semantics, in which induction on the syntax was always appropriate. An interleaving may fail even if its components (separately) succeed...

ACKNOWLEDGEMENT

We are grateful to John C. Reynolds for a continued support and many stimulating discussions that affected both this paper and the first author's Ph.D. thesis. David Gries had several suggestions that improved the presentation and thanks also to L. Morris.

REFERENCES

[ADA] Preliminary ADA reference manual. SIGPLAN notices 14, 6 (June 1979).

[AFRI] K.R. Apt, N. Francez, W.P. de Roever: A proof system for communicating sequential processes, ACM-TOPLAS, 2, 1, (July 1980).

[BH] P. Brinch Hansen: Distributed processes - a concurrent programming concept. CACM 21, 11 (November 1978).

[CC] P. Cousot, R. Cousot: Semantic analysis of communicating sequential processes. Proceedings of the 7-th Colloquium, Automata, Languages and Programming, Nordwijkerhout, July 1980.

[CH] Z.C. Chen, A.A.R. Hoare: Partial correctness of communicating sequential processes. Proc. 2nd Int. Symp. on Distributed Systems, Paris (April 1981).

[CM] K.M. Chandy, J. Misra: Proofs of networks of processes. IEEE-TSE, SE-7, No. 4 (July 1981).

[D] E.W. Dijkstra: A Discipline of Programming. Prentice Hall, Englewood Cliffs, New Jersey, (1976).

[E] Tz. Elrad: Ph.D. thesis, in preparation.

[FE] J.A. Feldman: High level programming for distributed computing. CACM 22, 6 (June 1979).

[FHLR] N. Francez, C.A.R. Hoare, D.J. Lehmann, W.P. de Roever: Semantics of nondeterminism, concurrency and communication. JCSS 19, 3 (December 1979).

[FLP] N. Francez, D.J. Lehmann, A. Pnueli: A linear history semantics for distributed leanguages. Proc. FOCS Conf. (October 1980).

[FS] L. Flon, N. Suzuki: Nondeterminism and the correctness of parallel programs. IFIP working conf. on Formal Description of Programming Concepts, Saint Andrews, 1977.

[H] C.A.R. Hoare: Communicating sequential processes. CACM 21, 8 (August 1978).

[LG] G. Levin, D. Gries: A proof technique for communicating sequential processes. Acta Informatica 15 (1981).

[LS] A. Van Lamsweerde, M. Sintzoff: Formal derivation of strongly correct concurrent programs. Acta Informatica, Vol. 12, Fasc. 1, (1979).

[MM] G. Milne, R. Milner: Concurrent processes and their syntax. JACM 26, 2 (April 1979).

[OG] S.S. Owicki, D. Gries: An axiomatic proof technique for parallel programs I. Acta Informatica, 6 (1976).

[MI] R. Milner: A Calculus of Communicating Processes. Lecture Notes in Computer Science, No. 92, Springer-Verlag (1980).

[P] G.D. Plotkin: An operational semantics for CSP. Technical Report, Dept. of Computer Science, University of Edinburgh, October 1981.

From abstract model to efficient compilation of patterns

Pär Emanuelson

Software Systems Research Center
Linköping University
S-581 83 Linköping
Sweden

Abstract

Pattern matching is a technique which is used in many application areas such as text manipulation in editors, manipulation of arithmetic formulas in computer algebra systems and in artificial intelligence applications. In programming systems it can be a built-in language facility as string matching in SNOBOL4 or a language extension for matching of list structures as in INTERLISP.

This paper presents a strategy for achieving a pattern match facility with the following properties (1) it is based on a simple model of pattern matching in order to give a good understanding for the pattern matching process (2) it is powerful, that is, it contains the union of the facilities commonly found in pattern matchers (3) it provides compilation of patterns to efficient code.

Available implementations are oriented towards providing either a clear and extensible definition of pattern matching or towards good performance at execution. The underlying problem is that good optimizing compilers are too complex to also serve as a modifiable definition of the language.

Our strategy is based on the development of a simple formal definition of the problem. Then a pattern match interpreter in Lisp is developed as an extension of the formal definition and thus serves to reach the second goal. Powerful program manipulation tools are then used to transform the interpreter according to the partial evaluation principle. The Lisp code which is the result from partial evaluation is regarded as compiled patterns.

The stepwise development of a suitable model is described and the resulting Lisp program is shown. The partial evaluation of the program with respect to one given pattern is demonstrated. Examples of optimization in the pattern language is shown and similarities between partial evaluation and lazy evaluation are pointed out. Performance results of the full implementation are given. Other approaches to pattern matching systems are briefly described and related to our approach. Finally the effects of partial evaluation on the pattern matcher are characterized and their relative importance is evaluated. The outcome of applying this strategy to similar problems is discussed.

1. Introduction

There are many requirements that general purpose pattern match implementations must meet. In editors patterns are normally typed in by the user and then executed by an interpreter and discarded. In other situations a compilation of the pattern is preferred since the pattern match is incorporated in a program and hence executed several times. In some applications sophisticated patterns are needed but the generality of the pattern matcher must not imply low performance for simple patterns. The set of potentially useful patterns is quite large, so it is difficult to provide a set which is large enough for a wide variety of problems. Therefore pattern languages frequently provide a way to define and name new patterns in terms of existing ones, but in many situations this is not enough and there is a need to define new patterns in terms of the implementation language.

In this paper we will argue that a simple formal definition and powerful program manipulation tools can provide a pattern matching facility with the following properties:

1. It is based on a simple model of pattern matching in order to give a good understanding of the pattern matching process.
2. It is powerful, that is, it contains the union of the facilities commonly found in pattern matchers.
3. It provides compilation of patterns to efficient code.

One or two of these goals can be fulfilled by most strategies, but achieving all three is nontrivial. Our strategy is as follows:

1. An abstract and simple mathematical model is developed and patterns are defined within this model. This model is suitable for studying and proving properties of patterns such as associativity and distributivity. The model is then further developed into two more expressive and algorithmic models.

2. The most concrete model is then translated into a Lisp program which will be an interpreter of patterns. The translation process is in our case fairly straightforward since the target language is Lisp. This interpreter is extended with additional capabilities which make definitions of additional patterns possible. Some of the added patterns concern the communication between the pattern and the surrounding host language program (including side-effects). Other such patterns build a structure to be returned as the result of the match process.

3. Given patterns can then be translated into Lisp code by partial evaluation of the interpreter with respect to the pattern. Partial evaluation here amounts to a simplification of the interpreter given that the pattern to be interpreted is known but not the subject to match. The Lisp code can then be further compiled into machine code by a Lisp compiler.

With our approach no special purpose compiler has to be built. We can take advantage of interpretation which is preferable for defining new pattern primitives and for debugging, while compilation is delayed until efficiency is demanded. Normally both a compiler and an interpreter have to be built to achieve these properties and then the extra problem of keeping these consistent arises. Since optimization is done via partial evaluation and is not included in the model, the model can be kept simple.

In this paper we will only deal with pattern matching in list structures, which however is very similar to string pattern matching. The differences are more of the pragmatic kind and will not be stressed. In related work on formal definitions and theory for patterns [GIM73, STE75] theorems are proved about the properties of patterns within a model essentially the same as the ***transformational*** model in this paper. Our work goes further by providing a more abstract and intuitive model, the ***matval*** model, and formally derive the ***transformational*** and ***algorithmic*** models.

There is a rich material for comparisons and evaluation of our strategy since there are many approaches for implementing backtracking and generating alternative matches. In our implementation backtracking and handling of alternatives is carried out by recursive function calls. Function calls make backtracking easy since there are no side effects which must be undone during backtracking.

In some implementations the handling of alternatives is carried out by generators, as in the SL5 and Icon languages [GRI76, GRI80] and by a graph interpreter with explicit stacks for SNOBOL4 [GRI71]. In the Qlisp and Lisp70 programming systems [SAC76, TES73] mechanisms for automatic backtracking are used. Our pattern interpreter copies the state of the match at each step during the match via a recursive call. This is less efficient than working with a global state, but since simple mechanisms such as recursive function calls are well understood and easier to analyze than for example generators, partial evaluation of the interpreter can be performed. The interpreter has much of the "applicative" structure of the abstract model which is useful in partial evaluation.

A compilation involves more than a translation of the program to a different language. It also involves optimizations which can be performed since properties of the program have been bound at compile time. We will show that nontrivial optimizations in the pattern language can be performed by partial evaluation on the Lisp level. Also the need for special versions of general patterns which are used for efficiency reasons is decreased since partial evaluation discovers and simplifies general mechanisms.

Chapter 2 introduces the formal models and ends with the derived pattern interpreter. Chapter 3 introduces partial evaluation and the effects of applying partial evaluation to the pattern interpreter is described. Conclusions including a brief description of the full implementation and performance comparisons is given in chapter 4. An appendix shows an example of partial evaluation of the full scale interpreter.

2. Pattern matching

2.1 Informal

A pattern *p* is a list $\langle p_1\ p_2 \ldots p_n \rangle$ where p_i are ***elementary patterns***. The pattern *p* matches the subject *s* (an arbitrary list) if each elementary pattern of *p* matches some (zero, one or more) elements of *s* such that these ***segments***, taken together in order make up the whole list, without overlapping of segments. If the pattern matches the subject the match ***succeeds*** otherwise it ***fails***. The actual segment of a subject which is matched by an elementary pattern will be called the ***matchvalue*** of the elementary pattern.

We will define only three elementary patterns for the purpose of demonstrating the models, namely & (the ***element*** pattern) which matches one arbitrary element, 'x (the ***quote*** pattern) which matches the expression x, and -- (the ***segment*** pattern) which matches zero, one or more arbitrary elements of the list.

Examples: The pattern <& 'A> matches any list with two elements where the second element is an A such as <B A> or <<C D> A> but not <A> or <B A B>. The pattern <-- 'C> matches lists ending in C and <-- 'A --> matches lists that contain at least one A (it performs the Lisp function member).

The full implementation which is briefly described in chapter 4, contains 43 different elementary patterns including binding of variables, applying arbitrary Lisp predicates, patterns that restrict backtracking, control-patterns such as and, or, sequence, optional order etc.

2.2 Formal models

We will present three formal models, the first being the simplest. The later models are steps towards an implementation and they will also provide the basis for extensions of the pattern language. A full description of the models and proofs of consistency can be found in [EMA80b]. We will use the four Lisp functions car, cdr, null and append which are defined by:

$\mathrm{car}(\langle x_1 \ldots x_n \rangle) = x_1$

$\mathrm{cdr}(\langle x_1 \ldots x_n \rangle) = \langle x_2 \ldots x_n \rangle$

$\mathrm{null}(x) = (x = \langle\rangle)$

$\mathrm{append}(\langle x_1 \ldots x_m \rangle, \langle y_1 \ldots y_n \rangle) = \langle x_1 \ldots x_m, y_1 \ldots y_n \rangle$

Let EP be the set of all elementary patterns, P be the set of patterns, S be the set of S-expressions and let L be the set of all lists. <> and nil both denote the empty list.

2.3 The Matval model

This is the simpliest and most abstract model. A function ***matval*** maps elementary patterns into sets of lists which are the set of possible matchvalues for each elementary pattern.

matval: EP $\rightarrow$ powerset(L)

The ***quote***, ***element*** and ***segment*** patterns can then be defined as follows

$\mathrm{matval}('x) = \{\langle x \rangle\}$

$\mathrm{matval}(\&) = \{\langle x \rangle \mid x \in S\}$

$\mathrm{matval}(--) = L$

matval for patterns (lists of elementary patterns) is defined by:

matval(<>) = {<>}

$$\text{matval}(\langle p_1 \ldots p_n \rangle) = \bigcup_{\substack{x \in \text{matval}(p_1) \\ y \in \text{matval}(\langle p_2 \ldots p_n \rangle)}} \{\text{append}(x, y)\}$$

The function ***match*** which is true iff the pattern matches the subject is then defined by:

match(p, s) = s ∈ matval(p)

Examples:

matval(<& 'A>) = the set of all lists with two elements where the second element is an A.

matval(<& -->) = the set of lists with at least one element.

The Matval model provides simple and compact definitions for elementary patterns. The definitions however involve infinite sets, such as the set of all lists, and are therefore difficult to implement. There are also several elementary patterns commonly found in pattern matchers that cannot be defined within this model since they depend on the context and not only the elements which they match. One such example is the SNOBOL4 pattern BREAK(X) which matches all elements up to, but not including, X.

2.4 The Transformational model

The function ***trans*** is defined in terms of matval by:

trans: EP x powerset(L) → powerset(L)

trans(e, sl) = {x ∈ L | (∃y)(∃z) y ∈ matval(e) ∧ z ∈ sl ∧ append(y, x) = z}

The following definitions can then be derived from the corresponding matval-definitions above.

trans('x, sl) = {y ∈ L | (∃z) z ∈ sl ∧ z ≠ <> ∧ car(z) = x ∧ cdr(z) = y}

trans(&, sl) = {x ∈ L | (∃y) y ∈ sl ∧ y ≠ <> ∧ cdr(y) = x}

trans(--, sl) = {x ∈ L | (∃y) (∃i) i ≥ 0 ∧ y ∈ sl ∧ $\text{tail}^i(y)$ = x}

where $\text{tail}^0(x) = x$

$\text{tail}^i(x) = \text{tail}^{i-1}(\text{cdr}(x))$

match(<$p_1 \ldots p_n$>, s) = <> ∈ trans(p_n, trans(p_{n-1}, ... trans(p_1, {s}) ...))

This model hence associates a transformation with each of the elementary patterns and these transformations are applied sequentially to a set of subjects by the function ***match***. Most common and useful elementary patterns such as the previously mentioned BREAK(X) pattern can be defined within this model. The elementary patterns are not defined in terms of infinite sets in the same extent as for the matval model; see for example the segment pattern above. This model however does not provide a program, since for example the sequence pattern (which matches any number of occurrences of a given pattern) yields infinite sets. A scheme for lazy evaluation could however be used to evaluate the elementary patterns that yield infinite sets. Such a scheme would also prevent redundant computation when only one or a few alternatives and not all are asked for. The following model does not require lazy evaluation.

2.5 The Algorithmic model

A function *ematch* is defined in terms of trans by:

$\text{ematch}: EP \rightarrow (P \times L \rightarrow \text{boolean})$

$\text{ematch}(e)(p, s) = (\exists x \in \text{trans}(e, \{s\})) \wedge \text{match}(\text{cdr}(p), x)$

where match is defined by:

$\text{match}: P \times L \rightarrow \text{boolean}$

$\text{match}(p, s) = (p = \langle\rangle \wedge s = \langle\rangle) \vee (p \neq \langle\rangle \wedge \text{ematch}(\text{car}(p))\ (p, s))$

It is proved in [EMA80b] that this definition of match is consistent with the previous and the following definitions can be derived from the transformational model.

$\text{ematch}('x)\ (p, s) = s \neq \langle\rangle \wedge \text{car}(s) = x \wedge \text{match}(\text{cdr}(p), \text{cdr}(s))$

$\text{ematch}(\&)\ (p, s) = s \neq \langle\rangle \wedge \text{match}(\text{cdr}(p), \text{cdr}(s))$

$\text{ematch}(--)\ (p, s) = \text{match}(\text{cdr}(p), s) \vee (s \neq \langle\rangle \wedge \text{match}(p, \text{cdr}(s)))$

The function match is the ***pattern interpreter***, and ematch(e) is called the ***pattern function*** associated with e. The "$\exists x \in \text{trans}(e, \{s\})$" expression implies a loop over the elements of trans(e, {s}), which obtains the alternatives for e. When there are no more alternatives the elementary pattern fails, that is, the pattern function returns false. This is a model which is suitable for translation into a Lisp program. The definitions are compact and simple although not as simple as for the matval model. The ordering of alternatives is defined and the generation of alternative matches stops when the match has succeeded.

2.6 Implementation

The FP conditional expression: $p_1 \rightarrow e_1; \ldots ;p_n \rightarrow e_n; e_{n+1}$ is used.

The resulting Lisp pattern matcher will be:

```
m-quote(p, s) = null(s) → nil;
                car(s) = cadar(p) → match(cdr(p), cdr(s)); nil
m-element(p, s) = null(s) → nil; match(cdr(p), cdr(s))
m-segment(p, s) = prog((ns)
                       ns ← s
                   lp: match(cdr(p), ns) → return(t);
                       null(ns) → return(nil); ns ← cdr(ns)
                       goto(lp)
match(p, s) = null(p) → null(s); ematch(car(p)) (p, s)
```

ematch(e) returns the name of the pattern function of e (m-quote, m-element ...).

The function ***prog((x) ... lp: ...)*** binds the local variable ***x*** and ***lp*** is a label. The prog function is exited via the ***return*** statement.

This interpreter is not the full implementation, but it is large enough to illustrate the compilation process that will follow.

3. Partial evaluation of the interpreter

The essence of partial evaluation can be described as:

> "Suppose S is a procedure of n arguments $x_1, x_2, \ldots, x_n$ and the values of the first m arguments are known as $v_1, v_2, \ldots, v_m$. A new procedure S' can then be generated by partial evaluation such that $S'(x_{m+1}, \ldots, x_n) = S(v_1, \ldots, v_m, x_{m+1}, \ldots, x_n)$ for all x_i, $i = m+1,n$".

In the procedure body of S the arguments x_i, $i = 1,m$ are replaced by corresponding values v_i and simplifications in the procedure body are performed. The goal is to achieve a new version S' which is more efficient to execute than S. This can be generalized to any piece of code C combined with any knowledge we have about C which holds in a particular situation: we can generate a specialized version C' where this knowledge has been used to affect optimizations in C.

Let P denote a function which performs partial evaluation. In our case P will take two arguments, a function to be partially evaluated (the pattern interpreter ***match***) and an argument to that function (the pattern ***p***) which has a known value. The subject ***s*** will generally not have a known value at partial evaluation time. If ***p*** has a known value the following relation holds:

match(p, s) = P(match, p) (s) = match'(s)

Here match' is a specialized version of match which evaluates ***p*** (and no other patterns) in different environments.

The partial evaluation can be carried out by a program manipulation system. The main transformations necessary for partial evaluation are constant computation; constant propagation; dead code elimination and opening of functions where procedure calls are replaced by the corresponding procedure bodies after replacing formal parameters with actual ones. Partial evaluation has been studied by several researchers [ERS77, HAR80, WEG76] and its connection to interpretation and compilation was first mentioned by Futamura [FUT71]. The program manipulation aspects of this work are further described in [EMA80a].

3.1 An example

In this section we will follow an example of how partial evaluation is achieved through a number of program transformations for the match:

match(<& 'A -- 'B>, x)

1. Opening of the function match gives:

null(<& 'A -- 'B>) → null(x); ematch(car(<& 'A -- 'B>)) (<& 'A -- 'B>, x)

2. Evaluation of null and ematch and simplification of the conditional expression gives:

m-element(<& 'A -- 'B>, x)

3. Opening of m-element gives:

null(x) → nil; match(cdr(<& 'A -- 'B>), cdr(x))

3.2 Partially known subjects

If the subject is partially known, which is often the case when a pattern match is performed in a program, the generated code may be further simplified. Special purpose compilers normally do not provide this feature since it requires special analysis of the subject. Partial evaluation however considers information for all arguments of the interpreter in the same way.

Partial evaluation of:

match(<'A & 'B>, cons(x, cons(y, cons(z, nil))))

yields: x = 'A → z = 'B; nil

In this case some simple syntactic transformations were used, such as:

car(cons(x, y)) → x

null(cons(x, y)) → nil

Partial evaluation of: match(<'A & 'B>, cons(x, cons(y, nil))) yields nil (that is, that the match always fails).

3.3 Optimizations

The previous examples show that the code of the interpreter will be simplified and optimized. However no optimizations on the pattern level have been performed, that is, all elementary patterns result in some code and the order of evaluation during interpretation is preserved. But partial evaluation of the interpreter level also has effects on the pattern level as the following example will show.

Some problems with efficiency of pattern combinations occur, especially for patterns containing the segment pattern (--). These problems arise since the full generality of some patterns is not needed in combination with certain other patterns (or at the end or beginning of the whole pattern). One such simple case is the pattern <'A --> for which the following code is generated:

```
null(x) → nil;
car(x) = 'A →
   (prog((ns)
         ns ← cdr(x)
      lp: null(ns) → return(t); ns ← cdr(ns)
         goto(lp));
nil
```

The generated loop will traverse the list to the end and then return t. A slightly more advanced analysis will however replace the whole loop with t. This can be done since no interfering side effects occur and the loop has to stop and return t (since our lists always end in nil). The conditional is then simplified and the result is:

```
null(x) → nil; car(x) = 'A
```

4. Opening of match gives:

```
null(x) → nil;
(null(<'A -- 'B>) → null(cdr(x)); ematch(car(<'A -- 'B>)) (<'A -- 'B>, cdr(x)))
```

5. The two conditionals are combined into one and evaluation of ematch gives m-quote which is opened and simplified:

```
null(x) → nil;
null(cdr(x)) → nil;
cadr(x) = 'A → match(<-- 'B>, cddr(x)); nil
```

6. Now focus on the call match(<-- 'B>, cddr(x)), and open:

```
prog((ns)
     ns ← cddr(x)
  lp: match(cdr(<-- 'B>), ns) → return(t);
     null(ns) → return(nil); ns ← cdr(ns)
     goto(lp))
```

7. Two further openings of match give:

```
prog((ns)
     ns ← cddr(x)
  lp: (null(ns) → nil;
      car(ns) = 'B → null(cdr(ns)); nil) → return(t);
     null(ns) → return(nil); ns ← cdr(ns)
     goto(lp))
```

8. The predicate null(ns) occurs in two places and under current circumstances the two conditionals are merged into one. The final result is then:

```
null(x) → nil;
null(cdr(x)) → nil;
cadr(x) = 'A →
  (prog((ns)
        ns ← cddr(x)
     lp: null(ns) → return(nil);
        and(car(ns) = 'B, null(cdr(ns))) → return(t); ns ← cdr(ns)
        goto(lp)));
nil
```

This code will compute whether x matches the pattern <& 'A -- 'B> or not.

The same optimization can be performed when the segment pattern is only followed by non-advancing patterns (that is, patterns that always match the empty list when successful).

In some cases the analysis cannot be done on the Lisp code level. One such case is when the segment pattern is followed by elementary patterns which match a constant (and known) number of elements such as the example in 3.1. One fast algorithm is to skip the number of elements required to reach the tail with the given length. In this case the program analysis problem would be to examine a piece of Lisp code and given that the value of this code is non-nil find out if the length of the list s has to take a certain value, and if so, determine that value. We have no method for such an analysis.

We use two methods for optimization of pattern combinations. If it is known that there is an efficient algorithm for the pattern combination P_1 P_2, then P_1's pattern function can be modified to inspect the following pattern and in case of P_2 choose the special algorithm. The second approach is to define P_3 to perform the special algorithm and then to analyze the pattern prior to execution and replace P_1 P_2 by P_3. Both of these approaches (interpreter versus compiler oriented) go well together with partial evaluation and both methods have their merits.

Other implementations also use these methods. In the Clisp pattern compiler [MAS78] pattern combinations are detected by the compiler. In the interpreter FLIP [TEI67] special cases are discovered during interpretation. In SNOBOL4 several combinations also exist as separate patterns which should be chosen by the user in the interest of increased efficiency.

In some cases partial evaluation has the "lazy" effect of lazy evaluation [HEN76, FRI76] with the essential difference that the laziness in our case occurs at compile time. When a function call is opened the actual arguments of the call are substituted into the body of the function and thus "move". Thus the evaluation of these expressions is delayed. Since opening of functions in our case is frequent, computations can be delayed more than might be expected.

The pattern <* 'A *> collects the two segments around an A in the subject and append these. When the pattern is interpreted the first * will cause segments of increasing length to be appended to the result variable until an A is found. Each time an A does not follow this effect will be undone during backtracking and a segment with one additional element will then be attempted. In the evaluation of the result from partial evaluation, the appending is however not done until the whole match is certain to succeed and then the segment matched by the first * is determined.

4. Conclusions

The main goals

The three goals stated in the introduction were achieved on the whole. The abstract models provide a strong formal basis for the implementation. The implementation was however not derived formally from the most abstract model for all the elementary patterns, but the knowledge gained in developing the models gave the clean structure which was needed in order to allow user extensions and to perform partial evaluation. It is also valuable to be able to do proofs and be convinced of correctness in difficult cases.

It has been demonstrated that a pattern matcher which saves its environment in each step of the interpretation also can be efficient. The advantage with saving the environment is that backtracking is more easily handled. When user extensions to the pattern matcher are allowed mistakes in the handling of backtracking increases and this can be disastrous as pointed out in [GRI80].

The full implementation

The full implementation contains as many as 43 different elementary patterns, which include ***control*** patterns, which take other patterns as arguments and ***backtrack-control*** patterns which restrict the normal backtracking. It also contains patterns which build a structure which will be the result of the pattern match. The design is thus general enough to provide a powerful pattern language; for a comparison with other pattern matchers, see [EMA80b]. In the full implementation the match values are remembered rather than just "skipped over". The match function is extended to take three extra arguments, namely (1) the ***match-value-of-preceding-pattern***, which can be assigned to Lisp variables in the surrounding program or appended to the value of the match (2) the ***synthesized-result*** which is a list structure to be returned in case of success and (3) the ***subject-stack*** which is used for constructing match values for control patterns.

The ***Redfun*** program manipulation system [HAR77] has been used to perform partial evaluation. The results from partial evaluation are the same as for the small pattern matcher in this paper. The full pattern matcher is however more inefficient in interpretation since matchvalues are computed but not used etc. so the difference in efficiency between interpretation and evaluation of partially evaluated patterns is radically increased in the full implementation.

Performance

Performance was compared to the Clisp pattern compiler [MAS78], which emphasizes efficiency of the object code rather than generality. The speed was equal but the translations were double in space for our pattern matcher and partial evaluation took 25 times longer than compilation in Clisp. Evaluation of results from partial evaluation compared to interpretation of patterns was a factor 50 faster for the patterns used in the Clisp comparison. Since Clisp does not provide more sophisticated patterns involving control patterns such patterns were only compared with the interpreter, and results from partial evaluation proved to be a factor 375 faster on average. Thus the more complex patterns, the more is gained from partial evaluation. These measurements were made with compiled INTERLISP code on a DEC-20/40, that is, the pattern interpreter was compiled and the results from partial evaluation and the Clisp compiler were further compiled by the Lisp compiler. Unrestricted recursion in patterns (a pattern defined in terms of itself) was however not possible to partially evaluate to an efficient form. In that case the result from partial evaluation is the unmodified call to the interpreter.

Thus, our strategy does not give us a pattern match facility which is more efficient than Clisp, but it gives us much richer and flexible pattern language with equal efficiency except for compilation time.

What transformations contributed most to efficiency

The effects of partial evaluation can be divided into the following categories:

1. Elimination of decoding, that is, the examination of the pattern in order to determine which function to call.
2. Elimination of error tests (when performed on a known pattern).
3. Unwinding of the control structure in order to create one block of code.
4. Elimination of redundant computation. Computations that are not referenced may be eliminated.
5. Elimination of state saving. That is, elimination of parameters in function calls.

We estimate that 3 contributed most to increased efficiency followed by 4 and 5. There are consequently only small gains in efficiency if just 1 and 2 were performed.

The code of the interpreter had to be adapted to the restrictions implied by the partial evaluation system. We however rarely had change to more "low level" code, but rather to high level and clear code, which is quite unusual when optimization is involved.

Extending our strategy to other, similar, problems

Unification differs from the pattern matching described here in that two patterns are matched instead of a pattern and a subject. We think that our approach could be applied also to that problem without major difficulties. Another problem is the matching of many patterns against many subjects which occurs in production systems where a database of facts is matched against a set of rules. For this problem our style of partial evaluation would not be sufficient since a ***reordering*** of the straightforward match order is required to get efficient matching. Efficient solutions to this problem only exist for simple pattern languages.

Language features used

Interpretation requires many of Lisp's features including EVAL and dynamic scope for variables. EVAL is used in order to avoid the simulation of facilities available in Lisp (such as variable binding). Calls to EVAL are however eliminated during partial evaluation since enough information can be derived from the given pattern. Partial evaluation also unrolls function calls in a way that no free variables occur in the final code. The "compiled" patterns thus require simple Lisp subset and can be translated to almost any language.

Partial evaluation is a complex task for large applications and uses much resources. One way of speeding up the compilation is to apply the partial evaluator onto itself with respect to the interpreter. The result will be a compiler for the language. The problem is discussed in [BEC76] but results for real-life programs have not yet been achieved.

Acknoledgements

Thanks to Anders Haraldsson, Jan Maluszynski and Jim Goodwin for reading the manuscript and suggesting improvements.

References

[BEC76] Beckman, L., Haraldsson, A., Oskarsson Ö., Sandewall, E., A partial evaluator and its use as a programming tool, ***Artificial Intelligence Journal***, Vol. 7, Number 4, 1976, 319-357.

[EMA80a] Emanuelson, Pär, Haraldsson, Anders, On Compiling Embedded Languages in Lisp, ***Proc. 1980 Lisp Conference***, 1980.

[EMA80b] Emanuelson, Pär, Performance enhancement in a well-structured pattern matcher through partial evaluation. Ph.D. thesis. Software Systems Research Center, Linköping University, Sweden, 1980.

[ERS77] Ershov, A.P., On the partial computation principle, ***Information Processing Letters***, Number 2, 1977.

[FRI76] Friedman, D.P., Wise, D.S., CONS Should Not Evaluate Its Arguments, In ***Automata, Languages and Programming***, S Michaelson and R. Milner (eds), Edinburgh University Press, 1976.

[FUT71] Futamura, Y., Partial evaluation of computer programs: An approach to a compiler-compiler, ***J. Inst. Electronics and Communication Engineers***, 1971.

[GIM73] Gimpel, J. F., A Theory of Discrete Patterns and Their Implementation in SNOBOL4, ***Comm. ACM***, Vol. 16, Number 2, 1973.

[GRI71] Griswold, R. E., The SNOBOL4 programming language, Bell Telephone Laboratories Inc., 1971.

[GRI76] Griswold, Ralph E., String Scanning in SL5, SL5 Project Document S5LD5a, The University of Arizona, Tucson, Arizona, 1976

[GRI80] Griswold, Ralph E., Hanson, David R., An Alternative to the Use of Patterns in String Processing, ***ACM Transactions on Programming Languages and Systems***, Vol 2, No 2, 1980.

[HAR77] Haraldsson, Anders, A Program Manipulation System Based on Partial Evaluation, Ph. D. Thesis, Informatics Laboratory, Linköping University, Sweden, 1977.

[HAR80] Haraldsson, Anders, Experiences From a Program Manipulation System, Informatics Laboratory, Linköping University, Sweden, 1980.

[HEN76] Henderson, Peter, Morris, James H., A Lazy Evaluator, In ***Conf Rec. third Annu. ACM Symp. Principles of Programming Languages***, Jan 1976.

[MAS78] Masinter, Larry, The Clisp Pattern Compiler, printed in [TEI78].

[SAC76] Sacerdoti, Earl D., Fikes, Richard E., Reboh, Rene, Sagalowicz, Daniel, Waldinger, Richard J., Wilber, B. Michael, Qlisp: A Language for the Interactive Development of Complex Systems, Technical Note 120, Stanford Research Institute, 1976.

[STE75] Stewart, G.F., An algebraic model for string patterns. In ***Conf Rec. 2nd Annu. ACM Symp. Principles of Programming Languages***, Jan 1975, pp 167-184.

[TEI67] Teitelman, Warren., Design and implementation of FLIP, a Lisp format directed list processor. Bolt Beranek and Newman Inc, 1967.

[TEI78] Teitelman, Warren., INTERLISP reference manual, Xerox Palo Alto Research Center, Oct 1978.

[TES73] Tesler, Lawrence G., Enea, Horace J., Smith David C., The LISP70 Pattern Matching System, ***Proc. Third International Joint Conference on Artificial Intelligence***, 1973.

[WEG76] Wegbreit, B., Goal-directed Program Transformation, ***Third ACM Symposium on Principles of Programming Languages***, Atlanta, Georgia, 1976.

Appendix: A more complex example

The or-pattern takes a number of patterns as argument and succeeds if any of the arguments succeed. Each argument of the or-pattern implies a recursive call to ***match***. Since the arguments are limited in number these calls can be recursively opened and the resulting code will be a conditional expression. The seq-pattern (sequence) succeeds for any number (0 - ∞) of matches of its arguments and the pattern function is called each time the arguments of seq are matched. The number of calls is then bounded only by the length of the subject, which generally is unknown. Therefore the pattern function cannot be recursively opened. However each time the pattern function is called the pattern will be the same although the other arguments might have changed. This gives the possibility for a special kind of opening where a special version of the pattern function is generated and the body is specialized with respect to the pattern. The arguments of the seq-pattern can then be partially evaluated and calls to the pattern function will be replaced by calls to the generated function. In the following example the pattern :x matches one element and bind this to x, the pattern =form matches the value of form.

The pattern <<seq <or <:x =x> <:x @numberp =<add1 x>>>> 'alfa --> matches a list which begins with a sequence of elements which are pairwise equal or the first of the pair is a number and following element is one greater. This sequence must be followed by the atomic symbol alfa. This pattern matches for instance <alfa a b> or <a a di di alfa> or <1 2 a a 55 56 alfa>.

Partial evaluation of the match of the given pattern against the variable x yields seq/3(x), where seq/3 is a specialized version of seq's pattern function. The function seq/3 is defined by:

```
seq/3(s) =
null(s) → nil;
car(s) = 'alfa → t;
null(cdr(s)) → nil;
cadr(s) = car(s) → seq/3(cddr(s));
numberp(car(s)) → (cadr(s) = add1(car(s)) → seq/3(cddr(s)); nil);
nil
```

The program manipulation system automatically generates the above code with the exception that two arguments of the generated function have been removed manually. This cleaning-up procedure (the values in the recursive call are the same as for the first call of the function for both arguments) does not require human thought but has not yet been implemented.

COMPUTER-BASED SYNTHESIS OF LOGIC PROGRAMS

Agneta Eriksson
Anna-Lena Johansson
UPMAIL
Computing Science Department
Uppsala University
Sweden

1 Introduction.

Synthesis as well as other formal reasoning about programs is not only difficult, but also practically hard to perform depending on the great complexity of the proof, even when the programs are rather small. A computerized system can eliminate some of these problems and an automated system where the user creates the deductions interactively is a realistic solution to problems, where automatic systems have failed.

The purpose of our semi-automatic deductive system is to offer possibilities for reasoning at a higher level without losing the safety of the formal reasoning. The system should support the user during the derivation process so she can follow and control the proof and keep a good understanding as the proof is built up.

In section 2 follows a short introduction to the deductive method we use. In section 3 we present a synthesis of a program for a partition relation of three lists. The synthesis is performed interactively on a system, NATDED, developed for proof-making and program reasoning in a natural deduction system (10).

2 The deductive method.

The program synthesis method we use is developed by Clark & Tarnlund (2), and Hansson & Tarnlund (3, 4, 5).

The basis of the method is a calculus where the data structures are axiomatized and the specifications of the executable objects are defined in first order predicate logic. To synthesize programs in this calculus we derive theorems from the specification, for example by an inductive argument over the data structures. The derivations are performed in natural deduction, where the set of inference rules consists of rules for introduction and elimination of the logical connectives and quantifiers. The language of the program synthesized is Horn Clauses, a subset of first order predicate logic, that efficiently can be run by PROLOG systems, (9).

This work is supported by the National Swedish Board for Technical Development (STU)

We could compare other deductive approaches to program synthesis to ours, notably Manna & Waldinger (8), Hogger (6), Kowalski (7), and Clark & Darlington (1). The first three use resolution and transformation rules or equivalence substitution for the reasoning. Clark and Darlington use symbolic execution and logical manipulation together with "folding" to get their programs.

3 Facilitating proof-making using an interactive system.

Deductions can be edited by a set of inference rules and validity is provided by checking the correct use of these rules. The deduction-steps are stored and can be presented in a clear and lucid way using brackets to illustrate the dependencies in the proof. Basically there are administrative operations such as saving, killing, getting, and logging a deduction or parts of a deduction.

In addition the system contains features for facilitating the proof-making. The complexity of a formal proof due to the number of small steps hides the essentials of the proof. The user wants be able to keep the general lines of the proof, and work according to those without getting lost in the bushes.

A partial solution to this problem is to design composite inference rules making it possible to go through the deduction in larger steps. Composite inference rules can be defined in a hierarcy and is a user-programmed deduction.

Another partial solution is to let the system outline the structure of a proof. In this way the system breaks up a deduction in sub-deductions easier to grasp. This eliminates trivial considerations.

We shall now take up outlines of deductions and compositions of rules.

4 An example: synthesis of a partition relation.

The partition relation between three data structures U,V, and W together with an element X, where the structure U can be partitioned into two structures V and W with respect to X, can formally be defined like this:

Definition 4:1.

```
(X)(U)(V)(W)
(partition(U,X,V,W) <-> (Y)(member(Y,V) -> Y ≤ X) &
                        (Y)(member(Y,W) -> Y > X) &
                        (Y)(member(Y,U) <-> member(Y,V) or member(Y,W)))
```

Let the structures U, V, and W be list structures. The empty list is represented by 'nil' and a list where z is the first element and u is the rest, is represented by z.u, using the list-constructor '.'.

The membership relation for lists is defined in the following way:

Definition 4:2.

```
(X)(U)
(member(X,U) <-> (e Z)(e V)(U=Z.V & (X=Z or member(X,V))))
```

From this definition we can derive more useful lemmas.

Lemma 4:1.

```
(X) not member(X,nil)

(X)(Z)(U)
(member(X,Z.U) <-> X=Z or member(X,U))
```

From the above definitions we want to derive a theorem that can be executed as a program. The idea is to derive the program by induction on the data structure. The induction schema for lists is:

Definition 4:3.

```
P(nil) & (X)(U)(P(U) -> P(X.U)) -> (U)(list(U) -> P(U))
```

This divides the synthesis into two cases: a derivation for the induction base and another for the induction-step.

Let us first look at the induction-step. From the hypothesis partition(u,x,v,w) we shall try to derive partition(z.u,x,v1,w1) where the list z.u contains one more element than the list u.

According to the normal form theorem (Hauptsatz) by Prawitz (10) for natural deduction systems, a deduction is roughly carried out by decomposing the premises and assumptions into parts using the elimination rules and from these parts constructing the theorem using the introduction rules.

The premises for this deduction are the definition of partition, the lemmas for member, and the induction hypothesis partition(u,x,v,w).

Our aim is to complete the definiens of partition(u,x,v,w) to yield the definiens for partition(z.u,x,v1,w1). This cannot be directly acheived, so we have to examine the subformulas of the definiens. Decomposing partition's definition given the hypothesis partition(u,x,v,w) by an application of the elimination rule corresponding to the main logical constant, gives us the following steps:

```
(1)  partition(u,x,v,w)

(2)  partition(u,x,v,w) <->
             (Y)(member(Y,v) -> Y ≤ X) &                        all_elim def 1.
             (Y)(member(Y,w) -> Y > X) &
             (Y)(member(Y,u) <-> member(Y,v) or member(Y,w)))

(3)  (Y)(member(Y,v) -> Y ≤ X) &                                subst
     (Y)(member(Y,w) -> Y > X) &
     (Y)(member(Y,u) <-> member(Y,v) or member(Y,w)))

(4)  (Y)(member(Y,v) -> Y ≤ X)                                  & elim 3.

(5)  (Y)(member(Y,w) -> Y > X)                                  & elim 3.

(6)  (Y)(member(Y,u) <->                                        & elim 3.
          member(Y,v) or member(Y,w))

(7)  member(y,v) -> y ≤ x                                       all_elim 4

(8)  member(y,w) -> y > x                                       all_elim 5

(9)  member(y,u) <->                                            all_elim 6
          member(y,v) or member(y,w)
```

In an informal argument we would probably directly reach steps 7-9 from the assumptions without the detour to steps 2-6. This way of using the definition is straightforward when we do inductive reasoning. Therefore, it seems worthwhile to define a composite rule to the editor that from the definiendum can extract the parts in the definiens. Such a rule starts to instantiate the outermost quantifiers, eliminates the equivalence sign, and if, after instantiating the quantifiers of the definiens, the remaining formula is a conjunction it can be divided into subformulas whose quantifiers can be eliminated.

We define a composite inference rule by a Horn clause, and we can identify definition-head and body separated by a implication sign. The body consists of rules separated by conjunction or disjunction. We describe the composite rules in a relation named rule, which has tree arguments: the name of the rule, the arguments to the rule in a list, and the result from the rule. The rule from_def extracts the definiens parts (Formulas) from the definition (Def).

```
rule(from_def,Def.Definiendum,Formulas) <-
        rule(elim,Def,UnquantDef) &
        rule(subst,Definiendum.UnquantDef,Definiens) &
        rule(elim,Definiens,UnquantDefiniens) &
        rule(repeat_&_elim,UnquantDefiniens,List_of_formulas) &
        rule(repeat_elim,List_of_formulas,Formulas).
```

If the rules in the body are conjoined together it means that all of them have to be performed in sequence. If the body is disjunctive, as for the composite rule elim, defined below, either of the rules in the disjunction can be tried. Two definitions with the same name in the head also expresses alternation, either of the definitions can be performed. The composite rules can be used for trying out different compositions of rules for obtaining a desired result.

In the rule from_def, the rules in the body are composite rules. We can formulate the definition of the composite rule elim as follows:

```
rule(elim,Formula1,Formula2) <-
      (rule(all_elim,Formula1,Formula3) or                          (NR)
       rule(exist_elim,Formula1,Formula3)) &                        (NR)
      rule(elim,Formula3,Formula2).

rule(elim,Formula,Formula).
```

In the definition all_elim and exist_elim are basic inference rules in NATDED denoted by (NR). The definitions for the composite rules subst, repeat_&_elim, and repeat_elim are given in appendix I.

If we construct the definiens of the partition(z.u,x,v1,w1) then we can conclude the deduction by a similar composite rule (only opposite) as from_def. The construction of the definiens is performed by a successive use of introduction rules. The final step (l) and its premises (i)-(k) are given in our next outline of the proof.

The deduction when the composite rules from_def and from_def_2 are used have the following appearance:

```
(1)  partition(u,x,v,w)

(2)  member(y,v) -> y ≤ x                                      from_def

(3)  member(y,w) -> y > x

(4)  member(y,u) <-> member(y,v) or member(y,w)

   ...
(i) INFER: member(y,v1) -> y ≤ x

   ...
(j) INFER: member(y,w1) -> y > x

   ...
(k) INFER: member(y,z.u) <-> member(y,v1) or member(y,w1)

(l) partition(z.u,x,v1,w1)                                     from_def_2
```

The steps connecting the parts of the two definiens are still missing, the steps (i)-(k) are still to be deduced and are therefore marked with the text 'INFER:'. The formulas to be inferred are implications and an equivalence. An implication is derived by assuming the antecedent and deducing the consequence, and finally an application of the ->_introduction rule. Utilizing knowledge like this, extractable from the inference rules we can obtain a proof-structure for these steps.

The proof-structure:

```
┌    member(y,v1)                                              hypothesis
│    ...                                                       (Infer 1)
│    INFER: y ≤ x
└──────────────────────
 (i) member(y,v1) -> y ≤ x                                     ->_intro.

┌    member(y,w1)
│    ...                                                       (Infer 2)
│    INFER: y > x
└──────────────────────
 (j) member(y,w1) -> y > x                                     ->_intro.

┌──  member(y,v1) or member(y,w1)                              hyp.
│┌   member(y,v1)                                              hyp.
││   ....                                                      (Infer 3)
││   INFER: member(y,z.u)
│└──────────────────────
│    member(y,v1) -> member(y,z.u)                             ->_intro.
│┌   member(y,w1)                                              hyp.
││   ...                                                       (Infer 4)
││   INFER: member(y,z.u)
│└──────────────────────
│    member(y,w1) -> member(y,z.u)                             ->_intro
│    member(y,z.u)                                             or_elim.
└───────────────────────
     member(y,v1) or member(y,w1) -> member(y,z.u)             ->_intro.

┌    member(y,z.u)                                             hyp.
│    ...                                                       (Infer 5)
│    INFER: member(y,v1) or member(y,w1)
└──────────────────────────
     member(y,z.u) -> member(y,v1) or member(y,w1))            ->_intro.
 (k) member(y,z.u) <-> member(y,v1) or member(y,w1)            <->_intro.
```

From the definition of partition we can identify two separate cases : z ≤ x and z > x. We continue the deduction by the case, z ≤ x. The added element z has to be present in one of the lists v1 or w1. If z is less than or equal to x, then z has to be present in v1 together with the elements in v i.e. v1 is equal to z.v, and then w1 has to be equal to w. Let us include these hypotheses in the deduction.

```
┌─(5) z ≤ x                                                    hyp.
│┌(6) v1=z.v & w1=w                                            hyp.
```

appendix II).

Let us look at (Infer 4) where we want to derive member(y,z.u) from the hypothesis member(y,w1). Informally we can reason like this: use the identity w1=w to get member(y,w), complement this to (member(y,v) or member(y,w)), use the equivalence in step 4 to get member(y,u). Continuing by an or_introduction to (y=z or member(y,u)) and using the lemmas for member gives member(y,z.u). We see that we twice do an or_introduction followed by the use of an equivalence formula. The composite rule, or_from_def (see appendix I), accomplishes this.

When filled in (Infer 4) will look like this.

```
┌    member(y,w1)                                hyp.
│
│    member(y,w)                                 id
│
│    member(y,u)                                 or_from_def
│
│    member(y,z.u)                               or_from_def
└──────────────────

     member(y,w1) -> member(y,z.u)               ->_intro
```

The rule or_from_def can be used at several places in the deduction. For reasons of space we leave out the rest of the deduction (see appendix II).

The deduced program statement is:

```
partition(z.u,x,v1,w1) <-
        z ≤ x & v1= z.v & w1 = w &
        partition(u,x,v,w)
```

The case where z > x is derived similarly. Together with the base case the resulting program have this appearance:

```
partition(nil,x,nil,nil) <-

partition(z.u,x,z.v,w) <-
        z ≤ x & partition(u,x,v,w)

partition(z.u,x,v,z.w) <-
        z > x & partition(u,x,v,w)
```

5 Implementation.

The implemantation language used for the system is Edinburgh-PROLOG (9). In this section we will make some comments on the implementation.

The inference rules are internally defined in a relation where the rule, the antecedent formulas and the consequent formulas are represented. The relation also contains knowledge about restriction for the use of the rule. The set of inference rules can interactively be increased by the user-defined composite inference rules. These rules are represented and applied in the same way as the predefined inference rules.

NATDED uses the inference rules to compose and decompose formulas, and the corresponding inference relation is therefore called in different ways. Given the rule and the antecedent formulas the system can create new formulas which continue the deduction. Furthermore, given the consequent formula the inference rule suggests a deduction structure consisting of a rule and antecedent formulas for the given formula-pattern. An outline of a proof structure suggestion does not have to be fully instantiated; PROLOG's ability to return incomplete structures makes the outlining facility more useful. The inference rule is thus used in multiple ways, making no distinction between input and output arguments.

The structuring is done in interaction with the user who can let the system outline a derivation to a specific level. If the user is not content with the presented structure, she can reject it and the system can be asked to come up with an alternative proof.

I. More composite rules.

The composite rule subst:

```
rule(subst,Part.Def,OtherPart) <-
    rule(<->_elim,Def,(Part -> OtherPart) & (OtherPart -> Part)) &       (NR)
    rule(&_elim,(Part -> OtherPart) & (OtherPart -> Part):1,
                Part -> OtherPart) &                                       (NR)
    rule(->_elim,(Part -> OtherPart).Part,OtherPart).                      (NR)

rule(subst,Part.Def,OtherPart) <-
    rule(<->_elim,Def,(OtherPart -> Part) & (Part -> OtherPart)) &       (NR)
    rule(&_elim,(OtherPart -> Part) & (Part -> OtherPart):2,
                Part -> OtherPart) &                                       (NR)
    rule(->_elim,(Part -> OtherPart.Part),OtherPart).                      (NR)
```

The composite rule repeat_&_elim:

```
rule(repeat_&_elim,Formula1:P1,Formula2) <-
    rule(&_elim,Formula1:P1,Formula2).                                     (NR)

rule(repeat_&_elim,Formula1:P1.Formulas,Formula2.Rest) <-
    rule(&_elim,Formula1:P1,Formula2) &                                    (NR)
    rule(repeat_&_elim,Formulas,Rest).
```

The composite rule repeat_elim:

```
rule(repeat_elim,Formula:P1.Formulas,Formula1)  <-
    rule(elim,Formula:P1,Formula1).

rule(repeat_elim,Formula:P1.Formulas,Formula1.Rest) <-
    rule(elim,Formula:P1,Formula1) &
    rule(repeat_elim,Formulas,Rest).
```

The composite rule or_from_def:

```
rule(or_from_def,Part:Def,DefPart) <-
    rule(extract_def,DefPart:Def,OtherDefPart) &
    rule(or_intro,Part:CompPart,DefPart).                                  (NR)
```

The composite rule extract_def:

```
rule(extract_def,Part.Def,OtherPart) <-
    rule(elim,Def,UnquantifiedDef) &
    rule(subst,UnquantifiedDef,OtherPart).
```

II. The entire deduction.

Definition of partition:

```
(X)(U)(V)(W)
(partition(U,X,V,W) <-> (Y)(member(Y,V) -> Y ≤ X) &
                        (Y)(member(Y,W) -> Y > X) &
                        (Y)(member(Y,U) <-> member(Y,V) or member(Y,W)))
```

Deduction for the induction step:

```
(1)  partition(u,x,v,w)
(2)  member(y,v) -> y ≤ x                                   from_def
(3)  member(y,w) -> y > x
(4)  member(y,u) <-> member(y,v) or member(y,w)
(5)  z < x                                                  hyp.
(6)  v1=z.v & w1=w                                          hyp.
(7)  member(y,v1)                                           hyp.
(8)  y < x

(9)  member(y,v1) -> y ≤ x                                  ->_intro.
(10) member(y,w1)                                           hyp.
(11) y > x

(12) member(y,w1) -> y > x                                  ->_intro.
(13) member(y,v1) or member(y,w1)                           hyp.
(14) member(y,v1)                                           hyp.
(15) member(y,z.u)

(16) member(y,v1) -> member(y,z.u)                          ->_intro.
(17) member(y,w1)                                           hyp.
(18) member(y,w)                                            id
(19) member(y,u)                                            or_from_def
(20) member(y,z.u)                                          or_from_def

(21) member(y,w1) -> member(y,z.u)                          ->_intro
(22) member(y,z.u)                                          or_elim.

(23) member(y,v1) or member(y,w1) -> member(y,z.u)
(24) member(y,z.u)
(25) y=z or member(y,u)
(26) y=z -> member(y,v1) or member(y,w2)
(27) member(y,u) -> member(y,v1) or member(y,w1)
(28) member(y,v1) or member(y,w1)                           or_elim.

(29) member(y,z.u)->member(y,v1) or member(y,w1)
(30) member(y,z.u) <-> member(y,v1) or member(y,w1)         <->_intro.
(31) partition(z.u,x,v1,w1)                                 from_def_2

(32) partition(u,x,v,w) & z ≤ x & v1=z.u & w1=w ->
            partition(z.u,x,v1,w1)
```

REFERENCES

(1) Keith Clark and John Darlington.
Algorithm Classification through Synthesis.
Computer Journal, No 1 , 1980.

(2) Keith Clark and Sten-Ake Tarnlund.
A First Order Theory of Data and Programs.
Proceedings IFIP-77, Toronto , 1977.

(3) Ake Hansson and Sten-Ake Tarnlund.
A Natural Programming Calculus.
Proceedings IJCAI-79, Tokyo , 1979.

(4) Ake Hansson and Sten-Ake Tarnlund.
Derivations of Programs in a Natural Programming Calculus.
Proceedings Electrotechnical Laboratory, Tokyo , 1979.

(5) Ake Hansson.
A Formal Development of Programs.
Department of Information Processing and Computer Science, 1980.

(6) C. J. Hogger.
Derivation of Logic Programs.
JACM, Vol 28, No 2 :372-392, 1981.

(7) Robert Kowalski.
Logic for Problem Solving.
Elsevier North Holland, 1979.

(8) Zohar Manna and Richard Waldinger.
A Deductive Approach to Program Synthesis.
SRI International, Menlo Park, California, 1978.

(9) Luis Moniz Pereira, Fernando Pereira and David Warren.
User's Guide to DecSystem-10 PROLOG.
Department of Artificial Intelligence, University of Edinburgh, 1978.

(10) Dag Prawitz.
Natural Deduction.
Almqvist & Wiksell, Stockholm, 1965.

ON SOME SYNTACTIC EQUIVALENCES OF PROGRAM SCHEMAS AND RELATED TRANSFORMATIONS

M.P. FLE - G. ROUCAIROL
Université P. et M. Curie
Institut de Programmation
4, place Jussieu - 75230 PARIS CEDEX 05

INTRODUCTION

Between node-splitting equivalence (identity of set of computations) [LED 75] and equivalence by identity of results under any interpretation [PAT 67], a wide range of syntactic equivalences of program schemas can take place. Each of these equivalences can be used either to characterize some particular differences among programs or to validate some transformations which allow for instance to optimize a program, to modify its structure in order to improve its readability or to point out further semantic transformations.

Herein, we introduce (section 2) a lattice of five equivalences which allow to compare program flowcharts from the point of view of their size, their set of variables, the ordering of their operations. Basically, these equivalences are build by composing an equivalence defined by L. Logrippo [LOG 75] which allows variable-renaming, with node-splitting equivalence and an extension of the latter dealing with reordering of operations.

The use of these equivalences in order to validate various program transformations is then illustrated in section 3 and 4. More precisely, we characterize in section 3 a transformation which renames by a unique name a given set of variables used at given places in a program. This characterization distinguishes the case where the structure of the program has not to be modified from the case where some "unfoldings" of the loops of the program are necessary.

In section 4, we consider the problem of anticipating the execution of an operation of a program. This transformation formalizes some moves of instructions used by J. Arsac [ARS 77] and generalizes a transformation defined by R. Keller [KEL 73] for parallelization purposes under an equivalence stronger than the ones we are concerned with. For this transformation, we again characterize the case where the program structure is not deeply changed from the case where some variable-renamings and unfoldings of loops are necessary.

1. PROGRAM SCHEMAS

A program schema over a set of operations O which is partitionned into a set O_a of assignment and read or write operations and a set O_t of test operations, is a finite automaton $S_O = (Q, q_o, \tau, Q_f)$ where :

(i) Q is the finite set of states, $q_o \in Q$ the initial state and $Q_f \subset Q$ the set of terminal states (without successors).

(ii) $\tau : Q \times (O \cup \{T, F\}) \to Q$ is a partial mapping called the transition function such that : (labelling of test branches) for every state q, if there exists a test operation a and a state q' such that $\tau(q', a) = q$ then $\tau(q, F)$ and $\tau(q, T)$ are defined otherwise none of them is defined ; we call a state like q a choice-state.

In the following, we shall consider the usual extension of τ as a mapping

$\tau : Q \times (O \cup \{T, F\})^* \to Q$.

An operation is a triple a = (F(a), D(a), R(a)) where :

(i) F(a) is the function symbol corresponding to the operation a.
(ii) $D(a) = \{e_1,\ldots,e_{d(a)}\} \subset \mathbb{N}$ is either an ordered set of d(a) input variables, the ith $(1 \le i \le d(a))$ of them being referred as $D(a)_i$ or the empty set.
(iii) R(a) is either the empty set (it is always the case for test operations), or a singleton specifying the output variable of a. In this case, R(a) will denote the set R(a) as well as the only element of R(a).

Example 1.1. :

Figure 1.1. illustrates a program schema corresponding to the following Algol-like program which computes the expression x^p/A_n^{p+1} where x is a real, n and p are integers, and A_n^{p+1} is the number of permutations of p+1 items among n.

```
Input (X, N, P) ;
U := N ; D := X ; Y := 1 ; Z := 1 ;
While Y ≤ P-1 do D := D * X ; Y := Y+1 ; Z := Z * U ; U := U-1 od ;
H := Z * U ; U := U-1 ; R := D/H * U ;
Output(R)
```

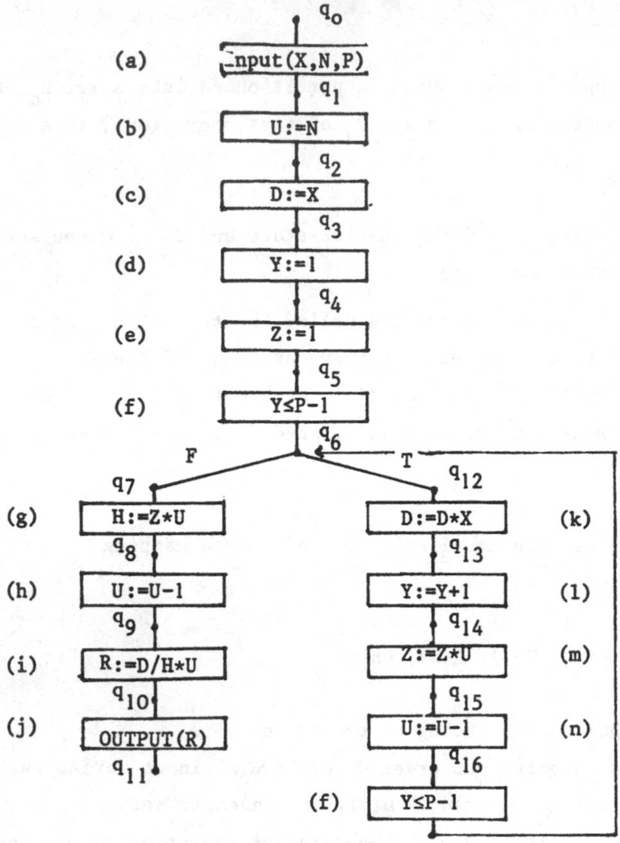

FIGURE 1-1

The behaviour of a program schema S_0 is characterized by its set of computations, $C(S_0)$, which is the language accepted by S_0

$C(S_0) = \{x \in (O \cup \{T, F\})^* \mid \tau(q_o, x) \in Q_f\}$.

The set of computations of the schema of figure 1-1 is given by the regular expression : a b c d e f $(T\ k\ l\ m\ n\ f)^*$ F g h i j.

Notations

Let $P(S_0)$ be the set of prefixes of computations of $S_0(C(S_0) \subseteq P(S_0))$ and x an element of $P(S_0)$; x [k] will denote the kth symbol of x, x[1,k] its prefix of length k, $|x|$ the length of x and $|x|_a$ the number of occurrences of symbol a in x.

In the sequel, we shall consider only those schemas which meet the following restrictions, each of them corresponding either to the satisfaction of an elementary correctness property or to a proper presentation of a schema used for sake of simplicity.

Restrictions

. Sequentiality and determinism : for every state q the cardinal of the set $\{q' \mid \exists\, a \in O \cup \{T,F\}, \tau(q,a) = q'\}$ is at most 2 and for every symbol $a \in O_a$, there exists at most one state such that $\tau(q,a)$ is defined.

. <u>Connectivity</u> : for every state q, there exists an $x \in P(S_0)$ such that $\tau(q_0,x) = q$.

. <u>Expansion</u> : if there exist two different ways to reach one state then this state is a choice state -i.e- for every pair of states (q,q') and every pair of symbols (a,b) in $O \cup \{T,F\}$, $\tau(q,a) = \tau(q',b)$ implies that $\tau(q,a)$ is a choice state. It is obvious that any schema can be transformed into a new schema with this property, without modifying its set of computations.

. <u>Initialization of variables</u> : all the used values are produced -i.e- $\forall x \in P(S_0), \forall h \in \mathbb{N}, d(x[k]) \neq 0 \Rightarrow \forall n \in D(x[k]), \exists h < k$ s.t $n \in R(x[h])$.

. <u>Usefulness of computed values</u> : every produced value is used -i.e- $\forall x \in P(S_0)$, $\forall k \in \mathbb{N}, R(x(k)) \neq \emptyset \Rightarrow \exists h > k, R(x[k]) \in D(x[h])$ and $\forall l, k<l<h, R(x[l]) \cap R(x[k]) = \emptyset$. (If a computed value is not used by further instructions in a program, then it is always possible to consider it as used by some ending instruction).

. <u>Consistency of operations</u> :
$\forall (a,b) \in O \times O, (F(a)) = F(b)) \Rightarrow (|D(a)| = |D(b)|$ and $|R(a)| = |R(b)|)$

2. SYNTACTICAL EQUIVALENCES OF PROGRAM SCHEMAS

We introduce successively five definitions of equivalences between schemas so-called N, R, R_N, U_N, $U_{N,R}$ - equivalences which form the following lattice where I-equivalence means isomorphism between schemas up to a renaming of their states.

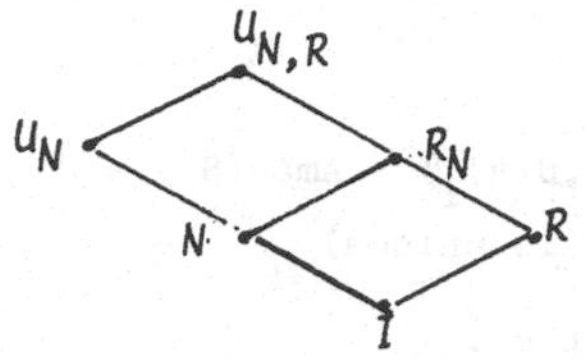

For each equivalence, it can be obviously shown that under any interpretation, two equivalent schemas compute identical sets of values.

2.1. <u>N-equivalence</u> ("Node splitting equivalence" [LED 75])

Two schemas S_0, S'_0 are said N-equivalent iff they have an identical set of computations. $(C(S_0) = C(S'_0))$.

2.2. <u>R-equivalence</u> [LOG 75]

This equivalence allows to compare schemas which are isomorphic up to a renaming of the variables used by the operations. It is based on the notion of <u>route</u> of one variable which defines one longuest path beginning at a state where this variable receives a new value and ending in a state after which this value is no longer used. In other words, the route of a variable m from a state q is the set of the elements of the maximal sequence of consecutive states $(q_1 = q, q_2, \ldots, q_n)$ such that :

(i) m is assigned at q -i.e- $\exists (a,q') \in O \times Q$ s.t. $\tau(q',a) = q$ and $R(a) = m$

(ii) m is used at q_n -i.e- $\exists (b,q'') \in O \times Q$ s.t. $\tau(q_n,b) = q''$ and $m \in D(b)$.

(iii) m is not assigned between q and q_n -i.e-
$\forall i \in [1, n-1], \forall a \in O, (\tau(q_i,a) = q_{i+1} \Rightarrow m \notin R(a))$.

Let us call the domain of the variable m from q, $\Delta(m,q)$, the union of routes starting at q, and let us say that two domains $\Delta(m,q)$ and $\Delta(m,q')$ are connected iff their intersection is not empty. Then, we call the area of m containing q, $A(m,q)$, the union of domains linked to $\Delta(m,q)$ by a chain of connected domains.

Example 1.2. In fig. 1.1., the set $\{q_5,q_6,q_{12},q_{13},q_{14}\}$ is a route of Z from the state q_5, the set $\{q_5,q_6,q_7,q_{12},q_{13},q_{14}\}$ is the domain $\Delta(Z,q_5)$ and the set $\{q_5,q_6,q_7,q_{12},$ $q_{13},q_{14},q_{15},q_{16}\}$ is the area $A(Z,q_5)$.

Then the R-equivalence of two schemas can be defined by the existence of a so-called "renaming" function of the variables of one schema which establishes a one one correspondence between the areas of those schemas.

Let Amap (S_0) be the set : $\{(A(m,q),m) \mid q \in Q,\ m \in \mathbb{N},\ A(m,q) \text{ is defined}\}$

A schema $S'_{0'} = (Q',q'_o,\tau',Q'_\delta)$ is said R-equivalent to the schema $S_0 = (Q,q_o,\tau,Q_\delta)$, $S_0\ R\ S'_{0'}$, iff there exists a "renaming" function

$\gamma : \text{Amap}(S_0) \to \mathbb{N}$, and a bijection $h^Q : Q \to Q'$ such that :

- $\forall (M,m),\ (M',m') \in \text{Amap}\ (S_0),\ (M \cap M' \neq \emptyset \text{ and } m \neq m' \Rightarrow \gamma(M,m) \neq \gamma(M',m'))$.
- $q'_o = h^Q(q_o)$.
- $\forall q \in Q,\ \forall\ a \in \{T,F\}\ \tau'(h^Q(q),a) = h^Q(\tau(q,a))$
- $\forall q \in Q,\ \forall a \in O,\ \tau(q,a)$ is defined implies there exists $b \in Q'$ such that :
  - . $F(b) = F(a),\ d(b) = d(a),\ |R(b)| = |R(a)|$
  - . $\tau'(h^Q(q),b) = h^Q(\tau(q,a))$
  - . $\gamma(A(R(a),q),\ R(a)) = R(b)$
  - . $\forall i \in [1,d(a)],\ D(b)_i = \gamma(M,D(a)_i)$ where $(M,D(a)_i) \subset \text{Amap}(S_0)$ and $q \in M$ (from the definition of an area, such an M is unique)

Proposition 2.1 : [LOG 75] R is an equivalence relation.

In the schema of figure 1.1., since $A(H,q_8) \cap A(R,q_{10}) = \emptyset$ we may obtain an R-equivalent schema by replacing the operations $H := Z * U$ and $R = D/H * U$ by the operations $R := Z * U$ and $R := D/R * U$.

2.3. R_N-equivalence

Roughly speaking, this equivalence allows to compare two schemas whose set of computations are equal up to a renaming of the variables. It is obtained by composing the R and N equivalence on the tree schemas associated to the program schemas.

A tree $T = (Q^T,q^T_o,\tau^T,Q^T_\delta)$ is an automaton defined like a program schema but with a possibly infinite set of states and which satisfies the following point :

$\forall\ x,\ y \in (O \cup \{T,F\})^*\ ,\ \tau^T(q^T_o,\ x) = \tau^T(q^T_o,\ y) \Rightarrow x = y.$

Extending R and N equivalences to trees, the tree-schema $T(S_0)$ of a schema S_0 is the only tree N-equivalent to S_0 up to an I-equivalence.

Two schemas S_0 and $S'_{0'}$ are said R_N-equivalent, $S_0\ R_N\ S'_{0'}$, iff their associated tree schemas are R-equivalent.

Proposition 2.1 : R_N is an equivalence relation (obvious from transitivity of R).

Remark : It is possible to show [FLE 79] that R_N may be obtained by composing R and N equivalences over program schemas only -i.e- $S_0 \, R_N \, S_{0'}$, iff there exist two schemas S^1_0 and $S^2_{0'}$, such that $S_0 \, N \, S^1_0 \, R \, S^2_{0'} N \, S_{0'}$. Herein, we omit this proof for sake of place. The difficulty comes from the fact that a tree is not necessarily a tree-schema.

2.4. U_N equivalence

With this equivalence, schemas in which the order of operations is different can be compared. It is based upon an equivalence of computations [ROUC 74].

First we introduce a relation between two occurrences of operations characterizing a transmission of value between them. In a word x, the nth occurrence of an operation a is in relation u(x,i) with the pth occurrence of an operation b, (a,n)u(x,i)(b,p), iff :

(i) $R(a) = D(b)_i$;

(ii) $\exists k, h \in \mathbb{N}, k < h, \ |x[1,k]|_a = n$ and $|x[1,h]|_b = p$, $x \lfloor k \rfloor = a$, $x \lfloor h \rfloor = b$;

(iii) $\forall\, l \in \mathbb{N}, k < l < h, \ R(x[l]) \neq R(a)$

This means that p^{th} occurrence of b uses in its ith input variable a value produced by the nth occurrence of a.

In figure 1.1., we have the relation :

(1,1) u (x,1)(f,2) where x = a b c d e f T k l m n f F g h i j

ow, we can say that two computations x and y are U_N-equivalent (xU_Ny) iff they con-ain the same occurrences of operations as well as identical u-relation -i.e.-

i) $\forall \ \sigma \in O \cup \{T,F\}, \ |x|_\sigma = |y|_\sigma$

ii) $\forall a, b \in O, \forall i \in [1,d(b)], \forall n, p \in \mathbb{N}, (a,n) \ u(x,i)(b,p) \Leftrightarrow (a,n) \ u(y,i)(b,p)$

wo schemas S_0 and $S_{0'}$ are said U_N-equivalent ($S_0 \, U_N \, S'_0$) iff every computation of one chema is U_N-equivalent to one computation of the other.

.5. $U_{R,N}$-equivalence

his equivalence is obtained by composing the U_N and R_N equivalences in the following ay : two schemas S_0 and $S_{0'}$ are said $U_{R,N}$ equivalent iff there exists a finite se-uence of schemas $S^1_{0_1} = S_0, S^2_{0_2}, \ldots, S^n_{0_n} = S'_{0'}$, such that for all i, $1 \le i < n$, $S^i_{0_i}$ and $S^{i+1}_{0_{i+1}}$ re linked by the relations U_N or R_N.

he following figure shows the differences between schemas allowed by the equivalences e have described :

DIFFERENCES / EQUIVALENCES	SET OF VARIABLES	NUMBER OF STATES	ORDER OF OPERATIONS
I			
N		yes	
R	yes		
R_N	yes	yes	
U_N		yes	yes
$U_{R,N}$	yes	yes	yes

3. RENAMINGS OF VARIABLES

In this section, we characterize a class of renamings of variables which preserve either R or R_N equivalence. This class of renamings concerns the replacement by one variable, of a set of variables occuring in operations accepted at a given set of states.

3.1. Renaming under R-equivalence

As a straightforward consequence of R-equivalence we have :

THEOREM 3-1 :

Let $q_1,\ldots,q_n, q_{n+1},\ldots,q_{n+m}$ be n+m states of a schema $S_0 = (Q, q_o, \tau, Q_\delta)$.
Let $a_1,\ldots,a_n, a_{n+1},\ldots,a_{n+m}$, be n+m distinct operations and $v_1,\ldots,v_{n+1},\ldots,v_{n+m}$ be n+m (not necessarily distinct) variables such that :

1/ $\forall i \in [1, n+m]$, $\tau(q_i, a_i)$ is defined ;

2/ $\forall i \in [1, n]$ v_i is the output variable of a_i ;

3/ $\forall i \in [n+1, n+m]$ there exists an integer l_i such that v_i is the l_i^{th} input variable of a_i.

There exist an R-equivalent schema S_0', and a variable v such that :
$\forall i \in [1, n]$ (resp. $i \in [n+1,n+m]$) the operation accepted at state $h^Q(q_i)$ has v as output (resp. li^{th} input) variable ;
iff ;
$\forall h, k \in [1, n+m]$, $v_h \neq v_k \Rightarrow A_h \cap A_k = \emptyset$ where
$\forall i \in [1, n]$ $A_i = A(v_i, \tau(q_i, a_i))$
$\forall i \in [n+1, n+m]$ $(A_i, v_i) \in$ Amap (S_0) and $q_i \in A_i$ (from the definition of an area, such an A_i is unique). □

Example 3.1 :

In the schema of figure 1.1., we consider the states q_7 and q_{14} and the variables H and Z which are the output variables of the operations H := Z * U and Z := Z * U. For these elements, the conditions of theorem 3-1 are satisfied since $A(H, q_8) = \{q_8,q_9\}$ and $A(Z, q_{15}) = \{q_{15},q_{16},q_5, q_6,q_7,q_{12},q_{13},q_{14}\}$. Let V be a new variable ; by the transformation allowed by theorem 3-1, we obtain the schema modeling the following program :

Input (X, N, P) ;
U := N ; D := X ; Y := 1 ; V := 1 ;
while Y ≤ P-1 do D := D * X ; Y := Y+1 ; V := V * U ; U := U-1 od ;
V := V * U ; U := U-1 ; R := D/V * U ; OUTPUT(R)

3.2. Renaming under R_N-equivalence

In the previous transformation the renaming has been applied "in situ". In the new transformation we are going to describe, will be renamed, in the transformed schema, the variables occurring in operations accepted at states in some sense equivalent to the states $q_1,\ldots,q_{n+m}$.

Let us define recursively a notion of similarity (noted $\sim$) between the states of a schema and its tree schema.

- $q_o \sim q_o^T$,
- $\forall \sigma \in O \cup \{T,F\}, \forall q \in Q, q^T \in Q^T,$
  $\tau(q,\sigma) \sim \tau(q^T,\sigma)$ iff $q \sim q^T$

For some $q \in Q$, let $[q]_T$ be the set of states in Q_T similar to q.

Now the characterization theorem for renaming under R_N-equivalence is :

THEOREM 3-2 :

Let $q_1,\dots,q_n, q_{n+1},\dots,q_{n+m}$ be n+m states of a schema $S_0 = (Q, q_o, \tau, Q_\delta)$.
Let $a_1,\dots,a_n, a_{n+1},\dots,a_{n+m}$ be n+m distinct operations and $v_1,\dots,v_n, v_{n+1},\dots,v_{n+m}$ be n+m (not necessarily distinct) variables such that :

1/ $\forall i \in [1, n+m], \tau(q_i,a_i)$ is defined ;

2/ $\forall i \in [1,n]$ v_i is the output variable of a_i ;

3/ $\forall i \in [n+1, n+m]$ there exists an integer l_i such that v_i is the l_i^{th} input variable of a_i.

There exist a variable v and an R_N-equivalent schema S_0', whose tree-schema $T(S_0')$ is such that :

$\forall i \in [1,n]$ (resp. $i \in [n+1, n+m]$), the operations accepted at states belonging to the set $h^{Q^T}([q_i]_T)$ have v as output (resp. l_i^{th} input) variable.

Iff :

$\forall i, j \in [1,n], \forall k, l \in [n+1, n+m], \forall p, q \in Q,$

- $\tau(q_i, a_i) \notin \Delta(v_j, \tau(q_j, a_j))$
- $q_k \in \Delta(v_k,p) \Rightarrow (p \notin \Delta(v_i, \tau(q_i, a_i))$ and $\tau(q_i,a_i) \notin \Delta(v_k,p))$
- $q_k \in \Delta(v_k,p)$ and $q_l \in \Delta(v_l,q) \Rightarrow (p \notin \Delta(v_l,q)$ and $q \notin \Delta(v_k,p))$. $\sqcup$

Example 3-2 :

In the schema of figure 1-1, we consider the states q_3 and q_{15} and the variables Y and U which are respectively the output variables of the operations Y := 1 and U := U-1. For these elements, the conditions of theorem 3-2 are satisfied since $\Delta(Y,q_4) = \{q_4,q_5,q_6,q_{12},q_{13}\}$ and $\Delta(U, q_{16}) = \{q_{16},q_6, q_{12},q_{13},q_{14},q_{15},q_7, q_8\}$.
Let M be a new variable ; by the transformation allowed by theorem 3-2 we obtain the schema modeling the following program.

```
Input (X, N, P) ;
U := N ; D := X ; M := 1 ; Z := 1 ;
if M ≤ P-1 then D := D * X ; Y := M+1 ; Z := Z * U ; M := U-1 ;
                while Y ≤ P-1 do
                                D := D * X ;
                                Y := Y + 1 ;
                                Z := Z * M ;
                                M := M - 1 ;
                                od ;
```

$H := Z * M$; $U := M-1$; $R := D/H*M$; Output(R) ;

else $H := Z * U$; $U := U-1$; $R := D/H*U$; Output(R) ;

fi ;

The proof of theorem 3-2 is based upon the following lemmas :

Lemma 3-1. : In a tree, an area is a domain. □

Lemma 3-2 :

Let q, q' be two states of a schema S_0 and m, n two variables such that $\Delta(m,q)$ and $\Delta(n,q')$ are defined.

$q' \in \Delta(m,q)$ or $q \in \Delta(n,q')$ iff there exist two states p, p' of $T(S_0)$ such that $q \sim p$, $q' \sim p'$ and $\Delta(m,p) \cap \Delta(n,p') \neq \emptyset$. □

(On one hand this comes from the restriction of expansion and the fact that test operations have no output variable. On the other hand this is due to the unicity of a state to which states of a tree-schema are similar).

Sketch of proof of theorem 3-2

Two steps are needed. In the first one, we point a tree which satisfies the conditions of theorem 3-2 and which is $\mathcal{R}$-equivalent to $T(S_0)$. This tree is then proved to be the tree schema of a schema S_0', which is therefore $\mathcal{R}_N$-equivalent to S_0.

First step : we deduce from the previous lemmas that the necessary and sufficient condition of theorem 3-2 is equivalent to the one of theorem 3-1 applied to the tree $T(S_0)$ for states similar to q_i. Thus, the existence of a tree T' $\mathcal{R}$-equivalent to $T(S_0)$ is proved.

Let us explicit how T' may be obtained from $T(S_0)$.

For every state p of $T(S_0)$ we define a mapping $\mu_p : V \to \mathbb{N}$, $(V = \bigcup_{a \in O} D(a) \cup R(a))$, which renames all the variables occurring in the schema, in the following way :

$\forall i \in [n+1,n+m]$, let $P_i = \{p \in Q^T \mid \Delta(v_i,p) \cap [q_i]_T \neq \emptyset\}$ and $\Delta_i = \bigcup_{p \in P_i} \Delta(v_i,p)$

$\forall p \in Q^T$, $\forall m \in V$,

$$\mu_p(m) = \begin{cases} v \text{ if } \exists i \in [1,n+m],\ m = v_i \text{ and } p \in \bigcup_{i \in [1,n]} \Delta(v_i, \tau(q_i,a_i)) \cup \bigcup_{i \in [n,n+m]} \Delta_i \\ m \text{ otherwise} \end{cases}$$

It can be trivially verified that the function γ : Amap $(T(S_0)) \to \mathbb{N}$ defined by : $\forall (M,m) \in$ Amap $(T(S_0))$, $\forall p \in M$, $\gamma(M,m) = \mu_p(m)$, is a renaming function whose associated function h^{Q^T} satisfies the conditions of theorem 3-1.

Second Step : we must prove that there exists a schema S_0' $\mathcal{N}$-equivalent to T'.

Lemma 3-3 :

$\forall q \in Q, \forall p,p' \in Q^T$ $(p,p' \in [q]_T$ and $\mu_p = \mu_{p'})$, from $h^{Q^T}(p)$ and $h^{Q^T}(p')$, the same language is accepted (we say that p and p' are $\mathcal{N}$-equivalent). □

For all $p \in Q^T$, μ_p is a mapping from V into $V \cup \{v\}$ which are finite sets. So there is only a finite number, say k, of such mappings. By lemma 3-3, the $\mathcal{N}$-equivalence partitions Q^T into a most $k|Q|$ states and by elementary finite automata theory, T' is N-equivalent to a finite schema $S_{0'}'$, with at most $k|Q|$ states. (The arguments used in this step are similar to those attributed to E.A. ASHCROFT in [LOG 75] in order to build a schema with a minimal amount of variables).

4 - MOVE-UP OF AN OPERATION

In this section, we characterize, from the point of view of the U_N and $U_{N,R}$ equivalences, the transformation which consists in moving, just before an operation, an assignment operation which occurs always after the former without any test between them. Since the first operation may be a test, any move-up can be decomposed into several elementary ones.

Notations

In this section, we shall denote Before(q), for a state q of a schema $S_0 = (Q, q_o, \tau, Q_f)$, the set $\{a \in O |\ \exists q' \in Q : \tau(q',a) = q\}$.

For an operation b, we shall say that S_0 verifies P(b,q) iff the first occurrence of symbol b after q is before a test operation -i.e - $\forall x \in (O \cup \{T,F\})^*$, $\forall k \in \mathbb{N}$, $(\tau(q,x)$ is defined and $x[k] = b) \Rightarrow (\exists h \leq k : \forall 1 \leq j \leq h \ \ x[h] = b$ and $x[j] \notin O_t)$

4.1.- Move-up under U_N-equivalence

Let $S = \{Q, q_o, \tau, Q_f\}$ be a schema, b an operation, and q a state. Moving up b to q is obtained by the construction of a schema $S_{0'}' = \{Q', q_o, \tau', Q_f\}$ in which the operation b precedes the operations of the set Before(q) -i.e-

- $Q' = (Q-Q1) \cup Q2$ where
  - $Q1 = \{p \in Q : \tau(q, xb) = p$ and $b \notin x\}$
  - Q2 is a set of new states indexed by the predecessors of q -i.e.- $Q2 = \{q_p : \tau(p,a) = q$ and $a \in O\}$
- $\tau' : Q' \times (O \cup \{T,F\}) \rightarrow Q'$ is defined by :
  - $\forall p \ \ Q-Q1$, $\forall a \in O$,

$$\tau'(p,a) = \begin{cases} \tau(\tau(p,b),a) \text{ if } \tau(p,b) \in Q_1 \text{ and } \tau(\tau(p,b),a) \text{ is defined} \\ \tau(p,a) \text{ if } \tau(p,a) \text{ is defined, } \tau(p,a) \notin Q_1 \text{ and } \tau(p,a) \neq q \\ q_p \text{ if there exists } c \in O \text{ s.t. } \tau(p,c) = q \end{cases}$$

  - $\forall p \in O$, $\forall a \in O$, $\tau(p,a) = q \Rightarrow \tau'(q_p,a) = q$

Example 4-1 :

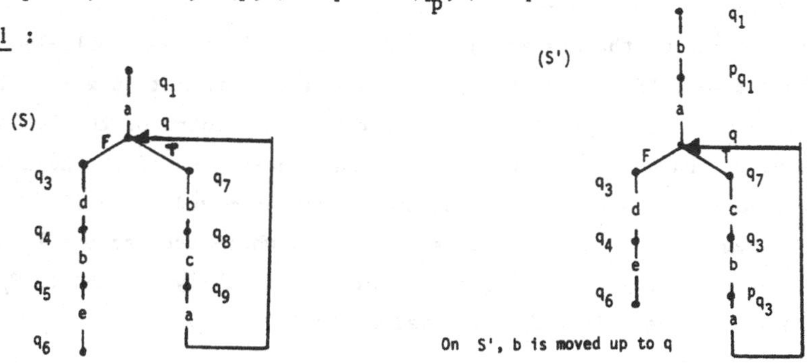

On S', b is moved up to q

THEOREM 4-1

Let $S_0 = (Q, q_o, \tau, Q_f)$ be a schema, b an operation and q a state such that P(b,q) is verified.

Schema S'_0 obtained by the construction described above is U_N-equivalent to S_0 iff the operation b satisfies the following "move-up" conditions :

$\forall x \in (O \cup \{T,F\})^*$ s.t. $\tau(q,x)$ is defined, $\exists\, k \in \mathbb{N}$

1/ $x\ [k] = b$,

2/ $\forall a \in \{x[j] \mid j<k\} \cup \text{Before}(q), D(a) \cap R(b) = \emptyset$, $R(a) \cap R(b) = \emptyset$ and $D(b) \cap R(a) = \emptyset$

Sketch of proof : It is clear that any computation in S'_0 going through q has the form $yba\ x_1x_2$; Condition 1/ is necessary and sufficient in order to insure that any computation going through q in S_0 has the form yax_1bx_2. Then, it is obvious that these computations are U-equivalent iff condition 2/ is satisfied. □

Example 4-2 :

In the schema of figure 1-1, any operation accepted between q_o and q_5 can be moved up until q_o. In example 3-1, the operation V := V * U satisfies the conditions to be moved up just before the "while loop". This leads to the following program :

```
Input(X,N,P) ;
U := N ; D := X ; Y := 1 ; V := 1 ; V := V * U ;
While Y ≤ P-1 do D := D * X ; Y := Y+1 ; U := U-1 ; V := V * U od ;
U := U-1 ; R := D/V*U ; output(R)
```

Then the operation U := U-1 may also be moved up just before the "while loop" :

```
Input(X,N,P) ;
U := N ; D := X ; Y := 1 ; V := 1 ; V := V*U ; U := U-1 ;
While Y ≤ P-1 do D := D*X ; Y := Y+1 ; V := V*U ; U := U-1 od ;
R := D/V*U ; output(R)
```

A very trivial semantic transformation finally leads to the program :

```
Input(X,N,P) ;
D := X ; Y := 1 ; V := N ; U := N-1 ;
While Y ≤ P-1 do D := D * X ; Y := Y+1 ; V := V * U ; U := U-1 od ;
R := D/V*U ; output(R)
```

4.2. Move-up under $U_{R,N}$ equivalence

In example 1-1 moving up the operation U := U-1 just before the "while-loop" is forbidden by theorem 4-1. In this section, we define a transformation which allows to do it providing some renamings of variables and some unfolding of the "while-loop". More precisely, we characterize a renaming of the tree-schema of a schema S_0 in order that operations with a given function symbol can be moved up until the states similar to a given state in S_0. If S'_0, is the schema whose tree schema is the renamed tree of S_0, then the move-up transformations will be actually applied to S'_0, in order to obtain a new schema S''_0, $U_{R,N}$ equivalent to S_0.

THEOREM 4-2 :

Let $S_0 = (Q, q_o, \tau, Q_f)$ be a schema, q a state and B a function symbol. There exists a schema $S''_{0'} = (Q'', q''_o, \tau'', Q''_f)$ $U_{R,N}$ equivalent to S_0 and a schema $S'_{0'} = (Q', q'_o, \tau', Q'_f)$ R_N equivalent to S_0 and U_N equivalent to $S''_{0'}$, such that : $\forall q' \in Q' \cap Q''$, if $[q']_{T(S'_0)} \subset h^{Q^T}([q]_{T(S_0)})$ then there exists an operation b such that P(b,q') is satisfied in $S'_{0'}$ and b is moved up to q' in $S''_{0'}$

iff : $\exists (n_i)_{i\in N}$, $n_i \in \mathbb{N}$, $\forall x \in (O \cup T,F)^*$: $\tau(q,x)$ is defined, $\exists k \in \mathbb{N}$. $\exists b \in O$:

1/ $F(b) = B$, $x[k] = b$

2/ $\forall i \in [1,d(b)]$, $D(b)_i = n_i$

3/ $\forall j \leq k$, $x[j] \notin O_t$

4/ $\forall a \in$ Before $(q) \cup \{x[j]/j < k\}$, $R(a) \cap D(b) \neq 0$

Sketch of proof :

Necessary condition : From the existence of schema $S'_{0'}$, 1/, 3/, 4/ are obvious. For every pair of operations (b,b'), F(b) = F(b') = B, occurring in different branches after q, let us assume that $D(b) \neq D(b')$. Then the areas to which the states accepting b and b' belong, intersect. Then it will be impossible to rename identically the input variables of b and b'. Hence b and b' cannot be transformed into the same operation and therefore cannot be moved up.

Sufficient condition :

Let us denote,

$\beta(B,(n_i)_{i\in \mathbb{N}}) = \{b \in O/\forall i \in [1,d(b)]\ F(b) = B \text{ and } D(b)_i = n_i\}$

For a state p of Q^T, we define :

$\Theta(B,p,(n_i)_{i\in \mathbb{N}}) = \{x \in O^*/\exists b \in \beta(B,(n_i)_{i\in \mathbb{N}}), \tau^T(p,xb)$ is defined and $\forall i \leq |x|\ \ x[i] \notin O_t$ and $x[i] \neq b\}$

We proceed in a way similar to the proof of theorem 3-2. For every state p of $T(S_0)$ we build partial mappings $\mu_p : V \to \mathbb{N}$, $(V = \bigcup_{a\in O} D(a) \cup R(a))$, by induction (the notation p^x means $\tau^T(p,x)$)

$\forall m \in V$,

$-\mu_{q_o}(m)$ is undefined

- Let $\tilde{q}$ a state similar to q, let $v_{\tilde{q}}$ the smallest element of the set $\{k \in \mathbb{N}-V/\forall s \in V\ \mu_{\tilde{q}}(s) \neq k\}$

$$\mu_{q_o^{xa}}(m) = \begin{cases} \mu_{q_o^x}(m) \text{ if } R(a) \neq m \\ v_{\tilde{q}} \text{ if } R(a) = m,\ \tilde{q} \sim q,\ \exists y \in \Theta(\beta,\tilde{q},(n_i)_{i\in N}),\ q_o^{xa} = \tilde{q}^{yb} \\ m \text{ otherwise} \end{cases}$$

One can verify that mappings μ_p define a renaming function of $T(S_0)$ providing a tree T' such that after every state $h^{Q^T}(\tilde{q})$ (where $\tilde{q}$ is similar to q and h^{Q^T} the renaming function of the states of $T(S_0)$), an operation b(F(b) = B) appears in every branch issued from $\tilde{q}$, before a test and before an operation which uses an output variable of b.

The existence of $S'_{0'}$ comes from the two lemmas :

Lemma 4-1 :

The number of mapping μ_p is finite. □

We say that two states p and p' in $Q^{T'}$ are S-equivalent iff, $(h^{Q^T})^{-1}(p)$ and $(h^{Q^T})^{-1}$ (p') are respectively reachable from choice-states t and t' such that $\mu_t = \mu_{t'}$ and t, t' are similar to a same state in Q.

Lemma 4-2 :

Two states p and p' of T', S-equivalent, accept the same language □

To prove lemma 4-1, we must show that :

$\exists k \in \mathbb{N}-V,\ \forall \tilde{q} \in Q^T,\ \forall x \in \Theta(B,\tilde{q},(n_i)_{i\in \mathbb{N}}),\ \forall b \in \beta(B,(n_i)_{i\in \mathbb{N}})$

$\tilde{q} \sim q,\ \tau^T(\tilde{q}, xb)$ is defined, $\exists i < k,\ i \in \mathbb{N}-V,\ \mu_{\tilde{q}xb}(R(b)) = i$

Let us suppose that :

$\forall k \in \mathbb{N}-V,\ \exists \tilde{q} \in Q^T,\ \tilde{q} \sim q,\ \exists x \in \Theta(B,\tilde{q},(n_i)_{i\in \mathbb{N}}),$

$\exists b \in \beta(B,(n_i)_{i\in N}),\ \tau(\tilde{q},xb)$ is defined, $\forall i < k,\ i \in \mathbb{N}-V,\ \mu_{qxb}(R(b)) \neq i$

Since $\mu_{\underset{q}{xb}}(R(b))$ is the smallest p such that $\forall s\in V\ \mu_{\tilde{q}}(s) = p$, we have :

$\forall i < k,\ i \in \mathbb{N}-V,\ \exists s\in V$ and $\mu_{\tilde{q}}(s) = i$.

This is impossible for k > 2xcard(V). □

Lemma 4-1 implies that there is a finite set of equivalence classes modulo the relation S.

Thus, the set of states of $S'_{0'}$ is the union of the set of representants of each class of the relation S and of the finite set of the states which are not reachable from a choice-state.

Lemma 4-2 implies that T' is the tree schema of $S'_{0'}$ and obviously schema $S'_{0'}$ satisfies the move up conditions of theorem 3-2. □

Example 4-3 :

On the schema of figure 1-1, move-up of operation U := U-1 just before the test Y ≤ P-1 needs to build the following intermediate program :

```
Input(X,N,P) ; U := N ; D := X ; Y := 1 ; Z := 1 ;
if Y ≤ P-1 then
   D := D * X ; Y := Y+1 ; Z := Z * U ; V1 := U-1 ;
   While Y ≤ P-1 do
         D := D * X ; Y := Y+1 ; Z := Z * V1 ; V2 := V1-1 ;
         if Y ≤ P-1 then D := D * X ; Y := Y+1 ; Z := Z * V2 ; V1 := V2-1
                    else H := Z * V2 ; V1 := V2-1 ; R := D/H * V1 ; Output(R) ; STOP
         fi
      od ;
```

```
   H := Z * V1 ; V2 := V1-1 ; R := D/H*V2 ;  Output(R)
        else
   H := Z * U ; V1 := U-1 ; R := D/H*V1 ; Output(R)
fi
```

In this program, operations of the form " " := " "-1 can be moved up just before the test Y ≤ P-1. This finally gives the following program :

```
Input(X,N,P) ; U := N ; D := X ; Y := 1 ; Z := 1 ; V1 := U-1 ;
if Y ≤ P-1 then
     D := D * X ; Y := Y+1 ; Z := Z * U ; V2 := V1-1 ;
     while Y ≤ P-1 do
               D := D * X ; Y := Y+1 ; Z := Z * V1 ; V1 := V2-1 ;
               if Y ≤ P-1 then D := D * X ; Y := Y+1 ; Z := Z * V2 ; V2 := V1-1
                          else M :=Z*V2; R := D/H*V1 ; output(R) ; stop
               fi
                  od ;
   H := Z * V1 ; R := D/H*V2 ; output(R)
       else
   H := Z * U ; R := D/H*V1 ; output(R)
fi
```

Remark :

By enforcing the conditions of theorem 4-2, it is possible to build a schema S'_0, $\mathcal{R}$-equivalent to S_0 and a schema S''_0, U_N-equivalent to S_0 such that there exists an operation b,E(b)=B,and b is moved up to $h^Q(q)$ where h^Q is the renaming function of the states of S.

The supplementary conditions are :

$\forall x,\ y \in \Theta(B,q,(n_i)_{i\in N}),\quad \forall b',\ b'' \in \beta(B,(n_i)_{i\in N})$

$\tau(q,xb')$ and $\tau(q,yb'')$ are defined implies

- $A(\tau(q,xb'),\ R(b')) \cap A(\tau(q,yb''),\ R(b'')) = \emptyset$
- $\forall a \in \mathrm{Before}(q) \cup \{x[j],\ j < |x|\},\ D(a) \cap (R(b') \cup R(b'')) = \emptyset$

(They derive directly from theorem 3-1)

The first program obtained in example 4-2 is an example of such a transformation applied ot the initial schema of figure 1-1.

Example 4-3 cont'd :

Let us consider the three states q_1, q_2 q_3 respectively corresponding to the first, the second and the third occurrence of the test Y ≤ P-1. The state q_1 (resp. q_2 and q_3) and the operator " "*" ":=" " verify the preceding conditions. The correponding transformations are applied successively to q_1, q_2 and q_3 and we finally obtain the $\mathcal{U}_{N,\mathcal{R}}$-equivalent program :

```
Input(X,N,P) : U := N ; D := X ; Y := 1 ; Z := 1 ; V1 := U-1 ; W1 := Z * U ;
if Y ≤ P-1 then
   D := D * X ; Y := Y+1 ; V2 := V1-1 ; W2 := W1 * V1 ;
   while Y ≤ P-1 do
         D := D * X ; Y := Y+1 ; V1 := V2-1 ; W3 := W2 * V2 ;
         if Y ≤ P-1 then D := D * Y ; Y := Y+1 ; V2 := V1-1 ; W2 := W3 * V1
                    else R := D/W3 * V1 ; output(R) ; stop
         fi
                 od ;
         R := D/W2 * V2 ; output(R)
       else
   R := D/W1 * V1 ; output(R)
fi
```

After a permutation of the operations of the form " ":=" "-1 (theorem 4-1) we are allowed to rename the variables U, V1, V2 by an unique variable, say V, and to rename Z, W1, W2, W3 by an unique variable, say W (theorem 3-1).

We finally obtain :

```
Input(X,N,P) ; V := N ; D := X ; Y := 1 ; W := 1 ; W := W * V ; V := V-1 ;
if Y ≤ P-1 then
   D := D * X ; Y := Y+1 ; W := W * V ; V := V-1 ;
   while Y ≤ P-1 do
         D := D * X ; Y := Y+1 ; W := W * V ; V := V-1 ;
         if Y ≤ P-1 then D := D * X ; Y := Y+1 ; W := W * V ; V := V-1
                    else R := D/W * V ; output(R) ; stop
                 od ;
   R := D/W * V ; output(R)
       else
   R := D/W * V ; output(R)
```

By replacing each occurrence of V by U and each occurrence of W by V, we obtain a program obviously N-equivalent to the one of example 4-2.

Remark :

All the transformations presented have been implemented in Basic language on an individual computer.

BIBLIOGRAPHY

[ARS 77] J. Arsac. Construction de programmes structurés. Dunod éd. 1977

[BER 67] A.J. Bernstein. Analysis of programs for parallel processing. IEEE. Trans. EC-15, n° 5, oct. 1967

[COU 77] G. Cousineau. Les arbres à feuilles indicées : un cadre algébrique pour l'étude des structures de contrôle. Thèse d'état, Université Paris VI

[FLE 79] M.P. Flé. Etude et mise en oeuvre de quelques transformations de programme. Thèse de 3ème cycle, Institut de Programmation Paris VI, 1979

[KEL 73] R.M. Keller. Parallel program schemata and maximal parallelism. JACM, vol. 20, n° 3, 4, 1973

[LED 75] H.F. Ledgard, M. Marcotty. A genealogy of control structures. CACM, vol. 18, nov. 1975

[LOG 75] L. Logrippo. On some equivalence-preserving transformations in program Colloque IRIA, proving and improving programs. juillet 1975

[LOG 78] L. Logrippo. Renamings and economy of memory in program schemata JACM, vol. 25, n° 1, 1978

[MIL 78] J.K. Millen. Construction with parallel derivations of the closure of a parallel program schema. IEEE Symposium on switching and automata theory, 1976

[PAT 67] M.S. Paterson. Equivalence problem in a model of computation. PHD, Cambridge university

[ROU 74] G. Roucairol. Une transformation de programmes séquentiels en programmes parallèles. Programming symposium, Paris, 1974, Lecture Notes in Comp. Sc. n° 19, Springer Verlag ed.

[WID 78] A. Widory. Etude du flot des données d'un programme. Application à la gestion des mémoires. Thèse de 3ème cycle, Institut de Programmation, Paris VI, 1978

PROCEDURES AND CONCURRENCY: A STUDY IN PROOF

Rob Gerth, Willem P. de Roever and Marly Roncken

affilation: University of Utrecht

the 2nd author was partially supported by the Dutch Organization for the Advancement of Pure Research (ZWO).

1. INTRODUCTION.

A commonly used model of distributed computing is the one in which a program consists of a fixed set of independently executing processes which may synchronize and communicate by means of procedure-like calls: each process may declare a number of *entry-procedures*, that can be called by other processes. In that case, execution of the caller is suspended until the caller has accepted the *external request* and has finished executing the associated code. Possible communication is established by the transmission of actual parameter values to the caller at the beginning of the synchronization-period and of computed values to the caller at the end of the period (hence, the parameter mechanism is call-by-value-result). Such an external request can be accepted when the caller arrives at a so-called *synchronization point*.

A well-known instance of this model in the *monitor*-concept, firstly axiomatically defined (although incompletely so) in [Hoa74]. In fact many parallel programming languages are based on the above model. Notably, Concurrent Pascal [BH75], Distributed Processes (DP) [BH78], ADA [ARM81], Mesa [La80] and Modula2 [Wi81].

In this paper, we develop a Hoare-style proof system w.r.t. safety-properties for the language DP.

We claim this proof system to be sound and relative complete, although we have no formal proof of this as yet.

The reason that DP has been chosen as vehicle for our research is twofold:

(1) DP is mini-language in that it admits the essential characteristics without being cluttered up by all the details which compromise a real-life language and

(2) in a sense, DP generalizes the concurrency sections of all of the above mentioned languages and it is straightforward to adapt the proof system for (a suitable subset of) any of them. In case of ADA, see [Ge81b].

The structure of the paper is as follows. In section 2 a subset of the language DP is introduced, which has one single synchronization primitive: the *entry-call* (and of course the ability to declare entry-procedures), besides the usual sequential constructs: the assignment, if and loop statements. For this subset, proof rules are developed; notably the *external request rule*, which characterizes partial correctness of an entry-call. Disregarding the synchronization involved, an entry-call is equivalent with an ordinary sequential procedure call. Hence, to describe the effect of executing the body of an entry-procedure (and the possible parameter-transfer) a (sequential) call-rule suffices. In order to capture additionally synchronization and communication, the notions of *general invariant* (GI) and *cooperation test* are adapted from the CSP proof system in [Apt80]. GI furnishes a global description of the communications that take place between the processes. The cooperation test checks, using GI, whether the assumptions on the communicated values, made in the *isolated* proofs of the component processes, are compatible. If so, these proofs may be tied together into a proof of the whole program. The resulting external request rule is the amalgamation of a sequential call-rule and this cooperation test. A salient fact is that, although the cooperation test enforces two checks for each communication-action (i.e., for each entry-call), the external request rule retains the idea of a single canonical proof of the body of an entry-procedure which suffices for all calls to that entry; this is the desired proof-theoretical pendant of the semantic notion of a procedure (-call) as an abstraction. This strategy is made possible by restricting the "range" of the cooperation test to a small *prelude* and *postlude* of an entry-procedure, which are not part of the body proper.

Section 3 introduces a new construct, thus defining full DP, which allows the programmer to define his own synchronization points (at which external requests may be accepted): the *when-statement*. This when-statement is a generalization of the *queues* of Concurrent Pascal and the *conditions* of Hoare's monitors. Using the when-statement, the internal execution of an individual process in general can be viewed as the concurrent execution of a varying number of sub-processes whose actions are interleaved. These sub-processes all have access to the variables of the original process, so that a process by itself is akin to programs in Owicki's *G*eneral *P*rogramming *L*anguage [OwG76]. In her proof system for GPL, Owicki introduces the notion of *interference freedom*: she proves each of the component processes correct in isolation and then, in a second stage, ties these separate proofs together. But, as the actions of each of the component processes can be interleaved, she is forced to show that the actions of one process do not interfere with the validity of the assertions in the component-proof of another one. Owicki however, is not forced to do so because in principle such a decomposition of proofs is not necessary as Ashcroft [Ash75] already has shown. In the current case, the reader will see the notion of interference freedom to be forced upon us indeed. The test will be formulated using a *process invariant*, PI (each process must be tested, hence each process receives his own PI). In fact, a number of alternative tests will be formulated. Interference freedom expresses the invariance of assertions over certain operations of the process. However in the current model there is more than one possible choice of these operations, hence the final choice of the formulation of the test, becomes a trade-off between the complexity of applying the test and the complexity of the necessary PI's.

We can now define what a valid proof is for some program (w.r.t. GI and the PI's of the constituent processes) or, equivalently, what a valid *proof-outline* is ([OwG76]); proof-outlines being somewhat easier to use in the next two sections.

In section 4, it is shown how these proof-outlines are used to prove safety-properties. This is not altogether trivial, because a major part of the assertions in the proof outline, namely that part associated with the bodies of the entry-procedures, consists of assertions which are canonical in the sense that they must hold for *any* call to the entry in question and thus do not reflect the actual states during execution. However, it will be shown how state-descriptions can be derived from these proof outlines. This suffices for the proof of safety-properties which amounts to showing that if a program is started in a correct initial state, a certain assertion will always remain true.

All this will be illustrated in section 5, in which a proof is given of a (corrected version of a) priority scheduler published in [BH78]. An appendix contains the list of axioms and proof rules which comprises the proof system.

2. PROCESS COMMUNICATION.

2.1. Introduction of the language.

A program consists of a fixed number of sequential processes that are executed concurrently. A process does not contain parallel statements and can access its own private variables only, i.e., there are no shared variables. The only form of process communication is calling an *entry-procedure* declared within another process. Such an *external request* can be accepted when the other process arrives at a *synchronization point*.

The syntax of a process is as follows:

```
process <name>
  <private variables>
  <entry-procedures>
  <initial statement>
end
```

If $P_1, P_2, \ldots, P_n$ denote n processes, the program is denoted as:

$[P_1 \parallel P_2 \parallel \ldots \parallel P_n]$.

2.1.1. Process execution.

A process starts by executing its initial statement. If this terminates, the process reaches a synchronization point, so another operation may be started by honouring an external request to one of its entry-procedures. If execution of the procedure-body terminates - another synchronization point - yet another external request may be accepted and so on. If no external requests are pending for some process and this process arrives at a synchronization point, it just waits until one is issued; hence, *processes do not terminate*. On the other hand, if a process has several external requests pending, it can choose one arbitrarily.

2.1.2. Entry procedures and procedure call.

Syntax of an entry procedure:

<u>proc</u> <name> (<value parameter list> # <variable parameter list>)

<statement>

<u>end</u>

Syntax of a call-statement in a process P, calling an entry-procedure qr, declared in a process Q:

<u>call</u> Q.qr(<expression list>, <variable list>)

where the variables in the expression and variable lists should be local to P.

The parameter transfer mechnism is call-by-value-result: before execution of an entry-procedure is started, the values of the expressions and variables in the actual parameter list of the call-statement are sent over to the process being called and are assigned to the formal parameters of the entry-procedure. After execution of the procedure, the values of the formal variable parameters are sent back to the caller and assigned to the actual variable parameters. Within an entry-procedure, none of its value-parameters may appear on the left hand side of an assignment statement.

If a process executes a call-statement, the process becomes idle until the caller has completed the external request. In particular, a process which is waiting for a call to finish does *not* accept external requests to one of its own entry-procedures. This includes the case of a process calling one of its *own* entry-procedures; i.e., the process deadlocks. Notice that a call-statement may also appear in the initial statement of a process; this in contrast with Hoare's monitor.

2.1.3. Sequential constructs.

The sequential language constructs are Dijkstra's *guarded commands* [Dijk76]:

(1) *guarded conditional*: <u>if</u> $b_1:S_1$ | ... | $b_n:S_n$ <u>end</u>
meaning: arbitrarily take one of the S_i's, whose boolean guard, b_i, evaluates to true, and execute it. Abort if there are no such guards.

(2) *guarded iteration*: <u>do</u> $b_1:S_1$ | ... | $b_n:S_n$ <u>end</u>
meaning: <u>while</u> $b_1 \vee \ldots \vee b_n$ <u>do</u> <u>if</u> $b_1:S_1$ | ... | $b_n:S_n$ <u>end</u> <u>end</u>.

2.1.4. Data-types.

For the formal proof system, we only allow the integer and boolean data-types. In practice, however, we will use in our examples (as usual) any data-type (and operations thereon), we deem necessary.

2.2. The proof theory of process communication.

2.2.1. The CSP-system of Apt, Francez and de Roever [Apt80].

We first give an overview of some ideas of this proof system, used in the sequel. The following three facts concerning the syntax and semantics of CSP suffice for our purpose:

(1) The basic command of CSP is $[P_1 \parallel \ldots \parallel P_n]$ expressing concurrent execution of the (sequential) processes $P_1 \ldots P_n$.

(2) Every P_i refers to a statement S_i: P_i::S_i. No S_i contains variables subject to change in S_j ($i \neq j$).

(3) Communication between P_i and P_j ($i \neq j$) is expressed by the receive and send primitives $P_j?x$ and $P_i!t$, respectively. Execution of $P_j?x$ (in P_i :: S_j and $P_i!t$ (in P_j :: S_j) is synchronized and results in the assignment of the value of expression t to the variable x (such a pair $P_i!t$, $P_j?x$, is called a (syntactically matching) *communication pair*).

In the proof system, the component processes are first proven correct in isolation. Because the processes communicate, two axioms are introduced to separate this first local stage of the proof from the second global stage:

(1) $\{p\}\ P_i!t\ \{q\}$ and (2) $\{p\}\ P_j?x\ \{q\}$.

This implies that the assumption on (i.e. the post-assertions of) the communication-actions in the component proofs must be tested for compatibility, in order for these proofs to be combined; this is the *cooperation test*. For this test a *general invariant* (GI) is needed which expresses globally, which of these communications occur, i.e., which of the syntactically matching communication pairs, match semantically; to define GI, *auxiliary variables* are introduced.

As the variables appearing free in GI have to be updated at times, GI cannot be expected to hold throughout the program. However, GI only concerns the communication actions, so updating of the GI-variables can be restricted to *bracketed sections*, $<S_1;\ \alpha;\ S_2>$, each of which is associated with a (unique) send or receive primitive α (the statements S_1 and S_2 perform the updating of the GI-variables). One of the functions of the cooperation test is to check whether GI is left invariant by the updating of its variables in each bracketed section. Basically, the test is the following:

Suppose we have proof outlines for the component processes of a CSP program. Then these proof outlines cooperate w.r.t. GI iff for any communication pair α, $\bar{\alpha}$ with associated bracketed sections and assertions $\{p\}<S_1;\ \alpha;\ S_2>\{q\}$, $\{\bar{p}\}<\bar{S}_1;\ \bar{\alpha};\ \bar{S}_2>\{\bar{q}\}$ in the respective proof outlines, the following condition holds:

$$\{p \wedge \bar{p} \wedge GI\}\ S_1;\ \bar{S}_1;\ x:=t;\ S_2;\ \bar{S}_2\ \{q \wedge \bar{q} \wedge GI\},$$

where x:=t is the result of performing the communication.

The definition can be paraphrased informally as follows: if execution in process P_i resp. P_j arrives at the communication α resp. $\bar{\alpha}$ (or rather, at the associated bracketed sections), as expressed by the validity of p resp. $\bar{p}$ and if additionally, these can occur simultaneously, as expressed by the validity of $p \wedge \bar{p} \wedge GI$, then the processes P_i and P_j communicate by executing α and $\bar{\alpha}$ and after this action (and after leaving the bracketed sections) both the assumptions q and $\bar{q}$, made about the value-transfer in the respective proof outlines, should be correct and GI should hold again.

For examples which show the *necessity* of something like GI and a cooperation test for a Hoare-style proof system for CSP (lest one wants to lose the idea of component proofs) the reader is referred to [Apt80]; these examples however are fully applicable to the current model.

In the next section of our paper, the analogues of the above ideas will be developed in the context of communication-by-entry-calls; in particular as the reader will notice, the cooperation test (re)appears in the external request rule.

2.2.2. The external request rule and the monitor invariant.

As was stated in the introduction, when synchronization is ignored, an entry-call behaves like an ordinary procedure call. Hence, to describe the effect of executing the body of an entry-procedure, we can look at ordinary procedure call rules.

A desirable property of procedure call rules is, that a single proof of the procedure body suffices for all applications of the call rule for this procedure. To be exact, we want the following:

For each declaration

<u>proc</u> $pr(\vec{u} \# \vec{v})$ T <u>end</u> ($\vec{u},\vec{v}$ denote the parameter lists)

in a process P and for each call-statement

<u>call</u> $P.pr(\vec{t},\vec{x})$:

if {p} T {q} holds, then {p[·]} <u>call</u> $P.pr(\vec{t},\vec{x})$ {q[·]} holds, where $[\cdot]\equiv[\vec{t},\vec{x}/\vec{u},\vec{v}]$ and denotes substitution of the actual for the formal parameters.

This implies that in order to prove {r} <u>call</u> $P.pr(\vec{t},\vec{x})$ {s}, one only has to prove the implications $r \rightarrow p[\cdot]$ and $q[\cdot] \rightarrow s$ (after having proved {p} T {q} once and for all). We can achieve this by placing the following restrictions on the actual parameters of a call (cf. [Apt81, 6.1]):

(i) the variable parameters x_i are pairwise disjoint,

(ii) $FV(\vec{t}) \cap \vec{x}=\emptyset$, i.e. no variable parameter appears free in a value expression,

(iii) $(Fv(\vec{t}) \cup \vec{x}) \cap FV(T) \subseteq \vec{u} \cup \vec{v}$, i.e. no variable in the actual parameter list may have the name of a variable appearing free in T, unless this is a formal parameter.

Only (ii) is a real restriction; the other two have to be made anyhow: firstly, our model does not specify a particular order in which the values computed in a procedure are assigned to the variables in the call-statement. Hence, if two of these variable-parameters are the same, their value is undefined after execution of the procedure, whence restriction (i). Secondly, because the proofs of the component processes will be combined at a later stage, variable-clashes must be avoided, so that the variables which appear in assertions of a proofoutline cannot appear in assertions of another proof outline. Hence a reasonable assumption is:

(iii') a variable appearing free in some process (and hence in the assertions of the corresponding proof outline) may not be subject to change in any other process.

This assumption implies restriction (iii) above. In the sequel we will assume (i), (ii) and (iii') to apply to each program.

Next we turn to the question of modelling synchronization. As in the CSP proof system, a *general invariant*, GI, is introduced to model synchronization globally and a set, AV, of *auxiliary variables*, in order to express GI:

AV is a set of variables such that $x \in AV$ if x appears only in assignments y:=t where $y \in AV$. (Notice that AV is defined relative to a particular program and that variables in AV do not influence the value of the 'real' program-variables during execution of the program).

Next, *bracketed sections* are introduced to which assignments of the GI-variables will be confined. First a (pseudo-)translation of an entry-call into CSP is given; using this translation, bracketed sections are defined:

	DP	translated CSP-version
P_i:	$\underline{call}\ P_j.pr(\vec{t},\vec{x})$	$P_j!(\vec{t},\vec{x});\ P_j?\vec{x}$
P_j:	$\underline{proc}\ pr(\vec{u}\ \#\ \vec{v})\ T\ \underline{end}$	$P_i?(\vec{u},\vec{v});\ T;\ P_i!\vec{v}$

The translation clearly shows that an entry-call results in *two* CSP-like communication actions. This suggests that *two* bracketed sections be associated with both the call and the procedure-body, which is essence is what we shall do:

A *bracketed section* is a construct of the form

(1) $<S_1;\ \underline{call}\ P_j.pr(\vec{t},\vec{x});\ S_2>$ or (2) $\underline{proc}\ pr(\vec{u}\ \#\ \vec{v})\ T_1;>\ T\ <;T_2\ \underline{end}$ such that S_1, S_2, T_1 and T_2 do not contain any call-statement. The T_1 resp. T_2-part of the procedure-body will also be referred to as the *prelude* resp. *postlude* of the body.

The pieces of program over which GI must be proven invariant for each call will then be: $S_1;\ \vec{u}:=\vec{t};\ \vec{v}:=\vec{x};\ T_1$ and $T_2;\ \vec{x}:=\vec{v};\ S_2$ (compare this with the CSP-translation of the entry-call).

Apart from what is suggested by the translation, there is a more pressing reason why the procedure-bodies have been extended by pre- and postludes; after all, why not show invariance of GI simply over $S_1;\ \vec{u}:=\vec{t};\ \vec{v}:=\vec{x};\ T;\ \vec{x}:=\vec{v};\ S_2$? This would reduce the number of cooperation tests and the procedure-body must be proven anyway. Moreover, the fact that two communication-actions are within the same bracketed section does not matter, because they take place during the *same* synchronization period. The catch is of course the appearance of other call-statements within the procedure-body. The idea is that GI must hold when (a new) synchronization-action takes place, i.e., at a new call-statement (or rather, at the entrance of the bracketed section surrounding it). Were the above suggestion to be accepted, the validity of GI would not have been assured for call-statements within the procedure-body, because GI would not have been required to hold within the body.

Before the *external request rule* and the cooperation test which is part of this rule can be formulated formally, one remaining detail must be filled in which has been glossed over until now. An entry-call can be accepted only if the process arrives at a synchronization point, i.e. at termination of the initial statement or of some procedure body. Consequently, the initial state in which an entry-procedure is executed, is the state at such a synchronization point. Hence, drawing upon an old idea of Hoare ([Hoa74]), for each process an invariant is introduced which must be proven to hold at each synchronization point, thus characterizing the intial state for entry-calls: the *monitor invariant*, MI.

As a last preparation, we mention that as a consequence of these restrictions on the actual parameters of a call, assignment of parameters is equivalent to substitution.

Hence:

<u>External request rule</u>:

$$\frac{\begin{array}{l}\{p \wedge MI_j \wedge GI\}\ S_1;\ T_1[\cdot]\ \{p_1[\cdot] \wedge p_2 \wedge GI\}\\ \{p_1\}\ T\ \{q_1\}\\ \{p_2 \wedge q_1[\cdot] \wedge GI\}\ T_2[\cdot];\ S_2\ \{q \wedge MI_j \wedge GI\}\end{array}}{\{p\}\ <S_1;\ \underline{call}\ P_j.pr(\vec{t},\vec{x});\ S_2>\ \{q\}}$$

where (1) the call-statement is contained in process P_i

(2) process P_j ($j \neq i$) contains a procedure declaration
$\underline{proc}\ pr(\vec{u}\ \#\ \vec{v})\ T_1;>\ T\ <;\ T_2\ \underline{end}$

(3) $[\cdot] \equiv [\vec{t},\vec{x}/\vec{u},\vec{v}]$

(4) MI_j is the monitor invariant of P_j

(5) $FV(p,q,p_2) \subseteq FV(P_i)$
$FV(p_2) \cap (FV(\vec{t}) \cup \vec{x}) = \emptyset$
$FV(p_1,q_1) \subseteq FV(P_j) \cup \vec{u} \cup \vec{v}$

In this rule, the first and third premiss (above the line) embody the cooperation test; the second premiss is the (canonical) proof of the procedure-body. However, notice that the Hoare-formula, $\{p_1\}\ T\ \{q_1\}$, which must be proven, does *not* refer to actual parameters. Hence, in spite of its appearance in the external request rule, *the body of the entry-procedure needs only to be proven once, and this proof suffices for each call to the procedure*. On the other hand, it can *not* be removed as premiss, because *if* calls are made, the procedure body must be proven correct (at least) once. Although a single proof suffices, the proof rule does not enforce this; it is not essential at this point. In section 3, when we extend the language and introduce an interference freedom test it will become essential to have single canonical proofs of the procedure-bodies as this will allow the interference freedom test to be canonical too, in a sense to be made precise. Consequently, the external request rule will then be changed: the second premiss will be removed to become part of a *process rule*.

In contrast, the cooperation tests are not canonical and must be proven anew, for each call. Of course this is only to be expected and besides that, the pre- and postludes of the bodies are rather trivial pieces of code.

Finally, we draw attention to the assertion, p_2, in the rule. This assertion characterizes the state of P_i when P_j has accepted the external request (i.e. the actual parameters have been sent over) but has not finished executing it yet. Assertion p_2 will play an essential part in the sequel, especially in the characterization of *calling-chains*, cfr. section 4.

3. PROOF THEORY OF PROCESS EXECUTION.

The language defined in the previous section has to be extended. Consider for example a bounded buffer (process). If this buffer is (still) empty, external requests to get an element *from* the buffer, clearly must be postponed until at least one external request has *put* something *into* the buffer. In other words, a facility is missing to define synchronization points oneself.

3.1. The when-statement.

The semantics of the when-statement **when** $b_1:S_1 \mid \ldots \mid b_n:S_n$ **end** is as follows: If $b_1 \vee \ldots \vee b_n$ holds, the when-statement resembles an ordinary guarded conditional; i.e., one of the S_i's whose boolean guard evaluates to true, is taken and executed. If however $b_1 \vee \ldots \vee b_n$ does not hold, the when-statement blocks and becomes a *waiting point*. A waiting point acts also as a synchronization point, so at a blocked when, new external requests can be accepted. Execution of such a request may cause the when-statement to become unblocked by making (at least) one of its guards true. Then, on arriving at another synchronization point, the process *may* continue execution at the when-statement instead of accepting another external request (but is not obliged to do so!).

Formally:

Within a process, control is at a *synchronization point*:

(1) at a when-statement which is blocked on arrival,

(2) upon termination of its initial statement,

(3) upon termination of a procedure body.

At these points, *synchronization* may take place as follows:

(1) an external request can be accepted, resulting in executing the appropriate procedure-body,

(2) execution can resume at a when-statement (having been blocked previously) as a result at some quard having become true.

The choice between these synchronization-actions is completely non-deterministic; this is also true for the possible choice between when-statements that can be resumed and between external request that can be accepted.

As when-statements can appear anywhere within a process, the description of process execution in section 2.1.1 needs refinement.

3.2. Process execution.

A process starts by executing its initial statement. This continues until control arrives at a synchronization point (either because the statement terminates or because a waiting point is encountered). Then another operation may be started by honouring an external request. In that case a new *procedure instance* is created and executed until a synchronization point is reached, in which case the process will either begin yet another operation (by honouring a new external request) or will resume an earlier operation (as a result of some when-statement having become unblocked in the meantime). This *interleaving* of statements from the initial statement and the procedure-instances continues until there is nothing left to be done anymore.

Notice that more than one procedure-instance can be 'active' at the same time within a process; this is a direct consequence of the possibility of procedure-bodies containing when-statements. The initial statement together with the active procedure instances can be viewed as a (varying) set of sub-processes which operate "in parallel" on the local variables of the main process. "In parallel" must be interpreted as in [OwG76]: In Owicki's model, it is assumed that at some level, viz. the memory-reference, the actions of the program are indivisible. As memory-references roughly correspond with assignments in a program, Owicki can simulate true parallelism by an interleaving of these assignments. This is similar to the current model, in which the indivisible actions extend from one synchronization point to another. Hence, each *process* in this model can be compared with a *program* in Owicki's model.

3.3. <u>The when-rule</u>.

If a when-statement is not blocked, it acts as a guarded conditional; so, one premiss of the when-rule is the same as for a guarded conditional. However, how do we characterize the case that the when-statement is blocked? Two problems arise:
(1) what assertion can be assumed, when execution resumes at the when-statement, and
(2) as external requests may be accepted, the monitor invariant of the process must hold (see section 2.2.2). To start with the latter problem, this is trivially solved by demanding MI to hold if a when-statement blocks, as a premiss in the when-rule. In fact, this also solves our first problem: if a when-statement blocks, the only way that execution can proceed at this when-statement is when execution 'comes' from another synchronization point, at which MI holds by definition. This leads to the following version of the

<u>when-rule</u>:

$$\frac{\begin{array}{l}\{p \wedge b_1\}\ S_1\ \{q\},\ \ldots,\ \{p \wedge b_n\}\ S_n\ \{q\} \\ p \wedge \neg(b_1 \vee \ldots \vee b_n) \rightarrow MI \\ \{MI \wedge b_1\}\ S_1\ \{q\},\ \ldots,\ \{MI \wedge b_n\}\ S_n\ \{q\}\end{array}}{\{p\}\ \underline{\text{when}}\ b_1 : S_1 \mid \ldots \mid b_n : S_n\ \underline{\text{end}}\ \{q\}}$$

Sound as this rule is, it unfortunately leads to incompleteness of the proof system. Consider the following process-fragment:

```
process P
  u:int
  proc a(#x) x:=u; b:=false; when b : x:=x-u end {x=0} end
  ....
end
```

As indicated, we want to have {x=0} as post-assertion of the procedure-body. This implies that {x=u} must hold when execution resumes at the when-statement. But as the when-statement is blocked, this means (see the when-rule above) that {x=u} must be implied by $\{MI \wedge b\}$ (with MI the monitor invariant of process P). However, x is a *local* variable of the procedure-instance (since x is a formal parameter), so x should not appear in assertions not belonging to the proof of the procedure-body, and can therefore certainly not appear free in MI which must hold at every synchronization point.

There is a second difficulty. One may consider DP-program as having terminated once all its component processes have finished executing their initial statements (since no activity can henceforth occur). Hence, when proving partial correctness properties, this resulting program-state has to be characterized. Unfortunately however, the only assertion which is required to hold up till now in a process at this point, is the process's MI. But MI does not fully characterize termination of the initial statement as it must hold at *each* synchronization point (within the process).

As is indicated by the two problems above, it is not sufficient to associate only an invariant with the synchronization points; specific assertions must be attached to some of them. In the next section, these special assertions together with MI, will be combined into a *process invariant* PI; one for each process. Anticipating the notation to be developed, the final form of the when-rule becomes:

when-rule:

$$\frac{\{p \wedge b_1\}\ S_1\ \{q\},\ \ldots,\ \{p \wedge b_n\}\ S_n\ \{q\} \qquad p \wedge \neg(b_1 \vee \ldots \vee b_n) \rightarrow PI{:}at('S') \qquad \{PI{:}at('S') \wedge b_1\}\ S_1\ \{q\},\ \ldots,\ \{PI{:}at('S') \wedge b_n\}\ S_n\ \{q\}}{\{p\}\ \underline{when}\ b_1{:}S_1\ |\ \ldots\ |\ b_n{:}S_n\ \underline{end}\ \{q\}}$$

The term PI:at('S') denotes the conjunction of those assertions which (must) hold at this particular when-statement, i.e., the conjunction of MI and the special assertion attached to the when-statement (i.e., to the associated synchronization point).

3.4. The process invariant.

In the previous section, we argued that special assertions must be associated with specific locations, viz.: certain when-statements. As these assertions play an important part in the next sections, they are collected into a *process invariant* PI; one for each process.

To this end, notation must be developed to refer to (syntactical) locations within a process. Firstly, for each (syntactic) occurrence of an entity S within a program, a unique *name* is introduced, denoted by 'S'. This will not be done formally; one may think of some form of labeling. In the sequel the following standard names are used:

'W', 'W_i',	- (the name of) some occurrence of a when-statement
'C', 'C_i'	- some occurrence of a call-statement
'<C>', '<C_i>'	- some occurrence of the bracketed section associated with 'C' or 'C_i'
P.pr.body	- the body of entry-procedure pr, declared in process P

P.pr - the body proper of pr; i.e. the body of pr (P.pr.body) without its pre- and postlude (see section 2.2.2)

$Init_Q, Init_i$ - the intial statement of process Q resp. P_i

If no confusion arises, reference to the process-name is omitted (and Init, pr.body and pr are used).

With this notation, the following *location specifiers* are introduced:

at('S') - denoting the point just before 'S'

after('S') - denoting the point immediately following 'S'

Now, we can define the *process invariant* PI_j of some process P_j by the following expression

$$MI_j \wedge \bigwedge_{'W_i'} at('W_i'):p_i \wedge \bigwedge_{pr_i} (at(pr_i):pre_i \wedge after(pr_i):post_i) \wedge at(Init_j):q_1 \wedge after(Init_j):q_2$$

where (i) the first conjunction ranges over all occurrences of all when-statements within the procedure-bodies in P_j,

(ii) the second one over all entry-procedures in P_j,

(iii) q_1 and q_2 denote the pre- and post-assertions of the initial statement,

(iv) MI_j is the monitor invariant of P_j and q_1, q_2, all p_i, pre_i and $post_i$ are assertions,

(v) loc:p denotes the association of assertion p to the location specified by loc,

(vi) only the assertions associated with locations within a procedure-body may contain formal parameters of that procedure.

In practice, some simplifications will be made in the specification of a PI: terms like loc:true (where loc is at(Init), after(Init) or at('W_i')), at(pr_i):MI and after(pr_i):MI will not be mentioned explicitly.

The process-invariant specifies more than the assertions at synchronization points. The pre-assertion of the initial statement is specified but more importantly, it specifies the pre- and post-assertions of the procedure-bodies. After introducing interference freedom tests in the next paragraph, it will turn out to be essential that precisely one canonical proof be given of an entry-procedure, which sufficies for every application of pre- and post-assertions.

Now, how are the PI's used in the proof system? Although written as formulae in some predicate logic, the PI's themselves are *not* assertions. Within the proof system, only expressions s.a. PI:at('W') will occur inside assertions, to denote the assertion(s) (as specified in PI) which should hold at that location. In general, the following convention is used (see PI's definition above):

<u>expression</u>	<u>meaning</u>
PI:at(Init)	q_1
PI:at(pr_i)	pre_i
PI:after(pr_i)	$post_i$

PI:at('W_i') MI $\wedge\ p_i$

PI:after(Init) MI $\wedge\ q_2$

Thus, the PI's are a purely notational device. This is also the case with the location specifiers, and contrasts with Lamport's location *predicates* ([Lam81]) which have the same appearance and are used to associate assertions with locations too. Lamport's predicates however, have an operational meaning. For instance, the location *predicate* at('S') is a syntactically correct assertion in his proof system, being valid when control resides just before 'S'. We emphasize that this is not the case in our formalism.

3.5. Interference freedom.

3.5.1. Owicki's proof system [OwG76].

We first review Owicki's proof system for her *G*eneral *P*rogramming *L*anguage. Parallelism is introduced in GPL by the *cobegin*-statement: cobegin S_1 ‖ ... ‖ S_n coend. Where S_1 through S_n are sequential statements, which are called the component processes of this statement. A set of variables is *shared* between S_1 ... S_n, and the processes are executed in parallel. However, Owicki makes an essential restriction on the parallelism in GPL. To simplify matters, this restriction is paraphrased as follows: *the assignments within the S_i's are executed as atomic, indivisible actions.* This means that the execution of a cobegin-statement amounts to an arbitrary *interleaving* of the assignments within the component processes.

In the GPL proof-system, the components of a cobegin-statement are proven correct in isolation and, as in the CSP-system of [Apt80], a consistency check is therefore needed when these separate proofs are combined. This check is in fact straightforward.

Consider the program cobegin x:=1; x:=x+1 ‖ x:=2 coend, and the (valid) isolated proof-outlines {true} x:=1 {x=1} x:=x+1 {x=2} and {true} x:=2 {x=2}. A quick inspection of the program shows that after termination, the value of x is either 2 or 3. However, restricting one's attention to these component proofs in isolation, might lead one to conclude that {x=2} holds after termination. Now consider the pre-assertion {x=1}, of the action x:=x+1, which is also the post-assertion of x:=1. This assertion holds immediately after the assignment x:=1 has terminated, but this does not imply that {x=1} holds, whenever the second assignment x:=x+1 is executed; the statement x:=2 could have been executed first. Hence, the necessary consistency check simply is the test whether each assertion in the proof outline of a component process is invariant over all atomic actions of the other processes which can be interleaved at that point. This check implies that the post-assertion of some action can safely be taken as the pre-assertion of the following action in the component process. The following *interference freedom test* formalizes this idea:

Consider a program cobegin S_1 ‖ ... ‖ S_n coend and proof-outlines for the component processes. For each statement T, let pre(T) resp. post(T) denote the pre resp. post-assertions of T within the proof outline. For any assignment A in S_i and assignment B in S_j ($i \neq j$) the following Hoare-formulae should be valid

(1) {post(A) ∧ pre(B)} B {post(A)}

(2) $\{pre(S_i) \wedge pre(B)\}$ B $\{pre(S_i)\}$

The pre-assertions in this test may be interpreted as stating the possibility to be both at(A) and at(B) (resp. at(S_i) and at(B)).

In Owicki's case this test is complicated by the presence of await-statements (which resemble when-statements somewhat).

3.5.2. Interference freedom in DP.

In section 3.2 we showed that process-execution in our model may be viewed as the execution of a GPL-cobegin-statement, in which the component processes are both the initial-statement and the various active procedure-instances. As 'location-dependent' assertions (which do not hold at every synchronization point) had to be introduced, an interference freedom test (IFT) is needed here too, in order to check the validity of a proof outline of a process, or rather: of the corresponding PI in which all location-dependent assertions in the proof outline are collected.

Owicki's test is a weak test in the sense that no unnecessary checks are made. An interference freedom test of similar strength in our model is difficult to formulate and also complicated to apply (see [Ge81a] in which such a test is defined. Hence, in the proof system a stronger test will be used; easier to formulate and apply but enforcing superfluous tests. Of course, this may be an invitation for incompleteness of the proof system. This problem is discussed at the end of the section.

An important characteristic of *our* IFT is its canonical nature. We have seen in section 2.2.2. that by suitably restricting the actual parameters of each procedure-call, it becomes possible to construct a canonical proof of the procedure-body which specifies the behaviour of the procedure for *all* calls within the program. Therefore it is not necessary to check every two coexisting procedure-instances for interference freedom of the associated assertions; rather, *a test on the canonical proofs suffices.*

While developing the IFT, we shall see that some changes and extensions to the rest of the proof system are necessary.

As stated in section 3.2, the operations which can be interleaved at some synchronization point, are all delimited by other synchronization points. These operations would also be the atomic actions over which assertions must be checked for invariance in the IFT. However, in the IFT which will be developed below, we allow these operations to end at a when-statement *even though this when-statement is not blocked.* The effect is, that these operations now become syntactically determined so that the IFT is easier to formulate. The price we have to pay is, that the assertions in a proof-outline may become more complicated; this decision will be discussed at the end of the section.

We now turn to the actual formulation of the IFT. While checking interference freedom of the proof outline of some process, the environment of the process has to be taken into account: whether some assertion, associated with a synchronization point, has to be checked for invariance over the operations of some procedure of the process, depends on whether an instance of the procedure can be active at this point. Hence, given two statements 'S_1' and 'S_2', at('S_1') being (or having been) a synchronization point and 'S_2' being a potentially 'interleavable' atomic action; find an assertion which expresses whether control within the processes can be both at('S_1') and at('S_2'), so that 'S_2' can indeed be interleaved at('S_1') (or vice versa); notation: 'S_1' ‖ 'S_2'.

In Owicki's GPL system the required assertion simply is pre('S_1') ∧ pre('S_2') (see section 3.5.1). For the current case it can shown that the assertion pre('S_1') ∧ pre('S_2') ∧ Gi works (see [Ge81a]) provided 'S_1' and 'S_2' are different. In this model, however, the situation that 'S_1' and 'S_2' denote syntactically the same statement can occur, because they may be part of different instances of some procedure and hence differ semantically. In this case, the above assertion degenerates into pre('S_1') ∧ GI, so that we cannot distinguish between one instance being active or two instances being active concurrently of a procedure. Owicki does not have this problem because in GPL, interleavable operations must differ syntactically.

To solve it, the proof system must express the coexistence of more than one incarnation. Therefore the system is extended with

incarnation counters:

With each entry procedure pr in each process P, an (incarnation) counter, P.pr'c (or pr'c) is associated, under the following restrictions:

(1) they may not appear in any program text (in particular, they may not be assigned to), and

(2) a counter P.pr'c may only appear free in GI and in the assertions of the proof outline of process P.

The idea is of course, that these counters are implicitely updated whenever an instance is created or destroyed. As these counters may appear in GI, it is clear that the external request rule too will need modification, to reflect the updatings of the counters.

To characterize 'S_1' ‖ 'S_2', the following auxiliary predicate is used:

#('S_1', 'S_2')≡P.pr_1'c≥1 ∧ P.pr_2'c≥1	if	'S_1' within P.pr_1 and 'S_2' within P.pr_2,
P.pr'c≥1	if	'S_1' within P.pr and 'S_2' within the initial statement of P (or vice versa)
P.pr'c≥2	if	'S_1' and 'S_2' both in P.pr.

Finally we get:

'S_1' ‖ 'S_2' if the assertion pre('S_1') ∧ pre('S_2') ∧ #('S_1', 'S_2') ∧ GI holds.

Now, in the case of 'S' ‖ 'S', contradiction may be reached by the fact that #('S','S') implies P.pr'c≥2 (P.pr containing 'S') and GI implies P.pr'c≤1; clearly, *if* at most one instance of P.pr can be active at a time, P.pr'c≤1 is an invariant over the computation.

Before the IFT can be formulated, some technicalities must be dispensed with. Firstly, the proof outline of a procedure must (in general) be tested 'against itself'. The problem is, that the assertions to be checked may contain formal parameters which are *local* w.r.t. the procedure-instance; hence there are variable-name clashes to be avoided. Secondly, there is a problem with the preludes of procedure-bodies. We have argued that invariance of pre('S_1') over 'S_2' is expressed by {pre('S_1') ∧ pre('S_2') ∧ X} S_2 {pre('S_1')}(where X ⇔ #('S_1', 'S_2') ∧ GI). Now, if 'S_2' is an initial part of a procedure-body, say 'S_2'≡'T;>S', pre('S_2') does not exist, because the proof outline of a procedure-body does not extend to the prelude (and postlude) of that procedure-body. On the other hand, the prelude *must* be taken into account, because pre('S_1') may contain variables which are changed in the prelude.

The first problem is solved, simply by substituting new variable-names for the possible formal parameters. The second one is solved as follows: instead of checking invariance of pre('S_1') over 'S_2' (remember: 'S_2'≡'T;>S') we check the formula {q ∧ pre('S') ∧ X} S {pre('S_1')} where q is the strongest post-condition (w.r.t. partial correctness) s.t. {pre('S_1')} T {q}; q is notated as pre('S_1') → T. I.e., we simply incorporate the effect on pre('S_1') of executing the prelude T, in the pre-assertion of S in the above formula. Using strongest post-conditions does not complicate matters unduly, because a prelude typically consists of one or two assignments.

The following definition formalizes these ideas:

Let p be an assertion within a proof outline of process P. Let $\vec{x}$ denote the (possibly empty) set of formal parameters in p and $\vec{y}$ a set variables (of the same cardinality and type of $\vec{x}$) which are not used in P. Furthermore, let 'S' denote some statement in P.

Then $\overline{p}$≡p[$\vec{y}/\vec{x}$] and p('S')≡$\overline{p}$ → R

where R≡T if 'S' is the body proper of some procedure in P with prelude 'T',

≡<u>skip</u> otherwise

In our definition of the IFT, we will not specify the interference freedom condition for each atomic action separately (as in the corresponding definition in section 2.5.1). Instead we define interference freedom w.r.t. a procedure body or the initial statement as a whole; this being somewhat easier to formulate. In the following definition, this is embodied in the predicate INV.

interference freedom test:

Let process P have procedure(-bodies) pr_1, ..., pr_n and a process invariant PI. Assume we have a proof outline (w.r.t. PI and a GI) for P. For any 'S' in P, let pre('S') denote the (sequential) pre-assertion of 'S' in P's proof outline. Define the predicate INV(p,'S') for any assertion p, associated with a statement 'R', and statement 'S' as follows:

INV(p,'S') is true if and only if a valid proof outline can be constructed for the Hoare-formula

{p('S') ∧ PI:at('S') ∧ #('R', 'S') ∧ GI} S {$\overline{p}$},

s.t. (1) the process invariant used in this new proof-outline is PI' ≡

$MI \wedge \widehat{_{'W_i' \text{ in } 'S'}}$ at('W_i'):($\overline{p}$ ∧ PI:at('W_i') ∧ #('R', 'S') ∧ GI) and

(2) for each 'W_i' in 'S' with pre-assertion r in the new proof outline:

$$r \Leftrightarrow \overline{p} \wedge pre('W_i') \wedge \#('R', 'S') \wedge GI$$

Then PI is defined to be *interference free* w.r.t. a proof-outline of P if

(1) for each 'term' in PI of the form at('W_i'):p_i the formula $INV(p_i,pr_1) \wedge \ldots \wedge INV(p_i,pr_n) \wedge INV(p_i,Init)$ holds, and

(2) for the (possible) term at('W_i'):q in PI the formula $INV(q,pr_1) \wedge \ldots \wedge INV(q,pr_n)$ holds.

The invariance check for some assertion p, is expressed by the predicate INV. It tells us to construct a proof outline, showing the invariance of p over the whole statement. If this statement contains any when-statements, the proof outline must show that p holds at each when-statement, blocked (restriction(1)) or not (restriction(2)). The assertions which must be proven to hold at each when-statement seems rather formidable. In fact they are not: GI holds by definition (a when-statement cannot be inside a bracketed section) and validity of pre('W_i') and PI:at('W_i') at when-statement 'W_i' has already been proven in the regular process proof outline. However, they must be specified because every time we must check anew if interleaving is possible.

This IFT depends essentially on the existence of a single canonical proof for each entry-procedure. In the current system (i.e., in the external request rule) this is not enforced, so we have to change it. This is in fact straightforward: the (second) premiss in the external request rule, requiring a proof of the procedure body proper, is removed and a new rule, the *process rule*, enforcing single canonical procedure-proofs (with the help of PI), is introduced.

The new external request rule also reflects the introduction of instance counters in the proof system:

<u>external request rule</u>:

$$\frac{\{p \wedge MI_j \wedge GI\}\ S_1;\ pr'c\ +:=1;\ T_1[\cdot]\{PI_j:at(pr)[\cdot] \wedge p_2 \wedge GI\} \quad \{p_2 \wedge PI_j:after(pr)[\cdot] \wedge GI\}\ T_2[\cdot];\ pr'c\ -:=1;\ S_2\ \{q \wedge MI_j \wedge GI\}}{\{p\}<S_1;\ \underline{call}\ P_j.pr(\vec{t},\vec{x});\ S_2>\{q\}}$$

for the restrictions, the reader is referred to section 2.2.2.

<u>process-rule</u>:

$$\frac{\{PI:at(pr_i)\}\ pr_i\ \{PI:after(pr_i)\}\ i=1\ldots n \quad \{PI:at(Init)\}\ Init\ \{PI:after(Init)\} \quad \text{PI is interference free}}{\{PI\}\ P\ \{PI\}}$$

where (i) PI is the process invariant of process P,

(ii) $pr_1 \ldots pr_n$ denote the bodies proper of all entry-procedures of P,

(iii) {PI} P {PI} is an informal notation, just denoting the validity of the premisses above the line.

Now, what about alternatives to the above IFT? The obvious candidate is obtained by requiring that invariance is only checked over operations which can actually be interleaved. The problem is the dynamic nature of these operations.

Consider a procedure body S≡if d:S_1 | ¬d:S_2; when e:S_3 end end. Depending on the state in which this procedure is executed, the following operations can be atomic and hence can be interleaved: (1) S, (2) S_2, (3) S_3 and (4) S_2;S_3. So, a method must be found to generate all these atomic operations. Qualitatively this may be done as follows: Informally a statement 'T' within a procedure body or the initial statement 'S' of some process is atomic if (1) at('T') is a point at which the process starts or resumes execution when coming from a synchronization point, (2) after('T') is a synchronization point and (3) control cannot leave 'T' in between, i.e., no when-statement in 'T' is blocked. These conditions are partly of a syntactic and partly of a semantic nature. For any statement 'T' which obeys the syntactic restrictions, an assertion atom('T') is associated which characterizes the state in which 'T' has to be executed, in order for it to be atomic. For instance, in the case above, atom('S') ≡ d ⊃ (S_3→e) (where R → s denotes the weakest pre-condition, w.r.t. partial correctness, s.t. {R → s} R {s} holds). Invariance of an assertion p (associated with 'S') over 'T' is then expressed by validity of

$$\{p('T') \wedge PI{:}at('T') \wedge atom('T') \wedge \#('S', 'T') \wedge GI\}\ T\ \{\overline{p}\}.$$

Following up on a suggestion of Amir Pnueli's, the assertion atomic('T') can be expressed for any 'T' using dynamic logic. A major drawback however is, that (1) in general there will be many statement-sequences which can be executed atomically and (2) the necessary dynamic logic expressions become complicated ([Ge81a]).

The above shows the problems which are encountered when constructing a weaker IFT. On the other hand, by adopting our stronger IFT these problems cannot have disappeared; they must raise their head elsewhere. In fact, the assertions that we need in the proof outlines in general will be more complicated than the ones that would be needed in case a weaker IFT was used. I.e., assertions in a procedure-body must be invariant over operations which will not, in fact, be interleaved (because they are not atomic). This is the trade-off alluded to in the introduction.

Consequently, the question arises whether such assertions can be expressed indeed; i.e., whether the IFT leads to incompleteness of the proof system. Of course, this question can only be answered convincingly by proving completeness of the system, which is beyond this paper. However, some indication of completeness can be given.

The question boils down to whether the occurrence of waiting points can be encoded within the assertions of the proof outline. We will give an example of such an encoding, using the program below (ℓ_1,ℓ_2, and ℓ_3 are labels and 'i' an auxiliary variable).

```
process P
  a:int;
  proc pr₁(#x)
    x:=a; ℓ₁:when b: c:= true end
  end
  proc pr₂
    a-:=1; b:=true; i:=0;
    ℓ₂:when b: a+:=1 end; c:=false;
    i:=1; ℓ₃:when c: skip end
  end
  a:=0; b:=false; i:=0
end
```

Both $P.pr_1$ and $P.pr_2$ are assumed to be called once. Now, consider $P.pr_1$. We would like assertion {x=a} to hold just before termination. A quick inspection of the program shows that associating {x=a} with the waiting point ℓ_1 would be correct; i.e., this assertion is invariant over all operations which can be interleaved at this point. Unfortunately, *not* according to our IFT which also forces us to show invariance over the operation ending at(ℓ_2).
Therefore an auxiliary variable '*i*' is introduced, which is zero initially and is set to one on arrival at(ℓ_3); the assertion $\{i=1 \supset x=a\}$ is associated with ℓ_1 and {i=0} with ℓ_2. It is easy to see that these assertions are invariant, also according to our IFT. However, the strongest assumption that can be made about the value of x now is: $i=1 \supset x=a$, which is too weak. Hence, the introduction of a monitor invariant $MI \equiv b \supset i=1$. Remembering the when-rule, the assertion which may be assumed when execution returns to ℓ_1 becomes $MI \wedge (i=1 \supset x=a) \wedge b$ which reduces to x=a. To give some insight into the nature of this encoding, the assertion $i=1 \supset x=a$ can be interpreted as "if control reaches the (waiting) point at(ℓ_3) then x=a", and MI as "execution can continue at(ℓ_1) only if ℓ_3 has been reached". {i=0} has been chosen to trivialize, when applying the when-rule to ℓ_2, the proof of the third premiss of that rule.

The IFT as presented here, is in a sense the most complicated part of our proof system. It is also the most dissatisfying part, because its introduction forced us to develop a lot of purely technical machinery. However, it has been demonstrated that we cannot do without one; moreover we emphasize that the necessity of an IFT and its complexity is *not* a pecularity of the language DP. It is the proof-theoretical consequence, for any language, of allowing a similar interleaving of operations within a process as in DP; hence for languages such as Concurrent Pascal, Mesa and Modula2 (but not ADA). Perhaps this section should be taken as (another piece of) evidence against allowing a programmer to much liberty in introducing parallelism into his programs.

4. SAFETY PROPERTIES.

We can now define what a valid proof (or proof outline) for a program is: For each process P_i we give separate proofs for its initial statement and its procedure-bodies, using the usual sequential proof rules together with the when rule and the external request rule. Before these separate proofs can be combined into a proof of the process, we must show that there is a GI and, per process, a single PI_i of P_i, used in all applications of the when rule within the component proofs of P_i, which is interference free (this is incorporated in the process rule). At a next level, the process-proofs must be combined and for this it is necessary to show the existence of a single GI, used in all applications of the external request rule in the program (and which is hence invariant over all communication-actions). If this is done, a valid proof (outline), w.r.t. a GI and the PI's of the component processes, results. The question is, how to draw conclusions from such outlines; i.e., what is the parallel composition rule? If we are only interested in partial correctness properties this is straightforward:

$$\frac{\{PI_i\}\ P_i\ \{PI_i\}\ i=1...n,\ \text{"using one GI"}}{\{\bigwedge_i PI_i:at(Init_i) \wedge GI\}[P_1 \parallel ... \parallel P_n]\{\bigwedge_i PI_i:after(Init_i) \wedge GI\}}$$

However this class of properties is too limited for concurrent programs. Firstly, non-terminating concurrent programs are perfectly respectable and secondly, even if a program terminates, we may still be interested in intermediate stages, e.g., in the states at the various synchronization points where new external requests may be accepted. Therefore, *safety-properties* are introduced, expressing that, in Lamport's parlance ([Lam80]), "during the computation of some program nothing bad happens". This neatly generalizes partial correctness properties, which state that a program does not terminate in an incorrect state. In general, safety properties are invariants over the computation of a program.

The principal question which must be answered next is: at which points should such an invariant hold? In other words, if we take snapshots of the execution of a program, we get a sequence of *frontiers of computation*. Which frontiers should be charaterized by the safety-invariant?

A first choice might be: the invariant should hold before and after each assignment, i.e., everywhere. However, the semantics in our model is such that the statements between two synchronization points are executed as indivisible atomic actions; which implies (although things can go wrong during the execution of such an operation) that the place at which an observer is confronted with the result of this operation, may logically be taken as the synchronization point terminating it. Hence a more reasonable choice is: such an invariant should hold at each synchronization point. And this is basically what we shall use.

As a safety-assertion describes the program state at certain locations during the computation (the frontiers of computation), first some notation must be introduced to describe these frontiers. This is not altogether trivial, because specifying that one process is at some synchronization point within a procedure may imply that a second process is suspended on a call to the first process, and, in case this call took place within a procedure-body of the second process, that there is a third process waiting for the second process to finish and so on. So, there is a set of processes which all are 'on the calling chain' to a specific procedure-instance within the first process, which must be specified too. This places syntactic constraints on a potential specification of a frontier of computation. These constraints will be embodied in the following definitions.

To denote within a single process the location in which we are interested, we introduce the concept of

control-point (c.p.):

x is a c.p. iff it is a location specifier of one of the following forms

(1) at ('W_i') ('W_i' some when-statement)

(2) at ('C_i') ('C_i' some call-statement)

(3) at(Init)

(4) after(Init)

Control-points of type(2) are needed to describe processes on a calling chain. Because of this fact, it makes sense to combine the control point specifications of such processes into a *multi-control-point*, as they clearly are interdependent. First we define a

calling chain (c.c.):

at('C_1'), at('C_2'), ..., at('C_k') is a c.c. in a program iff

(1) each at('C_i') refers to a call within a different process of the program,

(2) 'C_1' is a call within some initial statement; 'C_2', ..., 'C_k' are calls within procedures,

(3) ($1 \leq i \leq k-1$): 'C_i' is a call to the procedure containing 'C_{i+1}'.

Notice that a calling chain of some program is always of finite length, because a process on a chain cannot honour an external request before its own request has been executed. A calling chain determines (or is determined by) an instance of the procedure called by the last specifier in the chain. Now we can define a

multi-control-point (m.c.p.):

$<x_1, x_2, \ldots, x_m>$ is an m.c.p. iff

(1) m=1: x_1 is a c.p. *not* of type(2) within some initial statement,

(2) m>1: $x_1, \ldots, x_{m-1}$ is a calling chain;

x_m is a c.p. of type(1) and contained in the procedure 'called' by x_{m-1}.

Finally, to specify a frontier of computation of some program, one multi-control-point will in general not be enough, because not all processes within the program need take part in one calling chain; simultaneously, there may be other processes on another calling chain within the program. However, not every combination of multi-control-points specifies a frontier of computation.

For instance, a process can be part of one calling chain only. So, here too, are (syntactical) restrictions.

frontier of computation (f.o.c.):

$[x^{(1)}, x^{(2)}, \ldots, x^{(k)}]$ is a f.o.c. of some program $[P_1 \| \ldots \| P_n]$ iff

(1) each $x^{(i)}$ is a m.c.p.

(2) all $x^{(i)}$'s are different

(3) [syntactic consistency and completeness of the specification]

(Notation: $x_i \in A$ means that x_i references a location within A; this includes at(A) or after(A))

For each process P the following should hold:

Let $\bar{x}_1 \ldots \bar{x}_s$ be the list (with repetition) of all c.p.'s within the m.c.p.'s of the f.o.c., s.t. $\bar{x}_i \in P$.

(a) there is precisely one $\bar{x}_i \in Init_P$ (in the list),

(b) there is at most one $\bar{x}_i$ of type(2),

(c) if there is an $\bar{x}_i \in P.pr$ (pr some procedure of P) then the (unique) c.p. $\bar{x}_j \in Init_P$ must reference a location which is either at or after a (potential) synchronization point.

The syntactic constraints in this definition are all quite natural: as the initial statement of a process is always executed, a location in it (or after it) should be specified, hence constraint (a); a call is not a synchronization point, so a process cannot be at more than one call at the same time, hence constraint (b); finally, an external request cannot be honoured before a synchronization point in the initial statement has been reached, hence constraint (c). However, in this set-up the following may occur: execution of the procedure-instance (caused by accepting the external request) lead to a second synchronization point after which control switched back to the initial statement which was executed until the call was reached at which the process is at present waiting. These possible frontiers we have in mind, when stating in constraint (c) that the control point must refer to a location which is either at or *after* a potential synchronization point.

Now that the set of legal frontiers of computation of some program has been described, we can turn to our next assignment: Given a proof outline of a program, state-descriptions must be generated for the frontiers of this program. There is a problem to be solved here, because assertions belonging to the proof outlines of the procedure bodies are not assertions on the actual states during execution, since they are canonical. Hence, these assertions must be modified to describe the states of particular instances of the procedures. Instances are determined by multi-control-points, so the question is, how to construct a *multi-control-point-assertion*.

Consider the m.c.p. $\langle at('C_1'), \ldots, at('C_k'), at('W') \rangle$.

If 'S' is some statement within a program P, the pre-assertion of 'S', pre('S'), in a proof-outline of P, expresses in general that there is a computation-history leaving control in process P just before 'S'. A first approximation to the multi-control-point-assertion might therefroe be:

pre('C_1') $\wedge$ pre('C_2') $\wedge$ ... $\wedge$ pre('C_k') $\wedge$ PI:at('W')

i.e., the conjunction of the pre-assertions of the call's and the when-statement. As in the situation we are attempting to characterize, the call-statements in the calling-chain are actually being executed, the assertions in the corresponding calling-chain-assertion should indeed be the pre-assertions of the call-statement (i.e. the "p_2-assertion" of the external request rule), rather than the pre-assertion of the surrounding bracketed section.

There are however two refinements that must be incorporated in the definition. Firstly, the pre-assertions all encode *local* computation-histories, which therefore should be checked for compatibility with the global calling-history which is encoded in GI. Secondly, in the proof outlines, no specific incarnations are considered, hence the assertions interspersed in the procedure bodies and in particular the pre-assertions of the various call-statements are canonical w.r.t. the various incarnations. In the multi-control-point-assertions however, we do consider specific incarnations, so the assertions making up the multi-control-point-assertion must be modified by substituting for the formal parameters of each common procedure the actual parameters of the corresponding call-statement (bearing in mind that the actual parameters of a call 'C_i' ($2 \le i \le k$) may contain formal parameters of the procedure containing 'C_i', called by 'C_{i-1}'). Hence the following definition:

multi-control-point-assertion (m.c.p.a.):

$<x_1, \ldots, x_m>$: p is a m.c.p.a. iff

(i) $<x_1, \ldots, x_m>$ is a m.c.p.

(ii) m=1: p $\Leftrightarrow$ PI:x_1 (where PI is of course the process invariant of the process containing x_1)

m>1: let $x_i \equiv$ at('C_i') ($1 \le i \le m-1$), denote the actual parameters of 'C_i' by $\bar{y}_i$ and the formal parameters of the procedure called by 'C_i', $\bar{u}_i$. Then

$$p \Leftrightarrow \text{pre}('C_1') \wedge \text{pre}('C_2')[y_1/u_1] \wedge \text{pre}('C_3')[y_2/u_2][y_1/u_1] \wedge \ldots$$
$$\wedge\ \text{pre}('C_{m-1}')[\bar{y}_{m-2}/\bar{u}_{m-2}]\ldots[\bar{y}_1/\bar{u}_1] \wedge \text{PI}:x_m[\bar{y}_{m-1}/\bar{u}_{m-1}]\ldots[\bar{y}_1/\bar{u}_1]$$

The state at a frontier of computation is now simply described by the conjunction of m.c.p.a.'s:

frontier-of-computation-assertion (f.o.c.a.):

$[X^{(1)}, \ldots, X^{(m)}]$: p is a f.o.c.a. iff

(1) $[X^{(1)}, \ldots, X^{(m)}]$ is a f.o.c.

(2) let $p^{(i)}$ denote the m.c.p.a. associated with $X^{(i)}$ (notice that a m.c.p.a. is determined up to equivalence by a proof-outline). Then $p \Leftrightarrow p^{(1)} \wedge \ldots \wedge p^{(m)}$.

Notice, that GI is part of a f.o.c.a. because it is part of the constituent m.c.p.a.'s.

Now, how does one prove some safety-assertion p? Informally, this is now straightforward: One finds appropriate PI's and a GI, and constructs a valid proof-outline w.r.t. these PI's and GI). Then one finds the f.o.c.a.'s corresponding with the .o.c.'s specified in the safety-assertion p and checks if these f.o.c.a.'s imply the orresponding state-descriptions in p.

This must be formalized. First a definition

Ashcroft-invariant (AI):

$[P_1 \| \ldots \| P_n]$ is some program, with a (valid) proof-outline w.r.t. GI and $PI_1 \ldots PI_n$. Then

$AI(GI, PI_1 \ldots PI_n) \equiv \bigwedge_i X_i$, where

(1) each X_i denotes a f.o.c.a.

(2) the conjunction ranges over all f.o.c.'s within the program.

.e., in AI we simply collect all f.o.c.a.'s of a program. Notice, that due to their yntactical definition, there are only finitely many f.o.c.'s for a (finite length) rogram and hence, only finitely many f.o.c.a.'s within an AI. It is called the shcroft-invariant because Ashcroft was the first to consider these kind of invariants, lbeit in a different setting and using a different formalism ([Ash75]).

hen

parallel-composition-rule:

$$\frac{\{PI_i\}\ P_i\ \{PI_i\}\ i=1\ldots n,\ \text{"using one GI"}}{AI(GI, PI_1, \ldots, PI_n)}$$

inally, to derive the correct safety-assertion, we must define a consequence and sub- titution-rule for AI; and also a (new) auxiliary variable rule. However, this is traightforward, because implication and substitution for safety-assertions is simply efined on the constituent assertions. The reader is referred to the list of proof ules in the appendix for this.

In this section we showed how to extract state-information from a proof-outline. erhaps somewhat surprisingly, we have not changed the rest of the proof system, i.e. e have not changed the structure of the proof outline and in particular we still do ot consider procedure-instances separately in the proof-outline. Hence, *the proof ystem works only with canonical proofs and assertions*. The question whether for each alid safety-assertion, a (canonical) proof-outline can be given, is part of the (rela- ive) completeness proof of the system, which is projected as part of the first author's h.D-thesis.

5. Correctness proof of a distributed priority queue.

In this section we give a correctness proof of a priority queue, based upon Brinch Hansen's sorting algorithm [BH78]. Brinch Hansen claimed that his algorithm could be used as priority scheduler, but when trying to prove it, we discovered an error. This was mended by replacing the guard len<2 in procedure put by len=1 ∨ (len=0 ∧ rest=0) (for an explanation, the reader is referred to the program-description below).

5.1. Description of the program.

For the description of the algorithm an array of n processes is introduced, denoted by sort⟦n⟧. The i-th process in sort⟦n⟧ is called sort[i]. To describe the process in a uniform way, the expressions 'sort[succ]' and 'this' are used to denote the successor and index, respectively, of the process in consideration.
Furthermore, Brinch Hansen's cycle-statement is used:

<u>cycle</u> b_1:S_1 | ... | b_n:S_n <u>end</u>

with meaning <u>do</u> <u>true</u> : <u>when</u> b_1:S_1 | ... | b_n:S_n <u>end</u> <u>end</u>. (Note that this statement never terminates!).

The priority queue can sort ≤n elements. The items are input through process sort[1], that stores the smallest item so far and passes the rest to its successor, process sort[2]. The latter keeps the second smallest item and passes the rest to process sort[3], and so on. The items are output in increasing order through process sort[1]. After each output a process receives one of the remaining items from its successor. A sorting process is in equilibrium when it holds a single item. When the equilibrium is disturbed (by its predecessor) a process takes the following action:

(1) If the process holds two items (len=2) it keeps the smallest one and passes the larger one to its successor.

(2) If the process holds no items, but its successor does (len=0 ∧ rest>0) then it takes the smallest item from its successor.

```
process sort[[n]]
   here:seq[2]int; rest, temp:int
proc put(c:int)
   when len=1 v (len=0 ^ rest=0); len +:=1; here[len]:=c end end
proc get(#v:int)
   when len=1: v:=here[1]; here:=[]; len:=0 end end
begin
   here:=[]; rest:=0; len:=0;
   cycle
     len=2:
        if this <n:
             if here[1] ≤ here[2]: temp:=here[2]; here:=[here[1]]
              | here[1] > here[2]: temp:=here[1]; here:=[here[2]]
            end
```

```
        call sort[succ].put(temp); rest +:=1; len:=1
      | this≥n: skip
     end
  | len=0 ∧ rest>0:
      if this<n: call sort[succ].get(temp); rest -:=1
                 here:=[temp]; len:=1
       | this≥n: skip
     end
  end
end
```

Suppose, the guard in the when-statement of procedure put, is replaced by len≤2 (as in the original algorithm in [BH78]).

Consider the following situation: firstly, two values, 1 and 2, are sent to process sort[1], then a value is extracted and another value, 3, is put in (which is accepted because $len_1<2$). After the third call sort[1] contains no elements and sort[2] contains the element 2. After the last call, sort[1] contains 3 and sort[2] contains 2. Hence, although the sort-processes are in equilibrium, the elements in the queue are not ordered. This mistake is mended by forcing sort[i] to accept elements only if it already contains an element, or none at all and neither its successors, i.e. $len_i=1 \vee (len_i=0 \wedge rest_i=0)$. The only thing that can still go wrong is that more elements are put in than sort[n] can deal with. To handle this case smoothly, the calls in the processes are embedded in if-statements.

5.2. Correctness proof.

The invariance property we want to prove is the following: "the element output by the program (via sort[1]) is the smallest among all elements currently present inside the queue". If so, the program satisfies the specifications of a priority scheduler. This implies that the frontiers of computation we are interested in, are those for which control in process sort[1] resides at the cycle-statement with len=1, i.e., those for which sort[1] is able to honour and execute a request to its procedure get. Hence, for these frontiers we must prove that $here_1[1]$ is the smallest item currently available in the process-queue.

5.2.1. Proof outlines.

In the sequel, the auxiliary variable $kept_i$ denotes the bag of elements which are kept in process sort[i] at any time during the computation and the auxiliary variable $away_i$ denotes the bag of elements which have been sent on to its successor sort[i+1]. (A bag is a set in which the same element may have multiple occurrences. We will use + for the union and - for the splitting of bags. Notice that with a union, no elements are thrown away).

The general invariant GI expresses the telescopic behaviour of the priority queue:

$$GI \equiv \bigwedge_{i=1}^{n-1} away_i = away_{i+1} + kept_{i+1}$$

The monitor invariant MI_i of sort[i] expresses among other things the crucial property that makes the process-queue a priority scheduler, i.e.

$(len>0 \wedge rest>0) \supset here[1] \leq min(AWAY)$:

$$MI \equiv 0 \leq len \leq 2 \wedge rest \geq 0 \wedge rest=|away| \wedge len=|here| \wedge$$
$$kept=\{here[1]\} + \{here[2]\} \wedge (len>0 \wedge rest>0) \supset here[1] \leq min(away)$$

$$PI \equiv MI \wedge after(put):MI[kept+\{c\}/kept] \wedge$$
$$\wedge\ after(get):MI[kept-\{v\}/kept] \wedge$$
$$at(Init):(kept=\emptyset \wedge away=\emptyset)$$

The proof outline of the i-th process, denoted by sort[i]', is given below (the proof-outline of the other processes are similar):

```
process sort[i]'
  here: seq[2] int; rest, temp:int; kept, away:bag[2] int
proc put(c:int)
{MI} begin> {MI}
     when len=1 ∨ (len=0 ∧ rest=0):
        {MI ∧ (len=1 ∨ (len=0 ∧ rest=0))}
        len +:=1; here[len]:=c
     end
     {MI[kept+{c}/kept]}
     <kept +:={c}
    end {MI}
proc get(#v:int)
{MI} begin> {MI}
     when len=1:
        {MI ∧ len=1}
        v:=here[1]; here:=[]; len:=0
     end
     {MI[kept-{v}/kept]}
     <kept -:={v}
    end {MI}
```

```
{kept=away=∅}
begin here:=[]; rest:=0
{MI} cycle {MI}
        len=2:{MI ∧ len=2}
           if i<n:{MI ∧ len=2 ∧ i<n}
                if here[1] ≤ here[2] : temp:=here[2]; here:=[here[1]]
                |  here[1] > here[2] : temp:=here[1]; here:=[here[2]]
                end
                {len=|here|=1 ∧ rest≥0 ∧ rest=|away| ∧ kept={here[1]} + {temp} ∧
                here[1]≤min(away+{temp}) ∧ i<n}
                <call sort[succ]'.put(temp); rest +:=1; len:=1
                away +:={temp}; kept -:={temp}> {MI}
             |i≥n: skip {MI}
            end {MI}
      |len=0 ∧ rest>0:{MI ∧ len=0 ∧ rest>0}
           if i<n:
              <call sort[succ]'.get(temp) end; rest -:=1
              away -:={temp}; kept +:={temp}
              here:=[temp]; len:=1> {MI}
             |i≥n: skip {MI}
          end {MI}
     end
end
```

5.2.2. Correctness of the proof-outlines.

We will restrict attention to the first call-statement within the cycle-statement. The second call-statement is proven analogously and all other formulae can be verified easily from the proof-outline, using the assignment axiom and the composition, consequence, if and when rule.

To verify the first call-statement, we must prove:

```
{len=|here|=1 ∧ rest≥0 ∧ rest=|away| ∧ kept={here[1]}+{temp} ∧
                                   ∧ here[1]≤min(away+{temp}) ∧ this<n}
<call sort[succ]'.put(temp); rest +:=1; len:=1
away +:={temp}; kept -:={temp}>
{MI}
```

Name the pre-assertion p. By the external request rule, this reduces to proving:

(i) $\{p \wedge MI_{succ} \wedge GI\}$ skip $\{MI_{succ} \wedge p \wedge GI\}$ and

(ii) $\{p \wedge MI_{succ}[kept_{succ}+\{temp_{this}\}/kept_{succ}] \wedge GI\}$

$kept_{succ}$ +:=$\{temp_{this}\}$; $rest_{this}$ +:=1; len_{this}:=1;
$away_{this}$ +:=$\{temp_{this}\}$; $kept_{this}$ -:=$\{temp_{this}\}$
$\{MI_{this} \wedge MI_{succ} \wedge GI\}$

The first clause is trivial, the second one follows from the proof-outline and the third clause holds by the assignment axiom and consequence rule.

5.2.3. Interference freedom test.

This part is trivial, because there are no special assertions attached to waiting points. The proof-outlines of the procedure-bodies and the initial statement are sequentially correct w.r.t. PI_i; PI_i is trivially interference-free. So, the process rule deduces the validity of $\{PI_i\}$sort[i]'$\{PI_i\}$. As we have used a single GI, the program proof-outline is correct.

5.2.4. Invariance property: sort[n]' is a priority queue.

There remains the verification of the specifications for a priority scheduler, As we have reasoned in section 5.2, this means that for all frontiers of computation with control in sort[1] at the cycle-statement, here[1] is minimal. In the other processes sort[i]' in such frontiers, control resides at a waiting point or at a call-statement. The reader can check from the proof outline that in these cases $kept_i=\{here_i[1]\}+\{here_i[2]\}$ holds. This will turn out to be the assertion we need:

Control at a desired frontier of computation $\supset$

$$GI \wedge MI_1 \wedge len_1=1 \wedge \bigwedge_{i=2}^{n} kept_i=\{here_i[1]\}+\{here_i[2]\} \supset$$

$$\bigwedge_{i=1}^{n-1}(away_i=away_{i+1}+kept_{i+1}) \wedge here_1[1]\leq min(away_1) \wedge \bigwedge_{i=1}^{n} kept_i=\{here_i[1]\}+\{here_i[2]\} \supset$$

$here_1[1]\leq min\{here_i[j],\ i=1...n,\ j=1...2\}$, i.e.

$here_1[1]$ is the smallest item currently available in the process-queue; which was to be proven.

ACKNOWLEDGEMENTS.

We would like to thank Amir Pnueli for the helpfull discussions during the second author's stay in Israel last summer and the members of the working group on semantics and program correctness for the privilege of presenting earlier versions of this paper to them. Finally, special thanks goes to Joke Pannekoek, who did a wonderfull job of typing under a considerable time pressure.

REFERENCES.

[Apt80] Apt, K., N. Francez, W.P. de Roever; A proof system for Communicating Sequential Process. TOPLAS 2-3, p. 359-385, 1980.

[Apt81] Apt, K.; Ten years of Hoare's logic: A survey - Part 1. TOPLAS 3-4, p. 431-484, 1981.

[ARM81] The programming language ADA. Reference manual. LNCS 106, Springer Verlag, New York, 1981.

[Ash75] Ashcroft, E.; Proving assertions about parallel programs. JCSS 10, p. 110-135, 1975.

[BH75] Brinch Hansen, P.; The programming language concurrent Pascal. IEEE TSE 1, p. 99-207, 1975.

[BH78] Brinch Hansen, P.; Distributed Processes: A concurrent programming concept. CACM 21-11, p. 934-941, 1978.

[Ge81a] Gerth, R.; M.Sc. thesis. Vakgroep Informatica, University of Utrecht, 1981.

[Ge81b] Gerth, R.; A proof system for a subset of the concurrency section of ADA. Technical report RUU-CS-81-17, Vakgroep Informatica, University of Utrecht, 1981.

[Hoa74] Hoare, C.A.R.; Monitors, an operating system structuring concept. CACM 17-10, p. 549-557, 1974.

[La80] Lampson, B.W., D.D. Redell; Experience with processes and monitors in MESA. CACM 23-2, p. 105-117, 1980.

[Lam80] Lamport, L.; The Hoare's logic of concurrent programs. Acta Inf. 14, p. 21-37, 1980.

[OwG76] Owicki, S., D. Gries; An axiomatic proof technique for parallel programs I. Acta Inf. 6, p. 319-340, 1976.

[Wi81] Wirth, N.; Modula2. Report 36, Institut für Informatik, ETH, Zürich, 1981.

APPENDIX.

This appendix contains the list of axioms and proof rules which make up the system. AI is the Ashcroft-invariant; we sometimes write AI(P) to denote that AI is associated with the program $P \equiv [P_1 \| \ldots \| P_n]$. Finally, if X denotes some f.o.c., AI:X denotes (as usual) the state-description given by AI at this f.o.c., and AI[X:q] denotes the AI in which the assertion associated with X has been replaced by q.

Axioms

assignment :

$$\{p[t/x]\}\ x{:=}t\ \{p\}$$

skip :

$$\{p\}\ \underline{\text{skip}}\ \{q\}$$

Rules

composition :

$$\frac{\{p\}\ S_1\ \{q\}\ ,\ \{q\}\ S_2\ \{r\}}{\{p\}\ S_1;S_2\ \{q\}}$$

consequence :

$$\frac{p \supset p_1,\ \{p_1\}\ S\ \{q_1\},\ q_1 \supset q}{\{p\}\ S\ \{q\}}$$

$$\frac{p \supset AI{:}X,\ AI{:}Y \supset q}{AI[X{:}p,\ Y{:}q]},$$

provided $X \equiv [at(Init_1), \ldots, at(Init_n)]$ and Y is a f.o.c.$\neq$X.

conjunction :

$$\frac{\{p\}\ S\ \{r\},\ \{q\}\ S\ \{r\}}{\{p\ q\}\ S\ \{r\}}$$

substitution :

$$\frac{\{p\}\ S\ \{q\}}{\{p[z/x]\}\ S\ \{q\}},\quad \text{provided } x\notin \text{free}(S,q)$$

$$\frac{AI(P)}{AI(P)[X:(AI:X[z/x])]},$$

provided $X=[at(Init_1),\ \ldots,\ at(Init_n)]$ and $x\notin \text{free}(P,AI:Y)$ for any f.o.c. $Y\neq X$.

$$\frac{\{p\}\ \langle S_1;\ \underline{call}\ P_j.pr(x,y);\ S_2\rangle\ \{q\}}{\{p[r/s]\}\ \langle S_1;\ \underline{call}\ P_j.pr(x,y);\ S_2\rangle\ \{q[r/s]\}},\ \text{provided } r\in \text{free}(P_i) \text{ and } (r\cup s)\cap(\text{free}(x,S_1,S_2)\cup y)=\emptyset$$

where P_i contains the bracketed section

if :

$$\frac{\{p_1\wedge b_1\}\ S_1\ \{q\},\ \ldots,\ \{p_n\wedge b_n\}\ S_n\ \{q\},\ p\rightarrow \bigvee_{i=1}^{n} b_i}{\{p\}\ \underline{if}\ b_1\ :\ S_1|\ldots|b_n\ :\ S_n\ \underline{end}\ \{q\}}$$

do :

$$\frac{\{p_1\wedge b_1\}\ S_1\ \{p\},\ \ldots,\ \{p_n\wedge b_n\}\ S_n\ \{p\}}{\{p\}\ \underline{do}\ b_1\ :\ S_1|\ldots|b_n\ :\ S_n\ \underline{end}\ \{p\wedge\neg\bigvee_{i=1}^{n} b_i\}}$$

when :

$$\frac{\begin{array}{l}\{p_1\wedge b\}\ S_1\ \{q\},\ \ldots,\ \{p_n\wedge b\}\ S_n\ \{q\},\\ p\wedge\neg\bigvee_{i=1}^{n} b_i\rightarrow PI{:}at(\text{'}S\text{'}),\\ \{b_1\wedge PI{:}at(\text{'}S\text{'})\}\ S_1\ \{q\},\ \ldots,\ \{b_n\wedge PI{:}at(\text{'}S\text{'})\}\ S_n\ \{q\}\end{array}}{\{p\}\ \underline{when}\ b_1\ :\ S_1|\ldots|b_n\ :\ S_n\ \underline{end}\ \{q\}}$$

external request rule :

$$\frac{\begin{array}{l}\{p\wedge MI_j\wedge GI\}\ S_1;\ pr'c{+}{:=}1;\ T_1[\cdot]\{PI_j{:}at(pr)[\cdot]\wedge p_2\wedge GI\}\\ \{p_2\wedge PI_j{:}after(pr)[\cdot]\wedge GI\}\ T_2[\cdot];\ pr'c{-}{:=}1;\ S_2\ \{q\wedge MI_j\wedge GI\}\end{array}}{\{p\}\langle S_1;\ \underline{call}\ P_j.pr(\vec{t},\vec{x});\ S_2\rangle\{q\}}$$

where (1) the call-statement is contained in process P_i,

(2) process P_j $(j\neq i)$ contains the declaration proc $pr(\vec{u}\#\vec{v})\ T_1;\rangle T\langle;\ T_2$ end,

(3) $[\cdot]\equiv[\vec{t},\vec{x}/\vec{u},\vec{v}]$,

(4) MI_j is the monitor invariant of process P_j,

(5) $\text{free}(p,q,p_2)\subseteq \text{free}(P_i)$

$\text{free}(p_2)\cap(\text{free}(\vec{t})\cup\vec{x})=\emptyset$

$\text{free}(p_1,q_1)\subseteq \text{free}(P_j)\cup\vec{u}\cup\vec{v}$

process-rule :

$\{PI:at(pr_i)\}\ pr_i\ \{PI:after(pr_i)\}\ i=1...n$

$\{PI:at(Init)\}\ Init\ \{PI:after(Init)\}$

PI interference free

$$\frac{}{\{PI\}\ P\ \{PI\}},$$

where $pr_1...pr_n$ are all entry procedures within P.

parallel composition rule :

$\{PI_i\}\ P_i\ \{PI_i\}\ i=1...n$

"Using one GI"

$$\frac{}{AI(GI,PI_1...PI_n,P)},$$

where $P=[P_1 \| ... \| P_n]$

AV rule :

$$\frac{AI(P')}{AI(P)},$$

provided no f.o.c.a. in AI other than the one associated with $[after(Init_1), ..., after(Init_n)]$ contains variables from AV, and P is obtained from P' by deleting all assignments $x:=t$ with $x\in AV$.

ANOTHER CHARACTERIZATION OF WEAKEST PRECONDITIONS

Pedro Guerreiro

Departamento de Informática
Faculdade de Ciências e Tecnologia
Universidade Nova de Lisboa
Quinta da Torre
2825 Monte da Caparica
PORTUGAL

ABSTRACT

We present an approach to the study of nondeterministic programs, consisting essentially in using binary relations as semantic objects representing the input-output behaviour of programs. These relations include an explicit representation of non--terminating computations. Based on the relational model we introduce a weakest precondition total correctness predicate transformer. We then show how to build up this predicate transformer starting from others of a more elementar kind. Finally, we obtain a characterization of its healthiness properties in terms of set-theoretical properties of the relations involved.

1. INTRODUCTION

Usually, a deterministic program is viewed as a representation, or description, in a given language of a certain partial function from a suitable set of states into itself. Putting forward the semantics of the program consists essentially in presenting the associated function, or relevant properties of it, in some, hopefully sufficiently widespread, standard formalism.

Generalizing this idea, a nondeterministic program, that is, a program that can produce several outputs for some of its inputs, can be considered to be a representation of a function from the set of states to the set of sets of states, or, alternatively, of a binary relation over that set of states. In fact, using relations instead of functions is perhaps more convenient because, the source and target spaces being the same, relations are more comfortable to compose, to invert, etc., than the corresponding functions.

The operational meaning of the semantic relation of a program must reflect the input-output behaviour of the program. Therefore, whenever there exists a possibility that an execution of the program initialized in a state a terminates in a state b the pair (a,b) will appear in the relation. However, special attention must be paid to those cases in which the execution may not terminate. This situation of non-termination must be somehow recorded in the semantics, otherwise it will be impossible to distinguish, for example, the two following programs (written in Dijkstra's guarded command language,(Dij75)):

```
r1 :: if true → skip fi          r2 :: if true → skip
                                      □ true → abort
                                      fi
```

If we consider terminating computations only, the input-output behaviours of r1 and r2 are the same. However, r1 and r2 definitely should not be regarded as "equivalent".

In order to distinguish two programs like the ones above two techniques can be used:

i - to exclude from the relation all pairs whose first elements are also starting points of non-terminating computations. This is justified if we are only interested in total correctness semantics, as in this case we regard the possibility of non-termination as "bad" as guaranteed non-termination. Therefore, the loss of information caused by deleting those pairs appears to be of no consequence. Using this technique the semantic relation of program r1 is the identity relation whereas that of r2 is the empty relation.

ii - to enlarge the state space with a special element to be used as a "final" state for non-terminating computations. If we choose this alternative the relation for program r1 is still the identity relation, but for program r2 we now have, denoting by ω the special element and by Q the state space, the union of the identity relation and the cartesian product $Q \times \{\omega\}$.

We believe that the second approach is more interesting, for several reasons. First, it is independent of any notion of correctness, which, anyway, can easily be introduced later. Besides, putting in total correctness right from the start causes some loss of information, namely the possibility of termination in presence of the possibility of non-termination. This loss of information is inconvenient in that it hinders us from using composition of relations to represent sequential composition of commands. Take, for example, the two following commands, where b is a boolean variable:

```
s1 :: if b → b:=false            s2 :: if b → skip fi
      □ b → skip
      fi
```

Using the first approach in the state space of the truth values {true, false} the semantic relation of command s1 is {(true,true), (true,false)} and that of s2 is {(true, true)}. Relational composition yields {(true,true)}, whereas the command s1;s2 is never guaranteed to terminate and hence its semantic relation is empty. On the other hand, following the second approach with an enlarged state space {true,false,ω}, we obtain for s1 {(true,true),(true,false),(false,ω), (ω,ω)}, and for s2 {(true,true), (false,ω),(ω,ω)}. Relational composition now gives {(true,true),(true,ω),(false,ω),

$(\omega,\omega)\}$, which in fact corresponds to s1;s2, telling us not only that termination is never guaranteed but also that termination with b=true is possible in the case where we had initially b=true.

Another advantage in taking approach ii. is that semantic relations are constructed mainly by set-theoretical union, whereas the first approach implies frequent use of intersection and complementation also. It turns out that the algebraic properties of the union operation are nicer than those of the intersection. For example: let R and S be relations over Q and A a subset of Q. Denoting by R(A) the "image" of A by R (formally defined by $R(A)=\bigcup_{a\in A} R(a)$ where $R(a)=\{b:(a,b)\in R\}$), it is easy to see that we have $(R\cup S)(A)=R(A)\cup S(A)$, but concerning the intersection all we can say is that $(R\cap S)(A)\subseteq R(A)\cap S(A)$.

In the last few years several interesting papers were devoted to the study of nondeterminacy and its relation with total correctness. Wand treats nondeterminacy following the first of the two relational approaches described above, providing a first relational characterization of Dijkstra's weakest precondition predicate transformer (Wan 77). deRoever points out the need for explicit representation of non-termination (Roe 76). Hoare models nondeterminacy in terms of sets of program traces and studies several kinds of correctness for nondeterministic programs (Hoa 78). Harel's model is that of computation trees, which allows him to define several "execution methods" for nondeterministic programs, each method implying a different total correctness predicate transformer (Har 79). Back investigates problems posed by considering also unboundedly nondeterministic commands (Bac 79). Sifakis presents a systematic approach to the study of properties of nondeterministic systems using so-called transition systems (Sif 79). The author, in a paper presented at a previous edition of this colloquium, proposed a semantics for the language of guarded commands using relations of the type suggested above in the second relational approach to nondeterminacy (Gue 80).

In this paper we are mainly interested in developping that study, by considering a more convenient framework for studying a total correctness weakest precondition predicate transformer. Basically we are looking for a characterization of the "healthiness" properties of that predicate transformer in terms of set-theoretical properties of the semantic relations involved.

This paper is organized as follows: in section 2 we introduce the class of binary relations we shall be using; next, in section 3 we define our weakest precondition total correctness predicate transformer; in section 4 we build up some useful predicate transformers starting from the elementary notion of "image of a set by a relation"; these predicate transformers are then used in sections 5 and 6 to assist us in the study of the total correctness predicate transformer defined previously.

2. PROGRAMMABLE RELATIONS

Let Q be an (arbitrary) set (of states) and ω a distinguished element of Q. Assume r is a (nondeterministic) program whose state space is the set $Q-\{\omega\}$. We shall use ω to represent the final state of a non-terminating computation of r, as suggested in the Introduction. The semantic relation of r (i.e., the relation represented by program r), denoted R, (throughout this paper we use capital letters R, S, ... to denote semantic relations of programs r, s, ...) is obtained as follows:

for $a,b \in Q$ we have:

i - $(a,b) \in R$, $b \neq \omega$, if there exists a computation of r initialized in state a and terminating in state b.

ii - $(a,\omega) \in R$, if there exists a non-terminating computation of r starting in state a.

The special meaning of state ω tells us immediately that not all relations in Q will be of use to us. In fact, a relation such that ω might have a successor other than itself would be semantically meaningless. Therefore we may focus our attention only on so-called ω-relations:

Definition 2.1. ω-relation. A relation R is called a ω-relation if $R(\omega) \subseteq \{\omega\}$. □

Using ω-relations allows us to restrict further the class of semantic relations for nondeterministic programs. We can, in fact, say that a computation of a command will always produce an output, no matter how the command was initialized. (The output may be ω if the computation is infinite, which is what should happen if the command was not supposed to be initialized in the given initial state). We conclude that semantic relations of programs are total:

Definition 2.2. Totality. A ω-relation is total if $\underline{A} a \in Q \; R(a) \neq \emptyset$. □

The programs that we want to deal with here are those that can be written in the guarded command language. As Dijkstra explained (Dij 76) they are boundely nondeterministic, that is, whenever for a given initial state there is an infinite number of terminating computations there is also a non-terminating computation for that initial state. Relationally, this property may be expressed by the following definition:

Definition 2.3. Bounded nondeterminacy. A ω-relation is boundedly nondeterministic if $\underline{A} a \in Q \; (\underline{E} k \in N \;\; |R(a)| \leq k \vee (a,\omega) \in R)$. □

We may conclude that the semantic relations of programs are ω-relations enjoying at least the properties of totality and bounded nondeterminacy. Such relations are called programmable relations:

Definition 2.4. Programmable relation. A programmable relation is a ω-relation that is total and boundedly nondeterministic. □

3. A WEAKEST PRECONDITION TOTAL CORRECTNESS PREDICATE TRANSFORMER

A predicate (over Q) is a mapping from Q into the set of truth values {true, false}. Let $\mathcal{P}$ denote the set of predicates over Q. A predicate transformer (pt) (over Q) is a mapping from $\mathcal{P}$ into $\mathcal{P}$. A pt associated to a program r is said to be total correctness if it "transforms" a target predicate P1 in a source predicate P0 such that if the program r is initialized in a state verifying P0 then termination is guaranteed in a state where P1 holds. This idea of a total correctness pt can be very pleasantly expressed in terms of semantic relations.

Let R be a ω-relation, and for each predicate P consider the predicate $\lambda a.\underline{A}b\ (a,b)\epsilon R \Rightarrow P(b) \wedge b \neq \omega$. This predicate characterizes the largest set of states such that all their successors by R satisfy P while remaining different from the special element ω. In particular all the states which have no successors by R belong to that set. We conclude that in those cases where R is total, and this includes all programmable relations, the formula presented defines indeed a weakest precondition total correctness pt.

We therefore propose the following general definition:

Definiton 3.1. wpr(R). Let R be a ω-relation. The predicate transformer wpr(R) is defined by the equation $wpr(R)(P)=\lambda a.\underline{A}b\ (a,b)\epsilon R \Longrightarrow P(b) \wedge b \neq \omega$. □

We now want to study the properties of wpr(R), to answer questions such as is wpr(R) continuous?, do we have wpr(RoS)=wpr(R)owpr(S)?, etc.. We shall see that the answers turn out to be as we would like them to be, at least when the relations involved are programmable relations.

4. OTHER PREDICATE TRANSFORMERS

It is more interesting to study wpr(R) in terms of other pt's of a more elementar kind than to manipulate directly the defining formula.

Note: Although we are mainly interested in ω-relations the results presented in this section (except theorem 4.16) are valid for any binary relation in Q.

The following are well-known properties of the operation "image of a set by a relation"; their proofs are quite trivial.

Properties 4.1. Let R and S be relations, A a subset of Q, and {Ai}i a family of subsets of Q. We have:

1. $R(\bigcup_i Ai) = \bigcup_i R(Ai)$
2. $(R \cup S)(A) = R(A) \cup S(A)$
3. $(RoS)(A) = S(R(A))$
4. $R \subseteq S$ iff $\underline{A}A\ R(A) \subseteq S(A)$ □

The following are particular cases, or consequences, of properties 4.1.1.:

Properties 4.2. Let R be a relation and A and B subsets of Q. We have:

1. $R(\emptyset) = \emptyset$
2. $R(A \cup B) = R(A) \cup R(B)$
3. $A \subseteq B \Longrightarrow R(A) \subseteq R(B)$

4. $R(A\cap B)\subseteq R(A)\cap R(B)$ □

If R is the semantic relation of a program and A is a set of initial states for the program then R(A) is the set of possible final states. Obviously, if $\omega\varepsilon R(A)$ then it is also possible that the program does not terminate.

Usually, reasoning about programs is made with predicates and predicate transformers, rather than directly with sets and relations. We now introduce some of these predicate transformers.

In the sequel, for a predicate P, we denote by $\underline{P}$ the set $\{a:P(a)\}$, and for a pt F we abbreviate $\underline{F(P)}$ by $\underline{F}(P)$. We define $\top=\lambda a.$ true and $\bot=\lambda a.$ false, (i.e., $\underline{\top}=Q$ and $\underline{\bot}=\phi$). We denote by $\cup$, $\cap$ and $\neg$ the operations of, respectively, sum, product and complementation of predicates; they can be formally defined by: $P1\cup P2=\lambda a.P1(a)\vee P2(a)$; $P1\cap P2=\lambda a.P1(a)\wedge P2(a)$; $\neg P=\lambda a.\neg(P(a))$. We define a partial order, $\subseteq$, in the set of predicates, by: $P1\subseteq P2$ if $\underline{A}a$ $P1(a)\Longrightarrow P2(a)$, (that is, if $\underline{P1}\subseteq\underline{P2}$, set-theoretically). We also define a partial order in the set of predicate transformers, and we denote it by the same symbol $\subseteq$: $F\subseteq G$ if $\underline{A}$ P $F(P)\subseteq G(P)$. Finally we denote by $\tilde{F}$ the dual of the pt F : $\tilde{F}=\lambda P.\neg F(\neg P)$.

The set-theoretical notion of image of a set by a relation corresponds to the following predicate transformer :

Definition 4.3. The predicate transformer image(R). Let R be a relation. The pt image (R) is defined by:

$\underline{\text{image}}(R)(P)=R(\underline{P})$. □

The following is an alternative definition of image(R):

$\text{image}(R)(P)=\lambda b.\underline{E}a\ P(a)\wedge(a,b)\varepsilon R$

Properties of image(R) are a mere translation of properties 4.1 and 4.2 into predicate transformer notation:

Properties 4.4. Let R and S be relations, P a predicate, and {Pi}i family of predicates. We have:

1. $\text{image}(R)(\bigcup_i Pi) = \bigcup_i \text{image}(R)(Pi)$
2. $\text{image}(R\cup S)(P) = \text{image}(R)(P) \cup \text{image}(S)(P)$
3. $\text{image}(RoS)(P) = \text{image}(S)(\text{image}(R)(P))$
4. $R\subseteq S$ iff $\text{image}(R)\subseteq\text{image}(S)$ □

Properties 4.5. Let R be a relation and P1 and P2 predicates. We have:

1. $\text{image}(R)(\bot) = \bot$
2. $\text{image}(R)(P1\cup P2) = \text{image}(R)(P1) \cup \text{image}(R)(P2)$
3. $P1\subseteq P2 \Longrightarrow \text{image}(R)(P1)\subseteq\text{image}(R)(P2)$
4. $\text{image}(R)(P1\cap P2) \subseteq \text{image}(R)(P1) \cap \text{image}(R)(P2)$ □

Not all pt's can be written in the form image(R) for some relation R. In fact:

Proposition 4.6. For a given pt F there exists a relation R such that F=image(R) iff F is such that, for any family of predicates $\{Pi\}i$, $F(\underset{i}{\cup}Pi)=\underset{i}{\cup}F(Pi)$. □

The operational meaning of image(R)(P) is analogous to that of R(P̲) : it caract̲erizes the set of all possible final states of program r, provided r is initialized with P holding. If image(R)(P)(ω) is true then non-termination is possible also.

image(R) is a "forward" pt. Usually "backwards" pt's are preferred. We may consider the following:

Definition 4.7. The predicate transformer pre(R). Let R be a relation. The pt pre(R) is defined by:

$$pre(R) = image(R^{-1}).$$ □

The following equation may be seen as an alternative definition of pre(R):

$$pre(R)(P) = \lambda a.\underline{E}b\ P(b) \wedge (a,b) \epsilon R$$

Quite naturally, properties of pre(R) are similar to those of image(R); the only exception is property 4.8.3. below.

Properties 4.8. Let R and S be relations, P a predicate, and $\{Pi\}i$ a family of predicates. We have:

1. $pre(R)(\underset{i}{\cup}Pi) = \underset{i}{\cup} pre(R)(Pi)$

2. $pre(R \cup S)(P) = pre(R)(P) \cup pre(S)(P)$

3. $pre(R \circ S)(P) = pre(R)(pre(S)(P))$

4. $R \subseteq S$ iff $pre(R) \subseteq pre(S)$ □

Properties 4.9. Let R be a relation, and P1 and P2 predicates. We have:

1. $pre(R)(\perp) = \perp$

2. $pre(R)(P1 \cup P2) = pre(R)(P1) \cup pre(R)(P2)$

3. $P1 \subseteq P2 \implies pre(R)(P1) \subseteq pre(R)(P2)$

4. $pre(R)(P1 \cap P2) \subseteq pre(R)(P1) \cap pre(R)(P2)$ □

Proposition 4.10. For a given pt F there exists a relation R such that F=pre(R)   iff F is such that, for any family of predicates $\{Pi\}i$, $F(\underset{i}{\cup}Pi) = \underset{i}{\cup}F(Pi)$.

The operational meaning of pre(R) is the following: if P(ω) is false then pre(R)(P) is the predicate characterizing the set of initial states for which computa̲tions exist that terminate with P holding. If P(ω) is true then the initial states of the non-terminating computations are also included in pre(R)(P); in other words, if the program is initialized outside p̲r̲e̲(R)(P) and P(ω) is true, then termination outside P̲ can be guaranteed.

The double negation implicit in the preceeding phrase suggests the introduction of the dual pt of pre(R):

Definition 4.11. The predicate transformer p̃re(R). Let R be a relation. The pt p̃re(R) is defined by

$\tilde{pre}(R)(P) = \neg pre(R)(\neg P)$. □

The equation in this definition may be rewritten as:

$\tilde{pre}(R)(P) = \lambda a.\underline{A}b\ (a,b)\varepsilon R \Longrightarrow P(b)$

The properties of $\tilde{pre}(R)$ are the duals of the properties of pre(R):

Properties 4.12. Let R and S be relations, P a predicate, and {Pi}i a family of predicates. We have:

1. $\tilde{pre}(R)(\bigcap_i Pi) = \bigcap_i \tilde{pre}(R)(Pi)$
2. $\tilde{pre}(R\cup S)(P) = \tilde{pre}(R)(P) \cap \tilde{pre}(S)(P)$
3. $\tilde{pre}(RoS)(P) = \tilde{pre}(R)(\tilde{pre}(S)(P))$
4. $R\subseteq S$ iff $\tilde{pre}(S)\subseteq\tilde{pre}(R)$ □

Properties 4.13. Let R be a relation, and P1 and P2 predicates. We have:

1. $\tilde{pre}(R)(\top) = \top$
2. $\tilde{pre}(R)(P1\cap P2) = \tilde{pre}(R)(P1) \cap \tilde{pre}(R)(P2)$
3. $P1\subseteq P2 \Longrightarrow \tilde{pre}(R)(P1)\subseteq\tilde{pre}(R)(P2)$
4. $\tilde{pre}(R)(P1) \cup \tilde{pre}(R)(P2) \subseteq \tilde{pre}(R)(P1\cup P2)$ □

Proposition 4.14. For a given pt F there exists a relation R such that $F=\tilde{pre}(R)$ iff F is such that, for any family of predicates {Pi}i, $F(\bigcap_i Pi) = \bigcap_i F(Pi)$ □

A pt F is said to be continuous if for every ascending sequence of predicates $\{Pi\}i\varepsilon N$, $Pi\subseteq Pi+1$, F is such that $F(\bigcup_i Pi) = \bigcup_i F(Pi)$.

Property 4.8.1. implies continuity of pre(R), for all R. For $\tilde{pre}(R)$ we have the following result (Gue80):

Theorem 4.15. The pt $\tilde{pre}(R)$ is continuous iff R is image-finite, (i.e., if for all $a\varepsilon Q$, R(a) is a finite set). □

If the computation of program r is initialized in $\tilde{pre}(R)(P)$ and $P(\omega)$ is false, then termination of that computation with P holding can be guaranteed,and reciprocally. If $P(\omega)$ is true only termination in P or non-termination can be guaranteed. This suggests that the pt $\tilde{pre}(R)$ is closely related to our original wpr(R), In fact, the following theorem provides an alternative definition for wpr(R). The symbol Ω denotes the predicate $\lambda a.a=\omega$.

Theorem 4.16. Let R be a ω-relation. We have:

$wpr(R)(P) = \tilde{pre}(R)(P-\Omega)$. □

The study of the properties of wpr(R) is the subject of the restof the paper.

5. GENERAL PROPERTIES OF THE PREDICATE TRANSFORMER wpr(R)

Some properties of wpr(R) hold for every ω-relation R. Other interesting properties appear only if restrictions are imposed on the relations considered. The following belong to the first group.

Properties 5.1. Let R and S be relations, P a predicate, and {Pi}i a non-empty family of predicates. We have:

1. $wpr(R)(\bigcap_i Pi) = \bigcap_i wpr(R)(Pi)$
2. $wpr(R \cup S)(P) = wpr(R)(P) \cap wpr(S)(P)$ □

Properties 5.2. Let R be a relation, and P1 and P2 predicates. We have:

1. $wpr(R)(P1 \cap P2) = wpr(R)(P1) \cap wpr(R)(P2)$
2. $P1 \subseteq P2 \implies wpr(R)(P1) \subseteq wpr(R)(P2)$
3. $wpr(R)(P1) \cup wpr(R)(P2) \subseteq wpr(R)(P1 \cup P2)$ □

In order to obtain a result similar to property 4.12.4 we would like to define a partial order $\preccurlyeq$ on relations, such that $R \preccurlyeq S$ iff $wpr(R) \subseteq wpr(S)$. Unfortunately, that is not possible, as anti-symmetry would imply wpr(R) = wpr(S) iff R=S, which is a false assertion, as the following example shows:

We have $R \neq S$ but $wpr(R) = wpr(P) = \lambda P.\bot$.

Therefore all we can hope is that $\preccurlyeq$ is a pre-order, (i.e., a reflexive and transitive relation).

It is more comfortable to treat this question with the help of the predicate transformer $\widetilde{wpr}(R)$, dual of wpr(R), and to "dualize" the results at the end, using the fact that for pt's F and G we have $F \subseteq G$ iff $\tilde{G} \subseteq \tilde{F}$.

Consider the following definition:

Definition 5.3. Pre-order << . Let R and S be ω-relations. We define R << S if $R \subseteq S \cup S^{-1}(\omega) \times Q$. □

The meaning of this definition is described in the following proposition:

Proposition 5.4. Let R and S be relations. We have R << S iff
$\underline{A}\, a,b\ (a,b) \in R \implies (a,b) \in S \vee (a,\omega) \in S$. □

The result we are looking for is the following, (Gue 81):

Proposition 5.5. Let R and S be ω-relations. We have R << S iff $\widetilde{wpr}(R) \subseteq \widetilde{wpr}(S)$.
It is now easy to obtain the corresponding result for wpr(R). □

Definition 5.6. Pre-order >> . Let R and S be ω-relations. We define R >> S if S << R. □

Proposition 5.7. Let R and S be ω -relations. We have
$R >> S$ iff $\underline{A}a,b\ (a,b)\varepsilon S \Longrightarrow (a,b)\varepsilon R \vee (a,\omega)\varepsilon R$. □

Proposition 5.8. Let R and S be ω-relations. We have $R >> S$ iff $wpr(R) \subseteq wpr(S)$. □

Starting from a pre-order, an equivalence relation can be defined in a standard way:

Definition 5.9. Total correctness equivalence, $<<>>$. Let R and S be ω-relations. We say that R and S are total correctness equivalent, and write $R <<>> S$ if $R << S$ and $R >> S$.

The notion of total correctness equivalence is important on account of the following theorem:

Theorem 5.10. Let R and S be ω-relations. We have $R <<>> S$ iff $wpr(R) = wpr(S)$. □

6. HEALTHINESS

Following Dijkstra (Dij 76) a "good" total correctness predicate transformer must satisfy five properties, called "healthiness criteria".

Definition 6.1. Healthiness criteria. Let F be a predicate transformer. We say F is healthy if F satisfies the following five properties:

H1. $F(\Omega) = \perp$ (recall that Ω denotes the predicate $\lambda a.a{=}\omega$).

H2. $F(\bigcap_i Pi) = \bigcap_i F(Pi)$, for every non-empty family of predicates $\{Pi\}i$.

H3. $P1 \subseteq P2 \Longrightarrow F(P1) \subseteq F(P2)$

H4. $F(P1) \cup F(P2) \subseteq F(P1 \cup P2)$, for predicates P1 and P2.

H5. F is continuous. □

Notes: Criteria H1 to H4 were introduced by Dijkstra in (Dij 75); H5 appears in (Dij 76) only. Criterium H2 is Hoare's version (Hoa 78) of the one presented by Dijkstra, which applies only to finite families of predicates. H1 is the version in our model with the state ω of the "law of the excluded miracle", presented by Dijkstra in the form $F(\perp)=\perp$.

It is easy to see that criteria H3 and H4 are implied by H2. Hence, in order to check if a pt is healthy is suffices to consider H1, H2 and H5.

Property 5.1.1. tells us immediately that wpr(R) satisfies H2, for every ω-relation R□
Concerning the law of the excluded mirecle we have the following result:

Proposition 6.2. Let R be a ω-relation. We have $wpr(R)(\Omega) = \perp$ iff R is total.
Proof: The equation in def. 4.11 can be rewritten $\tilde{pre}(R)(P)=\lambda a.R(a)\underline{\subseteq P}$. Using 4.16 we get $wpr(R)(\Omega)=\tilde{pre}(R)(\perp)=\lambda a.(R(A)=\emptyset)$, and the result follows. □

As for continuity of wpr(R), we have (Gue 80):

Theorem 6.3. Let R be a ω-relation. The predicate transformer wpr(R) is continuous iff R is boundedly nondeterministic. □

The pleasant conclusion we can draw is that for all programmable relations R, and this includes all semantic relations of programs, the predicate transformer wpr(R) is healthy. The question we want to discuss now is the following: does every healthy predicate transformer correspond to the pt wpr associated to some programmable relation? In other words, is the set {wpr(R) : R is a programmable relation} equal to the set {F : F is a healthy pt} ? The answer to this question is provided by the following fundamental theorem:

Theorem 6.4. For a given pt F there exists a programmable relation R such that $F = wpr(R)$ iff F is healthy and such that $F(\top) = F(\neg\Omega)$ and $F(\top) \subseteq \neg\Omega$.

Proof. (=>) Trivial, on account of 6.2. (H1), 5.1.1(H.2), 6.3.(H.5), 4.16.($F(\top)=F(\neg\Omega)$), and 3.1.($F(\top)\subseteq\neg\Omega$).

(<=) $\tilde{F}$, the dual pt of F, is such that $\tilde{F}(\bot)=\tilde{F}(\Omega)$, and $\Omega\subseteq\tilde{F}(\bot)$ and, for a non-empty family of predicates $\{Ai\}i$, $\tilde{F}(\underset{i}{\cup}Ai)= \underset{i}{\cup}\tilde{F}(Ai)$. Let <a> be the predicate $\lambda q.q=a$, and for a predicate P let $\underline{\tilde{F}}(P)$ be an alternative notation for $\underline{\tilde{F}(P)}$. Let us define a relation S by:

$$S(a) = \begin{cases} \underline{\tilde{F}}(\bot) & \text{if } a=\omega \\ \\ \underline{\tilde{F}}(<a>)-\{\omega\} & \text{if } a\neq\omega. \end{cases}$$

$\Omega\subseteq\tilde{F}(\bot)$ implies that $S^{-1}(\omega) = \{\omega\}$.

Now, let P be a predicate such that $P\subseteq\neg\Omega$; if $P\neq\bot$, we have:

$$\begin{aligned} S(\underline{P}\cup\underline{\Omega}) &= S(\underline{P})\cup S(\underline{\Omega}) \\ &= S(\underset{a\in \underline{P}}{\cup}\{a\})\cup S(\omega) \\ &= \underset{a\in\underline{P}}{\cup} S(\{a\})\cup \underline{\tilde{F}}(\bot) \\ &= \underset{a\in\underline{P}}{\cup}((\underline{\tilde{F}}<a>)-\{\omega\})\cup \underline{\tilde{F}}(\bot), && \text{(recall that } \omega\notin\underline{P}) \\ &= (\underset{a\in\underline{P}}{\cup}\underline{\tilde{F}}(<a>)) - \{\omega\}\cup\underline{\tilde{F}}(\bot) \\ &= \underline{\tilde{F}}\ (\underset{a\in\underline{P}}{\cup}<a>) - \{\omega\}\cup\underline{\tilde{F}}(\bot) \\ &= \underline{\tilde{F}}(P) - \{\omega\}\cup\underline{\tilde{F}}(\bot) \\ &= \underline{\tilde{F}}(P)\cup\tilde{F}(\bot), && \text{since } \Omega\subseteq\tilde{F}(\bot) \\ &= \underline{\tilde{F}}(P)\ ; \end{aligned}$$

if $P = \bot$ we have, trivially:

$S(\underline{P}\cup\underline{\Omega}) = S(\underline{\bot}\cup\underline{\Omega}) = S(\underline{\Omega}) = \underline{\tilde{F}}(\bot) = \underline{\tilde{F}}(P)$.

Suppose now that P is such that $P \not\subseteq \neg\Omega$; if $P\neq\Omega$ we have:

$S(\underline{P} \cup \underline{\Omega}) = S((\underline{P-\Omega}) \cup \underline{\Omega})$

$= S(\underline{P-\Omega}) \cup S(\underline{\Omega})$

$= \underline{\tilde{F}}(P-\Omega) \cup \underline{\tilde{F}}(\Omega)$, (using the first part of the proof, since $P-\Omega \subseteq \neg\Omega$, plus the hypotheses that $\tilde{F}(\perp) = \tilde{F}(\Omega)$)

$= \underline{\tilde{F}}(P)$;

if $P=\Omega$ we have trivially

$S(\underline{P} \cup \underline{\Omega}) = S(\underline{\Omega} \cup \underline{\Omega}) = S(\underline{\Omega}) = \underline{\tilde{F}}(\perp) = \underline{\tilde{F}}(\Omega)$.

We conclude that, for all P, we have $S(\underline{P} \cup \underline{\Omega}) = \underline{\tilde{F}}(P)$, or image $(S)(P \cup \Omega) = \tilde{F}(P)$, using 4.3. Let $R=S^{-1}$. Then $pre(R)(P \cup \Omega) = \tilde{F}(P)$. By duality we get $\tilde{pre}(R)(P-\Omega) = F(P)$. Remarking that $R(\omega) = \{\omega\}$, which means that R is a ω-relation, we arrive at $wpr(R)(P)=F(P)$, using 4.16.

Therefore, wpr(R) also satisfies criteria H1 and H5 which implies by 6.2 and 6.3 that R is total and boundedly nondeterministic. □

This theorem suggests that, in our model the properties $F(\top) = F(\neg\Omega)$ and $F(\top) \subseteq \neg\Omega$, should be considered as extra healthiness criteria:

Definition 6.1'. Healthiness criteria. To the list in definition 6.1 we add:

H6. $F(\top) = F(\neg\Omega)$

H7. $F(\top) \subseteq \neg\Omega$. □

Criterium H6. together with criterium H2 implies that for all P $F(P) = F(P-\Omega)$: $F(P) = F(P \cap \top) = F(P) \cap F(\top) = F(P) \cap F(\neg\Omega) = F(P-\Omega)$; this is not surprising, on account of theorem 4.16. This criterium may be interpreted as stating a triviality: to guarantee that a program terminates $(F(\top))$ is to guarantee that it does not go on for ever $(F(\neg\Omega))$. Criterium H7 is perhaps more interesting: it may be regarded as a second law of the excluded miracle. In fact it should be interpreted as follows: in order to be able to guarantee that a program terminates $(F(\top))$ we must guarantee that it does start $(\neg\Omega)$. Of course these kind of properties are not necessary in Dijkstra's original context, for non-termination is not explicitly formalized there.

We may remark, in passing, that the first law of the excluded miracle, which by property 6.2 is equivalent to the totality of the ω-relation involved, means in fact that any program that starts must either terminate or not terminate. The excluded miracle in this case in the existence of a third possibility. Besides, from this point of view, H5 is also a law of excluded miracle: by property 6.3 it expresses that it is impossible for a program to produce an infinite number of results from a given initial state and yet be guaranteed to terminate for that initial state. We see that criteria H1, H5 and H7 (the "laws of excluded miracles") express properties intrinsic to kind of relations used to represent programs whereas criteria H2 (and H3 and H4) and H6 are inherent to the definition of the predicate transformer wpr(R), (cf. 4.16), for they hold for arbitrary ω-relations.

Considering the similarity between H6 and H7 one might wonder whether in the presence of the remaining criteria they are indeed independent. In other words, can we find a pt G1 satisfying H1, H2, H5 and H6 but not H7, and a pt G2 satisfying H1, H2, H5 and H7 but not H6? The following examples show that we can. Let $Q = \{1,\omega\}$; then $\neg\Omega$ is the predicate $\lambda q.q=1$. Define G1 by:

$G1(\top) = \top$, $G1(\neg\Omega) = \top$, $G1(\Omega) = \bot$, $G1(\bot) = \bot$; and define G2 by:

$G2(\top) = \neg\Omega$, $G2(\neg\Omega) = \bot$, $G2(\Omega) = \bot$, $G2(\bot) = \bot$.

Related to the question of healthiness is the so-called "law of composition" (Hoa 78): do we have $wpr(RoS)(P)=wpr(R)(wpr(S)(P))$? Although this property is not valid for ω-relations in general it holds for programmable relations:

Proposition 6.5. Let R and S be ω-relations. If $S(\omega) = \{\omega\}$ then $wpr(RoS)(P) = wpr(R)(wpr(S)(P))$. □

This proposition, along with propositions 6.2 and 6.3, makes it easy to prove the following important result:

Proposition 6.6. If R and S are programmable relations then RoS is a programmable relation. □

7. CONCLUSION

Theorem 6.4, which is the main result in this paper, supports our conviction that programmable relations are an interesting concept in the study of nondeterminacy. They were used, in particular, to introduce a relational weakest precondition total correctness predicate transformer. In order to prove that this predicate transformer corresponds indeed to the one proposed by Disjkstra (Dij 75, Dij 76) it is necessary to provide a semantics of the language of guarded commands in terms of programmable relations, and then to derive the associated predicate transformers and show that they coincide with Dijkstra's axiomatic definition. This problem was treated in (Gue 80) and (Gue 81). Other issues that can be dealt with satisfactorily with programmable relations are the study of so-called invariants and the characterization of the termination of repetitive commands. These questions are considered in detail in (Gue 81).

REFERENCES

(Bac 79) R.-J,Back, "Semantics of unbounded nondeterminism". Proceedings ICALP 80, Lect. Notes Comp. Sci. 85, Springer (1980).

(Dij 75) E.W.Dijkstra, "Guarded commands, nondeterminacy and formal derivation of programs". CACM 18,8 (August 1975), pp. 453-457.

(Dij 76) E.W.Dijkstra, "A Discipline of Programming". Prentice Hall (1976).

(Gue 80) P.Guerreiro, "A relational model for nondeterministic programs and predicate transformers". Fourth International Colloquium on Programming, Paris, Lect. Notes Comp. Sci. 83, Springer (1980), pp. 136-146.

(Gue 81) P.Guerreiro,"Semantique Relationnelle des Programmes Non-deterministes et des Processus Communicants". These de 3eme Cycle, Univ. Grenoble I, (July 1981).

(Har 79) D.Harel, "On the total correctness of nondeterministic programs". IBM Research Report RC7691 (1979).

(Hoa 78) C.A.R.Hoare, "Some properties of predicate transformers". JACM 25,3 (July 1978), pp. 461-480.

(Roe 76) W.P.de Roever, "Dijkstra's predicate transformer, non-determinism, recursion and termination". Math. Found. Comp. Sci. 1976, Lect. Notes Comp. Sci. 45, Springer (1976), pp.472-481.

(Sif 79) J.Sifakis. "A unified approach for studying properties of transition systems". Rapport de Recherche 179, IMAG, Grenoble, (December 1979). To appear in Theoretical Computer Science.

(Wan 77) M.Wand, "A characterization of weakest preconditions". Journal of Computer and Systems Sciences 15, (1977), pp. 209-212.

POWERDOMAINS AND NONDETERMINISTIC RECURSIVE DEFINITIONS

M.C.B. Hennessy
Dept. of Computer Science
University of Edinburgh
Edinburgh EH9 3JZ
Scotland

Abstract

A nondeterministic Language for recursive definitions, L, is defined. It includes simple functions for manipulating data values, in this case the natural numbers, a choice operator OR and recursive procedures. Various kinds of parameter-passing mechanisms are allowed: the well-known call-by-value, run-time choice which models the Algol60 substitution rule and call-time choice in which no nondeterminism is allowed in the actual parameters once the procedure has been called.

An operational semantics is defined for this language in the form of a next state relation. Using this relation three different operational preorders are defined between programs. The difference in these orders reflect different views of divergent computations.

On the other hand we define three different mathematical models, in the sense of Scott-Theory and show that they are fully-abstract; that is programs are identified in the model if and only if they are identified by the corresponding operational preorder. The three different models are defined using three different powerdomains and these are shown to arise naturally by considering different properties of the semantic counter-part of the operator OR.

Finally we discuss the suitability of L for defining elements of the various domains. An element of a domain is computable if it is the least upper bound of a recursively enumerable set of finite elements. We show that for certain domains all computable elements are definable in L and point to difficulties in extending L so as to define all such elements in the remaining domains.

Introduction

Nondeterminism is implicit in many aspects of programming. A typical example is an operating system where the response to a user depends on such factors as workload, number of other users, etc. If all the parameters are known then the response is determined uniquely. But usually the relationship between the various parameters is so complicated that from the point of view of the user the response may be taken to be nondeterministic. Another example is a data base system where a query made at different points in time can have different responses. As a final example the behaviour of a distributed computing system in general depends on the relative speeds of the different processors. If these systems are examined at a level of abstraction which ignores time then the behaviour will be nondeterministic. It follows that an adequate model of the behaviour of programs in general must be capable of representing nondeterminism.

Explicit nondeterminism has appeared in programming languages under varying disguises over the last ten to fifteen years. See for example [5],[9]. More recently Dijkstra has popularised nondeterministic features of programming languages in [4], where under-specification of the behaviour of a program is reflected in nondeterministic computations. Various semantic models of this language have appeared in the literature ([12]). In this paper we investigate another language with explicit nondeterminism. The language of recursive definitions (for example in [16]) is augmented by adding a choice operator OR. Then T_1 OR T_2 can behave as T_1 or as T_2. The exact definition of the syntax of the language is taken from [6], where three different types of parameter-passing mechanisms are allowed: call-by-value, as in Algol60, run-time choice which models the substitution rule of Algol60 and finally call-time choice in which the actual parameters to a procedure must be deterministic. The operational semantics of call-time choice is somewhat different than that of [6], in that we use <u>bindings</u> [1] to associate the actual parameters to the formal parameters.

Three different operational preorders are defined for this language. Indeed the main point of this paper is that there is no one correct or incorrect model for nondeterministic programs. Such programs may be used in many different ways and different models reflect the different uses. The three different preorders arise from the different views one may have on divergent computations and we argue that these preorders arise quite naturally from consideration of desired input-output behaviour of programs.

On the other hand we consider mathematical models for this language, in the sense of Scott [19]. In this approach mathematical functions from <u>domains</u> are associated with every program. In [11],[14], the theory of domains is extended so as to model nondeterministic features of languages. The two different definitions of <u>power-domains</u> are given which are intended to play the role of the "set of subsets of a set". Here we show that three different powerdomains can be defined in a natural way by considering the desirable properties of the semantic counterpart of the operator OR. Using these powerdomains three models are defined for the language and are shown to be fully abstract with respect to the operational preorders. This means that programs are identified in the model if and only if they are equivalent under the corresponding preorder. It should be emphasised that we only consider the case of unstructured data, in particular the set of integers, and the corresponding data domains are simply <u>flat</u> cpos. It remains to see how suitable powerdomains are for modelling languages with more complicated data structures. More generally it would be interesting to give a connection between the powerdomain approach and the theory of algebraic semantics [8]. A first step in this direction is given in [3].

In the final part of the paper we study the class of functions definable by programs in this language. This problem has already been studied for deterministic languages in [15],[13]. In [10] a simple nondeterministic language for defining functions over truth values is investigated but since the semantic domain is finite neither the results nor the proof techniques carry over to our language. Following [13] we define an element of a domain to be computable if it is the least upper bound of a recursively enumerable set of finite elements. If we confine our attention to call-by-value definitions it turns out that all computable elements of the relevant domain are definable in the language, except in the case when we use the Smyth Powerdomain. There is a difficulty in relating definable to computable in this case which seems to stem from the incompatibility of the Smyth partial order with the natural computational order. In the remaining cases, e.g. call-time choice definitions and run-time choice definitions not all computable elements are definable and we discuss remedies, either by augmenting the language or restricting the model.

§1. The Language L

§1.1 Syntax

The language L, considered in this paper is essentially that of [6]. For simplicity we allow only one kind of data type, the natural numbers. Apart from §3, all our results still hold if we allow various data types within the language, but it is essential that they be unstructured. The language then consists of recursive definitions over natural numbers, using some predefined constant function symbols, such as IF...THEN...ELSE, SUCC, PRED, etc. As in [6] we allow three kinds of parameter-passing mechanisms, call-by-value, call-time choice and run-time choice: the first is the familiar mechanism of Algol60 [20], whereby all parameters to a procedure call must be evaluated before it can be called. Run-time choice is the analogue of body-replacement rule of Algol60 and call-time choice is when we ensure that each parameter to the procedure is deterministic, in the sense that it can be evaluated to at most one value. To specify the operational behaviour of this parameter-passing mechanism we use bindings.

We now proceed with the definition of the syntax. This is parameterised over the following sets:

i) $X = \{X_1,\dots,X_k\}$ a finite set of data-variables

ii) $F = \{F_1,\dots,F_n\}$ a finite set of procedure-variables.

For simplicity we assume that each F_i has arity k. The five syntactic categories of L are defined using a BNF like notation as follows:

i) Constants - the set of constants or values, ranged over by K, and given by

$K ::= K_n, n \in N \mid KB$

ii) Terms - the set of terms, ranged over by P,T, and given by

$T ::= X_i \mid K \mid ZERO(T) \mid SUCC(T) \mid PRED(T) \mid TB \mid IF(T_1,T_2,T_3)$
$\mid T_1 \text{ OR } T_2 \mid F_i^m(T_1,\ldots,T_k)$, $m=r,c$ or v

iii) Bindings - the set of bindings, ranged over by B and given by

$B ::= <T_1,\ldots,T_k>$

iv) Declarations - the set of declarations, ranged over by D:

$$\begin{aligned} D ::= F_1(X_1,\ldots,X_k) &<= T_1 \\ &\vdots \\ F_n(X_1,\ldots,X_k) &<= T_n \end{aligned}$$

v) Programs - the set of programs, ranged over by Pr:

$Pr ::= <F_1^m(X_1,\ldots,X_k),D>$, $m = r,c$ or v.

In the sequel we will also be interested in two subsets of Program, CVPrograms - those programs of the form $<F_1^v(X_1,\ldots,X_k),D>$, where D contains no occurrences of F_i^c, F_i^r or TB, and CCPrograms - those of the form $<F_1^c(X_1,\ldots,X_k),D>$, where D contains no occurrence of F_i^v, F_i^r.

Since we are assuming that each F_i has arity k it will be convenient to let $F_i(\underline{T})$ denote $F_i(T_1,\ldots,T_k)$, where $\underline{T}$ denotes the vector $(T_1,\ldots,T_k)$. We also let $\underline{X}$ denote the vector $(X_1,\ldots,X_k)$.

If B is the binding $<T_1,\ldots,T_k>$ we let $B(i)$ denote T_i. We also use $B(i \rightarrow T')$ to denote the binding which is the same as B except its ith component is T'. In the term TB every occurrence of the variable X_i is bound to the term $B(i)$. This gives rise to free and bound data-variables in a term, which we leave the reader to define in the usual way. Note that in the term TB free variables can only occur in B since every variable in T is bound to some term in B. Then a term is closed if it contains no free variables. Let CTerms denote the set of such terms. We also let $[\underline{T}/\underline{X}]S$ denote the term which results from substituting T_i for each free occurrence of X_i in S.

§ 1.2 Operational Semantics

The operational semantics is essentially that of [6], with a modification of the operation call-time choice. It is essentially a binary operation $\overset{D}{\rightarrow}$ which specifies how terms should behave when the procedure variables are bound by the declaration D: $T \overset{D}{\rightarrow} T'$ means that T can evolve to T' in the presence of the declaration D. We give some examples by way of explanation.

Since run-time choice is meant to model Algol substitution the following rule is reasonable:

$F_i^r(\underline{T}) \overset{D}{\rightarrow} [\underline{T}/\underline{X}]P_i$ if $F_i <= P_i$ is in D.

Similarly call-by-value is captured by the following two rules

i) $F_i^v(\underline{K}) \overset{D}{\rightarrow} [\underline{K}/\underline{X}]P_i$ if $F_i <= P_i$ is in D

ii) $T_j \overset{D}{\to} T'_j$ implies $F^v_i(\underline{T}) \overset{D}{\to} F^v_i(\underline{T}')$

where $\underline{T}'$ is obtained from $\underline{T}$ by substituting T'_j for T_j.

In English we say that the procedure F_i can be called if all the parameters are constants. Otherwise to proceed with the computation we must evaluate the parameters.

In a similar manner we can attempt to specify call-time choice in which the actual parameters to a procedure must be "deterministic". Indeed this is the approach in [6], with the two rules:

i) If $\underline{T}$ is deterministic then

$F^c_i(\underline{T}) \overset{D}{\to} [\underline{T}/\underline{X}]P_i$ if $F_i \Leftarrow P_i$ is in D

ii) Otherwise $T_j \overset{D}{\to} T'_j$ implies $F^c_i(\underline{T}) \overset{D}{\to} F^c_i(\underline{T}')$

where $\underline{T}'$ is obtained by substituting T'_j for T_j in $\underline{T}$.

The problem arises when we try to define a suitable syntactic notion of deterministic. Intuitively we wish to say that no choices will ever be made when T is evaluated. Any syntactic definition can at most approximate this and consequently problems arise.

Example 1: Let D_1 be the following definition:

$F_1(X) \Leftarrow F^c_2(F^r_3(K_0))$

$F_2(X) \Leftarrow K_1$

$F_3(X) \Leftarrow F^r_3(X)$ OR $F^r_3(X)$

Then if the definition of nondeterministic does not decree that $F^r_3(K_0)$ is deterministic, $F^r_1(K_0)$ will diverge whereas intuitively it should evaluate to K_1. The problem arises because F_2 does not require its actual parameters to return a value, whereas the rules insist that these parameters must be reduced so as to eliminate possible nondeterminism. ◻

To overcome this problem we have borrowed an idea from [1] and introduced the class of bindings. We then get the rule:

$F^c_i(\underline{T}) \overset{D}{\to} P_iB$ if $F_i \Rightarrow P_i$ is in D and $B(j) = T_j$.

In turn to evaluate PB we merely evaluate P until we need the value bound to X_i, whereupon we start evaluating B(i). The value obtained will remain bound to each occurrence of X_i in P. In this approach the only extra machinery required is to know when the value of the value X_i is needed. This is given by the following predicates:

For $1 \leq i \leq k$ let $Stuck_i$ be the least predicate over terms which satisfies

i) $Stuck_i(X_j)$ if i=j

ii) $Stuck_i(T)$ implies $Stuck_i(IF(T, T_2, T_3))$ and $Stuck_i(G(T))$, where G is SUCC, PRED or ZERO.

iii) $Stuck_i(T_j)$ implies $Stuck_i(F^v(\underline{T}))$, $1 \leq i,j \leq n$

iv) $Stuck_i(B(j))$, and $Stuck_j(T)$ implies $Stuck_i(TB)$, $1 \le i,j \le n$.

With the aid of this predicate we can now define the operational semantics. Throughout it is convenient to identify the constant K with the constant KB.

For any declaration D let $\overset{D}{\to}$ be the least relation between terms which satisfies:

I a) $SUCC(K_n) \overset{D}{\to} K_{n+1}$

b) $T \overset{D}{\to} T'$ implies $SUCC(T) \overset{D}{\to} SUCC(T')$

II a) $PRED(K_{n+1}) \overset{D}{\to} K_n$, $PRED(K_0) \overset{D}{\to} K_0$

b) $T \overset{D}{\to} T'$ implies $PRED(T) \overset{D}{\to} PRED(T')$

III a) $ZERO(K_0) \overset{D}{\to} K_0$

$ZERO(K_{n+1}) \overset{D}{\to} K_1$

b) $T \overset{D}{\to} T'$ implies $ZERO(T) \overset{D}{\to} ZERO(T')$

IV) a) $IF(K_0,T,T') \overset{D}{\to} T$

$IF(K_{n+1},T,T') \overset{D}{\to} T'$

b) $T \overset{D}{\to} T'$ implies $IF(T,T_1,T_2) \overset{D}{\to} IF(T',T_1,T_2)$

V T_1 OR $T_2 \overset{D}{\to} T_1$

T_1 OR $T_2 \overset{D}{\to} T_2$

VI $F_i^r(\underline{T}) \overset{D}{\to} [\underline{T}/\underline{X}]P_i$ if $F_i \Leftarrow P_i$ is in D

VII a) $F_i^v(\underline{K}) \overset{D}{\to} [\underline{K}/\underline{X}]P_i$ if $F_i \Leftarrow P_i$ is in D

b) $T_j \overset{D}{\to} T_j'$ implies $F_i^v(\underline{T}) \overset{D}{\to} F_i(\underline{T}')$,

where $\underline{T}'$ is obtained from $\underline{T}$ by replacing T_j with T_j'.

VIII $F_i^c(\underline{T}) \overset{D}{\to} P_iB$ if $F_i \Leftarrow P_i$ is in D and $B(j) = T_j$, $1 \le j \le k$.

IX a) $T \to T'$ implies $TB \to T'B$

b) $Stuck_i(T)$, $B(i) \overset{D}{\to} R$ implies $TB \overset{D}{\to} TB(i \to R)$

c) $Stuck_i(T)$, $B(i) = K$ implies $TB \overset{D}{\to} ([K/X_i]T)B$.

With these rules we now have that

$$F_1^r(K_0) \overset{D_1}{\to} F_2^c(F_3^r(K_0))$$
$$\overset{D_1}{\to} K_1B, \text{ where B is defined by } B(1) = F_3^r(K_0).$$

Since we identify K_1B with K_1 this means that the computation has finished with output K_1. □

The difference between run-time choice and call-time choice is given in the following example.

<u>Example 2</u>: Let D_2 be the declaration

$F_1(X) \Leftarrow IF(ZERO(X),X,K_2)$

Then $F_1^r(K_0$ OR $K_1)$ can be reduced to any of the values K_0,K_1,K_2. However $F_1^c(K_0$ OR $K_1)$ can only be reduced to $IF(ZERO(X),X,K_2)$ $\{K_0$ OR $K_1\}$ where $\{T\}$ denotes the binding

$B(1) = T$.

This in turn has only two possible reduction sequences

$$IF(ZERO(X),X,K_2)\{K_0 \text{ OR } K_1\} \overset{D_2}{\rightarrow} IF(ZERO(X),X,K_2)\{K_0\} \overset{D_2}{\rightarrow} \ldots\ldots \overset{D_2}{\rightarrow} K_0\{K_0\}$$

or

$$IF(ZERO(X),X,K_2)\{K_0 \text{ OR } K_1\} \overset{D_2}{\rightarrow} IF(ZERO(X),X,K_2)\{K_1\} \overset{D_2}{\rightarrow} \ldots \overset{D_2}{\rightarrow} K_2\{K_0\}. \quad \square$$

§1.3 Operational Preorders

There are various ways in which we could use the operationalsemantics of §1.2 to give meanings to programs. For example we could associate with every program $Pr = \langle F_1^m(\underline{X}),D\rangle$ the relation Com_{Pr}, defined by:

$\langle\underline{K},K'\rangle \in Com_{Pr}$ if and only if $F_1^m(\underline{K}) \rightarrow^* K'$.

However by focusing attention on the relation computed by a program we are ignoring relevant behaviour. For example let $Pr = \langle F_1^v(X),D\rangle$ and $Pr' = \langle F_1^v(X),D')$ where D,D' are given by:

$F_1(X) \Leftarrow K_1$ — D

$F_1(X) \Leftarrow K_1 \text{ OR } F_1(X)$ — D'.

Then $Com_{Pr} = Com_{Pr'}$ but clearly if a program is required to return the value 1 always then Pr is preferable to Pr'.

We now define three different methods for comparing programs using the operational semantics. The differences arise by treating different types of behaviour as significant. Throughout these explanations we let Pr,Pr' denote $\langle F_1^m(\underline{X}),D\rangle$, $\langle F_1^{m'}(\underline{X}),D'\rangle$ respectively.

I Ignoring Divergence

$Pr <_1 Pr'$ if for every vector of closed terms $\underline{T}$,

$F_1^m(\underline{T}) \overset{D}{\rightarrow}^* K$ implies $F_1^{m'}(\underline{T}) \overset{D'}{\rightarrow}^* K$.

This corresponds to the traditional notion used by formal language theorists when discussing nondeterministic machines.

II Possible Divergence is Catastrophic

Here we take the view that if a program can diverge it is of no use. For a given input it must be guaranteed to halt.

For a closed term T and declaration D let $T{\downarrow}D$ (i.e. T converges on D) if there is no infinite sequence

$T \overset{D}{\rightarrow} T_1 \overset{D}{\rightarrow} \ldots\ldots \overset{D}{\rightarrow} T_n \rightarrow \ldots\ldots$

Then Pr $<_2$ Pr' if for every vector of closed terms $\underline{T}$,

$F_1^m(\underline{T})\downarrow D$ implies a) $F_1^{m'}(\underline{T})\downarrow D'$

and b) $F_1^{m'}(\underline{T}) \xrightarrow{D'} K$ implies $F_1^m(\underline{T}) \xrightarrow{D} K$.

This relation $<_2$ is consistent with the idea that nondeterminism constitutes under-specification. The <u>less</u> nondeterminism there is the more 'defined' the program becomes. This is the view taken by Dijkstra in [4].

III <u>Divergence is not Catastrophic</u>

Here we take into consideration the possible divergence of computations. As in the work of Scott [19], divergence constitutes under-specification and elimination of diverging computations makes a program more 'defined'. For a given input a program is fully defined and cannot be improved upon if it does not diverge.

Pr $<_3$ Pr' if for every vector of closed terms $\underline{T}$

i) $F_1^m(\underline{T}) \xrightarrow{D}{}^* K$ implies $F_1^{m'}(\underline{T}) \xrightarrow{D'}{}^* K$

ii) $F_1^m(\underline{T})\downarrow D$ implies a) $F_1^{m'}(\underline{T})\downarrow D'$

b) $F_1^{m'}(\underline{T}) \xrightarrow{D'} K$ implies $F_1^m(\underline{T}) \xrightarrow{D} K$

Note that this is the preorder used in [6].

There are many other comparisons we could make between the behavioural aspects of programs. However the three chosen here seem to have special significance, as we will now see.

Let R,S range over predicates on vectors of closed terms, constants respectively. So for example R is a total mapping from $(\underline{\text{CTerms}})^k$ to {tt,ff}. We write $\underline{T} \in R$, $K \in S$, to mean $R(\underline{T}) = tt$, $S(K) = tt$, respectively. For any program Pr = $\langle F_1^m(\underline{X}),D\rangle$, let R{Pr}S if:

$\underline{T} \in R$ implies $K \in S$ for some K such that $F_1^m(\underline{T}) \xrightarrow{D}{}^* K$.

This is one possible generalisation to nondeterministic programs of the usual notion of partial correctness with respect to the predicates R,S.

Similarly let R[Pr]S if:

$\underline{T} \in R$ implies ($F_1^m(\underline{T})\downarrow D$ and $F_1^m(\underline{T}) \xrightarrow{D}{}^* K$ implies $K \in S$).

In this case Pr is said to be <u>totally correct</u> with respect to the predicates R,S, or R is said to be a <u>precondition</u> of S.

<u>Prop. 1.3.1</u> a) Pr $<_1$ Pr' if and only if R{Pr}S implies R{Pr'}S

b) Pr $<_2$ Pr' if and only if R[Pr]S implies R[Pr]S

c) Pr $<_3$ Pr' if and only if Pr $<_1$ Pr' and Pr $<_2$ Pr'

<u>Proof</u>: Omitted. □

We leave the reader to use this proposition to establish a connection between $<_2$ and the weakest precondition semantics of [4]. This is discussed at length in [12]. Apart from the inclusions implied by c), the three relations are incomparable.

§2. Denotational Semantics

In this section we assume that the reader is familiar with the usual mathematical constructs and notions of Scott theory: partial order (po), complete partial order (cpo), directed set, finite element, algebraic, consistently complete, continuous function, strict function, etc. Details may be found in [21], [22]. For any set S let $S_\perp$ denote the flat cpo obtained by adding the 'undefined' symbol $\perp$ beneath S. Let S^k denote $S\times\ldots\times S$ (k-times) and note that if S is a cpo then so is S^k under the pointwise ordering. For cpos (or domains) S_1, S_2 let $[S_1 \to S_2]$ ($[S_1 \to S_2]_\perp$) denote the cpo of continuous functions (strict continuous functions) from S_1 to S_2, under the pointwise ordering.

§2.1 Definition of the Models

We define the mathematical semantics of programs by giving three domains X_i, $1\leq i\leq 3$ and three mappings:

$$\mathcal{V}_i: \underline{\text{Programs}} \to [X_i^k \to X_i],\ 1\leq i\leq 3.$$

These should be defined in such a way that

$$Pr <_i Pr' \text{ if and only if } \mathcal{V}_i [[Pr]] < \mathcal{V}_i [[Pr']].$$

Such $\mathcal{V}_i$ are called <u>fully abstract</u> with respect to $<_i$ since they model these relations exactly.

Certain requirements of X_i are apparent. For example it should be a cpo in order to handle the recursion. It should also contain an embedding of $N_\perp$ in order to handle deterministic definitions in the usual way. We also need a binary function, which we call $\cup: X_i \times X_i \to X_i$. This is to mimic set-theoretic union. Thus a program which on a given input can output K_0 or can output K_1 can be handled within the theory using the object $0 \cup 1$.

However the properties required of this binary function $\cup$ vary according to the index. For example in X_1 we should have $\perp \cup x = x$ but not in X_2, X_3 and $\perp \cup x = \perp$ in X_2 but not in X_1 or X_3. If $\cup$ is to act in any way like set-theoretic union it should at least satisfy the equations:

$$\begin{aligned} x \cup x &= x \\ x \cup y &= y \cup x \\ (x \cup y) \cup z &= x \cup (y \cup z) \end{aligned} \qquad \text{E3}$$

<u>Definition 2.1.1</u>: If E is a set of equations over the binary symbol $\cup$ then N_E-cpo is the collection of pairs <D,$\cup$> where

a) D is an algebraic cpo

b) $\cup$ is a continuous binary function over N which satisfies E.

A typical element of N_E-cpo will be denoted by N_E-cpo. We choose three sets of equations:

i) E3

ii) E3 with $x \cup y < x$ E2

iii) E3 with $x < x \cup y$ E1

It is easy to see that an N_{E3}-cpo satisfies $\bot \cup x = \bot$ if and only if it is an N_{E2}-cpo. Also it satisfies $\bot \cup x = x$ if and only if it is an element of N_{E1}-cpo. As stated above we also need an embedding of $N_\bot$. The construction of the required N_{Ei}-cpo is given in the next proposition. We say a function f is <u>linear</u> if it preserves $\cup$, i.e. if $f(x \cup y) = f(x) \cup f(y)$.

<u>Prop. 2.1.2</u> For every algebraic cpo D there exists a unique (up to isomorphism) N_E-cpo, called $\wp_E(D)$ such that

i) there is a continuous function in $\in [D \to \wp_E(D)]$

ii) given any continuous function $f \in [D \to D']$, where $D' \in N_E$-cpo, there exists a unique linear extension $ext(f) \in [\wp_E(D) \to D']$ such that the following diagram commutes:

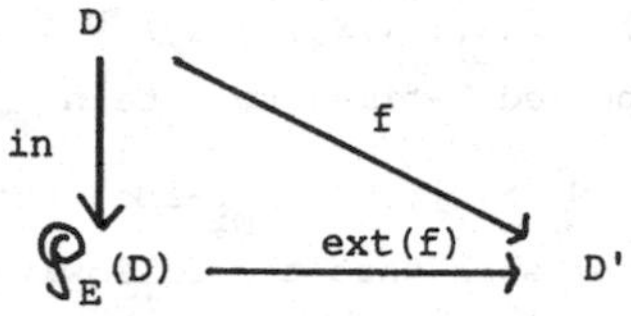

Furthermore the mapping ext is continuous.

Proof: See [7]. □

We are interested in three particular cases of this theorem, when D is $N_\bot$ and E is E1,E2 or E3. In these cases $\wp_E(N_\bot)$ is particularly easy to describe.

I Let $\wp_1 = \langle 2^N, \cup \rangle$, where 2^N is the set of subsets of N ordered by set inclusion and $\cup$ is the usual set-theoretic union. Then $\wp_1$ satisfies the requirements of $\wp_{E1}(N_\bot)$ and therefore is isomorphic to it.

II Let P_S be the set of subsets of $N_\bot$ which satisfy the following

$X \in P_S$ implies a) $X = N_\bot$

or b) $X \subseteq N$, X finite.

For $X, Y \in P_S$ let X   Y if $Y \subseteq X$.

Then P_S is a cpo under this ordering, usually called the <u>Smyth Powerdomain</u> of $N_\bot$. Let $\wp_2 = \langle P_S, \cup \rangle$ where   is the usual set-theoretic inclusion. Then 2 is isomorphic to $\wp_{E2}(N_\bot)$.

III Let P_{EM} be the set of subsets of $N_\bot$ which satisfy the following requirements:

$X \in P_{EM}$ implies a) $\bot \in X$

or b) X is finite.

For $X, Y \in P_{EM}$ let $X \sqsubseteq Y$ if

a) $\forall x \in X \; \exists y \in Y. \; x \sqsubseteq y$

and b) $\forall y \in Y \; \exists x \in X. \; x \sqsubseteq y$.

This can also be defined as $X \sqsubseteq Y$ if

a) $X - \{\bot\} \subseteq Y$

b) $\bot \notin X$ implies $Y \subseteq X$.

Then P_{EM} is a cpo under this ordering. It is usually called the Egli-Milner Powerdomain of $N_\bot$. Let $\mathcal{P}_3 = \langle P_{EM}, \cup\rangle$ where $\cup$ is the usual set-theoretic inclusion. Then $\mathcal{P}_3$ is isomorphic to $\mathcal{P}_{E3}(N_\bot)$.

This completes the description of our three domains. In the next section we give the mappings

$\mathcal{V}_i$: Programs -> $[\mathcal{P}_i^k \to \mathcal{P}_i]$, i=1,3.

§2.2 The Denotational Semantics

We must first give a semantic counterpart of each of the syntactic constructs in the language. Let $\mathcal{F}_i = [\mathcal{P}_i^k \to \mathcal{P}_i]$, i=1,3. A function $f \in \mathcal{F}_i$ is said to be bilinear if it is linear in each argument, i.e.

$$f(x_1,\ldots,x_j \cup x_j',\ldots x_k) = f(x_1,\ldots,x_j,\ldots,x_k) \cup f(x_1,\ldots,x_j',\ldots,x_k),\ 1 \le j \le k$$

Proposition 2.1.2 can be applied k-times to obtain

Prop. 2.2.1 For every $f \in [N_\bot^k \to D]$, $D \in N_{Ei}$-cpo, there exists a unique bilinear extension $ext(f) \in [\mathcal{P}_i^k \to D]$ such that the following diagram commutes:

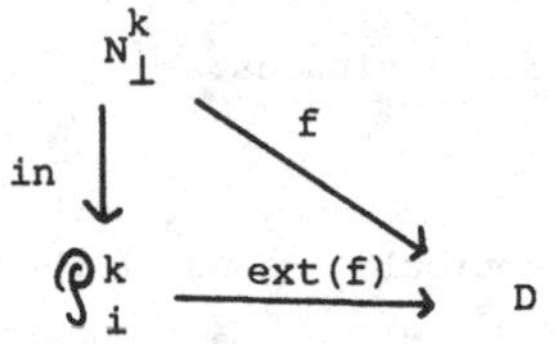

Furthermore the mapping ext is continuous. □

The injection mapping in: $N_\bot^k \to \mathcal{P}_i^k$ is simply the pointwise extension of the injection of $N_\bot$ into $\mathcal{P}_i$.

For $f \in [\mathcal{P}_i^k \to D]$, D as in the proposition, define the restriction $res(f) \in [N_\bot^k \to D]$ by:

$$res(f)(\underline{v}) = f(in(\underline{v})).$$

Note that res is itself continuous, since in is and composition preserves continuity. Finally define $cc \in [\mathcal{F}_i \to \mathcal{F}_i]$ by:

$$cc(f) = ext(res(f)).$$

Note that cc(f) is bilinear for every f. It is the semantic counterpart to call-time choice; in effect to apply cc(f) to an argument, a 'set', f is first applied to the 'elements' of the argument and then all the possible results are 'unioned'. For this reason it will be convenient to write cc(f) as f^c. Note also that if f is bilinear then $f = f^c$.

The semantic counterpart to call-by-value can be defined in a similar fashion. For $f \in [N_\bot^k \to D]$, D a cpo let $st(f) \in [N_\bot^k \to D]_\bot$ be defined by

$st(f)(\underline{v}) = \perp$ if $v_i = \perp$ for any i, $1\leq i\leq k$
$= f(\underline{v})$ otherwise.

Note that st is itself continuous. If we identify elements of $[N^k_\perp \to D]_\perp$ with their injections into $[N^k_\perp \to D]$ we can now define $cv \in [\mathcal{F}_i \to \mathcal{F}_i]$ by

$cv(f) = ext(st(res(f)))$.

Note that if f is strict and bilinear then $cv(f) = f$. We will also denote $cv(f)$ by f^v.

We now introduce some notation. If f denotes a total function from N^k to N we use the same symbol f to denote its extension to $[N^k_\perp \to \mathcal{P}_{i\perp}]_\perp$, defined by:

$f(\underline{v}) = \perp$ if $v_j = \perp$ for any j, $1\leq j\leq k$
$= in(f(v))$ otherwise.

We will also identify $f \in [N^k_\perp \to \mathcal{P}_{i\perp}]$ with its injection into $[N^k_\perp \to \mathcal{P}_i]$ and $f \in [N^k_\perp \to \mathcal{P}_i]$ with its bilinear extension $ext(f) \in [\mathcal{P}_i^k \to \mathcal{P}_i]$. If $f, g_1, \ldots g_k \in \mathcal{F}_i$, let $f \circ \langle g_1, \ldots, g_k\rangle \in \mathcal{F}_i$ be defined by:

$f \circ \langle g_1,\ldots,g_k\rangle(x) = f(g_1(x),\ldots,g_k(x))$.

For the sake of uniformity in the definitions below we also let f^r denote f.

We are now ready to define the semantic mappings $\mathcal{V}_i$, i=1,3.

Let ENV_i, the i-environments, be the set of mappings, e, which associates with every $F_j \in F$ an element of $\mathcal{F}_i$, $e(F_j)$. It will be convenient to let the vector $\underline{f}$ represent the environment given by $e(F_j) = f_j$. Then define

$\mathcal{J}_i$: Terms $\to ENV_i \to \mathcal{F}_i$, i=1,3

by structural induction:

i) $\mathcal{J}_i[\![X_j]\!](e) = \lambda\underline{x}.x_j$

ii) $\mathcal{J}_i[\![T \text{ OR } T']\!] = \mathcal{J}_i[\![T]\!] \cup \mathcal{J}_i[\![T']\!]$

iii) $\mathcal{J}_i[\![F_j^m(\underline{T})]\!](e) = e(F_j)^m \circ \langle \mathcal{J}_i[\![T_1]\!](e),\ldots, \mathcal{J}_i[\![T_k]\!](e)\rangle$

iv) $\mathcal{J}_i[\![TB]\!](e) = (\mathcal{J}_i[\![T]\!](e))^c \circ \langle \mathcal{J}_i[\![T_1]\!](e),\ldots, \mathcal{J}_i[\![T_k]\!](e)\rangle$
where $B(i) = T_i, 1\leq i\leq k$.

v) $\mathcal{J}_i[\![SUCC(T)]\!](e) = \lambda\underline{x}.succ(\mathcal{J}_i[\![T]\!](e)(\underline{x}))$
where succ: $N \to N$ is given by $n \to n+1$

vi) $\mathcal{J}_i[\![PRED(T)]\!](e) = \lambda\underline{x}.pred(\mathcal{J}_i[\![T]\!](e)(\underline{x}))$
where pred: $N \to N$ is given by $n+1 \to n$, $0 \to 0$

vii) $\mathcal{J}_i[\![ZERO(T)]\!](e) = \lambda\underline{x}.zero(\mathcal{J}_i[\![T]\!](e)(\underline{x}))$
where zero: $N \to N$ is given by $0 \to 0$, $n+1 \to 1$

viii) $\mathcal{J}_i[\![IF(T_1,T_2,T_3)]\!](e) = \lambda\underline{x}.if(\mathcal{J}_i[\![T_1]\!](e)(\underline{x}), \mathcal{J}_i[\![T_2]\!](e)(\underline{x}), \mathcal{J}_i[\![T_3]\!](e)(\underline{x}))$

where $if \in [N^3_\perp \to \mathcal{P}_i]$ is given by
$if(0,v,v') = v$, $if(k+1,v,v') = v'$, $if(\perp,v,v') = \perp$

Next define $\mathcal{D}_i$: Declarations $\to ENV_i$, i=1,3, by

$\mathcal{D}_i[\![D]\!](F_j) = Y_j(\underline{f}.\langle \mathcal{J}_i(T_1)(\underline{f}),\ldots \mathcal{J}_i(T_n)(\underline{f})\rangle)$

where D represents the declaration

$F_1(\underline{X}) \Leftarrow T_1$

$\vdots$

$F_n(\underline{X}) \Leftarrow T_n$

and Y_j denotes the j-th component of the least fixpoint. Note that this least fixpoint exists since the functional is continuous.

Finally define $\mathcal{V}_i$: Programs -> $\mathcal{F}_i$ by

$$\mathcal{V}_i[\![\langle F_1^m(\underline{X}),D\rangle]\!] = \mathcal{J}_i[\![F_1^m(\underline{X})]\!](\mathcal{D}_i[\![D]\!])$$

Theorem 2.2.2 $\mathcal{V}_i[\![Pr]\!] < \mathcal{V}_i[\![Pr']\!]$ if and only if $Pr <_i Pr'$, i=1,3. □

It was pointed out in [6] that in order to model run-time choice properly it is necessary to use the domains $[\mathcal{P}_i^k \to \mathcal{P}_i]$, as opposed to the simpler domains $[N_\bot^k \to \mathcal{P}_i]$.

However if Pr is in CVPrograms (CCPrograms) then $\mathcal{V}_i[\![Pr]\!]$ is in $[N_\bot^k \to \mathcal{P}_i]$ $([N_\bot^k \to \mathcal{P}_i]_\bot)$, considered as a subcpo of $\mathcal{F}_i$, and these restricted models as fully-abstract for the corresponding sublanguages.

§3. Definability

Theorem 2.2.2 shows that the domains $\mathcal{F}_i$ model the operational behaviour of the programs in a satisfactory manner. In this section we turn the question around. How good is the language L for defining elements of $\mathcal{F}_i$?

It is quite obvious that all elements of $\mathcal{F}_i$ are not definable since $\mathcal{F}_i$ is not denumerable. A more reasonable question to ask is whether or not all computable elements are definable, for some suitable notion of computable. We borrow the definition from [13] where an element of a domain is said to be computable if it is the least upper bound of a recursively enumerable set of finite elements.

Let CC_i, CV_i denote $[N_\bot^k \to \mathcal{P}_i]$, $[N_\bot^k \to \mathcal{P}_i]_\bot$, respectively. Then there are nine domains in all.

Definition 3.1.1: a) An algebraic cpo D is computable if there exists a recursive enumeration, fin_D, of its finite elements.

b) If D is a computable cpo then $d \in D$ is computable if $\{n \mid fin_D(n) \sqsubseteq d\}$ is recursively enumerable. □

Each of the nine domains are algebraic and consistently complete. Therefore we may use the method of [13] to recursively enumerate their finite elements. Due to lack of space we do not go through this process.

It turns out that even in the simple case of $CV\mathcal{F}_i$ there are computable functions which are not definable by programs from CVPrograms

Example: For every $n,k \geq 0$ let $t(n,k)$ be the step-function in $CV\mathcal{F}_2$ defined by:

$t(n,k) = n \Rightarrow \{0,1\}$, if the nth Turing machine with blank input has not halted in k steps

$= n \Rightarrow \{1\}$, otherwise.

We leave it to the reader to show that f = VS exists and is computable. Then $0 \in f(n)$ if and only if the nth Turing machine diverges with blank input. So the relation $0 \in f(x)$ is not re. If f were definable by Pr say, then it would be re since $0 \in f(n)$ if and only if $F_1^v(K_n) \rightarrow^* K_0$. □

The problem arises because the partial order in the Smyth Powerdomain is incompatible with the natural partial order generated by the computations: roughly speaking this relates the partial results of a computation to the new partial results obtained by extending the computation a little further. This computation relation is reflected exactly in the Egli-Milner Powerdomain.

In order to characterise the definable elements of $CV\mathfrak{F}_2$ we define the following functions:

$e_i : \mathcal{P}_3 \rightarrow \mathcal{P}_i$, i = 1,2 or 3 are defined by

a) $e_3(X) = X$

b) $e_2(X) = N_\perp$ if $\perp \in X$

$= X$ otherwise

c) $e_1(X) = X - \{\perp\}$

These mappings are surjective and they enable us to introduce a stricter order on $\mathcal{P}_i$ which reflects the computational order in $\mathcal{P}_3$. For $X,Y \in \mathcal{P}_i$ let

$X \sqsubseteq c\; Y$ if i) $X \sqsubseteq Y$ in $\mathcal{P}_i$

ii) $\exists X',Y' \in \mathcal{P}_3$ such that $X = e(X')$, $Y = e(Y')$ and $X' \sqsubseteq Y'$.

Then $\langle \mathcal{P}_i, \sqsubseteq c \rangle$ is a cpo which we denote by $e\mathcal{P}_i$.

Finally let $ECV\mathfrak{F}_i$, $ECC\mathfrak{F}_i$, $E\mathfrak{F}_i$ denote $[N_\perp^k \rightarrow e\mathcal{P}_i]_\perp$, $[N_\perp^k \rightarrow e\mathcal{P}_i]$, and $[\mathcal{P}_i^k \rightarrow e\mathcal{P}_i^k]$ respectively.

Now for i=1 or 3 $e\mathcal{P}_i$ is isomorphic to $\mathcal{P}_i$ and therefore $ECV\mathfrak{F}_i$, $ECC\mathfrak{F}_i$, $E\mathfrak{F}_i$ are isomorphic to $CV\mathfrak{F}_i$, $CC\mathfrak{F}_i$ and $\mathfrak{F}_i$ respectively. However $e\mathcal{P}_2$ is simply a flat domain obtained from the set of finite subsets of N. So $ECV\mathfrak{F}_2$ is a strict sub-cpo of $CV\mathfrak{F}_2$ and there are many functions which are computable in $CV\mathfrak{F}_2$ and not computable in $ECV\mathfrak{F}_2$.

<u>Theorem 3.1.2</u> For i = 1,2 or 3, f is computable in ECV_i if and only if there is a program Pr ∈ <u>CVPrograms</u> such that $\vartheta_i[[Pr]] = f$. □

In the case of $ECC\mathfrak{F}_i$ there are functions which are computable but not definable. A typical example is the parallel operator

$par(v_1,v_2) = \{0\}$ if $v_1 = 0$ or $v_2 = 0$

$= \{1\}$ if $v_1 = n+1$ and $v_2 = m+1$

$= \{\perp\}$ otherwise.

If we let $\underline{\text{CCPrograms}}_{PAR}$ be the set of $\underline{\text{CCPrograms}}$ definable in L augmented by a syntactic counterpart to par then we obtain

Theorem 3.1.3 For i = 1,2, or 3, f is computable in ECC_i if and only if there is a program $Pr \in \underline{\text{CCPrograms}}_{PAR}$ such that $\mathcal{V}_i[[Pr]] = f$. □

Instead of augmenting the language we might try to restict the domain $ECC\mathfrak{F}_i$. One obvious approach is to extend the notion of sequential, as used in [16]. Such an extension is given in [10]. Unfortunately there will still be computable sequential functions which are not definable in CCPrograms. One such function is given in [15], page 238.

The domains $E\mathfrak{F}_i$ will also contain computable functions which are not definable. If we let $x \subseteq y$ whenever $x \cup y = y$ then all definable functions preserve $\subseteq$ whereas it is easy to find functions in $E\mathfrak{F}_i$ which do not. Let $ME\mathfrak{F}_i$ be the cpo of $\subseteq$ preserving elements from $E\mathfrak{F}_i$. Then

Theorem 3.1.4 For i = 1,2,3, f is computable in $ME\mathfrak{F}_i$ if and only if there is a program $Pr \in \underline{\text{Programs}}_{PAR}$ such that $\mathcal{V}_i[[Pr]] = f$. □

Due to lack of space we have omitted all indication of proofs. These will appear in the final version of the paper together with a more detailed exposition of §3.

Acknowledgements

The research reported here was carried out with the financial support of the SERC. The author would like to thank G. Plotkin for helpful disaussions and E. Kerse for typing the manuscript.

References

[1] Astesiano, E., Costa, G., Sharing in Nondeterminism, 6th Int. Coll. on Algorithms, Languages and Programming, LNCS, 71, 1979.

[2] Berry, G. and Curien, P.L., Sequential Algorithms on Concrete Data Types, November 1979.

[3] Boudol, G., Semantique Operationelle et Algebrique des Programmes Recursifs Non-deterministes, These de Doctorat D'etat, Universite de Paris VII, 1980.

[4] Dijkstra, E.W., A Discipline of Programming, Prentice-Hall, Englewood Cliffs, 1976.

[5] Floyd, R.W., Nondeterministic Algorithms, JACM, 14, pp. 636-644, 1967.

[6] Hennessy, M.C.B., The Semantics of Call-by-Value and Call-by-Name in a a Nondeterministic Environment, SIAM J. Computing, Vol. 9, No. 1, 1980.

[7] Hennessy, M.C.B. and Plotkin, G., Full Abstraction for a Simple Programming Language, LNCS,74, 1979.

[8] Nivat, M., Nondeterministic Programs: An Algebraic Overview. In: S.H. Lavington (ed.) Proc. of IFIP Congress 1980, North Holland, 1980.

[9] McCarthy, J., A Basis for a Theory of Computation. In: B. Braffort and D. Hirschberg (eds.) Computer Programming and Formal Systems, North Holland, p. 33-70, 1963.

[10] Päppinghaus, P. and Wirsing, M., Nondeterministic Partial Logic: Isotonic and Guarded Truth-Functions, University of Edinburgh, 1980.

[11] Plotkin, G., A Powerdomain Construction, SIAM J. on Computing, 5, pp. 452-486, 1976.

[12] Plotkin, G., Dijkstra's Predicate Transformers and Smyth's Power Domains In: LNCS, 86, pp. 527-553, 1979.

[13] Plotkin, G., LCF considered as a programming language, Theoretical Computer Science, Vol. 5, pp. 223-255, 1977.

[14] Smyth, M.B., Powerdomains, JCSS, Vol. 16, pp. 23-26, 1978.

[15] Trakhtenbrot, M., Relationships between classes of Monotonic Functions, Theoretical Computer Science, Vol. 2, pp. 225-247, 1976.

[16] Vuillemin, J., Correct and Optimal Implementation of Recursion in a Simple Programming Language, JCSS, Vol. 9, No. 3, pp. 332-354, June 1974.

[17] Winskel, G., Events in Computation, Ph.D. thesis. University of Edinburgh, 1980.

[18] Astesiano, E., Costa, G., Nondeterminism and Fully Abstract Models, 1979.

[19] Scott, D., Outline of a Mathematical Theory of Computation, Oxford Monograph PRG-2, Oxford University Press, 1970.

[20] Naur, P., (ed.) Revised Report on the Algorithmic Language ALGOL 60, CACM, Vol. 6, 1963.

[21] Stoy, J., Denotational Semantics: The Scot-Strachey Approach to Programing Language Theory, MIT Press, 1977.

[22] Gordon, M., The Denotational Description of Programming Languages, Springer-Verlag, 1979.

[23] Courcelle, B., and Nivat, M., Algebraic families of interpretations. IRIA Rapport de Recherche 189, 1976.

Optimizing for a Multiprocessor: Balancing Synchronization Costs against Parallelism in Straight-line Code

Peter G. Hibbard and Thomas L. Rodeheffer

Abstract

This paper reports on the status of a research project to develop compiler techniques to optimize programs for execution on an asynchronous multiprocessor. We adopt a simplified model of a multiprocessor, consisting of several identical processors, all sharing access to a common memory. Synchronization must be done explicitly, using two special operations that take a period of time comparable to the cost of data operations. Our treatment differs from other attempts to generate code for such machines because we treat the necessary synchronization overhead as an integral part of the cost of a parallel code sequence. We are particularly interested in heuristics that can be used to generate good code sequences, and local optimizations that can then be applied to improve them. Our current efforts are concentrated on generating straight-line code for high-level, algebraic languages.

We compare the code generated by two heuristics, and observe how local optimization schemes can gradually improve its quality. We are implementing our techniques in an experimental compiler that will generate code for Cm*, a real multiprocessor, having several characteristics of our model computer.

This research is sponsored by the Defense Advanced Research Projects Agency (DOD), ARPA Order No. 3597, monitored by the Air Force Avionics Laboratory Under Contract F33615-78-C-1551.

The views and conclusions contained in this document are those of the authors and should not be interpreted as representing the official policies, either expressed or implied, of the Defense Advanced Research Projects Agency or the US Government.

1 Introduction

This paper reports on the status of a research project to develop compiler methods to optimize programs for execution on an asynchronous multiprocessor. In this paper, we present one part of this research, a method for transforming sequential, straight-line source code into parallel object code. This transformation is not a trivial task, because the cost of explicit interprocessor synchronization (which is required to guarantee a desired time order between operations on separate processors) must be balanced against any increase in speed gained by parallelism. Previous work has generally not considered synchronization costs.

1.1 Motivation

Although a multiprocessor has the ability to perform several independent operations at the same time, this advantage has been difficult to exploit. Programming a multiprocessor using parallelism is a difficult task and current optimizing compilers, designed for use on uniprocessors, do not provide much help. An optimizing compiler for a multiprocessor should be able to detect and exploit parallelism in a program automatically. The problem is how this is to be accomplished. We consider this problem restricted to optimizing programs written in an ordinary sequential language.

Because a sequential program contains no explicit parallelism, the compiler must exploit implicit parallelism. We feel that this is easier than analyzing programs containing explicitly specified parallelism. Such programs can have quite a convoluted structure. For example, semaphores can be used to simulate **goto** instructions. Moreover, a compiler for a parallel language would still want to search for implicit parallelism, because a programmer will certainly not specify all of the parallelism, down to the lowest level of expression evaluation. The mass of detail involved would make this task infeasible. The methods we develop depend only upon the construction of an acyclic operation dependency graph. Although we specifically consider the case of an ordinary sequential language, our methods would also apply to straight-line sections of programs written in a data-flow language.

An asynchronous multiprocessor is an interesting target architecture because it requires interprocessor synchronization to be performed explicitly if a chronological order is to be guaranteed between the execution of two operations on separate processors. A viable method for optimizing programs for a multiprocessor could be the first step on the path towards a treatment of less tightly-coupled parallel architectures, such as network systems, which have data communication as well as synchronization costs.

1.2 Related work

The problem of detecting latent parallelism in a program and exploiting it on a suitable architecture has been considered before. Gonzalez and Ramamoorthy [7] investigated the effect of task scheduling overheads in a multiprocessor's execution of an acyclic task dependency graph. By simulating the execution of dependency graphs of actual programs, they concluded that for best results the scheduling cost should be no more than one-fifth the cost of executing a task. In their model of execution, every task has a counter that holds the number of tasks that are not yet complete but must be finished before the task can start. When a task completes it decrements the counters of all of its dependent tasks. Tasks whose counters become zero are runnable, and a processor is dynamically assigned to execute the task.

Although their work resembles ours superficially, we are more interested in methods for reducing the inefficiencies caused by scheduling overheads. This can be done by binding more information at compilation time. Dynamic allocation of processors is a good approach if little is known about execution costs or about the instantaneous availability of processors. Given an estimation of execution costs and assuming that processors are available, however, the compiler can arrange a static allocation, with each processor executing a specific sequence of operations. Any dependencies that lie along the path of a given processor are guaranteed, without incurring any overhead: overhead is incurred only when synchronizing between processors. Arranging sequences of operations so that parallelism is exploited without incurring excessive synchronization overheads is for us the main topic of interest.

For the case of synchronous multiprocessors and array machines, Banerjee *et al.* [2] presented a methodology for analyzing and transforming loops that is based upon identifying the data dependencies between successive iterations of the loop as a type of recurrence. They developed transformations that can be applied in certain circumstances to improve the form of the recurrence: for example, interchanging the index variables in a doubly-nested loop. Although these transformations were designed with a synchronous parallel architecture in mind, they are still valid in the context of an asynchronous multiprocessor, provided that the cost of any necessary synchronization is considered when deciding whether a transformation would be beneficial.

Allan and Oldehoeft [1] considered the problem of transforming programs written in a sequential language into a language for a data-flow machine. Their treatment of loops is similar to that of Banerjee *et al.* Because a data-flow machine solves all of the problems of operator scheduling and synchronization in the hardware, these costs are not considered at the object code level.

2 Model of the Target Machine

In order to concentrate on the aspect of interprocessor synchronization, we adopt the following simplified model of a multiprocessor. A multiprocessor consists of several identical processors sharing access to a common memory. We assume that the processors can access the memory without imposing delays on each other. Each processor is independent, executing a sequence of operations that manipulates data and determines the control path. Interprocessor synchronization is provided by two special operations called **signal** and **wait**.

All operations take their arguments from the common memory and return any result back into it. The same location can be read by several processors at the same time, but simultaneous writes or a combination of reads and writes are not legal. The synchronization operations take a boolean semaphore as their argument: **signal** sets the semaphore to 1 and **wait** delays until the semaphore is 1, then sets it to 0 and continues.

In an asynchronous multiprocessor the individual processors need not proceed at exactly the same rate; however, we assume that each type of operation has an expected execution time that is the same for all processors. We call this the *cost* of the operation. For a **signal** operation, we assume that the cost is incurred in changing the semaphore value: the change takes effect at the completion of the operation. For a **wait** operation, some delay may occur waiting for the semaphore to be set, and then the execution cost is incurred in examining it and resetting it back to 0 This model of execution cost is used to evaluate the effects of different transformations on the object code.

The compiler can use the expected execution times only as a measure for approximating the execution behavior of the program; it cannot rely upon them to guarantee the relative execution order of operations on different processors. Signals must be used to ensure any particular desired order. Our object code programs will be correct even if the expected value of the operation costs is wrong, although of course performance will suffer.

This simple model of a multiprocessor contains no recognition of different memory classes. For example, in any real multiprocessor each individual processor will have some local memory, such as processor registers, which is much faster to operate upon than the common memory Although the problem does not yet arise in the treatment of straight-line code, handling parallel calls to a function subprogram will require some sort of local memory to hold an environment pointer. In this paper, however, we do not consider the problem of different classes of memory.

3 Methodology

The implicit parallelism that we extract from the program arises from the independent evaluation of operands in the flow of data values from definition to use. Our approach is to map a data-flow representation of the program onto the individual processors of a multiprocessor. Explicit interprocessor synchronization commands are inserted where necessary to guarantee the correct order of evaluation. This approach produces a parallel program whose computation does not depend upon the relative speeds of the individual processors. There are other methods of using parallelism to get an execution speedup, for example the chaotic relaxation algorithms of Baudet [3]. · We do not attempt to generate such parallel programs.

Our goal is to compile individual basic blocks—straight-line code sequences having a single entry and exit—into parallel code to be executed on a multiprocessor. The parallel code consists of a sequence of operations for each of *p* processors, where *p* is to be determined by the compiler as the greatest number of processors that can be used to advantage.

First we present two illustrations of arrangements of parallel code given an operation dependency graph. We indicate how to produce the dependency graph from the original source code. We then show how an exhaustive search could find the optimal arrangement. Finally we develop a heuristic method for generating and optimizing "good" arrangements.

3.1 Illustrations of parallel code

The difficulty in arranging an optimal assignment of operations to processors lies in the cost of interprocessor synchronization. If processor *a* must signal processor *b* to indicate that a result is available, then the subsequent operations of processor *a* are delayed by the time it takes to send the signal. However, if all of the immediately dependent operations are subsequently to be executed just by processor *a*, no interprocessor synchronization is needed and the signalling time is saved. Figure 1 shows a sample dependency graph for a segment of straight-line code and a possible arrangement for two processors, given that ordinary operations and **signal** and **wait** operations all cost one unit each. In this example, the dependency from node 10 to node 16 does not need a separate signal because it is guaranteed by the synchronization from node 3 to node 12.

r:= a * b
s:= r / (c + d)
t:= e /f
u:= (r + g) * (s + t)
v:= u * ((t + h) / i + j)
w:= (k + l) * (m + n)
x:= (w + u * u) / o + v

Sample straight-line code

Operation dependency graph

**Possible arrangement
for two processors**
total time = 14 units

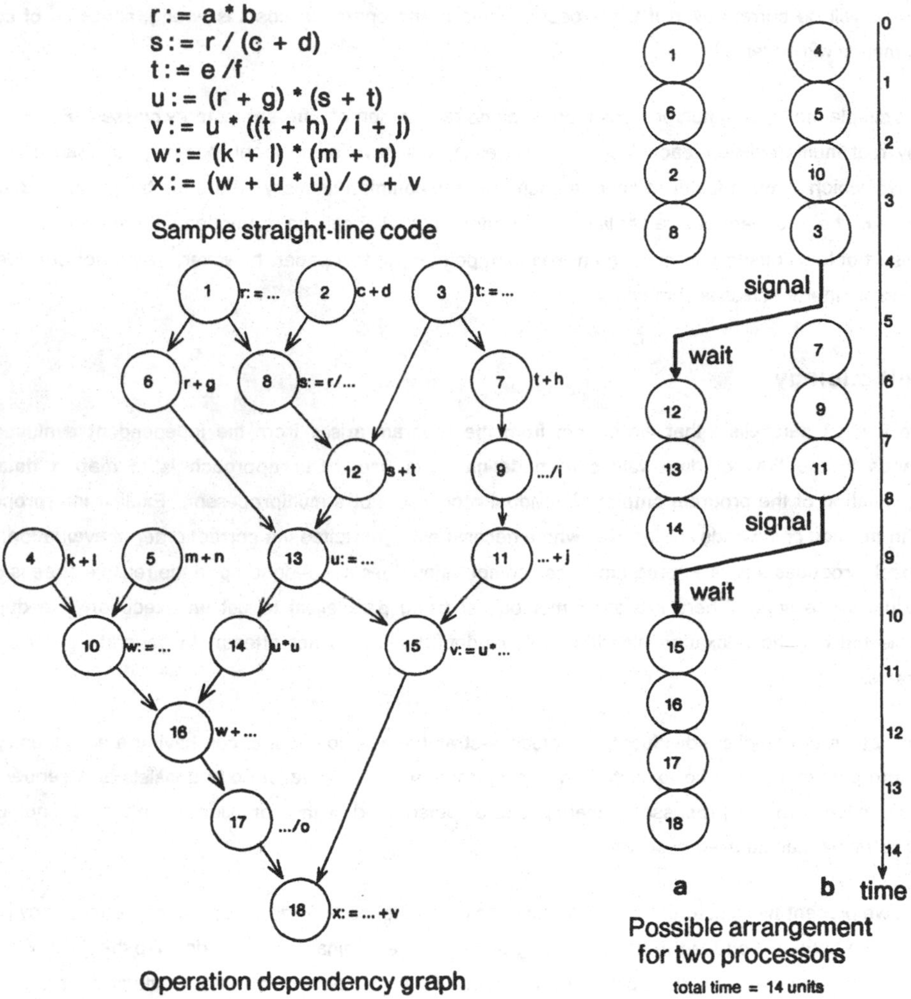

All ordinary operations cost one unit, **signal** and **wait** operations also cost one unit each.

Figure 1: Sample straight-line code, its operation dependency graph,
and a possible arrangement for two processors

Another feature of interest in figure 1 is the idle time in processor *a* after executing operation 8. Processor *a* cannot continue to operation 12 until it receives the signal from processor *b* indicating that operation 3 has been completed. In the sequence of operations performed by processor *b*, operation 3 could be executed earlier by promoting it over any of the operations 10, 5, and 4 (the dependency from 10 to 16 would still be guaranteed by the signal from 11 to 15), but no net gain would result because there would then be idle time after operation 14.

Using more processors in an arrangement does not always result in a shorter execution time. There may be too much interdependence between operations, requiring an excessive number of synchronization operations. For example, figure 2 shows a sample dependency graph in which using two processors is more expensive than using one.

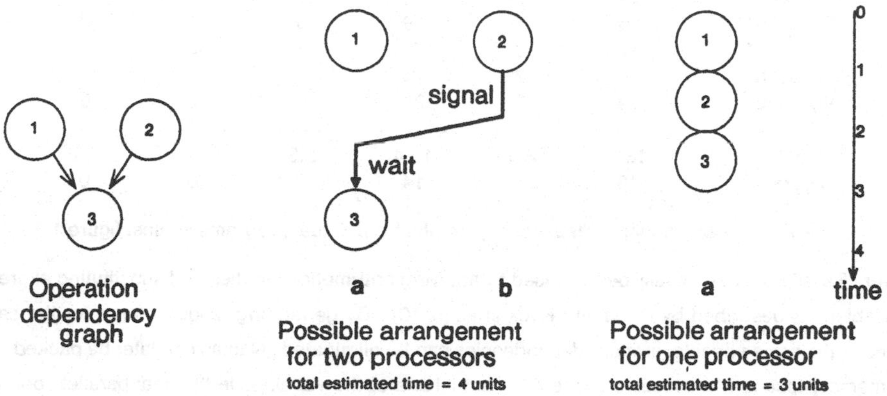

All ordinary operations cost one unit, **signal** and **wait** operations also cost one unit each.

Figure 2: Synchronization costs can cause two processors to take longer than one

An examination of programs appearing in *Communications of the ACM* shows that the dependency graph displayed in figure 1 is not exceptionally complicated. Fifteen different basic blocks from inner loops of the programs were translated by hand into data-flow graphs. These graphs were then examined to determine the number of immediate successors for each node. An operation that produces a value not used later in the basic block would have no successor nodes, for example. The results are presented in table 1.

3.2 Generating operation dependency graphs

The operation dependency graph shows the minimum sequencing constraint on the set of operations. For two adjacent operations, a sequencing constraint results from the use of memory locations. If memory locations are written into by either operation then the operations interfere with each other and must be executed in the sequential order specified originally in the program [4]. This interference can take either the form of a data dependency, in which the later operation uses a result computed by the earlier operation; or it can result from the two operations using the same memory location for two different purposes. The operation dependency graph is easily computed by employing the usual methods of data-flow analysis [8].

This initial dependency graph may not fully represent all of the parallelism implicit in the basic block,

graph	total nodes	nodes with 0 succ.	nodes with 1 succ.	nodes with 2 succ.	nodes with 3 succ.	nodes with 4 succ.
alg418bb1	30	8	14	7	1	0
alg418bb2	13	3	8	2	0	0
alg418bb3	8	3	4	0	1	0
alg418bb4	30	3	27	0	0	0
alg418bb5	14	4	8	1	0	1
alg487bb1	15	5	10	0	0	0
alg405bb1	13	1	10	2	0	0
alg405bb2	11	1	8	2	0	0
alg406bb1	18	2	13	3	0	0
alg406bb2	17	2	14	1	0	0
alg406bb3	14	3	7	3	1	0
alg407bb1	26	6	19	0	1	0
alg409bb1	12	2	7	3	0	0
alg409bb2	20	2	14	4	0	0
alg413bb1	39	6	25	6	2	0
average	18.7	3.4	12.4	2.3	0.4	0.1
figure 1	18	1	14	3	0	0

Table 1: Comparison of dependency graphs from actual programs against figure 1

however. Parallelism can usually be increased by applying arithmetic identities and substituting expressions for variables, as described by Brent and Kuck *et al.* [5, 10]. By generating unique names for the separate lifetimes of the same variable, artificial dependencies can be eliminated. Names can later be packed into the same memory location to conserve space if the actual use of the variables in the final parallel code can be proven not to overlap.

3.3 Exhaustive search for the optimal arrangement

A direct approach to finding the optimal arrangement involves an exhaustive search through all of the possibilities. This could be done as follows. Let g be the number of nodes in the graph. For a given number of processors p, consider all (unordered) assignments of operations to processors. There are p^g such assignments. For each assignment, the operations assigned to any particular processor have dependencies that must be observed. Any total ordering of the operations on a processor is legitimate provided that it completes the required partial order for the sub-graph of operations on that processor. All orderings for each assignment must be evaluated and the one with the least execution time retained. The number of total orders of a graph of g nodes can never exceed $g!$: this value is attained when all operations are independent. In the degenerate case of a completely linear graph, there is only one total order.

The number of possible total orders of a graph increases astronomically as the number of nodes increases. In table 2 we give the number of total orders of a few of the smaller of our test graphs. Although the search could be speeded up somewhat by pruning (rejecting a complete branch of the search if the cost of what is partially specified already exceeds the current best known), an exhaustive search is not feasible for graphs of any significant number of nodes. We propose instead a heuristic method.

graph	nodes	total orders
....	....	....
alg418bb3	8	48
alg405bb2	11	165
alg409bb1	12	31042
alg405bb1	13	1086
alg418bb2	13	10296
alg406bb3	14	49548
alg418bb5	14	66906
alg487bb1	15	>4592001

Table 2: Number of total orderings of various dependency graphs

3.4 Heuristic method for a good arrangement

Currently, we do not know how to determine *a priori* the number of processors for which the best final arrangement is produced, so we are looking at schemes for the initial allocation that operate with a given number of processors. If the cost of interprocessor synchronization is zero, then it is easy to produce an arrangement of nodes on processors that takes the maximum advantage of the parallelism in the graph. Call the number of processors needed for this arrangement *d*. Our experiments with a non-zero cost of synchronization show that usually the best arrangements also use *d* processors. Often, however, arrangements using fewer than *d* processors were just as good, and in two cases an arrangement using more than *d* processors was better. So far we have only experimented with one particular value for the cost of synchronization. The results are presented in more detail in section 4.

Our approach for obtaining a good arrangement is first to construct an initial arrangement and then to improve it through local transformations. We divide the construction of the initial arrangement into two stages: first the allocation of nodes to processors and then the placement of synchronization operations.

3.5 Initial allocation

We have studied two algorithms for the initial allocation of nodes to processors. Both of these algorithms are "greedy" algorithms that begin with all nodes unassigned and proceed by repeatedly selecting a best assignment of node to processor, until eventually no unassigned nodes are left. The nodes that are assigned to a particular processor form, in the order of assignment, the sequence of nodes that that processor is to execute. First some definitions:

If n is a node in the data-flow graph, let

cost(n) be the estimated execution cost associated with n,
prev(n) be the set of required predecessor nodes of n, and
next(n) be the set of required successor nodes of n.

An undirected path from n to m is a sequence of nodes $(n_0, n_1, \ldots n_k)$ such that $n_0 = n$, $n_k = m$, and for $1 \leq i \leq k$, either $prev(n_{i-1}) = .n_i$ or $next(n_{i-1}) = n_i$.

The weight of a path $(n_0, n_1, \ldots n_k)$ is the sum $cost(n_1) + \ldots + cost(n_{k-1})$. Note that this does not include the cost of the end nodes.

The distance between two nodes, *dist*(n,m), is the minimum weight of any undirected path from n to m.

The distance between two sets of nodes, *dist*(*N*,*M*), is the minimum over all distances *dist*(*n*,*m*), where $n \in N$ and $m \in M$. If either *N* or *M* is empty, then the distance is infinite.

The weight of a sequence, *weight*(*s*), is the sum of *cost*(*n*) for all nodes $n \in s$.

Now we can describe the outline of the allocation algorithms in more detail. The basic greedy algorithm for *p* processors, producing the sequences s_1 through s_p, proceeds as follows:

1. Initially, all sequences are empty. Let *U* be the set of unassigned nodes, initially the entire graph. While *U* is non-empty, repeat the following steps.

2. Let *E* be the set of all nodes $n \in U$ such that the intersection of *prev*(*n*) and *U* is empty. This is the set of nodes that are eligible to be selected next. Initially, this will be the set of nodes that have no predecessors.

3. A processor and an eligible node are selected; the node is assigned to the processor. Our two allocation algorithms differ in the heuristics used to determine this assignment.

Each repetition performs one assignment of a node to a processor. Because the dependency graph is acyclic, every node must eventually be assigned to some processor, whereupon the algorithm will finish.

Next we present the details of our two different allocation algorithms. The first algorithm (graph-distance algorithm) was designed to divide the data-flow graph into parallel sections that do not interact heavily. However, the algorithm takes no explicit account of the cost of interprocessor synchronization, and it was found to perform poorly. The second, simpler, algorithm (early-scheduling algorithm) makes explicit allowance for necessary synchronization costs when it produces its allocation. The performance of these two algorithms is compared in section 4.1.

3.5.1 Graph-distance algorithm

Given the set of eligible nodes *E*, and the existing sequences s_1 through s_p, the graph-distance algorithm determines the assignment of an eligible node to a processor as follows:

1. Choose the sequence with the least weight. Call it s_i. This is the sequence to which a node will be added.

2. Let *S* be the set consisting of the nodes in s_i, and let *S'* be the set consisting of the union of all of the nodes in s_k, for $1 \leq k \leq p$ and $k \neq i$.

3. Let A_1 be the set of all nodes $n \in E$ such that *dist*({*n*},*S*) is the minimum. The intent of this selection is to choose a node close to the nodes already in the sequence.

4. Let A_2 be the set of all nodes $n \in A_1$ such that *dist*({*n*},*S'*) is the maximum. The intent of this selection is to choose a node far away from the nodes being computed by the other sequences.

5. A node is chosen randomly from A_2 and assigned to s_i.

The most complicated part of the algorithm lies in steps 3 and 4, in the computation of *dist*({*n*},*T*) for a set *T* and each of the nodes *n* in some set. This computation can be performed for all nodes *n* simultaneously, with a minimum-path-weight-first traversal of the graph starting from *T*. If *g* is the number of nodes in the graph, this traversal cannot take more time than order of g^2. Since such a traversal is required twice per node selection, the running time of this heuristic method for assigning operations to processors is no more than order of g^3.

3.5.2 Early-scheduling algorithm

Given the set of eligible nodes E, and the existing sequences s_1 through s_p, the early-scheduling algorithm determines the assignment of an eligible node to a processor as follows:

1. For each node $n \epsilon E$ and each processor i, $1 \leq i \leq p$, compute an estimate of what the node's earliest finishing time could be if it were allocated to that processor. This is done as follows:

   a. Node n cannot start until the last node in s_i finishes. (If s_i is empty, then n could start at time 0.)

   b. Furthermore, for each $m \epsilon prev(n)$, if $m \epsilon s_i$, then no explicit synchronization is needed to guarantee the dependency. Otherwise, there will have to be an interprocessor synchronization to ensure that m is finished before n starts. In this case n will not be able to start until the time needed for a **signal** and a **wait** operation has elapsed after m finishes. The time needed to perform the **signal** and **wait** operations is treated here as a constraint: the interprocessor synchronization will have to be accomplished in some manner. However, the synchronization operations themselves are not actually inserted anywhere nor assigned to any processor.

   c. Adding *cost*(n) to its earliest starting time yields the earliest time at which n could finish.

2. From all of the possible assignments of eligible nodes to processors, we retain the set A of those that are estimated to have the earliest possible finishing time.

3. One assignment is selected at random from the set A.

3.6 Inserting synchronization operations

As it turns out, inserting synchronization operations into an existing allocation is itself a difficult task to do well. For example, a dependency from an early node on one processor to a late node on another may be redundant if there is also an intermediate dependency. There is no need to add an extra synchronization operation for a redundant dependency because the intermediate dependency will guarantee the order.

Our method for inserting synchronization operations into the initial allocation ignores redundant dependencies. The method operates by first constructing the minimum set of essential dependencies and then inserting explicit synchronization operations for each of them.

For all nodes n in the graph the set of required predecessor nodes, *reqprev*(n), containing those nodes in *prev*(n) for which an explicit synchronization operation seems essential, is constructed as follows:

1. Initially, for all nodes n, *reqprev*(n) = *prev*(n). For each node n, the following steps are performed for each $m \epsilon prev(n)$.

2. Tentatively remove m from *reqprev*(n).

3. If some guaranteed path still exists from n back to m, then the dependency with m is non-essential and can be ignored. Otherwise, m must be placed back in *reqprev*(n). (A guaranteed path steps from a node t back to any node that either preceeds t on the same processor, or is an element of *reqprev*(t). A path consists of one or more such steps.)

The remaining collection of *reqprev(n)* for all nodes *n* in the graph forms a minimum set of essential dependencies: this set is usually unique. (The case of three or more processors all being totally synchronized with a massive exchange of signals is an exception, however.) Taking in a random order each essential dependency, we insert a **signal** operation immediately after the required predecessor and a corresponding **wait** operation immediately before the required successor. When all the necessary synchronization operations are inserted, the arrangement becomes a legal translation of the source code

3.7 Improvements to the initial arrangement

Here we present two transformations that could be used to improve the initial arrangement of synchronization operations. The first transformation consists of splicing two interprocessor synchronizations into one. Suppose two early **signal** operations, s_1 and s_2, on processor *a*, send signals to two late **wait** operations w_1 and w_2, on processor *b*. If s_2 is early enough and w_1 late enough, it may be beneficial to delete s_1 and w_2 and change s_2 to send its signal to w_1. See figure 3.

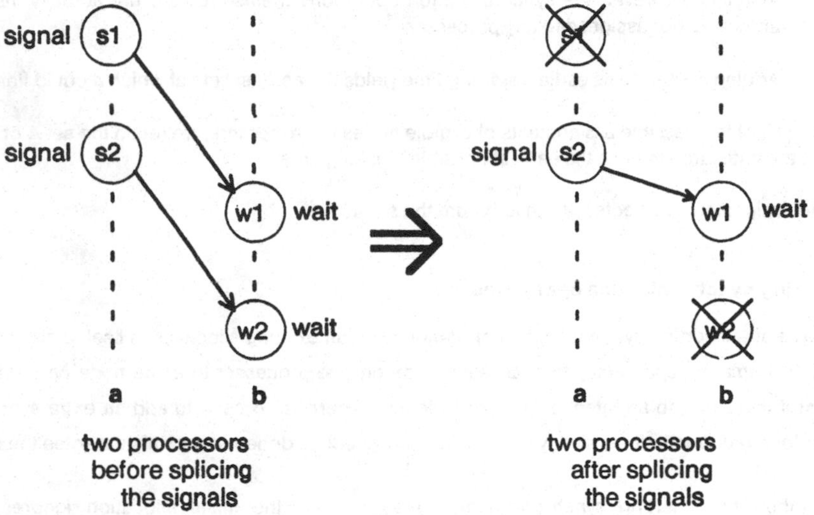

Figure 3: A transformation to improve the arrangement by splicing signal operations

The effect is to flatten the signalling arc so that it carries more information. An examination of several initial arrangements indicates that this transformation might be applicable fairly often.

The second transformation consists of "walking" a **signal** or **wait** operation around the arrangement until it hits an idle spot. Idle spots occur where a processor must wait for a signal to arrive. A **signal** operation can always be moved forward in an arrangement by stepping over the next operation on the same processor or even, if the next operation is itself a **signal**, stepping across the signal path to just after the **wait** operation on a different processor. Likewise, a **wait** operation can always be moved back. Depending on how flat the signalling arc is, there may be more or less freedom in where its actual endpoints need be. If the **signal** or **wait** operation can be moved into an idle spot, then the overhead of the operation is eliminated.

4 Experiments

In order to evaluate our heuristics for constructing an initial arrangement, we implemented them and ran them on our test graphs with a fixed cost assigned to all operations. Because the result of initial allocation is not a legal translation of the program until the necessary synchronization operations are inserted, the allocation heuristics cannot be evaluated in isolation. We are actually measuring the performance of the combination of a particular allocation heuristic with our heuristic for inserting synchronization operations To evaluate how well the insertion heuristic performs, we compare its results on a few allocations with the optimal synchronization pattern laboriously obtained by exhaustive search. The improvement obtained by the optimal synchronization search, although significant, is less than the difference in performance of the two allocation heuristics.

Each of our heuristics has a step in which one of a number of possible actions must be chosen at random because the heuristic provides no guide as to which choice would be better. If the same problem is run through the heuristic several times, a distribution of final arrangements is obtained. The best results in the distribution indicate how far the heuristic could be improved through the addition of further criteria to guide its selection of actions. The average result indicates how well the heuristic is performing in general.

4.1 Results of many trials

We applied our heuristics to each of the test graphs from table 1. In each graph the operation nodes were all assigned a cost of 10 and **signal** and **wait** nodes a cost of 5. Arrangements were constructed for each number of processors between two and seven. For some of the more interesting graphs we repeated the construction one hundred times for each number of processors; the rest we repeated only twenty times. The graph-distance allocation method was only applied to a few graphs when it became clear that it was not nearly as good as the early-scheduling method. The results are listed in tables 3 and 4.

These tables also contain the best execution time that could be obtained for each number of processors if there were no cost for synchronization. Values for a number of processors higher than the maximum degree of parallelism are omitted.

A better illustration of the comparison between the two allocation methods is given in figures 4 and 5. Here the distribution of final estimated execution times for one graph is shown for each number of processors from two to seven. The early-scheduling algorithm is clearly better.

4.2 Optimal synchronization patterns

For several allocations for one graph using two and three processors, we performed an exhaustive search and obtained the optimal synchronization pattern. The estimated execution time for the optimal pattern is compared with that obtained by our heuristic in table 5. In general it seems that our heuristic performs fairly well for two processors but not as well for three. We did not obtain any optimal patterns for four processors because of the amount of computer time required.

graph: figure 1, 100 trials

proc	w/o synch	early-scheduling min..max	early-scheduling avg	graph-distance min..max	graph-distance avg
1	180				
2	110	120..155	139	125..180	140
3	90	115..145	127	145..175	161
4	90	115..140	124	140..175	156
5	80	115..135	120	140..185	152
6	-	115..135	119		
7	-	115..130	120		

graph: alg406bb1, 20 trials

proc	w/o synch	early-scheduling min..max	early-scheduling avg
1	180		
2	120	125..155	138
3	-	125..125	125
4	-	125..125	125
5	-	125..125	125
6	-	125..125	125
7	-	125..125	125

graph: alg487bb1, 100 trials

proc	w/o synch	early-scheduling min..max	early-scheduling avg	graph-distance min..max	graph-distance avg
1	150				
2	80	85..120	103	120..140	135
3	70	75..110	89	95..125	103
4	70	70..100	82	85..115	95
5	60	65.. 95	79	90..130	103
6	50	65.. 95	74	80..120	97
7	-	65.. 85	70	80..110	95

graph: alg406bb3, 20 trials

proc	w/o synch	early-scheduling min..max	early-scheduling avg
1	140		
2	70	75..105	89
3	-	75.. 95	85
4	-	75.. 95	82
5	-	75.. 95	83
6	-	75.. 95	82
7	-	75.. 95	82

graph: alg406bb2, 100 trials

proc	w/o synch	early-scheduling min..max	early-scheduling avg	graph-distance min..max	graph-distance avg
1	170				
2	110	110..140	124	125..185	142
3	80	90..125	109		
4	70	90..120	102		
5	60	90..125	99		
6	-	85..125	98		
7	-	85..115	98		

graph: alg409bb1, 20 trials

proc	w/o synch	early-scheduling min..max	early-scheduling avg
1	120		
2	70	80.. 95	86
3	60	70.. 85	79
4	50	70.. 80	74
5	-	70.. 80	75
6	-	70.. 90	75
7	-	70.. 80	75

graph: alg407bb1, 20 trials

proc	w/o synch	early-scheduling min..max	early-scheduling avg
1	260		
2	150	150..185	165
3	110	110..150	123
4	90	105..135	116
5	-	105..120	109
6	-	105..125	110
7	-	105..115	108

graph: alg409bb2, 20 trials

proc	w/o synch	early-scheduling min..max	early-scheduling avg
1	200		
2	110	125..155	140
3	70	110..135	118
4	-	90..135	110
5	-	85..115	95
6	-	85..120	97
7	-	85.:105	92

w/o synch is the best expected execution time for zero synchronization cost.
For the heuristics, normal operations cost 10 units and **signal** and **wait** operations cost 5 units.

Table 3: Results of many arrangements for different graphs

graph: alg418bb1, 100 trials

proc	w/o synch	early-scheduling min..max	avg
1	300		
2	150	175..215	191
3	110	125..195	150
4	80	110..160	129
5	80	95..150	122
6	70	100..155	119
7	-	90..150	113

graph: alg418bb2, 20 trials

proc	w/o synch	early-scheduling min..max	avg
1	130		
2	80	80..100	91
3	70	80.. 90	83
4	-	80.. 85	83
5	-	80.. 90	84
6	-	80.. 90	84
7	-	80.. 90	84

graph: alg418bb3, 20 trials

proc	w/o synch	early-scheduling min..max	avg
1	80		
2	60	65.. 70	68
3	-	65.. 70	68
4	-	65.. 70	68
5	-	65.. 70	68
6	-	65.. 70	67
7	-	65.. 70	67

graph: alg418bb4, 20 trials

proc	w/o synch	early-scheduling min..max	avg
1	300		
2	180	165..190	171
3	120	120..120	120
4	-	120..120	120
5	-	120..120	120
6	-	120..120	120
7	-	120..120	120

graph: alg418bb5, 20 trials

proc	w/o synch	early-scheduling min..max	avg
1	140		
2	70	90..120	106
3	-	90..110	98
4	-	90..110	99
5	-	95..110	101
6	-	95..105	100
7	-	95..115	100

graph: alg405bb1, 100 trials

proc	w/o synch	early-scheduling min..max	avg
1	130		
2	80	90..115	93
3	70	85.. 90	86
4	-	85.. 90	88
5	-	85.. 90	88
6	-	85.. 90	88
7	-	85.. 90	88

graph: alg405bb2, 20 trials

proc	w/o synch	early-scheduling min..max	avg
1	110		
2	70	85..105	93
3	-	85..100	91
4	-	85..105	91
5	-	85..100	90
6	-	85.. 90	89
7	-	85..100	90

graph: alg413bb1, 20 trials

proc	w/o synch	early-scheduling min..max	avg
1	390		
2	200	250..280	264
3	130	195..230	212
4	130	170..215	187
5	110	150..210	175
6	-	160..195	170
7	-	145..175	161

w/o synch is the best expected execution time for zero synchronization cost.
For the heuristics, normal operations cost 10 units and **signal** and **wait** operations cost 5 units.

Table 4: More results of many arrangements for different graphs

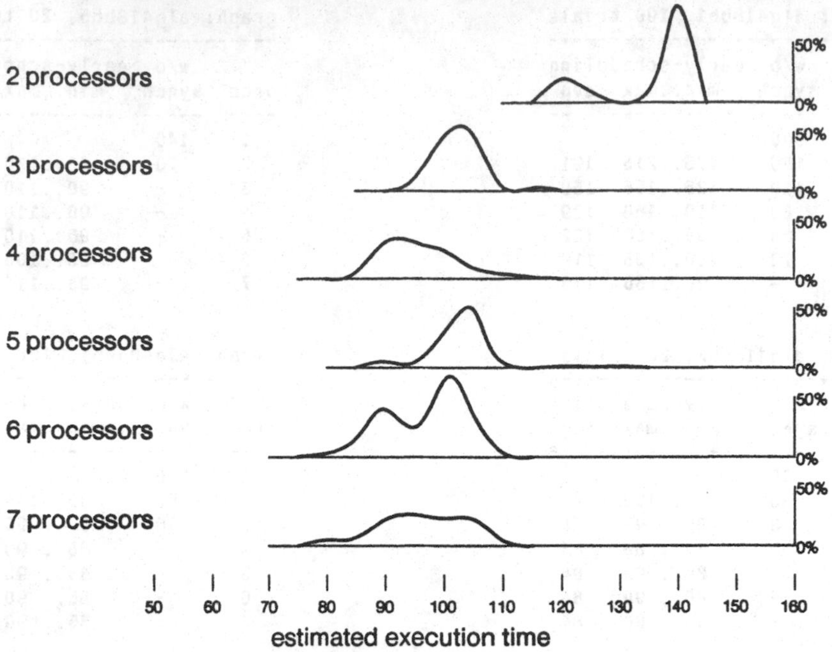

Figure 4:
Distribution of estimated execution times
for a random sample of arrangements of alg487bb1
produced by the graph-distance algorithm

4.3 Compilation for an actual multiprocessor

We intend to generate actual parallel machine code from the results of our heuristics and measure its performance on the multiprocessor Cm* [9]. On this machine, the execution time is 42 microseconds for a floating-point addition and 121 microseconds for a floating-point multiplication. We estimate that synchronization operations will cost between 30 and 340 microseconds, depending upon the primitives used. This estimate reflects the measured performance of various synchronization and communication mechanisms currently implemented by two operating systems on Cm*.

5 Future Work

The next steps in our research will be to refine our treatment of node allocation in basic blocks, and then to expand our treatment of the source language, first to include collections of basic blocks (single procedures), and then to entire programs composed of several procedures. We present below a summary of our current ideas on these points. Other future work includes expanding the model of the target machine to include separate memory classes with different accessing costs and capabilities.

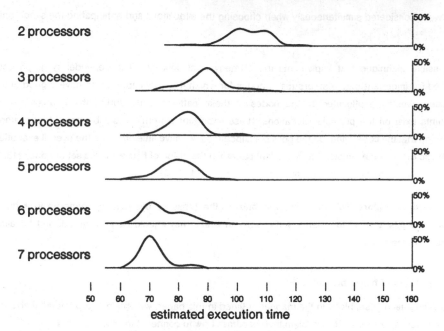

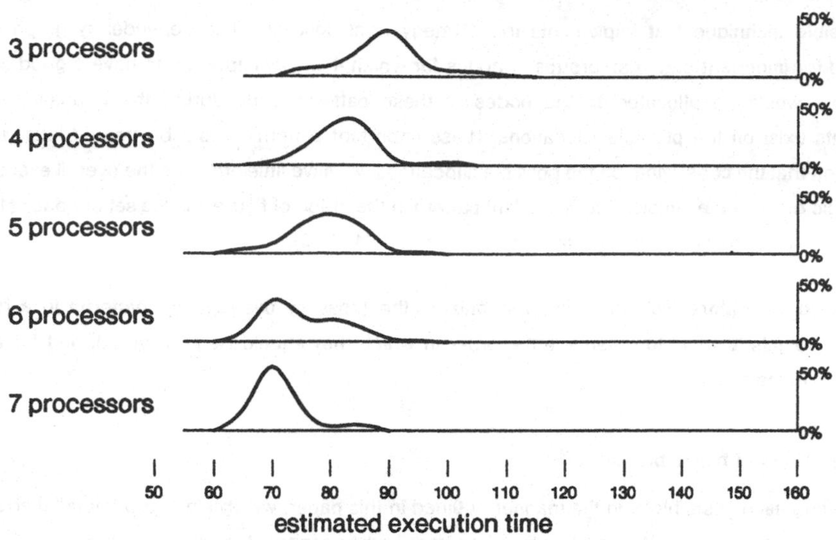

Figure 5:
Distribution of estimated execution times
for a random sample of arrangements of alg487bb1
produced by the early-scheduling algorithm

two processors		two processors		two processors		three processors	
heuristic	optimal	heuristic	optimal	heuristic	optimal	heuristic	optimal
140	135	145	145	140	135	120	120
140	135	145	140	140	140	140	125
145	140	140	130	145	145	120	115
150	150	155	145	145	140	130	125
135	135	140	135	145	140	130	120
150	145	145	145	140	135		
135	130	145	140	145	140		
135	135	150	140	155	155		
135	135	145	140	140	135		
150	140	150	140	140	135		

Table 5: Comparison of our heuristic against the optimal synchronization pattern for several allocations

5.1 Improved allocation heuristics

The results we have obtained from the two initial allocation heuristics indicate that the quality of the final allocation is strongly tied to how effectively the heuristic is able to anticipate the positions and costs of synchronization operations. The graph-distance algorithm, which pays scant attention to synchronization, is consistently worse than the early-scheduling algorithm, which anticipates possible synchronization costs when allocating a node to a processor. It seems clear that even better allocations could be done if several nodes were considered simultaneously when choosing the allocations and anticipating the synchronization costs.

A possible technique that implements this strategy is as follows. The dependency graph could be examined for important patterns: groups of nodes for which it is very important to have a good allocation. Processors would be allocated to the nodes of these patterns early during the heuristic, when few constraints exist on the possible allocations. Less important patterns would be treated later, under the assumption that the constraints on the possible allocations will have little effect on the overall execution time of the basic block. An example of an important pattern in the graph of figure 1 is the set of nodes (13, 14, 15, 16, 17, 18); an example of an unimportant pattern is the set (4, 5, 10).

We intend to explore techniques for recognizing the (possibly overlapping) patterns in a graph, for attaching weights to them to determine the order in which they should be considered, and for allocating processors to the nodes.

5.2 Collections of basic blocks

By treating each basic block in the manner outlined in this paper, we obtain a good parallel arrangement for each block individually. The problem then becomes how to connect the arrangements.

The simplest way to connect the blocks is to synchronize all processors at every control point. A conditional branch may actually require two complete synchronizations: one before the branch and one after, in order to guarantee that the value that decides the branch is seen by all processors before it is destroyed (as in a loop, for example). The drawback of this simple strategy is that much potential parallelism may be wasted in the complete synchronizations.

Currently, our idea is to produce an initial parallel program by connecting basic blocks in the straightforward manner and then to optimize it by improving the actions performed at the connections. In particular, the case of a loop whose body consists of a single basic block merits special treatment, for it may be possible to pipeline the decision that controls the branch. We are still investigating methods for improving the connection of basic blocks.

5.3 Collections of procedures

The problem with separate procedures is that it may be desirable for several invocations of the same procedure to execute in parallel. On a multiprocessor, this can be achieved by allocating an environment on entry to the procedure containing storage for this invocation's variables. Because processors could be in different environments at the same time, each processor would need its own environment pointer in local memory.

An analogous problem arises in the context of data-flow machines. Tokens that flow through separate iterations of the same loop or separate invocations of the same procedure must somehow be kept distinct. The standard solution [6] is to label each token with a color to which indicates the iteration or invocation that the token belongs. This is equivalent to constructing a separate environment in which distinct values are stored.

6 Conclusion

A multiprocessor can perform many independent series of operations at once, but any synchronization between separate processors requires overhead. The cost of this overhead affects the desirability of any particular arrangement of operations. This paper has presented two heuristics for creating a good initial allocation for straight-line blocks of assignment statements and a heuristic for inserting synchronization operations. Results of experiments indicate that one of the heuristics is far better than the other, but that further refinement is still required before an algorithm is obtained that is suitable for a compiler.

References

[1] S. J. Allan and A. E. Oldehoeft.
A Flow Analysis Procedure for the Translation of High Level Languages to a Data Flow Language.
In Oscar N. Garcia (editor), *Proceedings of the 1979 International Conference on Parallel Processing*, pages 26-34. IEEE Computer Society, Long Beach, California, 1979.

[2] U. Banerjee, S. C. Chen, D. J. Kuck, and R. A. Towle.
Time and Parallel Processor Bounds for Fortran-Like Loops.
IEEE Transactions on Computers C-28(9):660-670, September, 1979.

[3] G. Baudet.
Asynchronous Iterative Methods for Multiprocessors.
Technical Report, Department of Computer Science, Carnegie-Mellon University, 1976.

[4] A. J. Bernstein.
Analysis of Programs for Parallel Processing.
IEEE Transactions on Electronic Computers EC-15(5):757-763, October, 1966.

[5] R. P. Brent.
The Parallel Evaluation of General Arithmetic Expressions.
Journal of the ACM 21(2):201-206, April, 1974.

[6] A. J. Catto and J. R. Gurd.
Resource Management in Dataflow.
In *Proceedings of the 1981 Conference on Functional Programming Languages and Computer Architecture*, pages 77-84. Association for Computing Machinery, 1981.

[7] M. J. Gonzalez Jr. and C. V. Ramamoorthy.
Parallel Task Execution in a Decentralized System.
IEEE Transactions on Computers C-21(12):1310-1322, December, 1972.

[8] M. S. Hecht.
Programming Language Series: Flow Analysis of Computer Programs.
Elsevier, New York, New York, 1977.

[9] A. K. Jones and E. F. Gehringer.
The Cm Multiprocessor Project: A Research Review.*
Technical Report, Department of Computer Science, Carnegie-Mellon University, July, 1980.

[10] D. J. Kuck, Y. Muraoka, and S. C. Chen.
On the Number of Operations Simultaneously Executable in Fortran-Like Programs and Their Resulting Speedup.
IEEE Transactions on Computers C-21(12):1293-1310, December, 1972.

THE SIMPLE SEMANTICS FOR

COPPO-DEZANI-SALLÉ TYPES

J.R. Hindley
University College of Swansea
Wales, U.K.

ABSTRACT.

The Coppo-Dezani-Sallé type-language has "$\cap$" (intersection) and "ω" (universal type), besides the usual "$\rightarrow$" (exponentiation). Coppo, Dezani and Sallé have presented formal rules for assigning types to type-free λ-terms, and have proved metatheorems which give their system significance and interest. (Sallé 1978, Coppo et al. 1981.)

But no precise semantics has been given for their system yet, though the authors have made it fairly obvious informally what semantics they intended.

The present paper defines a precise semantics in an arbitrary model of type-free λ-calculus. The rules of Coppo, Dezani and Sallé turn out to be incomplete with respect to this semantics, but they become complete when three extra rules (two trivial, one not) are added. The completeness proof uses the term-model only.

INTRODUCTION.

In a series of manuscripts from 1977 onwards, Coppo, Dezani and Sallé have developed an extension of the usual Church-Curry type-language. They have added "$\cap$" (intersection) and "ω" (universal type) to the usual Church-Curry exponentiation connective (here denoted by "$\rightarrow$"). They have stated formal rules for assigning type-schemes to untyped λ-terms, which cover more terms than Curry's system, but still preserve the essential property of types; that the type should describe the term's functional behaviour in some significant way. (See for example Sallé 1978, Coppo et al. 1978, 1980, 1981.) A similar rule-system with "$\cap$" but not "ω" has been created independently by Pottinger, but not taken so far; Pottinger 1980.

The Coppo-Dezani-Sallé rules are motivated by a fairly obvious informal semantics. The present paper defines this semantics formally, in an arbitrary model of type-free λ-calculus; it is the same as the "simple semantics" of Hindley 1983.

The rules turn out to be incomplete with respect to this semantics; but they become complete when three extra rules (two trivial, one not) are added. Completeness is proved here using the term model, by the method of Hindley 1983.

A key lemma is the invariance of types under β-conversion; this will be proved via a translation into the system of Coppo et al. 1981, which will clarify the exact relation between that system and the present one.

The completeness problem has also been solved by Barendregt, Coppo and Dezani, independently of the present work and simultaneously with it (Spring 1980). Their version of the one non-trivial extra rule is a bit easier to handle than mine, so I shall use it below. The model they use is more complicated than the term-model used here, though it is interesting in its own right. (Barendregt et al. 198-.)

I thank Mariangiola Dezani and Mario Coppo for very helpful discussions, and the Italian C.N.R. who very generously financed a visit to Turin which made the discussions possible. I am also very grateful to Henk Barendregt for his comments on an earlier version of this paper; the present version owes something to all the above.

1. BASIC SYNTAX.

The reader is assumed to know at least the early parts of Coppo et al. 1980 or 1981. (1981 was written before 1980 and is the best reference for the basic ideas.) Also Hindley 1983 would be useful for motivation. The notation below is based on these papers, though with some changes.

Type-free λ*-terms* are built up as usual from *term-variables* (denoted by "x", "y", "z",...), but no atomic constants. Capital letters will denote type-free λ-terms. Identity will be called "=". The usual β-convertibility and reducibility relations will be called "$=_\beta$", "$\geq_\beta$". (Definitions are in Barendregt 1977 §1.) $\beta\eta$-reduction will not be considered here, nor will combinatory terms.

DEFINITION 1. Coppo-Dezani-Sallé type-schemes.

(i) An infinity of *type-variables* (a,b,c,d,...) are type-schemes. ω is a type-scheme.

(ii) If α and β are type-schemes, then so are $(\alpha\to\beta)$, $(\alpha\cap\beta)$. (Greek letters "α", "β", "γ", "∂" will denote arbitrary type-schemes. Informally, ω represents the universe, $\alpha\to\beta$ the set of all functions from α into β, and $\cap$ is intersection.)

Type-assignment statements are expressions αX (read as "assign α to X", or "X ε α"). X is called the *subject* of the statement.

A *basis* $\mathcal{B}$ is any finite or infinite set of statements whose subjects are variables (not necessarily all distinct; in fact one subject may occur infinitely often).

DEFINITION 2. *The pre-order* $\leq$ is defined by the following axioms and rules, taken from Barendregt et al. 198-. It formalizes the subset relation, and will be used in the non-trivial extra type-assignment rule.

(A1) $\alpha \leq \alpha$; (A4) $\alpha \leq \alpha\cap\alpha$;

(A2) $\alpha \leq \omega$; (A5) $\alpha_1\cap\alpha_2 \leq \alpha_i$ (i = 1,2);

(A3) $\omega \leq \omega\to\omega$; (A6) $(\alpha\to\beta)\cap(\alpha\to\gamma) \leq \alpha\to(\beta\cap\gamma)$;

(R1) $\alpha \leq \beta,\ \beta \leq \gamma \implies \alpha \leq \gamma$;

(R2) $\alpha \leq \alpha',\ \beta \leq \beta' \implies \alpha\cap\beta \leq \alpha'\cap\beta'$

(R3) $\alpha \leq \alpha',\ \beta \leq \beta' \implies \alpha'\to\beta \leq \alpha\to\beta'$.

Note the reversal in (R3); this is justified by thinking of $\leq$ as the subset relation. Note also (A3); (A3) says that every member of ω can be considered as a function on ω. This agrees with the semantics below. But there are other possible semantics, for example the F-semantics of Hindley 1983 §4, for which (A3) would have to be dropped.

DEFINITION 3. *The axioms and rules for type-assignment.* These are in the style of Gentzen's "Natural deduction"; cf. Hindley 1983 §1, or Coppo et al. 1981 §1.

Axioms (ω): ωX (one axiom for each term X);

Rules:

$$(\to i)\quad \frac{\begin{array}{c}[\alpha x]\\ \vdots\\ \beta Y\end{array}}{(\alpha\to\beta)(\lambda x.Y)} \qquad\qquad (\to e)\quad \frac{(\alpha\to\beta)U \quad \alpha V}{\beta(UV)}$$

$$(\cap i)\quad \frac{\alpha X \quad \beta X}{(\alpha\cap\beta)X} \qquad\qquad (\cap e)\quad \frac{(\alpha_1\cap\alpha_2)X}{\alpha_i X}\quad (i = 1,2)$$

$$(\leq)\quad \frac{\alpha X \quad \alpha\leq\beta}{\beta X}.$$

Note: each time rule ($\to$i) is used, we 'cancel' (shown above by "[ ]") all occurrences of αx at the tops of branches above βY, that have not previously been cancelled. We are allowed to use ($\to$i) even when there are no such occurrences of αx ("vacuous cancellation"). We must not use ($\to$i) when the uncancelled premises above βY include a γx with $\gamma \not\equiv \alpha$.

$\mathcal{B} \vdash \alpha X$ will mean that there is a deduction whose uncancelled premises are either axioms or members of $\mathcal{B}$, and whose conclusion is αX. (A deduction is a tree as usual.) If $\mathcal{B}$ is empty, we shall say $\vdash \alpha X$.

EXERCISE 1. (i) $\vdash ((a\cap(a\to b))\to b)(\lambda x.xx)$.

(ii) $\vdash (a\to\omega)(\lambda x.x)$

(iii) $\vdash (a\to(\omega\to a))(\lambda xy.x)$.

(Exercise 1 (i) shows how Coppo, Dezani and Sallé can give significant types to terms that Curry and Church could not. Exercise 1 (ii) and (iii) are examples of two different kinds of vacuous cancellation; (ii) can be done using (ω) and ($\to$i).)

REMARK 1. The type-language in Definition 1 is the same as that in Barendregt et al. 198-; it is more expressive than in Coppo et al. 1980, 1981. Coppo and Dezani deliberately restricted the language in their 1980, 1981 in order to simplify the metatheory. I shall take advantage of this simpler metatheory in the proof of the β-invariance theorem below, which proceeds by translating into the restricted language . The translation will also give a quick decision procedure for the relation $\leq$.

REMARK 2. The rules in Coppo et al. 1980, 1981 are not complete, even for the more restricted type-language used there. Moreover, the rules in 1980 differed in detail from the two sets of rules given in 1981; for example vacuous cancellation was allowed in the first set of rules in 1981, but restricted to a special case in the second set, and in 1980.

Rule ($\cap$e) was omitted from both papers. The authors remarked that adding ($\cap$e) would not give any more provable statements αX (X closed); but adding ($\cap$e) does give more deductions $\mathcal{B} \vdash \alpha X$ (X not closed), so it is included here.

Rule ($\leq$) was not included. But because of the restrictions on types, only a few special cases of ($\leq$) were relevant. The form of Rule ($\leq$) given above is due to Barendregt, Coppo and Dezani 198-; my original form was equivalent but clumsier.

DEFINITION 4. $\alpha \sim \beta$ iff $\alpha \leq \beta \leq \alpha$. (This is not the relation $\sim$ of Coppo et al. 1980.)

LEMMA 1.

(i)	$\alpha \sim \alpha$;	(vii)	$\alpha \cap \omega \sim \alpha$;
(ii)	$\alpha \sim \beta,\ \beta \sim \gamma \implies \alpha \sim \gamma$;	(viii)	$\alpha \to \omega \sim \omega$;
(iii)	$\alpha \sim \beta \implies \beta \sim \alpha$;	(ix)	$\alpha \cap \alpha',\ \beta \sim \beta' \implies \alpha \cap \beta \sim \alpha' \cap \beta'$;
(iv)	$\alpha \cap \beta \sim \beta \cap \alpha$;	(x)	$\alpha \sim \alpha',\ \beta \sim \beta' \implies \alpha \to \beta \sim \alpha' \to \beta'$;
(v)	$(\alpha \cap \beta) \cap \gamma \sim \alpha \cap (\beta \cap \gamma)$;	(xi)	$\alpha \leq \beta,\ \alpha \sim \alpha',\ \beta \sim \beta' \implies \alpha' \leq \beta'$;
(vi)	$\alpha \sim \alpha \cap \alpha$;	(xii)	$(\alpha \to \beta) \cap (\alpha \to \gamma) \sim \alpha \to (\beta \cap \gamma)$.

2. SEMANTICS.

The semantics is based on the concept of "model of the type-free $\lambda\beta$-calculus". The best way to define this concept is not yet agreed (some of the issues are discussed in Hindley and Longo 1980). But here only one model will be used, the term model, so the disagreements will not matter; everyone accepts the term model (I think). Type-schemes will be interpreted as subsets of models.

Models: Common to all definitions is that a model $\mathfrak{D}$ has a non-empty set D (its *domain*), a map $\circ : D^2 \to D$ (called *application*), and a map $[\![\ ]\!]$ which assigns a member $[\![X]\!]_\rho$ of D to each term X and each map ρ: term-variables $\to$ D. These satisfy

(i) $[\![x]\!]_\rho = \rho(x)$;

(ii) $[\![XY]\!]_\rho = [\![X]\!]_\rho \circ [\![Y]\!]_\rho$;

(iii) *if* $\sigma(x) = \rho(x)$ *for all* x *free in* X, *then* $[\![X]\!]_\sigma = [\![X]\!]_\rho$;

(iv) $X =_\beta Y \implies (\forall \rho)\ [\![X]\!]_\rho = [\![Y]\!]_\rho$.

The term model $\mathcal{TM}(\lambda\beta)$ has for its domain the set of all β-convertibility-classes of terms. (For all X let $[X] = \{Y : Y =_\beta X\}$.) Its map $\circ$ is defined by

$$[X] \circ [Y] = [XY].$$

And $[\![\ ]\!]$ is defined by

$$[\![X]\!]_\rho = [[Y_1,\ldots,Y_n/x_1,\ldots,x_n]X],$$

where $x_1,\ldots,x_n$ are the free variables of X, and $\rho(x_i) = [Y_i]$, and $[\ldots/\ldots]$ denotes simultaneous substitution.

The only ρ we shall need here is the simplest one, ρ_o, defined by

$$\rho_o(x) = [x].$$

It is easy to see that for all X,

$$[\![X]\!]_{\rho_o} = [X].$$

The simple semantics (Hindley 1983 §2). Given any model $\mathfrak{D}$, a *valuation of the type-variables* is any map V which assigns to each type-variable a subset of D. Any such V determines an interpretation $[\![\ ]\!]_V$ of all the type-schemes as follows:

(i) $[\![a]\!]_V = V(a)$;

(ii) $[\![\omega]\!]_V = D$;

(iii) $[\![\beta\to\gamma]\!]_V = \{d \in D : (\forall e)\ e \in [\![\beta]\!]_V \Longrightarrow d \circ e \in [\![\gamma]\!]_V\}$;

(iv) $[\![\beta\cap\gamma]\!]_V = [\![\beta]\!]_V \cap [\![\gamma]\!]_V$.

Satisfaction: A statement αX is *satisfied* by $\mathfrak{D}$, ρ, V iff $[\![X]\!]_\rho \in [\![\alpha]\!]_V$. Iff every $\mathfrak{D}$, ρ, V which satisfy all statements in $\mathcal{B}$ also satisfy αX, we say

$$\mathcal{B} \models \alpha X.$$

EXERCISE 2. $\alpha \le \beta \Longrightarrow (\forall\mathfrak{D})(\forall V)\ [\![\alpha]\!]_V \subseteq [\![\beta]\!]_V$.

(In particular, note that $[\![\omega\to\omega]\!]_V = D$. The converse of the above implication is also true, see later.)

3. MAIN RESULTS.

SOUNDNESS THEOREM. *If* $\mathcal{B} \vdash \alpha X$ *then* $\mathcal{B} \models \alpha X$.

Proof. Straightforward induction on $\vdash$, using the exercise at the end of §2. (By the way, this theorem holds even when one-member domains are counted as models; they were not excluded in §2.)

THE β-INVARIANCE THEOREM. *If* $\mathcal{B} \vdash \alpha X$ *and* $X =_\beta Y$, *then* $\mathcal{B} \vdash \alpha Y$.

Proof. By translating the present system into the simpler one of Coppo et al. 1981 and using their β-invariance proof, 1981 Theorem 1. (Details in §§4-5 below.)

REMARK 3. Contrast this theorem with Curry's type-assignment, e.g. in Hindley 1983. Curry's type-statements could only be made β-invariant by adjoining a rule

$$\text{(eq)} \qquad \alpha X,\ X =_{\beta} Y \vdash \alpha Y.$$

This rule is non-recursive. In contrast, all the Coppo-Dezani rules, even (≤), are recursive. (That is, there is an algorithm which, when given a finite tree of statements, will decide whether that tree is a deduction.) For recursiveness of (≤), see the corollary to Lemma 5. Of course the relation $\mathcal{B} \vdash \alpha X$ is non-recursive in both systems.

THE η-LEMMA. *If* $\mathcal{B}, \beta z \vdash \gamma(Yz)$ *and* z *is not in* $\mathcal{B}$ *nor free in* Y, *then* $\mathcal{B} \vdash (\beta \to \gamma)Y$.

Proof. See §5.

COMPLETENESS THEOREM. *If* $\mathcal{B} \models \alpha X$ *then* $\mathcal{B} \vdash \alpha X$.

Proof. (Cf. Hindley 1983 §3.) First extend $\mathcal{B}$ to a set $\mathcal{B}^+$ by adding an infinity of statements

$$\partial y_{\partial,i} \qquad (i = 1,2,\ldots)$$

for each type-scheme ∂ in the language. (The variables $y_{\partial,i}$ must all be distinct, and must not occur in $\mathcal{B}$ or X.)

If this extension is not possible (i.e. if only a finite number of term-variables are not subjects of $\mathcal{B}$), then list all the term-variables as $v_1, v_2, \ldots,$ and replace each v_i by v_{2i} in $\mathcal{B}$ and X. Let the results be $\mathcal{B}'$ and X'. By routine calculations,

$$\mathcal{B} \models \alpha X \iff \mathcal{B}' \models \alpha X',$$
$$\mathcal{B} \vdash \alpha X \iff \mathcal{B}' \vdash \alpha X'.$$

So we may assume the extension is possible.

Now take the term model $\mathcal{TM}(\lambda\beta)$, and define V thus:

$$V(a) = \{[Y] : \mathcal{B}^+ \vdash aY\}.$$

Then for all ∂, Y we have, by a proof to be given later,

(1) $\qquad [Y] \in [\![\partial]\!]_V \iff \mathcal{B}^+ \vdash \partial Y.$

Now $\mathcal{B} \models \alpha X$, so in particular for the V above, $[X] \in [\![\alpha]\!]_V$. Hence by (1), $\mathcal{B}^+ \vdash \alpha X$. Now the subject of any statement of $\mathcal{B}^+$ that occurs in this deduction will appear as a free variable in X. But no variable in $\mathcal{B}^+ - \mathcal{B}$ is free in X, so only statements in $\mathcal{B}$ are used in the above deduction. That is,

$$\mathcal{B} \vdash \alpha X,$$

as required for completeness. It only remains to prove (1).

Proof of (1). Induction on ∂. If ∂ is a variable, use the definition of V. If $\partial = \omega$, use the ω-axioms. If $\partial = \partial_1 \cap \partial_2$, use the induction hypothesis and rules $(\cap i)$, $(\cap e)$.

Finally let $\partial = \beta \to \gamma$. Then

$$\mathcal{B}^+ \vdash (\beta\to\gamma)Y \implies (\forall Z)\{\mathcal{B}^+ \vdash \beta Z \implies \mathcal{B}^+ \vdash \gamma(YZ)\} \text{ by } (\to e)$$
$$\iff (\forall Z)\{[Z] \in [\![\beta]\!]_V \implies [YZ] \in [\![\gamma]\!]_V\} \text{ by ind. hyp.}$$
$$\iff [Y] \in [\![\beta\to\gamma]\!]_V \text{ by definition of } [\![\ ]\!]_V.$$

To prove the converse of the first implication, suppose

$$(\forall Z)\{\mathcal{B}^+ \vdash \beta Z \implies \mathcal{B}^+ \vdash \gamma(YZ)\}.$$

Choose Z to be a variable $z = y_{\beta,i}$ not in Y. Then $\mathcal{B}^+ \vdash \beta z$, so

$$\mathcal{B}^+ \vdash \gamma(Yz).$$

Hence by the η-reduction lemma,

$$\mathcal{B}^+ \vdash (\beta\to\gamma)Y.$$

This proves (1) and the theorem.

NOTE. The β-invariance theorem was used implicitly throughout this proof. Because when selecting a member Y of a β-convertibility-class, it was assumed that all members had the same type.

COROLLARY (Barendregt, Coppo, Dezani).

(i) $\alpha \le \beta \iff (\forall\mathcal{D})(\forall V)\ [\![\alpha]\!]_V \subseteq [\![\beta]\!]_V$;

(ii) $\alpha \sim \beta \iff (\forall\mathcal{D})(\forall V)\ [\![\alpha]\!]_V = [\![\beta]\!]_V$.

Proof. For "$\Leftarrow$" in (i): if the right side of (i) holds, then $\alpha x \models \beta x$, so by completeness, $\alpha x \vdash \beta x$. Hence by checking all possible deductions, $\alpha \le \beta$.

4. THE TRANSLATION.

It remains to prove the β-invariance theorem and the η-lemma. This will be done via a translation into a system with a simpler metatheory, essentially the same as that of Coppo et al. 1981 §4.

DEFINITION 5. *Normal type-schemes (the set NTS).*

(i) Type-variables and ω are in NTS;

(ii) $(\sigma\cap\tau) \in$ NTS if $\sigma, \tau \in$ NTS$-\{\omega\}$;

(iii) $(\sigma\to\tau) \in$ NTS if $\sigma \in$ NTS and $\tau \in$ NTS$-\{\omega$, *intersections*$\}$.

NTS is the set of all σ such that: either $\sigma = \omega$, or $\sigma = \sigma_1\cap\ldots\cap\sigma_n$ with some bracketing and with each σ_i having form

$$\sigma_{i1}\to(\ldots(\sigma_{im_i}\to a_i)\ldots),\quad m_i \ge 0,\ n \ge 1.$$

NOTATION.

"α", "β", "γ" '∂' will denote arbitrary type-schemes of Def. 1;

"ρ", "σ", "τ" : members of NTS;

"$\alpha_1\cap\ldots\cap\alpha_n$", "$\sigma_1\cap\ldots\cap\sigma_n$", etc. : multiple intersections with parentheses determined by context, and with the convention that none of α_i, σ_j is an intersection. (Then every α can be written uniquely as $\alpha = \alpha_1\cap\ldots\cap\alpha_n$, $n \geq 1$, with the parentheses determined by the structure of α. Note that $\alpha_i = \alpha_j$ is permitted.)

DEFINITION 6. $\leq_N$ is the relation in $(NTS)^2$ obtained by restricting Definition 2 to NTS. (Later we shall see that

$$\sigma \leq_N \tau \iff \sigma \leq \tau ;$$

but this is not obvious, a priori, because there may exist $\beta \notin$ NTS such that $\sigma \leq \beta \leq \tau$.)

LEMMA 3. $\leq_N$ *behaves very nicely, thus:*

(i) $(\sigma_1\cap\ldots\cap\sigma_m) \leq_N (\tau_1\cap\ldots\cap\tau_n) \iff (\forall\tau_j)(\exists\sigma_i)\ \sigma_i \leq_N \tau_j$;

(ii) $\omega \leq_N \tau \iff \tau = \omega$;

(iii) $(\sigma_1\to(\ldots(\sigma_m\to a)\ldots)) \leq_N (\tau_1\to(\ldots(\tau_n\to b)\ldots)) \iff$

$a = b$ *and* $m = n$ *and* $(\forall i)\ \tau_i \leq_N \sigma_i$;

(iv) $(\sigma_1\to(\ldots(\sigma_m\to a)\ldots)) \leq_N \tau \iff$

either $\tau = \omega$, *or* $\tau = \tau_1\cap\ldots\cap\tau_k$ $(k \geq 1)$ *and*

$(\forall i)\ \tau_i = \tau_{i,1}\to(\ldots(\tau_{i,m}\to a)\ldots)$ *with* $\tau_{i,j} \leq_N \sigma_j$.

(v) The relation $\leq_N$ is recursive.

Proof. In each case "$\Leftarrow$" is trivial. For '$\Rightarrow$' in (i) - (iii), use induction on $\leq_N$. For (iv), use (i) and (iii). For (v), decide whether $\sigma \leq_N \tau$ by induction on σ, using (i) and (iv).

DEFINITION 7. *The translation.* Define α^* to be the NTS obtained by reducing α by the following replacement rules:

(i) $\beta\to(\gamma\cap\partial)$ *may be replaced by* $(\beta\to\gamma)\cap(\beta\to\partial)$;

(ii) $\beta\cap\omega$ *may be replaced by* β;

(iii) $\omega\cap\beta$ *may be replaced by* β;

(iv) $\beta\to\omega$ *may be replaced by* ω.

For any $\mathcal{B} = \{\alpha_1 x_1, \alpha_2 x_2, \ldots\}$, define $\mathcal{B}^* = \{\alpha_1^* x_1, \alpha_2^* x_2, \ldots\}$.

LEMMA 4. α^* *exists and is unique. Also* $(\beta\cap\gamma)^* = (\beta^*\cap\gamma^*)^*$ *and* $(\beta\to\gamma)^* = (\beta^*\to\gamma^*)^*$.

Proof. Call a replacement by one of (i) - (iv) a *contraction* ($\mapsto_1$), and a sequence a *reduction* ($\mapsto$). An ordinal number *degree* (α) will be assigned to each α, so that contraction strictly reduces degree. First define

$|\alpha|$ = *number of occurrences of symbols in* α.

(Contractions (ii) - (iv) reduce $|\alpha|$, but (i) does not.) Then define

$\mathscr{I}(e) = 0$ ($e = \omega$ *or a variable*);

$\mathscr{I}(\alpha_1 \to (\ldots(\alpha_m \to e)\ldots)) = \mathscr{I}(\alpha_1) + \ldots + \mathscr{I}(\alpha_m)$ $(m \geq 0)$;

$\mathscr{I}(\alpha_1 \to (\ldots(\alpha_m \to (\beta\cap\gamma))\ldots)) = m + \mathscr{I}(\alpha_1 \to (\ldots(\alpha_m \to \beta)\ldots)) + \mathscr{I}(\alpha_1 \to (\ldots(\alpha_m \to \gamma)\ldots))$.

It is easy to prove by induction on $|\alpha|$ that contractions (i) reduce $\mathscr{I}(\alpha)$; also that if α' is part of α, then $\mathscr{I}(\alpha') \leq \mathscr{I}(\alpha)$, so (ii) - (iv) do not increase $\mathscr{I}(\alpha)$.

Finally, take the ordinal ω and define

$$degree(\alpha) = \omega.\mathscr{I}(\alpha) + |\alpha|.$$

Contractions reduce degree, so all reductions must terminate. And when no further contraction is possible, α is obviously in NTS.

The uniqueness of α^* is proved by a Church-Rosser argument. First, by induction on *degree*(α), uniqueness follows from

(2) $\alpha \mapsto_1 \beta_1$ *and* $\alpha \mapsto_1 \beta_2 \implies (\exists\gamma)\ \beta_1 \mapsto \gamma$ *and* $\beta_2 \mapsto \gamma$.

Then (2) is proved by easy case-checking. For example, if

$$\alpha = (\beta \to (\omega\cap\partial)),$$

and α contracts to $((\beta\to\omega)\cap(\beta\to\partial))$ by (i) and to $(\beta\to\omega)$ by (iii), then we can choose

$$\gamma = \beta\to\omega.$$

LEMMA 5.

(i) $\alpha \sim \alpha^*$;

(ii) $\alpha \leq \beta \iff \alpha^* \leq_N \beta^*$;

(iii) $\alpha \sim \omega \iff \alpha^* = \omega$.

Proof. For (i), use Lemma 1. For (iii), use (ii) and Lemma 3(ii) and note that $\omega^* = \omega$.

For (ii) "$\Rightarrow$", use induction on Definition 2. (To prove $\alpha^* \leq \beta^*$ is easy, but to get $\leq_N$ we must check that all type-schemes involved are in NTS.) The only non-trivial case is rule (R3). Let $\gamma \leq \gamma'$, $\partial \leq \partial'$, and

$$\alpha = \gamma' \to \partial, \qquad \beta = \gamma \to \partial'.$$

By the induction-hypothesis,

$$\gamma^* \leq_N \gamma'^*, \qquad \partial^* \leq_N \partial'^*.$$

And by Lemma 4,

$$\alpha^* = (\gamma'^* \to \partial^*)^*, \qquad \beta^* = (\gamma^* \to \partial'^*)^*.$$

Consider ∂^*: if $\partial^* = \omega$, then by Lemma 3(ii) $\partial'^* = \omega$, and so $\beta^* = \omega$; then $\alpha^* \leq_N \beta^*$ by (A2). If $\partial^* \neq \omega$, then

$$\partial^* = \sigma_1\cap\ldots\cap\sigma_n \quad (n \geq 1),$$

$$\sigma_i = (\sigma_{i,1}\to\ldots(\sigma_{i,m_i}\to a_i)\ldots) \quad (1 \leq i \leq n).$$

If $\partial'^* = \omega$, then $\alpha^* \leq_N \beta^*$ as above. If not, then by Lemma 3,

$$\partial'^* = \tau_1\cap\ldots\cap\tau_p \quad (p \geq 1),$$

$$(\forall\tau_j)(\exists\sigma_i)\ \tau_j = (\tau_{j,1}\to\ldots(\tau_{j,m_i}\to a_i)\ldots) \ \textit{and}$$

$$(\forall k \leq m_i)\ \tau_{j,k} \leq_N \sigma_{i,k}.$$

Then

$$\alpha^* = (\gamma'^*\to\sigma_1)\cap\ldots\cap(\gamma'^*\to\sigma_n),$$

$$\beta^* = (\gamma^*\to\tau_1)\cap\ldots\cap(\gamma^*\to\tau_n).$$

So $\alpha^* \leq_N \beta^*$ by an easy calculation.

To prove (ii)"$\Leftarrow$", use induction on Definition 2. The only nontrivial cases are (R2) and (R3).

For (R2), let $\alpha^* \leq_N \alpha'^*$, $\beta^* \leq_N \beta'^*$. To show $(\alpha^*\cap\beta^*)^* \leq_N (\alpha'^*\cap\beta'^*)^*$. If the right-hand side is ω, the result is obvious. If the right side is α'^* or β'^*, the result comes from (A5) and (R1). Otherwise, none of $\alpha^*, \beta^*, \alpha'^*, \beta'^*$ is ω, and the result comes by (R2).

For (R3), let $\alpha^* \leq_N \alpha'^*$, $\beta^* \leq_N \beta'^*$. To show

(3) $$(\alpha'^*\to\beta^*)^* \leq_N (\alpha^*\to\beta'^*)^*.$$

If the right side is ω, the result is obvious. Otherwise, neither β^* nor β'^* is ω, and

$$\beta^* = \sigma_1\cap\ldots\cap\sigma_m,\ \beta'^* = \tau_1\cap\ldots\cap\tau_n \quad (m,n \geq 1;\ \sigma_i,\tau_j \neq \omega.)$$

Also the left side of (3) is

(4) $$(\alpha'^*\to\sigma_1)\cap\ldots\cap(\alpha'^*\to\sigma_m)$$

and the right side is

(5) $$(\alpha^*\to\tau_1)\cap\ldots\cap(\alpha^*\to\tau_n).$$

Now $\beta^* \leq_N \beta'^*$, so by Lemma 3(i), $(\forall j \leq n)(\exists i \leq m)\ \sigma_i \leq_N \tau_j$. From this we get (4) $\leq_N$ (5). This proves Lemma 5.

COROLLARY. *The relation* $\leq$ *is recursive.*

Proof. By (ii) above and Lemma 3(v).

LEMMA 6. $\sigma \leq \tau \iff \sigma \leq_N \tau$ *for* $\sigma,\tau \in$ NTS.

Proof. By Lemma 5(ii), since $\sigma^* = \sigma$ and $\tau^* = \tau$.

NOTATION. From now on, in NTS "≤" will be used for $\leq_N$.

DEFINITION 7. A deduction is called *moderately restricted* ($\vdash_{MR}$) when all its type schemes are in NTS.

LEMMA 7. *If* $\mathcal{B} \vdash \alpha X$, *then* $\mathcal{B}^* \vdash_{MR} \alpha^* X$.

Proof.

By induction on $\vdash$. The basis ($\alpha X \in \mathcal{B}$ or $\alpha = \omega$) is trivial. For rule (≤) or (∩e), use Lemma 5(ii).

Rule (∩i): easy, because $(\alpha \cap \beta)^*$ is either $\alpha^* \cap \beta^*$ or α^* or β^*.

Rule (→i): let $\mathcal{B}^*, \alpha^* x \vdash_{MR} \beta^* Y$. To show $\mathcal{B}^* \vdash_{MR} (\alpha^* \to \beta^*)^* (\lambda x.Y)$. If $\beta^* = \omega$, this is trivial by the ω-axiom. Otherwise

$$\beta^* = (\sigma_{1,1} \to (\ldots(\sigma_{1,m_1} \to a_1)\ldots)) \cap \ldots \cap (\sigma_{n,1} \to (\ldots(\sigma_{n,m_n} \to a_n)\ldots))$$

where $n \geq 1$ and $m_i \geq 0$. Hence

$$(\alpha^* \to \beta^*)^* = (\alpha^* \to (\sigma_{1,1} \to \ldots)) \cap \ldots \cap (\alpha^* \to (\sigma_{n,1} \to \ldots)).$$

Take the given deduction of $\beta^* Y$ and apply (∩e) n-1 times, then (→i), then (∩i) n-1 times.

Rule (→e): similar to (→i).

DEFINITION 8. A deduction is called *restricted* ($\vdash_R$) when all its type-schemes are in NTS and

(i) rule (∩e) never immediately follows (∩i),

(ii) (∩e) and (≤) are only used with atomic subjects.

TRANSLATION THEOREM. $\mathcal{B} \vdash \alpha X \iff \mathcal{B}^* \vdash_R \alpha^* X$.

Proof. For "⇐": use Lemma 5(i) and rule (≤).

For "⇒": by Lemma 7, it is enough to prove that $\mathcal{B} \vdash_{MR} \sigma X$ implies $\mathcal{B} \vdash_R \sigma X$. To do this, it is enough to prove

(6) $$\mathcal{B} \vdash_R \tau X \text{ and } \tau \leq \tau' \implies \mathcal{B} \vdash_R \tau' X.$$

(The elimination of (∩i)-(∩e) pairs is easy, and shortens deductions.)

Proof of (6).

Induction on $\vdash_R$. If τX is in $\mathcal{B}$, then X is an atom and rule (≤) is permitted.

Case (ω): If $\tau = \omega$, then by Lemma 3(ii), $\tau' = \omega = \tau$.

Case (→i): If τX comes from (→i), then $X = \lambda x.Y$, $\tau = \rho \to \sigma$, and

(7) $$\mathcal{B}, \rho x \vdash_R \sigma Y.$$

By Lemma 3(iv) applied to $\tau \le \tau'$, either $\tau' = \omega$, or

$$\tau' = \tau_1 \cap \ldots \cap \tau_k,\ k \ge 1,\ \tau_i = \rho_i \to \sigma_i,\ \rho_i \le \rho,\ \sigma_i \le \sigma.$$

If $\tau' = \omega$, then $\vdash_R \tau'(\lambda x.Y)$ by (ω). Now let $\tau' \neq \omega$. By the induction hypothesis applied to (7),

$$\mathcal{B},\ \rho x \vdash_R \sigma_i Y \qquad (\text{for } i = 1,\ldots,k).$$

And by rule $(\le)$ with atomic subject,

$$\rho_i x \vdash_R \rho x.$$

Hence $\mathcal{B},\ \rho_i x \vdash_R \sigma_i Y$; so by $(\to i)$,

$$\mathcal{B} \vdash_R \tau_i(\lambda x.Y) \qquad (i = 1,\ldots,k).$$

Then by $(\cap i)$,

$$\mathcal{B} \vdash_R \tau'(\lambda x.Y).$$

Case $(\to e)$: let $X = UV$ and $\mathcal{B} \vdash_R (\rho\to\tau)U$ and $\mathcal{B} \vdash_R \rho V$.

Since $\tau \le \tau'$, we have $\rho\to\tau \le \rho\to\tau'$. If $(\rho\to\tau') \in \mathrm{NTS}$, then apply the induction hypothesis to $(\rho\to\tau)U$, giving

$$\mathcal{B} \vdash_R (\rho\to\tau')U.$$

Hence by $(\to e)$,

$$\mathcal{B} \vdash_R \tau'(UV).$$

This assumed $\rho\to\tau' \in \mathrm{NTS}$. The only way this could fail would be $\tau' = \omega$ or an intersection.

If $\tau' = \omega$, then $\mathcal{B} \vdash_R \tau'(UV)$ by axiom (ω).

If $\tau' = (\tau'_1 \cap \ldots \cap \tau'_p)$ $(p \ge 2,\ \tau_i \neq \omega)$: since $\rho\to\tau \in \mathrm{NTS}$, τ is not an intersection, so by Lemma 3(iv), $(\forall i)\ \tau \le \tau'_i$. Hence $(\rho\to\tau) \le (\rho\to\tau'_i)$, and we get $\mathcal{B} \vdash_R \tau'_i(UV)$. Then $\mathcal{B} \vdash_R \tau'(UV)$ by $(\cap i)$.

Case $(\cap i)$: let $\tau = \tau_1 \cap \ldots \cap \tau_n$, $n \ge 2$, and let

$$\mathcal{B} \vdash_R (\tau_1 \cap \ldots \cap \tau_k)X, \quad \mathcal{B} \vdash_R (\tau_{k+1} \cap \ldots \cap \tau_n)X.$$

Now τ' has form

$$\tau' = \tau'_1 \cap \ldots \cap \tau'_p \qquad (p \ge 1).$$

And since $\tau \le \tau'$, by Lemma 3(i) we have

$$(\forall \tau'_j)(\exists \tau_i)\ \tau_i \le \tau'_j.$$

The result then follows by induction hypothesis.

Case $(\cap e)$ *or* $(\le)$: use the induction hypothesis.

This proves the theorem.

COROLLARY. *If all type-schemes in* $\mathcal{B}$ *are in* NTS, *then*

$$\mathcal{B} \vdash \sigma X \iff \mathcal{B} \vdash_R \sigma X.$$

5. PROOFS OF THE CONVERSION LEMMAS.

LEMMA 8. *If* $\mathcal{B}\vdash\alpha X$ *and* X *converts to* Y *by changing bound variables, then* $\mathcal{B}\vdash\alpha Y$. *Same for* $\vdash_R$.

THE β-INVARIANCE THEOREM. *If* $\mathcal{B}\vdash\alpha X$ *and* $X =_\beta Y$, *then* $\mathcal{B}\vdash\alpha Y$.

Proof. (Based on Coppo et al. 1981 Lemma 1 and Theorem 1.)

It is enough to prove

$$\mathcal{B}\vdash_R \sigma X,\ X =_\beta Y \implies \mathcal{B}\vdash \sigma Y.$$

(We only need to prove $\vdash$, because $\vdash_R$ will follow by the corollary to the translation theorem.) It is also enough to consider only the case that $=_\beta$ is one step, contraction or expansion.

Case 1: $X = (\lambda y.P)Q$, $Y = [Q/y]P$. We are given

(8) $\mathcal{B}\vdash_R \sigma((\lambda y.P)Q)$,

and we want to prove

(9) $\mathcal{B}\vdash \sigma([Q/y]P)$.

Subcase 1a: the last step in (8) is (ω). Then $\sigma = \omega$ and (9) follows by (ω).

Subcase 1b: the last step in (8) is (→e):

$$\frac{(\rho\to\sigma)(\lambda y.P)\quad \rho Q}{\sigma((\lambda y.P)Q)}.$$

The step above $(\rho\to\sigma)(\lambda y.P)$ must be (→i). (It cannot be (≤) or (∩e) because $\lambda y.P$ is composite.) So we have

$$\frac{\begin{matrix}[\rho y]\\ \vdots\\ \sigma P\end{matrix}}{(\rho\to\sigma)(\lambda y.P)}.$$

And $\mathcal{B}\vdash \rho Q$. Substitute the deduction $\mathcal{B}\vdash\rho Q$ for every premise ρy above σP. This will give a deduction (9).

Subcase 1c: the last step in (8) is (∩i). As we move up the deduction (8), there will be a finite number of (∩i)-steps, and above these the only possibility is (→e). (We cannot have (ω) because $\sigma \in$ NTS.) Hence

$$\sigma = \sigma_1\cap\ldots\cap\sigma_n \qquad (n \ge 2),$$

and

$$\mathcal{B}\vdash_R \sigma_i((\lambda y.P)Q) \qquad (i = 1,\ldots,n),$$

by deductions ending in (→e). Apply Subcase 1b to these deductions, giving $\mathcal{B}\vdash\sigma_i([Q/y]P)$, and then use (∩i) to get (9).

Case 2: $X = [Q/y]P$, $Y = (\lambda y.P)Q$

By Lemma 8, we may assume no variable free in yQ is bound in P. We have

(10) $\mathcal{B}\vdash_R \sigma([Q/y]P)$.

If y does not occur in P, then $[Q/y]P = P$, so we have $\mathcal{B}\vdash\sigma P$. Hence by

$(\to i)$ with vacuous cancellation,

$$\mathcal{B} \vdash (\omega \to \sigma)(\lambda y.P).$$

But $\vdash \omega Q$ by (ω), so by $(\to e)$, $\mathcal{B} \vdash \sigma((\lambda y.P)Q)$.

Now let y occur in P, and let $y_1,\ldots,y_n$ be its occurrences. In $[Q/y]P$ there will be corresponding occurrences $Q_1,\ldots,Q_n$ of Q. In the deduction (10), for each i, either Q_i will be part of a component $Z' = [Q/y]Z$ in $[Q/y]P$ such that $\omega Z'$ occurs in (10), or a sub-deduction $\mathcal{B} \vdash \rho_i Q_i$ occurs in (10) for some $\rho_i \neq \omega$. Say the former happens for $Q_1,\ldots,Q_k$, and the latter happens for $Q_{k+1},\ldots,Q_n$.

Take the deduction (10), and eliminate all the sub-deductions $\mathcal{B} \vdash \rho_i Q_i$ $(i \geq k+1)$, except for their last statements $\rho_i Q_i$. Then replace each Q_i by y, in these statements and in all statements below them. (By the nature of the rules in Definition 3, every statement below $\rho_i Q_i$ will contain a 'corresponding' occurrence of Q, in an obvious sense.)

For $i \leq k$, replace Q_i by y in the components Z'.

The result will be a deduction

$$\mathcal{B},\ \rho_{k+1} y,\ldots,\rho_n y \vdash \sigma P.$$

From this, by adding $(\cap e)$ at the top and $(\to i)$ at the bottom, we get

$$\mathcal{B} \vdash ((\rho_{k+1} \cap \ldots \cap \rho_n) \to \sigma)(\lambda y.P).$$

We had $\mathcal{B} \vdash \rho_i Q_i$ for $i \geq k+1$, that is $\mathcal{B} \vdash \rho_i Q$, so by $(\cap i)$ and $(\to e)$,

$$\mathcal{B} \vdash \sigma((\lambda y.P)Q).$$

Case 3: Y comes from X by an arbitrary contraction or expansion. Use induction on X, with Cases 1 and 2 in the basis. This proves the β-invariance theorem.

THE η-LEMMA. *If* $\mathcal{B}$, $\beta z \vdash \gamma(Yz)$ *and* z *is not in* $\mathcal{B}$ *nor free in* Y, *then* $\mathcal{B} \vdash (\beta \to \gamma)Y$.

Proof. Let $\mathcal{B}$, $\beta z \vdash \gamma(Yz)$. Then by the translation theorem,

(11) $$\mathcal{B}^*,\ \beta^* z \vdash_R \gamma^*(Yz).$$

The last rule in (11) may be (ω) or $(\to e)$ or $(\cap i)$.

Case (ω): $\gamma^* = \omega$. By Lemma 5(iii), $\omega \leq \gamma$. Hence

$$\omega \leq \omega \to \omega \leq \beta \to \omega \leq \beta \to \gamma.$$

So $\mathcal{B} \vdash (\beta \to \gamma)Y$ by (ω) and $(\leq)$.

Case $(\to e)$: we have, for some σ,

$$\mathcal{B}^*,\ \beta^* z \vdash_R (\sigma \to \gamma^*)Y; \quad \mathcal{B}^*,\ \beta^* z \vdash_R \sigma z.$$

In the first of these deductions, $\beta^* z$ cannot occur, because z is not free in Y. In the second, no member of $\mathcal{B}^*$ can occur, and the only rules possible are (ω), $(\cap e)$, $(\leq)$. Hence we have

$$\mathcal{B}^* \vdash_R (\sigma \to \gamma^*)Y, \qquad \beta^* \leq \sigma.$$

Therefore by $(\leq)$,

$$\mathcal{B}^* \vdash (\beta^* \to \gamma^*)Y.$$

Now $\beta \sim \beta^*$ and $\gamma \sim \gamma^*$, so again by $(\leq)$, $\mathcal{B} \vdash (\beta \to \gamma)Y$.

Case $(\cap i)$: This case can be reduced to Case $(\to e)$ just like Subcase 1c of the β-invariance theorem.

REFERENCES

BARENDREGT, H. (1977): "The type-free λ-calculus", *in* "Handbook of Mathematical Logic", edited by J. Barwise, North-Holland Co., 1977.

BARENDREGT, H., COPPO, M., DEZANI, M. (198-): "A filter lambda model and the completeness of type assignment", to appear, J. Symbolic Logic.

COPPO, M., DEZANI, M. (1978): "A new type-assignment for λ-terms", Archiv. Math. Logik 19, pp.139-156 (1978).

COPPO, M., DEZANI, M., VENNERI, B. (1980): "Principal type-schemes and λ-calculus semantics", *in* "To H.B. Curry", edited by J.P. Seldin and J.R. Hindley, Academic Press 1980.

COPPO, M., DEZANI, M., VENNERI, B. (1981): "Functional characters of solvable terms", Z. Math. Logik 27, pp.45-58 (1981).

HINDLEY, J.R. (1983): "The completeness theorem for typing λ-terms", to appear, Theoretical Computer Science 22 (1983).

HINDLEY, J.R., LONGO, G. (1980): "Lambda-calculus models and extensionality", Z. Math. Logik 26, pp.289-310 (1980).

POTTINGER, G. (1980): "A type assignment for the strongly normalizable λ-terms", *in* "To H.B. Curry", edited by J.P. Seldin and J.R. Hindley, Academic Press 1980.

SALLÉ, P. (1978): "Une extension de la théorie des types", Lecture Notes in Computer Science 62, pp.398-410, Springer-Verlag 1978.

PROVING THE CORRECTNESS OF IMPLEMENTATIONS OF SHARED DATA ABSTRACTIONS

L. Kozma

Enterprise for Computing Application
H-1536 Budapest P.O.B.227,Hungary

Abstract

A method is presented for proving the correctness of an implementation of shared abstract data types. The proposed correctness proof method is an extension of Hoare's method developed for proving the correctness of an implementation of abstract data types specified in a sequential programming environment. An example is given to illustrate the proposed proof method.

1. Introduction

This paper is concerned with proving the correctness of an implementation of shared data abstractions. A shared abstract data type can be specified, for instance, in the following way:

<u>type</u> typename ($\bar{p}$) : α
    <u>requires:</u> Requires ($\bar{p}$)
    <u>initially:</u> Init(α)
    <u>invariant:</u> I (α)
    <u>operations</u>
        operation name (<u>result</u> $\bar{x},\bar{y}$)
            $pre_a(\alpha',\bar{x}',\bar{y}')$
            $post_a(\alpha,\bar{x},\bar{y})$
        .
        .
        .
    <u>synchronization:</u> S(α)

where the data-related parts of an abstract object can be specified by Hoare's method [Hoare 72], and the synchronization can be specified by Laventhal's method [Laventhal 78].

A concrete implementation of a shared abstract data type takes the following form:

```
type classname ( p̄ )  shared class;
 begin declaration of local variables of class;
  procedures
   procedure name ( result x̄;ȳ);
    begin
     call m.procedure name-request ( x̄;ȳ);
     call m.procedure name-enter ( x̄;ȳ);
     (ζ,x) :=f_c(ζ;x̄;ȳ);
     call m.procedure name-exit ( x̄;ȳ )
    end
   .
   .
   .
mm(p̄):monitor;
 begin declaration of local variables of monitor;
  procedures
  :
  p_i-request (... list of formal parameters ...)
    begin
     :
      body of procedure
    end
  p_i-enter (... list of formal parameters ...)
    begin
     :
      body of procedure
    end
  p_i-exit ( ... list of formal parameters ...)
    begin
     :
      body of procedure
    end
  :
 Initialise local variables of monitor;
end mm
```

Initialise local variables of class;

<u>var</u> m: mm ($\bar{p}$)

<u>end</u> classname

where $f_c(\zeta, \bar{x}, \bar{y})$ implements the abstract operation $f_a(\alpha, \bar{x}, \bar{y})$ and ζ denotes the concrete objects defined by the local variables of the shared class. The focus of this paper is on proving the correctness of an implementation of a shared data abstraction.

Considerable effort has been devoted to issues related to verification of parallel processes [Lamport 77], [Owicki and Gries 76] , [Owicki 78] [Howard 76] or to derivation of correct concurrent programs [Lamsweerde and Snitzoff 79], [Kozma 81]. Numerous papers have dealt with verification problems of data abstractions but only in sequential programming environments [Hoare 72], [Shaw and et. al. 76], [Spitzen and Wegbreit 75], [Varga 80], [Wulf and et. al. 76], [Wulf and et. al. 77] Sharing an abstract data type among concurrent programs complicates both the specification and the verification. In [Owicki 76] proof techniques are suggested for verifying both partial and total correctness of concurrent programs with shared data, but these methods are too restrictive because an abstract data type can be implemented only by a single monitor. The proposed verification technique of this paper makes it possible to verify that a shared class correctly implements a shared abstract data type.

2. Proving correctness of an implementation

The specifications of a data abstraction form the interface between the program module implementing the abstract object and the programs which use it. So specification of an abstraction has to contain all the information needed for correct use of the concrete objects. Thus on the one hand it must be possible to verify that a particular implementation of an abstract data type is correct and on the other hand that the programs using abstract objects can be proved using only the specification of the abstract object. This paper considers only the first of these, the proof that the implementation satisfies the specification. The sufficent conditions for establishing the correctness of an implementation of an abstract data object in a sequential program are given in [Hoare 72] . In concurrent programs these conditions are no longer sufficient because now the correctness of synchronization code must be verified and a method is needed for verifying that an implementation constitutes a consistent system. Our proof method is an extension of Hoare's method for abstract data objects in sequential programs. In particular, we extend the set of correctness conditions in such a way that they are sufficient conditions for establishing correctness of an implementation of an abstract data object in a concurrent program. For the first step of verifying correctness of an implementation one must define the relation between the abstract object and the concrete data variables of the shared class implementing the abstract data type. If letter $\mathfrak{a}$ represents the abstract object and letter $\mathfrak{c}$ denotes the data variables of the shared class, the relationship is defined by a function such that

$$\mathfrak{a} = \varphi(\mathfrak{c}).$$

The second step in proving that a shared class correctly implements a data abstraction is to define the following pre - and post-conditions for every concrete procedure p_c: the pre-condition $pre_{f_c}(\mathfrak{c}, \bar{x}, \bar{y})$ and the post-condition $post_{f_c}(\mathfrak{c}, \bar{x}, \bar{y})$. Here $f_c(\mathfrak{c}, \bar{x}, \bar{y})$ denotes the data-related part of the code of the implementation of the abstract operation f_a, and the $pre_{f_c}(\mathfrak{c}, \bar{x}, \bar{y})$ is an assertion giving the conditions under which the concrete operation f_c performs correctly. The clause $post_{f_c}$ describes the effects of the concrete operation f_c supposing that the pre-condition pre_{f_c} holds before executing f_c.

The third step is to define the concrete invariant $I_c(\mathfrak{c}, ms)$, where ms denotes the local variables of the monitor describing the synchronization state of the concrete object. The invariant $I_c(\mathfrak{c}, ms)$ is an assertion defining the relation between the concrete data variables of the shared class and the local variables of the monitor.
Before describing the next step some definitions are given.

<u>Definition 1:</u> We say that a specification of a shared abstract data type is <u>consistent</u> if for every abstract operation p the following holds: whenever the synchronization specification $S(\mathfrak{a})$ holds before execution of abstract operation p, the pre-condition of the abstract operation p holds as well.

<u>Definition 2:</u> We say that a concrete shared class implementing a data abstraction is consistent if for every procedure p_c of the

shared class the following conditions hold:

a. $(I_c(\tau, ms') \wedge post_{p_c\text{-enter}}(ms) \wedge \underline{starting}) \supset$

$(pre_{f_c} \wedge I_c(\tau, ms) \wedge \underline{starting})$

b. $\{I_c(\tau, ms') \wedge \underline{finished} \wedge pre_{p_c\text{-exit}}\}$ p_c-exit

$\{I_c(\tau, ms)\}$

c. $\{I_c(\tau, ms') \wedge \underline{starting} \wedge pre_{p_c\text{-request}}\}$ p_c-request

$\{I_c(\tau, ms) \wedge \underline{starting}\}$

d. $\{I_c(\tau, ms') \wedge starting \wedge pre_{p_c\text{-enter}}\}$ p_c-enter

$\{I_c(\tau, ms) \wedge \underline{starting}\}$

Where p_c-request, p_c-enter and p_c-exit denote the monitor procedures implementing the event classes associated with every activation of procedure p_c. The pre-conditions $pre_{p_c\text{-request}}$, $pre_{p_c\text{-enter}}$ and $pre_{p_c\text{-exit}}$ are pre-conditions of monitor procedures.

The post - condition $post_{p_c}$-enter is the post-condition of the monitor procedure p_c-enter.

The keyword starting stands for the assertion such that $\underline{starting} \supset (\tau = \tau' \wedge \bar{x} = \bar{x}' \wedge \bar{y} = \bar{y}')$, other words the assertion starting implies that the procedure has not yet updated any values of data related variables. Similarly, the keyword finished stands for the assertion such that $post_{f_c}(\tau) \supset \underline{finished}$.

In other words, when the procedure has finished updating values of data-related variables, finished is true.

So the next step in proving that a shared class correctly implements a consistent specification of a data abstraction is to define the above pre- and post-conditions for every monitor procedure. Namely, for every operation p_c define the monitor pre-conditions pre_{p_c}-request, pre_{p_c}-enter and pre_{p_c}-exit, and the post-condition $post_{p_c}$-enter.

Let P be an abstract program having the following form:

P::Type T; parbegin P_1 ... P_n parend

where for every i $(1 \leq i \leq n)$ P_i contains only activations of operations of type T, and processes $P_1,\dots,P_n$ are synchronized by synchronization specification $S(\alpha)$ specified in type T.

Let CP denote a concrete implementation of the abstract program P:
CP::<u>Type</u> T: <u>shared</u> <u>class;</u> <u>var</u> t:T; <u>parbegin</u> $CP_1 \dots CP_n$ <u>parend</u> where for every i $(1 \le i \le n)$ CP_i contains only activitions of procedures of concrete type T and process CP_i is formed from P_i by replacement of all activations of abstract operations with activations of suitable concrete procedures $t.p_c$. The processes $CP_1,\dots,CP_n$ are synchronized by the monitor defined in shared class T.

We search for the sufficient conditions such that, if P and CP both terminate and the value of t on termination of concrete program CP will be τ then $\alpha=\varphi(\tau)$ will be true for the abstract object produced by the abstract program P.

The following conditions are required

(P.1.) The representation is correct

I. The representation of data-related parts is correct:

a. $I_c(\tau, ms) \supset I_a(\varphi(\tau))$

b. $\{Requires_a\}\ C_{init}\ \{Initially_a(\varphi(\tau)) \wedge I_c(\tau, ms)\}$

II. The representation of synchronization is correct:
For every abstract operation p the following holds: the synchronization specification $S(\alpha)$ holds before activation of p if and only if the pre-condition pre_{p_c}-enter holds before activation of monitor procedure p_c-enter.

Notes:

1/ Conditions required under point I ensure the correctness of the representation of data related parts, as in the case of sequential programs.

2/ Conditions required under point II for the monitor procedures hold automatically if the monitor is generated by the algorithm described in [Laventhal 78]. The equivalence of the abstract synchronization specification and the concrete synchronization specification can be formally proved. This proof can be found in [Laventhal 78].

(P.2.) The data-related parts and the synchronization code constitute a consistent system:

a. $(I_c(\tau, ms') \wedge post_{p_c\text{-enter}} \wedge \underline{starting}) \supset (pre_{f_c} \wedge I_c(\tau, ms) \wedge \underline{starting})$

b. $\{I_c(\tau,ms') \wedge \underline{finished} \wedge pre_{p_c\text{-exit}}\}$ p_c-exit $\{I_c(\tau,ms)\}$

c. $\{I_c(\tau,ms') \wedge \underline{starting} \wedge pre_{p_c\text{-enter}}\}$ p_c-enter $\{I_c(\tau,ms) \wedge \underline{starting}\}$

d. $\{I_c(\tau,ms') \wedge \underline{starting} \wedge pre_{p_c\text{-request}}\}$ p_c-request $\{I_c(\tau,ms) \wedge \underline{starting}\}$

Note:
On the one hand, the requirements of consistency say that if the concrete invariant I_c and the synchronization condition hold before activating a concrete procedure p_c and the procedure has not yet updated any values of data-related variables then the pre-condition pre_{f_c} of the concrete procedure holds as well. On the other hand they say that $I_c(\tau,ms)$ is also an invariant of the monitor and if the execution of a concrete operation f_c has finished the result of the operation f_c remains unchanged under execution of monitor procedure p_c-exit.

(P.3.) Every concrete operation f_c of a procedure p_c is correct

a. $\{I_c(\tau',ms) \wedge \underline{starting} \wedge pre_{f_c}(\tau')\}$ $f_c(\tau',\bar{x},\bar{y}')\{I_c(\tau,ms) \wedge post_{f_c}\}$

b. The proofs of all procedures p_c are interference-free in the sense of [Owicki 78] .

Notes:

1/ The conditions under point (P.3.a.) ensure that the body of every procedure is correct for the pre-condition pre_{f_c} and the post-condition $post_{f_c}$.

The condition under point (P.3.b.) ensures that the effect of operations executed concurrently is the same as if they had been executed one after the other /i.e. sequentially/.

2/ The interference-free property of two proofs

$\{R_i\}\ S_i\ \{Q_i\}$ and $\{R_j\}\ S_j\ \{Q_j\}$ for all i and j

automatically holds if S_i and S_j are mutually exclusive.

(P.4.) The connection is correct between the abstract and the concrete specifications.
For every abstract operation f_a and concrete operation f_c:

a. $(I_c(\tau, ms) \wedge pre_{f_a}(\varphi(\tau))) \supset pre_{f_c}(\tau)$

b. $(I_c(\tau', ms) \wedge pre_{f_a}(\varphi(\tau')) \wedge post_{f_c}(\tau)) \supset post_{f_a}(\varphi(\tau))$

Note:
Conditions required under points a and b ensure that the result of execution of the abstract operation f_a is equal to φ applied to the result of the execution of the concrete operation f_c.

<u>Theorem</u>

Let T be a consistent specification of a shared abstract data type and let t denote an implementation of the abstract type T. If the implementation t satisfies the conditions (P.1.) to (P.4.) and if, the abstract program P and the concrete program CP are constructed in the above way and both terminate, then they give results α and τ, respectively such that

$$\alpha = \varphi(\tau).$$

<u>Proof</u> /outline/
In the proof of our theorem we use the result of Hoare's theorem proved for sequential programs [Hoare 72].
An abstract program P is an ideal one and so it is interference-free according to the synchronization specification $S(\alpha)'$. This is why every execution sequence P_e of the abstract program P can be regarded as a sequential program S_a of abstract operations ordered in time according to the enter events associated with each abstract operation. From the view-point of the data-related parts of the concrete specification every execution sequence CP_e of the concrete program CP is equivalent to a sequential program S_c in which the form of every concrete operation is $f_c(\tau, \bar{x}, \bar{y})$ and the execution order of these operations is determined by the execution order of the appropriate enter procedures of the monitor.

This equivalence is ensured by conditions (P.2.) and by the fact that the proof of all operations f_c are interference-free, as required in condition (P.3.b.)
The conditions required under point (P.1. II.) ensure that for every execution sequence P_e of the abstract program P there exists an appropriate execution sequence CP_e of the concrete program CP, which is equivalent to a sequential abstract program S_a and a sequential concrete program S_c respectively.

Let us examine these "sequential" programs S_a and S_c.
The concrete program S_c fulfils the following conditions:

(C.1) a. $I_c(\tau, ms) \supset I_a(\varphi(\tau))$

b. $\{Requires_a\}\ \tau init\ \{Initially_a(\varphi(\tau)) \wedge I_c(\tau, ms)\}$

(C.2.) for every operation f_c:

$$\{I_c(\tau, ms) \wedge pre_{f_c}(\tau')\}\ f_c(\tau', \bar{x}; \bar{y};)\ \{I_c(\tau, ms) \wedge post_{f_c}(\tau)\}$$

(C.3.) for every abstract operation f_a and concrete operation f_c

a. $(I_c(\tau, ms) \wedge pre_{f_a}(\varphi(\tau)) \supset pre_{f_c}(\tau)$

b. $(I_c(\tau, ms) \wedge pre_{f_a}(\varphi(\tau')) \wedge post_{f_c}(\tau)) \supset post_{f_a}(\varphi(\tau))$

According to Hoare's theorem conditions (C.1.) to (C.3.) are sufficient conditions for $\alpha_{S_a} = \varphi(\tau_{S_c})$, where α_{S_a} denotes the abstract object after S_a terminates and τ_{S_c} denotes the concrete object after S_c terminates. But $\alpha_{S_a} = \alpha$ and $\tau_{S_c} = \tau$ since P_e is equivalent to S_a and CP_e is equivalent to S_c for the data-related part of the implementation. So $\alpha = \varphi(\tau)$ after both P_e and CP_e terminate, where α denotes the abstract object after P_e terminates and τ denotes the concrete object after CP_e terminates. This holds for every execution sequence of the abstract program P, so $\alpha = \varphi(\tau)$ holds after both P and CP terminate. This means that conditions (P.1.) to (P.4.) are sufficient conditions for our theorem.

In proving the correctness of an implementation we use Howard's method for proving monitors [Howard 76] but the proof rules must be extended with a rule for the <u>choose</u> statement and a rule for monitor procedure call.

3. Bounded shared stack - an example

The following is a specification of a bounded shared abstract stack:
<u>type</u> stack (n:integer):
    stack=sequence(e)

```
requires n >0
initially nullsequence ( e0)
invariant 0 ≤ length (stack)≤n
operations
 push (s:stack, y:elem)
  pre 0 ≤ length ( s)<n   post s=s'~y
 pop  (s:stack, result x)
  pre 0 < length (S) ≤ n  post x=last (s') ∧ s=leader (s')
synchronization
S: push[i].exit ——> pop[i].enter     ∧
   pop[i].exit  ——> push[i+n].enter  ∧
   push[i].exit ——> push[i+1].enter  ∧
   pop[i].exit  ——> pop[i+1].enter   ∧
  (push[i].exit ——> pop[k].enter     ∨
   pop[k].exit  ——> push[i].enter )
```

An implementation of the above specification is as follows:

```
type BS(n): shared class;
 begin
  BSvar: record c-stack: array 1...n of message;
                sp: integer
         end
  push: procedure (y:message);
         begin
          call m.push-enter;
            sp:=sp+1;
            c-stack[sp]:=y;
          call m.pop-exit
         end
  pop: procedure (result x: message);
         begin
          call m.pop-enter;
             x:=c-stack [sp];
            sp:=sp-1
          call m.pop-exit
         end
mm n :monitor;
        pushn, pushx, popn, popx: integer;
        pushentry, popentry: condition;
        push-enter: procedure;
        begin
```

```
     if(popx ≤ pushn-n ∨ pushn≠pushx∨popn≠popx)then
          condition ∦ wait (pushentry) end;
     pushn:=pushn+1,
   choose
     condition ∦ queue (pushentry)∧popx > pushn-n ∧
      pushn=pushx∧popn=popx:
     condition ∦ signal (pushentry);
     condition ∦ queue (popentry) ∧ pushx >popn ∧
      pushn=pushx∧popn=popx:
     condition ∦ signal (popentry);
   end
 end push-enter
 push-exit:procedure;
 begin
     pushx:=pushx+1;
     choose
       :
     end
 end push-exit
 pop-enter: procedure:
 begin
     if(pushx ≤ popn∨pushn≠pushx∨popn≠popx) then
          condition ∦ wait (popentry) end
     popn:=popn+1;
     choose
       :
     end
end pop-enter
pop-exit: procedure:
begin
      popx:=popx+1;
      choose
       :
      end
  end pop-exit
  pushn, pushx, popn, popx:=0,0,0,0;
end mm
sp:=0; var m (n):mm
end BS
```

The synchronization monitor mm was generated by the algorithm described in [Laventhal 78].
The proof of the correctness of the implementation of the bounded shared abstract stack is as follows.
The first step in the proof, is to define the relation between the abstract object and the concrete data variables:

$$\text{stack} = \varphi(\text{BSvar}) = \text{seq}(\text{c-stack}, 1, \text{sp})$$

where $\text{seq}(v,i,j) = \langle v_i, v_{i+1}, \ldots, v_j \rangle$ and

$$\text{seq}(v,i,j) = \langle\,\rangle \text{ if } i>j$$

Then we define the concrete invariant and pre-and post conditions of the concrete operations.
The concrete invariant $I_c(\mathcal{C},ms)$ is $: 0 \leq \text{pushx}-\text{popn} \leq \text{sp} \leq \text{pushn}-\text{popx} \leq n$
where sp is a data variable of the shared class and pushn, pushx, popn and popx are synchronization state variables of monitor m.

The pre- and post-conditions of the body of the concrete operations are the following:

pre_{push} : $\text{sp} < n$

$\text{post}_{\text{push}}$: $\text{c-stack} = \alpha(\text{c-stack}', \text{sp}, y) \wedge \text{sp} = \text{sp}'+1$

where $\alpha(v,i,y)$ denotes an array identical to v except that $v_i = y$.

pre_{pop} : $0 < \text{sp}$

post_{pop} : $\text{c-stack}' = \alpha(\text{c-stack}, \text{sp}', x) \wedge \text{sp} = \text{sp}'-1 \wedge x = \text{c-stack}[\text{sp}']$

To prove correctness of the implementation we must give the pre- and post-conditions of the monitor procedures as well, which are as follows:

$\text{pre}_{\text{push-enter}}$: <u>true</u>

$\text{post}_{\text{push-enter}}$: $\text{pushn} = \text{pushn}'+1 \wedge \text{pushn} = \text{pushx}+1 \wedge$
$\text{popn} = \text{popx} \wedge \text{popx} \geq \text{pushn}'+1-n$

$\text{pre}_{\text{push-exit}}$: $\text{pushn} = \text{pushx}+1 \wedge \text{pushx}-\text{popn} < \text{sp}$

$\text{pre}_{\text{pop-enter}}$: <u>true</u>

$\text{post}_{\text{pop-enter}}$: $\text{popn} = \text{popn}'+1 \wedge \text{pushx} > \text{popn}' \wedge \text{pushn} = \text{pushx} \wedge \text{popn} = \text{popx}+1$

$\text{pre}_{\text{pop-exit}}$: $\text{popn} = \text{popx}+1 \wedge \text{sp} < \text{pushn}-\text{popx}$

Now we can simply prove that the above implementation fulfils the conditions required in (P.1.) to (P.4.).

4. Conclusion

This paper presents sufficient conditions for proving correctness of an implementation of shared abstract data types. The presented technique is similar to Owicki's method [Owicki 76], but in our case abstract data types are implemented by shared classes instead of monitors. This fact makes the correctness proofs of implementations more complicated. But shared classes allow implementations with greater concurrency than monitors.

An open problem is: How can the abstract specification be used in correctness proofs of programs using the data objects specified by the above method? We think that the introduction of the notion of auxiliary variables helps us to solve this problem.

References

[Dijkstra 75] E.W. Dijkstra
"Guarded Commands, Nondeterminacy and Formal Derivation of Programs"
Comm. of the ACM 18, 8, pp. 453-457 /1975/

[Hoare 72] C.A.R. Hoare
Proofs of Correctness of Data Representations, Acta Informatica I. pp. 271-281. /1972/

[Hoare 74] C.A.R. Hoare
Monitors: an Operating System Structuring Concept
Comm. of the ACM 17. 10, pp. 549-556 /October 1974/

[Howard 76] J.H. Howard
Proving Monitors
Comm. of the ACM 19,5, pp. 273-279 /1976/

[Kozma 81] L. Kozma
A Transformation of Strongly Correct Concurrent Programs
In: Proceedings of Third Hungarian Computer Science Conference, pp. 157-170 /1981/

[Lamport 77] L. Lamport
Proving the Correctness of Multiprocess Programs
EIII Transactions on Software Engineering, Vol. SE-3, No. 2., /March 1977/

[Lamsweerde and Sintzoff 79] A. van Lamsweerde and M. Sintzoff
Formal Derivation of Strongly Correct
Acta Informatica 12, pp. 1-31. /1979/

[Laventhal 78] M.S. Laventhal
Synthesis of synchronization code for data abstracti abstractions
M.I.T. Laboratory for Computer Science /1978/

[Owicki 76] S. Owicki
An axiomatic proof technique for parallel programs
II. shared data abstractions
Stanford University /1976/

[Owicki and Gries 76] S. Owicki and D. Gries
An Axiomatic Proof Technique for Parallel Programs I.
Acta Informatica 6, pp. 319-340 /1976/

[Owicki 78] S. Owicki
Verifying Concurrent Programs with Shared Data Classes
In: Formal Description of Programming Concepts,
E.J. Neuhold /e.d./
North-Holland Publishing Company /1978/

[Shaw and et. al. 77] M.Shaw, W.A. Wulf, R.L. London
Abstraction and Verification in Alphard: Defining and Specifiying Iteration and Generators
Comm. of the ACM, 20, 8. pp. 353-364 /Aug. 1977/

[Spitzen and Wegbreit 75] J. Spitzen and B. Wegbreit
The Verification and Synthesis of Data Structures
Acta Informatica 4. pp. 127-144 /1975/

[Varga 80] L. Varga
Specification of Reliable Software
Operációs Rendszerek Téli Iskola
MTA Számitástechnikai és Automatizálási Kutató Intézet
Tanulmányok 113/1980 309-325

[Wulf and et. al. 76] W. Wulf, R. London and M. Shaw
"An Introduction to the Construction and Verification of Alphard Programs"
IEEE Transactions of Software Eng.
SE-2, pp. 253-264 /1976/

[Wulf and et. al. 77] W.A. Wulf, R.L. London and M. Shaw
Abstraction and Verification in Alphard:
A Symbol Table Example
In. Proceedings of IFIP TC2 Working
Conference, Novosibirsk /1977/

SPECIFICATION OF COMMUNICATING PROCESSES AND PROCESS IMPLEMENTATION CORRECTNESS

Philippe JORRAND
IMAG
BP 53X
38041 GRENOBLE CEDEX
FRANCE

In this paper, a communicating process is viewed as a device able to send and to receive messages through ports which constitute its only interface with its environment. The specification of a communicating process describes properties of this communication activity, independently of the internal structure and behavior of the process.

The specifications considered here are restricted to the description of the set of possible sequences of successive uses of the ports of a process. The chosen formalism, directly inspired from guarded commands, also applies to the description of sequences of communications inside a network of communicating processes.

This paper shows how process specifications can be combined to form networks and studies the conditions under which a given network or process can be said to be a correct implementation of another process. Directions for future research in this area are suggested at the end of the paper.

I. A SYNTAX FOR PROCESS AND NETWORK SPECIFICATIONS

For the purpose of this paper, a communication can be reduced to the instantatenous transmission of one message from one output port to one input port. The path followed by a message from output port a to input port b is an internal connector denoted by a.b. Some communications are simply said to be "from outside" or "to outside" and the dummy port name δ is used for referring to the corresponding external connectors : $a.\delta$ and $\delta.b$. If K_{IN} and K_{EX} are respectively the set of internal connectors and the set of external connectors, $K=K_{IN} \cup K_{EX}$ is the set of connectors.

Example

A buffer b(N) of capacity N can be viewed as a communicating process with an input port I and an output port O. Its specification describes the set of possible sequences of communications along $\delta.I$ and $O.\delta$. This can be done with a non deterministic automaton quite similar to a do..od iteration [DIJK 76] where one guarded command is labeled by $\delta.I$ and the other one is labeled by $O.\delta$; the set of possible sequences of "executions" of the commands thus defines the set of possible sequences of communications :

```
v:=0;
do
  {δ.I} v<N → v:=v+1 □
  {0.δ} v>0 → v:=v-1
od
```

End of Example

In order to define properly the network construction operators, there is a need for a formalization of such specifications. Let Var be a set of variable names and Val be a set of values. A "state" then belongs to $Q = Var \rightarrow Val$. A specification may be viewed as composed of two parts :

- an initialization function
- a set of "rules", each rule being a triple : <predicate on state, communications, state changing function>

More formally, we define :

$F = Q \rightarrow Q$ state changing functions

$F_0 \subseteq F$ constants $(\forall q,q' \in Q,\ \forall f_o \in Fo.\ f_o(q) = f_o(q'))$

$P = Q \rightarrow \{\underline{true},\underline{false}\}$ predicates on states

$E = 2^K$ events ($e = \{c_1, c_2, \ldots, c_p\}$ denotes the simultaneous occurrence of communications along $c_1, c_2, \ldots, c_p$)

$R = P \times E \times F$ rules

$S = F_o \times 2^R$ specifications

For making this structure of specifications appear clearly in our concrete syntax, we depart slightly from guarded commands. A specification s is written :

$s = \langle f_o,\ \{\langle p_i, e_i, f_i\rangle\}\ \rangle,\ i \in [n] = \{1,\ldots,n\}$

Examples

$b(N) = \langle\ v{:=}0,$
$\quad \{\ \langle v<N,\ \{\delta.I\},\ v{:=}v+1\rangle,$
$\quad\ \ \langle v>0\ \ \{0.\delta\},\ v{:=}v-1\rangle\}\ \rangle$

$c = \langle\ q{:=}Q_0,$
$\quad \{\ \langle q=Q_0,\ \{\delta.R\},\ q{:=}Q_1\rangle,$
$\quad\ \ \langle q=Q_0,\ \{\delta.S\},\ q{:=}Q_1\rangle,$
$\quad\ \ \langle q=Q_1,\ \{T.\delta, U.\delta\},\ q{:=}Q_0\rangle\}\ \rangle$

The process b(N) can be viewed as a buffer of capacity N whereas c accepts an input through either port R or port S, then sends outputs simultaneously through ports T and U before being ready again for input. These processes can be pictured as follows :

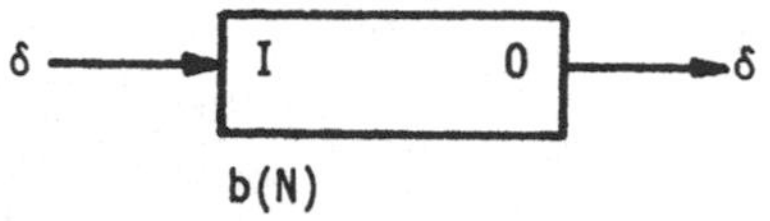

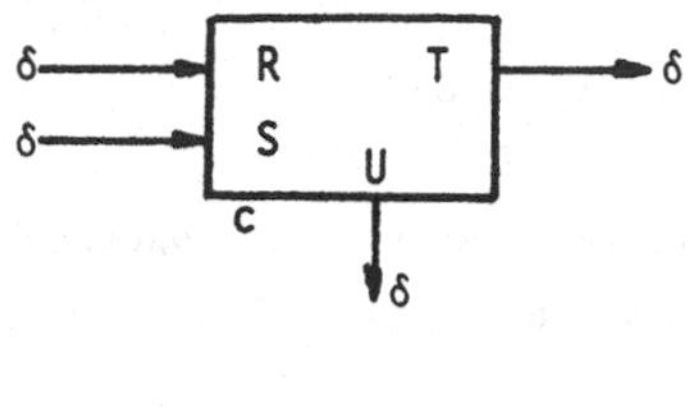

End of examples

II. CONSTRUCTION OF NETWORKS

We define three network construction operators :

$$\text{Union : } // \in S\times S \to S$$

$$\text{Connection : } + \in S\times K_{IN} \to S$$

$$\text{Abstraction : } [] \in S\times 2^{K} \to S$$

This approach has some similarity with [MILN 80]. A preliminary version of it has been presented in [JORR 80]. The main differences with the work of Milner are that the operations of union (juxtaposition of processes) and connection between ports are separated and that a connection may be established between any two ports, independently of their names, provided one of them is able to send messages and the other one is able to receive messages : the direction of communications is made visible. Furthermore, the connection operation allows multiple connections to and from any port. The abstraction operation may be used for preventing access to part or all of the structure of a network of processes : one of its applications is to make impossible further connections to or from specified ports. No renaming operation has been defined here, although it is clearly required in some cases (e.g. a network with several instances of identical processes) : it is a simple, superficial, syntatic operation and its definition has no interesting implications on the rest of the model.

An other related work is that of Hoare on a calculus of total correctness for communicating processes [HOAR 81], where he defines an algebra of processes. Here also, the difference lies in the choice of operators. Since we consider only the "black box" behavior of our processes, a number of Hoare's operators are not relevant to our approach. With respect to union, we consider that the result must also describe the possibilities of simultaneous communications, which is not the case with the disjoint parallelism of Hoare. When a connection is to be created between two processes P and Q, the union P and Q is built first and the connection is established in the result. Processes P and Q were independent and an important characteristic of our model is precisely that it maintains a distinction between communications which can only be interleaved and communications which are actually independent and which can be either interleaved or happen simultaneously. This distinction is introduced by our notion of event, and it is essential for a correct definition of the conditions under which a communication may actually happen between two processes. Furthermore, this notion of event also allows the definition of communications and synchronizations involving more than two processes.

II.1. The union operator

The union operator simply "puts together" two processes or networks and results in a specification which describes both the interleaving of the individual behaviors of its operands and the possible simultaneous occurrences of independent communications. Les s and s' be two specifications :

$$s = \langle f,h\rangle,\ h = \{\langle p_i,e_i,f_i\rangle\},\ i\in[n]$$

$$s' = \langle f',h'\rangle,\ h' = \{\langle p'_j,e'_j,f'_j\rangle\},\ j\in[n']$$

We assume, without any loss of generality, that s and s' do not use any identical variable name nor port name (a renaming operation could be introduced, precisely for that puspose).

The union of s and s' is then :

$$s//s' = \langle f\cdot f',\ h\cup h'\cup\{\langle p_i\wedge p'_j,\ e_i\cup e'_j,\ f_i\cdot f'_j\rangle \mid i\in[n],\ j\in[n']\}\rangle$$

where f•f' is the "union" of functions f and f' :

$$\begin{aligned} f\cdot f' = \lambda q\ .\ \lambda v\ .\ \underline{\text{if}}\ & q(v) \neq f(q)(v) \rightarrow f(q)(v)\ \square \\ & q(v) \neq f'(q)(v) \rightarrow f'(q)(v)\ \square \\ & q(v) = f(q)(v) \wedge q(v) = f'(q)(v) \rightarrow q(v) \\ \underline{\text{fi}} & \end{aligned}$$

Since the variables in s and s' are distinct, there is no danger of inconsistency in the definition of the function f•f'. We note also that f•f' = f'•f

II.2. The connection operator

Our hypothesis on the occurrence of a communication is similar to the "rendez-vous" hypotheses of CSP [HOAR 78], ADA [ICHB 79] and others : a communication along a.b is possible only when communications along a.δ and δ.b are simultaneously possible. Let s be a specification :

$$s = \langle f,h\rangle,\ h = \{\langle p_i,e_i,f_i\rangle\},\ i\in[n]$$

The connection of a to b in s is then :

$$s + a.b = \langle f,h \cup \{\langle p_i,e_i-\{a.\delta,\delta.b\} \cup \{a.b\},\ f_i\rangle \mid \{a.\delta,\delta.b\}\in e_i\}\rangle$$

II.3. The abstraction operator

Given a network or process specification $s = \langle f, \{\langle p_i,e_i,f_i\rangle\} \rangle$, $i\in[n]$, the abstraction operator can be used to hide part or all the internal structure of s, while keeping access, in the result, to a selected subset $\{k_1,\dots k_p\}$ of the connectors of s. The abstraction of s with access to $k_1,\dots,k_p$ is :

$$s[k_1,\dots,k_p] = \langle f,\{\langle p_i,e_i \cap \{k_1,\dots,k_p\},f_i\rangle \mid e_i\cap K_{EX} \subseteq \{k_1,\dots,k_p\}\}\rangle$$

II.4. Examples

Given b(N) and c defined above, we can write :

$$s(N) = ((b(N) \mathbin{//} c) + 0.S)\ [\delta.I,\ T.\delta,\ U.\delta]$$

The result is :

$$
\begin{aligned}
s(N) = <(&v:=0,\ q:=Q_0),\\
&\{<\ v<N,\ \{\delta.I\},\ v:=v+1>,\\
&\ <\ (v>0 \wedge q=Q_0),\ \emptyset,\ (v:=v-1,\ q:=Q_1)>,\\
&\ <q=Q_1,\ \{T.\delta, U.\delta\},\ q:=Q_0>,\\
&\ <\ (v<N \wedge q=Q_1),\ \{\delta.I, T.\delta,\ U.\delta\},\ (v:=v+1,,\ q:=Q_0)>\}>
\end{aligned}
$$

It can be pictured as follows :

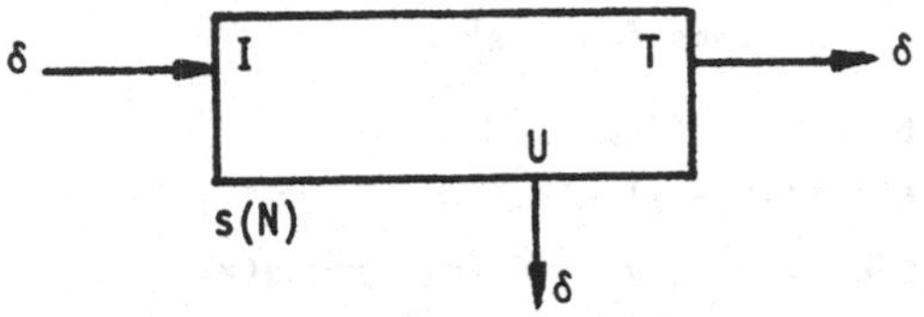

We could also write :

$$t(N) = ((b(N)//c) + T.I)\ [\delta.R, U.\delta, T.I, 0.\delta]$$

The result is :

$$
\begin{aligned}
t(N) = <\ &(v:=0,\ q:=Q_0),\\
&\{\ <\ q=Q_0,\ \{\delta.R\},\ q:=Q_1>,\\
&\quad <\ (q=Q_1 \wedge v<N),\ \{T.I, U.\delta\},\ (q:=Q_0,\ v:=v+1)>,\\
&\quad <\ v>0,\ \{0.\delta\}, v:=v-1>,\\
&\quad <\ (q=Q_0 \wedge v>0),\ \{\delta.R, 0.\delta\}, (q:=Q_1,\ v:=v-1)>\}\ >
\end{aligned}
$$

The corresponding picture would be :

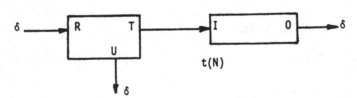

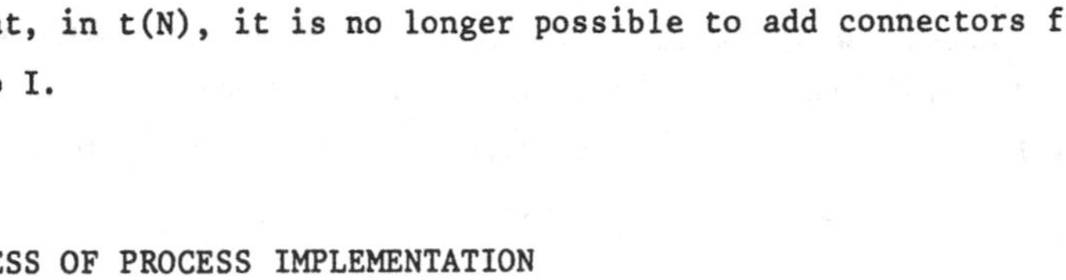

We notice that, in t(N), it is no longer possible to add connectors from T nor connectors to I.

III. CORRECTNESS OF PROCESS IMPLEMENTATION

Given a specification $s = <f, \{<p_i, e_i, f_i>\}>, i \in [n]$, we consider two categories of interesting questions about it :

i) Analysis questions. The design of the process or network s is supposed to produce an object with a dynamic behavior which has some desired properties. The analysis of its behavior is concerned with the study of situations where messages may or may not (will or will not) flow along some connectors and with the study of conditions which may or may not (will or will not) lead to such situations. The situations which are traditionally of interest are those of deadlocks and these of livelocks.

With our format of process and network specifications, the work of Sifakis [SIFA 80], Guerreiro [GUER 81] and Queille and Sifakis [QUEI 82] can be directly applied here : computation of invariants and trajectories as fixpoints of predicate transformers, definition of reachability properties and verification of desired properties expressed in terms of a temporal logic. The transposition of these tools to our specifications is described in [JORR 82]. It is quite straightforward and will not be further detailed here.

ii) Correctness questions. The process or network s, which may have been obtained by applying the network construction operators on more elementary processes or networks s_1, s_2, ..., is intended to be an implementation of some process r. The specification of r has been given as a goal to achieve in the design of s. The question is then : may someone use s, while believing he is actually using r ? If the answer is "yes", we say that r is correctly implemented by s.

We consider that such a question is much better answered by defining an order relation between r and s, rather than an equivalence or congruence relation as in CCS [MILN 80] : saying that r is correctly implemented by s is not the same as saying that s is correctly implemented by r. Our approach for defining that notion of correctness is to consider the infinite unwinding of specifications into trees and to define an appropriate order relation in the domain of those trees.

II.1. Trees and forests

We use a definition of trees analogous to that used, among others, by Guessarian [GUES 81].

For all $n \in \mathbb{N}$, we have $[n] = \{1,\ldots,n\}$. The set of finite words on $[n]$ is $[n]^*$ and $\epsilon[n]^*$ is the empty word. We call tree domain of degree n a part D_n of $[n]^*$ such that :

1) $\forall u \in D_n,\ v \in [n]^*.\ (v \leq u \implies v \in D_n)$

2) $\forall p,p' \in [n],\ u \in [n]^*.\ (up \in D_n \wedge p' < p \implies up' \in D_n)$.

Where, in $[n]^*$, $v \leq u$ means that v is a left factor of u. The elements of D_n are called the nodes of the tree domain.

Let X be an arbitrary set. A tree of degree at most n on X is a mapping $\sigma : [n]^* \to X$ such that $dom(\sigma)$ is a tree domain. The set of trees of degree at most n on X is $\Sigma_n(X)$. Given a node $u \in dom(\sigma)$, $\sigma(u)$ is called the label of u.

Given $\sigma\in\Sigma_n(X)$, the root of σ is $\sigma(\varepsilon)$ and, when $dom(\sigma) \neq \emptyset$, we have $a\in X$, $p\leq n$ and $\sigma_1,\ldots,\sigma_p \in \Sigma_n(X)$ such that :

1) $a = \sigma(\varepsilon)$
2) $dom(\sigma) \cap [n] = [p]$
3) $\forall i\in[p].\ dom(\sigma_i) = \{u \mid iu\in dom(\sigma)\}$
4) $\forall i\in[p].\ \sigma_i(u) = \sigma(iu)$

We write $\sigma=a<\sigma_1,\ldots,\sigma_p>$ and $son(\sigma) = <\sigma_1,\ldots\sigma_p>$. When $dom(\sigma) = \varepsilon$, we have $son(\sigma) = <>$. Finally, a forest is a finite sequence of trees $<\sigma_1,\ldots,\sigma_n>$. The set of forests of degree at most n on X is :

$$\Phi_n(X) = \bigcup_{i\in[n]} (\Sigma_n(X))^i$$

Thus, when $\sigma \in \Sigma_n(X)$, $son(\sigma) \in \Phi_n(X)$.

III.2. Tree semantics of processes and networks

With our restricted view of specifications, where we only describe all possible sequences of communications, we may represent these sequences in trees where the nodes are labeled by events. In the same way as program schemes have been used to represent programs and study their semantics [NIVAT 72] [DEBAK 76] [GUES 81], we associate a tree $T(s)$ (in fact, a forest) with a specification $s = <f, \{<p_i,e_i,f_i>\}>$, $i\in[n]$, where, given the initial state defined by f, every path originating at the root of a tree in $T(s)$ represents a possible sequence of events defined by s. The function we have to define is $T : S_n \to \Phi_n(E)$ where S_n is the set of specifications with at most n rules and $\mathbb{E}$ is the domain of events.

We define first the "unwinding" of $h = \{<p_i,e_i,f_i>\}$, $i\in[n]$:

$U : H_n \to \Phi_n(D)$ where H_n is the domain of sets of at most n rules and
$D = P\times E$, $P = Q \to \{\underline{true},\underline{false}\}$

We have $U(h) = <\sigma_1,\ldots,\sigma_n>$ where $\sigma_i : [n]^* \to D$, $dom(\sigma_i) = [n]^*$ and :

$\sigma_i(\varepsilon) = <p_i,e_i>$

$\sigma_i(k\ldots lm) = <p_m\circ f_l\circ\ldots\circ f_k\circ f_i, e_m>$

$U(h)$ is thus an "uninterpreted" forest. We interpret it by evaluating all the predicates on the initial state defined by f. This is done by the interpretation function :

$I : \Phi_n(D) \to (F\circ\!\!\to\Phi_n(\{\underline{true},\underline{false}\} \times E))$

Which, given $U(h)$ and f, builds $I(U(h))(f)$ where every predicate p in the labels $<p,e>$ of $U(h)$ is replaced by the value of the application of p to the initial state.

Finally, we need a low level "cleaning" function $R : \Phi_n(\{\underline{true},\underline{false}\} \times E)\to \Phi_n(E)$, which removes all subtrees rooted at nodes labeled by $<\underline{false},e>$, for any e. The function $\mathcal{R}$ also redefines properly the domain of the remaining trees.

Given s = <f,h>, the corresponding tree is thus :

$$T(s) = \mathcal{R}(\mathcal{I}(\mathcal{U}(h))(f))$$

The network construction operators can also be defined on forests, such that :

$$T(s) \;//\; T(s') = T(s//s')$$
$$T(s) + a.b = T(s+a.b)$$
$$T(s)\;[k_1,\ldots,k_p] = T(s[k_1,\ldots,k_p])$$

III.3. Comparison of specifications with implementations

We have given, at the begining of this paragraph, an intuitive idea of our notion of correct implementation of a process. The representation of specifications in terms of forests is used here as a basis for a formalizetion of this notion of correctness.

i) Visibility of events

An event $e_i = \{k_1,\ldots,k_p\}$ in a rule $<p_i,e_i,f_i>$ of a specification s is "enabled" when p_i is true. If at least one of the communications k_j in e_i is an external communication (i.e. of the form $\delta.a$ or $b.\delta$) then, when e_i is enabled, its occurrence requires a participation of the environment of s : we say that e_i is a visible event. On the contrary, if none of the communications in e_i is external (i.e. they are all internal or $e_i = \emptyset$), then the occurrence of e_i is out of the will of the environment and the network or process s decides alone whether it happens or not : e_i is then an invisible event. Thus we have $E = V \cup I$, where V is the set of visible events, $I=2^{K_{IN}}$ is the set of visible events and $V \cap I = \emptyset$.

Given e, e' $\in$ E, we say that e is correctly implemented by e', and we write $e \sqsubseteq e'$, iff :

$$(e\cap K_{EX} = e'\cap K_{EX}) \wedge (e\cap K_{IN} \subseteq e'\cap K_{IN})$$

ii) The case of visible events

Given $s\in S_n$ and $s'\in S_{n'}$, involving no invisible events, the corresponding forests are :

$$\phi = T(s)$$
$$\phi' = T(s'),\quad \phi,\phi'\in\Phi_p(V),\ p\leq \max(n,n')$$

It is possible to define preorder relations in $\Sigma_p(V)$ and in $\Phi_p(V)$, both denoted by $\leq_1$, in the following way :

$$\forall\sigma,\sigma'\in\Sigma_p(V).\ \sigma\leq_1\sigma' \Longleftrightarrow \sigma(\varepsilon) \sqsubseteq \sigma'(\varepsilon)$$
$$\wedge\ son(\sigma) \leq_1 son(\sigma')$$

$$\forall\phi,\phi'\in\Phi_p(V).\ \phi\leq_1\phi' \Longleftrightarrow \forall i\in[q].\ (\exists j\in[q'].\ \phi_i\leq_1 \phi'_j)$$

where $\phi = <\sigma_1,\ldots,\sigma_q>$ and $\phi' = <\sigma'_1,\ldots,\sigma'_{q'}>$.

If s and s' are two specifications such that :

$$T(s) = \langle e_1\langle\sigma_1,\sigma_2\rangle\rangle$$

$$T(s') = \langle e_2\langle\sigma_3\rangle,\ e_1\langle\sigma_2,\sigma_1,\sigma_2\rangle\rangle$$

it is indeed true that $T(s) \leq_1 T(s')$. This corresponds well to our intuitive definition of correctness considered from the user's point of view : one may use s' while believing he is using s. However, if we had :

$$T(s) = \langle e_1\langle e_2\langle\sigma_1,\sigma_2\rangle,\sigma_3\rangle\rangle$$

$$T(s') = \langle e_1\langle e_2\langle\sigma_1,\sigma_2\rangle,\ e_2\langle\sigma_1\rangle,\ e_2\langle\sigma_2\rangle,\ \sigma_3\rangle\rangle$$

it is also true $T(s) \leq_1 T(s')$. This is highly underisable : the specification s tells that after event e_1, event e_2 may occur and the user can then choose to proceed either on σ_1 or on σ_2. But the tentative implementation s' of s, which also allows e_1 followed by e_2, is such that it may take a unilateral decision forcing the user to proceed either on σ_1 or on σ_2 : the user of s' may thus be denied the ability to choose between σ_1 and σ_2. For this reason, s' cannot be considered as a correct implementation of s and the relation $\leq_1$ must be restricted to a new relation $\leq_2$ defined as follows :

$$\forall\sigma,\sigma' \in \Sigma_p(V).\ \sigma\leq_2\sigma' \Longleftrightarrow \sigma(\varepsilon) \sqsubseteq \sigma'(\varepsilon) \wedge \mathrm{son}(\sigma) \leq_2 \mathrm{son}(\sigma')$$

$$\forall\phi,\phi' \in \Phi_p(V).\ \phi\leq_2\phi' \Longleftrightarrow (\forall i\in[q].\ \exists j\in[q'].\ \sigma_i\leq_2\sigma'_j) \wedge \forall j\in q'\ .\ (\exists i\in[q].\ \sigma_i(\varepsilon) \sqsubseteq \sigma'_j(\varepsilon)) \Longrightarrow \exists k\in[q].\ \sigma_k\leq_2\sigma'_j)))$$

where $\phi = \langle\sigma_1,\ldots,\sigma_q\rangle$ and $\phi' = \langle\sigma'_1,\ldots,\sigma'_{q'}\rangle$.

We see that $\sigma\leq_2\sigma' \Longrightarrow \sigma\leq_1\sigma'$. However, as shown in the last section of the paper, a number of difficulties for a satisfying definition of implementation correctness remain with $\leq_2$.

iii) The case of invisible events

We consider now two specifications $s\in S_n$ and $s'\in S_{n'}$ such that :

$$\phi = T(s) \in \Phi_p(V)$$

$$\phi' = T(s') \in \Phi_p(E) \text{ where } p \leq \max(n,n') \text{ and } E = V \cup I.$$

It is therefore possible that some steps in the evolution of s' happen without any participation of the user. If we want to implement s by s', it is necessary that these invisible events happen without disturbing the belief of the user that he is using s while he is actually using s'. At some point, the user knows that, according to s, he may choose among a given set of events. If, in the meantime, invisible events occur in s', these must not modify the possibilities offered to the user. Hence the following definition of a relation "$\leq$" in $\Phi_p(V) \times \Phi_p(E)$ such that $\phi\leq\phi'$ can be read "ϕ is correctly implemented by ϕ'" :

$\forall\sigma\in\Sigma_p(V),\ \sigma'\in\Sigma_p(E).\ \sigma\leq\sigma' \iff (\sigma'(\varepsilon)\in V \wedge \sigma(\varepsilon) \sqsubseteq \sigma'(\varepsilon)$

$\wedge\ son(\sigma) \leq son(\sigma'))$

$\vee\ (\sigma'(\varepsilon)\in I \ \wedge\ \langle\sigma\rangle \leq son(\sigma\ ))$

$\forall\phi\in\Phi_p(V),\phi'\in\Phi_p(E).\ \phi\leq\phi \iff$

$(((\forall j\in[q'].\ \sigma'_j(\varepsilon)\in V) \wedge (\forall i\in[q].\ \exists j\in[q'].\ \sigma_i\leq\sigma'_j))$

$\vee((\exists j\in[q'].\ \sigma'_j(\varepsilon)\in I) \wedge (\forall j\in[q'].\ (\sigma'_j(\varepsilon)\in I \Longrightarrow \phi \leq son(\sigma'_j)))))$

$\wedge\forall j\in[q'].\ ((\exists i\in[q].\ \sigma_i(\varepsilon) \sqsubseteq \sigma'_j(\varepsilon)) \Longrightarrow (\exists k\in[q].\ \sigma_k\leq\sigma'_j))$

where $\phi = \langle\sigma_1,\ldots,\sigma_q\rangle$ and $\phi' = \langle\sigma'_1,\ldots,\sigma'_{q'}\rangle$. This definition clearly disallows infinite sequences of invisible events : this is the problem of "infinite chatter" also encountered by others (e.g. [HOAR 81] and [GUER 81]).

IV. DIRECTIONS FOR FUTURE WORK

In the domain of parallelism and communicating processes, much remains to be done. The specification formalism and the notion of correctness presented in this paper constitute an interesting basis for further studies in a variety of directions.

IV.1. Hidden choices

Let a, b, c and d be four events and let s and s' be two specifications such that (example suggested by [DARO 81]) :

$T(s) = \langle a\langle b\langle c\rangle,\ b\langle d\rangle\rangle\rangle$

$T(s') = \langle a\langle b\langle c\rangle\rangle,\ a\langle b\langle d\rangle\rangle\rangle$

With our definition of "≤", s and s' are not comparable. However, from the user's point of view, they are indistinguishable. The only difference is the point in the history of the systems when a choice is made between a sequence with c and a sequence with d. This choice is made by the system itself and is hidden from the user. But if we consider also s" such that :

$T(s") = \langle a\langle b\langle c,d\rangle\rangle\rangle$

we have $T(s) \leq T(s")$ and $T(s') \leq T(s")$, which is absolutely normal. Thus, we are in presence of a "restricted" distributivity rule where, in terms of regular expressions, we could have a(bc + bd) = (abc + abd) but also a(bc + bd) ≠ ab(c + d) and (abc + abd) ≠ ab(c + d). This can be formulated as follows, where $\phi = \langle\sigma_1,\ldots,\sigma_p\rangle$ and $\sigma_k = a_k\langle\sigma'_1,\ldots,\sigma'_{p'}\rangle$:

- If $\exists i,j\in[p'],\ i\neq j$, such that $\sigma'_i(\varepsilon) = \sigma'_j(\varepsilon)$, then ϕ can be rewritten :

$d(\phi) = \langle\sigma_1,\ldots,\sigma_{k-1},\sigma_{ki},\sigma_{kj},\sigma_{k+1},\ldots,\sigma_p\rangle$

where : $\sigma_{ki} = a_k<\sigma'_1,\ldots,\sigma'_{j-1},\sigma'_{j+1},\ldots,\sigma'_{p'}>$

$\sigma_{kj} = a_k<\sigma'_1,\ldots,\sigma'_{i-1},\sigma'_{i+1},\ldots,\sigma'_{p'}>$

If $\nexists i,j\in[p']$, $i\neq j$, such that $\sigma'_i(\varepsilon) = \sigma'_j(\varepsilon)$, then $d(\phi) = \phi$.

It would then be interesting to reduce all forests to a normal form by repeated application of this rewriting rule. However, we must first guarantee that such a normal form actually exists. The problem of hidden choices will then be solved without changing our definition of "≤".

IV.2. Proof of correctness

The order relation "≤" which has been described is defined on forests which contain infinite trees. If we want to prove correctness of implementation by computing that relation, we must do so on finite representations of these forests. First, we must guarantee that, given two such forests ϕ and ϕ', they can be considered as limits of chains $\{\phi_i\}$ and $\{\phi'_j\}$ of forests of finite trees and that if for every ϕ_i, there is a ϕ'_j such that $\phi_i \leq \phi'_j$, this implies that $\phi \leq \phi'$. If all of this holds, then we have to choose a subclass of forests such that we are able to find a ϕ_i and a ϕ'_j which characterize the complete chains. It seems that forest with regular trees will do. But then we must study which restrictions are necessary on the form of the p'_is and f'_is of the rules $<p_i,e_i,f_i>$ in a specification in order to guarantee that we produce such forests. This class of forest should also be closed under the operations of union, connection and abstraction.

IV.3. Full specifications

Clearly, "useful" specification of communicating processes and networks must contain further information about the communication activity than is present in the restricted form of specification considered in this paper. It appears that the framework presented in this paper can easily accomodate other aspects of specifications.

i) Types of messages. A type can be associated with every port in a process specification. This will define legal and illegal connections. Furthermore, process specifications can be generic, in the sense of [BERT 81] : a process specification can be parametrized by types. These formal types can be bound to actual types when an instance of the generic process is used. The actual types must satisfy properties attached to their corresponding formal types (e.g. have the operations + and < defined on objects of the type). These properties define an order relation between types with can then be used when extending our notion of correctness to take case of types : an event is now a set of pairs <connector,type> and only the order "$\sqsubseteq$" between events has to be redefined.

ii) Functions computed on output ports. In order to describe what a process actually "does", functions can be associated with output ports. Let $p_1,\dots,p_n$ be the output ports of a process, and $q_1,\dots,q_n$ be its input port. If we use the name of a connector to denote the sequential flow of messages having moved along that connector at some point in the history of the process, we can describe the functions of a sizeable subclass of processes by writing LUCID-like [ASHC 76] equations :

$$p_1.\delta = f_1(\delta.q_1,\dots,\delta.q_n)$$
$$p_2.\delta = f_2(\delta.q_1,\dots,\delta.q_n)$$
$$\vdots$$
$$p_m.\delta = f_m(\delta.q_1,\dots,\delta.q_n)$$

Three new operators are required to take care of properties of our communication networks :

- The shift operator λ : for a buffer of capacity N with input port I and outport O, we would say that $O.\delta = \lambda(\delta.I,N)$ to represent the fact that the flow $O.\delta$ is the same as $\delta.I$ at most N messages late.
- The choice operator γ : when $k>1$ connectors come out of a given port p_i, then the flow of messages through p_i is arbitrarily separated into k complementary subflows $p_i.r_1,\ p_i.r_2,\dots,p_i.r_k$. If we had :

  $$p_i.\delta = f_i(\delta.q_1,\dots,\delta.q_n)$$

  before establishing these connections, then we have :

  $$p_i.r_1 = \gamma_1(f_i(\delta.q,\dots,\delta.q_n))$$
  $$\vdots$$
  $$p_i.r_k = \gamma_k(f_i(\delta.q,\dots,\delta.q_n))$$

  after they are established (one of the r_j's may be δ).
- The shuffle operator σ : when $l>1$ connectors $s_1.q_i,\dots,s_l.q_i$ come into a given port q_i, then every occurrence of $\delta.q_i$ in the original equations defining the functions of the process is replaced by $\sigma(s_1.q_i,\dots,s_l.q_i)$ which denotes the shuffle of the corresponding flows. There is a relation between γ and σ, due to the complementarity of the subflows defined by γ : if a given f is separated into k subflows $\gamma_1(f),\dots,\gamma_k(f)$, then :

  $$\sigma(\gamma_1(f),\dots,\gamma_k(f)) = f$$

These equations on message flows are operated upon by the network construction operators extented to take care of such function definitions. In addition to the three special operators, these definitions may use any of the operations allowed by the types of messages, including the case where these are formal types in generic process specifications. The notion of correctness is naturally extented, events being now described by sets of triples <connector, type, function>.

iii) Delays between communications

Our model takes care of the ordering of communications in time. For real time applications, we must also describe and use distances between communications in time. This aspect of specifications also fits well on top of our basic tree model. For example, an elementary way of saying that the time elapsed between a communication on connector k_i and a communication on connector k_j lies in the internal $[t_1,t_2]$ is to write simply : $<k_i,k_j> \in [t_1,t_2]$. The notation $<k_i,k_j>$ can be interpreted as denoting all pathes in the forest of events which originate at an event containing k_i, which terminate at an event containing k_j and such that no event on the way does contain k_i nor k_j. Thus, for a process with connectors of the form $p_i.\delta$, $i\in[m]$ and $\delta.q_j$, $j\in[n]$, we may write a set of such delay conditions. From there, a number of problems must be solved :

- Given a specification s, we consider the forest $T(s)$ as describing the behavior of s free of timing considerations. When we adjoin the delay conditions, some pathes will become impossible to follow. How to characterize this forest with "trimmed" trees ? If the original trees were regular, are the trimmed trees still regular ?
- The network construction operators must be extended : they now have to build also the timing properties of the resulting network, using the timing properties of their operands.
- The correctness order relation has to be redefined : in addition to taking care of information attached to nodes (i.e. sets of triples <connector, type, function>), it must also take care of time intervals attached to finite pathes. If $[t_1,t_2]$ is the interval attached to a path in $T(s)$ and $[t_1',t_2']$ is the internal attached to the corresponding path in $T(s')$, then we must have $[t_1',t_2'] \subseteq [t_1,t_2]$ as a condition for having $s\leq s'$.

Other aspects of the behavior of communicating process (e.g. error recovery, reliability) can also be considered for inclusion in a specification formalism. In all cases, the framework proposed in this paper seems to constitute a basis which is well adapted to the expression and use of these properties and which can be used as a starting point for the design of a specification language and of a collection of analysis and validation tools.

ACKNOWLEDGEMENTS

The initial ideas on this work have originated during a stay of the author at the IBM San Jose Research Laboratory. I wish to thank my colleagues from this laboratory and especially Franco TURINI, now at the University of Pisa, without whom some of the essential ideas on process implementation correctness would have never been studied.

I wish also to thank Maurice NIVAT for this decisive contribution to the formalization of implementation correctness.

REFERENCES

[ASHC 76] ASHCROFT, E.A. and WADGE, W.W
Lucid - A formal system for writing and proving programs
SIAM Journal of Computing, Vol. 5, N° 3, September 1976

[BERT 81] BERT, D. and SOLER, R.
About data-type genericity
International Colloquium on Formalization of Programming Concepts, Peniscola, Lecture Notes in Computer Science, N° 107, Springer-Verlag, 1981

[DARO 81] DARONDEAU, Ph.
An enlarged definition and complete axiomatization of observational congruence of finite processes
IRISA Research Report, Rennes, October 1981

[DEBAK 76] DE BAKKER, J.W.
Semantics and termination of non deterministic programs
3rd. ICALP, Edited by S. Michaelson and R. Milner, Edinburgh
Edinburgh University Press, July 1976

[DIJK 76] DIJKSTRA, E.W.
A discipline of programming
Prentice Hall, 1976

[GUER 81] GUERREIRO, P.
Relational semantics of strongly communicating sequential processes
International Colloquium on Formalization of Programming Concepts, Peniscola, Lecture Notes in Computer Science, N° 107, Springer-Verlag, 1981

[GUES 81] GUESSARIAN, I.
Algebraic semantics
Lecture Notes in Computer Science, N° 99 , Springer-Verlag, 1981

[HOAR 78] HOARE, C.A.R.
Communicating sequential processes
CACM, Vol. 21, N° 8, August 1978

[HOAR 81] HOARE, C.A.R.
A calculus of total correctness for communicating processes
Science of Computer Programming, Vol. 1, N° 12, October 1981

[ICHB 79] ICHBIAH, J.D. et al.
Rationale for the design of the ADA programming language
SIGPLAN Notices, Vol. 14, N° 6, June 1979

[JORR 80] JORRAND, Ph.
Specification and analysis of communication protocols
IBM Research Report, RJ 2853, July 1980

[JORR 82] JORRAND, Ph.
Description and composition of communicating processes. Problems of analysis and correctness
IMAG Research Report, Grenoble, January 1982

[MILN 80] MILNER, R.
A calculus of communicating systems
Lecture Notes in Computer Science, N° 92, Springer-Verlag, 1980

[NIVAT 72] NIVAT, M.
Langages algébriques sur le magma libre et sémantique des schémas de programmes
1st. ICALP, Edited by M. Nivat, Paris
North-Holland, July 1972

[QUEI 81] QUEILLE, J.P. and SIFAKIS, J.
Specification and verification of concurrent systems in CESAR
IMAG Research Report, Grenoble, June 1981

[SIFA 80] SIFAKIS, J.
Deadlock and livelocks in transition systems
Mathematical Foundation of Computer Science
Lecture Notes in Computer Science, N° 88, Springer-Verlag, 1980

A SYSTEM FOR REASONING WITHIN AND ABOUT ALGEBRAIC SPECIFICATIONS *)

JALEK LESZCZYLOWSKI **)

MARTIN WIRSING ***)

*) This research was partially sponsored by the Sonderforschungsbereich 49, Programmiertechnik, Munich

**) Institute of Computer Science, Polish Acadamy of Sciences, P.O. BOX 22, 00-901 Warszawa, PKiN, Poland

***) Institut für Informatik, Technische Universität München, Arcisstrasse 21, D-8000 München 2, FRG

ABSTRACT

A machine-implemented system to support the reasoning about algebraic specifications is presented. The PAT-system is an attempt to ease design, analysis, and implementation of partial abstract data types. More precisely, the PAT-system

- allows to write "axiomatic abstract types", i.e. parameterised hierarchical algebraic specifications, as well as "domain types", i.e. abstract types defined by domain equations,
- introduces automatically the semantic conventions for the theory of partial abstract types including axioms for strictness (of partial functions) and for the validity of data type induction,
- facilitates proofs of derived properties: PAT provides (semiautomatic) strategies for using derived rules of inference as well as for simplifying conditional equations. It allows to use a metalanguage - Edinburgh-ML /LCF 79/ - for generating and performing proofs interactively;
- makes first attempts for analysing algebraic specifications by checking sufficient conditions for the existence of initial algebras (of hierachical specifications and/or parameterised specifications - for nonhierarchical and nonparameterised specifications initial algebras always exist) and for the existence of weakly terminal algebras,
- supports development and proof of correctness of implementations; in particular it is possible to verify implementations of "axiomatic types" by "domain types".

The PAT-system is implemented in Edinburgh-ML being part of an interactive verification system, Edinburgh-LCF, which seems particularly appropriate to support proofs with algebraic specifications.

The system PAT tries to use as much as possible the facilities and properties of the underlying Edinburgh-LCF system. Only necessary changes - such as "smash" product instead of "cartesian" product - and extensions - such as the introduction of certain induction schemata - are made.

A short characterisation of LCF and a description of the PAT-system is given. The PAT-system is shortly compared with other systems manipulating algebraic specifications. Finally, as an example for the reasoning with and about algebraic specifications priority queues over linearly ordered data types are described as a parameterised abstract type, PQ.

1. INTRODUCTION

Since the late seventies algebraic specification methods are considered as a tool for the formal specification of software systems (cf. e.g. /Liskov, Zilles 74/, /Guttag 75/, /ADJ 78/). In particular, the theory of partial abstract types allows to specify all partial-recursive functions (/Broy, Wirsing 80b/, /Hupbach 80/) and thus seems to be well-suited for the formal description of both, data structures and programming languages, as well as for the development of reliable programs by means of transformations (cf. e.g. /Reichel 79/, /Broy, Wirsing 80a, 81/, /CIP 81/).

Mainly two features have contributed that such specification methods found their way into programming: First, parameterisation techniques and hierarchy concepts allow to generalise descriptions to schemes of computational structures to decompose software systems into structures of manageable size. Second, the semantics of abstract data types is determined by axioms without referring to particular models. This model-independence increase the flexibility of implementation process. Moreover, the use of axioms supports the extensibility of e.g. specifications of programming languages (cf. /Mosses 81/); it allows to compare different concepts of similar specifications in a formal way (cf. /Broy, Wirsing 81b/). Finally, since axioms can be considered as transformations, abstract data types may build the basis for program development by transformations (cf. /Bauer, Wössner 81/, /Broy, Pepper 81/) and thus for program verification, too.

But carrying out formal proofs by hand is often lenghty and tedious. Writing axioms is difficult even for specialists: Since axioms cannot be proven to be correct wrt. the intuitive concepts, they have to be analysed, whether they are consistent and complete, what the classes of their models are and whether they imply a certain number of suitable properties.

The PAT-System (where PAT stands for "Partial Abstract Types") is designed as a machine-implemented system to support the reasoning about algebraic specifications. It is an attempt to ease design, analysis, and implementation of partial abstract data types. More precisely, the PAT-System provides the following facilities. It

- allows to write "axiomatic abstract types", i.e. parameterised hierarchical algebraic specifications, as well as "domain types", i.e. abstract types defined by domain equations,
- introduces automatically the semantic conventions for the theory of partial abstract types including axioms for strictness (of partial functions) and for the validity of data type induction,

- facilitates proofs of derived properties: PAT provides (semiautomatic) strategies for using derived rules of inference as well as for simplifying conditional equations. It allows to use a metalanguage - Edinburgh-ML /LCF 79/ - for generating and performing proofs interactively;
- makes first attempts for analysing algebraic specifications by checking sufficient conditions for the existence of initial algebras (of hierachical specifications and/or parameterised specifications - for nonhierarchical and nonparameterised specifications initial algebras always exist) and for the existence of weakly terminal algebras,
- supports development and proof of correctness of implementations; in particular it is possible to verify implementations of "abstract types" by "concrete types".

In order to achieve all these goals, the PAT-system is implemented on top of an interactive verification system, Edinburgh-LCF, which seems particularly appropriate for the following reasons:

- Edinburgh-LCF uses monotonic functions over cpo's. Thus partial functions - considered as strict functions over flat domains - are included and simple to implement.
- The logic of LCF and of the theory of partial abstract types correspond to each other: Strong equality and definedness predicate are predefined constructs of the logic of partial abstract types as well as of LCF.
- "Polymorphic LCF-theories with parent-theories" correspond exactly to parameterised hierarchical specifications: Signature and axioms of an abstract type can be considered as a "theory" of LCF. The modular decomposition of abstract types can be simulated by the "parent" and "daughter" theory-concepts. Finally, "polymorphism" of LCF-theories can support the parameterisation of algebraic specifications. Only the type instantiation has to be modified such that parameter requirements can be considered.
- LCF provides facilities for the use of equations as left to right term rewrite rules;
- the metalanguage ML allows to prove theorems in theories (by subgoaling methods) as well as metatheorems about theories (by ML-procedures).

The system PAT tries to use as much as possible the facilities and properties of the underlying Edinburgh-LCF system. Only necessary changes - such as "smash" product instead of "cartesian" product - and extensions - such as the introduction of certain induction schemata - are made.

In the following sections, a short characterisation of LCF , a description of the PAT-system and remarks on the implementation of PAT are given (section 2-4). In section 5 the PAT-system is shortly compared with other systems manipulating algebraic specifications. Finally, as an example for the reasoning with and about algebraic specifications priority queues over linearly ordered data types are described as a parameterised abstract type, PQ .

This type PQ is (weakly) sufficiently complete. It has initial and weakly terminal models as it is shown by the procedures EXIN (short for "EXistence of INitial algebras") and EXTL (short for "EXistence of weakly Terminal algebras"). Finally, a domain type SEQ specifying sequences is given. SEQ is extended to an implementation of (the terminal algebras of) PQ and the machine support for the correctness of the implementation is outlined.

2. A SHORT CHARACTERISATION OF LCF

An extensive presentation of LCF can be found in /LCF 79/. The following is mainly based on /Cohn 80/.

Edinburgh-LCF is an interactive theorem-proving system (where LCF stand for "Logic of Computable Functions). LCF is composed of a meta-language ML, and a formal logic PPLAMBDA (which stands for "Polymorphic Predicate LAMBDA-calculus). The meta-language is used for talking about and manipulating the logic. The logic is designed for reasoning about computation.

2.1. PPLAMBDA

PPLAMBDA is a language with two principal syntax classes: *terms* and *formulae*. The terms are those of *typed* lambda-calculus, and each class of objects includes a least defined element UU and an implicit partial ordering << within the class. The formulae are drawn from the predicate calculus.

The only basic types are tr, the type of truth values, and ·, the type with a single member, UU. There are four basic type operators (i.e. *parameterised sorts*) for building up new types. Suppose *,** are (variables for) types. Then *u adds a new minimum element to *; *×** denotes the cartesian product of * and **, *+** the disjoint sum, and *→** the class of continuous functions from * to **. It is worth mentioning that for a variable type * every type can be instantiated - e.g. types with a finite number of elements as well as types of the form $\tau 1 \rightarrow \tau 2$. This is different from the semantics of parameterised algebraic specifications and has to be taken into account for the implementation of the PAT-system.

There exists a number of predefined *constants* (in ADT-terminology predefined *function symbols*) the meaning of which is defined by inference rules of the logic. Among those are the constants TT, FF of type tr, a pairing function (.,.) and selector functions FST ("first"), SND ("second") for the cartesian product, a fixpoint operator FIX and a definedness predicate DEF from every type to tr. For every term t DEF t yields TT, if t is (semantically) different from UU, and UU, otherwise.

The terms of PPLAMBDA are built from variables, constants, function application t(t'), lambda abstraction λx.t and the constraining of a term to a type t:τ where t,t' are terms, x is a variable and τ a type.

The formulae are built from atomic formulae by the normal predicate calculus connectives - conjunction .&, implication IMP and universal quantification !. The atomic formulae are either equalities t==t' or inequalities t << t'. Axioms and proved *facts* are called *theorems*. Theorems are produced by rules of inference such as Modus Ponens and Computation Induction.

2.2. METALANGUAGE ML

ML is a general purpose programming language. Some of the main features are the possibilities to construct new logical theories and to conduct interactively goal-directed proofs.

Logical *theories* are introduced in ML by declaring new types or type operators, new constants and new axioms (i.e. in ADT-terminology by sorts or parameterised sorts, functions symbols and axioms) - in addition, to those already existing in PPLAMBDA.

Theories are arranged in *hierarchies* so that if a theory T1 is a *parent* of theory T2 all types, constants, and axioms of T1 are known in T2.

There are two ways of introducing a theory: implicitly by axioms (as e.g. LINORD and PQ in the appendix), and directly via a representation (as e.g. SEQ). In the following we will call the former theories *axiomatic types* and the latter ones *domain types* (in LCF-terminology both forms are called abstract types).

Domain types are defined in terms of basic or other types. Thus if these other types are not inconsistent, domain types cannot be inconsistent either. Therefore, there are safer than axiomatic types where the consistency must always be proven. But using axiomatic types one has the possibility to specify theories the (finitely generated) models of which are not all isomorphic. This is, in general, not the case with domain types; e.g. the type PQ cannot be specified using only domain types. In fact, domain types can be considered as implementations of axiomatic types; e.g. the type SEQ is a possible implementation of PQ.

2.3. PROOFS IN LCF

Proofs in LCF are based on natural deduction methods and are done in a goal-directed way. This means that inference rules play a dominant role instead of axioms and that - given a formula w to be proved - we want to transform w into "simpler" formulae (which in turn have to be proved) and a proof of w from the simpler formulae.

The LCF-system supports this style of proving via three predefined types : goals, proofs and tactics. A *goal* is a triple consisting of the formula to be proved, a set "simpset" of simplification rules and a list of formulas representing the assumptions. A *proof* is a function which maps a list of theorems to a theorem and a *tactic* maps a goal to a list of ("simpler") goals together with a proof. An example of a tactic is the "simplification tactic" SIMPTAC; applied to any goal (w, ss, A) SIMPTAC produces a list of goals [(w', ss, A)] and a proof p such that w' is the simplification of w by ss and p justifies all the simplifications made. Another specific tactic is INDTAC deriving automatically the structural induction tactic (see APPENDIX).

Such tactics can also be combined to form larger ones - by ML-prodedures called *tacticals*. For example see e.g. /LCF 79/ or /Leszczylowski 81a/.

3. THE PAT SYSTEM

Like other systems for specification and verification the PAT-system has its own paradigm for specification and programming:

An algebraic specification of a problem builds the "contract" for the development of a software system. In order to understand better this "contract" and to get an idea of the variety of possible solutions the specification is analysed by deriving properties and metaproperties from the axioms - such as consistency, sufficient completeness, or existence of initial and terminal algebras. From the specification an implementation is developed and verified using program and data type transformation techniques (cf. /Dosch et al. 80/, /Laut, Partsch 81/).

The underlying theory of partial abstract types is described in /Broy, Wirsing 80a/, /Wirsing, Broy 81/, the semantics of the implementation concepts (including implementation of parameterised types is treated in /Broy et al. 80/ and /Sannella, Wirsing 81/). Therefore the PAT-system has a fully defined formal semantics. The syntax of PAT is made in an LCF-like style in order to have compatibility with the LCF-system in which the proofs are carried out.

A first version of the PAT-system is implemented in Edinburgh-LCF running on the Edinburgh DEC-system-10. Apart from EXTL and CORREP all following commands are already implemented. At the Technical University of Munich a second, extended version of PAT is currently being built on top of the CIP-system (cf. /CIP 81/) together B. Brass, A. Laut, R. Steinbrüggen, H. Poetzsch-Heffter and H. Hussmann.

3.1. PARTIAL ABSTRACT TYPES

The basic ideas of partial abstract types are simple: A partial abstract type consists of a set of sorts, a set of (possibly partial) operations and a set of axioms. Axioms are formulae of the predicate calculus which are built just as in LCF. Usually axioms are of the form

t1 == t1' & ... & tn == tn' IMP u1 == u1' & ... & um == um'

where only free first-order variables are allowed. The semantics of an abstract type T is the class of all finitely generated models, i.e. the class of all algebras with the same signature as T which are finitely generated from the operations named in the signature and which satisfy the axioms of T.

The PAT commands for writing such a type include

THEORY? <specname>

After the initial THEORY? which is provided by the system (a name of) an abstract type specname is designated in which the following components are placed.

PATin <specname>

Introduces automatically names for all axioms in the specification to be developed. The names of the axioms have the form <specname>n where n is a positive integer.

newtype <sort name> <list of <parameter sort name>>

Declares a new sort (operator) <sort name>. The second argument determines the list of formal parameter sorts of <sort name>. Such parameter sorts may be built by a sequence of * just as in LCF or by *<identifier list> if particular functions or axioms are required for the parameter (cf. 4.3). E.g. a sort "seq" of sequences could have a parameter sort * or *data . Moreover, this command ensures the flatness of the sort <sort name> by introducing the axiom

```
FLAT "DEFx == TT & DEFy == TT & x<<y IMP x == y
```

strictconstant <function symbol> <functionality>

Declares an operation <function symbol> together with its <functionality>. It introduces automatically axioms for ensuring the strictness of the function being defined. The names of the axioms are of the form UUn where n is a positive integer. E.g. the operation cons which adds a new element to a sequence would have the declaration

```
strictconstant(`cons`, ": * x * seq → * seq")
```

and the strictness axioms

```
UU1  cons(UU,x) == UU
UU2  cons(x,UU) == UU
```

strictolinfix <function symbol> <functionality>

Behaves just as strictconstant, except that the <function symbol> may be infixed between two arguments.

CONSTRUCTORSdec <list of <function symbol><functionality>>

Behaves just as strict constant for a list of function symbols and introduces the axiom and rule for structural induction over partial algebras (see section 4). E.g. for sequences with the constructors emptyseq and cons the system introduces

```
INDseq  !F: * seq → tr
        (DEF emptyseq == TT  IMP  F emptyseq == TT)
        & (!x. !q. DEF (cons(x,q)) == TT  &  F q == TT  IMP F (cons(x,q)) == TT)
        IMP  !q. DEF q == TT  IMP  F q == TT
```

defaxiom <formula>

Introduces an axiom for the specification. An axiom name is automatically created (by PATIN). All variables of <formula> are automatically quantified by universal quantifiers the domain of which is restricted to defined objects; i.e. every subfomula

!x.w

of <formula> is compiled to

!x. DEF x == TT IMP w

if the definedness of x cannot be inferred from w.

E.g. defaxiom("isempty(cons(x,q)) == FF") yields

PQi !x. !q. DEF x = TT & DEF q == TT IMP isempty(cons(x,q)) == FF

whereas

defaxiom("isempty q == FF IMP DEF(top q) == TT ")

has simply to be closed by universal quantification (since the definedness of q can be inferred from the strictness of isempty

PQj !q. isempty q == FF IMP DEF(top q) == FF

3.2. MODULARISATION OF ABSTRACT TYPES

The PAT system supports two concepts of modularisation of abstract types: Parameterisation and hierarchical structure.

Parameterisation is expressed by the "generic" types of LCF, i.e. the new sorts may be considered as type operators for which any other sort (type) may be instantiated. E.g. for the sort *1seq one may get nat seq, int seq by instantiation.
In contrast to LCF certain sorts may be excluded from instantiation. In particular

- all instantiated sorts have to be flat and
- (the corresponding abstract types) have to satisfy the parameter restrictions.

Parameter restrictions are written in the form of an abstract type as well.

The hierarchical structure is expressed by the "parent theory" concept of LCF. Every abstract type is hierarchically based on its "parent" types. From the semantic point of view the parent types introduce a "hierarchy constraint" on the models of a type (cf. /Wirsing et al. 80/):

An abstract type T with parent P accepts a finitely generated algebra satisfying the axioms of T as a model only if the restriction of A to P is a finitely generated model of P as well. This means that every model (viz. implementation) of the overall type can be constructed from a model of the parent type which is built without any knowledge of T. (For theoretical consequences of hierarchy constraints cf. /Bergstra et al. 81/.)

Parameterisation and hierarchical structure are modelled by PAT as follows:

newparent <specname>

> Makes an abstract type <specname> to a parent of the current specification. Thus all sorts, function symbols and axioms of <specname> and its ancestors are introduced and become accessible. All functions of the current abstract type with range in (the new sorts of) <specname> are considered as "output functions".

newparameter `<specname>`

> Makes the abstract type <specname> to a parameter of the current type T. That is the sorts and function symbols and ancestors of <specname> are accessible in T. The axioms of <specname> become assumptions for any type instantiation of a parameter sort.

3.3. DOMAIN TYPES

Domain types are specified by domain equations on the standard type operators of PPLAMBDA. E.g. a type of sequences may be introduced by the isomorphism (cf. /LCF 79/)

    * seq ≃ .u + (* x * seq) u

That is, sequences are represented in terms of sums, products, and lifting. A sequence can either be an empty sequence (the left summand) or (recursively) an object of sort * paired with a sequence. The abstract type (with sort) * seq is *isomorphic* to the type on the right hand side. To express this isomorphism two function symbols

    seqREP : * seq → (.u + (* x * seq) u
    seqABS : (* u + (* x * seq) → * seq

are introduced to map objects of sort * seq to their representations, and back again. The axioms about seqABS and seqREP are

!s. DEF s == TT IMP seqABS(seqREP s) == s

!r. DEF r == TT IMP seqREP(seqABS r) == r .

The PAT-system allows to specify such domain types as follows (based on Robin Milners file):

beginAXIOMSof <sort name> <integer>

Behaves just as newtype <sorts name> [*1;...;*n] (if <integer> is n) and prepares the definition of domain equations.

CONSTRUCTORS <list of <function symbol, term> >

Introduces a domain type:

- Declares function symbols together with their functionality which is derived from the functionality of the corresponding terms.
- Introduces specifications of the function symbols derived from the corresponding term representation.
- Introduces REPresentation and ABStraction function together with the above isomorphism axioms.
- Introduces axioms ensuring the validity of structural induction.

3.4. ANALYSIS OF PARTIAL ABSTRACT TYPES

For the understanding of the axioms as well as for an overview over possible implementations of an abstract type it seems useful to analyse an algebraic specification by means of methods from universal algebra. There the existence of initial and terminal models plays a prominent role. By different authors both isomorphism classes of models have been considered as <u>the</u> semantics of abstract types (cf. /ADJ 78/, /Wand 79/). Initial and (weakly) terminal algebras of partial abstract types can be characterised as follows (cf. /Broy, Wirsing 80a/, /Wirsing, Broy 81/).

- Initial algebras I are minimally defined, i.e. a term is defined in I iff it is defined in all algebras of the type, and two terms are identified in I iff they must be identified i.e. iff they are identified in all models.

- Weakly terminal algebras Z are also minimally defined but two terms are identified in Z iff they can be identified (i.e. there exists at least one model identifying them). Weakly terminal models are often *fully abstract* (/Milner 77/), i.e. they identify exactly those terms which have the same *visible behaviour* wrt. its parent types (cf. /Broy, Wirsing 81a/).

The first version of the PAT-system has incorporated two procedures which check sufficient conditions whether an abstract type has initial and/or fully abstract weakly terminal models:

EXIN <specname> <list of <function symbols>>

Considers the <list of <function symbols>> as the "output functions" of the type <specname> and returns true if these functions satisfy the following sufficient conditions for the EXistence of INitial algebras. Otherwise it returns false.

- all *proper* axioms (i.e. the axioms which are not automatically introduced by the system) are of the form

  tl == tl' & ... & tn == tn' IMP ul == ul' & ... & um == um' .

- every free variable x occurring in a proper axiom is first order and ensured to be defined
- every term ui or ui' in the succedent of a proper axiom is in *output-normal form* (cf. /Broy, Wirsing 80a/, /Wirsing, Broy 81/) i.e. every element of <list of function symbols> may occur at most in outermost position of ui or ui'.

EXTL <specname> <list of <function symbols>>

Considers just as EXIN the <list of <function symbols>> as the output functions of type <specname> and checks whether specname satisfies sufficient conditions for the EXistence of weakly TerminaL algebras (wrt. the above output functions). Otherwise it returns false.

In particular, EXTL checks whether

- EXIN returns true and
- every equation ti == ti' in the antecedent of a proper axiom is of sort tr or has the form t == x where x is a free variable not occurring elsewhere in the antecedent of that axiom.

3.5. PROOFS IN PAT: STRUCTURAL INDUCTION AND CORRECTNESS OF IMPLEMENTATIONS

Proving in the PAT system is based on natural deduction and term rewriting just as in LCF (cf. section 2.3). In fact, all proofs are done using a modified version of the LCF-system.

All tactics and tacticals of LCF are available as well as the (more convenient) extensions of LCF by the Mate-system /Leszczylowski 81b/. We only note that a structural induction tactical INDTAC : {<specname>} → tactic is valid for every abstract type <specname> of PAT.

One of the principal aims of the system is to give a formal support for the development of implementations. In general, an implementation T^+ of an algebraic specification T is defined via restriction and identification of certain classes of terms of T^+ (cf./Ehrich et al. 80/,/Ehrich 81/,/Sannella, Wirsing 81/). At the moment, in the PAT-system a somewhat simpler notion is considered involving only restriction:

An abstract type T^+ (with sorts S^+ and operations T^+) is an *implementation* of T (with sorts S and operations F) if there exists a representation function $rep : S \times F \rightarrow S^+ \times F^+$ such that T^+ restricted to terms of form rep(x) satisfies the images rep(Ax) of the axioms of T.

The command CORREP ("correct representation")

```
CORREP <implname> <specname> <specname> <list of (type × type)>
       <list of (function symbol × function symbol)>
```

produces the representation functions which are induced by rep and the axioms rep(Ax):

If T is an abstract type with sorts {si} and operations {fi} and if si^+ and fj^+ are sorts and operations of T, then

$$\text{CORREP I } T^+ \text{ T } [(si,si^+)] \; [(fj,fj^+)]$$

gives the name I to the implementation, declares representation functions $Irepsi : si \rightarrow si^+$ and defines them inductively by the axioms

$$Ireps(fj(x)) == fj^+(Ireps'(x)) \qquad \text{for every} \quad fj : s' \rightarrow s$$

Moreover, CORREP introduces the axioms rep(Ax) by

$$Ax[\ldots\ Iresps(x)/x\ \ldots\ ,\ \ldots\ si^+/si\ \ldots\ ,\ \ldots\ fj^+/fj\ \ldots]$$

for every axiom Ax of T where every first order variable x of sort s is substituted by Ireps(x) and all si and fj are replaced by si^+ and fj^+.

4. IMPLEMENTATION OF PAT

The PAT-system is implemented in Edinburgh-LCF running on the Edinburgh DECsystem-10. Axioms and formulae are compiled into LCF-like axioms and formulae. Then proofs of properties are done within the LCF-system.

For this purpose, LCF has been modified as follows.

4.1. SMASH-PRODUCT

The PAT-system uses the smash product instead of normal cartesian product. The syntax FST, SND, PAIR of LCF for the cartesian product is adopted by hiding the "ordinary" cartesian product. A disadvantage is that users are not able to have both products while developing their theories in LCF.

The rules SELCONV, PAIRCONV and destpair differ from the LCF-manual /LCF 79/ as follows

```
SELCONV "FST(t,u)"  |---> "DEF u == TT  IMP  FST(t,u) == t"
SELCONV "SND(t,u)"  |---> "DEF t == TT  IMP  SND(t,u) == t"
PAIRCONV "(UU,u)"   |---> "(UU,u) == UU"
PAIRCONU "(t,UU)"   |---> "(t,UU) == UU"
```

Moreover, the function destpair fails on (t,UU) and (UU,u) in order to avoid to give a wrong intuition.

4.2 STRUCTURAL INDUCTION

An inference rule for structural induction is indroduced:

INDUCT : $\{\langle specname\rangle\}_T \to formula_w \to$ thm list $\to$ thm

$$\frac{A_i \cup \{w[x_{i1}/x],\dots,w[x_{ik}/x]\}\ \ ]\!-\ !x_1{:}s_1\dots !x_n{:}s_n.\mathrm{DEF}(f(x_1,\dots,x_n)){==}\mathrm{TT}\ \mathrm{IMP}\ w[f(x_1,\dots,x_n)/x] \qquad \text{for all constructors } f \text{ of } T}{\bigcup_i A_i\ \ ]\!-\ !x{:}s.\ \ \mathrm{DEF}\ x == \mathrm{TT}\ \ \mathrm{IMP}\ \ w}$$

where s is a new sort of the abstract type T and for every constructor f holds {il, ..., ik} = {i | si = s} i.e. the set of indices for which the domain of f is the new sort s.

The failure conditions are analogous to those of computational induction (cf. /LCF 79/).

4.3. TYPE INSTANTIATION

In the PAT-system type variables are considered as variables for parameter sorts. Thus in contrast to LCF, type instantiation has to be protected wrt. to the parameter restrictions.

Given a parameterised type the "actual" abstract type ACT which is instantiated for the formal parameter PA has to satisfy the axioms of the formal parameter PA. Thus for PAT the type instantiation rule of LCF is changed such that after instantiation with ACT the instantiations of all axioms of PA occur among the assumptions. Then the only way to get rid of these parameter restrictions is to prove them (involving the axioms of ACT). The modified inference rule is defined as follows:

PARINSTTYPE : $(\text{type}_{ti} \times \text{type}_{vti})$ list → theorem → theorem

$$\frac{A]\text{- } w}{A \cup \ldots Ax_{vti}\,[ti/vti] \ldots\ ]\text{- } w[\ldots ti/vti \ldots]}$$

where Ax_{vti} are the axioms of the parameter with sort vti. The failure conditions of INSTTYPE (cf. /LCF 79/) hold analogously.

5. COMPARISON WITH OTHER SYSTEMS

In the past years several systems and languages have been developed for supporting design and verification of algebraic specifications. In the following we try to give short (and very subjective) characterisations of some of these systems.

Probably the most advanced system is the AFFIRM system at ISI (/Gerhart et al. 80/). It supports equational specifications of abstract data types and verification of PASCAL-like programs using these types. Not much attention seems to be paid to the modularisation of data types. No formal semantics is defined either; since AFFIRM is based on Guttag's ideas all finitely generated models should be admitted, but the rewrite rule approach seems to favour an initial algebra semantics. Apart from that the AFFIRM system provides many facilities e.g. for rewriting expressions, proving confluence and sufficient completeness, and theorem proving (in an LCF-like style).

On top of AFFIRM a tool for a stepwise specification of data types is implemented - the ALGORITHMIC SPECIFICATIONS /Loeckx 80/. These specifications are comparable with domain types and are written as recursive schemata involving fixed point operators.

Similarly, Klaeren's STRUCTURAL RECURSIVE SCHEMATA /Klaeren 80/ are a constructive approach for specifying abstract software module. For these schemata an interpreter has been implemented which can "run" specifications.

OBJ (/Goguen, Tardo 80/) allows for parameterised specifications (without parameter restrictions) and partitions the axioms into OK- and ERROR-axioms. As in most other systems specifications can be tested for consistency by means of a rewrite-rule based operational semantics.

The APE-system /Seki 81/ even tries to find automatically implementations of algebraic specifications (with some user-provided knowledge). It admits parameterised specifications with hidden operators based on an initial algebra semantics.

The only system which considers also terminal algebras is that of /Bergman, Deransart 81/. It comprises a "terminal data type induction" and a method for proving equalities in terminal algebras. It uses PROLOG as underlying language and thus provides also facilities for theorem proving.

Two languages are very similar to our ideas of modularisation: JOTA and CLEAR. JOTA /Nakajima et al. 80/ includes hierarchical algebraic specifications with first order axioms as well as ALGOL-like programming concepts and supports interactively the verification of programs wrt. abstract types.

CLEAR (/Burstall, Goguen 77, 80/) is a specification language with two modularisation concepts: Parameterisation and data constraints. The latter requirements are stronger than hierarchy constraints: Informally data constraints ensure initiality and hierarchy. Also types without any constructors (such as LINORD) can be written in CLEAR. Recently a theorem prover (using LCF) has been connected to CLEAR (/Sannella 81/). An interactive programming system, CAT, is currently designed on top of CLEAR for constructing large programs (/Goguen, Burstall 80/). The idea is that program development has a two-dimensional structure: a *horizontal* one which corresponds to the structure of the specification and a *vertical* one which corresponds to the sequence of successive implementations towards the actual code.

This is also one of the mottos of the CIP-system (/Bauer, Broy 79/). The CIP-language (cf. /CIP 81/) comprises tools for writing modularised algebraic specifications as well as programs over ("concrete") computational structures. The CIP-system supports the development of programs from specifications by transformations.

Our PAT-system could be understood as a tool providing necessary information to guide such a transformation process.

It can be seen as an extension of LCF. Thus in contrast to most other systems (apart from /Loeckx 80/) its syntax is written in an LCF-like style. As CAT, it is designed to support a horizontal and a vertical structure for modularisation and implementation. The difference is that PAT has a partial algebra semantics considering all models whereas CAT (extending CLEAR) has a total algebra semantics based on initial algebras. Apart from PAT only /Bergman, Deransart 81/ consider both, initial and terminal algebras. In PAT it is not intended to find implementation automatically as APE does, but to support an intuition guided stepwise development of implementations. The possibility of writing both, axiomatic abstract types as well as domain types, exists also in Loeckx'system since he uses LCF, too.

REFERENCES

/ADJ 78/
J.A. Goguen, J.W. Thatcher, E.W. Wagner: An initial algebra approach to the specification, correctness and Implementation of abstract data types. In: Current Trends in Programming Methodology IV. Prentice Hall, 80-144, 1978

/Bauer, Broy 79/
F.L. Bauer, M. Broy (eds.): Program Construction. LNCS 69

/Bauer, Wössner 81/
F.L. Bauer, H. Wössner: Algorithmic language and program development. Berlin: Springer 1981

/Bergman, Deransart 81/
M. Bergman, P. Deransart: Abstract data types and rewriting systems: application to the programming of algebraic abstract data types in Prolog. 6th CAAP, Genova, March 1981. LNCS 112

/Bergstra et al. 81/
J.A. Bergstra, M. Broy, J.V. Tucker, M. Wirsing: On the power of algebraic specifications. 10th MFCS, 1981, LNCS 118

/Broy et al. 80/
M. Broy, B. Möller, P. Pepper, M. Wirsing: A model-independent approach to implementations of abstract data types. In: A. Salwicki (ed.): Algorithmic logic and the programming language LOGLAN. August 80. To appear in LNCS

/Broy, Pepper 81/
M. Broy, P. Pepper: Program development as a formal activity. IEEE Transactions of Software Engineering 7:1 (1981)

/Broy, Wirsing 80a/
M. Broy, M. Wirsing: Partial abstract types. To appear in Acta Informatica. Preliminary version: TUM-I8018, 1980

/Broy, Wirsing 80b/
M. Broy, M. Wirsing: Partial recursive functions and abstract data types. Bull. EATCS 11, June 1980

/Broy, Wirsing 81a/
M. Broy, M. Wirsing: On the algebraic extensions of abstract data types. In J. Diaz, I. Ramos (eds.): Formalization of programming concepts. LNCS 107, 244-251

/Broy, Wirsing 81b/
M. Broy, M. Wirsing: On the algebraic specification of nondeterministic programming languages. In: E. Astesiano, C. Böhm (eds.): 6th CAAP, Genova, 1981. LNCS 112, 162-179.

/Burstall, Goguen 77/
R.M. Burstall, J.A. Goguen: Putting theories together to make specifications. Proc. IJCAI, MIT, Cambridge, Mass. 1045-1058, 1977

/Burstall, Goguen 80/
R.M. Burstall, J.A. Goguen: The semantics of CLEAR: a specification language. Proc. Copenhagen Winter School on Abstract Software Specifications, 1980

/CIP 81/
Report on a wide spectrum language for program specification and development. TUM-I8104, May 1981

/Cohn 80/
A. Cohn: Abstract types in LCF. Unpublished manuscript

/Dosch et al. 80/
W. Dosch, M. Wirsing, G. Ausiello, G.T. Mascari: Polynomials - the specification, analysis and development of an abstract data type. 10. GI-Jahrestagung, Saarbrükken, Oktober 1980, Informatik-Fachberichte 33, 306-320 (1980)

/Ehrig 81/
H.P. Ehrig: On realization and implementation. 10th MFCS. LNCS 118

/Ehrig et al 81/
H. Ehrig, H.J. Kreowski, J.W. Thatcher, E.G. Wagner, J.B. Wright: Parameterized data types in algebraic specification languages. 7th ICALP, LNCS 85, 157-168, 1980

/Gerhart et al. 80/
S.L. Gerhart, D.R. Musser, D.H. Thompson, D.A. Baker, R.L. Bates, R.W. Erickson, R.L. London, D.G. Taylor, D.S. Wile: An overview of AFFIRM: A specification and and verification system. IFIP 80

/Goguen, Tardo 79/
J.A. Goguen, J. Tardo: An introduction to reliable software. In: Specification of relaible software, IEEE 1979

/Goguen, Burstall 80/
J.A. Goguen, R.M. Burstall: CAT, a system for the structured elaboration of correct programs from structured specifications. SRI, Techn. Rep. CSL-118, Oct. 1980

/Guttag 75/
J.V. Guttag: The specification and application to programming of abstract data types. Ph. D. thesis, Univ. of Toronto, 1975

/LCF 79/
M. Gordon, R. Milner, C. Wadsworth: Edinburgh LCF, LNCS 78 (1979)

/Leszczylowski 81a/
J. Leszczylowski: An experiment with Edinburgh LCF. 5th Conf. on Automated Deduction, France, 1980

/Leszczylowski 81b/
J. Leszczylowski: The MATE-system. In preparation

/Liskov, Zilles 74/
B. Liskov, S. Zilles: Programming with abstract data types. Proc. ACM Sigplan Conference on Very High Level Languages, Sigplan Notices 9:4, 55-59, 1974

/Loeckx 80/
J. Loeckx: Proving properties of algorithmic specifications of abstract data types in AFFIRM. ISI, AFFIRM Memo, July 1980

/Mosses 81/
P. Mosses: A semantic algebra for binding constructs. Proc. Formalization of Programming Concepts, LNCS 107, 408-419, 1981

/Nakajima et al. 80/
R. Nakajima, T. Yusa, K. Kojima: the IOTA programming system - a support system for hierarchical and modular programming. IFIP 80

/Reichel 79/
H. Reichel: Theorie der Aequoide. Dissertation B. Humboldt Universität Berlin, 1979

/Sannella 81/
D. Sannella: Proving theorems in CLEAR theories. In preparation

/Sannella, Wirsing 81/
D. Sannella, M. Wirsing: Implementations of parameterised algebraic specifications. 9th ICALP, Aarhus (1982). To appear.

/SEKI 81/
U. Bartels, W. Althoff, P. Raulefs: APE: An expert system for automatic programming from abstract specifications of data types and algorithms. Universität Bonn, Institut für Informatik III, Memo SEKI-BN-81-01 (1981)

/Wand 78/
M. Wand: Final algebra semantics and data type extensions. Indiana University TR65, 1978

/Wirsing et al. 80/
M. Wirsing, P. Pepper, H. Partsch, W. Dosch, M. Broy: On hierarchies of abstract data types. Institut für Informatik, TU München, TUM-I8007, 1980

/Wirsing, Broy 81/
M. Wirsing, M. Broy: An analysis of semantic models for algebraic specifications. Int. Summer School on Theoretical Foundations of Programming Methodology, August 1981

APPENDIX

EXAMPLE: PRIORITY QUEUES

In this section we illustrate how to set up a parameterised algebraic specification of priority queues in PAT and how to use PAT for proving an implementation of priority queues over ordered sequences.

Priority queues are finite collections of data for which a linear ordering is defined. Characteristic operations for priority queues are that on request one may get or delete the least element of a queue.

These priority queues can be specified as a parameterised abstract type with the requirement that for the parameter, *1 say, a linear ordering relation is defined.

To start with, we enter the LCF-system as usual /LCF 79/ and begin a draft of the parameter called LINORD. To define LINORD we load first the PAT-system using mlin, prepare the names of axioms by PATIN, declare the variables occurring in the axioms and define the axioms using defprecond (lines typed by the user are designated by $):

```
$    `/. PARAMETER LINORD `/.
$    mlin (`PAT`, false);;
$    PATin `LINORD` ;;
$    strictolinfix(`less`, ":*1x*1 → tr" ) ;;
$    "x:*1", "y:*1;, "z:*1"
$    map defaxiom
$         [ "DEF(x less y) == TT  &  x less x ==  TT" ];;
$    map defaxiom
$         [ "x less y == TT  & y less z ==  TT IMP  x less z ==  TT " ;
$           "x less y == FF   IMP  y less x  ==  TT "
$           "x less y == TT   &  y less x ==  TT  IMP  x == y "] ;;
```

The PAT-system closes these axioms by universal quantification, names the axioms by LINORDi and introduces axioms for flatness of *1 (FLAT) and strictness axioms for less (UU1,UU2) :

```
NEWAXIOMS() ;;
FLAT      " !x:*1. !y:*1.  DEF x == TT  &  x << y  IMP  x == y "
UU1       " !x2:*1.(UU:*1)less x2 == UU:tr "
UU2       " !x1:*1.x1 less (UU:*1)== UU:tr "
LINORD1   " !x:*1. !y:*1.  DEF x == TT  &  DEF y == TT  IMP
                           DEF (x less y) == TT  &  x less x == TT "
LINORD2   " !x:*1. !y:*1. !z:*1. x less y == TT  &  y less z == TT  IMP
                                                   x less z == TT "
LINORD3   " !x:*1. !y:*1. x less y == FF  IMP y less x == TT "
LINORD4   " !x:*1. !y:*1. x less y == TT  &  y less x == TT  IMP  x == y "
```

Now we can define the abstract type PQ of priority queues with parameter LINORD which is introduced using the command newparameter. The sort of PQ has one parameter *1. The operations emptyq and add are chosen as constructors for structural induction.

```
$          '/.  THEORY PQ '/. .
$          newparent `LINORD`
$          newtype 1 `pq`
$          PATin `PQ`
$          CONSTRUCTORSdec [ `emptyq`   ":*1 pq";  `add`" : *1 x *1 pq →*1 pq" ];;
$          map strictconstant
$             [ `isempty`,  ": *1 pq  → tr"        ";
$                 `remove`,  ": *1 pq  → *1 pq"      ;
$                 `min`,     ": *1 pq  → *1 "        ];;
```

For the axioms we need two variables x and q. We need two axioms for defining isempty. Also the operations min (for getting the least element of a queue) and remove (for deleting the least element of a queue) are inductively defined. Note that there are no axioms for min(empty) and remove(empty). Thus these terms will be undefined in minimally defined models such as initial or weakly terminal ones. Also, there are no axioms relating directly the constructors add and emptyq. The type PQ is specified by its "visible behaviour" only (cf. /Broy, Wirsing 81a,b/). We divide the axioms into two groups: for the first group the system has to ensure the definedness of variables whereas for the second this definedness can be inferred automatically.

```
$    "x: *1", "q: *1pq" ;;

$    map defaxiom
$        [ "isempty emptyq      == TT" ;
$          "isempty(add(x,q))   == FF" ;
$          "min(add(x,emptyq)) == x"  ;
$          "remove(add(x,emptyq)) == emptyq" ] ;;

$    map defaxiom
$        [ "isempty q == FF  &  x less(min q) == TT  IMP
$           min(add(x,q)) == x  &  remove(add(x,q)) == q" ;

$          "isempty q == FF  &  x less(min q) == FF  IMP
$           min(add(x,q)) == min q  &  remove(add(x,q)) == add(x,remove q)" ] ;;
```

As for LINORD the system introduces axiom names as well as flatness and strictness axioms (for better readability we do not write all sorts of variables which are inferred by the system

```
NEWAXIOMS()
FLAT "!x: *1 pq. !y *1 pq. DEF x == TT  &  x << y  IMP  x == y"
UU1PQ  "isempty  UU == UU"
UU2PQ  "remove   UU == UU"
UU3PQ  "min      UU == UU"
UU4PQ  "add(UU:*1x*1)== UU"
INDpq   "! F: *1 pq → tr.
           DEF emptyq == TT  IMP F emptyq ==  TT  &
          (!x. !q. DEF(add(x,q)) ==  TT  &  F q ==  TT  IMP
                                  F(add(x,q)) == TT)  IMP
           !q. F q ==  TT"
PRIOQ1  "isempty emptyq == TT "
PRIOQ2  "!x. !q. DEF x == TT  IMP  isempty(add(x,q)) == FF"
PRIOQ3  "!x.     DEF x == TT  IMP  min(add(x,emptyq)) == x"
PRIOQ4  "!x.     DEF x == TT  IMP  remove(add(y,emptyq)) == emptyq"
PRIOQ5  "!x. !q. isempty q == FF  &  x less(min q) == TT  IMP
          min(add(x,q)) == x  &  remove(add(x,q)) == q"
PRIOQ6  "!x. !q. isempty q == FF  &  x less(min q) == FF  IMP
          min(add(x,q)) == min q  &  remove(add(x,q)) == add(x,remove q)"
```

E. g. termination of min can be expressed by the formula

"!q. isempty q == FF IMP DEF (min q) == FF.

To prove this we have to construct a composed tactic

T = (INDTAC `PQ` `pq`) THEN (REPEAT CASETAC) THEN SIMPTAC

where INDTAC is a tactic for structural induction, CASETAC a tactic for analysing cases and SIMPTAC a tactic for the simplification of terms and formulae. More details about these tactics and the construction of composed tactic are given in /leszczylowsky 81b/.

To check the existence of initial and weakly terminal algebras we apply EXIN to EXTL to the output functions min and isempty

```
$    EXIN `PQ` [ `min` ; `isempty` ] ;;
$    true : bool

$    EXTL `PQ` [`min` ; `isempty`]
$    true : bool
```

Thus PQ has initial and weakly terminal algebras. In fact, the equality between constructor terms of the form add(x1, ..., add(xn, emptyq) in the initial algebras is the syntactic equality. Therefore, initial algebras correspond to unordered sequences. In the weakly terminal algebras two terms are equal if they contain the same *1-elements x1, ..., xn. Thus such algebras may be represented by ordered sequences as we will do in the following.

We specify a type SEQ of sequences as a domain type for which we have only to give the name of its sorts and of the constructors together with their representations as PPLAMBDA types (cf. 3.3):

```
$    '/. DRAFT SEQ '/.
$    newparent  LINORD
$    mlin(`PAT`, false) ;;
$    beginAXIOMSof `seq` 1 ;;
$    CONSTRUCTORS [ `emptyseq`, "UP()                ; "
                    `cons`, "(X: * , S: * seq) u" ] ;;
```

Then the system (working with R. Milner's file except that it uses the smash product) responds by defining abstraction and representation operations seqABS and seqREP as well as an operation seqFUN ensuring the validity of structural induction (cf. /LCF 79/):

```
DRAFT SEQ

newtype 1 `seq` ;;

newconstant(`seqABS`, ": . u + (* x * seq) u → * seq") ;;
newconstant(`seqREP`, ": * seq → . u + (* x * seq)") ;;
newconstant(`emptyseq`, ": * seq") ;;
newconstant(`cons`, ": * x *seq → * seq") ;;
newconstant(`seqFUN`, ": (* seq → * seq) → (* seq → * seq)") ;;

NEWAXIOMS() ;;

seqABS       "!ABS.  seqABS(seqREP ABS) == ABS"
seqREP       "!REP.  seqREP(seqABS REP) == REP"


emptyseq     "emptyseq == seqABS(INL(UP()))"
cons         "!X. !S. cons(X,S) == seqABS(INR(UP(X,S)))"


seqUU        "!F. seqFUN F UU == UU
seqemptyseq  "!F. seqFUN F emptyseq == emptyseq
seqcons      "!F. !X. !S. seqFUN F cons(X,S ) == cons(X,F S)
seqFix       "!ABS. FIX seqFUN ABS == ABS
```

To complete the abstract type we introduce selector functions and a test for emptyseq:

```
$    map strictconstant

$        [ `null`, ": * seq → tr"     ;
$          `head`, ": * seq → *"      ;
$          `tail`, ": * seq → * seq" ] ;;
```

with axioms in the usual LCF-style (without introducing definedness requirements:

```
$          "s: * seq" ;;

$    map defaxiom

$        [ `NULL`, "null s == ISL(seqREP s)" ;
$          `HEAD`, "head s == FST(DOWN(OUTR(seqREP s)))" ;
$          `TAIL`, "tail s == SND(DOWN(OUTR(seqREP s)))" ] ;;
```

For the implementation of priority queues by ordered sequences we have to insert a new element in a sequence at the right place. Therefore, we introduce a new operation insert on parameter sorts *1:

```
$    strictconstant(insert, ": *1x *1seq → *1seq")
$    "x: *1", "s: *1seq"
$    map defaxiom
$        [ "insert(x, emptyseq) == add(x, emtpyseq)" ;
$          "x less(head s) == TT  IMP  insert(x,s) == cons(x,s)" ;
$          "x less(head s) == FF  IMP  insert(x,y) == cons(head s, insert(x, rest s))" ] ;;
```

Now the operation add of PQ can be represented by insert and the other operations isempty, empty, ... by null, emptyseq, ... A call of CORREP produces the equations which have to be checked for the correctness of this implementation:

```
$     '/. IMPLEMENTATION PS '/.
$     CORREP `PS` `PQ` `SEQ` `(`pq`, `seq`)`
$           [ (`isempty`, `null`) ; (`emptyq`, `emptyseq`) ;
$             (`remove`, `tail`) ; (`min`, `head`) ; (`add`, `insert`) ];;
```

Then the system produces a new constant PSREPpq : *1 pq → *1 seq, new axioms such as

```
pq seq REPpq2  "PSREPpq(emptyq) == emptyseq;
pq seq REPpq5  "!x1: *1 . !x2: *1 pq. PSREPpq(add(x1,x2)) == insert(x1, PSREPpq x2));;
```

and goals of the form

```
PQSEQREP1 = "null emptyseq == TT" ,-, [] : goal
PQSEQREP2 = "!x. !q. DEF x == TT  IMP null(insert(x, PSREPpq q)) == x" ,-,[] : goal
```

For the correctness of the implementation these formulae have to be checked which can be done as usual in LCF.

TUNING ALGEBRAIC SPECIFICATIONS BY TYPE MERGING *)

A. Laut, H. Partsch **)

Abstract

Although modularized algebraic specifications consisting of a number of types hierarchically based on each other are well comprehensible, they often have the disadvantage of being too much decomposed and hence not directly suited for finding efficient implementations. The paper presents a formal method for overcoming this drawback by combining suitable hierarchical types while simultaneously specifying new (combined) operations.

*) This research was carried out within the Sonderforschungsbereich 49, Programmiertechnik, Munich.

**) Technische Universität München, Institut für Informatik, Postfach 20 24 20, 8000 München 2, Germany

0. Introduction

Recent developments in connection with algebraic data types (for short: types) provide structuring mechanisms (e.g. "theory-building operators" in /Burstall, Goguen 77, 80/ or "hierarchical types" in /Wirsing et al. 80/), with allow for an agreeable specification even of relatively large, complex problems. In such a specification of a certain type T it often happens that T is hierarchically based on another type P which is only introduced for the sake of a more transparent specification. (In particular this will happen if predefined, available type schemes are used for constructing new types adapted to specific requirements.) Although this situation is perfectly good with respect to understandability, for an efficient implementation the distinction between T and P should vanish when developing T by appropriate data type transformations towards an implementation.

In the following we introduce such a data type transformation called "type merging" (in order to stress the asymmetry of this operation), which may be sketched as follows: Suppose we have a type T based on a primitive type P which in turn is based on some other primitives. We aim at a general rule for transforming this hierachical definition of T into an equivalent one which does not use the definition of P . The first step towards this goal consists of "expanding" P in T, i.e. of inserting the specification of P into that of T, such that the operations of P are amenable to further manipulations. Then we enrich this expanded type by new operations which result from suitably composing particular operations from T with particular ones from P. These new operations allow to "simulate" the old ones from P such that sorts and operations of P can be hidden without changing the semantics. In a final step we deduce a new independent axiom system for the new operations such that the old operations even can be eliminated.

The paper starts by repeating the notions of a (hierachical) type and its models, which will serve as the formal basis for all subsequent definitions and theorems. We then introduce some simple combinators for operations and types as the basic constituents of type merging. The intuitively required properties of type merging, viz. right-commutativity and associativity (i.e. "horizontal" and "vertical associativity" with respect to the hierarchy) will be proved as the main theorems. Another theorem introduces the notion of "equivalence" mentioned above and provides the formal basis for finally dropping the old operations. For the proofs in the paper only the basic idea is sketched; detailed proofs can be found in a more comprehensive paper (/Laut, Partsch 82/) on the same topic.

All the theoretical considerations and results are illustrated by the simple accompanying example of specifying bit matrices as vectors of bit vectors. Similarly a number of algebraic types occurring in the literature can be derived by merging basic types, e.g. the symbol table in /Guttag 77/ by merging stacks with arrays, the blocks world in /Burstall, Goguen 77/ by merging arrays with stacks, or the attributed trees in /Bauer et al. 81b/ by merging trees with arrays. Further examples are treated in /Laut, Partsch 82/.

1. Hierarchical Types

As a formal basis for our subsequent considerations we recap the notions of a (hierarchical) type and its models.

Definition D1

A (hierarchical) type T is a triple $(\Pi_T, \Sigma_T, \Lambda_T)$ where

- Π_T is a set of primitive types
- the signature $\Sigma_T = (S_T, F_T, S_T^h, F_T^h)$ consists of the pairwise disjoint sets S_T of visible sorts, F_T of visible operation symbols, S_T^h of hidden sorts, F_T^h of hidden operation symbols (for signatures we assume the usual set operations to be defined component-wise)
- Λ_T is a set of laws

such that

(i) $\forall P, Q \in \Pi_T^* : P \neq Q \Rightarrow \Sigma_P \cap \Sigma_Q = \emptyset$ where $\Pi_T^* =_{def} \{T\} \cup \Pi_T^+$ and $\Pi_T^+ =_{def} \Pi_T \cup \bigcup_{P \in \Pi_T} \Pi_P^+$ (i.e. no name clashes in the transitive closure of the primitive types)

(ii) every $f \in F_T \cup F_T^h$ is associated with a functionality, i.e. arity, domain and range, in the form $f : \times_{i=1}^{n(f)} \underline{s}_f^i \rightarrow \underline{s}_f^{n(f)+1}$ such that $n(f) \geq 0$ and $\forall_{k=1}^{n(f)+1}\ \underline{s}_f^k \in S_T^r \wedge (f \in F_T \Rightarrow \underline{s}_f^k \notin S_T^h)$ where $S_T^r =_{def} S_T \cup S_T^h \cup \bigcup_{P \in \Pi_T} S_P$

(i.e. all sorts involved must be among the "reachable" sorts S_T^r of T and the functionality of visible operation symbols must not contain hidden sorts).

(iii) every $L \in \Lambda_T$ is a closed first-order formula over equations between terms (of the sorts of S_T^r) built from operation symbols of F_T^r where $F_T^r =_{def} F_T \cup F_T^h \cup \bigcup_{P \in \Pi_T} F_P$ (the "reachable" operation symbols of T) ■

Note that due to the inductive definition the "hierarchy condition" $T \notin \Pi_T^+$ is always fulfilled. The outermost universal quantifier of a law is often omitted since it can be reconstructed by quantifying over all free variables.

The semantics of a type is given by its (hierarchy-preserving, finitely generated) models:

Definition D2

A model of a type T is a partial heterogeneous algebra A of the signature Σ_T^* where $\Sigma_T^* =_{def} \bigcup_{P \in \Pi_T^*} \Sigma_P$ such that

(i) for every $P \in \Pi_T$ the reduct of A to Σ_P^* (short: A/Σ_P^*, i.e. the carrier sets and operations associated with the sorts and operation symbols of Σ_P^*) is a model of P

(ii) for every $\underline{s} \in S_T \cup S_T^h$ the carrier set $\underline{s}_A$ is finitely generated by the operations of A

(iii) the laws of Λ_T hold in A (note that the equality in the laws is interpreted as stron equality; thus the first-order formulas can be interpreted as in ordinary two-valued logic). ■

The definitions in principle follow /Wirsing et al. 80/, /Bauer, Wössner 81/ and /Bauer et al. 81a/. Whereas /Wirsing et al. 80/ considers hierarchical types with only one primitive type, /Bauer et al. 81a/ also admits type schemes, "overloaded" operation symbols and name clashes between the hidden sorts and operation symbols of the primitive types. For our considerations type schemes have been excluded since they are still subject of current research (cf. e.g. /Wirsing, Broy 81/, /Ganzinger 81/, /Ehrig 81/). Overloading and name clashes would technically complicate the presentation; they could be coped with by suitably indexing the respective sorts and operation symbols.

For the presentation of examples we use the notation of CIP-L (cf. /Bauer et al. 81a/): A type T (with finite Π_T, Σ_T, Λ_T) is denoted by

<u>type</u> T ≡ << headline >> : << body >> <u>endoftype</u>

In the headline the (names of the) elements of $S_T \cup F_T$ are listed. The body contains the

$P \in \Pi_T$	in the form	<u>based on</u> P
$\underline{s} \in S_T \cup S_T^h$	in the form	<u>sort</u> $\underline{s}$
$(f : \times_{i=1}^{n(f)} \underline{s}_f^i \to \underline{s}_f^{n(f)+1}) \in F_T \cup F_T^h$	in the form	<u>funct</u> $(\underline{s}_f^1, \dots \underline{s}_f^{n(f)})\ \underline{s}_f^{n(f)+1} f$
$L \in \Lambda_T$	in the form	id_L : L

The example we will use for demonstrating the theoretical results specifies matrices in terms of vectors where the respective indices are integral numbers and the components of a vector are supposed to be bits (denoted by the truth values). This simple example has the advantage of having not too many operations, which are moreover totally defined. The theory, of course, is applicable to partial operations without any restrictions (cf. /Laut, Partsch 81/).

Presupposing a usual definition of the types INT and BOOL (cf. e.g. /Bauer et al. 81b/), we specify:

```
type BITVECTOR ≡ vector, initv, putv, getv :
    based on INT, based on BOOL ,
    sort vector ,
    funct(bool) vector initv ,
    funct(vector, int, bool) vector putv ,
    funct(vector, int) bool getv ,
        GV1 : getv(initv(x), i) = x ,
        GV2 : getv(putv(v, i, x),i) = x ,
        GV3 : i ≠ j ⇒ getv(putv(v, i, x), j) = getv(v, j) ,
        PV1 : putv(initv(x), i, x) = initv(x) ,
        PV2 : putv(putv(v, i, x), i, y) = putv(v, i, y) ,
        PV3 : i ≠ j ⇒ putv(putv(v, i, x), j, y) = putv(putv(v, j, y), i, x)
                                                              endoftype

type BITMATRIX₀ ≡ matrix, initm, putm, getm :
    basedon INT, basedon BITVECTOR ,
    sort matrix ,
    funct(vector) matrix initm ,
    funct(matrix, int, vector) matrix putm ,
    funct(matrix, int) vector getm ,
        GM1 : getm(initm(x), i) = x ,
        GM2 : getm(putm(m, i, x), i) = x ,
        GM3 : i ≠ j ⇒ getm(putm(m, i, x), j) = getm(m, j) ,
        PM1 : putm(initm(x), i, x) = initm(x) ,
        PM2 : putm(putm(m, i, x), i, y) = putm(m, i, y) ,
        PM3 : i ≠ j ⇒ putm(putm(m, i, x), j, y) = putm(putm(m, j, y), i, x)
                                                              endoftype
```

Using type schemes, BITVECTOR and BITMATRIX could also be defined by instantiating the type scheme TOTALGREX (cf. /Bauer et al. 81b/) first with BOOL and then with BITVECTOR.

2. Type Expansion

As to the formal definition of the data structure, there is no objection against the above sample specification. But as soon as we try to formulate algorithms for matrices, e.g. multiplication, we will immediately find out that we are primarily interested in selecting and updating single bits of a matrix and not vectors as a whole. If, moreover, vectors are not part of the problem, i.e. only serve for structuring the specification, it is desirable (especially with respect to a later implementation) to merge BITVECTOR with BITMATRIX_0. A similar need for merging types will arise whenever we want to implement such a composite data structure on a von Neumann machine, since it is generally impossible to push a composite object (like a vector above) all at once through the "bottle-neck" cpu.

As a first step towards type merging we introduce the (textual) expansion of types:

Definition D3

Let T be a type and $P \in \Pi_T$ such that for all $Q \in \Pi_T : P \notin \Pi_Q^+$. (*)

Then we define the expansion of P in T (short: T □ P) by

$$T \,\square\, P =_{def} ((\Pi_T \setminus \{P\}) \cup \Pi_P,\ \Sigma_T \cup \Sigma_P,\ \Lambda_T \cup \Lambda_P) \qquad \blacksquare$$

The condition (*) in D3 serves to avoid name clashes in T □ P; if it does not hold a priori, it can easily be established by (consistently) renaming P and its constituents before the expansion.

If T itself is primitive in another type, T □ P has to be renamed T after the expansion has been performed.

For our example the expansion of BITVECTOR in BITMATRIX_0 yields:

> <u>type</u> BITMATRIX_1 ≡ <u>matrix</u>, initm, putm, getm, <u>vector</u>, initv, putv, getv :
> <u>basedon</u> INT, <u>basedon</u> BOOL ,
> << signature and laws of BITVECTOR >>
> << signature and laws of BITMATRIX_0 >>
>
> <u>endoftype</u>

For type expansion some useful properties can be proved which will be needed later on:

Lemma L1 : Under the assumptions of D3 the following holds:

a) T □ P is a well-defined type

b) Every model of T is a model of T □ P, but not necessarily vice versa.

c) Type expansion is right-commutative, i.e.

$P, P' \in \Pi_T$, $P \neq P'$, $(\forall Q \in \Pi_T : P, P' \notin \Pi_Q^+ \; (*))$

$\Rightarrow$ $(T \,\square\, P) \,\square\, P'$ and $(T \,\square\, P') \,\square\, P$ are both defined and equal

d) Type expansion is associative, i.e.

$P \in \Pi_T$, $P' \in \Pi_P$ $(\forall Q \in \Pi_T : P \notin \Pi_Q^+ \; (*)) \wedge (\forall Q \in \Pi_P \cup (\Pi_T \setminus \{P\}) : P' \notin \Pi_Q^+)$

$\Rightarrow$ $(T \,\square\, P) \,\square\, P'$ and $T \,\square\, (P \,\square\, P')$ are both defined and equal

(Note that $P \,\square\, P'$ must be renamed P in order to construct $T \,\square\, (P \,\square\, P'))$

Proof:

a) Straightforward by showing that $T \,\square\, P$ fulfills the conditions of D1.

b) b1) By applying D3 it can be shown that $\Sigma_T^* = \Sigma_{T \square P}^*$;
using D2 to show $(\forall Q \in \Pi_{T \square P} = \Pi_T \setminus \{T\} \cup \Pi_P : A/\Sigma_Q^*$ is a model of $Q)$ is straightforward.

b2) Counterexample:

<u>type</u> P ≡ <u>p</u> : <u>sort</u> <u>p</u> <u>endoftype</u>

<u>type</u> T ≡ x : <u>basedon</u> P, <u>funct</u> <u>p</u> x <u>endoftype</u>

The algebra A with $p_A = \{0\}$, $x_A = 0$ obviously is a model of $T \,\square\, P$, but not of T , since $A/(\{\underline{p}\}, \emptyset)$ is not finitely generated by the operations of P .

c), d) Again straightforward from the respective definitions. ■

The above lemma states that the order in which types are expanded is irrelevant, no matter whether the types are situated horizontally (c) or vertically (d) in the hierarchy. Similarly type expansion commutes with "operational enrichment" of the type:

Definition D4

Let T be a type, $f \notin \Sigma_T^*$, $\overset{n(f)+1}{\underset{k=1}{\forall}} \; \underline{s}_f^k \in S_T^r$, and L_f be a law of the form

$f(\vec{x}) = \tau[\vec{x}]$ where τ is a term built from the operation symbols of F_T^r and the typle of free variables x.

Then the <u>operational enrichment</u> of T by f is the type

$T + f =_{def} (\Pi_T, (S_T, F_T \cup \{f\}, S_T^h, F_T^h), \Lambda_T \cup \{L_f\})$. ■

This notion of operational enrichment, which agrees with the "enrichment by derived operators" of /Goguen et al. 78/, suffices for our purposes. A more general notion allowing for recursion has been introduced in /Broy et al. 80/.

Lemma L2 : Under the assumptions of D4 the following holds:

a) $T+f$ is a well-defined type

b) Operational enrichment is right-commutative, i.e. if additionally $g \notin \Sigma_T^* \cup \{f\}$, $\forall_{i=1}^{n(g)+1} \underline{s}_g^i \in S_T^r$ and L_g is of the form $g(\vec{x}) = \tau'[\vec{x}]$ (τ' term over F_T^r and $\vec{x}$), then $(T+f)+g$ and $(T+g)+f$ are both defined and equal

c) Operational enrichment commutes with type expansion, i.e. $P \in \Pi_T \wedge \forall Q \in \Pi_T : P \notin \Pi_Q^+$
$\Rightarrow (T \square P) + f$ and $(T+f) \square P$ are both defined and equal

Proof: Obvious from the respective definitions ■

3. Operation Merging

In order to have direct access to the single elements in a matrix, for our example $BITMATRIX_1$, we would like to merge getv with getm. Generally we aim at merging all "output" operations of the hierarchically lower type with those of the higher type. Similarly the "input" operations of the higher type will be merged with those of the lower one. Since we assume that the type to be merged defines "large" composite objects which we intend to manipulate piecewise, we presuppose that the operations of this type have at most one parameter of the "sort of interest" (otherwise piecewise manipulation would be much more difficult). Moreover we presuppose for the operations to be merged that exactly one parameter sort of the first coincides with the result sort of the second. (If also operations with more than one result were admitted, a similar restriction would have to be imposed on the result sorts.)

In order to formally state these restriction, we use the following notions:

Definition D5

Let T be a type, $f \in F_T$, $S \subseteq S_T$. We say that

- f is nullary in S iff $\forall_{k=1}^{n(f)} \underline{s}_f^k \notin S$,

- f is <u>unary</u> in S iff $\exists_1{}_{k=1}^{n(f)} \ \underline{s}_f^k \in S$,

- f is <u>at most unary</u> in S iff f is nullary or unary in S .

As an abbreviation we will also write "F is nullary in S" etc. for $F \subseteq F_T$ and analogously for $S = \{\underline{s}\}$. ■

Now we are able to formalize what we mean by merging an operation with another one, which in this simple case amounts to ordinary functional composition.

<u>Definition D6</u>

Let T be a type and $f, f' \in F_T^r$ such that f is unary in $\underline{s}' =_{def} \underline{s}_{f'}^{n(f')+1}$.

Then we define the type $T + f \circ f'$ resulting from T by <u>merging f' with f</u> by

$T + f \circ f' =_{def} (\Pi_T, (S_T, F_T \cup F_{f \circ f'}, S_T^h, F_T^h), \Lambda_T \cup \Lambda_{f \circ f'})$ where

- $F_{f \circ f'} =_{def} \{f \circ f' : \mathop{\times}_{i=1}^{j-1} \underline{s}_f^i \times \mathop{\times}_{i=1}^{n(f')} \underline{s}_{f'}^i \times \mathop{\times}_{i=j+1}^{n(f)} \underline{s}_f^i \rightarrow \underline{s}_f^{n(f)+1}\}$

where $f \circ f'$ is a new operation symbol

- $\Lambda_{f \circ f'} =_{def} \{f \circ f'(\vec{y}_1, \vec{x}, \vec{y}_2) = f(\vec{y}_1, f'(\vec{x}), \vec{y}_2)\}$ ■

In our current example, BITMATRIX_1 + getv o getm + initm o initv is the following type (with get for getv o getm and init for initm o initv):

<u>type</u> BITMATRIX_2 ≡ <u>matrix</u>, initm, putm, getm, <u>vector</u>, initv, putv, getv, init, get:

  << primitives, signature, and laws of BITMATRIX_1 >> ,

  <u>funct</u>(<u>bool</u>) <u>matrix</u> init ,

    I : init(x) = initm(initv(x)) ,

  <u>funct</u>(<u>matrix</u>, <u>int</u>, <u>int</u>) <u>bool</u> get ,

    G : get(m, i, j) = getv(getm(m, i), j) <u>endoftype</u>

Note that the operations being merged will eventually be hidden (cf. D10).

Again some properties can be stated in connection with the merging of operations:

<u>Lemma L3</u>: Under the assumptions of D6 the following holds:

a) $T + f \circ f'$ is a well-defined type

b) Extending T by expansion or merged operations is right-commutative

c) The merging of operations is associative, i.e.

$f, f', f'' \in F_T$, f is unary in $\underline{s}' =_{def} \underline{s}_{f'}^{n(f')+1}$ and nullary in

$\underline{s}'' =_{def} \underline{s}_{f''}^{n(f'')+1}$, f' is unary in $\underline{s}''$

$\Rightarrow$ $T + f \circ f' + (f \circ f') \circ f''$ and $T + f \circ f'' + f \circ (f' \circ f'')$ are both defined and $(f \circ f') \circ f''$ and $f \circ (f' \circ f'')$ are specified equivalently.

Proof: a) and b) follow from D6 and L2

c) i) Since f' is unary in $\underline{s}''$ and f is nullary in $\underline{s}''$, $f \circ f'$ is unary in $\underline{s}''$ and hence $(f \circ f') \circ f''$ is defined. Since f is presupposed to be unary in $\underline{s}'$, $f \circ (f' \circ f'')$ is also defined

ii) The equality of the signatures follows immediately from D6

iii) The coincidence of the laws is a consequence of the associativity of functional composition

■

4. Update Operations

In order to be able to hide the sort of interest of the primitive type, similarly to the input and output operations also the "transput" operations such as e.g. putv must be merged with some operations of the higher type. Certainly, such a transput operation will be applied to the result of an output operation of the higher type such as getm in our current example. This would lead to operations such as

funct (matrix, int, int, bool) vector put_o

specified by the law

$put_o(m, i, j, x) = putv(getm(m, i), j, x)$.

But what is to be done with the result of put_o? Intuitively, it is to "update" the element selected by the output operation, leading in the example to

funct (matrix, int, int, bool) matrix put

specified by the law

$put(m, i, j, x) = putm(m, i, putv(getm(m, i), j, x))$

Thus we have to generalize the relation between putm and getm , which will be called "putm updates (the element yielded by) getm" and then define the merging of transput operations.

First we make the notions in/trans/output of a certain sort precise:

Definition D7

Let T be a type and $\underline{s} \in S_T$. Partition $F_{\underline{s}} =_{def} \{f \in F_T : \overset{n(f)+1}{\underset{k=1}{\exists}} \underline{s}_f^k = \underline{s}\}$

into $F_{\underline{s}}^{in}$, $F_{\underline{s}}^{trans}$, $F_{\underline{s}}^{out}$, $F_{\underline{s}}^{com}$ such that $\forall f \in F_{\underline{s}} : (f \in F_{\underline{s}}^{out} \Leftrightarrow \underline{s}_f^{n(f)+1} = \underline{s})$,

$F_{\underline{s}}^{in}$ is nullary in $\underline{s}$, $F_{\underline{s}}^{trans}$ is unary in $\underline{s}$ and the $f \in F_{\underline{s}}^{com}$ are neither nullary nor unary in $\underline{s}$. (According to the restriction mentioned in the beginning of section 3 the "combining" operations of $F_{\underline{s}}^{com}$ can be disregarded here). ∎

Obviously for $BITMATRIX_o$ we have

$$F_{\underline{matrix}}^{in} = \{initm\} , \quad F_{\underline{matrix}}^{out} = \{getm\}, \quad F_{\underline{matrix}}^{trans} = \{putm\}.$$

Now we can define what we mean by "a transput operation updates an output operation":

Definition D8

Let T be a type and $\underline{s} \in S_T$. $g \in F_{\underline{s}}^{trans}$ updates $f \in F_{\underline{s}}^{out}$ iff the following holds:

(i) g has the functionality $g : \overset{n(f)+1}{\underset{i=1}{X}} \underline{s}_f^i \rightarrow \underline{s}$

(ii) With $\underline{s}_f^k = \underline{s}$ the following law is valid :

$$\forall \vec{x} \in \overset{n(f)}{\underset{i=1}{X}} \underline{s}_f^i , \quad y \in \underline{s}_f^{n(f)+1} : f(\vec{x}) \text{ is defined} \Rightarrow$$

$$g(\vec{x}, f(\vec{x})) = x_k \wedge f(x_1,\ldots,x_{k-1}, g(\vec{x}, y), x_{k+1}, \ldots, x_{n(f)}) = y$$

Note that stating (i) in the restricted form as above is just to ease the formulation, more generally, the domain of g can be any permutation of the sorts occurring in the functionality of f . The left equation in the conclusion of the last line states that updating with the original value does not change the argument of sort $\underline{s}$; the right equation requires that after the updating the output operation yields the new value. Note also that the equality in $g(\vec{x}, f(\vec{x})) = x_k$ may be weakened to "visible equivalence" (cf. /Laut, Partsch 82/). ∎

In our current example,

<u>funct</u>(<u>matrix</u>, <u>int</u>, <u>vector</u>) <u>matrix</u> putm

updates

<u>funct</u>(<u>matrix</u>, <u>int</u>) <u>vector</u> getm ,

since (i) holds obviously and the following law is valid:

$$\forall \underline{\text{matrix}}\ m, \underline{\text{int}}\ i, \underline{\text{vector}}\ y, z :$$
$$y = getm(m, i) \Rightarrow (putm(m, i, y) = m \wedge getm(putm(m, i, z), i) = z)$$

Whereas the second equation of the conclusion is the law GM3 of $BITMATRIX_o$, the first one has to be proved by structural induction on m :

(I) Let $m = initm(x)$ for some <u>vector</u> x. Then

$$putm(initm(x), i, getm(initm(x), i)) = putm(initm(x), i, x) = initm(x)$$

(II) Let $m = putm(m_o, j, x)$ for some <u>matrix</u> m_o, <u>int</u> j, <u>vector</u> x . Then

$$putm(putm(m_o, j, x), i, getm(putm(m_o, j, x), i)) =$$

<u>case a</u> : $i = j$: $= putm(putm(m_o, i, x), i, x) = putm(m_o, i, x)$

<u>case b</u> : $i \neq j$: $= putm(putm(m_o, j, x), i, getm(m_o, i)) =$
$= putm(putm(m_o, i, getm(m_o, i)), j, x) =$ (ind. hyp.)
$= putm(m_o, j, x)$

The merging of update operations is now defined by

<u>Definition D9</u>

Let T be a type, $\underline{s} \in S_T$, $g \in F_{\underline{s}}^{trans}$ update $f \in F_{\underline{s}}^{out}$, and $h \in F_{\underline{s}'}^{trans}$ with $\underline{s}' =_{def} \underline{s}_f^{n(f)+1}$ and $\underline{s}_h^k = \underline{s}'$.

Then we define the type $T+g \bullet h \bullet f$ resulting from T by <u>merging h with f and g</u> by

$$T + g \bullet h \bullet f =_{def} (\Pi_T, (S_T, F_T \cup F_{g \bullet h \bullet f}, S_T^h, F_T^h), \Lambda_T \cup \Lambda_{g \bullet h \bullet f}) \text{ where}$$

- $F_{g \bullet h \bullet f} =_{def} \{ g \bullet h \bullet f : \mathop{X}\limits_{i=1}^{k-1} \underline{s}_h^i \times \mathop{X}\limits_{i=1}^{n(f)} \underline{s}_f^i \times \mathop{X}\limits_{i=k+1}^{n(h)} \underline{s}_h^i \rightarrow \underline{s} \}$

  where $g \bullet h \bullet f$ is a new operation symbol

- $\Lambda_{g \bullet h \bullet f} =_{def} \{ g \bullet h \bullet f(\vec{y}_1, \vec{x}, \vec{y}_2) = g(\vec{x}, h(\vec{y}_1, f(\vec{x}), \vec{y}_2)) \}$ ∎

For our current example $BITMATRIX_2$ + putm • putv • getm is the following type (where putm • putv • getm is abbreviated by put) :

<u>type</u> $BITMATRIX_3$ ≡ <u>matrix</u>, initm, putm, getm, <u>vector</u>, initv, putv, getv, init, put, get :
<< primitives, signature, and laws of $BITMATRIX_2$ >> ,
<u>funct</u>(<u>matrix</u>, <u>int</u>, <u>int</u>, <u>bool</u>) <u>matrix</u> put,
P: put(m, i, j, x) = putm(m, i, putv(getm(m, i), j, x)) <u>endoftype</u>

Now the sort <u>vector</u> and its operations could be hidden.

For the merging of transput operations, too, some properties can be shown.

<u>Lemma L4</u>: Under the assumptions of D9 the following holds:

a) T + g • h • f is a well-defined type

b) The merging of transput operations is right-commutative and also commutes with the ordinary merging of operations and with type expansion

c) The merging of transput operations is "associative" and "associates" also with the ordinary merging of operations, i.e.

(i) $\underline{s}, \underline{s}', \underline{s}'' \in S_T$ such that $\underline{s} \neq \underline{s}''$, $g \in F^{trans}_{\underline{s}}$ updates $f \in F^{out}_{\underline{s}}$, $\underline{s}_f^{n(f)+1} = \underline{s}'$, $g' \in F^{trans}_{\underline{s}'}$ updates $f' \in F^{out}_{\underline{s}'}$, $\underline{s}_{f'}^{n(f')+1} = \underline{s}''$, f' is nullary in $\underline{s}$, and $h' \in F^{trans}_{\underline{s}''}$ is nullary in $\underline{s}'$

$\Rightarrow$ $T_1 =_{def} T + g \bullet g' \bullet f + f' \circ f + (g \bullet g' \bullet f) \bullet h' \bullet (f' \circ f)$ and

$T_2 =_{def} T + g' \bullet h' \bullet f' + g \bullet (g' \bullet h' \bullet f') \bullet f$ are both defined and the resulting transput operations are specified equivalently

(ii) $\underline{s}, \underline{s}', \underline{s}'' \in S_T$ such that $\underline{s} \neq \underline{s}'$ and $\underline{s}' \neq \underline{s}''$, $g \in F^{trans}_{\underline{s}}$ updates $f \in F^{out}_{\underline{s}}$,

$\underline{s}_f^{n(f)+1} = \underline{s}'$, f is nullary in $\underline{s}''$, $h \in F^{trans}_{\underline{s}'}$ is unary in $\underline{s}''$,

$f'' \in F_T$ with $\underline{s}_{f''}^{n(f'')+1} = \underline{s}''$ is nullary in $\underline{s}'$

$\Rightarrow$ $T + (g \bullet h \bullet f) \circ f''$ and $T + g \bullet (h \circ f'') \bullet f$ are both defined and equivalently specified

Proof: a) and b) follow from D9 and L2.

c) i) According to D9, $g' \bullet h' \bullet f'$ is defined. Since f is unary in $\underline{s}'$ and h' is nullary in $\underline{s}'$, $g' \bullet h' \bullet f' \in F^{trans}_{\underline{s}'}$. Hence with the assumptions of L4 T_2 is defined.

For proving the definedness of T_1 we have to verify that

- $f' \circ f \in F^{out}_{\underline{s}}$ and $\underline{s}^{n(f' \circ f)+1}_{f' \circ f} = \underline{s}''$,
- $h =_{def} g \bullet g' \bullet f \in F^{trans}_{\underline{s}}$,
- h updates $f' \circ f$.

The equivalence of the resulting transput operations in T_1 and T_2 can be seen by constructing the respective signatures and applying D9 to the respective laws.

ii) similarly ∎

In order to make the property c)i) of L4 more concrete, we extend our current example by

> <u>type</u> $BITSPACE_0$ ≡ <u>space</u>, inits, puts, gets :
>
> <u>basedon</u> INT, <u>basedon</u> $BITMATRIX_0$,
>
> << vector of matrices, analogous to BITVECTOR and $BITMATRIX_0$ >>
>
> <u>endoftype</u>

Let $BITSPACE_1 =_{def} (BITSPACE_0 \;\square\; BITMATRIX_0) \;\square\; BITVECTOR$ (which according to L1 is the same as $BITSPACE_0 \;\square\; (BITMATRIX_0 \;\square\; BITVECTOR)$).

$BITSPACE_1$ + putm • putv • getm contains

> <u>funct</u>(<u>matrix</u>, <u>int</u>, <u>int</u>, <u>bool</u>) <u>matrix</u> putmv ,
>
> putmv(m, i, j, x) = putm(m, i, putv(getm(m, i), j, x))

The type corresponding to T_2 of c)i) further contains

> <u>funct</u>(<u>space</u>, <u>int</u>, <u>int</u>, <u>int</u>, <u>bool</u>) <u>space</u> putsmv,
>
> putsmv(s, i, j, k, x) = puts(s, i, putmv(gets(s, i), j, k, x)).

This equation is equivalent to

(*) putsmv(s,i,j,k,x) = puts(s,i, putm(gets(s,i),j, putv(getm(gets(s,i),j), k,x)))

$BITSPACE_1$ + puts • putm • gets + getm o gets contains

> funct(space, int, int, vector) space putsm,
> putsm(s,i,j,v) = puts(s,i, putm(gets(s,i), j, v)) ,
> funct(space, int, int) vector getsm ,
> getsm(s,i,j) = getm(gets(s,i), j).

The type corresponding to T_1 of c)i) further contains

> funct(space, int, int, int, bool) space putsmv ,
> putsmv(s,i,j,k,x) = putsm(s,i,j, putv(getsm(s,i,j), k, x)).

This equation is again equivalent to (*) above.

5. Type Merging

As already pointed out in the beginning of section 3, some restrictions will be imposed on a type P to be merged with its superposed type T , which all result from the intention of piecewise manipulating the objects it defines. Thus we presuppose that P introduces exactly one sort s and that no operation of P has more than one parameter of sort s . Moreover, the output operations of T are not allowed to have parameters of sort s in order not to confuse the embedding of the s -objects in T with the calculation of output from T .

First we define the notions in/out/transput of a type analogously to those concerning a sort (cf. D7) in order to capture types definingmore than one sort:

Definition D10

Let T be a type. Partition F_T into F_T^{in}, F_T^{out}, F_T^{trans}, F_T^{com}, F_T^{null} such that $\forall f \in F_T : (f \in F_T^{out} \cup F_T^{null} \Leftrightarrow \underline{s}_f^{n(f)+1} \notin S_T)$, F_T^{in} and F_T^{null} are nullary in S_T, F_T^{out} is at least unary in S_T, F_T^{trans} is unary in S_T, and the $f \in F_T^{com}$ are neither nullary nor unary in S_T. Furthermore, for $\underline{s} \in S_P$, $P \in \Pi_T$, and $\alpha \in \{in, trans, com, out, null\}$ we use $F_{T,\underline{s}}^{\alpha} =_{def} F_T^{\alpha} \cap F_{\underline{s}}$, and $F_{T,\underline{s}}^{par} =_{def} \{f \in F_T \mid f$ is not nullary in $\underline{s}\}$. ∎

Note that the result sort of an operation $g \in F_T^{trans}$ that updates some $f \in F_T^{out}$ is uniquely determined, since it is in S_T , it coincides with a parameter sort of g , and g is unary in S_T.

Now we define

Definition D11

Let the type P be mergeable with the type T, i.e. $P \in \Pi_T$, $S_P = \{\underline{s}\}$, $\forall Q \in \Pi_T : P \notin \Pi_Q^+$, both F_T and F_P are at most unary in $\underline{s}$, F_T^{out} is even nullary in $\underline{s}$, $\forall f \in F_{T,\underline{s}}^{out} : \exists_1\, up(f) \in F_T^{trans} : up(t)$ updates f, and finally $F_{T,\underline{s}}^{null} = \emptyset$.

In order to define the merging of P with T (short: $T \circ P$), we first introduce the auxiliary type

$$\overline{T \circ P} =_{def} T \square P + \sum_{f \in F_{T,\underline{s}}^{par},\; f' \in F_P^{\overline{in}}} f \circ f' + \sum_{f \in F_{T,\underline{s}}^{out},\; f' \in F_P^{out}} f' \circ f + \sum_{f \in F_{T,\underline{s}}^{out},\; h \in F_P^{trans}} up(f) \bullet h \bullet f$$

(The sum operator "Σ" is understood to repeat the "+"-operations introduced by D4; according to L2 the order of the summation is irrelevant.)

$T \circ P$ then evolves from $\overline{T \circ P}$ by hiding the sort $\underline{s}$ and the operations involved in the merging (note that the new operations do not touch $\underline{s}$ any longer):

$$\Sigma_{T \circ P} =_{def} (S_{\overline{T \circ P}} \setminus \{\underline{s}\},\ F_{\overline{T \circ P}} \setminus F_{\underline{s}},\ S^h_{\overline{T \circ P}} \cup \{\underline{s}\},\ F^h_{\overline{T \circ P}} \cup F_{\underline{s}})$$ ■

For our current example we thus get first

$\overline{BITMATRIX_0 \circ BITVECTOR}$ = BITMATRIX □ BITVECTOR + initm o initv + putm o initv + getv o getm + putm • putv • getm =
= $BITMATRIX_3$ + putm o initv

and then (with reinit for putm o initv) :

type $BITMATRIX_4$ ≡ **matrix**, init, put, get, reinit :
  << primitives, signature, and laws of $BITMATRIX_3$ >> ,
  funct(**matrix**, **int**, **bool**) **matrix** reinit ,
  R : reinit(m, i, x) = putm(m, i, initv(x))   **endoftype**

The new operation reinit re-initializes a line/column of a matrix. As in this case, it is often not necessary to merge the input operations with the update operations. Thus in the first sum of D11 f could be restricted to $F^{par}_{T,\underline{s}}$ without the image set of up. In some examples, however, the updating is not defined unless the corresponding component has been initialized (cf.the type GREX /Bauer et al. 81b/ specifying non-initialized arrays).

Now we can state our main theorems on type merging.

Theorem T1 Under the assumptions of D9 the following holds:

a) $T \circ P$ is a well-defined type

b) $T \circ P$ is an operative enrichment of T.

Proof: a) $\overline{T \circ P}$ is a well-defined type according to L1, L3, and L4 ; $\underline{s}$ may be hidden in $T \circ P$, since all operations of $T \circ P$ involving $\underline{s}$ are hidden (cf. D1).

b) Obvious from L2. ∎

Theorem T2 Type merging is right-commutative, i.e.

P, P' mergeable with T, $P \neq P'$

$\Rightarrow$ $(T \circ P) \circ P'$ and $(T \circ P') \circ P$ are both defined and their visible operations are specified equivalently.

Proof: i) The definedness of $(T \circ P) \circ P'$ is ensured by showing along the respective definitions that P' is mergeable with $T \circ P$ ($(T \circ P') \circ P$ analogously).

ii) Since according to L3 and L4 all the single steps leading to $T \circ P$ can be performed in arbitrary order, it remains to show that for all operations newly introduced by $T \circ P$, i.e.

$$\underbrace{\qquad\qquad\qquad\qquad}_{f \in F^{par}_{T,\underline{s}} \cap F^{par}_{T,\underline{s}'},\ f' \in F^{in}_{P}} f \circ f' ,$$

which are to be merged with all $f'' \in F^{in}_{P'}$, $(f \circ f') \circ f''$ is defined. But this can simply be done by applying the respective definitions (Analogously we proceed for $T \circ P'$). ∎

Type merging ist not only right-commutative, but also associative :

<u>Theorem T3</u> Type merging is associative, i.e.

P' mergeable with P, P mergeable with T, $\forall Q \in \Pi_T \setminus \{P\} : P' \notin \Pi_Q^+$
$\Rightarrow$ $(T \circ P) \circ P'$ and $T \circ (P \circ P')$ are both defined and their visible operations are specified equivalently.

<u>Proof:</u> i) Again the definedness of $(T \circ P) \circ P'$ and $T \circ (P \circ P')$ is proved by verifying the conditions of D11.

ii) For showing the equivalent specification of the operations in $F_{(T \circ P) \circ P'}$ and $F_{T \circ (P \circ P')}$ we first derive (using D11) explicit definitions for them (depending on the different kinds of merged operations from F_T, F_P, and $F_{P'}$). In this way we e.g. get

$$
\begin{aligned}
F_{(T \circ P) \circ P'} = (F_T \setminus F_{\underline{s}})
& \cup \{f \circ f' : f \in F^{par}_{T,\underline{s}},\ f' \in F^{in}_P \setminus F_{\underline{s}'}\} \\
& \cup \{f' \circ f : f \in T^{out}_{T,\underline{s}},\ f' \in F^{out}_P \setminus F_{\underline{s}'}\} \\
& \cup \{up(f) \bullet h \bullet f : f \in F^{out}_{T,\underline{s}},\ f' \in F^{trans}_P \setminus F_{\underline{s}'}\} \\
& \cup \{(f \circ f') \circ f'' : f \in F^{par}_{T,\underline{s}},\ f' \in F^{in}_{P,\underline{s}'},\ f'' \in F^{in}_{P'}\} \\
& \cup \{(up(f) \bullet h \bullet f) \circ f'' : f \in F^{out}_{T,\underline{s}},\ h \in F^{trans}_{P,\underline{s}'},\ f'' \in F^{in}_{P'}\} \\
& \cup \{f'' \circ (f' \circ f) : f \in F^{out}_{T,\underline{s}},\ f' \in F^{out}_{P,\underline{s}'},\ f'' \in F^{out}_{P'}\} \\
& \cup \{(up(f) \bullet up(f') \bullet f) \bullet h \bullet (f' \circ f) : f \in F^{out}_{T,\underline{s}},\ f' \in T^{out}_{P,\underline{s}'},\ h \in F^{trans}_{P'}\}
\end{aligned}
$$

and a similar definition (also consisting of 8 subsets) of $F_{T \circ (P \circ P')}$. Now some of the subsets in $F_{(T \circ P) \circ P'}$ and $F_{T \circ (P \circ P')}$ are equal; for the remaining ones the equivalency of their operations can be inferred from L3 and L4. ∎

According to T1 , all terms over $T \circ P$ can be reduced to terms over T . However, it is not sure whether all terms over T that one is still interested in after the merging, can be generated by the visible operations of $T \circ P$. The following theorem states that this holds under certain conditions for all terms that are not of the sort defined by P . One condition is "sufficient completeness" of T and P (cf. /Guttag, Horning 78/ und /Wirsing et al. 80/), i.e. all terms of primitive sorts are reducible to a primitive term or to "undefined".

Theorem T4 : Let T be a type, $P \in \Pi_T$, both sufficiently complete, P mergeable with T, $S_P = \{\underline{s}\}$, and $F_P^{null} = \emptyset$. Further we presuppose that

i) for all $f \in F_{T,\underline{s}}^{in}$ the parameter of sort $\underline{s}$ is restricted to images of F_P^{in} . (Note that usually $F_{T,\underline{s}}^{in} = \emptyset$, anyhow.)

ii) $\forall f \in F_{T,\underline{s}}^{trans} : \exists\, up^{-1}(f) \in F_{T,\underline{s}}^{out} :$ f updates $up^{-1}(f)$

Then for every defined term t over $T \square P$ which is not of sort $\underline{s}$ there exists a term t' over $T \circ P$ such that $t = t'$ is provable in $T \circ P$ and t' contains no operation symbol of $F_{T \circ P} \setminus F_{T \circ P}$.

Proof: W.l.o.g. we assume that $\forall f \in F_{T,\underline{s}}^{par} \cup F_P^{trans} : \underline{s}_f^1 = \underline{s}$.

a) If t contains no subterm of sort $\underline{s}$ we choose $t' =_{def} t$.

b) Otherwise we consider the outermost subterm s of sort $\underline{s}$ and the operation symbol f that immediately applies to s .

b1) $f \in F_{T,\underline{s}}^{in}$. Then according to presupposition i) the outermost symbol of s is some $f' \in F_P^{in}$. According to D11 and D5 the subterm $f(f'(\ldots),\ldots)$ reduces to $f \circ f'(\ldots)$ with $f \circ f' \in F_{T \circ P}$.

b2) $f \in F_{T,\underline{s}}^{trans}$. Since T and P are sufficiently complete, s can be reduced such that it consists of $n \geq 0$ symbols $f_1,\ldots,f_n \in F_P^{trans}$ applied to some $f_0 \in F_P^{in}$.

b2 α) $n = 0$. Then $f(f_0(\ldots$ reduces to $f \circ f_0(\ldots$ with $f \circ f_0 \in F_{T \circ P}$.

b2 β) $n > 0$. Then according to presupposition ii) and D8 $f(f_n(f_{n-1}(\ldots$ can be expanded to $f(f_n(up^{-1}(f)(f(f_{n-1}(\ldots$, which reduces to $f \circ f_n \circ up^{-1}(f)\,(f(f_{n-1}(\ldots$ with $f \circ f_n \circ up^{-1}(f) \in F_{T \circ P}$. ∎

6. Simplifying merged types

Up to now, the merged type still contains the original operations (although they are hidden), and the new, combined operations are specified in terms of those hidden ones. If one aims at an independent specification of the new type, one has to derive laws for the new operations which are independent of the original operations, such that the latter can be dropped (together with the laws specifying them). Provided that the original types are sufficiently complete, the sufficient completeness of the new one can be achieved by applying the method of /Guttag, Horning 78/. The crucial step of this method, viz. finding an adequate partition of the operations, is simplified by doing it in analogy to those partitions implicitly present in the previous type definitions, i.e. by exploiting the relations (established by the type merging) between the operations in T and P and their "associated" ones in T∘P. A more formal treatment may be found in /Laut, Partsch 82/.

Starting with BITMATRIX_3 (since we are not interested in the operation reinit) we can e.g. derive the new laws

$$\text{get(init(x), i, j)} \overset{G}{=} \text{getv(getm(init(x), i), j)} \overset{I}{=} \text{getv(getm(initm(initv(x)),i),j)} = \overset{GM1}{=} \text{getv(initv(x), j)} \overset{GV1}{=} \text{x}$$

$$\text{put(init(x), i , j, x)} \overset{I,P}{=} \text{putm(initm(initv(x)), i, putv(getm(initm(initv(x)),i),j,x))} = \overset{GM1}{=} \text{putm(initm(initv(x)), i, putv(initv(x), j, x))} = \overset{PV1}{=} \text{putm(initm(initv(x)), i, initv(x))} = \overset{PM1}{=} \text{initm(initv(x))} \overset{I}{=} \text{init(x)}$$

In the same way we can derive the further laws appearing in the final version BITMATRIX5 :

```
type  BITMATRIX5 ≡ matrix, init, put, get :
      based on  INT, based on  BOOL ,
      sort matrix ,
      funct(bool) matrix init ,
      funct(matrix, int, int, bool) matrix put ,
      funct(matrix, int, int) bool get ,

         get(init(x), i, j) = x ,
         get(put(m, i, j, x), i, j) = x ,
         (i, j) ≠ (k, l) ⇒ get(put(m, i, j, x), k, l) = get(m, k, l) ,
         put(init(x), i, j, x) = init(x) ,
         (i, j) ≠ (k, l) ⇒ put(put(m,i,j,x),k,l,y) = put(put(m,k,l,y),i,j,x)
                                                             endoftype
```

7. Conclusion

In contrast to algorithmic specifications where a lot of tools are available for performing "equivalence-preserving" transformations, the area of algebraic specifications nearly completely lacks these specific tools. Most of the activities in transforming algebraic types are rather directed to finding implementations, although very frequently a slightly different form of a specification is a better starting-point for a smooth and elegant later development (cf. /Pepper, Partsch 80/). Although type merging as introduced above can be motivated by looking for implementations, its main purpose should be seen as an equivalence-preserving type transformation and thus as an attempt to contribute to the aforementioned set of tools.

However, there are still some open problems that are subject of current and future research: It is to be checked whether the method can be generalized for a less restricted type concept, e.g. allowing parameterized types. It might also be interesting to investigate whether the particular way of eliminating hidden functions as in section 6 can be extended to the general problem of deriving a new axiom system for a given type. Whereas a model of the merged type simply evolves by operatively enriching models of the original types, the question how procedural implementations (cf. /Laut 80/) are to be combined still has to be answered. This question is rather interesting since the types derived by merging are particularly suited for procedural implementations which selectively update small components of large structured objects.

Acknowledgement: We gratefully acknowledge valuable discussions with our colleagues B. Möller, R. Obermeier, P. Pepper and M. Wirsing.

8. References

/Bauer, Wössner 81/
Bauer, F.L., Wössner, H.: Algorithmische Sprache und Programmentwicklung. Berlin-Heidelberg-New York: Springer 1981

/Bauer et al. 81a/
Bauer, F.L., Broy, M., Dosch, W., Gnatz, R., Geiselbrechtinger, F., Hesse, W., Krieg-Brückner, B., Laut, A., Matzner, T., Möller, B., Partsch, H., Pepper, P., Samelson, K. (†), Wirsing, M., Wössner, H.: Report on a Wide Spectrum Language for Program Specification and Development. Institut für Informatik der TU München, Report TUM-I8104, 1981

/Bauer et al. 81b/
Bauer, F.L., Broy, M., Dosch, W., Gnatz, R., Krieg-Brückner, B., Laut, A., Luckmann, M., Matzner, T., Möller, B., Partsch, H., Pepper, P., Samelson, K. (†), Steinbrüggen, R., Wirsing, M., Wössner, H.: Programming in a Wide Spectrum Language: a Collection of Examples. Science of Computer Programming 1, 73-114 (1981)

/Broy et al. 80/
Broy, M., Möller, B., Pepper, P., Wirsing, M.: A Model-Indeoendent Approach to Implementations of Abstract Data Types. 2nd Workshop on Algebraic Methods in Programming, Rocquencourt, 27.-29.10.1980.

/Burstall, Goguen 77/
Burstall, R.M., Goguen, J.A.: Putting Theories Together to Make Specifications. Proc. of 5th. Int. Joint Conf. on Art. Int., Cambridge, Ma, 1977, 1045-1058

/Burstall, Goguen 80/
Burstall, R.M., Goguen, J.A.: The Semantics of CLEAR, a Specification Language. Proc. of 1979 Copenhagen Winter School on Abstract Software Specifications, 1980. Lecture Notes in Computer Science, Berlin-Heidelberg-New York: Springer 1980

/Ehrig 81/
Ehrig, H.: Algebraic Theory of Parameterized Specifications with Requirements. Proc. 6th CAAP, Genova 1981

/Ganzinger 81/
Ganzinger, H.: Parameterized Specifications: Parameter Passing and Optimizing Implementation. Institut für Informatik der TU München, Report TUM-I8110, 1981

/Goguen et al. 78/
Goguen, J.A., Thatcher, J.W., Wagner, E.G.: An Initial Algebra Approach to the Specification, Correctness, and Implementation of Abstract Data Types. In: Yeh, R.T. (ed.): Current Trends in Programming Methodology, Vol. 3: Data Structuring. Englewood Cliffs, NJ: Prentice-Hall 1978, 80-149

/Guttag 77/
Guttag, J.V.: Abstract Data Types and the Development of Data Structures. Comm. ACM 20:6, 396-404 (1977)

/Guttag, Horning 78/
Guttag, J.V., Horning, J.J.: The Algebraic Specification of Abstract Data Types. Acta Informatica 10, 27-52 (1978)

/Laut 80/
Laut, A.: Safe Procedural Implementations of Algebraic Types. Inf. Proc. Letters 11 :45, 147-151 (1980)

/Laut, Partsch 82/
Laut, A., Partsch, H.: Merging Algebraic Types. Institut für Informatik der TU München, Technical Report, to appear

/Pepper, Partsch 80/
Pepper, P., Partsch, H.: On the Feedback between Specifications and Implementations. Institut für Informatik der TU München, Report TUM-I8011, 1980

/Wirsing, Broy 81/
Wirsing, M., Broy, M.: An Analysis of Semantic Models for Algebraic Specifications. Working Material for the Int. Summer School on Theoretical Foundations of Programming Methodology, Marktoberdorf 1981

/Wirsing et al. 80/
Wirsing, M., Pepper, P., Partsch, H., Dosch, W., Broy, M.: On Hierarchies of Abstract Data Types. Institut für Informatik der TU München, Report TUM-I8007, 1980

COMMUNICATING AGENTS FOR APPLICATIVE CONCURRENT PROGRAMMING

Alberto Pettorossi
IASI - CNR
Via Buonarroti 12
00185 Roma (Italy)

Andrzej Skowron
Institute of Mathematics
Warsaw University PKiN IX/907
00-901 Warszawa (Poland)

Abstract

A good program methodology should allow easy proofs of program correctness and should also incorporate methods for improving program efficiency. We try to achieve both aims by proposing, in the framework of the applicative programming style, a language by which one can specify a system of computing agents, which communicate by sending and receiving messages.

The contents of these messages are "facts", or "pieces of truth" about computations. They are formally defined in the paper.

When communications occur, the system of agents achieves better performances in executing programs, and the task of showing correctness of the resulting computations remains relatively simple. We will give some examples for illustrating these points.

The proposed language supports a program methodology for writing concurrent programs in a reliable way. A basis for a theory of communications is introduced, together with a method for using it in specifying behaviours of agents and proving them correct.

Introduction

In writing programs two main objectives should be achieved: correctness and efficiency. Failing in achieving either of those aims would result in a program of no use in practice. Therefore programming languages for which correctness proofs are easy, should be provided to the programmer, and for those languages, methodologies for increasing efficiency of programs should also be suggested.

The problem we addressed in this paper is how to achieve those goals in the framework of the applicative programs, where correctness proofs are often relatively simple. We also allow parallel execution of distinct function evaluations, for better program performances, taking advantage of the possibilities offered by the new hardware technologies and related VLSI design techniques.

Concurrent agents may communicate with each other by sending and receiving "messages", which in general allow a fruitful cooperation among those agents, saving computational resources. In this case it could be difficult in general to prove the correct behaviour of a system of agents. Therefore in order to overcome that difficulty we adopt a technique derived from the program transformation approach à la Burstall-Darlington [2]. The programmer is first urged to be concerned with program correctness only and then at later stages with program efficiency, and he improves it by establishing some communications among agents (and not only by inventing new suitable "eureka functions" as in [2]).

In functional programming the major problem of proving correctness of programs when communications occur, does not seem to be easily solvable using techniques similar to those suggested by Owicki [9], because of the peculiar features of such programming style. We will propose our own methods for solving this problem: they rely on the property that messages basically are "pieces of truth", and if received, they cannot modify the correct behaviour of a system of computing agents.

The whole theory of communications we will introduce, is based on a notion of "computing agent" which we will define with respect to the syntax and the semantics of our language constructs. Agents are indeed semantical notions which have their corresponding syntactical counterpart: the programmer can see them "statically" and have also a firm grasp on their dynamical generation, when concurrent activation of function evaluations is performed.

Our approach is similar to Milner's [8] in the following respect: syntactic terms denote agents which are capable of performing actions. The main difference consists in the fact that we distinguish between the agents themselves and the task they have to perform, and we do this for reasons we will explain later.

2. Basic ideas for the Language of Communicating Agents

The first basic idea of the language we are proposing is the functional approach: we like functional languages, like LISP [7], HOPE [4], etc..., because during the evaluation of terms, side-effects do not occur. Therefore the programmer may rely on a "transparent" environment, where the terms are evaluated. Indeed the value of any term directly appears to the programmer from the same syntactical representation of it. On the contrary, imperative languages, like PASCAL or ADA and the like, allow assignments and side-effects to be generated in evaluating expressions: this makes correctness proofs quite difficult to be performed, especially in the case in which procedure calls are involved.

In particular our language can be considered as a subset of HOPE, extended for incorporating the notion of "computing agents" and for expressing "communications" among them.

In what follows we assume that the reader is familiar with HOPE or other functional languages, but this is not a strong requirement for an easy reading of the paper.

Now we will explain the two central ideas of our language which are, in some sense, new: namely, the "agents" and the "communications". We will give an informal introduction to those concepts and later on we will be more precise by defining the operational semantics for the whole language.

Agents are thought as unspecified entities which perform tasks and in particular function evaluations. For example, if the term f(a1,...,an) occurs in the program, we consider that at a certain moment in time, the evaluation of the function f applied to the arguments a1,...,an is done by a computing agent. The evaluation may take place in the central processing unit of a traditional computer or in a microprocessor of a multi-micro computer architecture. We may consider that such a microprocessor is distinct from the ones used for other function evaluations and therefore many agents in a multiprocessor system can evaluate terms in a concurrent way. In our language we would like to make visible to the programmer the existence of those evaluation processes, via the syntactic definition of agents as elements of a data domain. For instance the programmer may declare, as a usual HOPE data domain:

<u>data</u> agname == num

whereby agents are named by natural numbers. Then, for instance, in defining a recursive function f, the programmer may write:

```
--- <p,m>::f(a1,a2) <= ... <l,m1>::f(a1,a2-1)...<r,m2>::f(a1-1,a2)...
```

In this definition the agent whose name is p has to evaluate f(a1,a2), while the agents l and r have to evaluate f(a1,a2-1) and f(a1-1,a2) respectively, and they may do so concurrently or in parallel. m,m1 and m2 specify elements of a <u>message domain</u>, which we will define later on.

Therefore, in general, instead of writing simply a term,one could write the following syntactic structure:

<agent-name, message>::term, by which it is possible to name, using an agent-name, the process of evaluating a term and it is possible to associate a value, i.e. a message, with that process. But why would we like to do so? This corresponds to the introduction in the programming language of a way of denoting executions of programs. Therefore it is a "higher level" construct like the introduction of meta-linguistic notions in a language. However we think that in dealing with concurrent programs and communicating systems, a syntactic notion of an agent via its name should be introduced for preserving the idea of "referential transparency" which is central in any functional language.

One could say that the idea of making computing agents to be expressions of the language is analogous to Strachey's idea of making functions as "first class citizens" in functional programming. We could also compare our approach to that of Milner [8]: in CCS in fact, a computing agent (possibly parameterized) is denoted by a term, where other computing agents are possibly involved. For instance:

ASK p = ix.<u>if</u> p(x) <u>then</u> $\bar{\sigma}_1$ x.(ASK p) <u>else</u> $\bar{\sigma}_2$ x.(ASK p)

(see [8] p. 53), which defines the behaviour of a "unary predicate agent".

However we do not follow Milner in that we would like the programmer to have control over the various instantiations of the agents. For instance, in our example, we want the programmer to be able to distinguish between two subsequent executions of the agent ASK p. Therefore he could write a program for the same computation as follows:

```
data agname == ε + agname.0 + agname.1
    .
    .
    .
---<s,...>::ASK(p) <= ...<s.0,...>::ASK(p)...<s.1,...>::ASK(p)
```

The ability of distinguishing among different recursive calls is not really necessary from the point of view of proving correctness of programs, but it is essential in controlling the efficiency of program executions by suitable communications. The examples we will give in the following sections will clarify this point.

The second central idea of our language is the "communication" idea. Communications are performed via sending values of expressions and receiving values by binding them to variables. In this sense our approach is similar to Hoare's one [5] and Milner's one [8]. However, we would like the programmer to define explicitly a data domain for the possible content of communications, or messages as we say. The reason for that is our desire to allow the programmer to deal with messages as data which are "first class citizens". In particular, messages domains occur in the programs as algebras with their internal and external operations. Therefore messages will be used by agents in a controlled way and they can be structured as modules (in HOPE terminology).

However, a danger is hidden in this approach: namely the fact that the programmer may be induced to think only in terms of communications among agents and specify computations using messages only. The possible outcome of this way of thinking is an excessive abundance of communications in the programs, and the recursive structure of the programs would no longer reflect the structure of the data.

Therefore we propose a discipline for the programmer: it consists in specifying agents mainly for recursive function calls and having exactly one possible message for each of them, at each instant in time. This, for instance, implies that values, which are all messages for the same agent, are not waiting in queues. A message will be used for expressing properties of computations, so that efficiency may be improved, as we will see in the examples. Moreover we assume that there exists a function from agent-names to messages and we force the programmer to represent by this function a "piece of truth", possibly time depending, i.e. depending on the step of the computation. Using that "piece of truth" or "fact", as we say, the agent should preserve his correct behaviour. From a semantical point of view, a fact is an equality between terms in a given algebra.

In what follows we will give a formal semantic definition of communications and facts and the reader will have a clear mathematical understanding of what we mean by sending or receiving messages.

The notion of "facts" plays a very interesting role in our language because it makes correctness proofs relatively easy and it also allows a quite simple way of showing that some communications, when realized, improve program efficiency. The programmer may in fact code in the <agent-name,message> pairs the properties of the computations which are useful for increasing efficiency.

So far, we have given an informal description of the syntactic structures which we use in our language for specifying computing agents, their tasks (i.e. the evaluations of terms) and their messages by the construct <agname,message>::term . In the following sections we will give a concrete example where we will make extensive use of these structures and we will also use sending and receiving operations for exchanging messages among agents. We will then give the formal definition of the syntax and the semantics of our language.

3. The notions of agents and messages through an example

In this section we will give an example of a program written in our proposed programming language, which we will call HOPE-C, short for "HOPE and Communications".

Suppose that we are given a binary tree whose leaves are labelled by natural numbers, and we will like to compute the set of all leaf-values which are inside a given closed interval [lb,ub], defined by the two natural numbers, lb for the lower bound, and ub for the upper bound. We also suppose that the leaves of the given binary tree are ordered, so that if t1 ∧ t2 is a binary tree then all leaf-values in t1 are not larger than the leaf-values in t2. We have given a similar example in a previous paper [10]; we apologise for the repetition, but we hope that in this way the reader may more easily appreciate the novel approach we have taken here.

A program for solving the proposed problem may be written as follows:

```
                                                                Program P0
data  btree(num) == niltree ++ tip(num) ++ btree(num) ∧ btree(num)

dec intleaves:btree(num) × num × num -> set(num)
--- intleaves(niltree,lb,ub) <=  {}
--- intleaves(tip(l),lb,ub)  <= {l}                        if lb≤l≤ub
                              else  {}
--- intleaves(t1 ∧ t2,lb,ub) <= intleaves(t1,lb,ub) U intleaves(t2,lb,ub)
```

This is a usual HOPE program: no agents and no communications occur in it. But the programmer may realize that an increase of efficiency is possible because, if a leaf-value smaller than lb has been found in a right subtree, then the leaves in the left subtree are smaller than lb and therefore they cannot contribute to the set of leaf-values to be computed. An analogous situation occurs in the symmetric case if a leaf-value greater than ub is found. The following program realizes that increase of efficiency.

```
                                                              Program P1
data  agname == ε ++ agname.0 ++ agname.1

dec left:agname -> agname              dec right:agname -> agname
--- left(ε) = ε                        --- right(ε) = ε
--- left(a.0) = a.0                    --- right(a.0) = a.1
--- left(a.1) = a.0                    --- right(a.1) = a.1

data  mess == GOON ++ STOP   init GOON

data  btree(num) == niltree ++ tip(l) ++ btree(num) ∧ btree(num)

dec <agname,mess>::intleaves1:btree(num) × num × num -> set(num)
--- <agn,m>::intleaves1(niltree,lb,ub) <= {}
--- <agn,m>::intleaves1(tip(l),lb,ub) <= {}  if z!receivefrom(agn,true)!=STOP
              else {l}                           if lb≤l≤ub
              else {}                            if l<lb
                   /sendto(left(agn),STOP)/
              else {}                            if ub>l
                   /sendto(right(agn),STOP)/
--- <agn,m>::intleaves1(t1∧t2,lb,ub) <= {}  if z!receivefrom(agn,true)!=STOP
    else <agn.0,m>::intleaves1(t1,lb,ub) U <agn.1,m>::intleaves1(t2,lb,ub)
```

In this program the domain of the agent names is an algebra, whose operations are: ε, .0 , .1 , left and right with the obvious arities. The domain of the message values is also an algebra. There are only two constants: GOON and STOP and one of them is qualified as initial value by init, so that when agents are first generated they have GOON as corresponding message. (This is necessary to force the correspondence between agentnames and messages to be a function, as we assume).

In the Program P1 there are three annotations to denote communications among agents: /sendto(left(agn),STOP)/, /sendto(right(agn),STOP)/ and !receivefrom(agn,true)!. Let us informally explain the first one (the second one is analogous). By the operation sendto(left(agn),STOP) a given agent, which has found a leaf-value l smaller than lb, sends to the agent which has to operate in the corresponding left subtree, the message STOP. That message will force it to immediately return {} as result (see the definition of intleaves1).

The communication sendto(left(agn),STOP) is optional and we wrote it between slashes to denote the optionality. The correctness of the program should be independent from the realization of optional communications. The general form of such sending operation is: sendto(agentname,expression) and their meaning is to make the association of the specified agentname with the value of the specified expression. The third annotation !receivefrom(agn,true)! denotes a compulsory communication and for that reason we wrote it between exclamation marks. A receivefrom operation binds the received value to a variable, which is local in the clause where the annotation occurs. Its general form is:

```
var     !receivefrom(agentname,function from messages to boolean values)!
```

The specified function is used as a "filter" for messages, in the sense that the binding of the variable to the message of the specified agentname is realized only if that function assumes the value <u>true</u> for that message.

We can use m as a syntactic abbreviation of

z !receivefrom(agn,<u>true</u>)! when such an annotation should be evaluated by the agent agn, which has m as message.

In the following section we will exactly specify the concepts related to the communications we have now introduced, by giving the formal definition of the syntax and the semantics of the whole language.

Notice that Program P1 allows a high degree of parallelism, since agents agn.0 and agn.1 can operate in parallel. But the increase of efficiency is not very high because in Program P1 we have not provided any mechanism to propagate the STOP message through various agents, as it would be necessary in a situation like the one in fig. 1.

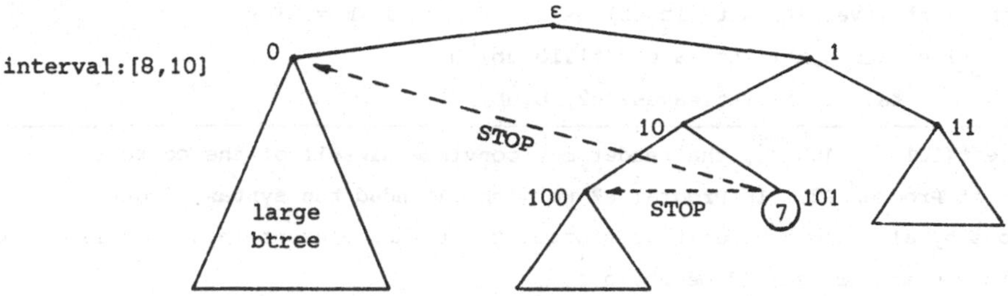

<u>fig. 1. A binary tree with a large btree with small leaf-values</u>

In that case we would like to have the message STOP sent from the agent 101 to the agent 100 and 0 also. This is done by Program P2.

<u>Program P2</u>

```
data  agname == ε ++ agname.0 ++ agname.1

dec upleft:agname -> set(agname)
--- upleft(ε) <= {0}
--- upleft(n.0) <= upleft(n)
--- upleft(n.1) <= {n.0} U upleft(n)     if 1in(n)
                   else {n.0}
```

```
dec  upright:agname -> set(agname)
--- upright(ε) <= {1}
--- upright(n.0) <= {n.1} U upright(n)   if 0in(n)
                   else {n.1}
--- upright(n.1) <= upright(n)

dec 1in:agname -> bool
--- 1in(ε) <= false
--- 1in(n.0) <= 1in(n)
--- 1in(n.1) <= true

dec  0in:agname -> bool
--- 0in(ε) <= false
--- 0in(n.0) <= true
--- 0in(n.1) <= 0in(n)

data  mess == GOON ++ STOP      init GOON
data  btree(num) == niltree ++ tip(num) ++ btree(num) ∧ btree(num)
dec <agname,mess>::intleaves2:btree(num) × num × num -> set(num)
--- <agn,m>::intleaves2(niltree,lb,ub) <=  {}
--- <agn,m>::intleaves2(tip(l),lb,ub)  <=  {}        if m = STOP
          else {l}                                   if lb≤l≤ub
          else {}                                    if l<lb
              /for i ∈ upleft(agn) do  sendto(i,STOP)/
          else {}                                    if l>ub
              /for i ∈ upright(agn) do sendto(i,STOP)/
--- <agn,m>::intleaves2(t1 ∧ t2,lb,ub) <= {}         if m = STOP
          else <agn.0,m>::intleaves2(t1,lb,ub) U
                 <agn.1,m>::intleaves2(t2,lb,ub)
```

Since upleft(101) = {100,0}, the reader may convince himself of the correct behaviour of Program P2. In Program P2 we also extended the syntax of our annotations by allowing a repetitive statement for each element in a specified set; its intended semantics should be obvious.

The notion of messages has been introduced as expressing facts about the computations. In the case of Program P2, the fact denoted by the association of an agent-name and the message STOP is the equality of the term which should be computed by that agent and the empty set.

The role played by the messages in our language for applicative concurrent programming, could have been played in the traditional way of writing programs, by an extra argument associated to the function to be computed [10]. For example, instead of declaring intleaves2 as:

```
dec <agname,mess>::intleaves2:btree(num) × num × num -> set(num)
```

one could have declared in standard HOPE:

```
dec intleaves3:btree(num) × num × num × mess -> set(num) × mess
```

In that case the effect achieved by Program P1 could have been partially simulated by the following Program P1.1:

```
                                                          Program P1.1
dec intleaves3:btree(num) ×num ×num ×mess -> set(num)× mess
--- intleaves3(bt,lb,ub,STOP) <= <{},STOP>
--- intleaves3(niltree,lb,ub,GOON) <= <{},GOON>
--- intleaves3(tip(l),lb,ub,GOON) <= <{l},GOON>          if lb≤l≤ub
                  else <{},STOP>                         if  l<lb
                  else <{},GOON>
--- intleaves3(t1 ∧ t2,lb,ub,GOON) <= [<c U a,d & b>
                                  where <c,d> = intleaves3(t1,lb,ub,b) ]
                                  where <a,b> = intleaves3(t2,lb,ub,GOON)
dec &:mess × mess -> mess
--- &(m1,m2) <= GOON            if m1 = GOON and m2 = GOON
          else STOP
```

In this program we have used the <u>where</u> clause, whose semantics can be informally described as follows: the evaluation of "term1 <u>where</u> z=term2" forces the evaluation of term2 first, and then the evaluation of term1 where the variable z has the value of term2. Therefore intleaves3(t1 ∧ t2,...) simulates the behaviour of intleaves2(t1 ∧ t2,...), avoiding the visit of the whole left subtree t1, when a leaf-value smaller that lb has been found in the corresponding right subtree t2, by using the first clause of the definition of intleaves3. However, this simulation is achieved by losing the parallel evaluation of intleaves3 for the two subtrees t1 and t2. Forcing sequentiality makes it impossible to use the same simulation for stopping the evaluation process for the subtree t2, when in the corresponding left subtree t1 a leaf-value larger than ub has been found. This is one of the reasons which stimulated us to study the present extension of the HOPE language by allowing agents and communications among them.

Given the btree t1 ∧ t2, when the parallel evaluation of

<agn.0,m0>::intleaves2(t1,...) and <agn.1,m1>::intleaves2(t2,...)

are performed, changes of the messages m0 and/or m1 may occur. In order to realize the possible improvement in efficiency evoked by those messages, we will assume that the agents will try to evaluate again their associated terms when their messages change. This policy forces us to make the agents, so to speak, look at their messages, as long as they are in the process of performing their tasks.

We need also to create agents with "empty" tasks, when messages are sent to them and they have not yet been generated by the usual mechanism of recursive function calls. Notice that, if we assume such creation of agents under communication instances, the system has to perform some extra activities connected with the association of the messages to the agents, when they are indeed generated by recursive calls evaluation.

We will be more specific about these issues in the next section, when specifying the semantics of our language.

4. The formal definition of the language: syntax, semantics and proof theory

In this section we will define the syntax of our language HOPE-C in terms of usual HOPE notions, as data domains, constructor functions, etc. The semantics will be specified using an operational approach via a system of non-deterministic transition rules and the proof theory via a simple logical theory.

Agentnames and Messages are defined by HOPE data declarations with their constructor functions and their operations: they can be considered as algebras. There is a distinguished message, denoted by the constant KILLED, which has an important role from a semantic point of view: we will speak about it later on.

Now, in order to define the syntax of HOPE-C, we will introduce some important notions. They are:

TN is the set of terminal nodes, which is the set of terms used for expressing the input and output values of a computation (e.g. natural numbers, boolean values, etc.). We will denote by tn a generic element of TN.

TN_X, where X is a generator set, is the set of all terms in TN where variables from the set X are also allowed. We will denote by $\underline{tn}$ a generic element of TN_X.

N is the set of HOPE-C expressions, called nodes. We will denote by n,n1,... the elements of N. They are of the following form:

1.1 <agn,m>:: τ (τ is the empty task) 1.2 ε (empty node)

2.1 <agn,m>::$\underline{tn}$ 2.2 $\underline{tn}$

3.1 <agn,m>::g(n1,...,nr) 3.2 g(n1,...,nr)

where g is a basic function whose arity is r and g ∈ G

4.1 <agn,m>::f(n1,...,nr) 4.2 f(n1,...,nr)

where f is a recursively defined function and f ∈ F

5.1 n !sendto(agn2,$\underline{tn2}$)! 5.2 n /sendto(agn2,$\underline{tn2}$)/

6. z !receivefrom(agn2,predic)!

where predic is a predicate over Messages

7. n where z=n1

8. $COND[ni1 \Rightarrow ni2]_1^k$ (which stands for the usual if-then construct with k conditions).

In these definitions : agn ∈ Agentnames, m ∈ Messages and $F \cap G = \emptyset$.

A term of a node is also called "task" for the agent named in that node.

For a sequence of optional communications we can write /a1,...,an/ instead of /a1/.../an/. Analogously for compulsory communications, using exclamation marks.

A program is a function from F to N, which should be well-formed in the usual HOPE sense. In general we assume that any program defines for a recursive function f, whose arity is r, a COND-node, where only the variables x1,...,xr may occur free. The <u>semantics</u> of HOPE-C constructs is defined by the following conditional transition system, by which a graph of given nodes is transformed into a new graph of nodes, by transforming nodes as specified by the following rules R1,...,R6.

For instance the graph: <agn,m>::intleaves2(t1∧t2,lb,ub) (which is single node) can be transformed into the following graph with three nodes and two arcs:

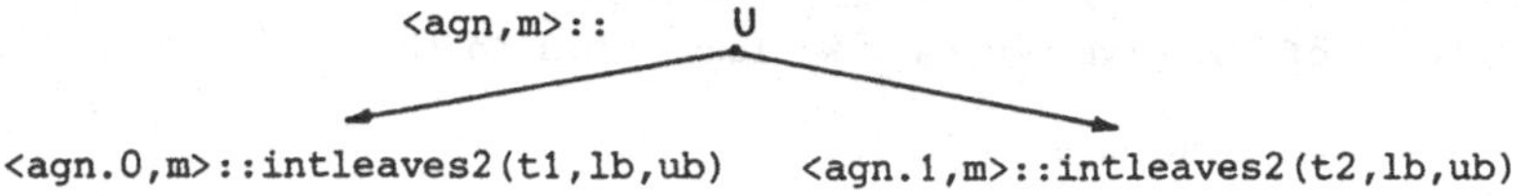

Arcs in a graph denote the recursive calls activations and, in general, the generation of agents. In transforming nodes, arcs are consistently transformed.

R1. <agn,KILLED>::n → ε

R2. All reduction rules in the algebras of the Agentnames, Messages and basic functions in G. Using these rules, normal forms of the terms in those algebras may be computed. (A term is said to be in normal form when only constructors occur in it.)

R3.1 <agn,m>::f(<u>tn</u>1 ...,<u>tn</u>r) → <agn,m>::(COND[ni1 => ni2]$_1^k$) [$^{xj}/_{\underline{tnj}}$]$_1^r$

R3.2 <agn,m>::COND[ni1 => ni2]$_1^k$ $\xrightarrow{\text{ni1=true}}$ <agn,m>::ni2

R3.3 and R3.4 as R3.1 and R3.2, without the pair <agentname,message> in both sides.

R4.1 n <u>where</u> z = n1 $\xrightarrow{\text{n1} \rightarrow \text{n2}}$ n <u>where</u> z = n2

R4.2 n <u>where</u> z = tn ⟶ n[$^z/_{tn}$]

R5.1 tn !sendto(agn2,tn2)! ⟶ tn [[messof(agn2) = tn2]]

R5.2.a tn /sendto(agn2,tn2)/ ⟶ tn

R5.2.b tn /sendto(agn2,tn2)/ ⟶ tn [[messof(agn2) = tn2]]

R6 z !receivefrom(agn2,p)! $\xrightarrow{\text{p(messof(agn2)) = true}}$ messof(agn2)

Some explanations are necessary for clarifying the meaning of the given rules:

- for rule R.2: we mean that, for instance, the node + (4,3) can be transformed into the node 7, and the node <3-2,STOP>::+(4,3) can be transformed into the node <1,STOP>::7.
- the function "messof" gives the message associated to each agentname. For instance, given <1,STOP>::7 we have messof(1) = STOP.
- in the substitutions occurring in rules R3.1 and R4.2, if tn is of the form <agn,m>::tn', then by n[$^z/_{tn}$] we mean n[$^z/_{tn'}$] together with a unique node like tn itself (see the following rule M2).
- by [[messof(agn2) = tn2]] we mean that, when we apply the corresponding rule to the node in question, we have also to change the message of the agent agn2, which becomes tn2 (or tn2' if tn2 is of the form <agn,m>::tn2'), for all subsequent evaluations of the function messof. If agent agn2 does not exist,it is created with the message tn2 and the empty task τ. Notice the way in which we express optionality of a sendto communication by the rules R5.2a and R5.2b.

To complete our semantics definition, we add also some extra rules which may be considered as metarules:

M1. α-conversion can be used in applying rule R3.1

M2. A node of the form <agn,mess>::tn, if mess ≠ KILLED, cannot be deleted in applying the rewriting rules. For instance:
<1,GOON>:: +(<2,GOON>::3,5) → <1,GOON>::8
together with the node <2,GOON>::3

Semantics of other constructs, like n !<u>for</u> a ∈ A <u>do</u> sendto(...)!, can be easily expressed in terms of the given rules. We leave this to the reader.

Now we will give a well-known example [2] for illustrating the use of rules R1,...,R6. The following program computes the Fibonacci function in linear time.

Program P4

```
data  agname == num
data  mess == num ++ GOON    init GOON

dec is-num:mess -> bool
--- is-num(m) <= false     if m=GOON
         else true

dec <agname,mess>::fib:num -> num
--- <n,m>::fib(n) <= 1    !sendto(0,1), sendto(1,1)!    if n=0 or n=1
         else  z   !sendto(n,z)!
           where z =<n-1,m>::fib(n-1) + y  !receivefrom(n-2,is-num)!
```

Notice that a program like the following:

Program P5

```
      .  (as in Program P4)
      :
dec <agname,mess>::fib:num -> num
--- <n,m>::fib(n) <= 1                  if n=0 or n=1
         else <n-1,m>::fib(n-1) + <n-2,m>::fib(n-2)
```

cannot be considered as an efficient program because an exponential number of computing agents is created. If an algorithm, in fact, requires an exponential number of computing resources, it cannot be acceptable, in general, for any practical use.

The following rewriting is a possible computation of fib(4) according to Program P4:

```
<4, GOON>::fib(4) → <4, GOON>::COND[n=0 or n=1 => ...] [n/4] → ...
→ <4, GOON>::z  !sendto(4,z)!
   where z = <3,GOON>::fib(3) + y  !receivefrom(2,is-num)! → ...
→ <4,GOON>::z   !sendto(4,z)!
   where z = <3,GOON>::z1    !sendto(3,z1)! + y  !receivefrom(2,is-num)!
        where z1=<2,GOON>::fib(2) + y1  !receivefrom(1,is-num)! → ...
   (using rule M1 for replacing z by z1 and y by y1)
→ <4,GOON>::z  !sendto(4,z)!
   where z=<3,GOON>::z1   !sendto(3,z1)! +y  !receivefrom(2,is-num)!
     where z1=<2,GOON>::z2   !sendto(2,z2)! +y1   !receivefrom(1,is-num)!
      where z2=<1,GOON>::fib(1) +y2   !receivefrom(0,is-num)! → ...
→ <4,GOON>::z  !sendto(4,z)!
                      :  (as before)
   where z2=<1,GOON>::1   !sendto(0,1),sendto(1,1)! + y2   !receivefrom(0,is-num)!

... → <4,GOON>::z  !sendto(4,z)!
                         :  (as before)
   where z2=<1,1>::1 + y2    !receivefrom(0,is-num)!
   <0,1>:: τ  (by rule R5.1, agent 0 is created with the message 1 and the empty
               task τ)
→ <4,GOON>::z    !sendto(4,z)!
                      :  (as before)
    where z1=<2,GOON>::z2    !sendto(2,z2)! +y1   !receivefrom(1,is-num)!
          where z2=<1,1>::1 +1
  <0,1>:: τ
→ <4,GOON>::z    !sendto(4,z)!
                      :  (as before)
   where z1=<2,GOON>::2   !sendto(2,2)! +y1   !receivefrom(1,is-num)!
   <1,1>::1    (by rule M2)
   <0,1>:: τ
... → <4,GOON>::z    !sendto(4,z)!
        where z =<3,GOON>::z1   !sendto(3,z1)! +y !receivefrom(1,is-num)!
         where z1=<2,GOON>::2    !sendto(2,2)! +1
   <1,1>:: 1
   <0,1>:: τ
... → <4,5>::5      <3,3>::3  <2,2>::2  <1,1>::1  <0,1>:: τ
```

Now we have the answer 5 from the agent 4 which had to compute fib(4).

We see that only a linear number of agents has been created (not an exponential one), but unfortunately we were not able in Program P4 to destroy those agents which were no longer useful for subsequent computations. In order to be able to do so, we may consider by convention that an extra constant, called KILLED, is always present in the message domain. The programmer can use it to destroy agents which are no longer useful (as shown in Program P6). Without using that "killing" feature, we may otherwise consider that, at the end of the computation, all agents not in the node which carries the output value, are destroyed, as in a garbage collection process.

```
                                                                  Program P6

              :  (as for Program P4)
dec <agname,mess>::fib:num -> num
--- <n,m>::fib(n) <= 1      !sendto(0,1),sendto(1,1)!      if n=0 or n=1
              else  z       !sendto(n,z),sendto(n-2,KILLED)!
              where z=<n-1,m>::fib(n-1) + y  !receivefrom(n-2,is-num)!
```

We will close this section by giving some preliminary notions of a simple theory for proving correctness of programs with communications.

As our semantic rules suggest, the <u>computation process</u> of a program for a given term is essentially a graph rewriting process (not simply a term rewriting process, because some extra nodes may be generated by rules R3.1 and R5's, as we saw in our Fibonacci example). In each graph, which represents one step of the computation, there is a <u>distinguished node</u>, i.e. the node with the agent which has to compute the result of the computation itself.

Given a term t to be evaluated and a program, possibly with communications, the non-deterministic computation process, according to our rewriting rules, generates a <u>partial order</u> of graphs, whose smallest graph is the graph with the node t only. In that partial order there will be one or many final graphs, i.e. graphs for which no rewritings are possible. We may depict the situation like in fig. 2.

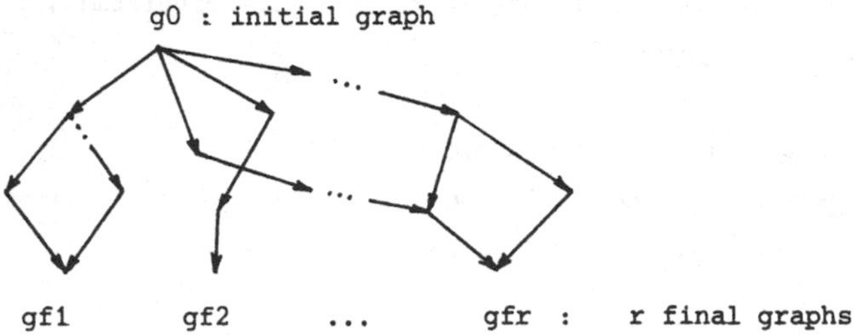

fig. 2. Non-deterministic computation as partial order on graphs.

We write g1 -> g2 if we can obtain the graph g2 from the graph g1, by applying a particular semantic rule. There will be an obvious notion of sequence of graphs, derived from the relation ->. Given a sequence s = g1 -> g2 -> ... -> gn, a sequence s' = gi1 $\overset{+}{\rightarrow}$ gi2 $\overset{+}{\rightarrow}$ ... $\overset{+}{\rightarrow}$ gik is a subsequence of s iff $1 \le i1 < i2 < \ldots < ik \le n$

and $1 \leq k \leq n$.

We assume that for any given computation, if there are r final graphs gf1,...,gfr then there exists a function val such that: val(gf1) =... =val(gfr), defined as follows: if a final graph gfi has m nodes and the node <agn,m0>::tn0 is the distinguished one, then we assume that val(gfi)=tn0.
The existence of such a function val masters non-determinism and extracts a unique output value as result of a computation.

We say that two programs P1 and P2 are equivalent iff for any given term t there exist two graphs g1 and g2 such that for i=1,2 gi is a final graph of the computation evoked by program Pi for evaluating t, and val(g1) = val(g2).

Now we give some auxiliary definitions which will allow us to present a method for showing that a program PC with communications is equivalent to a program P without communications. This method may also be considered as a way of proving correctness of program PC with respect to the specifications as given by program P. We will consider here only the case in which the messages occurring in the communications are results of computations performed by agents, when evaluating the associated terms.
We say that a sequence of graphs ss2 corresponds to a sequence of graphs ss1 with respect to the communication in the node na such that:

na ≡ z!receivefrom(agb,pr)! iff

if ss1 = <g11,g21,...,gn1> and ss2 = <g12,g22,...,gn2> then for any i, $1 \leq i \leq n$, gi2 is obtained from gi1 by replacing the node na by the node of the agent agb. (For this respect two graphs are considered to be equal regardless of the occurrence of <agent-name,message> pairs in their nodes). □

Given two sequences s1 and s2 of graphs, s.t. no communications exist in the graphs of s2, we say that s2 simulates s1 iff:

1. s1 = s2 if s1 and s2 are sequences of length one,i.e. with only one graph;
2. if in the sequence s1 there is a subsequence ss1 starting from the graph g1a and ending in the graph g1b s.t. in g1a occurs for the first time in the sequence s1 the node na with the term:

   z !receivefrom(agb,pr)!

   and the graph g1b is obtained by performing such "receivefrom" communication, i.e. g1b is obtained by application of the rule R6, then in s2 there is a subsequence of graphs ss2 s.t. ss2 corresponds to ss1 with respect to the communication in the node: z !receivefrom(agb,pr)! □

In order to prove that a program PC with communications is equivalent to a program P without communications we need to prove that: for any computation of PC,

(A) for each node na, with a term of the form z !receivefrom(agb,pr)! in a graph of the computation of PC, in the same computation the message of the agent agb is either initialized or updated by a sending operation so that, for the resulting value m, we have pr(m)=true (it means that sooner or later the message from agb will be accepted), and

(B) for each sequence s1 of graphs for PC there exists a sequence s2 of graphs for P s.t. s2 simulates s1.

As an exercise we will show the correctness of Program P4 with respect to the Program P5. Program P5 could also be considered as the formal specification of P4.

It is easy to prove by induction on n that property (A) holds for the computation of fib(n).

We also use induction on n for proving property (B). If n=0 then property (B) vacuously holds, because no node with a receivefrom communication occurs. If we assume that property (B) holds for k=n-1, then it is obvious that, for any sequence of graphs for Program P4, we can simulate in the node y !receivefrom(n-2,is-num)! the transformations of the node <n-2,m>::fib(n-2) until the "receivefrom" communication is realized. Thus we obtain a sequence of graphs for P5 from a sequence of graphs for P4. For the other nodes of any sequence of graphs in the computation of Program P4, where "receivefrom" communications occur, we use the induction hypothesis.

5. Conclusions

We defined a language, called HOPE-C, for applicative concurrent programming. It is derived from the HOPE language [1] which is a functional language under development at Edinburgh University, and incorporates the notions of computing agents and messages for achieving high efficiency in concurrent evaluations of terms through communications. As HOPE itself, our language is suited for writing programs which can be improved using the program transformation technique [2], in a very simple and natural way. Problems still remain to be solved in this direction, but some preliminary results appear to be quite promising. We have methods which, for a certain class of programs, allow to transform a program with communications into a pure applicative program à la HOPE. We will discuss these issues in a forthcoming paper.

We gave the definition of both syntax and semantics of our language. They are not definitive yet and indeed we will extend the language for including broadcast communications as well.

We also briefly introduced a theory for proving program correctness when communications among computing agents take place.

An analysis of the language constructs and their possible hardware implementations using VLSI design techniques will be done in the development of our project: this study will give a rigorous framework in which we can measure the efficiency of the programs.

In the area of concurrent programming many other approaches are known in the literature, and as a conclusion, we would like to make a brief comparison between our approach and those ones. This comparison also will underline the basic ideas of our language.

The main feature of the language is the notion of "fact", which is quite novel. Facts are realized by a function which relates agents and their messages. Those messages do not represent variable values, but properties of computations, so that correctness proofs of concurrent programs are made easier. Using facts the program transformation methodology for improving program efficiency can be applied in an easy way, as suggested in [10].

Comparing our language to data flow languages [3] à la Dennis, our messages are not sent by an agent always to the same one(s) and they do not necessarily correspond to computed intermediate values, which are needed for computing output values.

Analogous remarks hold for Kahn-MacQueen's approach [6].

Hoare's approach [5] is also different from ours in that we may easily incorporate broadcast communications. Moreover our notion of agents and their creation is a dynamic run-time notion.

Milner in CCS [8] makes values to be passed available to any receiver at particular places, while we name the receiver explicitly and this may be simulated by extending CCS and passing names of ports as parameters.

Hewitt's et al [4] idea of actors is very similar to ours, but we make a clear distinction between the task, which an actor or a computing agent has, and the message structure associated with it. We think that this distinction is very important from a programming methodology point of view, so that in our approach the recursive structure of the programs executions is preserved, while the communication facilities are introduced in a disciplined way, as we analyzed in section 2.

Acknowledgements

The first author would like to thank Professor R. Burstall and R. Milner at Edinburgh University for their help and encouragement in studying applicative parallel programming, and for their generous hospitality at the Computer Science Department during 1980.

The second author thanks his colleagues at Warsaw University for many stimulating conversations on semantics of concurrent systems.

The National Research Council of Italy and Warsaw University (Poland) provided the financial support and allowed the authors to work together both in Rome and in Warsaw. Many thanks to Eleanor Kerse for her excellent typing.

References

[1] Burstall, R.M., D.B. MacQueen and D.T. Sannella: "HOPE: an experimental applicative language", Proc. LISP Conference, Stanford University (1980).

[2] Burstall, R.M. and J. Darlington: "A transformation system for developing recursive programs", JACM, Vol. 24, No. 1 (1977), 44-67.

[3] Dennis, J.B.: "First version of a data flow procedure language", LNCS 19 Springer-Verlag (1974).

[4] Hewitt, C. and H. Baker, Jr: "Actors and continuous functionals" in: Neuhold, E.J. ed., Formal Descriptions of Programming Languages, North-Holland, Amsterdam (1978).

[5] Hoare, C.A.R.: "Communicating sequential processes", CACM, 21, 8 (1978).

[6] Kahn, G. and D.B. MacQueen: "Coroutines and network of parallel processes" in: Gilchrist, B. ed., Information Processing 1977, North-Holland, Amsterdam (1977) pp. 993-998.

[7] McCarthy, J. et al: "LISP Programmer's Manual", MIT Press, MIT, Cambridge, Mass. (1962).

[8] Milner, R.: "A calculus for communicating systems", LNCS 92, Springer-Verlag (1980).

[9] Owicki, S.: "Axiomatic proof techniques for parallel programs", Computer Science Department, Cornell University, Ph.D. thesis (1975).

[10] Pettorossi, A.: "A transformational approach for developing parallel programs", CONPAR Conference Nürnberg (1981), LNCS 111, pp. 245-258.

ON EFFECTIVE COMPUTATIONS OF NON-DETERMINISTIC SCHEMES

Axel Poigné
Informatik II
Universität Dortmund
Postfach 500 500
D-4600 Dortmund 50

0. INTRODUCTION

The meaning of a recursive program may be defined with regard to different points of view:

- *operational semantics* are defined via syntactical rules such as the copy rule of Algol 60. Starting with a procedure call application of these rules yields a possible infinite computation sequence for any combination of arguments. By attaching a "result" to each computation sequence a mapping from the arguments to the results is defined which constitutes the meaning of a recursive program.
- in *denotational semantics* a set of recursive programs is understood as a system of equations in a function space, the meaning is defined as a solution of the equations.
- *algebraic semantics* provide an intermediate step; the recursive program is split into a formal equation - a recursive program scheme - and an interpretation. Meaning now is given by extending the interpretation to formal solutions of the recursive program schemes.

In case of deterministic programs all these approaches are thoroughly investigated using fixpoint techniques (based on Knaster-Tarski's theorem in case of ordered sets and Banach's theorem in case of metrical spaces) and the coincidence of the three semantics is shown [14].

The situation gets more complicated if non-deterministic recursive programs are considered. Results similar to those in the deterministic case are obtained by Arnold and Nivat for non-deterministic program schemes being Greibach by an approach using metrical spaces [3], [4]. In [15] we posed the question why it should not be possible to achieve the equivalence of operational and denotational semantics by means of order semantics and least fixpoints. We are motivated by the feeling that Scott's thesis that infinite information is to be approximated by finite information, should hold in the non-deterministic case. In [16] we give a positive answer for formal computations or computations with respect to Herbrand interpretations. We now extend our approach to so called effective computations. As in [15] we restrict our attention to the case of non-deterministic equations in order to develop our methods in a structure simpler than that of non-deterministic program schemes. But all our results may be extended to non-deterministic recursive programs - as in the case of formal computations [16].

Our approach is axiomatic. We exploit an idea to be found in many papers on non-determinism, namely that semilattices are appropiate structures to model finitary non-determinism. In fact we enrich algebras by (ω-complete) partial orders and semilattice structure to what we call an ω-complete OI-algebra [16].

An operational semantics is defined by means of successful computation sequences which are maximal elements in a ω-complete algebra of computation sequences. The equivalence of operational and algebraic semantics is established.

To define fixpoint semantics a "power domain algebra" or free continuous OI-algebra is constructed. We prove the equivalence of **semantics** with respect to the power domain algebra ("P_c-equivalence") which seems to be the best possible way to compare the semantics. The result is unsatisfactory because the notion of P_c-equivalence is rather weak. This is due to the power domain construction which identify too many subsets of the given continuous algebras. We shall discuss this problem. In general it should be asked which kind of continuous algebras allow stronger results, respectively if there are more elaborate methods which allow stronger results for all continuous algebras. This question will be postponed to future work. For the case of continuous Ω-algebras over a flat poset we already showed a stronger equivalence in [15].

Our work seems to be closely related to the results of Boudol (as cited in [13], we do not yet have a copy of Boudol's dissertation). We acknowlegde [3], [4], [7] as a source of inspiration. For category theory we refer to [10], [11]. We only sketch the ideas of the proofs, full proofs shall be given elsewhere.

1. Operational Semantics

We assume the notion of Ω-algebras to be well known. As notation we use Ω for operator domains, $a: \Omega \to \mathbb{N}$ for arity functions, $T_\Omega(X)$ for the canonical free term algebra over a set X [1]. For $n \in \mathbb{N}$ let $\underline{n} := \{0,\dots,n-1\}$.

Let $\Omega+$ be an operator domain Ω plus an additional binary operator $\underline{or}$. A function

$$S: X \to T_{\Omega+}(X)$$

is called *system of non-deterministic equations* or *non-deterministic scheme*. It is common to state that the set X of recursive variables is finite.

Let $A = (A,(\delta_\omega | \omega \in \Omega))$ be a Ω-algebra. An *(elementary) computation* with the non-deterministic scheme $S: X \to T_{\Omega+}(X)$ in A then has one of the following forms:

- replacing a recursive variable by the right hand side of the respective equation
- making a non-deterministic choice
- evaluating one of the operations of the algebra A.

Formally, a relation $\to_{S,A} \subseteq T_{\Omega+}(X+A) \times T_{\Omega+}(X+A)$ is defined by (X+A denotes coproducts, here in the category of sets)

$t \to_{S,A} t'$ iff (i) $t = x$ and $t' = S(x)$ or

(ii) $t = \underline{or}(t_0,t_1)$ and ($t' = t_0$ or $t' = t_1$) or

(iii) $t = \omega(a_0,\dots,a_{a(\omega)-1})$ with $a_i \in A$ for all $i \in \underline{a(\omega)}$ and $t' = \delta_\omega(a_0,\dots,a_{a(\omega)-1})$ or

(iv) $t = \omega(t_0,\dots,t_i,\dots,t_{a(\omega)-1})$ and there exists a t_i' such that $t_i \to_{S,A} t_i'$ and $t' = \omega(t_0,\dots,t_i',\dots,t_{a(\omega)-1})$.

Let $\to^r_{S,A}$ be the reflexive and $\to^*_{S,A}$ be the reflexive and transitive closure of $\to_{S,A}$. The index "S,A" shall be omitted if the context is obvious.

A computation is called *formal* if $A = T_\Omega(\emptyset)$, the initial Ω-algebra.

A *computation sequence* is a sequence $(t_n | n \in \omega)$ with $t_n \in T_{\Omega+}(X+A)$ such that $t_n \to^* t_{n+1}$ for all $n \in \omega$. If for some $n \in \omega$ and all $i \in \omega$ $t_n = t_{n+i}$ the a computation sequence is called *finite* otherwise *infinite*. We shall use c as notation for computation sequences, c_n denotes the n-th element of c. Terms $t \in T_{\Omega+}(X+A)$ may be understood as constant computation sequences $(t | n \in \omega)$.

.1 *Example:* Let $\{a,b\}$ be a set. Then $(\{a,b\}^*, conc, \lambda, a, b)$ with concatenation and empty word and nullary operators a,b is a algebra of typ $\{\cdot, e, 0, 1\}$. The non-deterministic scheme (using infix notation)

$$S(x) := (0\cdot 1)\cdot x \ \underline{or}\ e \qquad X=\{x\}$$

generates for instance

$x \to (0\cdot1)\cdot x \ \underline{or}\ e \to (0\cdot1)\cdot x \to (a\cdot1)\cdot x \to (a\cdot b)\cdot x \to (a\cdot b)\cdot((0\cdot1)\cdot x \ \underline{or}\ e) \to$
$\to (a\cdot b)\cdot e \to (a\cdot b)\cdot\lambda \to ab\cdot\lambda \to ab$

$x \to (0\cdot1)\cdot x \ \underline{or}\ e \to (0\cdot1)\cdot x \to (0\cdot1)\cdot((0\cdot1)\cdot x \ \underline{or}\ e) \to (0\cdot1)\cdot e$

There are infinite computation sequences

$x \to^* ab\cdot x \to^* ab\cdot(ab\cdot x) \to^* ab\cdot(ab\cdot(ab\cdot x)) \to^* \dots$

A computation sequence is called successful if, intuitively, all possible computations are executed. In the example the first and third computation sequence is successful while the second is not successful, the computation $(0 \cdot 1) \cdot \lambda \to^{*} ab$ is not executed. To give a formal definition we need some preparation:

An Ω-algebra is called *ordered* (ω-*complete*) if the carrier is a (ω-complete) partial ordered set and if the structure maps are monotone (ω-continuous). With monotone (ω-continuous) homomorphisms these data define categories $\underline{\Omega\text{-alg-pos}}$ resp. $\underline{\Omega\text{-alg-}\omega\text{-pos}}$. These are enriched categories in the sense of [12] which live in the category $\underline{\text{pos}}$ of posets resp. in the categoy $\underline{\omega\text{-pos}}$ of ω-complete posets.

Let $t,t' \in T_{\Omega}(X)$. An ordered algebra is said to *satisfy the inequation* (t,t') if for all mappings $\sigma: X \to A$ (A being the carrier of the ordered algebra) we have that $\sigma^{\#}(t) \leq \sigma^{\#}(t')$ with $\sigma^{\#}: T_{\Omega}(X) \to A$ being the unique homomorphic extension [1].

Let $\Omega_{\perp}$ be an operator domain Ω plus an additional nullary operator $\perp$. Then all ω-complete Ω-algebras satisfying the inequation $\perp \leq x$ are usually called *continuous Ω-algebras* [2]. Notation is $\underline{\text{c-}\Omega\text{-alg}}$ and $\underline{\text{cpo}}$ if $\Omega = \emptyset$.

We now observe that $T_{\Omega+}(X+A)$ with the relation $\to^{*}_{S,A}$ is a quasi-ordered $\Omega+$-algebra and that the induced ordering may be extended to computation sequences yielding a ω-complete Ω-algebra. In fact this "ω-complete Ω-algebra of computation sequences" is obtained by a free construction:

Let $\underline{\Omega\text{-R-alg}}$ be the category with objects being Ω-algebras A plus a binary relation $R_A \subseteq A \times A$. Morphisms are homomorphisms $h: A \to B$ preserving the relations, i.e. $\{(h(a),h(a')) \mid (a,a') \in R_A\} \subseteq R_B$.

1.2 *Proposition* : The forgetful functor $\underline{\Omega\text{-alg-}\omega\text{-pos}} \to \underline{\Omega\text{-R-alg}}$ has a left adjoint (or less technically free construction functor) we shall denote by $C: \underline{\Omega\text{-R-alg}} \to \underline{\Omega\text{-alg-}\omega\text{-pos}}$.

Free objects are obtained as ω-completion of the smallest congruent (wrt. the algebra structure) partial order.

The free algebra of computation sequences is given as follows:

Let the relation $R_{S,A}$ over $T_{\Omega+}(X+A)$ be defined by

$$(*) \qquad R_{S,A} := \{(x, S(x)) \mid x \in X\} \cup \{(\underline{or}(t_o,t_1),t_o) , (\underline{or}(t_o,t_1),t_1) \mid t_o,t_1 \in T_{\Omega+}(X+A)\} \cup \{(\omega(a_o,\ldots,a_{a(\omega)-1}), \delta_{\omega}(a_o,\ldots,a_{a(\omega)-1})) \mid a_i \in A, \ i \in \underline{a(\omega)}, \ \omega \in \Omega\} \ .$$

On computation sequences a quasi-order is defined by

$$c \le c' \quad \text{iff} \quad \forall m \in \omega \ \exists n \in \omega: \ c_m \to^* c_n \ .$$

Factorization by antisymmetry yields a free ω-complete Ω-algebra over $(T_{\Omega+}(X+A),\ R_{S,A})$, the algebra of computation sequences with carrier

$$\text{comp}(S,A) := (\ \{[c]\ |c \text{ comp. sequ. for } S \text{ and } A\ \},\ \le\ )$$

and operations

$$\mu_\omega([c_o],\ldots[c_{a(\omega)-1}]) = [(\ \omega(c_{o,n},\ldots,c_{a(\omega)-1,n})\ |n \in \omega)]\ .$$

1.3 *Definition:* A computation sequence c is called *successfull* if c is maximal in comp(S,A).

(In a partial ordered set X an element t is called maximal if for all $t' \in X$ $t \le t'$ implies $t = t'$)

Now let A be a continuous Ω-algebra. A is extended to a $\Omega+$-algebra A by adding a binary operation $\perp: A \times A \to A$, $(a,a') \to \perp$. Let $[\perp,id_A]: X+A \to A \in$ set be the mapping which sends all variables to $\perp$ and which is the identity on A. As the homomorphic extension $[\perp,id_A]!: T_{\Omega+}(X+A) \to A$ preserves the relation $R_{S,A}$ (cf (*)) we have a unique ω-continuous homomorphic extension $[\perp,id_A]^\#: \text{comp}(S,A) \to A$. Explicitly, computation sequences c are mapped to $\bigsqcup_n \bar{c}_n$, where $\bar{c}_n$ is the element of A obtained from c_n by replacing all variables and all subterms of the form "or(t_o,t_1)" by the symbol $\perp$ and then evaluating the resulting term in A.

1.4 *Definition:* The *set of results of a non-deterministic scheme* S *in a continuous algebra* A *starting in a term* $t \in T_{\Omega+}(X)$ is defined by

$$\text{Res}(S,A)(t) := \{[\perp,id_A]^\#(\ c\ )\ |c \quad \text{comp}(S,A) \text{ successful and } \quad t \le c\ \}$$

The *operational semantics* then is a vector $\text{Res}(S,A): X \to A, \quad x \to \text{Res}(S,A)(x)$.

It should be noted that our proceeding is similar to that to be found in [14] only that we point out the underlying free construction of which we shall make use.

1.5 *Example* (continued): In $\{a,b\}^*$ let $v \le w \iff \exists v' \in \{a,b\}^*: vv' = w$. Let $\{a,b\}^\infty$ be the ω-completion of $\{a,b\}^*$under the above ordering. With operations be extended properly

$$\text{Res}(S,(\{a,b\}^\infty,\text{conc},\lambda,a,b))(x) = \{ab^n|n \in \omega\} \cup \{ab^\omega\}$$

2. Algebraic Semantics

We have two possibilities to define algebraic semantics; one is to consider formal computations and to interpret them in a continuous algebra, the second is to take the results in the initial continuous algebra and to interpret them by unique homomorphisms.

Let $[\bot,i]: X+T_\Omega(\emptyset) \rightarrow A$ be the mapping which maps variables to $\bot$ and which is the initial homomorphism on $T_\Omega(\emptyset)$. It is easy to see that the unique extension $[\bot,i]!: T_{\Omega+}(X+T_\Omega(\emptyset)) \rightarrow A_\bot$ preserves the relation $R_{S,T_\Omega(\emptyset)}$ and thus induces a ω-continuous homomorphic extension $[\bot,i]^{\#}: comp(S,T_\Omega(\emptyset)) \rightarrow A_\bot$.

2.1 *Definition:* $Res'(S,A)(t) := \{[\bot,i]^{\#}(c) \mid c \in comp(S,T_\Omega(\emptyset))$ successful, $t \leq c\}$

is called *set of results of formal computation sequences in* A *starting in* $t \in T_{\Omega+}(X)$.

2.2 *Theorem:* Let $I: CT_\Omega(\emptyset) \rightarrow A$ be the initial morphism in c-Ω-alg. Then for all $t \in T_{\Omega+}(X)$

$$Res(S,A)(t) = Res'(S,A)(t) = Res(S,CT_\Omega(\emptyset))_I(t)$$

where $Res(S,CT_\Omega(\emptyset))_I(t) := \{I(t') \mid t' \in Res(S,CT_\Omega(\emptyset))(t)\}$. $CT_\Omega(\emptyset)$ is the initial continuous Ω-algebra of infinite trees [2].

The proof is diagrammatic. The diagram

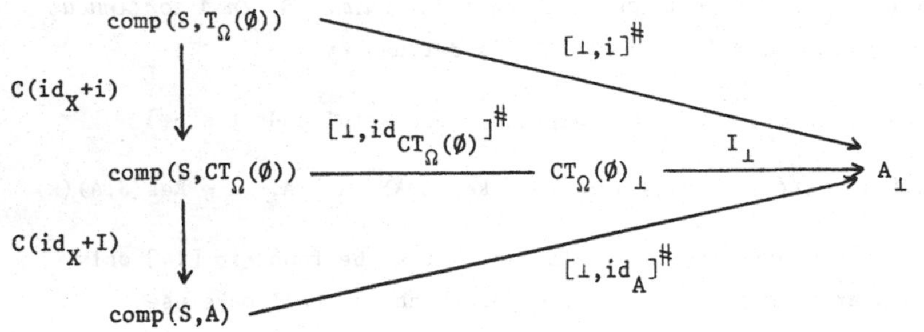

commutes due to the freeness of structures and due to the fact that the morphisms $C(id_X+i)$ and $C(id_X+I)$ preserve maximal elements. (we remind that C: Ω-R-alg → Ω-alg-ω-pos is the left adjoint). The latter fact may easily derived from

2.3 *Lemma:* Let $f: A \rightarrow A'$ be a homomorphism of Ω-algebras. f extends to a Ω+-homomorphism $\bar{f}: T_{\Omega+}(X+A) \rightarrow T_{\Omega+}(X+A')$.
For all $s \in T_{\Omega+}(X+A)$, if $\bar{f}(s) \rightarrow_{S,A'} t'$ then there exists a $t \in T_{\Omega+}(X+A)$ such that $s \rightarrow_{S,A} t$ and $\bar{f}(t) = t'$.

3. Non-Deterministic Algebras and Denotational Semantics

To define the denotational semantics in the standard way by means of fixpoints we have to choose some appropiate non-deterministic domain. Several authors [7], [8] use semilattices (or commutative idempotent semigroups) to model finitary non-determinism. This is motivated by the fact that the finite power set functor P_f: <u>set</u> $\to$ <u>sl</u>, $X \to (\{Y \subseteq X \mid Y \text{ finite, non empty}\}, \cup)$ provides us with free semilattices, and that the mappings $f: X \to P_f(Y)$ are understood as non-deterministic functions (<u>sl</u> denotes the category of semilattices and linear homomorphisms). Thus to deal with non-determinism the algebra structure should be suitably enriched by the semilattice structure. The following definition was proposed in [16].

3.1 *Definition:* A *(non-deterministic) OI-Ω-algebra* consists of a semilattice (A,+) and a Ω-indexed family of mappings $\delta_\omega : A^{a(\omega)} \to A$ which are linear in each component. With Ω-homomorphisms being linear this defines a category <u>OI-Ω-alg</u>.

The following arguments are borrowed from category theory. Basically we show that for the construction of free OI-Ω-algebras over a given Ω-algebra we only need to know how free semilattices are constructed; a free OI-Ω-algebra then is obtained as the image of the given algebra under the functor constructing free semilattices. The same idea will be used later to construct free ω-complete OI-Ω-algebras (see below). Free ω-complete OI-algebras shall be used as non-deterministic domains where denotational semantics are defined.

We note that OI-Ω-algebras are exactly Ω-algebras which are defined with respect to the tensor product of semilattices [15].

3.2 *Proposition:* The left adjoint P_f: <u>set</u> $\to$ <u>sl</u> maps finite products in <u>set</u> to tensor products in <u>sl</u>, i.e. $P_f(X \otimes Y) = P_f(X) \times P_f(Y)$.

The proof depends on the fact that <u>set</u> is cartesian and <u>sl</u> monoidal closed [9] and to the well known chain of natural isomorphisms

$$\underline{sl}[P_f(X) \otimes P_f(Y), Z] \cong \underline{sl}[P_f(X), P_f(Y) \to Z] \cong \underline{set}[X, U_f(P_f(Y) \to Z)] \cong \underline{set}[X, Y \to U_f(Z)]$$
$$\cong \underline{set}[X \times Y, U_f(Z)] \cong \underline{sl}[P_f(X \times Y), Z]$$

where U_f: <u>sl</u> $\to$ <u>set</u> is the forgetful functor. It should be remarked that the isomorphism $\underline{set}[X, U_f(P_f(Y) \to Z)] \cong \underline{set}[X, Y \to U_f(Z)]$ holds because we have $\underline{sl}[P_f(Y), Z] \cong set[X, U_f(Z)]$ on the level of sets.

The observation now is that because of 3.2 P_f maps Ω-algebras to OI-Ω-algebras, in fact to free ones [9].

3.3 *Corollary*: The forgetful functor $\underline{OI\text{-}\Omega\text{-alg}} \to \underline{\Omega\text{-alg}}$ has a left adjoint P_f given by

$$P_f(A) := \{Y \subseteq A \mid Y \text{ finite, non empty}\}$$

$$Y + Y' := Y \cup Y'$$

$$\mu_\omega(Y_o,\dots,Y_{a(\omega)-1}) := \{\delta_\omega(a_o,\dots,a_{a(\omega)-1}) \mid a_i \in Y_i \text{ for } i \in \underline{a(\omega)}\} \quad .$$

To apply the Knaster-Tarski fixpoint theorem the structure has to be enriched by some complete order. There are several possibilities (compare [8]), we choose the following:

3.4 *Definition*: Semilattices may be understood as posets such that any finite, non empty subset has a least upper bound (lub). With morphisms preserving the lubs this defines a category $\underline{\omega\text{-pos}}$ which clearly is isomorphic to $\underline{sl}$. The isomorphism is given by $(X,+) \to (X,\leq)$ with $x \leq y$ iff $x+y = y$. If the carrier (omitting the isomorphism) is ω-complete, we refer to a ω-complete semilattice. With linear mappings being ω-continuous this defines a category $\underline{\sqcup\text{-}\omega\text{-pos}}$.

ω-complete OI-Ω-algebras then are OI-Ω-algebras with structure mappings being ω-continuous. With OI-Ω-algebra homomorphisms being ω-continuous this gives a category $\underline{\omega\text{-OI-}\Omega\text{-alg}}$.

We would like to find a left adjoint to the forgetful functor $\underline{\omega\text{-OI-}\Omega\text{-alg}} \to \underline{\Omega\text{-alg-}\omega\text{-pos}}$ along the lines of 3.2/3.3. This leads us to the well known power domain discussion: Hennessy and Plotkin [8] have proved the existence of a left adloint "power domain" P_c: $\underline{\omega\text{-pos}} \to \underline{\sqcup\text{-}\omega\text{-pos}}$, As an immediate consequence of the V-Yoneda lemma in [6] for $V = \underline{\omega\text{-pos}}$ (compare also [12]) we have

3.5 *Lemma*: The natural isomorphism $\underline{\sqcup\text{-}\omega\text{-pos}}[P_c(X),Y] \cong \underline{\omega\text{-pos}}[X,U_c(Y)]$ to the adjunction $P_c \dashv U_c : \underline{\sqcup\text{-}\omega\text{-pos}} \to \underline{\omega\text{-pos}}$ is an isomorphism of ω-complete posets (with function space ordering).

As $\underline{\sqcup\text{-}\omega\text{-pos}}$ is monoidal closed wrt. tensor products we obtain as a corollary

3.6 *Proposition*: (i) P_c maps products to tensor products.

(ii) A left adjoint P_c: $\underline{\Omega\text{-alg-}\omega\text{-pos}} \to \underline{\omega\text{-OI-}\Omega\text{-alg}}$ is defined by

$$P_c((A,(\delta_\omega \mid \omega \in \Omega)) := (P_c(A),\ (P_c(\delta_\omega) \mid \omega \in \Omega)) \quad .$$

3.7 *Remark*: All results hold if we consider $\Omega_\perp$-algebras satisfying the inequation $\perp \leq x$. Thus continuous Ω-algebras are mapped by P_c to what may be called continuous OI-Ω-algebras, i.e. ω-complete OI-Ω-algebras with a least element $\perp$.

Now we are able to define the denotational semantics of a non-deterministic scheme in the power domain algebra $P_c(A)$.

3.8 *Definition*: Let A be a continuous Ω-algebra. Then $P_c(A)$ is a continuous Ω+-algebra ($\delta_{\underline{or}}$ is the binary lub). Thus every mapping $f: X \to P_c(A)$ has a unique homomorphic extension $f^{\#}: T_{\Omega+}(X) \to P_c(A)$. For a non-deterministic scheme $S: X \to T_{\Omega+}(X)$ we define a ω-continuous (!) mapping

$$\hat{S}_A: P_c(A)^X \to P_c(A)^X \ , \quad f \to f^{\#} \cdot S \ .$$

The least fixpoint of $\hat{S}_A$ is caled the *denotational semantics* of S in A and is given by $\mathrm{Fix}(\hat{S}_A) = \bigsqcup \hat{S}_A^n(\bot)$.

4. Comparison Of Operational And Denotational Semantics

A serious difficulty to compare operational and denotational semantics is that operational semantics is defined on the level of subsets of a continuous algebra A while denotational semantics is defined as an element of the continuous OI-algebra $P_c(A)$. So we need some devices to compare the semantics "as good as possible". Bad enough this requires some understanding of the power domain construction. To dbtain this understanding we recall several well known definitions and facts.

4.1 *Facts*: Let X be a poset, $Y,Y' \subseteq X$. Then

$$Y \sqsubseteq Y' \ :\Longleftrightarrow\ \forall y \in Y\ \exists y' \in Y': y \leq y' \qquad (\textit{Cofinality})$$

$$Y \approx Y' \ :\Longleftrightarrow\ Y \sqsubseteq Y' \text{ and } Y' \sqsubseteq Y \ .$$

$\sqsubseteq$ is a quasi ordering, $\approx$ an equivalence relation.

$Z_f(X) := \{Y \subseteq X \mid Y \text{ finite, non empty}\}_{/\approx}$ with ordering induced from $\sqsubseteq$ is a free semilattice over X. This defines a left adjoint Z_f: $\underline{\text{pos}} \to \underline{\text{sl}}$.

On ω-chains $c,c': \omega \to X$ cofinality is introduced via the images: $c \sqsubseteq c' :\Longleftrightarrow \mathrm{Im}(c) \sqsubseteq \mathrm{Im}(c')$. The *Chain closure* of X is given by

$$Z_\Omega(X) := \{c \mid c \ \ \omega\text{-chain}\}_{/\approx}$$

$Z_\omega(X)$ with induced ordering is a free ω-complete poset over X. This defines a left adjoint Z_ω: $\underline{\text{pos}} \to \underline{\omega\text{-pos}}$.

If X is ω-complete $\sup_X: Z_\omega(X) \to X,\ \ c \to \sqcup c$ is a monotone mapping. In the special case of $Z_\omega(X)$ $\sup_{Z_\omega(X)}: Z_\omega(Z_\omega(X)) \to Z_\omega(X)$ is defined as follows (for sake of notation we shall argue on represetants here and in the following)

Let $c_o \sqsubseteq c_1 \sqsubseteq \dots \sqsubseteq c_n \sqsubseteq \dots$ be a cofinal chain of ω-chains. We define a ω-chain $c\colon \omega \to X$ by induction

$$c(0) := c_o(0) \qquad c(n+1) := c_{n+1}(\max\{n+1, i_n\})$$

where $\quad i_n := \min\{\, i \in \omega \mid c(n) \leq c_{n+1}(i)\}$.

Then $\quad \sup_{Z_\omega(X)}([([c_n] \mid n \in \omega)]) = [c]$.

4.2 *Lemma:* Given a poset X $Z_\omega(Z_f(X))$ is a free ω-complete semilattice over X.

The proof is straightforward.

We shall now use that for a ω-complete poset X the power domain $P_c(X)$ may be obtained from $Z_\omega(Z_f(X))$ by factorization. The arguments are an application of Beck's theorems on distributive laws [5].

Let X be a ω-complete poset. Then the mapping $Z_\omega(Z_f(\sup_X))\colon Z_\omega(Z_f(Z\ (X))) \to Z_\omega(Z_f(X))$ is a <u>⊔-ω-pos</u> - homomorphism. Explicitly it is given by

$$Y_o \sqsubseteq Y_1 \sqsubseteq \dots \sqsubseteq Y_n \sqsubseteq \dots \quad \to \quad \{c \mid c \in Y_o\} \sqsubseteq \{c \mid c \in Y_1\} \sqsubseteq \dots \sqsubseteq \{c \mid c \in Y_n\} \sqsubseteq \dots \quad .$$

A second mapping $g\colon Z_\omega(Z_f(Z_\omega(X))) \to Z_\omega(Z_f(X))$ is given as the composition of the mappings

$$g_o\colon Z_\omega(Z_f(Z_\omega(X))) \to Z_\omega(Z_\omega(Z_f(X)))$$

$$Y_o \sqsubseteq \dots \sqsubseteq Y_n \sqsubseteq \dots \quad \to \quad \bar{Y}_o \sqsubseteq \dots \sqsubseteq \bar{Y}_n \sqsubseteq \dots$$

where $\bar{Y}_n(m) := \{c(m) \mid c \in Y_n\}$ for $m \in \omega$, and

and

$$g_1 := \sup_{Z_\omega(Z_f(X))}\colon Z_\omega(Z_\omega(Z_f(X))) \to Z_\omega(Z_f(X)) \quad .$$

4.3 *Proposition* (Beck [5]): A free ω-complete semilattice $P_c(X)$ over a ω-complete poset X is given as coequalizer object of f and g in <u>⊔-ω-pos</u>,

$$Z_\omega(Z_f(Z_\omega(X))) \overset{f}{\underset{g}{\rightrightarrows}} Z_\omega(Z_f(X)) \xrightarrow{\ \pi\ } P_c(X)$$

Existence of coequalizers is ensured in [12]. The argument then is as follows: Given a ω-continuous morphism $h\colon X \to Y$ where $Y \in$ <u>⊔-ω-pos</u> there is a unique extension $h!\colon Z_\omega(Z_f(X)) \to Y \in$ <u>⊔-ω-pos</u> defined by $Y_o \sqsubseteq \dots \sqsubseteq Y_n \sqsubseteq \dots \to \bigsqcup_n (\bigsqcup Y_n)$. It is an easy exercise to ensure $h! \cdot f = h! \cdot g$. Thus h! induces a unique homomorphism $h^{\#}\colon P_c(X) \to Y$.

e need one more

.4 *Observation:* (i) For $X \in \underline{pos}$ let $Y \subseteq X$ be called *finitely generated* if there exists a chain $(Y_n | n \in \omega)$ of finite, non empty subsets $Y_n \subseteq X$ with $Y_n \sqsubseteq Y_{n+1}$ for all $n \in \omega$ such that $Y \underset{\sim}{\sqsubset}_n Y_n$. Then

$$Z_\omega(Z_f(X)) \cong \{Y \subseteq X \mid Y \text{ finitely generated}\}_{/\underset{\sim}{\sqsubset}} =: \bar{P}(X)$$

(ii) Let A be a continuous Ω-algebra, $S: X \to T_{\Omega+}(X)$ be a non-deterministic scheme. Then Res(S,A)(t) is finitely generated. The generating sets are

$$T_n(t) := \{[\bot, id_A]^\#(t') \mid t \overset{r}{\underset{S,A}{\to}}{}^n t'\}$$

(where R^n is the n-th iteration of a relation R, t' understood as comp. sequ.)

fter these (inherently lengthy) preliminaries we are able to state what we mean by quivalence of operational and denotational semantics. The following seems to be the est possible way to generate an element of $P_c(A)$ from a set of results Res(S,A)(t).

.5 *Definition:* Given a non-deterministic scheme $S: X \to T_{\Omega+}(X)$ and a continuous Ω-algebra A operational and denotational semantics are P_c*-equivalent* if for all $x \in X$

$$Fix(S_A)(x) = \pi(Res(S,A)(t))$$

(the isomorphism of 4.4(i) used implicitly).

e feel that this definition is somewhat unsatisfactory as the connection between perational and denotational semantics is rather weak. The blame is to be put to the ower domain construction: the order of the algebra A may be much finer than it is eeded to obtain a homomorphic extension $[\bot, id_A]^\#$: comp(S,A) $\to$ A . This shall be disussed below. But first we state the

.6 *Proposition:* Operational and denotational semantics are P_c-equivalent.

ne proof is based on the standard observation that computation by "parallel substiution" yields the same results as "substitution at one point" as defined above. In act, parallel substitution is defined by

$$\hat{S}_\Omega: T_{\Omega+}(X+A)^X \to T_{\Omega+}(X+A)^X \quad , \quad f \to f^\# \cdot S$$

here $f^\#: T_{\Omega+}(X+A) \to T_{\Omega+}(X+A)$ is induced from f.
sing freeness of $T_{\Omega+}(X)$ we immediately conclude the commutativity of the diagram

$$\begin{array}{ccccc}
T_{\Omega+}(X+A)^X & \xrightarrow{\Gamma^X} & \bar{P}(A)^X & \xrightarrow{\pi^X} & P_c(A)^X \\
\hat{S}_\Omega \downarrow & & \hat{S}_{\bar{P}(A)} \downarrow & & \hat{S}_A \downarrow \\
T_{+}(X+A)^X & \xrightarrow[\Gamma^X]{} & P(A)^X & \xrightarrow[\pi^X]{} & P_c(A)^X
\end{array}$$

where $\hat{S}_{\bar{P}(A)}$ is defined in analogy to 3.8 and $\Gamma : T_{\Omega+}(X+A) \to \bar{P}(A)$ is uniquely induced by $\gamma: X+A \to \bar{P}(A)$ which maps elements of X to $[\{\bot\}]$ and elements of A to $[\{a\}]$ (3.6 works as well for <u>Ω-alg-pos</u> → <u>ω-OI-Ω-alg</u>, that is why $\bar{P}(A)$ can be understood as a ω-complete OI-algebra).

Essentially by simulation of computations one can conclude that $T_n(x) \sqsubseteq \Gamma \cdot (\hat{S}^n_\Omega(\eta))(x)$ for all $n \in \omega$, with $\eta: X \to T_{\Omega+}(X+A)$ being the embedding, and that for all $m \in \omega$ there exists a $n \in \omega$ such that $\Gamma \cdot (\hat{S}^m_\Omega(\eta))(x) \sqsubseteq T_n(x)$. This implies

$$\mathrm{Res}(S,A)(x) \underset{\sim}{\sqsubseteq} \bigcup_n T_n(x) \underset{\sim}{\sqsubseteq} \bigcup_n \Gamma \cdot (\hat{S}^n_\Omega(\eta))(x) \quad .$$

But due to $\eta \cdot \Gamma = \bot : X \to \bar{P}(A)$, $x \to [\{\bot\}]$

$$\Gamma \cdot (\hat{S}^n_\Omega(\eta))(x) = \hat{S}^n_{\bar{P}(A)}(\bot)(x)$$

and

$$\mathrm{Res}(S,A)(x) \underset{\sim}{=} \bigcup_n \hat{S}^n_{\bar{P}(A)}(\bot)(x) \overset{!}{=} \mathrm{Fix}(\hat{S}_{\bar{P}(A)})(x) \quad .$$

At last because of ω-continuity of π and the above diagram we conclude

$$\pi^X(\mathrm{Fix}(\hat{S}_{\bar{P}(A)})) = \mathrm{Fix}(\hat{S}_A)$$

and

$$\pi(\mathrm{Res}(S,A)(x)) = \mathrm{Fix}(\hat{S}_A)(x)$$

5. Discussion And Outlook

The aim of our paper has been to establish the equivalence of semantics for effective computations of non-deterministic schemes. The definition of operational and algebraic semantics was straightforward using the notion of computation sequences- which to our opinion are a very basic tool for analysis of programming features. Demonstration of coincidence of operational and algebraic semantics was - as always - an easy exercise in algebra.

With denotational semantics we encountered two problems. First we need an appropiate non-deterministic domain, second we had to introduce a notion of equivalence of operational and denotational semantics. Both problems required considerable efforts and may be understood as the heart of this paper.

The proof of P_c-equivalence of semantics is technically somewhat envolved but as a result unsatisfactory. The reason for this is implicit in the definition of P_c-equivalence: The sets $T_n(t)$ not only generate Res(S,A)(t) but also $\{[\bot, id_A]^{\#}(c) \mid c \in \mathrm{comp}(S,A)$ and $t \leq c\}$, i.e. the results of all computation sequences and not necessarily the successful ones. P_c-equivalence thus characterizes the computational power of a non-deterministic scheme up to all computation sequences. The situation is even worth:

Let ω+1 be the set of natural numbers plus a limit point, order is the canonical one. As operations we have the constant 0 and the successor function which is the identity at the limit point. This is a {s,e}-algebra. We consider the schemes

S_1: $x \to e \ \underline{or} \ s(x)$

S_2: $x \to e \ \underline{or} \ s(s(x))$.

Then

$$Res(S_1,(\omega+1,succ,0))(x) = \{n|n \in \omega\} \cup \{\omega\}$$

$$Res(S_2,(\omega+1,succ,0))(x) = \{2\cdot n|n \in \omega\} \cup \{\omega\}$$

but

$$\{n|n \in \omega\} \cup \{\omega\} \ \underset{\sim}{\sqsubseteq} \ \{2\cdot n|n \in \omega\} \cup \{\omega\} \ \overset{!}{\underset{\sim}{\sqsubseteq}} \ \{0,\omega\}$$

Even if the equivalences are correct with respect to infinitary behaviour we feel that the schemes should not be considered as equivalent.

If we are only interested in formal computations, i.e. computations in the initial algebra $CT_{\{s,e\}}(\emptyset)$, the result is different. Then the sets

$$\{s^n(e)|n \in \omega\} \cup \{s^\omega(e)\} \qquad \text{and} \qquad \{s^{2\cdot n}(e)|n \in \omega\} \cup \{s^\omega(e)\}$$

are incomparable. Thus the mapping $P_c(CT_{\{s,e\}}(\emptyset)) \to P_c((\omega+1,succ,0))$ identifies too much information. The reason is obvious, the order structure of $\omega+1$ is much finer than the ordering inherited from the computation sequences.

The above arguments suggest that there are several notions of equivalence of semantics. P_c-equivalence seems to be the weakest one while equivalence on the level of sets, i.e. $Fix(S_A)(x) = Res(S,A)(x)$ as sets, is the strongest one. In [15] we showed that this strong equivalence holds if formal computations of non-deterministic schemes being Greibach are considered. We conjecture that strong equivalence only holds for quotients of free continuous algebras $CT_\Omega(X)$ over flat posets X.

In general it seems to be worthwile to investigate different notions of equivalence and to look for classes of algebras, in which the respective equivalence holds. Connections of this kind should give some insight in the interaction of poset ordering and ordering of computation sequences. Problems of this kind shall be discussed in future work.

REFERENCES

[1] ADJ-group: A junction between computer science and category theory. IBM research report RC-4526, 1973

[2] ADJ-group: Some fundamentals of order algebraic semantics. MFCS'76, LNCS 45, 1976

[3] Arnold,A.,Nivat,M.: Metric interpretations of infinite trees and semantics of non deterministic programs. Techn. Rep. Lille 1978

[4] Arnold,A.,Nivat,M.: Formal computations of non deterministic recursive program schemes. Math. Syst. Th. 13, 1980

[5] Beck,J.: Distributive laws. Lect. Notes Math. 80, 1969

[6] Dubuc,E.: Kan extensions in enriched category theory. Lect. Notes Math. 145, 1970

[7] Hennessy,M.C.B.,Plotkin,G.: Full abstraction of a simple parallel programming language. MFCS'79, LNCS 74, 1979

[8] Hennessy,M.C.B., Ashcroft,E.A.: The semantics of non-determinism. 3rd ICALP, Edinburgh 1976

[9] Huwig,H.,Poigné,A.: Continuous and non-deterministic completions of algebras. 3rd Hungarian Comp. Sci. Conf., Budapest 1981

[10] MacLane,S.: Kategorien. Berlin-Heidelberg-New-York 1972

[11] Manes,E.G.: Algebraic Theories. Berlin-Heidelberg-New-York 1976

[12] Meseguer,J.: On order-complete universal algebra and enriched functorial semantics. FCT')), LNCS 56, Poznan 1977

[13] Meseguer,J.: Order completion monads. Math. Dpt. UCLA, Berkeley, 1979

[14] Nivat,M.: Non deterministic programs: an algebraic overview. Lab. Informatique Theorique et Programmation, Paris 1980

[15] Poigné,A.: Using least fixed points to characterize formal computations of non-deterministic equations. Proc. Conf.Formalization of programming concepts. LNCS 107, Peniscola 1981

[16] Poigné,A.: An order semantics for non-deterministic program schemes. 11.GI-Jahrestagung, Fachber. Informatik 50, 1981

SPECIFICATION AND VERIFICATION OF CONCURRENT SYSTEMS IN CESAR

J.P. Queille and J. Sifakis
Laboratoire IMAG, BP 53X
38041 Grenoble Cedex, France

Abstract :

The aim of this paper is to illustrate by an example, the alternating bit protocol, the use of CESAR, an interactive system for aiding the design of distributed applications.
CESAR allows the progressive validation of the algorithmic description of a system of communicating sequential processes with respect to a given set of specifications. The algorithmic description is done in a high level language inspired from CSP and specifications are a set of formulas of a branching time logic, the temporal operators of which can be computed iteratively as fixed points of monotonic predicate transformers. The verification of a system consists in obtaining by automatic translation of its description program an Interpreted Petri Net representing it and evaluating each formula of the specifications.

1. INTRODUCTION

The aim of this paper is to illustrate by an example the use of the system CESAR for the analysis of the properties of parallel systems.
CESAR is a system for aiding the design and integration of distributed applications. Its input language is a high level language, inspired from CSP [Hoare 78], for the algorithmic description of systems of communicating sequential processes. CESAR allows a progressive validation during the design process by considering two complementary aspects in a description :
- coherence in data manipulation (static characteristics of data and exchanged variables, visibility and access rights...)
- validation of the dynamic behaviour of a description with respect to its specifications.

Behavioural analysis of a system described by a program in the input language is based on the study of a representation of it in terms of Interpreted Petri Nets (IPN). Figure 1 illustrates the general principle of the system CESAR : given an algorithmic description of a system by a program in a high level language, a model representing some aspects of the described functioning is obtained by automatic translation. This model (an IPN) is treated by an analyzer in order to verify the conformity of the described system to given specifications. Specifications are a set of formulas of a branching time logic and express correctness properties which must be satisfied by the system. Using branching time logic instead of linear time logic as it has often been done [Gabbay 80] [Lamport 80] [Manna 81], is one of the peculiarities of our approach. It is shown that in this logic it is possible to compute

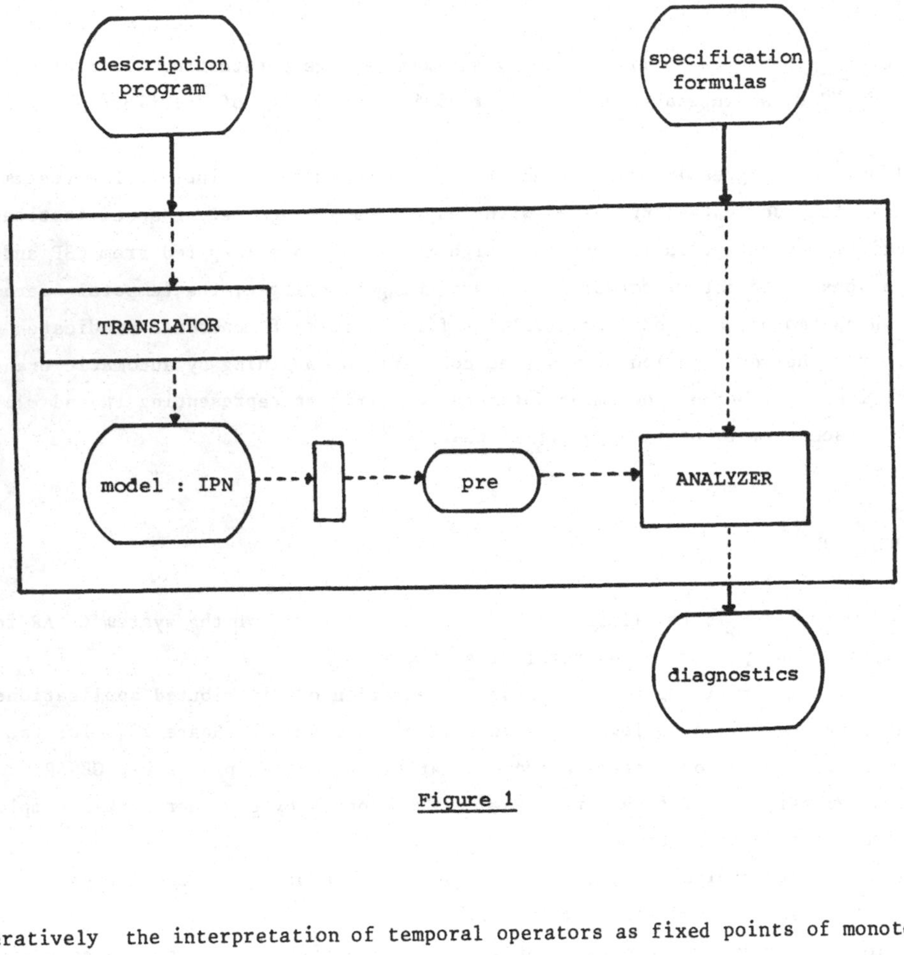

Figure 1

iteratively the interpretation of temporal operators as fixed points of monotonic predicate transformers.

Our approach presents some similarities to these followed in [Jensen 79] [Lauer 75] as far as the use of Petri nets as a model for the semantical analysis is concerned. The example considered throughout this paper is the alternating bit protocol. We have chosen this example because protocol modelling and verification is one of the principal application domains for CESAR. Furthemore, as protocols have been the object of many studies and especially the alternating bit protocol [Bartlett 69] [Bremer 79]

[Schwartz 81] [SIGPN 81], a rather precise comparison between the different approaches can be done.

This paper is organized in four parts. In part 2, the features of the description language are given and an illustration of its use for the description of the AB-protocol. After presenting the specification language, a part of the specifications of this protocol is given (part 3). In part 4 are exposed the analysis principle applied in CESAR and the theoretical results on which it is based.

2. DESCRIPTION IN CESAR

2.1. The description language

A system is described as a set of communicating sequential processes. Communications are declared as names of "exchanged variables". Exchange is done by rendez-vous between two processes, the one executing an output operation !V:=exp and the other an input operation ?V where V is the exchanged variable. The process executing the input operation has a local copy of the exchanged variable also denoted by V (not preceded by ?).

In addition to exchanged variables, processes have internal variables (which cannot be used for communication). Internal and exchanged variables are typed. Usual standard types and type constructors are available but the user can also introduce non-specified types for which it is not necessary to make manipulation rules explicit.

The basic statement of the language is the vectorial assignment. An input or output operation can be executed simultaneously with a vectorial assignment. We denote by nop the assignment whose right member is the identity function.

Besides the usual control structures, the CESAR description language provides the two following non-deterministic composed statements :

$\underline{\text{if}}\ b_1 \rightarrow s_1 \ // \ b_2 \rightarrow s_2 \ // \ \dots \ \underline{\text{fi}}$

$\underline{\text{do}}\ b_1 \rightarrow s_1 \ // \ b_2 \rightarrow s_2 \ // \ \dots \ \underline{\text{od}}$

where the b_i's are boolean conditions (guards) and the s_i's are sequences of statements. Their meaning is the following.

- IF : wait until one of the conditions is true and execute the corresponding sequence of statements.
- DO : repetition of an IF statement until a statement EXIT is encountered during the execution of some s_i.

For both of these constructs, if more than one conditions are true, the choice is non-deterministic. If a statement s_i begins with an input or output operation, the condition "the exchange can be executed" (i.e. the rendez-vous is possible) implicitely strengthens the guard b_i. The interpretation of the IF and DO constructs are the same as the interpretation of the WHEN and CYCLE statements in [Brinch Hansen 78].

2.2. Translation of description programs into interpreted Petri nets

Given a program in the input language, the translator generates an Interpreted Petri Net (IPN) representing the main aspects of its behaviour. It performs also the type verification and deletes the internal variables of non-specified types.

The IPN corresponding to a program is obtained by composing the IPN's representing its sequential processes. The translation method of the process uses a graph grammar, every rule of which is associated with a rule of the grammar of the description language [Queille 81].

An IPN is a Petri net with :

- a vector of variables X,
- a mapping associating with each transition of the net a guarded command $c_i \rightarrow a_i$ where c_i is a condition on X and a_i is a vectorial assignment $a_i = (X:=\alpha_i(X))$.

Functioning rules of an IPN are those of standard Petri nets, with the addition of the following rules :

- a transition can fire only when its associated condition is true,
- when a transition fires, its associated action is executed.

IPN's are a useful tool for representing parallel programs in a non-deterministic way [Keller 76]. They can be graphically represented by the corresponding Petri net, the transitions of which are inscribed by the associated guarded commands. By convention, the always true condition and the identity assignment can be omitted. Thus, if a transition has no inscription its firing rule is the same as in a standard Petri net.

The translation method is such that each net representing a sequential process is a safe state graph. The composition rule expresses the rendez-vous by merging transitions and so, it preserves safety of each process. This property is used by the analyzer in order to simplify predicate manipulations.

2.3 Example : The Alternating Bit Protocol

2.3.1 Presentation of the protocol

The Alternating Bit Protocol (AB-Protocol) introduced in [Barlett 69] to provide a reliable full-duplex transmission over half-duplex links, is a protocol where the control information of each transmitted message or acknowledgement is a single control bit which can be used to detect loss of messages or acknowledgements and recover from them. In this paper, we are not interested in transmission errors which at the protocol level are not distinguished from losses. Since this protocol is completely symmetrical we suppose transmission of data in a single direction and describe it by considering a Sender and a Receiver as follows :

:he Sender sends messages to the Receiver, which answers by sending acknowledgements. 'he Sender associates with each message a control bit which takes alternating values. ıfter sending a message, the Sender does not change the control bit and does not send .he next message before the reception of the corresponding acknowledgement (an acknow-edgement with the same control bit). To recover from loss of messages or of acknow-edgements, the Sender awaits the acknowledgement during a finite delay (measured by ın arbitrary local clock) and then repeats the same message (without changing the :ontrol bit).

:he Receiver behaves symmetrically. After receiving a message, it sends an acknowled-ement with the same control bit and then awaits the next message (with a control bit f alternate value). If the next message does not arrive within an arbitrary local delay, he Receiver repeats the previous acknowledgement.

f we assume that the line cannot loose all the messages and acknowledgements (i.e. he line is not cut), this protocol ensures the correct transmission of each message fter a sufficient number of repetitions. Message duplication does not cause any pro-lem because the protocol guarantees that any sequence of received messages with the ame control bit are duplications of the same message and the bit is changed by the ender for all new messages. Thus, the Receiver has just to skip all the messages of uch sequences except the first one. Symmetrically, the Sender has to skip duplica-ions of acknowledgements in the same way.

:.3.2 Description programs and IPN's for the AB-protocol

/e introduce two non-specified types :

- data to represent the data part of the messages
- pattern to represent the pattern of bits which is recognized as an acknow-ledgement.

'sing the standard type boolean, we can define both the type msg for the messages ınd the type ack for the acknowledgements as two structures :

```
type msg = ( MESSAGE : data ;
             B : boolean ) ;
type ack = ( ACKNOWLEDGEMENT : pattern ;
             B : boolean ) ;
```

he program for the sender is given in the following page (T means true ; ^ is the omplementation operator).

```
process SENDER
   ( output M : msg ;
     input A : ack ) ;

X : data ;
Y : boolean := 0 ;                                        -- initial value

begin

                          loop
send:                        !M := (X, Y) ;               -- send the message
                             do
receiveack:                     T -> ?A ;                 -- receive acknowledgement
                                   if
acceptack:                            A.B = Y -> Y := ^Y ;      -- expected acknowledgment
                                                exit //
skipack:                              A.B ≠ Y -> nop            -- else skip
                                   fi //
repeat:                         T -> !M := (X, Y)         -- repeat the message
                             od
                          end loop

end SENDER ;
```

The program for the Receiver is the following :

```
process RECEIVER
   ( input MM : msg ;
     output AA : ack ) ;

Z : boolean := 0 ;                                        -- initial value

begin

                          loop
                             do
receive:                        T -> ?MM ;                -- receive message
                                   if
accept:                               MM.B = Z -> exit //       -- expected message
skip:                                 MM.B ≠ Z -> nop           -- else skip
                                   fi //
repeatack:                      T -> !AA := ("ack", ^Z) -- repeat previous acknowledgement
                             od;
sendack:                     !AA := ("ack", Z), Z := ^Z -- send acknowledgement
                          end loop

end RECEIVER ;
```

The transmission line is described by the two following processes :

```
process SENDTORECEIVE
   ( input M : msg ;
     output MM : msg ) ;

begin

                          loop
get:                         ?M ;                         -- message is sent
                                if
transmit:                          T -> !MM := M //       -- message is transmitted
loose:                             T -> nop               -- message is lost
                                fi
                          end loop

end SENDTORECEIVE ;
```

```
process RECEIVETOSEND
   ( input AA : ack ;
     output A : ack ) ;

begin

                        loop
getack:                    ?AA ;                          -- acknowledgement is sent
                               if
transmitack:                      T -> !A := AA //        -- acknowledgement is transmitted
looseack:                         T -> nop                -- acknowledgement is lost
                               fi
                        end loop

end RECEIVETOSEND ;
```

Figure 2 presents the IPN obtained by translation of the description program.

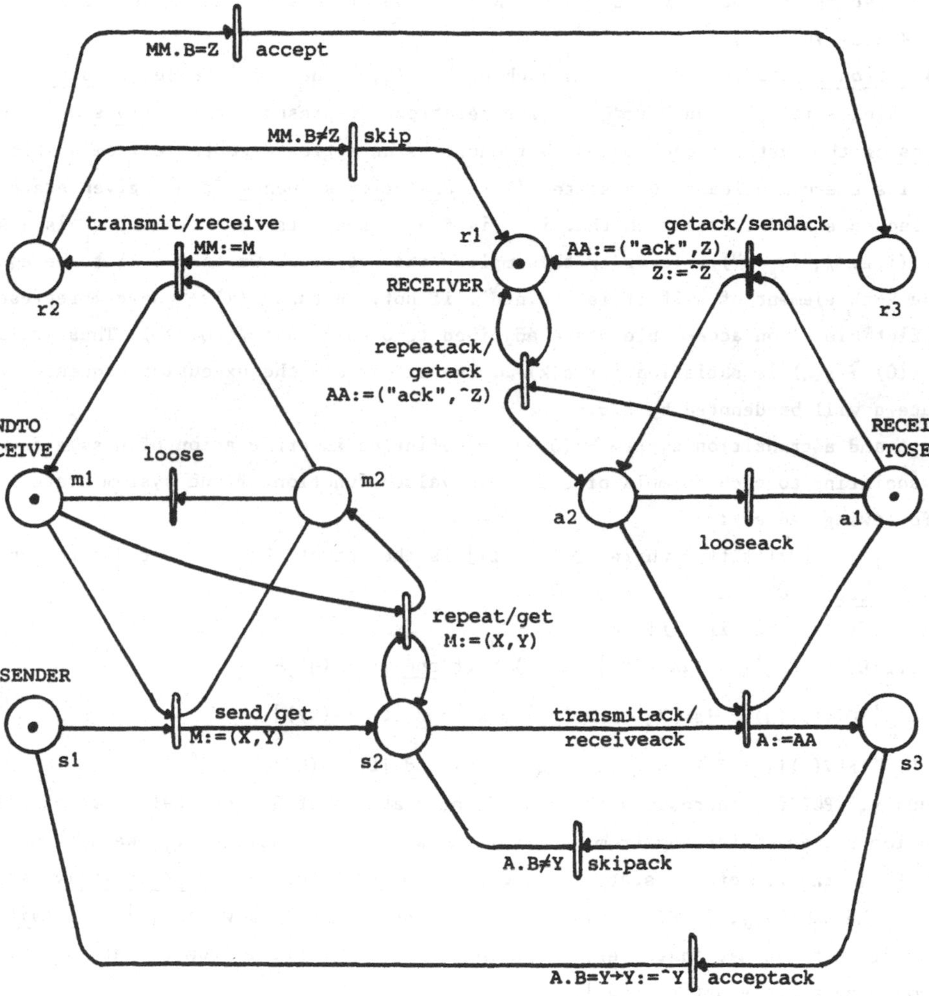

Figure 2

3. SPECIFICATION IN CESAR

3.1 The specification language

The specification language of CESAR is a branching time logic L [Lamport 80] [Rescher 71] constructed from a set of propositional variables F and the constants true, false, by using the logical connectives, $\neg$, $\wedge$, $\vee$, $\Longrightarrow$ and the unary temporal operators POT and INEV. The abbreviations ALL(f) and SOME(f) are used for respectively $\neg$POT($\neg$f) and $\neg$INEV($\neg$f).

The formulas of L represent assertions about the functioning of a given system if we consider that propositional variables represent predicates on its state and give a precise meaning to the operators POT and INEV. In order to do this, we consider transition systems as a model for L since IPN's can be given a semantics in terms of them [Keller 76].

A transition system is defined as a doublet $S = (Q,\rightarrow)$ where Q is a set of states and $\rightarrow$ is a binary relation on Q ($\rightarrow\subseteq Q\times Q$). The relation $\rightarrow$ represents the actions or transitions of the system : $q\rightarrow q'$ means that there is an action executable from q which after its execution leads to a state q'. An execution sequence from a given state q_0 is a sequence s of states such that if s is finite then its last element q_t is a sink state (i.e. $\nexists q''(q_t\rightarrow q'')$). In order to simplify the notations we take s(k) to be equal to the k-th element of s if it is defined ; if not, we take $s(k)=\omega$ where ω represents some ficticious non accessible state adjoined to Q such that $\nexists q\in Q(q\rightarrow\omega)$. Thus, relation $s(0) \xrightarrow{k} s(k)$ is satisfied iff $s(k)\neq\omega$. The set of all the execution sequences from a state q will be denoted by EXq.

Given L and a transition system $S=(Q,\rightarrow)$ we define an interpretation of L as a function $|\;|$ associating to each formula of L a truth-valued function of the system state in the following manner :

- $\forall f\in F \quad |f| \in [Q\rightarrow\{tt,ff\}]$ where $[Q\rightarrow\{tt,ff\}]$ is the set of the unary predicates on Q
- $\forall q\in Q \quad |\underline{true}|\ (q) = tt$
- $\forall f\in L \quad |\neg f|(q) = tt$ iff $|f|\ (q) = ff$
- $\forall f_1,f_2\in L \quad |f_1\wedge f_2|(q) = tt$ iff $|f_1|\ (q) = tt$ and $|f_2|\ (q) = tt$
- $\forall f\in L \quad |POT(f)|(q) \equiv \exists s\in EXq\ \exists k\in\mathbb{N}\ [q \xrightarrow{k} s(k)$ and $|f|\ (s(k))]$
- $\forall f\in L \quad |INEV(f)|(q) \equiv \forall s\in EXq\ \exists k\in\mathbb{N}\ [q \xrightarrow{k} s(k)$ and $|f|\ (s(k))]$

Obviously, $|POT(f)|$ represents the set of the states q of S such that there exists an execution sequence starting from q containing a state satisfying $|f|$. We say that $|POT(f)|$ is the set of the states from which some state of $|f|$ is potentially reachable. In the same way, $|INEV(f)|$ is the set of the states from which $|f|$ is inevitably reachable in the sense that every execution sequence starting from a state of this set contains a state satisfying $|f|$.

The interpretation of the dual operators ALL and SOME is,

$$|ALL(f)|(q) \equiv \forall s \in EXq\ \forall k \in \mathbb{N}\ [q \overset{k}{\to} s(k)\ \underline{\text{implies}}\ |f|\ (s(k))]$$

$$|SOME(f)|(q) \equiv \exists s \in EXq\ \forall k \in \mathbb{N} [q \overset{k}{\to} s(k)\ \underline{\text{implies}}\ |f|\ (s(k))]$$

Remark that if the state q of a transition system satisfies |ALL(f)| then all the states of all the execution sequences from q verify |f|. Also, if a state q satisfies |SOME(f)| then there exists some execution sequence from q such that all its states verify |f|.

The properties of a branching time logic similar to L have been studied in [Ben-Ari 81] where a decision procedure and a complete deduction system are given.

3.2 Example

In this section we give examples illustrating the use of the specification language for expressing system properties. The formulas of this languages are constructed from the following set of propositional variables :

- propositional variables representing predicates on the variables of the description program (only program variables of specified types are considered),
- the propositional variable Init which characterizes the set of all the possible initial (control and data) states,
- propositional variables on the control of the system referring to names of actions (labels) defined in the description program ; for each labelled action a, the propositional variables enable a and after a are introduced such that |enable a| and |after a| characterize respectively the set of the states from which this action can be executed and the set of the states reached just after the termination of this action. The following abbreviations are used :

  . enable $(a_1,\ldots,a_k) = \bigvee_{i=1}^{k}$ enable a_i, where $\{a_1,\ldots,a_k\}$ is a set of actions,

  . enable P = enable A(P) where P is a process the set of the actions of which is A(P),

  . after $(a_1,\ldots,a_k) = \bigvee_{i=1}^{k}$ after a_i, where $\{a_1,\ldots,a_k\}$ is a set of actions.

Obviously, a large number of properties can be formulated concerning the behaviour of a system. For methodological reasons, it is interesting to classify the most important of them as this has already been done for linear time logic in [Gabbay 80] [Lamport 80] and [Manna 81]. Hereafter we introduce three families of properties and give specifications of the AB-protocol in terms of them.

Invariant properties

Invariant properties express the fact that a predicate P, constructed by using only logical operators, is always true.

They are formulas of the type : Init ⟹ ALL(P)

In the case of the AB-protocol such formulas can be used to express :

* Init ==> ALL(after(send,repeat) ==> (M.B=Y))

  i.e. after the emission of a message the value of the control bit emitted M.B is equal to the control bit Y of the SENDER.

* Init ==> ALL(after receive ==> (MM=M))

  i.e. after the reception of a message the value of the received message MM is equal to the value of the emitted message M, i.e. the line does not modify the transmitted information.

* Init ==> ALL(after receive ==> (MM.B=Y))

  i.e. after reception of a message the value of the received control bit MM.B is equal to the value of the control bit of the SENDER at the same time.

Liveness properties

These properties express the fact that an action can always be executed.

- Liveness of an action a : from every state q, successor of a state satisfying Init, there exists an execution sequence of EXq containing a state which enables a. This is expressed by the formula : Init ==> ALL POT enable a
- Liveness of a set of actions $\{a_1,\ldots,a_k\}$: each one of the actions a_i is live. This can be expressed by the formula : Init ==> $\bigwedge_{i=1}^{k}$(ALL POT enable a_i).

Or, by distributivity of ALL with respect to $\wedge$: Init ==> ALL($\bigwedge_{i=1}^{k}$ POT enable a_i).

- Absence of deadlock for a set of actions $\{a_1,\ldots,a_k\}$: from every state q, successor of a state satisfying Init, there exists an execution sequence of EXq which contains a state enabling at least one of the actions a_i. This is expressed by : Init ==> ALL POT enable $(a_1,\ldots,a_k)$.

Some interesting liveness properties of the given example are (starting from the weakest ones) :

* Init ==> ALL POT enable (SENDER), i.e. absence of deadlock for the SENDER
* Init ==> ALL POT enable (RECEIVER), i.e. absence of deadlock for the RECEIVER
* Init ==> ALL POT enable send, i.e. the action of emitting a new message is live
* Init ==> ALL POT enable accept, i.e. the action of receiving a new message is live.

Properties of response to an action

They are properties expressing the fact that an action b is a consequence of an action a.

- Possible response : if an action a is executed then it is possible that an action b becomes executable. This is expressed by the formula :

  Init ==> ALL(after a ==> POT enable b)

- Inevitably possible response : if an action a is executed then necessarily b becomes executable. This is expressed by the formula :

  Init ==> ALL(after a ==> INEV enable b)

Some interesting properties of this family for the given example are :

* Init ==> ALL (after (send,repeat) ==> POT enable receive)

  i.e. the line from the SENDER to the RECEIVER is able to transmit messages.
* Init ==> ALL (after(sendack,repeatack) ==> POT enable receivack)

  i.e. the line from the RECEIVER to the SENDER is able to transmit acknowledgements.
* Init ==> ALL(after(send,repeat) ==> INEV enable receivack)

  i.e. after sending a message the SENDER waits for an acknowledgement.
* Init ==> ALL[(after accept ==> INEV(enable sendack)) $\wedge$

  (after sendack ==> AA.B=MM.B)]

  i.e. when the RECEIVER receives a new message, it will send the corresponding acknowledgement.

4. PROVING SPECIFICATIONS IN CESAR

4.1. The results used by the analyser

In this paragraph we present the basic theoretical results used by the analyser. The method consists in iteratively computing fixed points of predicate transformers obtained from the IPN under study. Fixed points are precisely the interpretations of temporal operators as it is shown by the following results proved in detail in [Sifakis 79].

Let $S = (Q,\rightarrow)$ be a transition system. It is convenient to identify any unary predicate on Q with its characteristic set. $(2^Q,\cup,\cap,\,^-)$ represents the lattice of predicates and $[2^Q \rightarrow 2^Q]$ the set of the internal mappings of 2^Q (predicate transformers). For $f,g\in[2^Q \rightarrow 2^Q]$, $f\cup g$, $f\cap g$, $\bar{f}$, $\tilde{f}$ and Id denote the functions $f\cup g = \lambda P.\ f(P)\cup g(P)$, $f\cap g = \lambda P.\ f(P)\cap g(P)$, $\bar{f} = \lambda P.\ \overline{f(P)}$, $\tilde{f} = \lambda P.\ \bar{f}(\bar{P})$, $Id = \lambda P.\ P$.

We also introduce the notations :

$$f^* = Id\cup f\cup f^2\cup\ldots f^k\cup\ldots = \bigcup_{i\in\mathbb{N}} f^i$$

$$f^x = Id\cap f\cap f^2\cap\ldots f^k\cap\ldots = \bigcap_{i\in\mathbb{N}} f^i$$

Definition 1 : Given $S = (Q,\rightarrow)$ a transition system, $P\in 2^Q$ and $q\in Q$, we define the predicate transformer pre : pre $P(q) \equiv \exists q'(q\rightarrow q'$ and $P(q'))$.

Proposition 1 :

Let f be a formula of L, $S = (Q,\rightarrow)$ a transition system such that $\rightarrow$ be image-finite and $|\,|$ an interpretation of L in S.

a) $|ALL(f)| = \widetilde{pre}^x|f|$

b) $|SOME(f)| = (Id\cap(pre\cup\widetilde{pre}))^x|f|$

Proposition 2 :

Let f be a formula of L, $S = (Q,\rightarrow)$ a transition system such that $\rightarrow$ be image-finite and $|\,|$ an interpretation of L in S.

a) $|POT(f)| = pre^*|f|$

b) $|INEV(f)| = (Id \cup pre\cap\widetilde{pre})^* \; |f|$

4.2 The principle of the verification method

According to the results of the preceding section, it is possible to compute iteratively the interpretation of the temporal operators. We present hereafter the principle of the verification method applied by the analyzer :

Let f be a formula to be verified on a given program PROG and N the IPN obtained by translation from PROG. Denote by $F = \{f_1,\dots,f_n\}$ the set of the propositional variables occuring in f.

- Associate a boolean variable with each place of N.
- For each after $a \in F$, express $|$after a$|$ as a predicate on these variables (if necessary, N is transformed by adding new places).
- For each enable $a \in F$, express $|$enable a$|$ as a predicate on the boolean control variables and program variables.
- Express Init as a predicate representing the set of all possible initial states (knowing the initial marking of the net and the initial values of program variables).
- Reduce N without transforming the places which are involved in the expression of the predicates of $|F| = \{|f_1|,\dots,|f_n|\}$. Reducing N consists in applying transformation rules preserving the property expressed by f in order to obtain an IPN of less complexity.
- Compute the predicate transformer pre associated to the reduced IPN and then, the interpretation of temporal operators following the evaluation order imposed by the formula f. During these computations simplification rules are applied, taking advantage of the fact that sequential processes correspond to state graphs. Given that there is no criterion on the speed of the convergence of these iterations, the user can impose a maximum number of iterations.
- If some iterative computation yields no result within the acceptable number of iterations then the analyzer fails to give an answer. If not, it evaluates $|f|$: the property described by f is verified iff $|f|\,(q) = tt$ for every state q.

4.3 Example

For the AB-protocol, the liveness property Init ==> ALL POT enable (SENDER) is verified by computing successively :

1) Init $= s_1 m_1 a_1 r_1 \overline{y} z$. Intersection operators are omitted. The boolean variables s_i, m_i, a_i, r_i, represent the fact that the places with the same name have a token (see figure 2).

2) enable(SENDER) $= s_1 m_1 \cup s_2 m_1 \cup s_2 a_2 \cup s_3$

3) the interpretation of POT enable (SENDER) as the limit of : $P_{k+1} = P_k \cup pre(P_k)$ with

P_0 = enable (SENDER).

The following relations are invariants generated by the translator expressing the fact that each process is a safe state graph and they are used to simplify the boolean expressions computed by the analyzer :

$s_1\bar{s}_2\bar{s}_3 \cup \bar{s}_1 s_2 \bar{s}_3 \cup \bar{s}_1 \bar{s}_2 s_3 = \top$ ($\top$ is the always true predicate)

$r_1\bar{r}_2\bar{r}_3 \cup \bar{r}_1 r_2 \bar{r}_3 \cup \bar{r}_1 \bar{r}_2 r_3 = \top$

$m_1\bar{m}_2 \cup \bar{m}_1 m_2 = \top$

$a_1\bar{a}_2 \cup \bar{a}_1 a_2 = \top$

The first step of the computation gives, $pre(P_0) = s_3 \cup r_2 \cup r_3 \cup a_2 \cup m_2$. Thus,

$P_1 = P_0 \cup pre(P_0) = \top$ and POT enable (SENDER) = $\top$.

) ALL POT enable (SENDER) = $\top$

) [Init ==> ALL POT enable (SENDER)] = $\top$ (the property is verified).

. CONCLUSION

We have tried to illustrate with an example, the AB-protocol, the analysis method applied in CESAR.

This method is based on the idea of translating the description of a system, given in some high-level formalism, into a model for which there exists a verification theory. This approach presents the advantage, on the one hand of abstracting from all the details which are not relevant to the verification of the behaviour (for example, data represented by variables of non-specified types), on the other hand, of displaying the control structure (invariants, for instance). In particular, the translation into a Petri net gives the possibility of naming control points which makes the expression of the properties easier.

The language of the formulas allows the expression of a great number of foundamental properties (invariant properties, liveness properties, properties of response to an action). The use of such a language is interesting from a methodological point of view as it provides the possibility of classification and comparison of the properties according to various criteria. Also, the representation of properties by formulas using temporal operators leads to mechanizable proofs provided that a method for obtaining from a given description the associated predicate transformer pre be given. Computing fixed points of monotonic functions is, from a practical point of view, a central problem and it determines the limitations of our approach. Appart from the limitations of theoretical nature (non-decidability of the "interesting" system properties) serious problems appear when applying iterative methods which require the manipulation, simplification and comparison of predicates on many variables. For this reason, the current version of CESAR can verify formulas with variables of type boolean, enumerated and integer with known bounds, only.In order to simplify computations, the analyzer

encodes the enumerated and bounded integer variables so that it manipulates only boolean variables ; this coding is completely transparent to the user.
However, in spite of these simplifications the problems due to the complexity of the analyzed system remain crucial. We intend to increase the efficiency of the applied method by working in the following directions :

- Use of methods for approximating fixed points of monotonic operators in a lattice [Cousot 78] [Clarke 80],
- Reduction of the complexity of the iterative computations by decomposing global assertions into a set of local assertions,
- Study of a methodology of description since the possibility of proving a property greatly depends on the way the description is built.

REFERENCES

[Bartlett 69] K.A. BARTLETT, R.A. SCANTLEBURY and P.T. WILKINSON "A note on reliable full-duplex transmission over half-duplex links" CACM, Vol. 12, N°5, May 1969, pp. 260-261.

[Ben-Ari 81] M. BEN-ARI, Z. MANNA and A. PNUELI "The temporal logic of branching time" Proc. 8th Annual ACM Symp. on Principles of Programming Languages, Jan. 1981, pp. 164-176.

[Bremer 79] J. BREMER and O. DROBNIK "A new approach to protocol design and validation" IBM research report RC 8018, IBM Yorktown Heights, Dec. 1979

[Brinch Hansen 78] P. BRINCH HANSEN "Distributed Processes : A concurrent programming concept" CACM, Vol. 21, N°5, Nov. 1978, pp. 934-941.

[Clarke 80] E.M. CLARKE Jr. "Synthesis of resource invariants for concurrent programs" ACM Trans. on Progr. Languages and Systems, Vol. 2, N°3, July 1980, pp. 338-358.

[Cousot 78] P. COUSOT and N. HALBWACHS "Automatic discovery of linear restraints among variables of a program" Proc. 5th ACM. Symp. on Principles of Programming Languages, Tucson, Ariz., 1978, pp. 84-96.

[Gabbay 80] D. GABBAY, A. PNUELLI, S. SHELAH and J. STAVI "On the temporal analysis of fairness" Conference Record of the 7th Annual ACM Symposium on Principles of Programming Languages, Jan. 1980, pp. 163-173.

[Hoare 78] C.A.R. HOARE "Communicating Sequential Processes" Comm. ACM 21-8, August 1978, pp. 666-667.

[Jensen 79] K. JENSEN, M. KYNG and O.L. MADSEN "A Petri net definition of a system description language" Semantics of Concurrent Computation in LNCS, Springer Verlag, July 1979, pp. 348-368.

[Keller 76] R.M. KELLER "Formal verification of parallel programs" Comm. ACM 19, 7 (July 1976), pp. 371-384.

[Lamport 80] L. LAMPORT ""Sometime" is sometimes "not never" - On the temporal logic of programs" Proc. of the 7th Annual ACM Symp. on Principles of Programming Languages, Las Vegas, Janv. 1980, pp. 174-185.

[Lauer 75] P.E. LAUER and R.H. CAMPBELL "Formal semantics of a class of high level primitives for coordinating concurrent processes" Acta Informatica 5, pp. 297-332 (1975).

[Manna 81] Z. MANNA and A. PNUELI "Verification of concurrent programs : The temporal framework" Intern. Summer School, Theoretical Foundations of Programming Methodology, Munich, July 1981.

[Queille 81] J.P. QUEILLE "The CESAR system : An aided design and certification system for distributed applications" Proc. 2nd Int. Conf. on Distributed Computing Systems, April 1981, pp. 149-161.

[Rescher 71] N. RESCHER and A. URQUHART "Temporal Logic" Springer Verlag, Vienna, 1971.

[Schwartz 81] R.L. SCHWARTZ and P.M. MELLIAR-SMITH "Temporal logic specification of distributed systems" Proc. 2nd Int. Conf. on Distributed Computing Systems, April 1981, pp. 46-454.

[Sifakis 79] J. SIFAKIS "A unified approach for studying the properties of transition systems" Research Report RR N° 179, IMAG December 1979 (Revised December 1980), to appear in TCS January 1982.

[SIGPN 81] Special Interest Group : Petri nets and related system models. Newsletter N° 7, Feb. 1981, p-. 17-20.

Proof of Separability

A Verification Technique for a Class of Security Kernels

J.M. Rushby

Computing Laboratory
University of Newcastle upon Tyne
Newcastle upon Tyne NE1 7RU
England

ABSTRACT

A formal model of `secure isolation´ between the users of a shared computer system is presented. It is then developed into a security verification technique called `Proof of Separability´ whose basis is to prove that the behaviour perceived by each user of the shared system is indistinguishable from that which could be provided by an unshared machine dedicated to his private use.

Proof of Separability is suitable for the verification of security kernels which enforce the policy of isolation; it explicitly addresses issues relating to the interpretation of instructions and the flow of control (including interrupts) which have been ignored by previous treatments.

INTRODUCTION

Systems with stringent security requirements such as KSOS [5], KVM/370 [11], and the various `Guards´ [12, 22] are amongst the very first computer systems to be produced under commercial contracts that require formal specification and verification of certain aspects of their behaviour. However, doubts have been expressed concerning whether the techniques used to verify these systems really do provide compelling evidence for their security [1, 19, 20]. The purpose of this paper is to develop and justify a new and, it is argued, more appropriate technique for verifying one class of secure systems.

A **secure** system is one which enforces certain restrictions on access to the information which it contains, and on the communication of information between its users. A precise statement of the restrictions to be enforced by a particular system constitutes its **security policy**. Secure systems are needed by the military authorities and by other agencies and institutions which process information of great sensitivity or value. In these environments, it is possible that attempts will be made to gain unauthorized access to valuable information by penetrating the defences of any computer system that processes it. It must be assumed that these attacks may be mounted by skilled and determined users with legitimate access to the system, or even by those involved in its design and implementation. Experience has shown that conventional operating systems cannot withstand this kind of attack, nor can they be modified to do so [2, 3, 13, 15, 21].

Accordingly, attention has now turned to the construction of **kernelized** systems: the idea is to isolate all (and only) the functions which are essential to the security of the system within a **security kernel**. If the kernel is `correct´ in some appropriate sense, then the security of the whole system is assured. The enthusiasm for this approach is due to the fact that a security kernel can be quite a small component of the total system (it is essentially an operating system nucleus) and there is, in consequence, some hope of getting it right. But since the security of the whole edifice rests on this one component, it is absolutely vital that it is right. Compelling evidence is therefore required to attest to the security provided by a kernel. **Verification**, that is a formal mathematical proof that the kernel conforms to an appropriate and precise specification of `secure behaviour´, is the evidence generally considered to be most convincing [17].

Two main approaches have been proposed for the verification of security kernels. These are **access control verification** [18] and **information flow analysis** [8, 16]. The first of these is concerned to prove that all accesses by users to the stored representations of information are in accord with the security policy. For military systems, however, it is not sufficient merely to be sure that users cannot directly access information to which they are not authorized; it is necessary to be sure that information cannot be leaked to unauthorized users by any means whatsoever.

This is the **confinement problem**. It was first identified by Lampson [14] who enumerated three kinds of channel that can be used to leak information within a system. **Storage channels** are those that exploit system storage such as temporary files and state variables, while **Legitimate channels** involve `piggybacking´ illicit information onto a legal information channel - by modulating message length, for example. The third type of channel is the **covert** one (also called a **timing channel**) which achieves communication by modulating aspects of the system´s performance (for example, its paging rate). Unlike access control verification, information flow analysis can establish the absence of storage and legitimate channels and for this reason it has been the verification technique preferred for certain military systems [9].

Although the properties established by access control verification and by information flow analysis are undoubtedly important ones, it is not clear that they amount to a complete guarantee of security. Both these verification techniques are applied to system descriptions from which certain `low level´ aspects of system behaviour have been abstracted away. Thus autonomous input/output devices - which can modify the system state asynchronously with program execution and which, by raising interrupts, can drastically change the protection state and the sequence of program execution - are absent from the system descriptions whose security is verified by these methods. This is despite the fact that penetration exercises indicate that it is precisely in their handling of these low level details that many computer systems are most vulnerable to attack - and, consequently, that these are the areas where verification of appropriate behaviour is to be most desired.

In a companion paper to this [19], I have distinguished between high and low level considerations in secure system design and have proposed that different mechanisms and verification techniques should be employed for each level.

At the high level, the system should be conceived as a distributed one where the significant issues are those of controlling access to information and the communication of information between conceptually separate single-user machines. The fact that all users actually happen to share the same physical machine should be masked at this level. It is precisely the task of the low level security mechanism to perform this masking and I have proposed a primitive type of kernel called a **separation kernel** to serve this purpose. Its function is to simulate the distributed environment assumed at the higher level of conceptualization. To this end it provides each system component with a **regime** (or `virtual machine´) whose behaviour is indistinguishable from that of a private machine dedicated to that component alone.

The fundamental property to be proved of a separation kernel is that it completely isolates its regimes from one another: there must be absolutely no flow of information from one regime to another. (In practice, controlled flow of information will be required between certain regimes. I will return to this point in the final section of this paper, but for the present I want to concentrate on the simplest case.)

For the reasons outlined earlier, neither of the established methods of security verification is adequate to the task of verifying a separation kernel: we really need a new method. The technique which I propose is a very natural one that is in accord with the intuition underlying the notion of a separation kernel. It is to prove that the system behaves as if it were composed of several totally separate machines - hence the name of this verification technique: `Proof of Separability´.

Although `separability´ is a straightforward notion, its formal definition in terms of a realistic system model is fairly complicated. Possibly, therefore, its own definition may contain errors. The primary purpose of this paper is to convince the reader that this is not the case and that the definition given at the end of this paper is correct. My tactic will be to start off with a specification of `secure isolation´ for a very simple system model and then to elaborate it until I arrive at the definition of Proof of Separability.

THE SPECIFICATION OF SECURE ISOLATION

To begin, we need some formal model of a `computer system´. In developing a verification technique based on information flow analysis, Feiertag and his co-workers used a conventional finite automaton for this purpose [7]. At each step, the automaton consumes an input token and changes its internal state in a manner determined by its previous state and by the value of the input token consumed. At the same time, it also emits an output token whose value is determined similarly. Each input and each output token is tagged with its security classification and the specification of security (for the case of isolation) is that the production of outputs of each classification may depend only on the consumption of inputs of that same classification.

While this is an appropriate model for a computer system viewed at a fairly high level of abstraction, it is less realistic as a model for a security kernel. A kernel is essentially an <u>interpreter</u> - it acts as a hardware extension and executes operations on behalf of the regimes which it supports. The identity of the regime on whose behalf it is operating at each instant is not indicated by a tag affixed to the operation by some external agent, but is determined by the kernel´s own state. Furthermore, this model does not capture the instruction sequencing mechanisms that seem, intuitively, to be of vital importance to the security of a kernel. Accordingly, I shall adopt a slightly different model. I shall suppose that a system comprises a set S of states and progresses from one state to another under its own internal control. The transition from one state to the next will be determined by a NEXTSTATE function solely on the basis of the current state: if s is the current state, then its successor will be NEXTSTATE(s).

Not only must a system have some means of making progress (modelled here by the NEXTSTATE function) but, in order to be interesting, it must interact with its environment in some way: it must consume inputs and produce outputs. For outputs, I shall suppose that certain aspects of the system's internal state are made continually visible to the outside world through a 'window' - modelled here by an OUTPUT function: OUTPUT(s) is the visible aspect of state s. Real-world interpretations of this 'window' are provided by the device registers of a PDP-11, for example.

In contrast to outputs, which are continuously available, I shall suppose, initially, that inputs are presented to the system just once, right at the start. The INPUT function takes an input value, say i, as its argument and returns a system state as its result. The system, once given this externally determined initial state, thereafter proceeds from state to state under its own internal control. Because INPUT(i) is the initial state of the system, the value of i may be considered to comprise, not merely an input in the conventional sense, but also the 'program' which determines the system's subsequent behaviour. The idea that all the input should be presented at one go is clearly artificial since it precludes genuine interaction between the system and its environment. Accordingly, I will extend the model later in order to overcome this objection - but readers should be aware that this extension causes something of a hiatus in the development.

Collecting the burden of the previous discussion together, and proceeding more formally, we may now say that a system or <u>machine</u> M is a 6-tuple

M = (S, I, O, NEXTSTATE, INPUT, OUTPUT)

where:

S is a finite, non-empty set of <u>states</u>,

I is a finite, non-empty set of <u>inputs</u>,

O is a finite, non-empty set of <u>outputs</u>, and

NEXTSTATE: $S \rightarrow S$,

INPUT: $I \rightarrow S$ and

OUTPUT: $S \rightarrow O$ are total functions. (The reason for assuming <u>total</u> functions will be explained later.)

The <u>computation</u> invoked by an input $i \in I$ is the infinite sequence

$$\text{COMPUTATION}(i) = \langle s_0, s_1, s_2, \ldots, s_n, \ldots \rangle$$

where $s_0 = \text{INPUT}(i)$ and $s_{j+1} = \text{NEXTSTATE}(s_j)$, $\forall\ j \geq 0$.

The result of a computation is simply the sequence of outputs visible to an observer, that is:

$$\text{RESULT}(i) = \langle \text{OUTPUT}(s_0), \text{OUTPUT}(s_1), \ldots, \text{OUTPUT}(s_n), \ldots \rangle. \quad (1)$$

As a notational convenience, I shall allow functions to take sequences as their arguments; the interpretation is that the function is to be applied pointwise to each element of the sequence. Thus, we may rewrite (1) as

$$\text{RESULT}(i) = \text{OUTPUT}(\text{COMPUTATION}(i)).$$

Now, in order to be able to discuss security, we must assume that our machine is shared by more than one user (or else there is no problem to discuss). I shall identify users with the members of a set $C = \{1,2, \ldots, m\}$ of `colours'. Each user must be able to make his own, personal, contribution to the machine's input and be able to observe some part of the output that is private to himself. We can model this formally by supposing that both the sets I and O (of inputs and outputs) are Cartesian products of C-indexed families of sets. That is:

$$I = I^1 \times I^2 \times \ldots \times I^m \quad \text{and} \quad O = O^1 \times O^2 \times \ldots \times O^m.$$

A machine whose input and output sets are of this form will be said to be C-shared. Notice that the components of these products are distinguished by superscripted elements of C. I shall use superscripts consistently for this purpose; subscripts, on the other hand, will be used exclusively to identify the components of sequences.

It is convenient to introduce a projection function, called EXTRACT, to pick out the individual components of members of Cartesian products of C-indexed sets. Thus, when $c \in C$, $i \in I$, and $o \in O$, EXTRACT(c,i) and EXTRACT(c,o) denote the c-coloured components of the input i and the output o, respectively. When a C-shared machine operates on an input $i \in I$, each user sees only his own component of the result. By the convention introduced previously, EXTRACT can be applied to sequences as well as to individuals and so the component of the output visible to user $c \in C$ is the sequence EXTRACT(c,RESULT(i)).

Now the simplest and most natural definition of secure isolation is surely that the results seen by each user should depend only on his own contribution to the input. Thus, we require,

$\forall c \in C, \forall i,j \in I:$

$$\text{EXTRACT}(c,i) = \text{EXTRACT}(c,j) \Rightarrow \text{EXTRACT}(c,\text{RESULT}(i)) = \text{EXTRACT}(c,\text{RESULT}(j)). \quad (2)$$

Further consideration, however, indicates that this requirement is too strong for our purposes. The real systems, whose salient characteristics we are trying to capture in these definitions, work in a `time-sharing' fashion. That is, they first perform a few operations on behalf of one user, then a few more on behalf of another and so on. While the system is operating on behalf of other users, user c should see no change in the outputs visible to him, but the length of time which he must wait before processing resumes on his behalf may well depend upon the activity of those other users. If user c' can influence the rate at which user c is serviced, and user c can sense his rate of service, then a communication channel exists between c' and

c. This is one of Lampson's 'covert channels' and while these channels constitute a security flaw and should be countered, their complete exclusion is beyond the scope of simple security kernel technology. Covert channels are typically noisy and of low bandwidth and are normally countered by ad-hoc techniques intended to increase noise and lower bandwidth still further. The threat which I want to completely exclude is that of storage channels and the trouble with (2) as a definition of security is that it requires the absence of covert as well as storage channels. There is little point in demanding the absence of covert channels when this cannot be achieved by the techniques under consideration. We should therefore weaken (2) so that only storage channels are forbidden and this can be done by restricting attention to the sequences of <u>changes</u> in the values of the outputs, rather than the output sequences themselves. To this end, I shall introduce a CONDENSE function on sequences. The CONDENSEd version of a sequence is just the sequence with every subsequence of repeated values replaced by a single copy of that value. For example:

CONDENSE(<1,1,2,2,2,3,4,4,3,3,6,6,6>) = <1,2,3,4,3,6>.

I shall give a precise definition of CONDENSE shortly but first I want to press on with the definition of security. Using CONDENSE, the revised definition of secure isolation, suggested above, becomes:

$$\forall c \in C, \forall i,j \in I,$$

$$\text{EXTRACT}(c,i) = \text{EXTRACT}(c,j) \Rightarrow \text{CONDENSE}(\text{EXTRACT}(c,\text{RESULT}(i))) = \text{CONDENSE}(\text{EXTRACT}(c,\text{RESULT}(j))). \quad (3)$$

Unfortunately, this definition is still too strong for our purposes. Suppose that certain inputs cause one of the users to crash the machine, or to loop endlessly when he gets control. This constitutes a type of security breach called 'denial of service'. Definition (3) requires the absence of such breaches. Like covert channels, denial of service should be excluded from a secure system - but, again like covert channels, the control of this type of security flaw is beyond the scope of the mechanisms being investigated here, for it concerns the fairness of scheduling procedures and the guaranteed termination of processes. Notice, however, that no attempt to defeat denial of service threats will succeed if any of the basic machine operations can fail to terminate. It is for this reason that I have required all the functions that comprise my machine definitions to be <u>total</u>. Clearly, this requirement must be verified during any practical application of techniques derived from these definitions. Cristian [6] discusses these issues in a wider context.

We can weaken the definition given by (3) so that it admits denial of service while still excluding storage channels if we require only that the condensed results should be equal <u>as far as they go</u>: we don't mind if one of them stops while the other carries on, so long as they are equal while they both survive. I shall, therefore, define a weaker form of equivalence on sequences, denoted by $\cong$, and defined by:

X $\cong$ Y if and only if either X = Y or the shorter of X and Y is an initial subsequence of the other.

My final definition of security is then:

$\forall c \in C, \forall i,j \in I,$

$$\text{EXTRACT}(c,i) = \text{EXTRACT}(c,j) \rightarrow$$
$$\text{CONDENSE}(\text{EXTRACT}(c,\text{RESULT}(i))) = \text{CONDENSE}(\text{EXTRACT}(c,\text{RESULT}(j))). \quad (4)$$

Given that we can accept (4) as a precise specification of secure isolation, our task now is to derive a series of testable conditions that are sufficient to ensure this property.

THE VERIFICATION OF SECURE ISOLATION

Before embarking on the main development, we need a precise definition of the CONDENSE function.

Let $X = \langle x_0, x_1, x_2, \ldots \rangle$, be a sequence (either finite or infinite) and let INDICES(X) denote the set of indices appearing in X.

Now define the total function f: INDICES(X) $\rightarrow \mathbb{N}$ by

$f(0) = 0$, and, for $j \geq 0$

$$f(j+1) = \begin{cases} f(j) & \text{if } x_{j+1} = x_j \\ f(j)+1 & \text{otherwise.} \end{cases}$$

$f(j)$ is the number of changes of value in the sequence X, prior to x_j; it is called the <u>condenser function</u> for X.

Let $\bar{f}$ be a right inverse for f. That is, any function such that $f(\bar{f}(j)) = j$, $\forall j$ in the range of f. (At least one such $\bar{f}$ exists - $\bar{f}(j)$ is the index of an element of X that is preceded by j changes of value.) Then define CONDENSE(X) to be the sequence:

$$\text{CONDENSE}(X) = \langle x_{\bar{f}(0)}, x_{\bar{f}(1)}, \ldots \rangle$$

Notice that this sequence is independent of the choice of $\bar{f}$.

We shall need the following result concerning condensed sequences. Its proof is elementary and is omitted.

Lemma 1

Let $X = \langle x_0, x_1, x_2, \ldots \rangle$ and $Y = \langle y_0, y_1, y_2, \ldots \rangle$

be sequences (each either finite or infinite) and let

$$f: \mathrm{INDICES}(X) \rightarrow \mathrm{INDICES}(Y)$$

be a total function such that

$f(0) = 0$ and $\forall\, j \geq 0\ x_j = y_{f(j)}$ and

either $f(j+1) = f(j)$

or $\quad f(j+1) = f(j)+1.$

Then CONDENSE(X) $\cong$ CONDENSE(Y). □

(Intuitively, this states that if Y is a 'slightly' condensed version of X, then X and Y both condense to the same value.)

We now return to the main thread of the argument. Given that we accept (4) as a definition of security, how might we establish the presence of this property? Essentially, (4) stipulates that each user of a C-shared machine must be unaware of the activity, or even the existence, of any other user: it must appear to him that he has the machine to himself. It is a natural and attractive idea, then, to postulate a 'private' machine which he does have to himself and to establish (4) by proving that user c is unable to distinguish the behaviour of the C-shared machine from that which could be provided by a private machine. I shall now make these ideas precise.

Let M = (S, I, O, NEXTSTATE, INPUT, OUTPUT) be C-shared machine where

$$I = I^1 \times I^2 \times \ldots \times I^n \quad \text{and} \quad O = O^1 \times O^2 \times \ldots \times O^n,$$

and let $c \in C$. A private machine for $c \in C$ is one with input set I^c and output set O^c, say

$$M^c = (S^c, I^c, O^c, \mathrm{NEXTSTATE}^c, \mathrm{INPUT}^c, \mathrm{OUTPUT}^c).$$

Denote the computation and result functions of M^c by $\mathrm{COMPUTATION}^c$ and RESULT^c, respectively. Then M^c is an M-compatible private machine for c if:

$\forall\, i \in I,$

$$\mathrm{CONDENSE}(\mathrm{EXTRACT}(c,\mathrm{RESULT}(i))) \cong \mathrm{CONDENSE}(\mathrm{RESULT}^c(\mathrm{EXTRACT}(c,i))) \qquad (5)$$

That is (roughly speaking), the result obtained when an M-compatible private machine is applied to the c-component of a C-shared input must equal the c-component of the result produced by the C-shared machine M applied to the whole input.

Obviously, we have:

Theorem 1

A C-shared machine M is secure, if for each $c \in C$, there exists an M-compatible private machine for c.

Proof Immediate from (4) and (5). □

Let us now consider how we might prove that a given private machine for c is M-compatible. Direct appeal to the definition (5) is unattractive since this involves a property of (possibly infinite) sequences and will almost certainly require a proof by induction. At the cost of restricting the class of machines that we are willing to consider, we can perform the induction once and for all at a meta-level and provide a more convenient set of properties that are sufficient to ensure M-compatibility.

The restriction on the class of machines considered is a perfectly natural one: I shall consider only those C-shared machines which `time share´ their activity between their different users. That is, each operation carried out by the the C-shared machine performs some service for just one user. In particular, it simulates one of the operations of that user´s private machine. The identity of the user being serviced at any instant is a function of the current state. Consequently I shall require a function COLOUR which takes a state as argument and returns the identity (colour) of the user being serviced (i.e. the user on whose behalf the next state transition is performed). I shall also require the notion of an `abstraction function´ between the states of a C-shared machine and those of a private one.

Theorem 2

Let M = (S, I, O, NEXTSTATE, INPUT, OUTPUT) be a C-shared machine and

COLOUR: $S \to C$ a total function.

Let $M^c = (S^c, I^c, O^c, NEXTSTATE^c, INPUT^c, OUTPUT^c)$ be a private machine for $c \in C$ and

$\phi^c: S \to S^c$ a total function such that $\forall s \in S, \forall i \in I$:

1) $COLOUR(s) = c \Rightarrow \phi^c(NEXTSTATE(s)) = NEXTSTATE^c(\phi^c(s))$,

2) $COLOUR(s) \neq c \Rightarrow \phi^c(NEXTSTATE(s)) = \phi^c(s)$,

3) $\phi^c(INPUT(i)) = INPUT^c(EXTRACT(c,i))$, and

4) $OUTPUT^c(\phi^c(s)) = EXTRACT(c,OUTPUT(s))$.

Then M^c is M-compatible.

Proof

For brevity, denote COMPUTATION(i) by P and COMPUTATION^c(EXTRACT(c,i)) by Q where

$$P = \langle p_0, p_1, p_2, \ldots \rangle \text{ and } Q = \langle q_0, q_1, q_2, \ldots \rangle.$$

Next, denote EXTRACT(c,RESULT(i)) by X and RESULT^c(EXTRACT(c,i)) by Y where

$$X = \langle x_0, x_1, x_2, \ldots \rangle \text{ and } Y = \langle y_0, y_1, y_2, \ldots \rangle.$$

By definition, x_j = EXTRACT(c,OUTPUT(p_j)), and

$$y_j = \text{OUTPUT}^c(q_j)$$

and we need to prove

$$\text{CONDENSE}(X) \cong \text{CONDENSE}(Y).$$

Define f: INDICES(P) $\rightarrow$ INDICES(Q) by

$$f(0) = 0, \text{ and } \forall j \geq 0$$

$$f(j+1) = \begin{cases} f(j) & \text{if COLOUR}(p_j) \neq c, \\ f(j)+1 & \text{if COLOUR}(p_j) = c. \end{cases}$$

By an elementary induction on j, it follows from parts 1), 2) and 3) of the statement of the theorem that

$$\Phi^c(p_j) = q_{f(j)}$$

and hence, by part 4) of the statement, that

$$\text{OUTPUT}^c(q_{f(j)}) = \text{EXTRACT}(c,\text{OUTPUT}(p_j)).$$

That is

$$y_{f(j)} = x_j.$$

Thus, f (regarded now as a function from INDICES(X) to INDICES(Y)) satisfies the premises of Lemma 1 and so we conclude

$$\text{CONDENSE}(X) \cong \text{CONDENSE}(Y)$$

and thereby the theorem. □

Let us take stock of our present position. We can prove that a C-shared machine M is secure by demonstrating the existence of an M-compatible private machine for each of its users. How might we demonstrate the existence of such M-compatible private machines? A highly `constructive´ approach would be to actually exhibit a private machine for each user and to prove its M-compatibility using Theorem 2. The conditions of Theorem 2 are straightforward and easily checked - it may even be possible to automate much of this checking. On the other hand, the `constructive´

aspect of the approach appears rather laborious: the construction of each private machine must be spelled out to the last detail.

A totally different approach would be a 'pure' existence proof. We could seek conditions on M which are sufficient to guarantee, à priori, the existence of M-compatible private machines - without ever needing to actually construct these machines at all. The problem here is to find a suitable set of conditions: conditions which can be easily checked without being overly restrictive on the class of machines that can be admitted. I doubt that these incompatible requirements can be reconciled in any single set of conditions and so conclude that the search for a 'pure' existence proof is not worthwhile.

Since both extreme positions (the fully constructive approach and the pure existence proof) have their drawbacks, it may prove fruitful to examine the middle ground. The idea will be to specify just the 'operations' of the private machine constructively and to constrain the behaviour of the C-shared machine so that we can guarantee that the construction of the private machine could be completed. To do this, we shall need to elaborate our model once more.

The machines we have considered until now, though very general, are rather unstructured. I now want to constrain them a little by adding more detail to the method by which a machine proceeds from one state to the next. At present, this happens as an indivisible step, modelled by the NEXTSTATE function. In any real machine, the process is more structured than this: first an 'operation' is selected by some 'control mechanism' and then it is 'executed' to yield the next state.

We can model this by supposing the machine M to be equipped with some set OPS of 'operations' where each operation is a total function on states. That is

$$OPS \subseteq S \rightarrow S.$$

Next we suppose the existence of a total function:

$$NEXTOP: S \rightarrow OPS$$

which corresponds to the 'control mechanism'. In each state s, NEXTOP(s) is the operation which is applied to s to yield the next state. Thus

$$NEXTSTATE(s) = NEXTOP(s)(s).$$

If machines are constrained to have this (more realistic) form, then the set OPS and the function NEXTOP may replace the monolithic NEXTSTATE function in their definition. We then have the following result (which guarantees the existence of a complete private machine, given a specification of only its operations and abstraction functions):

Theorem 3

Let M = (S, I, O, OPS, NEXTOP, INPUT, OUTPUT) be a (new style) C-shared machine and

COLOUR: $S \to C$ a total function.

Let $c \in C$ and suppose there exist sets

S^c of states, and

$OPS^c \subseteq S^c \to S^c$ of (total) operations on S^c

together with (total) abstraction functions:

$\phi^c: S \to S^c$ and

$ABOP^c: OPS \to OPS^c$,

which satisfy, $\forall c \in C, \forall s,s' \in S, \forall op \in OPS, \forall i,i' \in I$:

1) $COLOUR(s) = c \Rightarrow \phi^c(op(s)) = ABOP^c(op)(\phi^c(s))$,

2) $COLOUR(s) \neq c \Rightarrow \phi^c(op(s)) = \phi^c(s)$,

3) $EXTRACT(c,i) = EXTRACT(c,i') \Rightarrow \phi^c(INPUT(i)) = \phi^c(INPUT(i'))$,

4) $\phi^c(s) = \phi^c(s') \Rightarrow EXTRACT(c,OUTPUT(s)) = EXTRACT(c,OUTPUT(s'))$, and

5) $COLOUR(s) = COLOUR(s') = c$ and $\phi^c(s) = \phi^c(s') \Rightarrow NEXTOP(s) = NEXTOP(s')$.

Then there exists an M-compatible private machine for c.

Proof

Define the function $NEXTOP^c: S^c \to OPS^c$ by:

$NEXTOP^c(\phi^c(s)) = ABOP^c(NEXTOP(s)), \forall s \in S$ such that $COLOUR(s) = c$.

Condition 5) ensures that $NEXTOP^c$ is truly a (single-valued) function. If we define NEXTSTATE: $S \to S$ and $NEXTSTATE^c: S^c \to S^c$ by

$NEXTSTATE(s) = NEXTOP(s)(s) \; \forall s \in S$ and

$NEXTSTATE^c(t) = NEXTOP^c(t)(t) \; \forall t \in S^c$,

then conditions 1) and 2) above ensure these definitions satisfy conditions 1) and 2) of Theorem 2.

Next, define $INPUT^c: I^c \to S^c$ to be any total function which satisfies

$INPUT^c(EXTRACT(c,i)) = \phi^c(INPUT(i)), \forall i \in I$.

Condition 3) above ensures that such a function exists and that it satisfies condition 3) of Theorem 2.

Finally, define $OUTPUT^c: S^c \rightarrow O^c$ to be any total function satisfying

$$OUTPUT^c(\Phi^c(s)) = EXTRACT(c,OUTPUT(s)), \forall s \in S.$$

Condition 4) above ensures the existence of such a function and also that it satisfies condition 4) of Theorem 2.

We have now constructed a private machine

$$M^c = (S^c,I^c,O^c,NEXTSTATE^c,INPUT^c,OUTPUT^c)$$

which satisfies all the conditions of Theorem 2 and so conclude that M^c is M-compatible. □

We now need to make a final adjustment to the model. The present model accepts input only once and we really want something more realistic than this. Real I/O devices do not initialize the system state, they modify it (by loading values into device registers, or by raising interrupts, for example). It is natural, therefore, that the functionality of INPUT should be changed to:

$$INPUT: S \times I \rightarrow S.$$

We now need to decide when input occurs. On real machines, the state changes caused by I/O devices occur asynchronously, but not concurrently, with the execution of instructions. We could model this by supposing that the INPUT function is applied just prior to the NEXTSTATE function at each step. But with real machines, input does not always occur at every step: whether a device is able to deliver input at some particular instant may depend partly on its own state (whether it has any input available), partly on that of other devices (which may affect whether it can become the `bus master´), and partly on that of the CPU (which may lock out interrupts). We can model this by allowing the machine to make a non-deterministic choice whether or not to apply the INPUT function at each stage. (Actually, this non-determinism does not influence the choice of security conditions given below.) Thus, the machine is now understood to start off in some arbitrary initial state s_0 and to proceed from state to state by:

first) possibly accepting input from its environment, and

second) executing an operation.

That is, if the current value of the input available from the environment is i and the current state of the machine is s, then its next state will be $NEXTOP(\bar{s})(\bar{s})$, where $\bar{s} = INPUT(s,i)$ if the input is accepted, and $\bar{s} = s$ if it is not.

The problem with these changes is that the behaviour of the new model is not a simple variation on that of the old - it really is a new model altogether. For this reason, it is not possible to deduce the conditions that ensure secure behaviour of the new model from those that have gone before; we have to assert them. This is the hiatus in our orderly progress which I hinted at earlier. However, because the new model is similar to its predecessor, and because we have now gained considerable experience in formulating conditions of this sort, I believe that we can be confident of asserting the correct properties.

The conditions that I propose are just those of the statement of Theorem 3, but with its condition 3) replaced by the following pair of conditions which reflect the changed interpretation of the INPUT function (condition 3a is similar to the previous condition 3; condition 3b is new):

3a) $\text{EXTRACT}(c,i) = \text{EXTRACT}(c,i') \Rightarrow \Phi^c(\text{INPUT}(s,i)) = \Phi^c(\text{INPUT}(s,i'))$,

3b) $\Phi^c(s) = \Phi^c(s') \Rightarrow \Phi^c(\text{INPUT}(s,i)) = \Phi^c(\text{INPUT}(s',i))$.

The reader may wonder why I did not use a model with realistic I/O behaviour right from the start. The reason is that I can find no transparently simple specifications of security (corresponding, for example, to equations (2) to (4)) for such a model. The definition of Proof of Separability would have to be asserted 'out of the blue' and the goal of arguing its correctness would have been worse, rather than better, served.

PROOF OF SEPARABILITY

We have now derived the formal statement of the six conditions that constitute the security verificaton technique which I call 'Proof of Separability'. Using 'RED' as a more vivid name for the quantified colour c, these conditions may be expressed informally as follows:

1) When an operation is executed on behalf of the RED user, the effects which that user perceives must be capable of complete description in terms of the objects known to him.

2) When an operation is executed on behalf of the RED user, other users should perceive no effects at all.

3a) Only RED I/O devices may affect the state perceived by the RED user.

3b) I/O devices must not be able to cause dissimilar behaviour to be exhibited by states which the RED user perceives as identical.

4) RED I/O devices must not be able to perceive differences between states which the RED user perceives as identical.

5) The selection of the next operation to be executed on behalf of the RED user must only depend on the state of his regime.

Interpreted thus, I believe these six conditions have considerable intuitive appeal as a comprehensive statement of what must be proved in order to establish secure isolation between a number of users sharing a single machine. I hope the development that preceded their formulation has convinced the reader that they are the right conditions.

Of course, even the right conditions will be of no practical use if they are so strong that real systems cannot satisfy them. From this point of view, Proof of Separability suffers from a serious drawback: it is specific to the highly restrictive policy of isolation. Most real systems must allow some communication between their users and the aim of security verification is then to prove that communication only takes place in accordance with a stated policy. It is actually rather easy to modify Proof of Separability so that it does permit some forms of inter-user communication: we simply relax its second condition in a controlled manner. For example, if the RED user is to be allowed to communicate information to the BLACK user through use of the WRITE operation, we just delete requirement 2) of Theorem 3 for the single case where COLOUR(s) = RED, c = BLACK, and op = WRITE. Recent work by Goguen and Meseguer [10], which allows the precise description of a very general class of security policies, may allow this ad-hoc technique to be given a formal basis.

An elementary example of the application of this verification technique (and a comparison with some others) may be found in [20]. Present work is aimed at the verification of a complete security kernel described by Barnes [4]. The work described here actually grew out of an attempt to formalize the informal arguments used to claim security for this kernel.

REFERENCES

[1] Ames, S.R. Jr., "Security Kernels: Are they the Answer to the Computer Security Problem?", Presented at the 1979 WESCON Professional Program, San Francisco, CA. (September 1979).

[2] Anderson, J.P., "Computer Security Technology Planning Study", ESD-TR-73-51 (October 1972). (Two volumes).

[3] Attanasio, C.R., P.W. Markstein, and R.J. Phillips, "Penetrating an Operating System: a Study of VM/370 Integrity", IBM Systems Journal Vol. **15**(1), pp.102-116 (1976).

[4] Barnes, D., "Computer Security in the RSRE PPSN", Networks ´80, pp.605-620, Online Conferences (1980).

[5] Berson, T.A. and G.L. Barksdale Jr., "KSOS - Development Methodology for a Secure Operating System", AFIPS Conference Proceedings Vol. **48**, pp.365-371 (1979).

[6] Cristian, F., "Robust Data Types", Technical Report 170, Computing Laboratory, University of Newcastle upon Tyne, England (1981). (To appear in Acta Informatica).

[7] Feiertag, R.J., K.N. Levitt, and L. Robinson, "Proving Multilevel Security of a System Design", Proceedings of the Sixth ACM Symposium on Operating System Principles, pp.57-65 (1977).

[8] Feiertag, R.J., "A Technique for Proving Specifications are Multilevel Secure", CSL-109, SRI International, Menlo Park, CA. (January 1980).

[9] "KSOS Verification Plan", WDL-TR7809, Ford Aerospace and Communications Corporation, Palo Alto, CA. (March 1978).

[10] Goguen, J.A. and J. Meseguer, "Security Policies and Security Models", Internal Report, SRI International, Menlo Park, CA. (December 1981).

[11] Gold, B.D. et al., "A Security Retrofit of VM/370", AFIPS Conference Proceedings Vol. **48**, pp.335-344 (1979).

[12] Hathaway, A., "LSI Guard System Specification (type A)", Draft, Mitre Corporation, Bedford, MA. (July 1980).

[13] Hebbard, B. et al., "A Penetration Analysis of the Michigan Terminal System", ACM Operating Systems Review Vol. **14**(1), pp.7-20 (January 1980).

[14] Lampson, B.W., "A Note on the Confinement Problem", CACM Vol. **16**(10), pp.613-615 (October 1973).

[15] Linde, R.R., "Operating System Penetration", AFIPS Conference Proceedings Vol. **44**, pp.361-368 (1975).

[16] Millen, J.K., "Security Kernel Validation in Practice", CACM Vol. **19**(5), pp.243-250 (May 1976).

[17] Nibaldi, G.H., "Proposed Technical Evaluation Criteria for Trusted Computer Systems", M79-225, Mitre Corporation, Bedford, MA. (1979).

[18] Popek, G.J. and D.A. Farber, "A Model for Verification of Data Security in Operating Systems", CACM Vol. **21**(9), pp.737-749 (September 1978).

[19] Rushby, J.M., "The Design and Verification of Secure Systems", Proceedings of the 8th ACM Symposium on Operating System Principles, Asilomar, CA., pp.12-21 (December 1981).

[20] Rushby, J.M., "Verification of Secure Systems", Technical Report No. 166, Computing Laboratory, University of Newcastle upon Tyne (September 1981).

[21] Wilkinson, A.L. et al., "A Penetration Study of a Burroughs Large System", ACM Operating Systems Review Vol. **15**(1), pp.14-25 (January 1981).

[22] Woodward, J.P.L., "Applications for Multilevel Secure Operating Systems", AFIPS Conference Proceedings Vol. **48**, pp.319-328 (1979).

A METHOD FOR PROGRAM SYNTHESIS

Miklós Szőts and Sándor Csizmazia
Research Institute for Applied Computer Science
P.O. Box 227, Budapest, H-1536.

Abstract

Here we propose a program synthetising method. The method starts from a specially formed output condition written in predicate calculus, and it builds a correct program by simple rules. We think the idea might be developed to practical procedures.

1. *Introduction*

Usually a program verification method is considered complete, if for any input and output condition ρ,ψ and program p the inductive expression (ρ,p,ψ) is valid iff it can be verified. M.H. van Emden proposed a weaker notion of completeness. Let ρ,ψ be input and output condition respectively. Let us consider a method complete if there is a program p^* for which (ρ,p^*,ψ) can be verified, in the case where there exists a partial correct program p w.r.t. ρ and ψ (that is (ρ,p,ψ) is valid). This notion is called *weak completeness*, and is analyzed in [1].

Several of the results are negative, but also some positive ones are provided. Our research is based on one of these positive results. In the following section the theoretical facts are given, and in Section 3 we show a method for synthesis of correct programs. Logical notions are used as in [2] and notions connected to program verification as in [3].

For the formal discussion let us suppose, that we have a set of axioms Ax, which describes the data types. We interpret the programs in the models of Ax.

The notion of weak completeness as defined in the introduction is meaningless, since a program, which does not terminate for any input, suits as p^* for any input and output conditions. Therefore we give a modified definition. Let us call the models, whose universe is generated by the constants (that is the Herbrandt interpretations in [3]) H-models.

Definition 1

A program verifying method is *weak complete*, if for any input and output condition ρ,ψ it is true that: if there exists a partially correct program w.r.t. ρ,ψ then there exists such a program p^* that

(i) p^* is partially correct w.r.t. ρ and ψ in all models of Ax;

(ii) p^* terminates in all H-models of Ax for any input satisfying the input condition.

□

In the followings we define a special class of output conditions.

Definition 2

Let us consider formulas of the form $\exists x(\rho\wedge\psi)$ or $\forall x(\rho\rightarrow\psi)$. In these cases we say that ρ bounds x in ψ, and $\exists x, \forall x$ are called bounded quantifiers.

□

We introduce shorthands for bounded quantifiers:

$$\exists_\rho x\psi \quad \text{for} \quad \exists x(\rho\wedge\psi),$$

$$\forall_\rho x\psi \quad \text{for} \quad \forall x(\rho\rightarrow\psi).$$

It is easy to see that bounded quantifiers can be handled as unbounded ones.

Let us suppose that the programming language can manipulate on natural numbers, that is the type of the language of logic we use is arithmetic, and Ax can be any extension of Peano axion system. Let us introduce a notation for a set of formulas:

$w = \{x<\tau,\ \tau$ is a term which the variable x does not occur in$\}$.

Definition 3

A formula is called *w-cuttable* if every quantifier in the formula: $\exists x, \forall x$ is bounded by a formula of the form $x<\tau$, where x does not occur in the term τ.

□

Theorem 1 (cf. [1], Theorem 7.22)

The method of inductive assertions is weak complete w.r.t. w-cuttable output conditions.

□

The theorem says that if ρ, ψ are formulas of arithmetic, ψ contains only quantifiers in the form of $\exists x\{(x<\tau)\wedge \ldots\}$ or $\forall x\{(x<\tau\rightarrow \ldots\}$ and there exists a program partially correct w.r.t. ρ and ψ, then there also exists one that might be proved.

In the following section we show how the above theoretical construction can be the base of a program synthetising method.

3. *The method*

We use the well known algol-like language (see e.g. [3] ch. 3) as programming language, and suppose that the data types include the type of integers and booleans. We suppose that the input and output conditions contain only integer variables, the Boolean variables serve only as auxiliary ones for the program constructions. Let Ax be arbitrary axiom system of integers. We may suppose that Ax consists of open formulas (see e.g. [4]).

Let input condition ρ and output condition ψ be given with input variables $\bar{x}$ and output variables $\bar{y} = y_o, \ldots y_k$. In ψ the input and output variables occur freely, the bounded variables are marked by $y_{k+1}, \ldots y_n$. There exists program computing values according to the specifications iff

$$Ax \models \forall \bar{x}(\rho(\bar{x}) \rightarrow \exists y \psi(\bar{x}, \bar{y})).$$

We call the formula $\exists \bar{y} \psi(\bar{x}, \bar{y})$ closed output condition.

Let $\Phi \stackrel{d}{=} \{\tau_1 < y \leq \tau_2$ or $y = \tau_2$: y integer variable, τ_1 and τ_2 are terms of integer value, and y does not occur in τ_1 and $\tau_2\}$.

Definition 4

Let the set of *Φ-cuttable* formulas denoted by *C*. It is defined by recursion.

(a) quantifier-free formulas belong to *C*;

(b) if ψ_1 and ψ_2 belong to *C*, then also $\psi_1 \wedge \psi_2$ and $\psi_1 \vee \psi_2$ belong to *C*.

(c) Let x be an integer variable, and $\rho \in \Phi$, $\psi \in C$.
Then $\exists_\rho x\psi$ and $\forall_\rho x\psi$ belong also to *C*.

□

In Definition 4 (c) is the essential point. Note that according to (b) the negation sign may not occur outside of a quantifier, this condition is used only to gain more effective programs. In the followings we suppose that output condition is a Φ-cuttable formula.

Definition 5

We define a function with the Φ-cuttable formulas as domain and while-programs as range. The recursive definition can be seen in Table 1.. Note that the recursion runs according to the complexity of the formula.

□

If $\psi_i(\bar{x})$ is a Φ-cuttable formula, then $p(\psi_i)$ is a procedure to decide whether $\psi_i(\bar{x})$ is valid or not in the H-model of integers, for a given evaluation. The Boolean variable z_i gets the truth value of ψ_i.

Let $\rho(\bar{x})$, $\psi'(\bar{x},\bar{y})$ be input and output conditions, let ψ_o be the corresponding closed output condition in Φ-cuttable form.

	ψ_i	$p(\psi_i)$
1.	qantifier free formula	$z_i \leftarrow \psi_i$;

2.	$\psi_j \vee \psi_k$	$p(\psi_j)$
		if z_j *then* $z_i \leftarrow$ TRUE *else*
		begin
		$p(\psi_k)$
		$z_i \leftarrow z_k$;
		end;

3.	$\psi_j \wedge \psi_k$	$p(\psi_j)$
		if z_j *then*
		begin
		$p(\psi_k)$
		$z_i \leftarrow z_k$;
		end else $z_i \leftarrow$ FALSE;

4.	$\forall_{\tau_1 < y_i \le \tau_2} y_i \ \psi_j$	$(y_i, z_i) \leftarrow (\tau_1,$ TRUE);
		while $z_i \wedge (y_i < \tau_2)$ *do*
		begin
		$y_i \leftarrow y_i + 1$;
		$p(\psi_j)$
		$z_i \leftarrow z_j$;
		end;

5.	$\exists_{\tau_1 < y_i \le \tau_2} y_i \ \psi_j$	$(y_i, z_i) \leftarrow (\tau_1,$ FALSE);
		while $\sim z_i \wedge (y_i < \tau_2)$ *do*
		begin
		$y_i \leftarrow y_i + 1$;
		$p(\psi_j)$
		$z_i \leftarrow z_j$;
		end;

6.	$\exists_{y_i = \tau} y_i \psi_j$	$y_i \leftarrow \tau$; $p(\psi_j)$ $z_i \leftarrow z_j$;

Table 1

Theorem 2

The program $p(\psi_o)$ terminates in all H-models of Ax.

□

Theorem 3

Let us suppose that Ax $\models \rho \rightarrow \psi_o$. In this case:

(i) The program $p(\psi_o)$ is partially correct in all models of Ax.

(ii) If $p(\psi_o)$ terminates in a model of Ax ($\mathfrak{A}$) with the input vector $\bar{a}$, then the computed values ($\bar{b}$) are minimal that is if $\mathfrak{A} \models \psi(\bar{a},\bar{c})$, then $\bar{b} \leq_\alpha \bar{c}$. ($\leq_\alpha$ denotes the alfanumeric ordering of n-tuples).

First let us outline the proof of (i).

We define an input condition ρ_j for every subformula of ψ_o:

(i) $\rho_o(\bar{x}) \stackrel{d}{=} \rho(\bar{x})$;

(ii) if ψ_i is of the form $\psi_j \wedge \psi_k$ or $\psi_j \vee \psi_k$, then both ρ_j and ρ_k are identical to ρ_i;

(iii) if ψ_i is in the form $Q_\beta\ y_i\ \psi_j$, where Q stands for any quantor, $\rho_j \stackrel{d}{=} \rho_i \wedge \beta$.

For every subformula of ψ_o an inductive expression has to be proved, as it is shown in Table 2. The proof is done by induction, the base of it is case 1. . For the other cases

$$(\rho_j p(\psi_j), \psi_j \leftrightarrow z_j) \text{ and } (\rho_k, p(\psi_k), \psi_k \leftrightarrow z_k)$$

has to be supposed. Note that

$$(\beta \wedge \psi_j \wedge z_i) \vee (\sim \exists_\beta\ y_i \psi_j \wedge \sim z_i) \rightarrow [(\exists_\beta\ y_j \psi_j) \leftrightarrow z_i].$$

Each case can be proved by using the verification rules introduced by Hoare ([3], ch. 3.). It is only a question of techniques, therefore we do not detail here.

case	ψ_i	the provable inductive expression
1.	quantifier-free	
2.	$\psi_j \vee \psi_k$	$(\rho_i(\bar{x},\bar{y}'), p(\psi_i(\bar{x},\bar{y}')), \psi_i(\bar{x},\bar{y}') \leftrightarrow z_i$
3.	$\psi_j \wedge \psi_k$	
4.	$\forall_{\tau_1 < y_i \leq \tau_2} y_i \ \psi_j$	
5.	$\exists_{\tau_1 < y_i \leq \tau_2} y_i \ \psi_j$	$(\rho_i(\bar{x},\bar{y}'), p(\psi_i(\bar{x},\bar{y}')), [(\tau_1 < y_i \leq \tau_2) \wedge \psi_j(\bar{x},\bar{y}',y_i) \wedge z_i]$ $\vee [\sim \psi_i(\bar{x},\bar{y}') \wedge \sim z_i])$
6.	$\exists_{y_i = \tau} y_i \ \psi_j$	$(\rho_i(\bar{x},\bar{y}'), p(\psi_i(\bar{x},\bar{y}')), [y_i = \tau \wedge \psi_j(\bar{x},\bar{y}',y_i) \wedge z_i]$ $\vee [\sim \psi_i(\bar{x},\bar{y}') \wedge \sim z_i])$

Table 2

By the above outlined inference

$(\rho(\bar{x}),\ p(\psi_o(\bar{x})),\ (\sim \exists_\beta y\ \psi(\bar{x},\bar{y}) \vee \sim z_i) \vee (\beta \wedge \psi_j \wedge z_i))$

is obtained. Since Ax $\models \rho \rightarrow \psi_o$ is supposed, it is clear that

$$(\rho(\bar{x}),\ p(\psi_o(\bar{x})),\ \psi(\bar{x},\bar{y}))$$

holds.

As for the proof of (ii), we give only a hint. All the assignments occur in program segments defined by rule 5 or 6. Here the possible values are enumerated bottom up.

□

Note that the upper limit of the existentially quantified variables can be omitted. In this case Theorem 2 also needs the condition Ax $\models \rho \rightarrow \psi_o$.

Note that the map defined in Definition 5 is a constructive one, so for a formula ψ the program $p(\psi)$ can be constructed, as it can be seen in the following example

Example 1

Let us construct a program to compute the lowest common multiple. The usual specification:

$\rho = (0<x_1) \wedge (0<x_2)$

$$\psi = \exists y_1(y_1 \cdot x_1 = y_o) \wedge \exists y_2(y_2 . x_2 = y_o) \wedge$$

$$\forall y_3\{(\exists y_4(y_4 \cdot x_1 = y_3) \wedge \exists y_5(y_5 \cdot x_2 = y_3)) \rightarrow (y_o \leq y_3)\}$$

Here the subformula $\forall y_3(\dots)$ expresses that y is minimal, so it can be omitted (due to Theorem 3 (ii)).

The closed output condition in Φ-cuttable form:

$$\psi_o = \exists_{0<y_o \leq x_1 \cdot x_2}\ y_o(\exists_{0<y_1 \leq y_o}\ y_1 \cdot x_1 = y_o) \wedge (\exists_{0<y_2 \leq y_o}\ y_2 \cdot x_2 = y_o)$$

Let β_o denote $0<y_o \leq x_1 x_2$,
β_1 denote $0<y_1 \leq y_o$, and
β_2 denote $0<y_2 \leq y_o$.

The process of constructing $p(\psi_o)$:

Step 1 $\psi_o = \exists_{\beta_o} y_o \psi 1$

```
(yo,zo) ← (O,FALSE);
while ~ zo∧(yo<x1x2) do
   begin
      yo ← yo+1;
      p(ψ1)
      zo ← z1;
   end;
```

Step 2 $\psi_1 = \psi_2 \wedge \psi_3$

```
        (yo,zo) ← (O,FALSE);
        while ~ zo∧(yo<x1x2) do
           begin
             yo ← yo+1;
           ┌ p(ψ2)
           │ if z2 then
           │    begin
p(ψ1)      {       p(ψ3)
           │       z1 ← z3;
           └    end else z1 ← FALSE;
             zo ← z1;
           end;
```

Step 3 $\psi_2 = \exists_{\beta_2} y_1(y_1 \cdot x_1 = y_o)$ $\psi_3 = \exists_{\beta_2} y_2(y_2 \cdot x_2 = y_o)$

```
        (yo,zo) ← (O,FALSE);
        while ~ zo∧(yo<x1x2) do
           begin
              yo ← yo+1;
            ┌ (y1,z2) ← (O,FALSE);
            │ while ~ z2∧(y1<yo) do
            │    begin
p(ψ2)       {       y1 ← y1+1;
            │       z4 ← y1·x1 = yo;
            │       z2 ← z4
            └    end;
```

```
        if z2 then
           begin
              (y2,z3) ← (0,FALSE);
              while ~ z3∧(y2<yo) do
                 begin
p(ψ3)               y2 ← y2+1;
                    z5 ← y2·x2 = yo;
                    z3 ← z5;
                 end;
              z1 ← z3;
           end else z1 ← FALSE;
        zo←z1;
     end;
```

In Step 3 the final program is obtained.

□

The programs obtained this way are correct, but are hardly optimal. There are two ways to optimize them:

(1) To use transformation keeping correctness. This way the superfluous statements can be eliminated.

(2) Since the specification determines the program (our method is deterministic), to get a more effective algorithm, a new, equivalent specification is needed.

Example 2

Let us consider the specification of the above example, and let us suppose that from Ax we can obtain the following fact:

$$(\mathrm{rem}\ (u,v) = 0 \wedge \mathrm{div}\ (u,v) = w) \rightarrow w \cdot v = u \qquad (1)$$

From 1 follows that

$\exists! y_2 (y_2 \cdot x_1 = y_o)$ and

$\mathrm{rem}\ (y_o,x_1) = 0 \rightarrow \mathrm{div}\ (y_o,x_1) \cdot x_1 = y_o$

Similarly for y_2 and x_2. So the specification can be written:

$$\exists_{1<y_o\leq x_1 \cdot x_2} y\ \mathrm{rem}\ (y_o,x_1) = 0 \wedge \mathrm{rem}\ (y_o,x_2) = 0.$$

The corresponding program:

```
(y_o,z_o) ← (0,FALSE);
while ~ z_o∧(y_o≤x_1·x_2) do
 begin
   y_o ← y_o+1;
   z_1 ← rem (y_o,x_1) = 0 ∧ rem (y_o,x_2) = 0;
   z_o ← z
 end;
```

Using program transformations and omitting the upper limit we may get the following program:

```
y_o ← 1;
while ~ (rem(y_o,x_1) = 0 ∧(rem y_o,x_2) = 0) do y_o = y_o+1;
```

which is a program of acceptable complexity.

□

4. *Comparison*

We think that our method differs essentially from the other program synthetising methods. In all the logic based methods we know of, the construction of the program requires the proof of the output condition. In some cases a programming logic is used, where the programs are the terms of the logic. These methods are based on principles of program verification (see e.g. [5]). Other methods construct the program from the flow of proof (e.g. [6]). All these methods construct not only the code of the program but the algorithm too. Our method receives the algorithm hidden in the cuttable output condition, so it is sufficient to transform this condition in to the programming language, we do not need theorem proving. It is a bargain: we give up synthetising algorithm thus obtaining effectivity. Therefore we do not need a theorem prover, but only an easily programmable translator. Maybe it is more adequate to call our method *automatical coding* than *program synthesis*.

Remember R. Kowalsky's thesis:

ALGORITHM = LOGIC + CONTROL

(c.f. [7]). We start from the "logic of algorithm" (formulated in cuttable formula), and not from the "logic of problem". Therefore the method shown here is very close to the principle *logic as programming language* ([8], naturally it is very different from PROLOG). Really, the user may use the language of cuttable formulas as a high level programming language - he formulates his algorithm by this language.

5. *Prospects of the method*

Here we aimed only to outline the basic idea of the method, and to make it clear. Naturally, a lot of questions arise about its applicability. The most important one regards data types. If the method remains restricted to integer variables, it has no practical importance. Now we are working on the extension of this method to arrays and recursively definable data-types. Note that our method is highly structural, and serves modularity: if a subformula is equivalent to the specification of a module, the call of the module can be inserted into the place of the program segment corresponding to the subformula.

In the former section we pointed out that our method does not synthetise algorithm, the algorithm is formulated by the specification. So it can be only a component of a programming methodology, it automatises coding. However, it fulfills this task effectively.

Another important question is, whether the language of cuttable formulas is an adequate tool to describe algorithms. This problem is also under investigation. The practical importance of our idea depends mainly on the answer to this question.

References

[1] Gergely,T., Ury,L.: *Mathematical theories of programming* (in preparation)

[2] Schoenfiled,J.R.: *Mathematical logic* Reading, Addison - Wesley, 1967

[3] Manna,Z.: *Mathematical theory of computation* McGraw-Hill, 1974

[4] Gergely,T., Szőts,M.: *Logical foundation of problem solving* Proc. II. IMAI, Plenum P.O. (in preparation)

[5] Manna,Z., Waldinger,R.,J.: Towards Automatic Program Synthesis *C.ACM* Vol: 14, No.3 1971

[6] Gergely T., Vershinin,K.P.: Concept sensitive formal language for task specification. *Mathematical Logic in Computer Science* North Holland 1981

[7] Kowalsky,R.: Algorithm = Logic + Control *C.ACM* Vol.22, no 7, 1979

[8] Kowalsky,R.: Predicate Logic as a Programming Language *Proc. IFIP Congress'74* North Holland, 1974

The Use of Transformations to Implement an Algorithm

Judy A. Townley
Center for Research in Computing Technology
Harvard University
Cambridge, MA 02138

Abstract

Some years ago we developed a package for creating and applying transformation rules [Conrad 76]. The facilities in the package provide a way to transform user-defined language extensions into constructs in the base language EL1. We have used the facilities - and that approach to program refinement - extensively. Our experience led us to develop an integrated programming environment, the Harvard PDS, to support the methodology. In this paper we describe the use of transformation rules to refine the high-level specification of an algorithm. We use transforms to specify the meanings of high-level constructs and to encode special-purpose optimizations. We briefly discuss the PDS and its support for the methodology.

1. Introduction

Hopcroft developed an m·n·log(n) algorithm (where m is the number of input symbols and n is the number of states) for reducing a deterministic automaton [Hopcroft 71]. Gries then published a structured, top-down description of the algorithm [Gries 73], incorporating proofs of its correctness and its time bound into the description. Gries went on to write a PL/I program that implements the algorithm. We have taken Gries's description and, using transformation rules, produced an implementation of the algorithm by mechanical refinement of the specification. We use Gries's version of the algorithm as a high-level specification and develop two executable implementations from it. One is a prototype, which we use to test the overall correctness of the high-level specification; the other is a production version, in which we have implementations for the high-level constructs that meet the expected execution time bound of the algorithm.

We used the Harvard programming support environment, the PDS [Cheatham 81, Townley 81], for the project. It provides notational extension facilities, which we use to make our high-level specification correspond closely to Gries's version. The PDS has facilities for creating

---

This research was supported in part by the Defense Advanced Research Projects Agency, under contract N00039-78-G-0020 with the Department of the Navy, Naval Electronic System Command.

appropriate type abstractions and choosing underlying representations for them. It also has a transformation facility, which we used to refine many of the abstract constructs.

The high-level specification is a program and is on the machine. Each stage of refinement produces a program representing another level of definition of the algorithm. The PDS makes a record of the refinement steps so that, after a change, it can rederive the more concrete versions without the user's assistance. (The PDS allows a user to change only the high-level definitions - of procedures, data types, and transformation rules - not the more concrete versions.) The PDS records which modules are changed to reduce the amount of work it must do to rederive the more concrete versions.

The example provides a unifying theme for illustrating several points we wish to make: the usefulness of notational extension facilities to produce a readable, refinable specification, the usefulness of transformation rules for refinement and special-purpose optimization, and the usefulness of an integrated programming environment to support these activities. The two implementations are developed as a small program family - each executable version is derived by refinement of a common abstract model. The example also suggests some new directions for programming environments, in particular, the need for better pre-execution analysis tools.

2. Programming Environment

The PDS is a prototype programming support environment developed at Harvard University. It consists of

1. a software database containing the objects (called modules) that constitute the systems currently under development or maintenance;

2. a set of tools, including language-oriented editors, transformation facilities, a compiler, a loader, a symbolic debugger, a tracing facility, and a pretty printer;

3. an executive, which manages the software database, insures its integrity, and provides an interface to the user for calling the various tools.

The PDS is an integrated collection of tools that supports the interactive development and enhancement of large systems. The programming language, EL1 [ECL 74], around which the PDS is built is an interactive, interpreter-based language. The language has facilities that allow the user to introduce new control and type abstractions and notational abstractions. These features, supported by the PDS, allow the user to develop constructs and notation that are natural to his application. The resulting programs tend to be more readable than they would be if the programmer were constrained to use a language not tailored to his application.

The PDS supports the incremental refinement of abstractions. The refinement may be by conventional procedure definitions, by using the data type encapsulation facility, or by transformations. The transformation facility allows the user to provide pattern/replacement rules for refining abstractions. The user can control the order of application and the domain of application when such control is important, or he need not bother when it is not.

The PDS keeps a history of the refinement of each module. If a user changes an abstract module, the PDS automatically rederives the more concrete modules as they are needed.

The PDS has fine-grained version control. It keeps a record of exactly which parts of a module are changed. This allows the PDS to replay only those aspects of the derivation that are affected by the change. Such incremental rederivation is less costly than a rederivation based on version control only at the module level. This savings is significant in developing large systems.

The PDS supports program families. A program family is a collection of programs derived from a common ancestor, called a model. The model, which may consist of many modules, should be both general and precise. Family members are derived by mechanical refinement of the model, and each member typically serves a slightly different target or end-user environment. Thus the criterion of generality. The model also serves as an operational specification of the software system. It thus should be readable and precise.

The PDS has partitioning facilities for configuration management. A user associates partitioning attributes with a module, which may then be used to identify configurations. Partitions are used to distinguish the members of a program family and would be the basis for identifying releases of a system.

The tools in the PDS use a common representation of program modules. A module and its contents, called entities, are represented as attributes. Tools use the attributes as their input and their results are stored as attributes. As we add new tools, the set of attributes will grow. The use of attributes and the use of a common internal representation of program entities facilitates communication between tools and the construction of new tools using components of existing tools.

3. The Model

In [Hopcroft 71], Hopcroft gives an algorithm that minimizes the number of states in a finite automaton in an amount of time proportional to $m \cdot n \cdot \log(n)$, where m is the number of input symbols and n is the number of states. The algorithm produces a set of blocks $B_1, B_2, \ldots, B_p$ such that, in the end, two states are in the same block if and only if the states are equivalent. We briefly describe the algorithm in the paragraphs that follow. Our description is drawn from Gries's paper, which contains a complete development of the algorithm and its time bound.

Initially two blocks are created, B_1 and B_2, containing the final and nonfinal states of the automaton, respectively. If there are blocks B_i and B_j and a symbol "a" such that

$$s, t \in B_i, \delta(s, a) \in B_j \text{ but } \delta(t, a) \notin B_j, \quad (1)$$

then we must put s and t into separate blocks, which we accomplish by moving the states s whose transition on "a" is to a state in B_j to a new block, say, B_k. This step is called splitting B_i with respect to the pair (B_j, a), and B_k is called B_i's twin.

Checking every triple (a, B_i, B_j) to see if condition (1) is met would result in an expensive algorithm. The key to the algorithm's time bound is the discovery that we can ignore certain pairs (B_j, a). Hopcroft proves that if we split a block B_j into blocks $\bar{B}_j$ and $\tilde{B}_j$, then for some symbol "a", it is sufficient to split all blocks with respect to any two of the three pairs (B_j, a), $(\bar{B}_j, a)$, and $(\tilde{B}_j, a)$. He also shows that after all blocks have been split with respect to a pair (B_j, a), it is unnecessary to split any future block with respect to the pair. We thus maintain a list L of all pairs (B_j, a) wrt which some blocks may have to be split and use the fact that there are certain pairs that we need not put on the list L to come up with the m·n·log(n) algorithm. We keep on splitting until the list L is empty.

To initialize L, we consider each input symbol "a" and put either (B_1, a) or (B_2, a) on L, depending upon which of B_1 or B_2 is smaller. To prove the validity of this, let $B_j = S$ (the set of all states of the automaton), $\bar{B}_j = F$, and $\tilde{B}_j = S - F$. We know that $\delta(s, a) \in B_j$, so it it is unnecessary to split wrt (B_j, a). We need only split wrt either $(\bar{B}_j, a)$ or $(\tilde{B}_j, a)$, but not both.

To determine which blocks must be split (wrt some pair (B_j, a) on L), we make a list D of all the states that have a transition on "a" to a state in B_j. This is computed by an iteration

for each $s \in B_j$ **do** $D \leftarrow D \cup \delta^{-1}(s, a)$ **end**

We then process each state s in D, determining the block B_i in which s appears and determining whether B_i contains a state with a transition on "a" to a state not in B_j. If so, we create a twin for B_i – if one does not already exist – and move s to the twin.

Our rendering of Gries's version of the algorithm is shown in Figure 1. (Gries's version appears in Appendix I.) We do not claim that this is the only or the best translation of Gries's specification. Several members of the PDS project looked at Gries's paper; each person came up with a slightly different translation. The primary goals, we all agreed, were to produce something that is easy to understand, refine, and ultimately analyze. We differed on whether to be more explicit in the high-level specification or retain the flavor of Gries's more mathematical rendering. For example, we do not make explicit how we are able to execute the test

```
ThereExists t In Bi
    SuchThat Delta(fsa)(t, a) NotIn Bj
```

in constant time, choosing instead to stay close to Gries's version. On the other hand, we are more explicit than Gries in stating that we must keep track of blocks as we split them. We introduce a data structure, called BlocksSplit, and record blocks as we split them,

```
Add Bi To BlocksSplit.
```

```
Reduce ←
  EXPR(fsa:FiniteAutomaton; PartitionedStateSet)
    BEGIN
      Let B bea Sequence(Block) InitialSize 2 MaximumSize NumberOfStates(fsa);
      B[1] ← FinalStates(fsa);
      B[2] ← NonFinalStates(fsa);
      Let DeltaInverse bea Map(State, InputSymbol; Set(State)) WithValue
        InverseTransitionFunction(fsa);
      Let L bea Set(Pair(Block, InputSymbol)) Initially TheEmptySet;
      ForEach a In InputAlphabet(fsa)
        Do
          If (B[1] IsSmallerThan B[2]) Then Add < B[1], a > To L Else
            Add < B[2], a > To L;
        END;
      While NOT Empty L
        Do
          Pick < Bj, a > From L;
          /* 'Determine splittings of all blocks with respect to <Bj, a>';
          Let D bea Set(State) Initially TheEmptySet;
          ForEach s In Bj Do D ← D union DeltaInverse(s, a) END;
          Delete < Bj, a > From L;
          /* 'Split each block as determined above';
          Let BlocksSplit bea Set(Block) Initially TheEmptySet;
          Let Twin bea Map(Block; Block);
          ForEach s In D
            Do
              Let Bi be (BlockOf B containing s);
              If (ThereExists t In Bi SuchThat Delta(fsa)(t, a) NotIn Bj) Then
                BEGIN
                  If HasNoTwin(Bi) Then
                    [) Twin(Bi) ← CreateNewBlock(B); Add Bi To BlocksSplit (];
                  Move s From Bi To Twin(Bi);
                END;
            END;
          /* 'Fix L according to splits that occurred';
          ForEach Bi In BlocksSplit
            Do
              ForEach c In InputAlphabet(fsa)
                Do
                  Let Bk be Twin(Bi);
                  If (< Bi, c > In L) Then Add < Bk, c > To L Else
                    (If (Bi IsSmallerThan Bk) Then Add < Bi, c > To L Else
                      Add < Bk, c > To L);
                END;
            END;
        END;
      ReturnPartitionedStates(fsa, B);
    END;
```

Figure 1

Much of the notation in the high-level specification is invented for this program. We invented constructs, such as

- ForEach c In InputAlphabet(fsa) Do ... END

- Pick <Bj, a> From L

- Move s From Bi To Twin(Bi)

to correspond to the notation Gries uses. The first is an example of a new iterator, the second introduces nomenclature – Bj and a – and the third is a concise expression for what is actually several operations. Were we constrained to write the program in a language that did not allow us to use new notation, the high-level program would be less readable. Application-oriented notation allows us to preserve the clarity of the algorithm and hide the lower-level implementation decisions.

4. Refinement of the Model

We refine the model – provide meanings for the abstractions – using procedure definitions, type encapsulations, and transformation rules. The procedure definition and procedure application constructs are sufficiently conventional that we assume the reader can understand them without further explanation. The goals that motivated the design of the type encapsulation facility are similar to those for ALPHARD [Wulf 74] and CLU [Liskov 78]. The user may include as part of the definition of a new data type, the meaning of assignment, selection, conversion, generation, and printing.[1] When one of these operations is performed on an object of the type, the user's definition of the operation is used instead of the system's. The behavior of a data type is thereby not inextricably tied to its underlying representation. Unlike CLU and ALPHARD, other operations that involve objects of the new data type are defined externally to the type definition, often as generic procedures. Not all operations involving the data type are encapsulated in its definition, only the half dozen or so fundamental ones.

To test the program, we invent a representation for finite automata, using the type encapsulation facility to specify the behavior. To refine the algorithm, we need a representation for sets of states. We use the type encapsulation faculty for this as well. The set of states, for instance, is represented as a simple linked list in one implementation and as a doubly-linked list in another. The meaning of the abstraction – the set – remains the same. The execution time of the operations changes.

---

[1] There a few other aspects of the behavior of a data type that the user can control. The EL1 Manual [ECL 74] contains a complete description of the facility.

4.1. The transformation facility

We use transformation rules to give a meaning to many of the constructs. A transformation rule, or transform, consists of a pattern, an optional predicate, and a replacement

<pattern> {Where <predicate>} <-> <replacement>

Transforms typically include match variables, which are bound during pattern matching. Match variables may be of the form

$$ identifier

for matching a single expression or of the form

?? identifier

for matching a sequence of expressions.

An example of a notation that we add to EL1 for use in our model is the conditional expression If ... Then ... Else ... . EL1's builtin conditional statement

p => e

has the semantics

1. Evaluate p

2. If the result is TRUE, then exit the enclosing block or iteration. The result of evaluating e becomes the value of the construct exited.

3. If the result is FALSE, proceed to the statement following the conditional.

4. If the result is neither TRUE nor FALSE, then signal an error.

We introduce the If ... Then ... Else ... notation for our model and refine it by providing a transform

```
If $$ pred Then $$ action1 Else $$ action2 <->
   BEGIN $$ pred => $$ action1; $$ action2 END
```

In the refinement of the model, we use transforms to map the meaning of numerous abstractions to the base language EL1. EL1 has a single iterator, a REPEAT statement, with optional prefixes for introducing an integer iteration variable, its lower and upper limits, and its increment. We map various iterators

```
While $$ predicate Do ?? action END
```

ForEach $$ c In InputAlphabet($$ fsa) Do ?? action END

ForEach $$ bi In BlocksSplit Do ?? action END

into the single REPEAT construct.

We use transforms to refine abstractions that introduce nomenclature. The construct

Pick <Bj, a> From L

means pick a pair from L and introduce new local names Bj and a for the elements of the pair. The constructs

1. Let $$ identifier bea $$ mode WithValue $$ value

2. Let $$ identifier bea $$ mode Initially $$ value

3. Let $$ identifier be $$ value

also introduce names into the environment. In the first two instances, the identifier is declared to have a specific type and initial value; in the third instance, the type is deduced from the initial value. The difference between the first two is that in the first instance we do not expect the value to change, whereas in the second, we do. We could have used a single construct for all cases; we felt, however, that each of the variations conveyed the right amount of information for a particular situation.

We also use transforms to produce efficient realizations of abstract constructs. We take advantage, for instance, of the fact that the sets DeltaInverse(s, a) in the iteration

```
ForEach s In Bj
    Do D ← D union DeltaInverse(s, a) END
```

are disjoint and - choosing to represent D by a linked list - replace the union by an append operation. A mechanical program optimizer is unlikely to produce such optimizations, which requires facts about a program and a general understanding of high-level concepts. We expect, instead, that there will always be special-purpose optimizations that the programmer will want to incorporate; transformation rules are a convenient way to express them.

The PDS provides several ways to control the domain of application of a collection of transforms: the user may specify that a set of transforms is local to a scope or a module or he may request that a particular named set of transforms only be applied to a particular named set of entities.

4.2. Development of a prototype

We first implemented a prototype from the model to test its overall correctness. The prototype differs from the production version in the underlying representation of the set of states comprising a block. For the prototype, we used a library set package, whose underlying representation for any set is a simple linked list. Once we implemented and tested the prototype, it took little time to get the production version working. We defined a new data type – a doubly-linked list – and provided new meanings for three operations – adding an element to a set, deleting an element, and iterating over a set. We discuss the latter implementation in section 4.4.

4.3. Refinement criteria

Hopcroft's algorithm is noteworthy because of its execution time bound. It was critical that its implementation preserve the time bound. We present below the relevant refinements and discuss how they preserve the time bound. Appendix II contains a complete listing of the refinements.

4.3.1. Finite automata

The input to the program is a finite automaton. A user of the program need not conform to any particular representation of finite automata. All that we require is that the following operations have the indicated interpretations:

StateType bea Map(FiniteAutomaton; MODE)
 – yielding the data type of the states of the automaton

NumberOfStates bea Map(FiniteAutomaton; INT)
 – yielding the number of states of the automaton

InputSymbolType bea Map(FiniteAutomaton; MODE)
 – yielding the data type of the input symbols of the automaton

NumberOfInputSymbols bea Map(FiniteAutomaton; INT)
 – yielding the number of input symbols of the automaton

ForEach $$ c In Alpha($$ fsa) Do ?? action END
 – an iterator over the input symbols of the automaton

ForEach $$ s In Sigma($$ fsa) Do ?? action END
 – an iterator over the states of the automaton

FinalState($$ fsa)($$ state)

– returns true if the state is a final state

IsTransition($$ fsa)($$ state, $$ symbol)
  – returns true if there is a transition from the state on the symbol
    and false otherwise

Delta($$ fsa)($$ state, $$ symbol)
  – returns the state to which a transition is made

The last two constructs could be combined if we want to require that a value, such as 0, be returned when no transition is possible.

We create several auxilliary data structures to meet the time constraints of the algorithm. Three of them - NumberToBjOnA, MemberOfL, and DeltaInverse - are arrays that we want to index by a state, an input symbol, or both. (We describe these data structures in sections 4.3.2, 4.3.3, and 4.3.4, respectively.) Since we cannot assume that the user of the program will represent states and input symbols by integers, we create mappings from the integers to the user's values. We use the maps to transform the integer arguments in our calls on the functions FinalState, IsTransition, and Delta to the user's values. We also use an iterator for processing the input symbols

ForEach $$ c In InputAlphabet($$ fsa) Do ?? action END

that iterates over integers between 1 and the number of input symbols.

To test the program we chose a representation for finite automata and used the type encapsulation facility to specify its behavior. A finite automaton is a tuple with vectors of tokens for the set of states and the set of symbols, a bit-vector to indicate whether a state is a final state, and an n by m bit matrix (where n is the number of states and m is the number of symbols) to encode the transition function. We associate our own print function with the data type and provide meanings for the constructs listed above.

4.3.2. Blocks

A block is a set of states. The algorithm guarantees that if two states are equivalent they will end up in the same block. There are constraints on the execution time of several operations involving blocks.

1. To compare the number of states in two blocks can take no more than a constant amount of time.

2. The iteration

   ForEach s In Bj Do ... END

can take only an amount of time proportional to the number of states in Bj.

3. The body of the iteration

   ForEach s In D Do ... END

   can be repeated as many as m·n·log(n) times. Thus the operations in the body of the iteration, including the test

   ThereExists t In Bi SuchThat Delta(fsa)(t, a) NotIn Bj

   and the operation

   Move s From Bi To Twin(Bi)

   must be executable in constant time.

4. The iteration

   ForEach Bi In BlocksSplit Do ... END

   has an upper time bound that is proportional to the number of blocks split on the cycle.

We have chosen a representation for blocks that allows us to meet these constraints. The program builds a sequence of blocks, B, each block of which contains two pieces of information:

1. the number of states the block contains and

2. the set of states the block contains.

These records allow us to meet criteria (1) and (2) listed above, respectively.

Meeting criterion (3) is more complicated. We use an integer array, NumberToBjOnA, to help us compute the predicate

ThereExists t In Bi SuchThat Delta(fsa)(t, a) NotIn Bj

NumberToBjOnA[i] is the number of states in the block B[i] with a transition to block Bj on the symbol a. If NumberToBjOnA[i] equals the number of states in B[i], then the predicate is false. Otherwise it is true. This test takes a constant amount of time. We make sure that as we move states from one block to another, we update the array, and we have to clear the array before we split the states with respect to each pair <Bj, a>.

The other operation mentioned in criterion (3) involves moving a state from a block to its twin. This requires knowing which block is its twin. We could either store the index of the twin in another field of a block or use a separate data structure. We chose the latter. We use the index into B of a block as the index into an integer array named Twin. Twin[i] is the index of the block that is the twin for B[i]. We also must initialize the array Twin for each new pair <Bj, a>, which we do by declaring it in the body of the loop.

These two constructs, NumberToBjOnA and Twin, are sufficient to meet the third constraint.

The process of splitting a block – generating its twin – implies the ability to create new blocks. We have chosen to make B big enough initially to house all the blocks we could need. This is the number of states in the finite automaton. When we need a new block to serve as a twin, we use the next available slot in B. We have a variable BlockCount that tells us how many slots we have already used. Generating a twin involves incrementing BlockCount, initializing the new block, and recording its index in the array Twin.

Criterion (4) requires that we keep track of which blocks we split and that we be able to process them in an amount of time proportional to the number of blocks split. This is accomplished by recording the blocks that we split in a list named BlocksSplit. We then iterate through this list.

4.3.3. The list L

Gries points out that the operations involving L are critical to maintaining the algorithm's time bounds. In particular, the following constraints must be observed:

1. picking a pair <Bj, a> from L can take no more than a constant amount of time,

2. adding a pair <Bj, a> to L must be a constant-time operation, and

3. determining whether a pair <Bj, a> is in L must be a constant-time operation.

If we use a linked list to represent L and add and delete pairs from the head of the list, then criteria (1) and (2) are met. To meet criterion (3), we construct a boolean matrix, MemberOfL, such that MemberOfL[k, a] is true if the pair <B[k], a> is on the list L.

4.3.4. D and DeltaInverse

The set D is constructed during the iteration

```
ForEach s In Bj
    Do D ← D union DeltaInverse(s, a) END
```

where D is initially an empty set. Adding states to D must take at worst an amount of time proportional to the number of states added, and the iteration over D

ForEach s In D Do ... END

must be proportional to the number of states in D. The latter criterion suggests a linked list representation for D. We observe that the first criterion can also be met using a linked list, because the union operation in the iteration body always combines disjoint sets. The states in Bj are distinct and a state cannot have a transition to two different states in Bj on the same symbol, a. Thus we are assured that the map DeltaInverse produces entirely new states to add to D on each cycle of the iteration. We therefore represent D by a linked list and replace the union operation by an append operation, which meets the time bound.

We also have to make sure we can compute DeltaInverse(s, a) in a constant amount of time. To do this, we represent the function by an (n by m) array - named DeltaInverse - whose elements are lists of states. Thus an element of the array DeltaInverse[s, a] is the list of states that make transitions to s on input a.

We also must show that the operations inside the iteration

ForEach s In D Do ... END

take a constant amount of time. The first step computes the index of the block containing state s. We create an integer array called BlockContaining to store this information. The operation

Move s From Bi To Twin(Bi)

updates the array as it moves a state from one block to another. The second step inside the iteration is the test

If (ThereExists t In Bi SuchThat ...) Then ...

We have already shown (in section 4.3.2) that this operation takes a constant amount of time.

4.4. An efficient implementation of state sets

We used a set package in the first implementation, deferring the decision of how to represent the set of states comprising a block. We developed this implementation, a prototype, quickly and used it to test the structure of the model and concentrate on the implementation of the other data structures. Since the implementation in the set package did not meet our criteria that the addition and deletion of elements of the set of states comprising blocks be performed in constant time, we next propose a second implementation that does obey the constraints and produce a second refinement of the model using the implementation.

Recall that the operations involving the sets of states in a block are the following:

1. states are added to a block during the initialization of B[1] and B[2],

2. there is an iteration over the set of states in a block

   ForEach s In Bj Do ... END

   which must be performed in an amount of time at worst proportional to the number of states in the block, and

3. we move a state from one block to another, which must be accomplished in a constant amount of time.

We propose a doubly-linked list representation for the set of states in a block. By simply adding states to the head of the list in the initialization and using the obvious means for sequencing through a list, we meet criteria (1) and (2). Meeting criterion (3) is less straightforward, and it is the reason we resort to a doubly-linked list. We introduce an array CurrentPositionOfState whose i-th value points to the list element representing state i in some set. Moving an element from one block to another involves first deleting it from one block - since a state cannot be in more than one block at a time - and then adding it to the other block. We locate the state using the array and delete it by adjusting the predecessor and successor links. We add a state to the head of a list (and properly initialize its predecessor and successor links) and record its position in the array.

The refinements for this implementation are in Appendix III.

5. Future Directions in Tool Technology

The PDS - and its transformation facilities in particular - are useful and practical. We have used them in several large programming projects and would find it a hindrance to program without such facilities. While our experience has convinced us of their benefits, it has also revealed avenues for future work. Of course, we want the next generation of tools to be more efficient - perhaps through the use of dedicated, special-purpose hardware. We also want the tools to have more information about programs - through the incorporation of program analysis.

We have worked on program analysis, specifically, on the development of a symbolic evaluator called the SE [Cheatham 79], which is a static or pre-execution, analyzer that does value flow analysis - propagating symbolic expressions that represent the values of program expressions - as well as control flow analysis. We have implemented a prototype of the SE; our experience with it on test programs revealed that it would not be efficient enough for general use and suggested sources of its inefficiency. We also encountered issues on which we needed to do more research. We used recurrence relations to represent the values of variables changing inside a loop but found that not much work had been done to solve such recurrence relations. Also lacking were techniques for producing closed-form expressions to represent the values of arbitrary recursive procedures. We have worked on these problems [Brown 81, Ploedereder 80] and are now designing a new analyzer based on the symbolic evaluator.

Some type of static analyzer - whether it be a symbolic evaluator or something less powerful - is needed to do type-dependent transformation and pre-runtime error detection (semantic not syntactic). We could have used type-dependent transforms in the refinement of Reduce. The iterators and the constructs

Add <element> To <collection>

and

Delete <element> From <collection>

could have been implemented by type-dependent transforms. We also could have used a tool that reported what operations changed the value of an object. In particular, we wanted to know all places where B or any component of B is modified. This information would have revealed several errors in our first refinement.

We expect to work on these problems in the next few years and produce more powerful pre-execution analysis tools.

Acknowledgement

I would like to thank Thomas E. Cheatham and Glenn H. Holloway for their contributions to this paper. It was Tom Cheatham's idea to work on an implementation of this algorithm several years ago [Cheatham 75] to illustrate the usefulness of ECL for such tasks. That work is the basis of this paper and implementation. Glenn Holloway read the paper and the model many times, and each time provided numerous excellent suggestions.

I. Gries's Version of the Algorithm

```
Initialize: B1 ← F; B2 ← S − F; L = ϕ;

    for each c ∈ I do
        if b1 ≤ b2 then add (B1, c) to L else add (B2, c) to L
    end;
while L ≠ ϕ do

b: Pick one pair (Bj, a) ∈ L;

c: Determine splittings of all blocks wrt (Bj, a):
   D ← ϕ;
   for each s ∈ Bj do D ← D ∪ δ⁻¹(s, a) end;

d: L ← L − (Bj, a);

e: Split each block as determined in c:
   for each s ∈ D do
       BI ← block number in which s appears;
       if all s ∈ BI have δ(s, a) ∈ Bj then
       else begin if BI has no twin BK yet then
                  generate BI's twin BK and set BK ← ϕ;
                  Move s from BI to its twin BK
           end
   end;

f: Fix L according to splits that occurred:
   for each block BI split into BI and its twin BK do
       for each c ∈ I do
           if (BI, c) ∈ L then add (BK, c) to L
           else if bi ≤ bk then add (BI, c) to L
                else add (BK, c) to L
       end
   end f;
end
```

I. Refinements to the Model

(Appendix III contains the definition of a state set as a doubly-linked list.)

```
'Maps for the finite automaton:
';

State ← INT;

InputSymbol ← INT;

FinalState($$ fsa)($$ s) WHERE $$ s HasType State <->
  FinalState($$ fsa)(StateMap[$$ s]);

IsTransition($$ fsa)($$ s, $$ c) WHERE
  $$ s HasType State AND $$ c HasType InputSymbol <->
  IsTransition($$ fsa)(StateMap[$$ s], AlphabetMap[$$ c]);

Delta($$ fsa)($$ s, $$ c) WHERE
  $$ s HasType State AND $$ c HasType InputSymbol <->
  Delta($$ fsa)(StateMap[$$ s], AlphabetMap[$$ c]);

(ForEach $$ c In InputAlphabet($$ fsa) Do ?? body END) <->
  FOR $$ c TO NumberOfInputSymbols($$ fsa) REPEAT ?? body END;

(ForEach $$ s In SetOfStates($$ fsa) Do ?? body END) <->
  FOR $$ s TO NumberOfStates($$ fsa) REPEAT ?? body END;


'Blocks:
';

Block ← STRUCT(StateCount:INT, States:"StateSet");

BlockIndex ← INT;

Size($$ Blk) WHERE $$ Blk HasType BlockIndex <-> B[$$ Blk].StateCount;

Size(B[$$ Blk]) <-> B[$$ Blk].StateCount;

Let B bea Sequence(Block) InitialSize 2 MaximumSize $$ Num <->
  RAISE BEGIN
          DECL B:SEQ(Block) SIZE $$ Num;
          DECL BlockCount:INT;
          DECL BlockContaining:SEQ(BlockIndex) SIZE NumberOfStates(fsa);
          DECL StateMap:SEQ(StateType(fsa)) SIZE NumberOfStates(fsa);
          DECL AlphabetMap:SEQ(InputSymbolType(fsa)) SIZE
            NumberOfInputSymbols(fsa);
          DECL I:INT;
          ForEach s In Sigma(fsa) Do StateMap[I ← I + 1] ← s END;
          I ← 0;
          ForEach s In Alpha(fsa) Do AlphabetMap[I ← I + 1] ← s END;
        END;

CreateNewBlock($$ B) <-> BlockCount ← BlockCount + 1;
```

```
BlockOf B containing $$ s <-> BlockContaining[$$ s];

$$ Blk1 IsSmallerThan $$ Blk2 <-> Size($$ Blk1) LT Size($$ Blk2);

B[1] ← FinalStates($$ fsa) <->
  BEGIN
    CreateNewBlock(B);
    ForEach s In SetOfStates($$ fsa)
      Do FinalState($$ fsa)(s) -> Add s To TheBlock(1) END;
  END;

B[2] ← NonFinalStates($$ fsa) <->
  BEGIN
    CreateNewBlock(B);
    ForEach s In SetOfStates($$ fsa)
      Do NOT (FinalState($$ fsa)(s)) -> Add s To TheBlock(2) END;
  END;

Add $$ s To TheBlock($$ Blk) <->
  BEGIN
    Add $$ s To TheSet(B[$$ Blk].States);
    Size($$ Blk) ← Size($$ Blk) + 1;
    BlockOf B containing $$ s ← $$ Blk;
  END;

Delete $$ s From TheBlock($$ Blk) <->
  BEGIN
    Delete $$ s From TheSet(B[$$ Blk].States);
    Size($$ Blk) ← Size($$ Blk) - 1;
  END;

Move $$ s From $$ Blk1 To $$ Blk2 <->
  BEGIN
    /* 'a state can be in at most one block';
    Delete $$ s From TheBlock($$ Blk1);
    Add $$ s To TheBlock($$ Blk2);
    NumberToBjOnA[$$ Blk1] <- NumberToBjOnA[$$ Blk1] - 1;
  END;

(ForEach $$ s In Bj Do ?? body END) <->
  ForEach $$ s In TheSet(B[Bj].States) Do ?? body END;

Let Twin bea Map(Block; Block) <->
  RAISE [) DECL Twin:SEQ(INT) SIZE NumberOfStates(fsa) (];

Twin($$ Blk) <-> Twin[$$ Blk];

HasNoTwin($$ Blk) <-> Twin[$$ Blk] = 0;

Let BlocksSplit bea Set(Block) Initially TheEmptySet <->
  RAISE [) DECL BlocksSplit:List (];

(ForEach $$ bi In BlocksSplit Do ?? body END) <->
  ForEach $$ bi In TheList(BlocksSplit) Do ?? body END;

Add $$ Blk To BlocksSplit <-> Add $$ Blk To TheList(BlocksSplit);
```

```
ComputeNumberToBjOnA ←
  EXPR(Bj:BlockIndex, A:InputSymbol; SEQ(INT))
    BEGIN
      DECL Temp:SEQ(INT) SIZE BlockCount;
      ForEach s In Bj
        Do
          ForEach t In TheList(DeltaInverse(s, A))
            Do
              Temp[BlockOf B containing t] <-
                Temp[BlockOf B containing t] + 1;
            END;
        END;
      Temp;
    END;

ThereExists $$ s In $$ Blk SuchThat $$ pred <->
  NumberToBjOnA[$$ Blk] # Size($$ Blk);


'L:
';

Let L bea Set($$ mode) Initially TheEmptySet <->
  RAISE BEGIN
          DECL L:List;
          DECL MemberOfL:SEQ(SEQ(BOOL)) SIZE
            NumberOfStates(fsa), NumberOfInputSymbols(fsa);
        END;

Pick < $$ Bj, $$ a > From L <->
  RAISE BEGIN
          DECL NextPair:Pair(BlockIndex, InputSymbol) BYVAL
            PickNextElement(L);
          DECL $$ Bj:BlockIndex LIKE NextPair[1];
          DECL $$ a:InputSymbol LIKE NextPair[2];
          /* 'prepare to split wrt Bj and a';
          DECL NumberToBjOnA:SEQ(INT) BYVAL
            ComputeNumberToBjOnA($$ Bj, $$ a);
        END;

Add < $$ Blk, $$ c > To L WHERE $$ Blk HasType BlockIndex <->
  BEGIN
    Add CONST(Pair OF $$ Blk, $$ c) To TheList(L);
    MemberOfL[$$ Blk, $$ c] ← TRUE;
  END;

Add < B[$$ Blk], $$ c > To L <->
  BEGIN
    Add CONST(Pair OF $$ Blk, $$ c) To TheList(L);
    MemberOfL[$$ Blk, $$ c] ← TRUE;
  END;

Delete < $$ Blk, $$ c > From L <->
  [) DeleteNextElement(L); MemberOfL[$$ Blk, $$ c] ← FALSE (];

< $$ Blk, $$ InputSymbol > In L <-> MemberOfL[$$ Blk, $$ InputSymbol];
```

```
Empty L <-> EmptyList(L);


'D:
';

Let D bea Set(State) Initially TheEmptySet <-> RAISE [) DECL D:List ();

D union $$ l <->
  BEGIN
    DECL Result:List BYVAL D;
    ForEach s In TheList($$ l) Do Add s To TheList(Result) END;
    Result;
  END;

(ForEach $$ s In D Do ?? body END) <->
  ForEach $$ s In TheList(D) Do ?? body END;

'DeltaInverse
';

Let DeltaInverse bea Map(State, InputSymbol; Set(State)) WithValue
  InverseTransitionFunction(fsa) <->
  RAISE BEGIN
          DECL DeltaInverse:SEQ(SEQ(List(State))) BYVAL
            InverseTransitionFunction(fsa);
        END;

InverseTransitionFunction ←
  EXPR(fsa:FiniteAutomaton; SEQ(SEQ(List(State))))
    BEGIN
      DECL DeltaInverse:SEQ(SEQ(List(State))) SIZE
        NumberOfStates(fsa), NumberOfInputSymbols(fsa);
      FOR s TO NumberOfStates(fsa)
        REPEAT
          FOR sym TO NumberOfInputSymbols(fsa)
            REPEAT
              IsTransition(fsa)(s, sym) ->
                Add s To TheList(DeltaInverse[Delta(fsa)(s, sym), sym]);
            END;
        END;
      DeltaInverse;
    END;

DeltaInverse($$ State, $$ InputSymbol) <->
  DeltaInverse[$$ State, $$ InputSymbol];


'Pair:
';

Pair ← STRUCT(Comp1:BlockIndex, Comp2:InputSymbol);

Pair(BlockIndex, InputSymbol) <-> Pair;

'ReturnPartitionedStates:
';
```

```
PartitionedStateSet <-> SEQ(REF);

ReturnPartitionedStates ←
  EXPR(fsa:FiniteAutomaton, B:SEQ(Block); SEQ(REF))
    BEGIN
      DECL Result:SEQ(REF) SIZE BlockCount;
      FOR I TO BlockCount
        REPEAT
          Result[I] ← ALLOC(SEQ(StateType(fsa)) SIZE Size(B[I]));
          DECL J:INT;
          ForEach s In TheSet(B[I].States)
            Do Result[I, J ← J + 1] ← StateMap[s] END;
        END;
      Result;
    END;


'Lists:
';

List ← QL("List*", UPF(ListUPF)) :: PTR("ListElement*");

ListUPF ←
  EXPR(L:List, P:PORT; List)
    BEGIN
      PRINT('(', P);
      DECL Temp\\:List BYVAL L;
      REPEAT
        L = NIL => PRINT(')', P);
        PRINT(PickNextElement(L), P);
        L.Next # NIL -> PRINT(', ', P);
        DeleteNextElement(L);
      END;
      Temp\\;
    END;

ListElement ← "ListElement*" :: STRUCT(E:REF, Next:"List*");

EmptyList($$ L) <-> $$ L = NIL;

PickNextElement($$ L) <-> VAL(($$ L).E);

Add $$ e To TheList($$ L) <->
  $$ L ← ALLOC(ListElement OF ALLOC(ANY LIKE $$ e), $$ L);

DeleteNextElement($$ L) <-> $$ L ← ($$ L).Next;

(ForEach $$ e In TheList($$ L) Do ... END) <->
  BEGIN
    DECL Temp\\:List BYVAL $$ L;
    REPEAT
      EmptyList(Temp\\) => NOTHING;
      DECL $$ e:ANY BYVAL PickNextElement(Temp\\);
      ...;
      DeleteNextElement(Temp\\);
    END;
  END;
```

```
List($$ mode) <-> List;


'Finite automaton
';

FiniteAutomaton ←
  QL("FSA*", UPF(FSA\UPF), UGF(FSA\UGF), SUPUGF(TRUE)) ::
    STRUCT(AllStates:SEQ(SYMBOL),
           FinalStates:SEQ(BOOL),
           InputAlphabet:SEQ(SYMBOL),
           Delta:SEQ(SEQ(INT)),
           StateTable:HASHTABLE,
           SymbolTable:HASHTABLE);

FSA\UPF ←
  EXPR(fsa:FiniteAutomaton, P:PORT; FiniteAutomaton)
    BEGIN
      FOR J TO NumberOfStates(fsa)
        REPEAT
          PRINT('
', P);
          PRINT(J, P);
          PRINT('       ', P);
          fsa.FinalStates[J] -> PRINT('(', P);
          PRINT(fsa.AllStates[J], P);
          fsa.FinalStates[J] -> PRINT(')', P);
          DECL FIRST:BOOL BYVAL TRUE;
          FOR K TO NumberOfInputSymbols(fsa)
            REPEAT
              DECL T:INT LIKE fsa.Delta[J, K];
              T # 0 ->
                BEGIN
                  If FIRST Then FIRST <- FALSE Else
                    BEGIN
                      PRINT('
        ', P);
                      TO LENGTH(BASIC\STR(fsa.AllStates[J]))
                        REPEAT PRINT(' ', P) END;
                      fsa.FinalStates[J] -> PRINT('     ', P);
                    END;
                  PRINT('-- ', P);
                  PRINT(fsa.InputAlphabet[K], P);
                  PRINT(' ---> ', P);
                  fsa.FinalStates[T] -> PRINT('(', P);
                  PRINT(fsa.AllStates[T], P);
                  fsa.FinalStates[T] -> PRINT(')', P);
                END;
            END;
        END;
      fsa;
    END;
```

```
FSA\UGF ←
  EXPR(M:MODE, BC:SYMBOL, F\\:ANY; FiniteAutomaton)
    BEGIN
      BC # "OF" => BREAK('not handling other cases for this example
');
      DECL Result:FiniteAutomaton.UR BYVAL
        CONSTRUCT(FiniteAutomaton.UR, "OF", F\\);
      DECL ST:HASHTABLE BYVAL
        MAKEHASH(SYMBOL, INT, LENGTH(Result.AllStates));
      FOR I TO LENGTH(Result.AllStates)
        REPEAT FINDHASH(ST, Result.AllStates[I]) ← I END;
      Result.StateTable ← ST;
      ST ← MAKEHASH(SYMBOL, INT, LENGTH(Result.InputAlphabet));
      FOR I TO LENGTH(Result.InputAlphabet)
        REPEAT FINDHASH(ST, Result.InputAlphabet[I]) ← I END;
      Result.SymbolTable ← ST;
      LIFT(Result, FiniteAutomaton);
    END;

Alpha($$ fsa) <-> ($$ fsa).InputAlphabet;

Sigma($$ fsa) <-> ($$ fsa).AllStates;

StateType($$ fsa) <-> SYMBOL;

InputSymbolType($$ fsa) <-> SYMBOL;

NumberOfStates($$ fsa) <-> LENGTH(($$ fsa).AllStates);

NumberOfInputSymbols($$ fsa) <-> LENGTH(($$ fsa).InputAlphabet);

FinalState($$ fsa)($$ s) <->
  ($$ fsa).FinalStates[FINDHASH(($$ fsa).StateTable, $$ s)];

(ForEach $$ s In Sigma($$ fsa) Do ?? body END) <->
  FOR I\\ TO NumberOfStates($$ fsa)
    REPEAT DECL $$ s:SYMBOL BYVAL ($$ fsa).AllStates[I\\]; ?? body END;

(ForEach $$ c In Alpha($$ fsa) Do ?? body END) <->
  FOR I\\ TO NumberOfInputSymbols($$ fsa)
    REPEAT
      DECL $$ c:SYMBOL BYVAL ($$ fsa).InputAlphabet[I\\];
      ?? body;
    END;

IsTransition($$ fsa)($$ s, $$ InputSymbol) <->
  ($$ fsa).Delta[FINDHASH(($$ fsa).StateTable, $$ s),
                 FINDHASH(($$ fsa).SymbolTable, $$ InputSymbol)] # 0;

Delta($$ fsa)($$ s, $$ InputSymbol) <->
  ($$ fsa).Delta[FINDHASH(($$ fsa).StateTable, $$ s),
                 FINDHASH(($$ fsa).SymbolTable, $$ InputSymbol)];
```

III. Doubly-Linked List Refinements

```
/* 'Implementation of Set(State) using a doubly-linked list:
   ';

"StateSet" :: PTR("DoublyLinkedList");

PDLL <- "PDLL*" :: PTR("DoublyLinkedList");

DoublyLinkedList <-
  QL("DoublyLinkedList", UPF(PrintSet)) ::
    STRUCT(s:State, Predecessor:"PDLL*", Successor:"PDLL*");

RAISE [] DECL B:$$ m SIZE $$ number [] <--->
  RAISE BEGIN
          DECL B:$$ m SIZE $$ number;
          DECL CurrentPositionOfState:SEQ(PDLL) SIZE $$ number;
        END;

Add $$ s To TheSet($$ S) <->
  BEGIN
    DECL New:PDLL LIKE ALLOC(DoublyLinkedList OF $$ s, NIL, $$ S);
    $$ S # NIL -> ($$ S).Predecessor <- New;
    $$ S <- New;
    CurrentPositionOfState[$$ s] <- New;
  END;

Delete $$ s From TheSet($$ S) <->
  BEGIN
    DECL Pos:PTR(DoublyLinkedList) BYVAL CurrentPositionOfState[$$ s];
    BEGIN
      Pos.Predecessor = NIL => $$ S <- Pos.Successor;
      Pos.Predecessor.Successor <- Pos.Successor;
    END;
    Pos.Successor # NIL -> Pos.Successor.Predecessor <- Pos.Predecessor;
  END;

 (ForEach $$ s In TheSet($$ S) Do ?? body END) <->
  BEGIN
    DECL Temp\\:PTR(DoublyLinkedList) BYVAL $$ S;
    REPEAT
      Temp\\ = NIL => NOTHING;
      DECL $$ s:State BYVAL Temp\\.s;
      ?? body;
      Temp\\ <- Temp\\.Successor;
    END;
  END;
```

```
PrintSet ←
  EXPR(S:DoublyLinkedList, P:PORT; DoublyLinkedList)
    BEGIN
      PRINT('(', P);
      REPEAT
        S = NIL => PRINT(')', P);
        PRINT(S.s, P);
        S ← S.Successor;
        S # NIL -> PRINT(', ', P);
      END;
      S;
    END;
```

References

[Brown 81] Brown, D. W. *The solution of difference equations describing array manipulation.* Ph.D. Th., Harvard University, June 1981.

[Cheatham 75] Cheatham, T. E., Jr., and Townley, J. A. Implementing an algorithm of Hopcroft described by Gries. Center for Research in Computing Technology, Harvard University, 1975.

[Cheatham 79] Cheatham, T. E., Jr., Holloway, G. H., Townley, J. A. Symbolic evaluation and the analysis of programs. *IEEE Trans. Software Engineering SE-5*, 4 (1979), 402-417.

[Cheatham 81] Cheatham, T. E., Jr. Overview of the Harvard Program Development Systems. In Hunke, H, editor, *Software Engineering Environments.* North-Holland Publishing Co, 1981.

[Conrad 76] Conrad, William R. Rewrite User's Guide. Harvard University, Center for Research in Computing Technology, August 1976.

[ECL 74] *ECL Programmer's Manual*, Harvard University, Center for Research in Computing Technology, 1974.

[Gries 73] Gries, David. Describing an Algorithm by Hopcroft. *Acta Informatica 2* (1973), 97-109.

[Hopcroft 71] Hopcroft, J. An n log n algorithm for minimizing states in a finite automaton. In *Theory of Machines and Computation*, Academic Press, New York, 1971, pp. 189-196.

[Liskov 78] Liskov, B. H. CLU Reference Manual. Massachusetts Institute of Technology, 1978.

[Ploedereder 80] Ploedereder, E. O. *A semantic model for the analysis and verification of programs in general, higher-level languages.* Ph.D. Th., Harvard University, 1980.

[Townley 81] Townley, J. A. PDS User's Manual. Harvard University, Center for Research in Computing Technology, 1981.

[Wulf 74] Wulf, William A. ALPHARD: toward a language to support structured programs. Computer Science Department, Carnegie-Mellon Univerity, April 1974.

Vol. 107: International Colloquium on Formalization of Programming Concepts. Proceedings. Edited by J. Diaz and I. Ramos. VII, 478 pages. 1981.

Vol. 108: Graph Theory and Algorithms. Edited by N. Saito and T. Nishizeki. VI, 216 pages. 1981.

Vol. 109: Digital Image Processing Systems. Edited by L. Bolc and Zenon Kulpa. V, 353 pages. 1981.

Vol. 110: W. Dehning, H. Essig, S. Maass, The Adaptation of Virtual Man-Computer Interfaces to User Requirements in Dialogs. X, 142 pages. 1981.

Vol. 111: CONPAR 81. Edited by W. Händler. XI, 508 pages. 1981.

Vol. 112: CAAP '81. Proceedings. Edited by G. Astesiano and C. Böhm. VI, 364 pages. 1981.

Vol. 113: E.-E. Doberkat, Stochastic Automata: Stability, Nondeterminism, and Prediction. IX, 135 pages. 1981.

Vol. 114: B. Liskov, CLU, Reference Manual. VIII, 190 pages. 1981.

Vol. 115: Automata, Languages and Programming. Edited by S. Even and O. Kariv. VIII, 552 pages. 1981.

Vol. 116: M. A. Casanova, The Concurrency Control Problem for Database Systems. VII, 175 pages. 1981.

Vol. 117: Fundamentals of Computation Theory. Proceedings, 1981. Edited by F. Gécseg. XI, 471 pages. 1981.

Vol. 118: Mathematical Foundations of Computer Science 1981. Proceedings, 1981. Edited by J. Gruska and M. Chytil. XI, 589 pages. 1981.

Vol. 119: G. Hirst, Anaphora in Natural Language Understanding: A Survey. XIII, 128 pages. 1981.

Vol. 120: L. B. Rall, Automatic Differentiation: Techniques and Applications. VIII, 165 pages. 1981.

Vol. 121: Z. Zlatev, J. Wasniewski, and K. Schaumburg, Y12M Solution of Large and Sparse Systems of Linear Algebraic Equations. X, 128 pages. 1981.

Vol. 122: Algorithms in Modern Mathematics and Computer Science. Proceedings, 1979. Edited by A. P. Ershov and D. E. Knuth. XI, 487 pages. 1981.

Vol. 123: Trends in Information Processing Systems. Proceedings, 1981. Edited by A. J. W. Duijvestijn and P. C. Lockemann. XI, 349 pages. 1981.

Vol. 124: W. Polak, Compiler Specification and Verification. XIII, 269 pages. 1981.

Vol. 125: Logic of Programs. Proceedings, 1979. Edited by E. Engeler. V, 245 pages. 1981.

Vol. 126: Microcomputer System Design. Proceedings, 1981. Edited by M. J. Flynn, N. R. Harris, and D. P. McCarthy. VII, 397 pages. 1982.

Voll. 127: Y.Wallach, Alternating Sequential/Parallel Processing. X, 329 pages. 1982.

Vol. 128: P. Branquart, G. Louis, P. Wodon, An Analytical Description of CHILL, the CCITT High Level Language. VI, 277 pages. 1982.

Vol. 129: B. T. Hailpern, Verifying Concurrent Processes Using Temporal Logic. VIII, 208 pages. 1982.

Vol. 130: R. Goldblatt, Axiomatising the Logic of Computer Programming. XI, 304 pages. 1982.

Vol. 131: Logics of Programs. Proceedings, 1981. Edited by D. Kozen. VI, 429 pages. 1982.

Vol. 132: Data Base Design Techniques I: Requirements and Logical Structures. Proceedings, 1978. Edited by S.B. Yao, S.B. Navathe, J.L. Weldon, and T.L. Kunii. V, 227 pages. 1982.

Vol. 133: Data Base Design Techniques II: Proceedings, 1979. Edited by S.B. Yao and T.L. Kunii. V, 229–399 pages. 1982.

Vol. 134: Program Specification. Proceedings, 1981. Edited by J. Staunstrup. IV, 426 pages. 1982.

Vol. 135: R.L. Constable, S.D. Johnson, and C.D. Eichenlaub, An Introduction to the PL/CV2 Programming Logic. X, 292 pages. 1982.

Vol. 136: Ch. M. Hoffmann, Group Theoretic Algorithms and Graph Isomorphism. VIII, 311 pages. 1982.

Vol. 137: International Symposium on Programming. Proceedings, 1982. Edited by M. Dezani-Ciancaglini and M. Montanari. VI, 406 pages. 1982.

This series reports new developments in computer science research and teaching – quickly, informally and at a high level. The type of material considered for publication includes:

1. Preliminary drafts of original papers and monographs
2. Lectures on a new field or presentations of a new angle in a classical field
3. Seminar work-outs
4. Reports of meetings, provided they are
   a) of exceptional interest and
   b) devoted to a single topic.

Texts which are out of print but still in demand may also be considered if they fall within these categories.

The timeliness of a manuscript is more important than its form, which may be unfinished or tentative. Thus, in some instances, proofs may be merely outlined and results presented which have been or will later be published elsewhere. If possible, a subject index should be included. Publication of Lecture Notes is intended as a service to the international computer science community, in that a commercial publisher, Springer-Verlag, can offer a wide distribution of documents which would otherwise have a restricted readership. Once published and copyrighted, they can be documented in the scientific literature.

Manuscripts

Manuscripts should be no less than 100 and preferably no more than 500 pages in length.
They are reproduced by a photographic process and therefore must be typed with extreme care. Symbols not on the typewriter should be inserted by hand in indelible black ink. Corrections to the typescript should be made by pasting in the new text or painting out errors with white correction fluid. Authors receive 75 free copies and are free to use the material in other publications. The typescript is reduced slightly in size during reproduction; best results will not be obtained unless the text on any one page is kept within the overall limit of 18 x 26.5 cm (7 x 10½ inches). On request, the publisher will supply special paper with the typing area outlined.
Manuscripts should be sent to Prof. G. Goos, Institut für Informatik, Universität Karlsruhe, Zirkel 2, 7500 Karlsruhe/Germany, Prof. J. Hartmanis, Cornell University, Dept. of Computer-Science, Ithaca, NY/USA 14850, or directly to Springer-Verlag Heidelberg.

Springer-Verlag, Heidelberger Platz 3, D-1000 Berlin 33
Springer-Verlag, Tiergartenstraße 17, D-6900 Heidelberg 1
Springer-Verlag, 175 Fifth Avenue, New York, NY 10010/USA

ISBN 3-540-11494-7
ISBN 0-387-11494-7